Warfare in Europe 1650–1792

**The International Library of Essays on Military History**
*Series Editor: Jeremy Black*

**Titles in the Series:**

**Warfare in Europe 1650–1792**
*Jeremy Black*

**Warfare in the Middle East since 1945**
*Ahron Bregman*

**The English Civil War**
*Stanley Carpenter*

**Warfare in Latin America**
*Miguel A. Centeno*

**United States Military History 1865 to the Present Day**
*Jeffrey Charlston*

**Medieval Warfare 1300–1450**
*Kelly DeVries*

**Medieval Warfare 1000–1300**
*John France*

**Warfare in the Dark Ages**
*John France and Kelly DeVries*

**Naval History 1500–1680**
*Jan Glete*

**Byzantine Warfare**
*John Haldon*

**Warfare in Early Modern Europe 1450–1660**
*Paul Hammer*

**Naval Warfare 1680–1850**
*Richard Harding*

**Warfare in Europe 1919–1938**
*Geoffrey Jensen*

**Warfare in Japan**
*Harald Kleinschmidt*

**Naval History 1850–Present**
*Andrew Lambert*

**African Military History**
*John Lamphear*

**Warfare in China to 1600**
*Peter Lorge*

**World War I**
*Michael Neiberg*

**The Army of Imperial Rome**
*Michael Pavkovic*

**The Army of the Roman Republic**
*Michael Pavkovic*

**The American Civil War**
*Ethan Rafuse*

**The British Army 1815–1914**
*Harold E. Raugh, Jr*

**The Russian Imperial Army 1796–1917**
*Roger Reese*

**Medieval Ships and Warfare**
*Susan Rose*

**Warfare in Europe 1792–1815**
*Frederick C. Schneid*

**The Second World War**
*Nick Smart*

**Warfare in China Since 1600**
*Kenneth Swope*

**Warfare in the USA 1775–1861**
*Samuel Watson*

**The Vietnam War**
*James H. Willbanks*

**Warfare in Europe 1815–1914**
*Peter Wilson*

# Warfare in Europe 1650–1792

*Edited by*

Jeremy Black

*University of Exeter, UK*

ASHGATE

Published by
Ashgate Publishing Limited
Gower House
Croft Road
Aldershot
Hants GU11 3HR
England

Ashgate Publishing Company
Suite 420
101 Cherry Street
Burlington, VT 05401-4405
USA



Ashgate website: http://www.ashgate.com

**British Library Cataloguing in Publication Data**
Warfare in Europe 1650–1792. – (The international library of essays in military history)
1. Military art and science – Europe – History – 18th century 2. Military art and science – Europe – History – 17th century 3. Europe – History, Military – 1648–1789
I. Black, Jeremy
355'.0094'09033

**Library of Congress Cataloging-in-Publication Data**
Warfare in Europe 1650–1792 / edited by Jeremy Black.
p. cm. — (The international library of essays in military history)
Includes bibliographical references and index.
ISBN 0-7546-2464-1 (alk. paper)
1. Military art and science—Europe—History. 2. Europe—History, Military—17th century.
3. Europe—History, Military—17th century. I. Black, Jeremy. II. Series.

U42.E97 2005
355'0094'09032—dc22

2004048833

ISBN 0 7546 2464 1

Printed in Great Britain by The Cromwell Press, Trowbridge, Wiltshire

For Graham Gibbs
A good companion and a fellow tiller in eighteenth-century fields

# Contents

## PART IV WESTERN AND CENTRAL EUROPE



## PART V TECHNOLOGY

# Acknowledgements

The editor and publishers wish to thank the following for permission to use copyright material.

Canadian Slavonic Papers for the essay: John Keep (1987), 'Feeding the Troops: Russian Army Supply Policies during the Seven Years War', *Canadian Slavonic Papers*, **29**, pp. 24–44.

Copyright Clearance Center for the essays: Thomas M. Barker (1983–84), 'New Perspectives on the Historical Significance of the "Year of the Turk"', *Austrian History Yearbook*, **19–20**, Part 1, pp. 3–14; Alexander Balisch (1983–84), 'Infantry Battlefield Tactics in the Seventeenth and Eighteenth Centuries on the European and Turkish Theatres of War: the Austrian Response to Different Conditions', *Studies in History and Politics*, **3**, pp. 43–60; Daniel Stone (1983–84), 'Patriotism and Professionalism: The Polish Army in the Eighteenth Century', *Studies in History and Politics*, **3**, pp. 61–72; Dennis E. Showalter (1983–84), 'Tactics and Recruitment in Eighteenth Century Prussia', *Studies in History and Politics*, **3**, pp. 15–41.

Duke University Press for the essay: Steven T. Ross (1965), 'The Development of the Combat Division in Eighteenth-Century French Armies', *French Historical Studies*, **1**, pp. 84–94. Copyright © 1965 Society of French Historical Studies.

The Editors, War & Society for the essay: Bruce W. Menning (1984), 'Russian Military Innovation in the Second Half of the Eighteenth Century', *War & Society*, **2**, pp. 23–41.

Greenwood Publishing Group for the essay: Peter Paret (1978), 'The Relationship between the Revolutionary War and European Military Thought and Practice in the Second Half of the Eighteenth Century', in Don Higginbotham (ed.), *Reconsiderations on the Revolutionary War*, Greenwood Press, Westport, pp. 144–57 (original pagination pp. 208–10). Copyright © 1978 Greenwood Press.

Historical Society for the essay: Dennis Showalter (2003), 'Thinking about Military Revolution', *Historically Speaking*, **4**, pp. 1–3 (original pagination pp. 9–10).

Hodder Arnold for the essays: Peter H. Wilson (1996), 'German Women and War, 1500–1800', *War in History*, **3**, pp. 127–60. Copyright © 1996 Arnold; Christopher Storrs and H.M. Scott (1996), 'The Military Revolution and the European Nobility, c. 1600–1800', *War in History*, **3**, pp. 1–41. Copyright © 1996 Arnold; Peter H. Wilson (2000), 'Social Militarization in Eighteenth-Century Germany', *German History*, **18**, pp. 1–39. Copyright © 2000 German Society; Christopher Storrs (1997), 'The Army of Lombardy and the Resilience of Spanish Power in Italy in the Reign of Carlos II (1665–1700) Part I', *War in History*, **4**, pp. 371–97. Copyright © 1997 Arnold; Christopher Storrs (1998), 'The Army of Lombardy and the Resilience of Spanish Power in Italy in the Reign of Carlos II (1665–1700) Part II', *War in History*, **5**, pp. 1–22. Copyright © 1998 Arnold.

Johns Hopkins University Press for the essay: Brett D. Steele (1994), 'Muskets and Pendulums: Benjamin Robins, Leonhard Euler, and the Ballistics Revolution', *Technology and Culture*, **34**, pp. 348–82. Copyright © 1994 Society for the History of Technology.

Oxford University Press for the essay: Guy Rowlands (1999), 'Louis XIV, Aristocratic Power and the Elite Units of the French Army', *French History*, **13**, pp. 303–31. Copyright © 1999 Oxford University Press.

Sage Publications for the essays: James Michael Hill (1992), 'The Distinctiveness of Gaelic Warfare, 1400–1750', *European History Quarterly*, **22**, pp. 323–45. Copyright © 1992 Sage Publications; Peter H. Wilson (1998), 'War in German Thought from the Peace of Westphalia to Napoleon', *European History Quarterly*, **28**, pp. 5–50. Copyright © 1998 Sage Publications.

University of Minnesota Libraries and Bancroft Library for the essay: Gordon R. Mork (1967), 'Flint and Steel: A Study in Military Technology and Tactics in 17th-Century Europe', *Smithsonian Journal of History*, **2**, pp. 25–52.

Every effort has been made to trace all the copyright holders, but if any have been inadvertently overlooked the publishers will be pleased to make the necessary arrangement at the first opportunity.

# Series Preface

War and military matters are key aspects of the modern world and central topics in history study. This series brings together essays selected from key journals that exhibit careful analysis of military history. The volumes, each of which is edited by an expert in the field, cover crucial time periods and geographical areas including Europe, the USA, China, Japan, Latin America, and South Asia. Each volume represents the editor's selection of the most seminal recent essays on military history in their particular area of expertise, while an introduction presents an overview of the issues in that area, together with comments on the background and significance of the essays selected.

This series reflects important shifts in the subject. Military history has increasingly taken a cultural turn, forcing us to consider the question of what wins wars in a new light. Historians used to emphasise the material aspects of war, specifically the quality and quantity of resources. That approach, bringing together technological proficiency and economic strength, appeared to help explain struggles for mastery within the West, as well as conflicts between the West and non-West. Now, the focus is rather on strategic culture – how tasks are set and understood – and on how resources are used. It involves exploring issues such as fighting quality, unit cohesion, morale, leadership, tactics, strategy, as well as the organisational cultural factors that affect assessment and use of resources. Instead of assuming that organisational issues were driven by how best to use, move and supply weapons, this approach considers how they are affected by social patterns and developments.

Former assumptions by historians that societies are driven merely by a search for efficiency and maximisation of force as they adapt their weaponry to optimise performance in war ignored the complex process in which interest in new weapons interacted with the desire for continuity. Responses by warring parties to firearms, for example, varied, with some societies, such as those of Western Europe, proving keener to rely on firearms than others, for example in East and South Asia. This becomes easier to understand by considering the different tasks and possibilities facing armies at the time – when it is far from clear which weaponry, force structure, tactics, or operational method can be adopted most successfully – rather than thinking in terms of clear-cut military progress.

Cultural factors also play a role in responses to the trial of combat. The understanding of loss and suffering, at both the level of ordinary soldiers and of societies as a whole, is far more culturally conditioned than emphasis on the sameness of battle might suggest, and variations in the willingness to suffer losses influences both military success and styles of combat.

Furthermore, war is not really about battle but about attempts to impose will. Success in this involves far more than victory on the battlefield; that is just a pre-condition of a more complex process. The defeated must be willing to accept the verdict of battle. This involves accommodation, if not acculturation – something that has been far from constant in different periods and places. Assimilating local religious cults, co-opting local élites, and, possibly, today, offering the various inducements summarised as globalisation, have been the most important means of achieving it over the years. Thus military history becomes an aspect of total history; and victory in war is best studied in terms of its multiple contexts.

Any selection of what to include is difficult. The editors in this series have done an excellent job and it has been a great pleasure working with them.

JEREMY BLACK
*Series Editor*
*University of Exeter*

# Introduction

Moulding states and societies, economies and the arts, war played a major role in Europe in the period 1650–1792, but scholars have tended to underrate its importance and interest for military history. This reflects three linked factors. First, there is a sense that the periods before and after 1650–1792, both that of the so-called Military Revolution, dated by Michael Roberts (1956) to 1560–1660, and that of the French Revolutionary and Napoleonic Wars, were more consequential for military development and also characterized by a more urgent pursuit of victory. Second, the notion of consequence is related to that of stages in a pattern of military change with ideal forms and paradigmatic powers (Lynn, 1996). This, thirdly, leads to a focus on a small number of powers, with much of Europe ignored or discussed largely in terms of these powers – for example, with reference to the idea of the diffusion of best practice, through the emulation of their methods. For this period, the powers that receive most attention are France when under the personal rule of Louis XIV (1661–1715) and Prussia under Frederick II, the Great (r. 1740–86). A more sophisticated version also finds space for Austria and Russia in the early eighteenth century and for signs of military reform in France prior to the Revolution. Nevertheless, there is a general failure to appreciate the range and variety of warfare in Europe.

This volume sets out to address this problem. There is a deliberate choice of geographical example in order to probe the nature of warfare as part of a matrix that builds up to cover as much of Europe as space permits. This means not only a coverage of Eastern Europe, but also of Gaelic warfare, on which see the essay by J.M. Hill (Chapter 12). As Hill emphasizes, there was a stress on the tactical offensive by infantry in this warfare, and it therefore contrasts with the norm in Western European infantry tactics. In practice, the role of advances in the latter tends to be underrated by the stress on firepower (Parker, 1996). Neither Gaelic nor Eastern European warfare should be simplified, and, in particular, it would be as foolish to have an ideal account of Eastern European warfare as it is to have one of European warfare as a whole. The trajectory of Russian military development – the subject of the essays by Hellie, Keep and Menning (Chapters 8, 9 and 10) – was very different to that of the Ottoman Turks discussed by Barker (Chapter 6), the Austrians analysed by Balisch (Chapter 7), and the Poles considered by Stone (Chapter 11).

Allowing for this, there are clear contrasts between the general model of European development and the situation across much of Europe. This is linked to a problem of ranking, seen, for example, in the most influential book on the subject, Geoffrey Parker's *The Military Revolution* (1996). He argued that 'all the evidence for radical military change, whether in army size, fortifications, or firearms, comes from the lands of the Habsburgs or of their neighbours . . . That was the heartland of the military revolution'. Elsewhere, where the changes of the revolution do not take place, this is seen as failure:

> The *trace italienne* made slow progress, in Germany and elsewhere, not merely because of the cost . . . but also through the difficulties of keeping up to date . . . The position in Ireland during the 1640s illustrates the contrast between the old and new ways in warfare . . . the British Isles, then, were a

> zone where the transformation in fortification and siegecraft was incomplete, gradual and relatively tardy . . . The wars fought on the eastern half of the Great European Plain likewise remained deeply resistant to military innovation . . . The progress of the military revolution was no faster in Russia. (Parker, 1996, pp. 24, 26, 29, 37–38)

This approach, which is replicated at the global scale, is unhelpful as it assumes that there was a clear pattern of appropriate development predicated on an obvious best practice. The latter is seen in terms in infantry volley fire, with the view that there was only one theory concerning the effective use of muskets in the field and that the drill and discipline necessary to provide this became crucial to a distinctive Western way of war (Parker, 2003, p. 13).

This argument necessarily presents those who acted otherwise in terms of failure. This is an analysis that is questionable in itself as it is normal to adopt practices that seem appropriate, and societies at the time generally have a better idea of this than scholars writing with the condescension of posterity. Furthermore, it is empirically problematic. Work on the variety of military systems and methods seen in Europe indicate that they were fit for purpose within the constraints of the relevant social systems, the latter being an insight that had already been noted by writers of the period discussing, at least *en passant*, historical sociology – most obviously, Edward Gibbon and Adam Smith. Thus, the essays by Balisch, Barker and Menning serve as a reminder of the need for Eastern European forces to be able to respond to the Ottoman Turks. Furthermore, as is discussed in Paret's essay (Chapter 17), military experience on the European periphery, whether in the Balkans or in trans-oceanic colonies, existed in a dynamic relationship with practice within Europe.

If more attention is devoted to the variety that was European military activity, that in turn means challenging the standard baton-exchange account with its focus, for this period, on France and Prussia. That can be enhanced by two additional shifts in the historiography. First, there is a different Western Europe on offer. As Storrs' essays (Chapters 13 and 14) show, this includes a focus on Spain, no longer treated as the sick man of Europe. Aside from Spanish resilience in the late seventeenth century, it is necessary to note the success of Spanish intervention in Italy in the first half of the century, particularly the conquests of Sardinia, Sicily and Naples in 1717, 1718 and 1734 respectively. As yet there has been insufficient research in English (and not enough work in Spanish) on these campaigns, and this needs to be remedied. The situation in Italy is more promising, not least because the army of Savoy-Piedmont has attracted valuable attention (see Hanlon, 1998). Within Germany, there has similarly been considerable interest in the 'Third Germany' – states other than Austria and Prussia – and this provides the context for Wilson's essays on war in German thought (Chapter 15) and on social militarization (Chapter 5; see also Wilson, 2001).

Second, there is room for rethinking developments in the 'core' powers, especially France. Accounts that stress the sophistication, effectiveness, success and modernity of forces of the period – for example John Lynn's portrayal of Louis XIV's army in *Giant of the Grand Siècle 1610–1715* (1997), appear problematic both in their analysis of military developments and in their more general realization of the background socio-political situation. For the former, there is much work still to do, but a rewarding start is offered by Guy Rowlands, both in the essay in this collection and in his *The Dynastic State and the Army under Louis XIV* (2002). Rowlands sees a degree of continuity with the situation described by David Parrott in *Richelieu's Army. War, Government and Society in France, 1624–1642* (2002), not least in the important role of elite politics in constraining the choice of commanders. While there were certainly changes from the situation in the 1630s, it is important not to emphasize the transformation, a process that tends to be linked to a misunderstanding of the nature of 'absolutism' (Black, 2004a). In a parallel fashion, recent work on the development of the French navy suggests that, under Richelieu, it was less the case of major institutional innovations than of traditional methods of government through personal politics (James, 2004). This only changed to a certain extent under Colbert and his successors, and the central agencies of the French navy had scant control of the, in effect, autonomous naval bases: the agencies could move levers but, frequently, little happened.

The misunderstanding of 'absolutism' is related to the problematic use of the notion of modernity, as the variety of warfare in any one period acts as a qualification of any apparent clear-cut pattern of modernization. This is a problem with an important recent study that sees French warmaking in the 1670s as part of 'the birth of a more modern style of military operations' (Satterfield, 2003, p. 213). This is seen to lie in French operations emphasizing sieges and smaller actions of war that aimed at attrition, as a way of avoiding battle and the risks it contained. This assertion sits ill with the bulk of the study which instead addresses a generally underrated dimension of conflict, and, in doing so, shows how new fields can be profitably probed. Satterfield sees an ability to use the 'small' warfare he describes (and defines as partisan warfare) to serve operational goals. In particular, he discerns a more systematic approach to supplies and contributions in order to make it easier to support the burden of conflict than was the case earlier in the century, as well as to improve reconnaissance: the systematic gathering of intelligence by the French increased the possibilities for and of planning.

Raids took on a meaning within the calculus of supplies and also as a means of putting pressure on garrisons. There was an offensive–defensive character to French warmaking, with the French trying to protect their own northern frontier, as well as to put pressure on the Spaniards. It was impossible to seal off the frontier, but the French authorities dispatched war parties, prepared defences, issued ordinances, cajoled local officials and organized militia, all with the intention of slowing and disrupting the Spanish imposition and collection of contributions. In return, French reprisal raids and escalating demands for contributions were intended to inflict harm on the inhabitants of the Spanish Netherlands and to weaken their resolve. Satterfield shows that the French defences worked well, but that driving the Spanish garrisons from their fortresses was the only sure means of preventing Spanish raids. Blockades of fortresses were an important prelude to sieges. To Satterfield, they demonstrate the potency of French 'small war'. Blockades, he argues, wore down the Spaniards, enervating their garrisons or ensuring that sieges were concluded more rapidly. Crucially, blockades continued during the period of winter quartering in what was a war of outposts.

This was a particularly important part of French operations from 1676, and Satterfield is at pains to argue for its importance and novelty: 'The operational emphasis on blockades led Louis XIV and Louvois to perceive military actions in interrelated, and mutually supporting terms, rather than as discrete expeditions. It constituted a kind of "operational revolution"' (2003, p. 272) – a claim, however, that requires a wider assessment of other operations. Indeed, the extent to which there was a doctrinal shift is unclear, while, as so often in military history, it is helpful to think in incremental changes rather than a revolution.

The details of conflict in the 'small war' do not in fact suggest much change from earlier conflict. There was an emphasis on surprise and march security, and on cover. As a consequence, many actions took place around cemeteries, churchyards, villages and walled farms which one side had occupied for their defensive value. Most infantry actions were decided within minutes of the first volley, and Satterfield argues that partisan formations on foot fought using the same volley fire tactics employed by troops in large battles. Indeed, he suggests that large battles can be thought of as a series of small engagements in which men fought in relative isolation from one another, which is correct up to a point, although it minimizes the extent to which units did move on the battlefield; and there was a flow to many conflicts, one that was often very important to success. In small-scale conflict, as Satterfield points out, there was little 'all-out' pursuit because victorious detachments feared ambush. More generally, he indicates the limited ability of the Crown to control operations and events, and the serious financial problems that affected policy.

Alongside an emphasis on campaigning, as stages in the defeat of opposing forces, it is necessary to adopt a broader approach to victory and to underline the extent to which success had a symbolic value. From this perspective, decisiveness has to be reconceptualized, away from an emphasis on total victory, understood in modern terms as the destruction of opposing armies and the capture of their territory, and towards a notion that may have had more meaning in terms of the values of the period. This would present war as a struggle of will and for prestige, the ends sought being, first, a retention of domestic and international backing that rested on the gaining of *gloire*, and, second, persuading other rulers to accept a new configuration of relative *gloire*. This led, for example, to a concentration of forces on campaigns and sieges that were made important largely by the presence of the king as commander. Like other rulers, Louis XIV enjoyed both commanding and reviewing troops. His triumphs, such as the crossing of the Rhine in 1672 and the successful sieges of Maastricht (1673), Ghent (1678), Mons (1691) and Namur (1692), were celebrated with religious services and commemorative displays. In the Salon de la Guerre at the royal palace of Versailles, finished and opened to the public in 1686, Antoine Coysevox presented Louis as a stuccoed Mars, the God of War. By the 1690s, over 20 000 French nobles were serving in the army and navy, a bond that testified to aristocratic confidence in Louis.

Furthermore, alongside victories, it is necessary to consider the way in which conquered provinces, such as Artois and Franche-Comté, were assimilated. The same was true for Peter the Great with Estonia and Livonia, for Frederick the Great with Silesia, and so on.

If the development of the French army under Louis XIV can be debated, and a forthcoming book on the War of the Spanish Succession by Guy Rowlands is eagerly anticipated, there has been far less work on subsequent decades. The army was effective during both the War of the Polish Succession (1733–35) and the War of the Austrian Succession (1740–48), in which the French took part from 1741, but there has been very little research on this period, especially on the operational dimension.

As a consequence, work on Frederick II's Prussia lacks an adequate comparative dimension. Victory over the French at Rossbach in 1757 is used to assert a systemic Prussian advantage that is misleading, not least for the 1740s when French forces in the Low Countries were commanded by Saxe, an outstanding operational commander, as well as an imaginative thinker on the nature of war. First-rate work on Prussia – for example, the important essay by Dennis Showalter (Chapter 16) and his *The Wars of Frederick the Great* (1996), could profitably be integrated with that on other forces in order to gain a better grasp of the extent and limitations of Prussia's comparative advantages, which otherwise tend to be seen in isolation. This is true not only of battlefield criteria, but also of 'structural' elements such as logistics. For the

Seven Years' War, this is the topic of John Keep's essay in this collection (see Chapter 9), while Perjés' piece (Chapter 4), although written within the constraints of Marxist determinism, has much to offer on logistics for the late seventeenth century (see also Lynn, 1993a, 1993b).

Noting subjects that require study helps emphasize the dynamic character of the subject. Not only has it not been 'done', but there are also important intellectual questions that repay consideration. The essays in Part I of this book on War and Society, a much tilled but still valuable field, serve to remind us that it is an approach that is valid at all levels in society and for those who were combatants, as well as for others such as victims. Thus Wilson's essay on German women and war (Chapter 2) draws attention to the wide-ranging impact of military service and conflict. The war and society approach also offers a variety of ways to consider military history from the peripheries (see, for example, Mackillop and Murdoch, 2003). One area for future work is the treatment of prisoners and civilians across cultural boundaries – for example, in the Balkans, North America and India.

A developing field which offers much is that of warfare and science, not least from the technology and culture dimension. The questions in this field are changing, as can be seen in the essays by Mork (Chapter 19) and Steele (Chapter 20). The political context is also open to interrogation. Technological change occurs mostly in response to problems that need or, rather, apparently need, to be solved. This is an aspect of the extent to which broader cultural, social and organizational issues are at stake. There has to be a desire to change, and technological change is therefore affected by cultural responses to innovation, while the expectation of such change is important to developments in military capability and warmaking. Political contexts play a role. Thus, during the French Revolution, there was relatively little new science in French warmaking but, it has been claimed, there was a new 'political will to break with tradition and apply scientific knowledge to the needs of the military on a scale that would have been difficult to imagine in the France of Louis XVI' (Forrest, 2004), p. 153).

Indeed, alongside a perception of the essential socio-cultural foundations of technological success has come a view of technology as a direct 'social construct', with social-cultural forces shaping the technology. Once adopted, societies and cultural norms are themselves shaped by that technology – not least through the consequences of economic growth and change – but the underlying initial influences remain strong. From this perspective, warfare – the form and structure that it takes, and the technology it uses – emerges as a social construct. Dethroning technology from the central position in the narrative and explanation of military capability and change, does not, however, entail denying its importance. Instead, it is necessary to adopt a more nuanced approach to the different factors that play a role, considering them not as reified concepts that compete, but, rather, in a manner that allows for the multiple character of their interaction.

The role of research in clarifying the variety of factors that played a role in responding to suggestions for change emerges in Janis Langins' *Conserving the Enlightenment. French Military Engineering from Vauban to the Enlightenment* (2004), a work that not only emphasizes the importance of institutional conservatism, but also presents it as far from foolish. Montalembert, who advanced a series of bold fortification projects, was a man of great schemes but was not given to costing proposals or detailed design. Furthermore, local topography was secondary in his thinking. What was important was the basic design, which determined whether or not a fortification was capable of withstanding attack. For him, Reason was independent of Nature and dominated it: the accidents of terrain and specificities of location could be subordinated to the theoretical plan. Montalembert's drawbacks help explain opposition from engineers, but so also does the weight of the past, in the shape of Vauban's prestigious reputation. Rather than see themselves as individual inventors, as Montalembert did, engineers saw themselves as a corps.

Aside from theoretical discussion, on which see Dennis Showalter's essay at Chapter 21, the military history of the period will change as research extends, in particular to take advantage of the opportunities opened up by the fall of the Iron Curtain. Generally seen as a completed political development, this in fact is an incomplete cultural project, as the long-standing tendency to regard Eastern Europe as primitive remains all too potent (Woolf, 1994; Poe, 2001). The impact of the problems that Western European scholars face with Eastern European languages may well be lessened as research flourishes in Eastern Europe and is presented to the outside world in English. Topics that could be probed include the Saxon and Polish campaigns against the Turks in the 1690s and the War of Polish Succession in Poland itself, a subject that has been generally neglected. From the 1740s until the 1790s, the Prussian army enjoyed the highest reputation in Europe, but this led to an undervaluation of the achievement of the Russians, who had demonstrated fighting quality, unit cohesion, discipline and persistence on the battlefield against the Prussians in the late 1750s. In their wars with the Turks in 1768–74 and 1787–92, the Russians went on to display flexibility and success.

Research on developments in Eastern Europe needs, however, to abandon the conceptions framed on a Western European teleology, not least by addressing the extent of 'sub-state' violence. The imperial character of states in Eastern Europe was matched by an often only limited control over frontier regions, such as Transylvania and Ukraine, especially in the late seventeenth century, and it is necessary to devote appropriate attention to their military history. It is also important to consider elements that cannot be so readily seen as 'proto-states' (Subtelny, 1986; Longworth, 1969; Thomson, 1994).

An account of military activity that gives weight to warriors who were only imperfectly within state structures, and indeed were sometimes classed as brigands, can be matched by an (overlapping but not coterminous) reconceptualization of war so that it is not simply seen in terms of state-to-state conflict. Instead, the multiple concepts, causes and consequences of violence repay consideration (Ruff, 2001), not least so that the social dimension is understood not in terms only of war and society but, more generally, as violence and society.

Violence in society was mostly waged, handled and mediated without the intervention of the military, for both ideological/cultural and prudential/practical reasons. Nevertheless, the absence of police forces ensured that when it was considered appropriate for central authorities to act, then the response was to the military. The role of armies in social and political control is a subject that has received insufficient attention and deserves more consideration. The absence of police forces meant that troops were frequently used for policing purposes; but the limited nature of royal control in many, especially frontier, regions was such that the army was the appropriate solution anyway. Although there were fewer popular risings in the period 1650–1780 than in the previous 130 years, there were still many, and some, such as those in Brittany in 1675, Bohemia in 1680 and 1775, and Transylvania in 1784–85, were large-scale (Black, 1999, pp. 157–62). Troops were also used in response to urban disorder, as in London in 1780. This led to a role for fortified positions away from external frontiers. Louis XIV built a citadel at Marseille, while, after suppressing the rebellion of Messina in Sicily in 1678, Charles II of Spain imposed a substantial garrison in a new citadel.

This underlines the multiple nature of military tasking, which, as is generally the case, serves as a critique of the notion of best practice and a clear hierarchy in capability (Black, 2004b). The role of combating what was defined as disorder in society also highlights the issue of discipline within the military. There were mutinies (see Wilson, 1994) as well as the more commonplace, but underresearched, processes of desertion and evasion of instructions, but it is striking that rulers felt it safer to arm subjects, rather than, for example, following the more expensive, but socially less challenging, process of hiring mercenaries. This emphasizes the extent to which revolutionary sentiment among the majority of the population was limited, and also highlights the fact that the social politics of the military was not simply cooperation between the Crown and the élite, on which see the important essay by Storrs and Scott (Chapter 1).

The armies of the period were 'standing' (that is, permanent) forces under the direct control of rulers. The spread of conscription altered the social politics of military service, although systems of conscription were less effective than in the twentieth century, not least because of the limited amount of information at the disposal of the state and the weakness of its policing power. In 1693 each Prussian province was ordered to provide a certain number of recruits, which was achieved by conscription, largely of peasants. Such systems increased control over the peasantry, who were less able than mercenaries to adopt a contractual approach towards military service.

These recruitment practices were an important aspect of rising state military power. New recruitment systems were mediated by aristocratic officers, but they reflected an enhanced control on the part of government, and there was no longer a figure equivalent to Wallenstein – the independent entrepreneur who raised and commanded armies for Emperor Ferdinand II in the 1620s and 1630s, and was finally assassinated when his loyalty became suspect. Independent military entrepreneurship no longer undermined governmental political and operational control of the military, and this enhanced the ability to think and act effectively in strategic and operational terms. The increase in discipline, planning and organizational regularity and predictability made it less difficult to implement plans.

The greater effectiveness of military forces can be variously gauged – and there are counter-examples to most generalizations – but was certainly more marked by the late eighteenth century than it had been in the mid-seventeenth. For example, Austria's military culture became characterized more by regulation than by improvisation. A new transport corps was created in 1771, and the supply system was centralized (Hochedlinger, 2003, p. 304). Enhanced organizational capability was not simply a matter of financing, supplying or moving armies, but also improved the organizational and operational effectiveness of individual units. The Europeans moved mostly towards a large-scale rationalization of such units: they were to have uniform sieges, armaments, clothing, command strategies and so on. Such developments made it easier to implement drill techniques that maximized firepower. Allied and subsidized units could be expected to fight in an identical fashion with 'national units', and the Europeans extended this model to India, training local units to fight as they did. This was a marked contrast to the situation in the Asiatic empires where there were major differences between core and ancillary troops.

The social contours of military service are generally treated in broadbrush terms, but it is probable that, just as élite behaviour was affected by individual preference, factional politics, and family traditions and strategies, so there was considerable variety within the groups sometimes undifferentiated as soldiers and peasantry. The regional variations in recruitment found in France would have been seen elsewhere, while the complex web of assumptions and rituals that produced unit cohesion would have constrained as well as made possible the exercise of authority, and also ensured considerable variety in practice.

Underlining the need for research serves yet again to indicate that war and the military were both distinctive and also shared in wider social and political processes, especially shifts in the relationships between socio-political groups, and this has to be grasped if the intellectual challenge of the subject is to be addressed. Yet this dynamism does not match the search for another dynamism in the shape of change that concerns much scholarship. The extent to which there was change in particular portions of the period, and the causes and nature of this change, have been debated, with particular attention devoted to the implications of the transition from matchlock musket and pike to flintlock and bayonet (Black, 1994; Lynn 2001). Furthermore, the respective merits of the developments seen under Louis XIV, Peter the Great, Marlborough, Eugene of Saxony, Frederick the Great, and in the closing years of the *ancien régime* have all been discussed.

As already indicated, some of this literature is flawed because of its assumption of the paradigm power, clear hierarchy and obvious tasking model, but that does not lessen the challenge of assessing the quality of change. The resilience of Austrian forces in the 1790s, and the degree to which French warmaking in the 1790s and 1800s built on pre-Revolutionary developments (on which see Ross at Chapter 18), indicate that the French Revolution did not make redundant what had come earlier, a situation even more clearly exemplified by continued British success at sea. This suggests not only a strength of *ancien régime* structures and appropriateness of tactics with reference to the parameters of the period, but also that the politics of the 1790s bear a major responsibility for the failure to defeat Revolutionary France (Schroeder, 1994).

Furthermore, once the notions that conservative societies lack the capacity for reform, and that they are necessarily weaker than revolutionary counterparts, are challenged then the empirical can be joined to the conceptual in rejecting the notion of *ancien régime* redundancy. This offers another approach to the issue of earlier change. Rather than seeing a fundamental problem that required reform, it is possible to argue that the challenges – namely, the tasks of the moment and those seen as likely to arise – were far more specific and contingent in terms of what would subsequently be referred to as strategic culture. This may appear to offer a rather bitty and inconsequential account of the period, but in fact it reflects the absence of a dominant teleology.

As recently as two decades ago, when meta-narratives of military history were written in terms of such a teleology – specifically the move towards total war capability and doctrine, especially with the maximization of destructiveness through the enhancement of firepower – such a conclusion would appear lame and, indeed, as a recognition of irrelevance. Indeed, the period was seen as important largely in terms of the progenitors of modernity supposedly offered by the American War of Independence and the French Revolutionary Wars (Black, 2001, pp. 13–36). Now, as the multiple character of modern warfare can be better understood, so the very process of modernization can be seen to involve far more continuity or non-linear development than was hitherto appreciated. In addition, modern interest in limited warfare makes aspects of the doctrine and practice of *ancien régime* conflict appear important, although, in practice, its limited character (within the parameters of what was judged possible) should not be stressed.

Although it is planned that naval power and warfare will be covered as part of another volume, a number of points need to be made in the context of this one. First, the emphasis on variety seen here can be paralleled. This may appear surprising, as the focus on ships of the line in the literature appears to suggest a similarity, while the period saw the large-scale deployment of ships of the line in Mediterranean waters – for example, by the English in the 1650s and from the 1690s, and by the Dutch and the French in the struggle over control of Sicily during the Dutch War of 1672–78. Furthermore, the decision by Peter the Great to build up a navy of ships of the line similar to that of other European powers rested in part on direct emulation, not least through Peter's visit to shipyards in Western Europe and through the hiring of Western experts. It was also maintained by his successors, most prominently by Catherine the Great (r. 1762–96).

Nevertheless, there were other naval forces that need consideration. In shallow waters, such as the Gulf of Finland, galleys proved more useful, and warships of the type of ships of the line were similarly of little value in rivers. River gunboats are generally ignored by naval (and military) historians, both of this period and of others, but they were important, particularly on the rivers of the Balkans and southern Russia, such as the Danube and the Don, in conflicts between the Turks and their neighbours.

Even if the focus is solely on ships of the line, which were, indeed, the most important type of warship, it is necessary to note a parallel with land warfare in which the form, like that of musket–pike–cavalry cooperation in the late seventeenth century and musket plus bayonet–cavalry cooperation over the following century, could include important variations. As with land forces, these focused on specifications, particularly firepower, defensive strength, speed and manoeuvrability. These specifications arose largely in response to particular taskings. Thus, for warships, there were different emphases, including the extent to which ships were expected to cruise to the Indies and to take part in line-of-battle artillery exchanges. Command skills on both land and sea involved understanding and taking advantage of the capabilities arising from specifications, and these are lost from sight if only a uniform account of weaponry and tactics is offered.

This argument can be extended to the equations of defensive strength and offensive firepower that helped determine the potency of fortifications and the success of sieges. Rather than assuming a perfect state of fortification, it is necessary to evaluate systems not only with reference to the specifications that led to these equations, but also within the constraints of manpower and cost, each of which were also important in judging fitness for purpose. This returns attention from the theoretical and systemic to the particular. At the crudest level, the fortifications deemed necessary to withstand a major siege in Western Europe were more than were necessary for Eastern Europe, and far more than was required to defeat a rebellion. Thus, while fitness for purpose is a crucial concept when judging the applicability of weaponry and fortifications, such fitness is frequently misunderstood by putting the stress on the capacity for employing force, rather than the ends that are sought.

An element that emerges as of crucial importance is that of strategic culture, but, although the concept is clearly of value, the detailed work required in order to flesh it out has not been tackled for much of the world. That helps explain the importance of essays such as those by Rowlands (Chapter 3) and by Storrs and Scott (Chapter 1), for they probe the social politics of command that was significant in the framing of strategic culture.

Linked to the narrow range of knowledge is the popularity of the concept of *Zeitgeist* or spirit of the age. In asserting such a coherence, often on the basis of only limited work, this approach underplays diversity and is both empirically and conceptually questionable. Concepts as varied as *Zeitgeist*, national interest and strategic culture encourage reification (turning concepts into coherent causal factors) for reasons that can be actively misleading. Drawing on neo-Platonic assumptions about inherent reality, they assert a false coherence in order to provide clear building blocks for analytical purposes. This point can be taken further by challenging the notion that paradigm/diffusion models – the spread of the methods of an allegedly paradigm power – create either a cultural space in warmaking or, indeed, bridge such spaces as this spread takes place. Instead, the emphasis can be on how the selective character of borrowing, both within and between such spaces, reflected the limited validity of employing terms such as early modern and European, as if they described an inherent reality and/or a widespread practice.

This can be taken further by questioning the use of particular texts and writers to describe the ideas dominant in particular conjunctures, and thus the military culture of the period. Aside from the problems faced in establishing the textual history of particular works and the details of their writers, there is the issue of the typicality of what survives and the questionable nature of the relationship between literature and practice. Yet, it is necessary to consider texts in order to provide alternatives to the use of practice in order to understand assumptions. As the discussion of military culture focuses on perception – of norms, problems, opportunities, options, methods and success – this poses more serious analytical problems than those of establishing the nature of battle.

These points underline the looseness of the cultural description in military history, as well as the difficulty of employing the concept as either precise analytical term or methodology, but they do not undermine the value of the perspective. Instead, a synergy with the technological approach appears most attractive. Such a synergy would focus on issues such as the perception of improvement, as well as processes of learning and norm-creation. In this synergy, it will be necessary to be suggestive and descriptive, not assertive and prescriptive. However, that is in accord with the nature of scholarship: history as question and questioning, not history as answer.

Similarly, strategic culture offers a possible synergy with political dimensions, as the pressures arising from international relations are important in the setting of goals and the tasking that helps determine doctrine and procurement and that drives strategy. There has been no systematic study of strategic culture in the period, and indeed work on strategy is often limited: instead, the focus tends to be operational and tactical, or to take the war and society approach. The absence of such a study suggests not only a need for clear research but also a dimension that needs to be built into other perspectives. In particular, it is unclear how best to address the role of *gloire*, loosely translated as the pursuit of glory in military objectives. An emphasis on *gloire* appears to offer a non-rational account of policy – one in keeping with the dominant role of rulers and the prevalence of dynastic considerations – but this emphasis, role and prevalence were certainly rational as far as the political purpose, ethos and structure of states were concerned.

If this provides the wider context for strategic culture, it leaves more specific choices unclear. In particular, there is uncertainty about the normative character of war and territorial expansion. These brought exemplary purpose and glory to rulers and aristocracy, and success acted as a lubricant of obedience in crown–élite relations, but there were many occasions on which international crises did not lead to war: for example, the confrontation between the Alliances of Hanover and Vienna in 1725–29, between Britain, France, Spain and Austria in 1730, between Portugal and Spain in 1735–36, or between Prussia and Austria in 1790 and Prussia and Russia in 1791. The reasons for the avoidance of war require investigation from the perspectives of strategic culture and causes of war, while the war plans drawn up in such crises also need analysis. Indeed, a systematic listing and analysis of such plans would be a worthwhile project.

The war and society dimension offers the reflection that strategic culture can also be considered at different social levels, particularly in states such as Britain and the United Provinces (modern Netherlands) that had, in representative assemblies and a relatively free press, a means for such politics.

The extent to which 'the military' made a contribution to strategic cultures can be appreciated when it is realized that the military was not separate from political and social hierarchies, but intermixed with them. For example, the British Captain General in the mid-1740s was none other than William, Duke of Cumberland, the second (and favourite), son of George II and a player in ministerial politics. Particular socio-political groups clearly had distinctive goals, but the extent to which these could be advanced through the overlapping worlds of court, ministerial, aristocratic and military factions, and the consequences for military planning, are unclear, and largely unstudied. Yet, there were choices, most obviously when powers (that is, rulers or ruling groups) engaged on several fronts and had to decide how best to make a decision between commitments, and politics were clearly often involved. This was true, for example, of France in the Dutch, Nine Years', Spanish, Polish and Austrian Succession Wars and the Seven Years' War, and of successive Austrian Habsburgs commitments in Italy, the Empire (Germany) and the Balkans. Much of the discussion of the operational history of these conflicts is limited because of a failure to relate it to the strategic dimension in this fashion. For Britain, it is possible to see a public debate, as with the tension between 'blue water' policies and Continental interventionism, or with reference to sending troops to Germany in the Seven Years' War. Similar issues affected other states, but the discussion was less public.

Different strategic cultures also affected the perception of other states, and thus the dynamics of alliance diplomacy, both pre-war and wartime. This, in turn, had an influence on policies and on particular military goals, underlining the extent to which there was a dynamic character to strategic culture. This contributes to an indeterminate nature for military history that is anathema to those who seek the certainties of uniforms, drill and (at least apparently) tactical detail, but this indeterminacy matches the uncertainty of contemporaries. Indeed, the clarity of some modern treatments of historical developments sits uncomfortably with, for example, the uncertainty about best practice. Thus, action–reaction cycles in which one power sought to counter the advances made by another, as when the French responded to Marlborough's battlefield tactics in the 1700s, and the Austrians to Frederick the Great's oblique order attack in the 1750s, indicated the dynamic nature of the challenges facing generals. In the latter case, Frederick II in 1745 developed the attack in oblique order, so as to be able to concentrate overwhelming strength against a portion of the linear formation of the opposing army. Frederick devised a series of methods for strengthening one end of his line and attacking with it, while minimizing the exposure of the weaker end. This depended on the speedy execution of complex manoeuvres for which well-drilled and well-disciplined troops were essential. By the late 1750s, however, the Austrians had developed effective counter-tactics, retaining reserves that could be moved to meet the Prussian attack.

The challenges facing generals were not only a matter of responding to new developments, but also the more general problem of gaining comparative advantage. If armies were evenly matched, battles were either inconclusive encounters or were determined by other factors, such as terrain, the availability and employment of reserves, and the results of cavalry clashes on the flanks. The extent to which experienced and well-deployed infantry were usually safe against frontal attack threatened a tactical impasse in infantry warfare that led to a particular need for skills in generalship.

The dynamic nature of challenges was also true of the variety of environments that generals and their troops found themselves in. The large-scale English commitment in Spain during the War of the Spanish Succession was matched by the march of a large force to Blenheim in Bavaria in 1704, the furthest east commitment of such an English army on the European mainland. Russian troops moved into Mecklenburg in 1716–17, and French forces towards Vienna and into Prague in 1741. Unexpected tasks included the Austrians facing civil insurrection in the city of Genoa during the War of the Austrian Succession and the French conquering Corsica in 1769–70 in the face of popular opposition in its difficult mountains. Yet again, the variety and unpredictability of military tasks, and thus the difficulty of judging capability and establishing a clear hierarchy of military proficiency, are underlined.

The tension between research and theorization is a common one in history, and military history is no exception. The statements frequently made about *ancien régime* warfare and its 'locating' in terms of general theories appear misleading, if not glib, as any consideration of the excellent detailed work available suggests. Warfare within Europe in this period can be dismissed as rigid and anachronistic only if a very narrow and misleading view of it is taken. At the same time, its dynamism and flexibility should not detract attention from the variety of military systems and conflict elsewhere in the world. This comparative dimension is an important topic for research and discussion, and should not be reduced to a consideration only of warfare between Europeans and non-Europeans.

## References

Black, J.M. (1994), *European Warfare 1660–1815*, London: University College London Press.

Black, J.M. (1999), *Eighteenth-Century Europe* (2nd edn), Basingstoke: Macmillan.

Black, J.M. (2001), *Western Warfare, 1775–1882*, Bloomington: Indiana University Press.

Black, J.M. (2004a), *Kings, Nobles and Commoners. States and Societies in Early Modern Europe: A Revisionist History*, London: I.B. Tauris.

Black, J.M. (2004b), *Rethinking Military History*, London: Routledge.

Forrest, A. (2004), 'Enlightenment, Science and Army Reform in Eighteenth-Century France', in M. Crook, W. Doyle and A. Forrest (eds), *Enlightenment and Revolution: Essays in Honour of Norman Hampson*, Aldershot: Ashgate.

Hanlon, G. (1998), *The Twilight of a Military Tradition. Italian Aristocrats and European Conflicts, 1560–1800*, London: University College London Press.

Hill, J.M. (1986), *Celtic Warfare, 1595–1763*, Edinburgh: John Donald.

Hochedlinger, M. (2003), *Austria's Wars of Emergence: War, State and Society in the Habsburg Monarchy, 1683–1797*, London and New York: Longman.

James, A. (2004), *The Navy and Government in Early Modern France, 1572–1661*, London: Royal Historical Society.

Langins, J. (2004), *Conserving the Enlightenment: French Military Engineering from Vauban to the Enlightenment*, Cambridge, MASS: MIT Press.

Longworth, P. (1969), *The Cossacks*, London: Constable.

Lynn, J. (1993a), 'How War Fed War: The Tax of Violence and Contributions during the *Grand Siècle*', *Journal of Modern History*, **45**, pp. 286–310.

Lynn, J. (1993b), 'Food, Funds and Fortresses: Resource Mobilization and Positional Warfare in the Campaigns of Louis XIV', in J. Lynn (ed.), *Feeding Mars: Logistics in Western Warfare from the Middle Ages to the Present*, Boulder, CO: Westview Press.

Lynn, J. (1997), *Giant of the Grand Siècle: The French Army, 1610–1715*, Cambridge: Cambridge University Press.
Lynn, J. (2001), 'Forging the Western Army in Seventeenth-Century France', in M. Knox and W. Murray (eds), *The Dynamics of Military Revolution 1300–2050*, Cambridge: Cambridge University Press, pp. 35–56.
Mckillop, A. and Murdoch, S. (eds) (2003), *Military Governors and Imperial Frontiers c. 1600–1800: A Study of Scotland and Empires*, Leiden: Brill.
Parker, G. (1996), *Military Revolution. Military Innovation and the Rise of the West* (2nd edn), Cambridge: Cambridge University Press. First published 1988.
Parker, G. (2003), 'Random Thoughts of a Hedgehog', *Historically Speaking*, **4**(4), p. 13.
Parrott, D. (2002), *Richelieu's Army. War, Government and Society in France, 1624–1642*, Cambridge: Cambridge University Press.
Poe, M.T. (2001), *'A People Born to Slavery'. Russia in Early Modern European Ethnography, 1475–1748*, Ithaca, NY: Cornell University Press.
Roberts, M. (1956), 'The Military Revolution 1560–1660', lecture delivered at Belfast and reprinted in his *Essays in Swedish History*, London: Weidenfeld and Nicolson, 1967.
Rowlands, G. (2002), *The Dynastic State and the Army under Louis XIV: Royal Service and Private Interest, 1661–1701*, Cambridge: Cambridge University Press.
Ruff, J.R. (2001), *Violence in Early Modern Europe 1500–1800*, Cambridge: Cambridge University Press.
Satterfield, G. (2003), *Princes, Posts and Partisans: The Army of Louis XIV and Partisan Warfare in the Netherlands, 1673–1678*, Leiden: Brill.
Schroeder, P.W. (1994), *The Transformation of European Politics*, Oxford: Clarendon Press.
Subtelny, O. (1986), *Domination of Eastern Europe. Native Nobilities and Foreign Absolutism 1500–1715*, Gloucester: McGill-Queen's University Press.
Thomson, J.E. (1994), *Mercenaries, Pirates, and Sovereigns: State-Building and Extraterritorial Violence in Early Modern Europe*, Princeton, NJ: Princeton University Press.
Wilson, P.H. (1994), 'Violence and the Rejection of Authority in Eighteenth-Century Germany: The Case of the Swabian Mutinies in 1757', *German History*, **12**, pp. 1–26.
Wilson, P.H. (2001), 'War in Early Modern German History', *German History*, **19**, pp. 419–38.
Woolf, L. (1994), *Inventing Eastern Europe: The Map of Civilization on the Mind of the Enlightenment*, Stanford, CT: Stanford University Press.

# Part I
# War and Society

# [1]

# The Military Revolution and the European Nobility, c. 1600–1800

*Christopher Storrs and H.M. Scott*

## I

Warfare was a permanent and ubiquitous feature of early modern Europe, stimulating new developments in military technology and organization. Firearms became more important and, eventually, dominant, and armies more specialized and complex. By 1600 the proportions of infantry, artillery, and cavalry were roughly equal. Thereafter, the proportion of cavalry declined even more rapidly, while its nature also underwent fundamental change. The heavily armoured knights, the backbone of medieval warfare, came to be replaced by lighter horsemen, and the *mêlée* by the more disciplined – though less effective – *caracole*. New artillery made traditional fortifications redundant and necessitated much reconstruction along more modern lines. Armies were broken down into smaller units, while training and discipline became more important. Above all, the military forces of most states grew rapidly in size, reaching a peak in the first decade of the eighteenth century, and were composed increasingly of troops not provided directly by the nobility. Campaigns simultaneously became longer and forces continued in existence when peace was restored. The need to recruit, train, pay, and supply these enlarged standing armies demanded more effective military organization. This was mainly provided by the central authority, the state: increasingly (so it is argued) the only agency which could effectively mobilize society for war.[1]

The continuing debate on the 'Military Revolution' has concentrated upon its strategic, tactical, organizational, and administrative dimensions.

[1] The thesis of the 'Military Revolution' was originally outlined by Michael Roberts in an inaugural lecture, published as *The Military Revolution, 1560–1660* (Belfast, 1956), and reprinted in M. Roberts, *Essays in Swedish History* (London, 1967), pp. 195–225. It has frequently been restated and summarized, most authoritatively by G. Parker, *The Military Revolution: Military Innovation and the Rise of the West 1500–1800* (Cambridge, 1988), and most recently by B. Downing, *The Military Revolution and Political Change* (Princeton, NJ, 1991), ch. 3, and J. Black, *A Military Revolution? Military Change and European Society 1550–1800* (London, 1991), pp. 1 ff.

## 2 Christopher Storrs and H.M. Scott

Historians have neglected and even ignored the social and political aspects. Yet the transformation of warfare had immense implications for Europe's society and political organization. This was particularly true where the nobility was concerned. Since the central Middle Ages its *raison d'être* – the justification for its privileged position in state and society – had been that it was the fighting class (*defensores*). Whereas the First Estate, the clergy, prayed and the Third Estate worked (to provide for the other two in their more essential tasks), the Second Estate provided protection and military muscle. In some languages the very words for 'nobility' (or parts of it) derived from this function: for example *chevalerie* (French) and *cavalieri* (Italian). The European elite was in origin the men on horseback, the mounted knights who had dominated the battlefields of the Middle Ages. That special position was undermined by the Military Revolution. Thereafter the nobles were no longer the principal group who fought, nor were they primarily responsible for organizing and providing the means of defence and warfare. The commitment, in resources and time, now demanded of the would-be warrior noble was far greater than in the essentially seasonal and sporadic warfare of former centuries. Equipment now cost more and fighting was less seasonal than in the past, while the growth of standing armies tended to tie the noble officer to his particular unit for much of the year. There were fewer opportunities for the individual feat of valour typical of the medieval (noble) knight in larger, more impersonal armies. The expansion of state control meant, especially after 1660, the subordination of an increasingly professional, disciplined officer caste to governments less concerned with rank and hierarchy than with effectiveness and obedience. This, it is usually argued, meant the end of the nobility's claims to be the military profession *par excellence*.[2]

Similar perspectives are to be found in the growing literature on the early modern nobility. Its declining capacity and even willingness to play an effective military role were central to the theories elaborated from the 1960s of an early seventeenth-century crisis of the English and French nobilities, and to a lesser extent of the Spanish too, symbolized by the image of the anachronistic mounted knight, Don Quixote. According to some scholars, the nobles' failure to fulfil their military vocation obliged them to seek a new justification for their privileged social position. It was often found in birth and lineage, rather than in honour, merit, and function. Historians of other states – Denmark, Piedmont-Savoy and Portugal – have reached broadly similar conclusions, as have those of supranational military institutions such as the Knights of Malta, each new case

[2] Roberts, *Military Revolution*. There is an enormous literature on the society of 'orders': G. Duby, *The Three Orders: Feudal Society Imagined* (English trans., Chicago, 1980); O. Niccoli, *I sacerdoti, i guerrieri, i contadini: storia di un immagine della società* (Turin, 1979); P. Burke, 'The Language of Orders in Early Modern Europe' and W. Doyle, 'Myths of Order and Ordering Myths', in M. Bush, ed., *Social Orders and Social Classes in Europe since 1500: Studies in Social Stratification* (London, 1992), pp. 1–12, 218–29.

being fitted into a European pattern in which the Second Estate supposedly no longer finds its *raison d'être* in war.[3]

The nobility's loss of its military role and the growing gulf between itself and the profession of arms – in other words, its 'demilitarization' – by 1700 is now a commonplace of writing on early modern history. It has been restated recently by the leading British historian of the European elite, Michael Bush. According to Dr Bush, except where private noble military power survived, principally in Poland-Lithuania, Hungary and the Highlands of Scotland – all regions where the new military technology had a delayed and limited impact and where magnate power was in any case unusually strong – nobles were forced to adapt to the loss of armed might consequent on the growth of professional, national armies. In fact, as will be argued in this article, the nobility, far from losing its military function by 1700, probably enhanced this role. It was well entrenched in the upper ranks of all European armies on the eve of the French Revolution and continued to identify itself, and to be identified very closely, with the military profession, albeit in a redefined way. The precise degree of penetration varied from country to country, but the nobility's continued military pre-eminence represented an important achievement, with broader implications for its social and political role and for its enduring importance and power.[4]

Far from being the inevitable victims of the Military Revolution, noblemen were the principal agents of these changes and benefitted considerably from them. Above all, the rapid expansion of armies, particularly in the major continental states, and the simultaneous elaboration of more stratified and sophisticated command structures, created opportunities on a new scale for noblemen to find military careers and at least some income. These armies, moreover, were less modern and bureaucratic

[3] G. Parker, 'The Military Revolution – a Myth?', *Journal of Modern History* XLVII (1976), repr. in Parker, *Spain and the Netherlands 1559–1659: Ten Studies* (rev. edn., London, 1990), pp. 86–103; François Billaçois, 'La Crise de la noblesse européenne (1550–1650)', *Revue d'histoire moderne et contemporaine* XXIII (1976), pp. 258–77, esp. pp. 269–70; M.C. Mandlmayr and K.G. Vocelka, 'Vom Adelsaufgebot zum stehenden Heer', in G. Klingenstein and H. Lutz, eds., *Spezialforschung und 'Gesamtgeschichte': Beispiele und Methodenfragen zur Geschichte des frühen Neuzeit* (Vienna, 1981), pp. 112–25; L. Stone, *The Crisis of the Aristocracy 1558–1641* (Oxford, 1965), ch. 5; D. Bitton, *The French Nobility in Crisis, 1560–1640* (Stanford, CA, 1969), pp. 27 ff.; J.A. Maravall, *Poder, honor y elites en el siglo XVII* (Madrid, 1979), pp. 37 ff.; F. Pereira Marques, *Exercito e sociedade em Portugal no declino do Antigo Regime e advento do Liberalismo* (Lisbon, 1981), pp. 47 ff.; E. Schalk, *From Valor to Pedigree: Ideas of Nobility in France in the 16th and 17th Centuries* (Princeton, NJ, 1986), p. xiv, 202; K.J.V. Jespersen, 'Social Change and Military Revolution in Early Modern Europe: Some Danish Evidence', *Historical Journal* XXVI (1983), pp. 1–13; W. Barberis, *Le armi del principe: la tradizione militare sabauda* (Turin, 1988).

[4] H. Kamen, *European Society 1500–1700* (London, 1984), p. 98; Schalk, *From Valor to Pedigree*, pp. xiv, 202: M. Bush, 'An Anatomy of Nobility', esp. pp. 41–2. In the 1970s a number of studies in French attempted to redress the balance, but only one was translated into English: A. Corvisier, *Armées et sociétés en Europe de 1494 à 1789* (Paris, 1975), published in English as *Armies and Societies in Europe 1494–1789* (Bloomington, IN, and London, 1979), pt. 2; J.-P. Labatut, *Les Noblesses européennes de la fin du XV[e] à la fin du XVIII[e] siècle* (Paris, 1973); and J. Meyer, *Noblesses et pouvoirs dans l'Europe d'Ancien Régime* (Paris, 1973), pp. 43–4.

than often supposed and this enhanced the nobility's role. The assertion of state control after 1660 was everywhere incomplete. Government replaced the military enterprisers who had flourished particularly during the Thirty Years War (1618–48), but important aspects of the older contracting system persisted in the armies of the later seventeenth and even eighteenth centuries. The very speed of the numerical expansion was itself a considerable obstacle to the efforts of central governments to exert complete authority over their armies. Noble officers long remained responsible for important functions. The nature of these varied from country to country. In the French army, the provision of horses and equipment remained the responsibility of the 'captains' (that is to say, the officers who ran companies but who may not always have had that exact rank). Elsewhere, the captains or colonels were often responsible for the provision of clothing, while in some states recruitment long remained partly and even wholly in the hands of noblemen. In certain countries, notably Brandenburg-Prussia, the Habsburg Monarchy, and France, regiments were still the property of their noble officers well into the eighteenth century.[5] The consequence was that stronger links were forged between Europe's elite and its armies which would endure into the twentieth century. Far from 'demilitarizing' the Second Estate, the transformation of warfare professionalized the European nobility, redefining and perpetuating its military role. The elite's own hierarchy was directly transferred onto the officer corps. The numerically abundant lesser nobility found careers as lieutenants and captains, and sometimes rose higher, while the great families and the Court aristocracy dominated the High Command. The overall result was to be nothing less than the transformation of the Second Estate into a caste of military professionals.

## II

The Military Revolution undoubtedly affected the nobility's traditional power and function. The principal victim of these changes was the heavily armoured knight, whose importance had been eroded by English archers during the Hundred Years War and was subsequently destroyed by the gunpowder revolution and by changes in infantry tactics and weaponry. Cavalry long remained influential in the more mobile warfare of central, eastern, and south-eastern Europe, but everywhere its functions and thus its numbers were being severely reduced, both absolutely and even more as a proportion of total forces. By the eighteenth century, if not earlier, artillery and infantry dominated the battlefield, while the cavalry was used to provide mass and shock (*l'arme blanche*) against a broken enemy line, to pursue a defeated army from the field, and for a number of minor operational functions.

[5] There is much on this survival in F. Redlich, *The German Military Enterpriser and His Work Force* (2 vols., Wiesbaden, 1964–5) II, pp. 5–111 *passim*.

This transformation was accompanied by a striking and final decline in the importance of the feudal levy (principally the system of knights' service) as a means of providing armed forces. In southern Spain, the tradition of calling on the lesser nobility to perform such military service (the so-called *caballeros cuantiosos*) declined after the completion of the *Reconquista* in 1492, particularly after the middle of the sixteenth century, and was formally abolished in Philip III's reign in the early seventeenth century, following complaints from the Castilian Cortes that it was being abused by the Crown for fiscal purposes. After 1631, Philip IV of Spain allowed the greater nobility to commute the military service they owed for an annual payment, the so-called *lanzas*. This and the tensions provoked in England during the 1630s by Charles I's efforts to turn knights' service into fiscal income make clear that noble military obligations were often being exploited as a form of taxation and were valued less and less for any direct military contribution. In France, the feudal levy (the *ban* and *arrière-ban*), mainly composed of nobles, had long been in decline, and when it was summoned – as it was in 1623 – its uselessness became apparent. Louis XIV's efforts to revive it in a number of frontier provinces in 1674 during the Dutch War and again in 1685 and 1695 all proved disastrous. Thereafter, that service was commuted for cash, and it seems to have been abandoned altogether after 1697, although theoretically it might still be summoned in a crisis.

The same pattern can be seen in Denmark, where the seventeenth-century struggle with Sweden, together with the ill-fated intervention in the Thirty Years War, created a more modern army and navy supported primarily by taxation. The knights' service provided by the nobility (*rostjeneste*) had been one of the traditional elements in the royal army. It was now superseded as a source of military power by the conscript militia established in 1614 and by the large-scale use of mercenaries after 1637. The nobility's privileges, however, ultimately depended upon the knights' service which it performed, and this ensured that the levy was initially remodelled by the Danish crown. *Rostjeneste* was suspended after the introduction of absolute monarchy in 1660 and seems to have been formally abolished in 1679, after a short-lived revival in the emergency of the war against Sweden during the 1670s. A similar decline was apparent in the small state of Hesse-Kassel, where the *Ritterschaft* was permitted to give cash in 1654 and 1672 – the last two occasions when the levy was imposed, until its revival in the final decade of the eighteenth century.

An identical trend is evident in Piedmont-Savoy. By the end of the seventeenth century, the feudal levy (*cavalcata*) was only summoned in an emergency and even then commuted to cash payments: it was in practice a way of levying extraordinary taxation upon the nobility. By 1700 the feudal levy had become irrelevant from a purely military point of view. It was regarded virtually everywhere as an exceptional measure and even as a form of taxation, since it was almost always commuted:

6 **Christopher Storrs and H.M. Scott**

only in Poland-Lithuania and Hungary was the obligation even theoretically maintained during the eighteenth century. Indeed, the Hungarian army annihilated by Napoleon at Györ in 1809 consisted largely of noble levies. This was quite exceptional. Everywhere the principal instruments of warfare were now the more permanent forces raised, paid and controlled directly by the state.[6]

This trend was accompanied by a sharp decline in the nobility's own military potential. By the seventeenth century the private armies (or, as in England, retinues) which nobles had sometimes led to war, or employed in their private disputes, were disappearing. It was not that the elite was entirely losing its capacity to raise military forces on its own estates and in its own localities. Even in England, the peerage's capacity to raise men was far from negligible – witness its contribution to the Parliamentary and Royalist forces during the Civil War. This had its parallel on the Continent in the role of the grandees of Castile and the nobles of Naples in raising forces for Philip IV during the Thirty Years War. Another important reminder of the limitations of state power and the elite's continuing role as a provider of troops was the activities of the so-called German 'military enterprisers', almost all of them nobles, on behalf of the Austrian Habsburgs in particular during the same conflict. Yet these were increasingly the exception, as states sought to assume more and more direct responsibility for the enlarged forces they were maintaining. During the seventeenth century in most parts of Europe the nobility's private forces were declining numerically both in absolute terms and even more in proportion to those of the Crown. One of the earliest and clearest examples of this trend had come in the Papal States. Following the curbing of the nobility there shortly before 1600, their military retainers had been drafted into the papal army or forced into service abroad against the Turks. The principal exception to the general pattern was, once again, Poland-Lithuania. There the great magnates, especially in the eastern regions, sought to maintain substantial armed forces of their own, and certainly long retained a considerable military potential. The eighteenth-century

[6] Jespersen, 'Social Change'; L. Jespersen, 'The *Machtstaat* in Seventeenth-Century Denmark', *Scandinavian Journal of History* X (1985), pp. 271–304; A. Dominguez Ortiz, 'Caballeros cuantiosos', in M. Artola, ed., *Enciclopedia de historia de España* (Madrid, 1991) IV, p. 167; M. Artola, *La hacienda del Antiguo Regimen* (Madrid, 1982), p. 103; G.W. Pedlow, *The Survival of the Hessian Nobility 1770–1870* (Princeton, NJ, 1988), pp. 28–9; M.S. Anderson, *War and Society in Europe of the Old Regime 1618–1789* (London, 1988), pp. 131–2; A. Corvisier, ed., *Histoire militaire de la France* I: *Des origines à 1715*, ed. P. Contamine (Paris, 1992), pp. 250, 361, 395; S. Kettering, 'The Decline of Great Noble Clientage during the Reign of Louis XIV', *Canadian Journal of History* XXIV (1989), pp. 157–77, at p. 165; A. de Salucces, *Histoire militaire du Piémont* (Turin, 1818) I, p. 220; J.T. Lukowski, *Liberty's Folly: The Polish–Lithuanian Commonwealth in the Eighteenth Century, 1697–1795* (London, 1991), p. 34; N. Davies, 'The Military Traditions of the Polish *Szlachta* 1700–1864', in B.K. Király and G.E. Rothenberg, eds., *War and Society in East Central Europe* I: *Special Topics and Generalizations on the 18th and 19th Centuries* (New York, 1979), pp. 37–46, at p. 39; Zoltán Kramár, 'The Military Ethos of the Hungarian Nobility, 1700–1848', ibid. pp. 67–81, at pp. 70, 72.

Polish army was limited to 24 000 after 1717, but in the 1760s August Czartoryski theoretically could raise between 3000 and 4000 men, Karol Stanislaw Radziwill 5000, and his father, Michael Radziwill, (in 1750) a staggering 10 000.[7]

The decline of the nobility's private military potential was not simply a matter of numbers. Noble fortifications, and the large arsenals they sometimes contained, were also becoming a thing of the past. Here the mounting costs of warfare, for new defence works and equipment, were clearly important, especially at a time when the financial position of many noble families was being undermined. This was particularly important when the cost of private fortifications were also rising rapidly. The Duke of Gandia, the leading aristocrat of the Spanish realm of Valencia, was said in the 1560s to be able to arm fifty men-at-arms and 600 arquebusiers from his private arsenal; by the 1630s this was no longer the case. The fact that aristocrats like Gandia were increasingly absent from their estates, resident (especially after 1600) in Madrid, contributed to the decline of their personal retinues by reducing opportunities for contact with those who previously had flocked to their service. A similar evolution was apparent in England, where aristocratic arsenals were at their peak during the second half of the sixteenth century but declined after 1600.

Private fortifications were a special problem in France, where the later sixteenth-century Wars of Religion had provided an opportunity for widespread improvements to existing defences and even some new construction. These defence works came in all shapes and sizes, ranging from the addition of a few walls to fortify a village or a château to formidable and well-established private fortresses. One of the most remarkable of these was at Les Baux de Provence in southern France. Lying at the south-west of the Alpilles, it was a substantial and formidable natural fortress. The problem was tackled in the early decades of the seventeenth century, as the Crown's authority was slowly restored. Louis XIII and Richelieu ordered the demolition of a number of castles and numerous smaller fortifications in the localities, mainly belonging to the nobility: this was done on an especially large scale in Languedoc, after the suppression of the Montmorency rebellion in the early 1630s. One notable victim was the fortress of Les Baux in neighbouring Provence, finally destroyed in 1632 as a reprisal for its support for Gaston d'Orléans's rising in the previous year.

7 Stone, *Crisis of the Aristocracy*, esp. pp. 199–234; J.S.A. Adamson, 'The Baronial Context of the English Civil War', *Transactions of the Royal Historical Society*, 5th series, XL (1990), pp. 93–120; A. de Reumont, *The Carafas of Maddaloni* (London, 1854), p. 186; Redlich, *German Military Enterpriser*, esp. I, part 2; C.J. Jago, 'La Corona y la aristocracia durante el regimen de Olivares: un representante de la aristocracia en la Corte', in J.H. Elliott and A. Garcia Sanz, eds., *La España del Conde Duque de Olivares: encuentro internacional sobre la España del Conde Duque celebrado en Toro los dias 15–18 septiembre de 1987* (Valladolid, 1990), pp. 375 ff.; J.H. Elliott, *Europe Divided 1559–1598* (London, 1968), pp. 370 ff.; N. Davies, *God's Playground: A History of Poland* (2 vols., Oxford, 1981) I, p. 226; A. Zamoyski, *The Polish Way* (London, 1987), p. 199.

By that time, at least one of the medieval castles in the *stato* of the noble Caracciolo di Brienza, in the kingdom of Naples, was a ruin and the others were going the same way, fit only for storage space. One dimension of the growing authority of the Roman government over the nobility of the Papal States had been its assertion of ownership over many noble castles. Everywhere private fortifications were being destroyed and royal ones built in their place. Many private fortifications in England were 'slighted' in the 1650s and not restored after 1660. This was also done by Louis XIV in Luxembourg between 1684 and 1697. Not all such destruction and reconstruction was due to the actions of the state. Nobles were themselves reconstructing and reshaping them, or building anew, in styles which made far fewer concessions to military requirements. The period saw the appearance of more residential, palatial, and peaceful noble châteaux all over Europe: for example, the more luxurious Roman palaces of the nobility of the Papal States, increasingly resident in the capital rather than in the country, or the transformation of Beloeil, in the province of Hainault in the Austrian Netherlands by Field Marshal Charles-Joseph Lamoral, Prince de Ligne (1735–1814). By the eighteenth century, old-style defensive features were often a stylistic affectation with little real military purpose.[8]

This highlighted the way in which the military and political balance had, almost everywhere, swung decisively and permanently to the Crown and its agents. It was evident in the nobility's diminishing role in the political upheavals and even rebellions during the early modern period. Already by 1528 the Neapolitan baronage no longer provoked disorder in the kingdom. In Castile, there were no major noble revolts after 1516. Despite resenting the military and financial burdens imposed by Olivares in the 1630s, the Castilian grandees did not take up arms; instead, they attempted to increase their influence at Court, in an attempt to turn their obedience to account. A generation earlier, the Aragonese nobility had prudently resisted any temptation to become involved in the 'revolt' of Aragon in 1590, ensuring that it did not escalate. This was in sharp contrast with the Bohemian nobility's role in 1618, when it spearheaded the rebellion against Vienna. Yet barely two years later its abject military weakness had been revealed by the overwhelming defeat at the battle of White Mountain. In France,

[8] Anderson, *War and Society*, p. 31; Stone, *Crisis of the Aristocracy*, pp. 217–23; T. Astarita, *The Continuity of Feudal Power: The Caracciolo di Brienza in Spanish Naples* (Cambridge, 1991), p. 122; C. Hudemann-Simon, 'Une noblesse en déclin à la fin de l'ancien régime: le rôle des circonstances et les effets des comportements dans l'échec du second ordre luxembourgeois', *Histoire, économie, société* VI (1986), pp. 78–9; Elliott, *Europe Divided*, pp. 372–3; A. Barbey, ed., *Belgique–Luxembourg* (Hachette Guides Bleus) (Paris, 1987), pp. 246 ff. (This volume contains numerous entries on individual properties belonging to the greater and lesser nobility of the southern Netherlands.) For France cf. A. Mussat, 'Château-miroir ou la tradition architecturale de la noblesse française', in B. Kopeczi and E.H. Balàzs, eds., *Noblesse française, noblesse hongroise* (Budapest and Paris, 1981), pp. 99 ff.

Louis XIII's reign saw a series of conspiracies and rebellions, but the Frondes of 1648–53 proved the last real military revolt by the aristocracy. In Piedmont-Savoy, the last noble rebellion was a generation later: that of the marquis of Parella in 1682. Despite widespread noble resentment at Victor Amadeus II's policies, these failed to provoke an armed reaction even in the confused circumstances of his abdication and the accession of his son, Charles Emanuel III. By the second half of the eighteenth century, the main public-order problem in Piedmont-Savoy, as in many other parts of Europe, was no longer the nobility but the growing body of rural and urban poor.[9]

In all these ways the Military Revolution was accompanied by a sharp decline in the nobility's armed power. The disappearance of private forces and fortifications everywhere undermined the potential for noble violence – including the island of Mallorca, where nobles had used their own troops to pursue their vendettas and feuds, and areas such as Catalonia and Naples, where they protected local bandits in return for a share of their proceeds. This tradition of lawlessness was not stamped out overnight, persisting in some areas into the eighteenth century, but its foundations were considerably weakened. Though nobles still quarrelled among themselves and resented government actions, they were a far less violent elite, and were increasingly resorting to the courts – and to the Court – to obtain favourable decisions in disputes which might, before 1600, have been settled by their own men-at-arms, often in the most bloody manner. This new attitude to the law and violence was linked to the disappearance of many great noble families from the countryside, as their normal place of residence came to be the provincial or national capital or the ruler's Court, and it reinforced the dissolution of their military potential in the localities.[10]

The crucial development everywhere was the Crown's gradual assertion of a monopoly of military power. In France, the aristocratic provincial governors had been a central element in the sixteenth-century royal forces, but their military role was coming to be eclipsed as a state-controlled standing army slowly took shape. It was accompanied by the abolition of the old medieval offices, sometimes hereditary in certain noble families, which gave them the right to command the

[9] G. Symcox, *Victor Amadeus II: Absolutism in the Savoyard State 1675–1730* (London, 1983), p. 89; Jago, 'La corona y la aristocracia'; G. Ricuperati, 'Gli strumenti dell' assolutismo sabaudo: segreterie di stato e consiglio di finanze nel XVIII secolo', *Rivista storica italiana* CIII (1991), pp. 838 ff.; A. Lovett, 'Philip II, Antonio Perez and the Kingdom of Aragon', *European History Quarterly* XVIII (1988), pp. 131 ff.

[10] P. Molas Ribalta, *Edad moderna (1474–1808)*, vol. III of *Manual de historia de España* (Madrid, 1988), pp. 287, 345–6; J.H. Elliott, 'A Provincial Aristocracy: The Catalan Ruling Class in the 16th and 17th Centuries', in Elliott, *Spain and Its World 1500–1700* (New Haven, CT, 1989), pp. 71–91; R. Kagan, 'Pleitos y poder real: la chancilleria de Valladolid (1500–1700)', *Cuadernos de investigacion historica* II (1978), pp. 291 ff. (including p. 315, analysis of plaintiffs by social group); Astarita, *Continuity of Feudal Power*, pp. 212 ff.; Jago, 'La corona y la aristocracia'; Hudemann-Simon, 'Une noblesse en déclin', pp. 92–3.

Crown's forces: notably that of constable, effectively suppressed in 1627. Though this development also occurred elsewhere, it was far from general on the Continent. More important and certainly more widespread was the state's slow but determined emergence as recruiter, paymaster, organizer, and supplier of the new standing armies. Special government departments were established or elaborated with responsibility for the army, which was almost everywhere the largest item of expenditure.[11]

Armies were also becoming more national. In earlier centuries, soldiers – principally noblemen – had served freely beyond the borders of the country in which they lived. By the eighteenth century, however, this was starting to be much more difficult, as larger states expanded their armies, thereby creating a need for officers. Rulers such as the Habsburg Emperor Charles VI and Prussia's Frederick William I were making it harder for their subjects to serve abroad, and instead aiming to make them the backbone of their own officer corps. This reduced both the possibilities of service in their own armies for the subjects of other princes and the proportion of their forces represented by the surviving foreign corps: the Swiss Guards everywhere; the *Guardias Walonas* in Bourbon Spain. This development became quite pronounced towards the end of the eighteenth century. In Spain, Italians between 1713 and 1733 and Flemings and Walloons (even Frenchmen) between 1740 and 1790 still served in the upper reaches of the royal army, though their numbers fell considerably thereafter. The second half of the eighteenth century also saw a reduction in the proportion of foreigners in the officer corps of the multi-national Austrian Habsburg dominions, and in the Danish armed forces.[12]

The pace and extent of change were far from uniform. In many respects, at least before the eighteenth century, the French experience was untypical and precocious. Yet in one respect France was behind the times, at least by comparison with states such as Denmark, Prussia, and Russia. This was in the matter of recruitment, direct royal responsibility for which was only asserted at the close of the Seven Years War. Here France was comparable to the Habsburg Monarchy and Great

[11] Anderson, *War and Society*, pp. 99 ff.; G. Parker, *The Army of Flanders and the Spanish Road 1567–1659* (Cambridge, 1976); Symcox, *Victor Amadeus II*, pp. 190 ff.; I. Roy, 'The Profession of Arms', in W. Prest, ed., *The Professions in Early Modern England* (London, 1987), pp. 181–219; Corvisier, *Armies and Societies*, pt. 2; Corviser, ed., *Histoire militaire de la France* I, pp. 348, 436.

[12] J. Nicolas, *La Savoie au 18e siècle: noblesse et bourgeoisie* (2 vols., Paris, 1977–8) I, pp. 226 ff.; Anderson, *War and Society*, p. 116; F. Sanchez Marcos, 'Los oficios generales de Felipe V', *Cuadernos de investigacion historica* VI (1982), pp. 241–6; P. Molas Ribalta, 'Militares y togados en la Valencia borbonica', in P. Molas Ribalta, ed., *Historia social de la administracion española: estudios sobre los siglos XVII y XVIII* (Barcelona, 1980), pp. 165 ff.; C. Donati, 'Esercito e società civile nella Lombardia del secolo 18: dagli inizi della dominazione austriaca alla metà degli anni sessanta', *Società e storia* XVII (1982), pp. 527–54; G. Lind, 'Military and Absolutism: The Army Officers of Denmark-Norway as a Social Group and Political Factor 1660–1848', *Scandinavian Journal of History* XII (1987), pp. 224, 226–7; C. Hudemann-Simon, *La noblesse luxembourgeoise au XVIIIe siècle* (Paris, 1985), p. 162.

Britain. Despite growing state control over the Austrian army in the century following the Thirty Years War, only from the 1740s was dependence on 'military enterprisers' and foreigners to raise troops really ended. In Poland-Lithuania, the situation was even further removed from the models offered by its powerful Prussian and Russian neighbours, with their mass conscription of peasants and relatively efficient military administrations. The Polish magnates continued to maintain large private armies, officered by their clients among the indigent and numerous lesser nobility, and this, together with Russian opposition, prevented the Crown from developing a force of its own, which might impose a stronger central authority on the nobility. For most of the eighteenth century, the Polish army was limited to 24 000, in contrast with the much greater forces of Russia, Prussia, and the Habsburg Monarchy. Not until the later eighteenth century was any real attempt made to develop a centralized, royal, and professional army of the kind which existed in most states by that date. Developments in Poland-Lithuania, however, were clearly exceptional. Elsewhere, the Military Revolution had transformed and enlarged Europe's armies. And even Poland felt the influence of a new wave of military reform in the decades after 1763, when changes modelled on the successful Prussian army and furthering state control and monopoly were also introduced in a number of other countries, including Denmark, Portugal, and Hesse-Kassel.[13]

These changes had important implications for the nobility, its military role, and all that followed from it. The *mêlée* of mounted knights had become outmoded, and it was by no means certain that the traditionally independent knight/noble would submit to the discpline required by increasingly organized warfare, in which simple obedience appeared far more important than individual heroism. As early as the 1620s (if not before) contemporaries – notably Richelieu and Olivares – complained about the military incapacity and even disinclination of the French and Spanish elites, and sought to remedy the situation, principally through education (see below, Section IV). It seemed as if the very institution of nobility was itself under attack. The Thirty Years War provided the opportunity for a number of non-nobles, some of highly dubious origins, to push their way into the elite through military service – though these circumstances were excep-

[13] Lind, 'Military and Absolutism', pp. 224, 226–7; Roy, 'The Profession of Arms'; W. Majewski, 'The Polish Art of War in the 16th and 17th Centuries', in J.K. Fedorowicz, ed., *A Republic of Nobles: Studies in Polish History to 1864* (Cambridge, 1982), pp. 179–97; D. Stone, 'Patriotism and Professionalism: The Polish Army in the 18th Century', *Studies in History and Politics (1983–4*, special issue: Warfare and Tactics in the 18th Century), pp. 61 ff.; T.M. Barker, 'Absolutism and Military Entrepreneurship: Habsburg Models', *Journal of European Studies* IV (1974), pp. 19–42; idem Barker, 'Armed Forces and Nobility: Austrian Particulars', in Barker, *Army, Aristocracy, Monarchy: Essays on War, Society and Government in Austria, 1618–1780* (Boulder, CO, and New York, 1982), pp. 37–60.

tional, and ended in 1648.[14] A more serious and permanent challenge was in part an indirect consequence of the Military Revolution. This was the emergence of a nobility whose origin lay not in military service to the Crown but in administrative posts and – in a minority of states – even in the purchase of office. The process was accelerated by the development of bureaucratic cadres to run the new, enlarged, and permanent military structures, and by the spiralling costs of armies and warfare. A further dilution of the idea of nobility was the grant to commoners, often for non-military services, of the traditionally noble privilege of wearing a sword – the symbol and instrument of their military role – since it undermined the association between privileged nobility and warrior elite.[15]

These developments have been widely seen as a principal origin of the cult of the duel, or *la scienza cavalleresca*, which was most widely practised in France between the mid-sixteenth and mid-seventeenth centuries, although most writing on the subject came from Italy. The practice of duelling, which at times threatened to become an epidemic during these decades, emphasized the courage of the individual, defied ecclesiastical and civil authority – although their attitudes were always ambiguous – and was generally motivated by a desire to uphold noble honour – that which distinguished the elite from the unprivileged mass. It thus sought to perpetuate those very qualities which the Military Revolution threatened to remove from the nobility. A similar argument has been advanced to explain the development in later seventeenth-century Spain of *maestranzas*, socially exclusive riding clubs. According to their recent historian, these bodies filled the empty lives of nobles without a role, who needed them to maintain a social pre-eminence that seemed increasingly unjustifiable.[16]

[14] R. Kagan, 'Olivares y la educacion de la nobleza española', in Elliott and Garcia Sanz, eds., *La España del Conde Duque*, pp. 227 ff.; Anderson, *War and Society*, pp. 74–5; Lind, 'Military and Absolutism', pp. 228 ff.; S. Loriga, 'L'identità militare come aspirazione sociale: nobili di provincia e nobili di Corte nel Piemonte della seconda metà del Settecento', *Quaderni storici* LXXIV (1990), p. 445; B. Asker, *Officerarna och dit svenska samhalet 1650–1700* (Uppsala, 1983) (details obtained from review by L.B. Sather, *American Historical Review* LXXXIX (1984), p. 1345).

[15] Barberis, *Le armi del principe*, pp. 64 ff.; Nicolas, *La Savoie*, p. 454.

[16] V.G. Kiernan, *The Duel in European History: Honour and the Reign of Aristocracy* (Oxford, 1989); F. Billaçois, *Le Duel dans la société française des XVI–XVII^e siècles: essai de psychologie historique* (Paris, 1986); R. Liehr, *Sozialgeschichte spanischer Adelskorporationen: die Maestranzas de Caballeria (1670–1808)* (Wiesbaden, 1981); J.B. Owens, 'Diana at the Bar: Hunting, Aristocrats and the Law in Renaissance Castile', *Sixteenth Century Journal* VIII (1977), pp. 17–36; C. Donati, 'L'evoluzione della coscienza nobiliare', in C. Mozzarelli and P. Schiera, eds., *Patriziati e aristocrazie nobiliari: ceti dominante e organizazzione del potere nell'Italia centro-settentrionale dal XVI al XVIII. Atti del seminario tenuto a Trento il 9–10 dicembre 1977 presso l'Istituto Storico Italo-Germanico* (Trento, 1978), pp. 13 ff.; Nicolas, *La Savoie*, pp. 445 ff. Similar interpretations have lain behind research in recent decades on the (nobility's) new emphasis on birth rather than merit or virtue, to which reference has already been made: see Schalk, *From Valor to Pedigree*.

## III

Any wide-ranging account inevitably runs the risk of caricaturing the changes which took place during the early modern period. It would be wrong to imply some kind of overnight transformation from an entirely militarized nobility to its exact opposite. The European elite was never simply a military caste. In the first place, it had long included urban nobilities, like the patriciates of many Italian cities or the *ciutans honrats* of Barcelona. Far from all members of Europe's non-urban elites, moreover, were warriors or came from families with a tradition of military service. Secondly, the nobility's individual or group failure to fulfil traditional obligations could have specific causes little related to a loss of military inclination or capacity. The effective refusal of Castilian grandees to serve in 1640 has been widely produced as evidence for the decline of the martial character of Spain's nobility. But at least as important was the extent to which it was a temporary expression of some grandees' resentment at Olivares' monopoly of power and patronage. Their refusal to serve under his brother-in-law in Portugal in 1640 reflects the Conde-Duque's mishandling of the grandees, as much as – or rather than – the collapse of a warrior tradition. Much the same is true of the refusal of the Portuguese nobles summoned to accompany Philip IV to Catalonia in 1640. In any case, the entire responsibility did not always lie with the nobility: in the Iberian peninsula the Crown was reaping what it had sown. It had undermined the Military Orders' traditional role and effectiveness by granting *habitos* and *encomiendas* with little regard for the military service likely to be secured. The duel and the *maestranzas* – like the continued enthusiasm of nobles (and rulers) for hunting and, in Spain, for bullfighting – in fact reflected an interest in arms and horsemanship which were closely associated with a continued interest in and domination of military life. Where studies exist, for example of the Spanish frontier province of Estremadura during the war against Portugal (1640–68) or of individual nobles, it is clear that the elite – particularly the lesser nobles, but also some of the aristocracy – remained a warrior caste.[17]

[17] J. Amelang, *Honoured Citizens of Barcelona: Patrician Culture and Class Relations 1490–1714* (Princeton, NJ, 1986), pp. 24 ff.; C. Mozzarelli, 'Intervento', in Mozzarelli and Schiera. *Patriziati*, pp. 186 ff.; A. Dominguez Ortiz, 'La movilizacion de la nobleza castellana en 1640', *Anuario del derecho español* XXV (1995), pp. 799–824; J.H. Elliott, *The Count-Duke of Olivares: The Statesman in an Age of Decline* (New Haven, CT, 1986), p. 610; S.B. Schwartz, 'The Voyage of the Vassals: Royal Power, Noble Obligations and Merchant Capital before the Portuguese Restoration of Independence, 1624–1640', *American Historical Review* XCVI (1991), pp. 735 ff.; L.P. Wright, 'The Military Orders in 16th and 17th Century Spanish Society', *Past and Present* XLIII (1969), pp. 34–70; F.A. Dutra, 'Membership in the Order of Christ in the 17th century: Its Rights, Privileges and Obligations', *The Americas* XXVII (1970), pp. 3 ff.; J. Deleito y Pinuela, . . . *Tambien se divierte el pueblo* (Madrid, 1988), pp. 81 ff.; L. Clare, *La quintaine, la course de baque et le jeu des têtes* (Paris, 1983); L. White, 'War and Government in a Castilian province; Extremadura 1640–68' (PhD thesis, University of East Anglia, 1985); A. Rodriguez Villa, *Don Diego Hurtado de Mendoza y Sandoval, Conde de la Corzana* (Madrid, 1907) (military career in late seventeenth century, details of lesser nobles in officer posts); J.P. Le Donne, 'Outlines of Russian Military Administration 1762–1796', pt. 2: The High Command', *Jahrbücher für Geschichte Osteuropas* N.F. XXXIII (1985), pp. 175–204, underlines the nobility's near-complete dominance.

The opportunities for members of the nobility to serve in the army significantly increased during the seventeenth and eighteenth centuries as a direct consequence of the Military Revolution. Armies were multiplying in size, and needed ever-larger numbers of officers. In most states the nobility remained the most obvious, and sometimes the only, source of these. The scale of these opportunities varied from army to army, depending not only on total size but also on the ratio of officers to men, but it was everywhere considerable. It was especially so in eighteenth-century Prussia, where the army more than quadrupled in size, rising from around 40 000 at Frederick William I's accession in 1713 to 180 000 at Frederick the Great's death in 1786. There was a corresponding increase in the size of the Prussian officer corps, which had grown to around 3000 in 1740, 5500 by 1786, and between 7000 and 8000 by the beginning of the nineteenth century. An even more rapid rate of increase was apparent in the Russian officer corps, which more than quintupled in a century, rising from 5000 in 1725 (in itself a great increase on the numbers a few decades earlier) to 9000 in 1762, 16 000 in 1796, and 27 000 by 1825.

The opportunity was not missed by the continental elite. By the eighteenth century, the officer corps of Europe's armies were overwhelmingly noble in character – and becoming more so. This grip came to be especially strong on line regiments, both of infantry and cavalry: the growth of a noble caste of officers was most evident in the units that did the bulk of the fighting. The technial arms of artillery and engineers, the hussars and light infantry, and the garrison regiments all tended to be much more socially mixed in their upper ranks. This reflected both the need for considerable technical education in the artillery and engineers and the much lower prestige enjoyed by all these arms of the service. In the line infantry and cavalry, however, the officer corps was increasingly dominated by the nobility.

Developments in France here pointed the way forward. The massive increase in the size of the French standing army and the near-continuous warfare of the seventeenth century attracted an increasing proportion of noblemen into a military career. This was facilitated by the practice of selling commissions and even whole regiments, since these were mainly bought by members of the traditional high nobility and especially those with an established position at Court or who could secure access to the King and his ministers through an intermediary. While this general trend is apparent, however, it is much more difficult to provide statistical evidence to support it. Jean-Marie Constant's thesis on the nobility of the Beauce, an area lying to the south and east of Paris, provides some suggestive figures. The number of the region's noble families sending at least one son into the army almost doubled between the sixteenth and seventeenth centuries, rising from 97 to 186. During the same period, the percentage of noblemen undertaking a military career rose between three- and fourfold: from 4.45 per cent (1500–60) to 5.98 per cent (1560–1600), 8.78 per cent (1600–

60), and finally 16.10 per cent (1660–1700: the period of greatest expansion in the size of France's royal army).

There was a consequent change in the composition of the officer corps. In the early seventeenth-century French army, far from all officers had been noble, but by its closing decades the officer grades were dominated by the elite. The social hierarchy was here exactly replicated in the army. The unprivileged majority of the population was increasingly called upon to perform more or less compulsory military service in the ranks. The poorer families in the lesser nobility served in the lower grades of the officer corps and sometimes rose through it, while the aristocracy dominated the high command. Members of leading families could also expect to be promoted much more rapidly: in Louis XIV's France, it has been calculated that a titled nobleman could on average expect to rise to the rank of brigadier by the age of 34, after 19 years' service. By contrast, a member of the lesser nobility or a commoner would be 50 and would have served for 32 years.

This noble near-monopoly was widely apparent. In 1739 in Prussia, where there had been some looseness about social distinctions in the armed forces during the seventeenth century, 200 of all 211 staff officers were Junkers. By the final year of Frederick William I's life, all 63 generals in the Prussian army, 56 (out of 57) colonels, 44 (out of 46) lieutenant-colonels, and 100 (out of 108) majors were members of the nobility. Though there was a short-lived increase in non-noble officers during the emergency of the Seven Years War, such men were ruthlessly purged at its conclusion, and by 1786 there were only 22 non-nobles out of 689 majors and senior officers. In 1806, of a total of between 7000 and 8000 officers, only 695 were non-noble: less than one-tenth. By that point, some three-quarters of the nobility in the Hohenzollern heartlands of Brandenburg and Pomerania were active or retired officers. Even in East Prussia, where military service had always been less important for the elite, the figure was around 60 per cent. Yet, in keeping with the situation elsewhere, the noble monopoly did not extend beyond the line regiments. In 1774, the Prussian engineer corps had 38 officers who were commoners and only 6 noblemen, while six years later the artillery had 37 non-noblemen out of a total of 68 officers.

This strengthening of noble control over the line regiments was evident all across Europe. In France, from the middle of the eighteenth century only between 5 and 10 per cent of directly commissioned army officers were commoners, and during the last years of the *ancien régime* even this small number was all but eliminated: the Ségur Law of 1781 required proof of nobility over four complete generations for all officers. In Spain, by 1800 non-nobles only made up 25 per cent of the entire officer corps. A generation earlier it had been remarked that most Portuguese officers were members of the lesser nobility. In Sweden, the nobility's hold on the army strengthened in the course of the later seventeenth and eighteenth centuries. In 1684 the officer corps contained slightly more commoners (52 per cent) than noblemen, but by 1780 this proportion had fallen to around 20 per cent, concentrated mainly in the lower ranks and in the artillery, as the Swedish nobility consolidated its grip. In Hesse-Kassel, the nobility's presence in the officer corps (excluding the militia and garrisons) rose from 43 per cent (1764) to 57 per cent (1806) of posts. There – as elsewhere – only the extraordinary circumstances of the Revolutionary and Napoleonic Wars prompted an influx of commoners which tipped the balance against the nobility, and this proved short-lived. In Bavaria, in 1799, nobles and non-nobles had roughly the same share of officer posts. In Saxony, a majority of officers came from the nobility: in 1808, nobles held over two-thirds of the slightly more than 1000 officer posts. The elite also dominated the officer corps in major states such as Russia and the Austrian Habsburg lands as well as the middle-sized German principality of Württemberg. Even in England, 30 per cent of officers had titles in 1780.[18]

If the vast majority of officers were drawn from the lesser, generally untitled nobility, the senior ranks were equally the preserve of the titled, and often the Court, aristocracy, which dominated the high command almost everywhere. In France, for example, Louis XIV's generals were drawn overwhelmingly from this group and especially the older, established lineages. No less than 93 per cent of the aristocratic elite, the *ducs et pairs*, followed a military career: 41 per cent became generals and 11 per cent marshals of France. This pattern persisted and probably intensified over the following century. One historian has styled the 181 general officers – all members of the nobility – serving in 1758 in the German theatre of war 'almost a directory of the great

[18] A. Åberg, 'The Swedish Army from Lützen to Narva', in M. Roberts, ed., *Sweden's Age of Greatness* (London, 1973), pp. 265–87; O. Büsch, *Militärsystem und Sozialleben im alten Preussen 1713–1807* (Berlin, 1962), pp. 83, 94–6 and *passim*; Redlich, *German Military Enterpriser* II, pp. 18–19, 123; J.P. Le Donne, *Absolutism and Ruling Class: The Formation of the Russian Political Order 1700–1825* (Oxford, 1991), pp. 11–12, 42; J.-M. Constant, *Nobles et paysans en Beauce aux XVI^e et XVII^e siècles* (Doctorat d'état, University of Paris IV, 1978; published Lille, 1981), table 51, p. 159 bis, p. 160, and ch. 8 *passim*; A. Corvisier, 'La Noblesse militaire', *Histoire sociale/Social History* XI (1978), pp. 336–55, at p. 348; C. Jones, 'The Military Revolution and the professionalisation of the French army under the Ancien Régime', in M. Duffy, ed., *The Military Revolution and the State 1500–1800* (Exeter, 1980), pp. 29–48; Contamine, ed., *Histoire militaire de la France* I, pp. 373–4, 439 (this rightly emphasizes the variations from province to province, but the general pattern is clear); G. Best, *War and Society in Revolutionary Europe 1770–1870* (London, 1982), pp. 26–7; M. Martin, *Les Origines de la presse militaire en France à la fin de l'Ancien Régime et sous la Révolution (1770–99)* (Vincennes, 1975); K. Demeter, *The German Officer Corps* (English trans., London, 1965), pp. 3 ff. and 34; S.F. Scott, *The Response of the Royal Army to the French Revolution: The Role and Development of the Line Army 1787–93* (Oxford, 1978), pp. 19–20; C.J. Esdaile, *The Spanish Army in the Peninsular War* (Manchester, 1988), pp. 15–16; Pereira Marques, *Exercito*, p. 46; Dahlgren, 'Estates and Classes', in Roberts, *Sweden's Age of Greatness*, pp. 119 ff.; S. Carlsson, 'The Dissolution of the Swedish Estates 1700–1865', *Journal of European Economic History* I (1972), pp. 574–624, at pp. 585–8; Pedlow, *Hessian Nobility*, pp. 165 ff.; J.V. Beckett, *The Aristocracy in England, 1660–1914* (Oxford, 1986), pp. 408–9; Roy, 'The Profession of Arms', pp. 210–11.

noble families of France'. Two-thirds of these men were members of the titled nobility, with 3 princes of the blood, 5 other princes, 11 dukes, 44 counts, 38 marquises, 14 chevaliers, and 6 barons. On the eve of the French Revolution, the 11 marshals of France comprised 5 dukes, 4 marquises, one prince, and one count. A mere 9 out of 196 lieutenant-generals lacked a title.

This pattern was evident all across the Continent. In Russia, in 1730, of 125 men in the *Generalitet* (the first four military, Court, and civil ranks in Peter the Great's Table of Ranks), seventy-two held military posts. Proportionally the old service families were more represented in the military than in the civil ranks, and they monopolized over 90 per cent of the top positions in the army and navy. Even in England, in 1769, forty-three (of 102) colonels of regiments were peers or sons of peers, while 10 per cent of major-generals, 16 per cent of lieutenant-generals, and 27 per cent of full generals were themselves members of the peerage. The hold of the titled aristocracy on the upper ranks of the Spanish army also increased during the eighteenth century. By 1792, 80 generals (of a total of 327) were titled, although the latter constituted less than one-quarter of one per cent of Spain's entire population. The leading Portuguese noble family, the Tavoras, held a string of very senior military commands. In Sweden in 1654, 1672, and 1699, the only non-nobles present in the high command were in the fleet. In Hesse-Kassel, in 1806, only 17 of 80 officers of major and above were commoners. Four others were the sons of ennobled fathers. By 1800, nobles filled all ranks of colonel and above.

The nobility of these states seldom numbered more than a few per cent of the total population, and the titled nobility was an even smaller proportion. Everywhere the nobility's dominance of military command was substantially greater than a simple translation of that proportion into such posts might produce. This was even the case in those 'technical' branches in which noble officers were a minority. In Prussia in 1739, only in the engineers were the proportions of noble to non-noble roughly equal. The nobility's presence was even more strikingly at odds with its percentage of total population in some other states. In Piedmont-Savoy in 1767, nearly 75 per cent of infantry officers, 93 per cent of those in the cavalry, and 55 per cent of those of the provincial militia regiments were members of the elite. This virtual monopoly of the cavalry was evident in Portugal, Sweden, and most of Germany. In Hesse-Kassel, in 1800, excluding the militia and garrisons, the nobility provided 53 per cent of all officers but 72 per cent of those in the cavalry. By comparison, only 14 per cent of artillery and engineer officers were nobles, while in the militia and garrison regiments, nobles were also in a minority. In Piedmont-Savoy, Victor Amadeus III's Court-aristocratic reaction in the 1770s was accompanied by an expansion of the army and especially the cavalry regiments. Everywhere, nobility was in effect an entry requirement for the sovereign's personal corps of guards, for example the Hungarian royal bodyguard created by Maria Theresa in 1760.[19]

Some families and nobilities in maritime states, and particularly coastal provinces, saw action in their ruler's navy. Their numbers do not remotely compare with those serving in armies, even after the marked expansion of navies, particularly during the eighteenth century, but do demonstrate a similar service tradition. The Savoyard navy was largely officered by the nobilities of Nice and Savoy, including leading families like the de Sales. In later eighteenth-century France 90 per cent of the 1000-strong officer corps (and the great majority of 'reserve' officers) were nobles. The vast majority of these came from the ranks of the poorer provincial nobility. This was also true elsewhere. In Spain, the lesser noble Gortazar family of maritime Vizcaya sent sons into the navy. Yet even in those states with a substantial fighting navy, the vast majority of noblemen who followed a career in the armed forces did so in the officer corps of the army.[20]

Between 1650 and 1800, service as army officers was not universal among the nobility, but it was certainly widespread. In eighteenth-century Prussia, almost two-thirds of Junkers served as officers. It is usually impossible to produce more precise figures, though occasionally they can be found. This is so for the state of Piedmont-Savoy during the early part of Charles Emmanuel III's reign. Of 850 nobles from the provinces of Alessandria, Biella, Casale, and Vercelli in 1734, nearly two-thirds of the males aged 14 and above had an occupation and slightly more than 15 per cent were in the army. Nearly a third of the families involved had at least one son in the armed forces. A striking example of the growth of military service by the nobility is to be found in seventeenth-century Denmark, as the country's armed forces were modernized and expanded. In 1625, only 5 per cent of the nobility held military or civil office, while 84 per cent lived off the income

[19] Corvisier, *Armies*, p. 164; J.-P. Labatut, *Les ducs et pairs au XVIIe siècle* (Paris, 1972), p. 182; L. Kennett, *The French Armies in the Seven Years' War* (Durham, NC, 1967), p. 57: there were four grades of general officer – *maréchal de France, lieutenant général, maréchal-de-camp* and brigadier; ibid p. 54; Scott, *Response of the Royal Army*, pp. 22–3; Demeter, *German Officer Corps*, pp. 5–6 (Prussia); Sanchez Marcos, 'Los oficios generales', pp. 241 ff.; Esdaile, *Spanish Army*, pp. 17–18; J. Lynch, *Bourbon Spain, 1700–1808* (Oxford, 1989), pp. 232, 310–11; Pereira Marques, *Exercito*, p. 67; J. Cavallie, *De hoga officerarna: Studier i den svenska militara hierarkien under 1600-talets senare del* (Stockholm, 1981); B. Meehan-Waters, 'The Muscovite Noble Origins of the Russians in the *Generalitet* of 1730', *Cahiers du monde russe et soviétique* XII (1971), pp. 28–75; Beckett, *Aristocracy in England*, pp. 408–9; Roy, 'The Profession of Arms', pp. 210–11; Loriga, 'L'identità militare', p. 445; Pedlow, *Hessian Nobility*, pp. 165–6; Ricuperati, 'Gli strumenti', pp. 815 ff.; R.J.W. Evans, 'Maria Theresa and Hungary', in H.M. Scott, ed., *Enlightened Absolutism: Reform and Reformers in later Eighteenth Century Europe* (London, 1990), p. 203.

[20] C.A. Gerbaix de Sonnaz, *I savoiardi ed i nizzardi nella marina da guerra di Casa Savoia dal 1300 al 1860* (Turin, 1914), esp. p. 28 ff.; J. Pritchard, *Louis XV's Navy 1748–1762: A Study of Organization and Administration* (Kingston and Montreal, 1987), p. 64 and ch. 4 *passim*; J. Meyer, *La Noblesse française à l'époque moderne (XVIe–XVIIIe siècle)* (Paris, 1991), pp. 101–2; M. Basas Fernandez, 'Vida y fortuna de los Gortazar, caballeros ilustrados de Bilbao en el siglo XVIII', *Anuario de historia economica y social* I (1968), p. 435.

generated by their estates. By 1700, 41 per cent of the 'old' (that is, pre-1660) nobility were serving either in the army (35 per cent) or the civil service (6 per cent). Of the 'new' (i.e. post-1660) nobility, 17 per cent and 8 per cent respectively served in the army and civil service. In Hesse-Kassel, in almost every generation between 1730 and 1849, the army was the main career choice for young noblemen. This peaked at 67 per cent for those born between 1750 and 1769. About three-fifths of the lesser nobility (*Ritterschaft*) of Hesse-Kassel chose an army career during the eighteenth century, while among the titled upper nobility the proportion was at least as high.[21]

Although armies were increasingly national, this was less true for the officer corps than for the rank and file. For much of the eighteenth century, nobles could still be found serving other rulers. The best eighteenth-century example was Count Friedrich-Wilhelm von Schaumburg-Lippe-Bückeburg, who moved easily from army to army. He served with the Hanoverians at Dettingen (1743) and then with the Austrians in the Italian Peninsula (1745). During the Seven Years War he served with Ferdinand of Brunswick, and then in Portugal, during the war against Spain (1762–3), before returning to carry out some noted military reforms in his homeland.[22] Cosmopolitanism of this kind was especially likely in those countries where the state had not completely asserted its own monopoly over its armed forces. This was the situation in the Austrian Habsburg Monarchy before the 1740s, although it was in any case a particularly cosmopolitan political structure. Such foreign military service by the nobility was also common where there was a supply of experienced exiles available (such as English, Irish and Scots Jacobites), where there was a family tradition of serving certain princes, where the native elite was either unwilling or too small to meet the demand, or where foreign monarchs provided military opportunities not available at home. The French monarchy, for example, traditionally offered posts in certain regiments to 'foreign' nobles. Noblemen from the smaller German states were especially likely to serve outside their own territories, since these rulers could not provide the opportunities available in the handful of German states with substantial armies: notably Brandenburg-Prussia, Bavaria, Hesse-Kassel, Saxony, Württemberg, Hanover, and, of course, the Emperor's own lands. Hesse-Kassel's army included only a relatively small proportion of foreigners, while that of neighbouring Denmark offered openings to the nobles of the small North German principalities. In a similar way, members of northern Italian patrician families

[21] Loriga, 'L'identità militare', p. 445; J.P. Cooper, 'Patterns of Inheritance and Settlement by Great Landowners from the Fifteenth to the Eighteenth Centuries', in J. Goody *et al.*, eds., *Family and Inheritance: Rural Society in Western Europe 1200–1800* (Cambridge, 1976), pp. 192–327, at pp. 294–5; S.A. Hansen, 'Changes in the Wealth and Demographic Characteristics of the Danish Aristocracy 1470–1720', in *Third International Conference of Economic History* IV (The Hague, 1972), pp. 91–122, table p. 104; Pedlow, *Hessian Nobility*, pp. 165–6.

[22] There is a solid study of his later career by C. Banaschik-Ehl, *Scharnhorsts Lehrer: Graf Wilhelm von Schaumburg-Lippe in Portugal* (Osnabrück, 1974).

served in the larger armies of other princes. One example was Count Gian Luca Pallavicini, who was proprietor of his own infantry regiment and in 1742 was appointed commander-in-chief of the Austrian Habsburg forces in Lombardy by Maria Theresa. Members of Venetian patrician families also served abroad. By the later eighteenth century, however, these foreign noble officers were becoming increasingly marginalized, or, as in Spain, concentrated in the higher echelons. This was principally because in many states the native nobility had moved into the officer corps in such numbers by the mid- and later eighteenth century that the previous reliance upon foreigners to supply the lack of junior officers was no longer necessary.[23] Russia was an example of exactly this evolution.

The nobility of Europe's Catholic states also dominated the Military Orders, both 'national' where they existed (in Spain, Portugal, and parts of Italy) and international, above all the Knights of Malta. Membership of the latter remained, throughout the *ancien régime*, a roll-call of the continental elite, including members of individual nobilities, such as that of the kingdom of Naples (the Caracciolo di Brienza) and – at even a more elevated level – of distinguished sovereign princely houses such as that of the Dukes of Lorraine. Nobles also predominated in the newer, slightly different, and significantly more national military orders founded in various European states in the later seventeenth and eighteenth centuries.[24]

Many established families continued their traditions of army service in this period, while newcomers began to establish career patterns of their own. This was true throughout the elite, from aristocratic clans down to families in the lesser nobility. While some lineages such as the Lannoy in the southern Netherlands abandoned the military vocation, many and probably most continued to follow such a path down the generations. Army service was thus a prominent feature of many noble family strategies. This in itself is an additional reminder of the continued importance throughout the early modern period of such service for the elite in every continental country. In France, the Saulx-Tavannes supplied successive generations of soldiers, as did various branches of the Choiseul clan. There were many military dynasties among the middle ranks of the French nobility, such as the Scépeaux, who provided eighteen officers, nine of whom rose to be generals, between 1660 and 1790, while over exactly this period, fourteen members of the Lacger, a family of petty nobility from the region around Castres, served in the French army. In Piedmont, much the same could be said of the Cacher-

[23] Barker, 'Armed Forces and Nobility'; Barker, 'Absolutism and Military Entrepreneurship'; C. Duffy, *The Wild Goose and the Eagle: A Life of Marshal von Browne, 1705–57* (London, 1964); Pedlow, *Hessian Nobility*, pp. 165–73, and ch. 6, *passim*; Lind, 'Military and Absolutism', pp. 227–8; Donati, 'Esercito', p. 552.

[24] Astarita, *Continuity of Feudal Power*, pp. 169, 187; E. Stumpo, 'Vittorio Amedeo Costa', *Dizionario biografico degli italiani* (henceforth *DBI*) xxx (Rome, 1984), pp. 251–3; Corvisier, *Armies*, p. 153; information from an unpublished paper by Dr D.F. Allen on the Knights of Malta given to the Italian History Seminar at the University of London Institute of Historical Research, 1991.

ano di Bricherasio and the old-established Costa della Trinita family (dating from *c.* 1400). Elsewhere in Italy, successive generations of princely families – for example the Gonzaga of Mantua – continued to provide military commanders throughout the seventeenth century. At a less exalted level, some Milanese patrician families – notably the Arese – produced distinguished soldiers during the early modern period, while in the Seven Years War the cadet of one of the city's leading families, the celebrated enlightened thinker and reformer Pietro Verri, met scions of other Milanese Houses on various central European battlefields.

Mantua's richest noble House, the Cavriani, frequently served in the Austrian Habsburg armies following the Duchy's escheat to the Emperor at the beginning of the eighteenth century, while in Naples, families such as the Carafa also provided leading military figures in successive generations. In Spain, such army dynasties included those of lesser nobles like the Gortazar of Vizcaya and the Alos of Catalonia. One branch of the latter, ennobled shortly after 1700, devoted itself entirely to military service. In Portugal, examples of lineages with continuing traditions of military service can be found throughout the Second Estate: from the aristocratic Sao Paio to the lesser noble family of Carvalho, one of whose members was the father of the future prime minister, the marquês de Pombal. In the Austrian Habsburg lands, successive generations of the Daun family served in the Habsburg armies, culminating in Maria Theresa's favourite commander, the notably cautious and ineffective field marshal. In eighteenth-century Denmark, the growing proportion of officers' sons (including those of nobles) was such that by about 1850 one in two army officers was himself the son of an army officer. The sheer numbers of noblemen in Prussia and Russia serving in the army underlines the existence of numerous military dynasties in those states. In the Hohenzollern lands, for example, there were numerous families whose members served from one generation to the next: the Arnim, Below, Borcke, Bülow, and many more.[25]

[25] R. Forster, *The House of Saulx-Tavannes, Versailles and Burgundy 1700–1830* (Baltimore, 1971), pp. 1 ff.; Philippe Béchu, 'Noblesse d'épée et tradition militaire au XVIIIe siècle', *Histoire, économie et société* III (1983), pp. 507–48, at p. 545 (this article provides a detailed study of Jacques-Bertrand de Scépeaux, marquis de Beaupréau, 1704–78); R.A. Mentzer, Jr. *Blood and Belief: Family Survival and Confessional Identity among the Provincial Huguenot Nobility* (West Lafayette, IN, 1994), pp. 73 and 72–80 *passim*; Stumpo, 'Vittorio Amedeo Costa', pp. 251–3; A. Valori, *Condottieri e generali del Seicento* (Rome, 1943), under 'Gonzaga'; Donati, 'Esercito', pp. 552, 554; M. Vaini, *La distribuzione della proprietà terriera e la società mantovana dal 1785 al 1845* (Milan, 1973), pp. 180–1; M. de los Angeles Perez Samper, 'La familia Alos: una dinastia catalana al servicio del estado (siglo XVIII)', *Cuadernos de investigacion historica* VI (1982), pp. 195 ff.; Basas Fernandez, 'Vida y fortuna de los Gortazar', pp. 403 ff.; T.M. Barker, 'Military Nobility; The Daun family and the Evolution of the Austrian Officer Corps', in Barker, *Army*, pp. 128 ff.; Hudemann-Simon, *La Noblesse luxembourgeoise*, pp. 162 ff.; Lind, 'Military and Absolutism', p. 232; Butler, *Choiseul* I: *Father and Son, 1719–1754* (Oxford, 1980), pp. 6 ff.; Marques de São-Paio, 'O Tenente Geral lo marquês de São Paio (1762–1841); *Anais da Academia Portuguesa da Historia*, 2nd ser., VIII (1957), pp. 197 ff.; Pereira Marques, *Exercito e sociedade*, p. 67; Redlich, *German Military Enterpriser* II, p. 116. There were military families in the eighteenth-century British army as well: J.A. Houlding, *Fit for Service: The Training of the British Army, 1715–1795* (Oxford, 1981), p. 105 and n. 19.

The noble military dynasties shared many characteristics. Where venality was established, sons inherited their father's regiments, in which they often began to serve at an early age as a preparation for future command. Even when families lost control of these regiments to the state, or where they had never 'owned' a regiment at all, they and other noble clans continued to send their sons – and especially the eldest – into them rather than other regiments. Ten of the fourteen members of the Lacger family were commissioned into one regiment, that of Auvergne, where they constituted one of the three or four lineages who dominated the officer grades. The Auvergne regiment was drawn from Castres and the surrounding region, and the dominance of local families gave cohesiveness and unity to its command structure. Not all noblemen, however, entered national armies. Younger sons in particular entered the Order of St John of Jerusalem (the Knights of Malta): Victor Amadeus Costa's brother, Luigi, became a bailiff of the Order, as did various members of the Daun clan throughout the early modern era. Families with similar traditions frequently intermarried: one notable example was the marriage in the eighteenth century between a Daun and one of the Hungarian Palffy, with its own record of service in Habsburg armies. Since not all officers married, army service in some respects created an unofficial 'celibate' order reminiscent of medieval ideals of the military orders.

By the eighteenth century, some families were part of a distinct, endogamous military quasi-caste within the wider nobility. Despite the increasing barriers in the path of such service, many of these families continued to insert themselves into other armies, states, and societies, and contributed towards the cosmopolitanism of the upper ranks of both nobility and army. One celebrated example was the Italian Broglia family, which passed from the service of the House of Savoy into that of the French Crown in the seventeenth century, becoming as ducs de Broglie one of the great eighteenth-century French families – and also one of the leading aristocratic lineages in the Holy Roman Empire.[26]

To face these challenges, noble officers had to possess many qualities: self-discipline, leadership, inspiration, but above all courage and valour. The degree of commitment demanded was considerable. It was apparent in the heavy losses at times suffered by the officer corps in the wars of the seventeenth and eighteenth centuries. Contrary to the impression given by many accounts of *ancien régime* warfare, this service often meant battle action, injury, and death, particularly for the majority of lesser nobles in the more junior ranks but also for some

[26] Mentzer, *Blood and Belief*, p. 73; Stumpo, 'Vittorio Amedeo Costa', pp. 251–3; Barker, 'Military Nobility', p. 233; V. Castronovo, *DBI* XIV (1972), pp. 427–8 (Broglia); E. Stumpo, 'Tra mito, leggenda e realtà storica: la tradizione militare sabauda da Emanuele Filiberto a Carlo Alberto', *Rivista storica italiana* CIII (1991), pp. 560 ff.; J. Chagniot, 'The ethics and practice of war amongst French Officers during the 17th Century', *War and Society* X (1992), pp. 19 ff.

in more senior positions. This was so not least because noblemen officered the regiments that did the bulk of the fighting, rather than the less vulnerable militias and garrisons. The nobility who dominated the higher ranks of the French army suffered serious losses in the final war of Louis XIV's reign, that of 1702–13. Individual Houses also experienced such losses: members of successive generations of the Saulx-Tavannes family were killed in action during the conflicts of that era. Few families of the Savoyard nobility did not see service or 'sacrifice' one member in the wars of the seventeenth and eighteenth centuries. This is exemplified by the fortunes of the Costa della Trinita. Francesco Maria Costa della Trinita was killed at the siege of Alba (1617) while serving Charles Emmanuel I of Piedmont-Savoy. A century later, Victor Amadeus Costa saw action in the Wars of the Polish and the Austrian Successions in the service of Charles Emmanuel III. Luigi Costa had earlier fought in the Mediterranean on the galleys of the Knights of Malta. In Spain, casualties in the 1639 campaign included one-quarter of the Catalan nobility. At the end of this period, noble officers in the army of Hesse-Kassel, like their counterparts elsewhere in Europe, suffered major losses in the French Revolutionary and Napoleonic wars. Most striking, however, is the number of casualties among the Junkers during Frederick the Great's three Silesian wars and especially his struggle for survival in the Seven Years War. Prussia's officer corps in 1756 was around 5500: during the conflict which followed, at least 1500 were killed and some 2500 wounded, while still more were captured. Individual families with a strong military tradition suffered heavy losses during Prussia's mid-century wars: 24 Kleists, 19 Kameckes, and 20 (out of 23) Bellings perished in the carnage between 1740 and 1763. Even more remarkably, no fewer than 33 Prussian generals died in action between 1756 and 1759.[27] These figures were exceptional and due to Prussia's desperate plight, but they are an important reminder of the losses that could sometimes occur.

## IV

The nobility's continued and disproportionate pre-eminence in the officer corps of Europe's armies reflected both its own successful response to the challenge represented by the increased professionalism and technical expertise demanded by the age of the Military Revolution and the enduring importance of the idea that preference should always be given to birth and lineage in the choice of commanders and other officers. These new demands, together with the need for relevant

[27] Contamine, ed., *Histoire militaire de la France* I, pp. 542 ff.; Forster, *Saulx-Tavannes*, p. 12; Barberis, *Le armi del principe*; Stumpo, 'Tra mito . . .' (a response to Barberis); Pedlow, *Hessian Nobility*, p. 167; C. Duffy, *Frederick the Great: A Military Life* (London, 1985), p. 230; T. Schieder, *Friedrich der Grosse: ein Königtum der Widersprüche* (Frankfurt, 1983), p. 184.

education, were periodically articulated, for example by the French Huguenot François de la Noue in the sixteenth century and by Olivares in the seventeenth. The nobility was still assumed to possess a monopoly on courage, but now this had to be accompanied by an appropriate level of technical knowledge. As Louis XV remarked in 1743, after the French defeat at Dettingen: 'I have always been fully persuaded of the valour of our young nobles; but . . . you should study in them . . . the talents which they develop, in order that you may cultivate them so that they can become great generals.'[28]

From the close of the sixteenth century, the preoccupation of rulers and of the nobility itself with the education of the elite for the newly professionalized warfare led to the establishment of a number of academies, many restricted to the nobility and most with a distinctly military curriculum. A few informal, private institutions had briefly existed in Spain, France, and Germany before 1600, but the real expansion came thereafter. An academy was founded at Sedan (1606) by the duc de Bouillon, brother-in-law of the celebrated Prince Maurice of Orange. Between 1608 and 1610 the Venetian Republic helped establish four academies for nobles – at Padua, Treviso, Udine, and Verona – intended to produce skilled cavalrymen. These initiatives quickly inspired emulation. In 1617 Count John VII of Nassau founded a Kriegs- und Ritterschule at Siegen, though difficulties led to its closure even before the death of its founder six years later. Similar institutions were founded by Landgrave Maurice of Hesse-Kassel (1618), by Denmark's Christian IV at Sorø in 1623, and by the celebrated Imperial *generalissimo* Count Albrecht von Wallenstein at Gitschin (1624). Olivares was behind the opening of the Colegio Imperial as a kind of noble military academy in Madrid (1625). In 1658–9 the Danish noble Gunde Rosenkranz outlined an abortive scheme to revive the nobility's authority, and justify its continuing hold on office and power, which included military education. Ritterakademien were established in seventeenth-century Brandenburg-Prussia to train young nobles to be army officers. The Accademia Reale in Turin was founded in 1677, mainly to prepare the sons of the nobility for court service, while two decades later (1699) Duke Leopold of Lorraine founded an academy at Lunéville with a decidely military emphasis. Shortly after this, at the very beginning of the new century, Prussia's first King, Frederick I, established state-financed military academies in Berlin, Colberg, and Magdeburg.

In the second half of the eighteenth century the leading continental powers began to catch up, with a series of state foundations intended to train the sons of the nobility for a military career. In 1752 the military academy at Wiener Neustadt was founded by Maria Theresa for the nobility of the Habsburg Monarchy. In France, the comte d'Argenson

[28] C. Donati, *L'idea di nobiltà in Italia, secoli XIV–XVIII* (Bari, 1988), p. 279; Demeter, *German Officer Corps*, p. 67; Kagan, 'Olivares', pp. 227 ff.; Butler, *Choiseul*, p. 419; H. Speier, 'Militarism in the 18th Century', repr. in Speier, *Social Order and the Risks of War* (Cambridge, MA, 1969), p. 232.

founded the École Militaire in Paris (1751), with entrance restricted to boys from poor families of the traditional nobility. A quarter-century later, in 1777, it became a superior military academy for graduates of twelve provincial army colleges which had been founded in the previous year. Similar institutions were founded by the Bourbons in eighteenth-century Spain, while Portugal, too, had its training academies (from the 1780s), as did Poland (1765). In 1778 Landgrave Frederick II of Hesse-Kassel founded a military academy for young noblemen who, after a spartan existence which was intended to mask inequalities of wealth and birth, were commissioned as officers at 17 or 18. The first attempt at a more technical training for the duties of an officer in Württemberg was the Hohe Karlschule, raised to university status in 1782. Similar efforts in the later eighteenth century to create a military academy in the United Provinces, however, were not completely successful until after the Orange restoration of 1814.[29]

The success of such initiatives, and especially the early military academies, was extremely limited. Their failure was due not to any loss of military character by the nobility but to more prosaic considerations, above all finance. Both Olivares' initiative and the Venetian scheme quickly failed, largely due to the considerable cost of the education provided and to the consequent reluctance of young nobles to enter these institutions. In the case of Spain, the prospects of the Colegio Imperial were not helped by the degree of hostility towards the Conde-Duque. The Turin Accademia was also in frequent financial difficulty, most noble families instead sending their sons to the Jesuit Collegio dei Nobili. Indeed, neither the Turin nor Lorraine academies was an entirely military institution in the same way as the others listed above. Particularly by the eighteenth century they were, in effect, regarded as part of a broader preparation for life as a nobleman and at Court. Such institutions were also very expensive and therefore largely the preserve of Europe's noble elite. They were not to be found in certain countries, and where this was the case noblemen travelled abroad to study at established military academies. The Turin Accademia, for example, was the resort of young Polish and Russian nobles and the sons of English peers (who were also attracted to Lunéville) as well as the native nobility of Piedmont-Savoy, who went on to careers in the army command and at Court.

The curricula of these new institutions underlined the distinctly mili-

[29] J.R. Hale, 'The Military Education of the Officer Class in Early Modern Europe' and 'Military Academies on the Venetian Terraferma', both repr. in Hale, *Renaissance War Studies* (London, 1983), pp. 225–46 and 285–307; Demeter, *German Officer Corps*, pp. 67–8; Kagan, 'Olivares', pp. 227 ff,; Barberis, *Le armi del principe*, pp. 173 ff.; Butler, *Choiseul*, p. 57; A. Corvisier, ed., *Histoire militaire de la France* II: *De 1715 à 1871*, ed. J. Delmas (Paris, 1992), pp. 68–73; Pedlow, *Hessian Nobility*, pp. 154–6; J.A.M. Janssen, *Op weg naar Breda: De opleiding van officieren voor het nederlandse leger tot aan de oprichting van de Koninklije Militaire Academie in 1828* (The Hague, 1989) (as summarized in *Commission Internationale d'Histoire Militaire Comparée: bulletin de bibliographie* XI (1990), p. 39); W. Lisowski, *Polskie Korpusy Kadetow 1765–1956* (Warsaw, 1982) (as summarized in *Commission Internationale* ... VI (1984–5), p. 59); Scott, *Response of the Royal Army*, p. 24. Cf. also Pereira Marques, *Exercito e sociedade*, pp. 47, 79.

tary content in the education of a nobleman. Yet, as Castiglione had argued in his celebrated sixteenth-century treatise, the noble courtier should not simply be an otherwise uncouth expert in arms. He must instead be adept in all the courtly arts of pleasing. The Turin Accademia taught horsemanship, dancing, the handling of arms, military manoeuvres, history, geography, heraldry, French and Italian, and mathematics and drawing in preparation for siege warfare and the science of fortifications. Frederick II of Hesse-Kassel's academy taught French, military science, mathematics, riding, and fencing, while the Lorraine academy had a broadly similar curriculum.[30]

It must be emphasized that attendance at a military academy was extremely unusual among the nobility, and largely restricted to members of the aristocratic elite. The overwhelming majority of noblemen continued to prepare informally for a military career in the traditional ways: either by education within their own family or occasionally at Court, or by service with a celebrated commander or as a gentleman-volunteer. The sheer cost everywhere prevented the vast majority of noblemen from attending such institutions. In Piedmont-Savoy, fewer than 10 per cent of a total of 195 officers serving in the Vercelli regiment between 1713 and 1792 had any formal training: ten had attended the Turin Accademia, while a further seven had served as pages at Court. The high cost of military education, and the small numbers entering it, were precisely the reasons for the establishment and expansion in the eighteenth century of institutions which were intended to be cheap and therefore accessible to all young noblemen, whether by offering scholarships or by establishing very low fees and costs. But there simply were not enough places in these new academies to meet the demand. Most army officers from the lesser nobility therefore continued to enter the army without much vocational education, though they might receive lessons from local fencing and riding masters. They could also educate themselves by reading the growing military literature, as officers were advised to do in the Portuguese army in the period of reform during the second half of the eighteenth century. The great majority of Hesse-Kassel nobles who entered the army continued to do so as ensigns in their early teens, eventually becoming (at 17) lieutenant without any other, formal education. Though for most noblemen the academies were irrelevant, these initiatives and the curricula they sponsored make clear the new demands upon would-be officers. Military training was also offered by other institutions. Some

[30] Kagan, 'Olivares', 232 ff.; Barberis, *Le armi del principe*, pp. 173 ff.; Pedlow, *Hessian Nobility*, pp. 154–6; Castiglione, *The Courtier*, trans. and ed. G. Bull (London, 1967), pp. 57, 113–15, 124: Butler, *Choiseul*, p. 57; Nicolas, *La Savoie* I, pp. 394–6; cf. comments of Vittorio Alfieri: *Vita*, ed. A. Dolfi (Milan, 1987), pp. 67 ff. (1759); M. Motley, *Becoming a French Aristocrat: The Education of the Court Nobility, 1580–1715* (Princeton, NJ, 1990), pp. 123 ff.

nobles in Hesse-Kassel even attended military science courses at the University of Marburg before being commissioned.[31]

For most noblemen intending to be officers in the eighteenth century, training continued to be largely 'on the job' – exactly as it had been for earlier generations of noble volunteers. Such training was now more formal, however, sometimes related to the academies, sometimes an alternative to them. More and more it took place in the corps of cadets which proliferated in the eighteenth century and were also increasingly restricted to the nobility. These involved young men being trained for the officer corps, often by attachment to a regiment, performing some of the tasks of soldiers and officers for a certain period, before securing an established – and therefore paid – post. Cadet corps were founded not only in Prussia (1717: this was, in fact, an amalgamation of the three military academies established by Frederick I), Saxony (1725), and Russia (1731), but in Bavaria (1756), Portugal (1757), and France (1776, the *cadets-gentilshommes*). In Prussia, the cadet school proved to be a significant source of military talent. Between 1717 and 1740, some 1600 young noblemen were enrolled in it. Around 90 per cent of these received officers' commissions in the Prussian army, and forty rose to become generals. In the Hohenzollern lands, cadet schools were also founded for the sons of the nobility of Eastern Pomerania and (after its annexation in 1772) West Prussia, and after the Seven Years War a special class of the Berlin cadet corps was established by Frederick the Great under the name of the Académie des Nobles or Académie Militaire. In Piedmont-Savoy (1737), Spain (1738), and Bavaria (1778) each regiment contained cadet places reserved for young noblemen. In Saxony, the cadet corps, which until the nineteenth century provided the majority of officers, was overwhelmingly noble in character. Like the officer corps for which they were a preparation, the cadet corps, not surprisingly, included far more members of the nobility than the latter's proportion of total population might seem to justify. But not even the significant increase in the number of places for cadets could meet the demand from members of poorer noble families for whom they were intended. The crucial point is that nobles, great and small, continued to prepare themselves for a military career, as far as they could, and as far as was appropriate to their stations and prospects, though often in ways that were remarkably traditional.[32]

[31] Loriga, 'L'identità militare', pp. 451–2; Pereira Marques, *Exercito e sociedade*, pp. 50 ff.; Pedlow, *Hessian Nobility*, p. 154.

[32] *Op. cit.*, p. 156; Scott, *Response of the Royal Army*, p. 24; Pereira Marques, *Exercito e sociedade*, p. 76; Demeter, *German Officer Corps*, pp. 68, 95; Edgar Melton, 'The Prussian Junkers, 1600–1786', in H.M. Scott, ed., *The European Nobilities in the Seventeenth and Eighteenth Centuries* (2 vols., London, 1995) II, p. 96; G. Cardona. *El problema militar en España* (Madrid, 1988). p. 16: F. Andujar Castillo, *Los militares en la España del siglo XVIII: un estudio social* (Granada, 1991), pp. 121 ff. (noble cadets) and pp. 129ff. (for the creation of the post of *soldado distinguido* (1768) to give privileged promotion prospects to poor nobles serving in the ranks); Scott, *Response of the Royal Army*, p. 24. Cf. also C. Jones, 'The Military Revolution', pp. 30 ff., for cadet scheme established by Louis XIV.

## V

Military service was still seen by noble and non-noble alike as the elite's *raison d'être.* This was the main reason why large numbers of aristocrats and noblemen entered the officer corps and why the elite in general long pursued a military vocation. The connection between arms and gentility had been powerfully restated in Shakespear's *Henry V* (1599), and this view was echoed all across Europe throughout the seventeenth and eighteenth centuries. In a treatise of 1678 on arms – a typical product of the new technical literature – the French noble and soldier de Gaya declared that arms were the origin of true nobility. In Naples, the revolt of 1647 – itself in part directed against the nobility – was followed by a spate of publications of a historical rather than speculative-philosophical nature, emphasizing the military traditions and achievements of the realm's powerful baronage and so justifying their privileged status. Conversely, the attack on noble power in later eighteenth-century Naples was dominated by a critical debate about the elite's military obligations.

The connection between nobility and arms proved remarkably tenacious. In eighteenth-century Prussia, both Frederick William I and his more famous son believed that the Second Estate was the unique source of the kind of military virtue which officers must possess. As late as 1763 Frederick the Great, when refusing to sell noble lands and titles, declared that he would not debase the Second Estate. 'Noble status', he continued,

> can only be gained by the sword, by bravery and by other outstanding behaviour and services. I will tolerate as vassals only those who are at all times capable of rendering me useful service in the army, and those who because of exceptionally good conduct and exceptional service I choose to raise into the estate of the nobility.

The king's view was widely shared. A few years earlier the French maréchal-duc de Belle-Isle had proclaimed the Second Estate to be 'that precious portion of the state, its strength and its support'. In the early eighteenth century the Veronese noble Scipione Maffei scorned the cult of the duel of honour, but still cherished the nobility's military *métier.* Two generations before, in 1647, the Camara de Castilla had complained that Philip IV was granting nobility to men without military qualities. A hundred years later, in 1756, the martial character of the French nobility was forcibly restated by the Chevalier d'Arc in the course of a celebrated polemic, while shortly before a Portuguese treatise (1751) on the ideal infantry captain argued that nobles should command because their origin lay in arms and they alone possessed the associated virtues of loyalty and honour.

Many of these statements clearly reflect the nobility's sense of being under attack. Yet is is significant that the defensive ground adopted was the elite's traditional military function, together with an assertion of its established ideology as the fighting class. Such attitudes were reinforced by the continuing vitality of family military traditions. Most nobles derived their sense of self from an upbringing which emphasized the history of their own lineage. Particularly where the principal source of the family's previous glories was military service, subsequent generations would easily regard the army as their own most obvious destination. Such views were no doubt reinforced by a diet of reading which largely confined itself to history, and especially military history. A noble of Estremadura actually explained that he was inspired to join up in 1793 by his sense of his own lineage, as well as by honour and by revulsion against the French Revolution. The values which underlay the duel clearly played a part in the elite's continued dedication to the army. This enduring identification of nobility with military service was also apparent in the numbers still entering the Military Orders, dependent on proof of noble status.[33]

The link was reinforced by the fact that the army remained one of the most effective routes, albeit a slow one, to promotion within the nobility and to actual ennoblement: as in France, where over 75 per cent of new creations by the Crown between 1589 and 1723 were military in origin. This was also the case in the Habsburg Monarchy. During the Thirty Years War, many successful military enterprisers were promoted in the nobility through the award of the higher titles of baron, count, and (very occasionally) prince or, in some cases, ennobled for the first time by a grateful emperor. In the eighteenth century the same pattern was to be found: army officers received around one-third of the titles granted between 1711 and 1789, which numbered almost 2000. These grants were concentrated in periods of conflict, notably the Seven Years War. In some *ancien régime* states, military service recovered its previous position as the most prestigious form of service, eclipsing administrative office. In Bourbon Spain, for example, the proportion of sons of members of the Council of Castile going into the army was 14 per cent, three times the figure

[33] S. Aragon Mateos, 'La nobleza narcisista: ideologia nobiliaria en la España de la Ilustracion', *Mélanges de la casa de Velazquez* XXV (1989), pp. 279–301, esp. pp. 283–7; Castiglione, *The Courtier*, pp. 57, 113–15, 124; Shakespeare, *Henry V* (New Penguin edn., London, 1968), Act IV, sc. iii (the 'Agincourt' speech), pp. 132–4; L. de Gaya, *Traité des armes* (1678), ed. C. Ffoulkes (Oxford, 1911), pp. i ff.; Scott, *Response of the Royal Army*, p. 24; Redlich, *German Military Enterpriser* II, pp. 124–5; C.B.A. Behrens, *Society, Government and the Enlightenment: The Experiences of Eighteenth-Century France and Prussia* (London, 1985), quotation at p. 60; Kennett, *French Armies*, p. 59. C. Donati, 'Scipione Maffei e la "Scienza chiamata cavalleresca" ', *Rivista storica italiana* XC (1978), p. 30 ff.; (cf. also M. Berengo, 'Patriziato e nobilità: Il caso veronese', *Rivista storica italiana* LXXXVII (1975), p. 499); I. Atienza Hernandez, *Aristocracia, poder y riqueza en la España moderna: la casa de Osuna, siglos XV–XIX* (Madrid, 1987), p. 43; V.I. Comparato, 'Intervento', in Mozzarelli and Schiera, *Patriziati*, pp. 155–62; Astarita, *Continuity of Feudal Power*, pp. 17, 22, 27; R.F. Filamondo, *Il genio bellico di Napoli* (Naples, 1694); P. Villani, *Mezzogiorno tra riforme e rivoluzione* (Bari, 1974), pp. 155 ff.; Pereira Marques, *Exercito e sociedade*, pp. 38 ff.

(4.5 per cent) in the previous century. This was also the case in Piedmont-Savoy.[34]

Military service was not only important to established lineages. Newly ennobled families often adopted an army career as a form of self-legitimation, though this could often be fictitious, or at least grossly exaggerated. In Castile, those seeking royal letters declaring their nobility between 1500 and 1800 justified their requests in no less than three-quarters of all cases on the grounds of service done by themselves or their ancestors in the army, and frequently attempted to add a patina of military service to more civilian duties for the Crown. Even in the eighteenth century, those putting forward 'new' reasons for their nobility – above all utility and value – also advanced more traditional justifications, including careers spent in the army. In Piedmont-Savoy, the Gabaleone, ennobled in the early seventeenth century for their contribution to ducal finance and administration, had developed a military tradition by the eighteenth century, when a member of the family became director of the Turin *Accademia*. In a similar way the Riccardi of Florence, 'new' Medici nobles, sought military credibility by claiming an old condottiere for their ancestor, and in the seventeenth century members of the family actually did serve as soldiers. The same undoubtedly happened elsewhere. Entry into the Knights of Malta provided some emerging families – including, for example, the urban patricians of the Terra di Bari in the kingdom of Naples in the seventeenth and eighteenth centuries – with a point of contact with the old elite and thus further legitimation.[35]

The Danish nobility's increased adoption of military careers during the seventeenth century has been attributed partly to the economic difficulties it experienced between 1580 and 1660 and especially to their impact upon an increasingly landless lesser nobility. The trend was a general one throughout Europe. The majority of noble army officers were relatively poor and so forced to earn a living. Even in those families whose economic circumstances were more prosperous, but whose future well-being was protected by the practice of primogeniture (sometimes formally reinforced by a strict entail), younger sons had to be provided for in an 'acceptable' way: that is, in an occupation which yielded a

[34] Labatut, *Les ducs et pairs*, pp. 89 ff.; Redlich, *German Military Enterpriser* I, pp. 420–30; P.G.M. Dickson, *Finance and Government under Maria Theresia 1740–1780* (2 vols., Oxford, 1987), I, pp. 78–82; J. Fayard, *Les Membres du Conseil de Castile a l'époque moderne (1621–1746)* (Geneva and Paris, 1979) (figures cited by I.A.A. Thompson in 'The Rule of Law in Early Modern Castile', *European History Quarterly* XIV (1984), pp. 221–34, at pp. 228–9).

[35] I.A.A. Thompson, 'Neo-noble Nobility: Concepts of *hidalguia* in Early Modern Castile', *European History Quarterly* XV (1985), pp. 379 ff.; Barberis, *Le armi del principe*, pp. 80 ff., 173 ff.; P. Malanima, *I Riccardi di Firenze: una famiglia e un patrimonio nella Toscana dei Medici* (Florence, 1977), pp. 94, 154–5; A. Spagnoletti, *L'incostanza delle umane cose: il patriziato di Terra di Bari tra egemonia e crisi (XVI–XVIII secolo)* (Bari, 1981), pp. 109–10. We should like to thank Dr Roberto Mantelli for drawing our attention to this work and sending us a copy of it. Cf. C. Mozzarelli, 'Intervento', in Mozzarelli and Schiera, pp. 186 ff., on the increasing homogenization in the seventeenth century of different types of nobility/nobles (i.e. patrician and feudal).

reasonable income – and lifestyle – together with opportunities for advancement, without in any way compromising noble status. Since involvement in trade might theoretically threaten such status and was not always an available option in any case, the two principal careers open to nobles and their families (who often made the decision for a young son) were the Church – and especially the Roman Catholic Church – and the army: both traditional vocations for the elite. Where the Church provided an alternative, some families did not send sons into the army at all, or abandoned earlier military traditions, for example the Caracciolo di Brienza of Naples. But, even for them and as late as 1774, the army was viewed as a serious alternative for younger sons.[36]

The financial calculations involved were complex and uncertain. Military service was not always profitable and could be a source of serious financial losses. Army careers did not always flourish and only a minority prospered as they hoped. This is exemplified by the fortunes of the fourteen members of the Lacger family who made their careers in the French army between the 1660s and the Revolution. Three of these noblemen had long and successful careers: François de Lacger (1661–1758) served for forty-five years and reached the rank of lieutenant-colonel and brevet brigadier; his brother Louis (1680–1757) served for forty years, retiring as a battalion commander; while their cousin Jean-Jacques (d. 1748) also became a lieutenant-colonel, serving for no fewer than fifty-one years. Yet these were very much the exception. The remaining eleven members of the family who entered the royal army served for an average of around ten years, and none rose above the rank of lieutenant or captain.[37]

The financial burdens which military service could impose were everywhere a potential threat to the nobility's economic well-being. The frequent absences in the army of the dukes of Frias (hereditary constables of Castile) during the seventeenth century contributed to their economic difficulties. In eighteenth-century Spain, potential noble recruits were sometimes vetted to discover whether they – or their families – could bear the expense of being an officer. This was an especial problem for the poorer, lesser nobility, for whom the increasing cost of equipment and, even more, of a commission in those armies where venality was established were a considerable burden. The expenses involved in purchasing a command and in supporting an appropriate lifestyle often outran salary, especially in the elite forces stationed in the capital and near the Court. In the more obscure and isolated regiments, a careful officer of lesser means might just about get by, though it has been suggested that the considerable expense involved contributed to the Luxemburg nobility's relative lack of interest in army service during the eighteenth

[36] Cooper, 'Patterns of Inheritance', pp. 294–95; Astarita, *Continuity of Feudal Power*, pp. 186–7.

[37] Mentzer, *Blood and Belief*, p. 74 and 72–80 *passim*.

century. All across Europe, family estates were saddled with debt to launch and sustain military careers.[38]

Yet war had always been potentially profitable and it remained so, although in a different way. Broadly speaking, the Military Revolution theoretically transformed the army officer from freebooter into salaried state official. By 1700, for example, Sweden's noble-dominated officer corps had been turned into a body of paid and increasingly obedient Crown officials, and this model would eventually be widely followed. Officers' salaries were not always high, far less promptly paid, but often they were all that enabled poor noblemen to distinguish themselves from the rest of the population and so maintain their privileged status. This was particularly true in major powers such as Prussia or Russia, where the dramatic expansion of the military establishment during the eighteenth century provided careers and some income for many members of the numerous and often impoverished lesser nobility. The situation in the Prussian army was especially favourable to a successful noble officer. The system of *Kompagniewirtschaft*, by which captains owned their companies, provided many Junkers with a considerable income. It was even possible for senior officers to hold the proprietorship of whole regiments, with a profit to match. This was a legacy of the mercenary armies which had earlier served the Hohenzollerns. The noble proprietor received all the pay and expenses for his troops and the opportunities for profit legitimate and otherwise, were considerable.

Greater financial rewards would accompany any promotion, while the spread of a generally accepted hierarchy of ranks within most armies, such as that introduced in 1675 in France, offered at least the possibility of a career path and the financial rewards to accompany it. There is no doubt that military service could be profitable. François de Lacger used the income from a successful career in the French army to build up the family patrimony through purchases of property and investments in the early decades of the eighteenth century. But such success, though not exceptional, was probably unusual.[39] Towards the end of the eighteenth century the purchase system, which had tended to reinforce the grip of the greater nobility on the high command, was modified in some states, including France and Denmark. This ensured that more professional criteria, merit rather than wealth or favour, began to play a great role in promotion. The advance of professionalism in the Danish army culminated in the introduction of compulsory examinations for all officers at the very end of the eighteenth century. Yet this was exceptional: the overall picture remains confused. The dependence of most Hessian noble officers on their salaries explains their decision to remain in the army after 1806. Conversely, the rejection by the Piedmontese noble Vit-

[38] Aragon Mateos, 'La nobleza narcisista', p. 295; Scott, *Response of the Royal Army*, pp. 19 ff.; Hudemann-Simon, 'Une noblesse en déclin', 84–5; Hudemann-Simon, *La Noblesse luxembourgeoise*, pp. 162 ff. (examples of costs).

[39] Büsch, *Militärsystem und Sozialleben*, esp. pp. 113–34; Redlich, *German Military Enterpriser* II, pp. 77–88.

torio Alfieri of a military career was possible partly because of his great inherited wealth. After the enormous military sacrifices of the Prussian nobility in the Seven Years War, Frederick the Great first declared a five-year moratorium on all noble debts and then made available cheap credit through the *Landschaften* to enable the Junkers to retrieve their economic fortunes and restore their landed power.

Poorer, lesser nobles also valued army service for less material and often distinctly traditional reasons. These included opportunities not always available in the narrow provincial backwaters from which officers came: to see more of the world, for self-development (particularly to acquire the qualities connected with one's station, above all self-assurance, self-discipline, and the ability to command others), and to mix with people of one's own social status. The expansion of armies and the accompanying demand for noble officers also offered members of the lesser nobility the opportunity to advance through the officer grades on the basis of ability and merit, rather than simply birth and wealth. Though an increasing number of nobles were now seeking education as a preparation for army service, probably even more entered the army to obtain an education – and not a narrowly technical one. In many respects the officer corps of the *ancien régime* were finishing schools for the nobility. In the eighteenth century, questions of social rank were often less well defined and more open to dispute than was to be wished. Nobles were drawn to army service which confirmed their status, and also conferred the sanction of the ruler and his government, notably in the form of Tables of Ranks (see below, Section V).[40]

For the numerically small, but rich and powerful elite for whom such service was not an economic necessity, a military career often could be a different kind of family strategy. Service was given in return for a reward which might not be simply, or immediately, material. During the War of the Austrian Succession, the Milanese noble Count Antonio Giorgio Clerici sought favour in Vienna by raising his own regiment, much in the style of the old 'military enterprisers' a century before. Distinguished service in an Austrian Habsburg regiment in that same conflict by the Hungarian Ferenc Nadasy retrieved for his family the status and accompanying Court favour forfeited by an ancestor's treason as long ago as the 1670s. Such service was not always given willingly, especially as the nobles involved – unlike the poorer, lesser nobility who made up the bulk of the officer corps – often did not feel that it was either an economic necessity or their sole defining characteristic. Milanese patrician families who had served in the Austrian army abandoned this tradition in the later eighteenth century because, in the wake of Maria

[40] Mentzer, *Blood and Belief*, pp. 52, 72; J.L.H. Keep, *Soldiers of the Tsar: Army and Society in Russia, 1462–1874* (Oxford, 1985), pp. 233–4; R. Berdahl, *The Politics of the Prussian Nobility: The Development of a Conservative Ideology 1770–1848* (Princeton, NJ, 1988), pp. 14 ff., 78, 92, 97; Pedlow, *Hessian Nobility*, p. 167; cf. Alfieri, *Vita*, pp. 174 ff. (1749– ); Loriga, 'L'identità militare', pp. 452 ff.; Pereira Marques, *Exercito e sociedade*, pp. 35 ff.

Theresa's centralizing reforms, they were no longer obtaining the posts in the Duchy of Milan's administration that had been their traditional reward. More usually, however, such service was the price of favour increasingly demanded by rulers and Courts, and as a result, leading Houses now integrated it into their family strategies: for example, the marquis of Brienza (heir of the Caracciolo di Brienza) entered the Neapolitan royal cadets in 1782. Many aspects of government in the eighteenth century were increasingly militarized: the viceroyship of Sardinia was the preserve of noble soldiers for most of the period, as was the supreme command of Valencia, while the military element in Russian provincial government was also substantial. This was an additional reason for ambitious nobles to seek a military career, not least because it was also regarded as good preparation for the diplomatic service and eventually high office at home. For the Count of Aranda, a successful army career in Spain followed by a spell as ambassador to France ultimately led to political power under Charles III.[41]

The eighteenth-century army, of course, ultimately defended the *ancien régime,* that system of privilege out of which the nobility did so well. The military hierarchy reproduced the fundamental social hierarchy, with all its privileges and inequalities. This was one reason why the nobility provided the majority of the officer corps. The nobility's social superiority was both reflected in and reinforced by its military preeminence. The hold of the aristocracy on the senior posts and of lesser nobles on the bulk of the officers corps is an even more precise reflection of that social structure. It was, therefore, in the nobility's broader strategic interest to remain the military professionals *par excellence.*

Army service also enshrined the traditional, and privileged, personal link between the monarch and the individual officer and noble family. Noblemen everywhere still saw their ruler as a feudal lord to whom they and their kin were bound by ties of fealty.[42] This link could be reinforced by the oaths of loyalty to their king or prince which many high-ranking officers continued to take. In most countries, an army commission was sanctioned and sometimes personally approved by the monarch. In some states, such as Denmark, officers had privileged rights of access to the

[41] Donati, 'Esercito', p. 553; Evans, 'Maria Theresa and Hungary', p. 202; Loriga, L'identità militare', p. 460; Astarita, *Continuity of Feudal Power,* p. 187; Molas Ribalta, 'Militares'; 'Rafael Flaquer Montequi, Conde de Aranda', in Artola, ed., *Enciclopedia* IV, pp. 80–1; cf. the remarks of marquis de St Maurice on desirability of military experience for those sent to represent Duke of Savoy at French Court; D. Frigo, Principe, *Ambasciatori e jus gentium: l'amministrazione della politica estera nel Piemonte del Settecento* (Bologna, 1991), p. 126; those of Lord Chesterfield to his son – whom he was preparing for a diplomatic career – advising that he should acquire as much military intelligence in Berlin as possible because it was part of the conversation of courts. R.K. Root, ed., *Lord Chesterfield's Letters to His Son and Others* (London, 1969), p. 90 (10 January, 1749 OS); and C. Mozzarelli, 'Corte e amministrazione nel principato gonzaghesco', *Società e storia* V (1982), pp. 245 ff.; and S. Marchisio, 'Ideologia e problemi dell'economia familiare nelle lettere della nobiltà piemontese (XVII–XVIII secolo)', *Bolletino storico-bibliografico subalpino* LXXXIII (1985), pp. 78 ff.

[42] Redlich, *German Military Enterpriser* II, p. 145, for the situation in eighteenth-century Prussia.

king, while in Frederick the Great's Prussia, army officers dominated what court there was in Berlin and favoured commanders were admitted to the King's private society at Potsdam. Indeed, the triumph of centralized state control over traditionally independent noble officers could not always have been achieved without exploiting that special relationship with, and personal obligation to, the ruler. These personal ties were strengthened by the new Military Orders created in later seventeenth- and eighteenth-century Europe, whose predominantly noble membership reinforced the warrior ethos of at least part of the elite. The importance of personal service to a monarch was highlighted by Louis XVI's abortive flight from Paris in 1791, and the Revolutionary authorities' subsequent imposition on the French officer corps of an oath to themselves, which resulted in a mass exodus of noblemen who no longer felt obliged to serve.[43] Side by side with such traditional motives could be found rather more modern calculations, above all the opportunities for a relatively well-paid career.

A mixture of ideological and material reasons encouraged the European nobility to adapt to the Military Revolution, becoming military professionals in the new sense. This process, however, was also advanced and facilitated by the clear preference of rulers and governments for noblemen to command their expanding armies. Deliberate government policy was crucial in the continued and, indeed, intensified military role and the enduring identification of the Second Estate with the vocation of arms. Denmark, where the post-1660 absolute monarchy at first discriminated against the old nobility, was untypical in this respect, but much more typical in the subsequent emergence of a new nobility, partly based upon army service. Some monarchs imposed the obligation to serve in their armies directly – as did Peter the Great – or indirectly (by linking rank to service) in the Tables of Ranks introduced in states such as Russia, Denmark, and Sweden. Even where such measures were not taken, rulers like Charles III of Spain and Charles Emmanuel III of Piedmont-Savoy made clear their expectation that their noble subjects should serve in this way. Peter III's Manifesto (1762) freeing nobles from their service obligations still required those who left Russia to return to serve in times of crisis, on pain of forfeiture of their property. By then, in any case, many Russian nobles seem to have 'internalized' the idea of service that had been drummed into them during the previous half-century.[44]

Rulers eased the way for their noble subjects by creating cadet corps and founding military academies for them (see above, Section IV). These

[43] Lind, 'Military and Absolutism', pp. 223 ff.; Corvisier, *Armies*, p. 153; Scott, *Response of the Royal Army*, pp. 159–60.

[44] Lind, 'Military and Absolutism', pp. 224–5; Demeter, *German Officer Corps*, p. 34; Le Donne, *Absolutism and Ruling Class*, pp. 23, 42; Pedlow, *Hessian Nobility*, pp. 144–6; B. Meehan-Waters, 'The Development and the Limits of Security of Noble Status, Person and Property in 18th Century Russia', in A.G. Cross, ed., *Russia and the West in the 18th Century* (Newtonville, MA, 1983), pp. 295 ff. Before the Cortes removed the requirement (1813) aspiring entrants to the Spanish military academies were obliged to present proofs of their nobility: Atienza Hernandez, *Aristocracia*, pp. 44 ff.

advantages often continued once a noble had been commissioned. The Austrian Habsburgs were far from unique in deliberately favouring officers from old noble families rather than from the newly ennobled. Elector Ferdinand of Bavaria (1651–79) was not alone in promoting young noble officers more rapidly, and commissioning them with greater seniority than their non-noble colleagues. The final decades of the *ancien régime* saw a striking intensification of this discrimination in favour of the nobility all across Europe: in Russia, where Emperor Paul deliberately restricted access to the officer corps to nobles in the 1790s; in Prussia, where Frederick the Great was obliged to commission and to promote non-nobles to fill the enormous losses of Junker officers during the Seven Years War, but when peace was restored in 1763 immediately reverted to his earlier practice of advancing or selecting only Junkers; and in France (see below), Piedmont-Savoy, and elsewhere.[45]

Eighteenth-century monarchs certainly took a close and frequently personal interest in their armies. Their efforts sometimes went as far as the introduction of army uniform as an acceptable form of dress for the upper nobility who attended Court. But why did they prefer noblemen to command their forces? There is some suggestion that this preference even extended to preventing non-noblemen from becoming captains save in a minority of cases and not allowing these commanders to rise above the rank of lieutenant-colonel.[46] At one level, this was simply an attempt to buttress the developing discipline of the army: by transplanting the established social hierarchy into their military forces, rulers hoped to reinforce authority and encourage obedience in the ranks. A second, rather pragmatic motive was an attempt to utilize the nobleman's personal fortune and private credit in the interest of the state. When food, equipment, and pay were not provided on time by central government departments, as was frequently the case, a noble officer was expected to make up the shortfall and to expend his own money to keep his company supplied with the essentials of military life. The prince de Ligne would subsequently claim that his campaigns in Austrian service cost him more than 800 000 florins, 200 000 of which were devoted to the welfare of his own regiment and the other units under his command. In some measure rulers were only extending to their noble subjects, who were otherwise exempt, the military burdens being imposed on the rest of society in the form of conscription and taxation: it was simply a different form of service, which in many states was expected from everyone.[47]

More importantly, however, rulers, like many of their subjects, simply found it all but impossible to conceive of a military officer, and especially

[45] Hudemann-Simon, 'Une noblesse en déclin', p. 94; Demeter, *German Officer Corps*, p. 34; Le Donne, *Absolutism and Ruling Class*, pp. 42 ff. Cf. Ricuperati, 'Gli strumenti', pp. 816 ff., and Scott, *Response of the Royal Army*, pp. 19 ff.

[46] Redlich, *German Military Enterpriser* II, p. 121.

[47] *Op. cit.*, pp. 20, 121; John A. Lynn, 'A Pattern of French Military Reform, 1750–1790', in D.D. Horward, ed., *The Consortium on Revolutionary Europe 1750–1850: Proceedings 1974* (Gainesville, FL, 1978), pp. 113–28; Kennett, *French Armies*, p. 57; C. Duffy, *The Army of Maria Theresa* (London, 1977), p. 33.

a senior commander, who was not a nobleman. This no doubt explains why, in seventeenth-century Sweden, non-nobles who advanced beyond the rank of captain were automatically ennobled, reinforcing the link between the nobility and military professionalism. It also contributed to the issuing of Tables of Ranks. The ruler could also be harnessing the nobility's continuing local influence, especially as the state structure was not always as effective as night have been wished. This was especially important for matters such as recruitment and conscription, where a nobleman's local influence could compensate for the weakness of central authority in the provinces. As late as 1778 Prince Nicholaus Esterházy – the celebrated Maecenas and patron of Joseph Haydn – supplied the Austrian army with 200 hussars from his own vast estates. He also helped to persuade Ödenburg county – of which he was high sheriff – to furnish 2000 more men for the Habsburg cause in the War of the Bavarian Succession.[48]

There was seldom – particularly in eastern and central Europe – a social group sufficiently established and numerous to supply a credible alternative to the nobility as officers. At the same time, it was obviously better to have the armed forces in the hands of those with a stake in the status quo rather than in those of a military caste with no such stake, a view explicitly advanced by the British statesman Henry Pelham in 1744. Victor Amadeus III's Court-aristocratic reaction against the administrative cadre which had emerged in eighteenth-century Piedmont-Savoy reflected the belief that the aristocracy was the natural pillar of society and ally of monarchy. Many rulers also appreciated the value of the links established between themselves and the territorial nobility through the army. This was especially important when, as in Prussia and the Austrian Habsburg territories, there were few other common institutions, and military service might lead the nobleman to a greater identification with the prince.[49]

Last, but certainly not least, most rulers probably agreed with noble propagandists that the elite alone possessed an innate capacity for leadership together with virtues that were particularly appropriate for the military life, and therefore should be given special preference. Frederick the Great said as much. The celebrated *Allgemeines Landrecht* (1794), promulgated eight years after Frederick's death but very much bearing his imprint, unequivocally declared the nobility to be 'the first order in the

[48] Rebecca A. Gates, 'The Esterházy Princes, 1760–1790' (PhD thesis, University of Illinois at Urbana-Champaign, 1979), pp. 32–3.

[49] Anderson, *War and Society*, pp. 170–1; P. Mansel, 'Monarchy, Uniform and the Rise of the *Frac* 1760–1830', *Past and Present* XCVI (1982), pp. 103–32; Dahlgren, 'Estates and Classes', in Roberts, *Sweden's Age*, p. 127; Roy, 'The Profession of Arms', p. 212; Ricuperati, 'Gli strumenti', pp. 816 ff. Cf. Evans, 'Maria Theresa and Hungary', p. 202. The point should be stressed here, perhaps, that this concentration of military power in the hands of the civil elite is not in tune with Corvisier's thesis regarding a growing divide between civil and military society in the later 17th and 18th centuries, which is (temporarily) restored in the wake of the French Revolutionary Wars: *Armies*, pp. 195–7.

state. Its position [obliged it] to undertake to defend the state, to protect and uphold both its outward dignity and the fabric of its internal structure.' There were two dimensions to this. On the one hand, it was believed that the nobleman's sense of honour, family, and lineage would prevent him from failing to do his duty in front of his men and fellow officers. On the other, an important analysis of the thinking behind the narrowing by Louis XVI's government of entry into the officer corps to old noble families by the Ségur Law of 1781 – a development hitherto interpreted unfavourably by historians as the victory of social privilege, even at the expense of effectiveness – has revealed that those who pressed for these changes, and for the ending of the sale of commissions, were inspired less by a belief in the virtue of social exclusivity *per se* and hostility to a rising bourgeoisie than by the view that the older families, though generally poorer, were believed to be more likely to possess the correct military virtues, and to be capable of being moulded into good officers, than the more recently elevated, who were usually wealthier and more independent. Rulers and governments elsewhere evidently had similar ideas, since most of their military training and other projects were aimed at getting the vast mass of the poorer, provincial nobility (rather than the tiny noble elite – although the latter were not ignored in the process) into the officer corps, which the aristocracy alone simply could not have filled. We might conclude from this that, despite the Military Revolution and some officers' successful acquisition of the necessary technical education, nobles were valued as officers precisely because traditional qualities remained highly prized and because the noble 'ethic' remained fundamentally a fighting one.[50]

## VI

There was considerable variation in the responses of individuals, families, types of nobility, and states to the challenge of the Military Revolution. Yet despite differences of degree and in the extent to which governments used blandishments or coercion to get noblemen into their armies, the general picture seems clear. Far from all nobles were soldiers: the emergence of the term *noblesse militaire* in the mid-eighteenth century underlined that there were other types of nobility.[51] Yet many, and perhaps a majority, were – everywhere. Military service remained not an option but a defining quality which had to be maintained: especially in central and eastern Europe, but also among substantial sectors of the elite outside those regions. That continuity, however, did not preclude significant change.

[50] Demeter, *German Officer Corps*, pp. 6–7; *Die politischen Testamente der Hohenzollern*, ed. R. Dietrich (Cologne and Vienna, 1986), pp. 310 (1752 Testament) and 498–500 (1768 Testament); Roy, 'The Profession of Arms', pp. 211–12; D. Bien, 'The Army in the French Enlightenment: Reform, Reaction and Revolution', *Past and Present* LXXXV (1979), pp. 68 ff.; Best, *War and Society*, pp. 24 ff.

[51] This is the Chevalier d'Arc's term: Corvisier, *Armies*, p. 103; Corvisier, 'La Noblesse militaire', p. 336, for the suggestion that it was first used in 1750.

The early modern period and especially the eighteenth century saw the increased 'militarization' of noble life and culture. It was most apparent in the vast increase in the time demanded by the profession of arms. Whereas before the mid-seventeenth century military life was likely to be temporary and even occasional and sporadic, by the eighteenth century the typical noble officer was likely to be in uniform almost permanently, to be with his regiment more often than not, and to identify himself overwhelmingly with the army and military service. This was a remarkable change.

Equally remarkable was the nobility's success in remaining the leading military group or order in society in most states, until at least the end of the *ancien régime* (generally around 1800, but later in some parts of Europe). The two worlds of army officer and nobility were becoming ever more closely identified by the final decades of the eighteenth century. Indeed, their fusion may even have been becoming a defining feature of state and society at the end of the *ancien régime*. Some historians have even argued that the remarkable victories of the Revolutionary and Napoleonic armies over the established European powers during the 1790s and 1800s were facilitated by the enduring pre-eminence of ill-equipped and conservative officer corps in most of the states which fought France.

The nobility's continuing military role had implications for its political and social position. It undoubtedly contributed to the biological extinction of some families, whose sons entered the army and either were killed in combat or did not marry. But the overall verdict must be rather more positive. The nobility had survived the challenge represented by the Military Revolution and indeed had adapted remarkably successfully to the new circumstances. This involved a reshaping of the nature of its military service by 1800, revealing that there was no inherent contradiction between nobility and military professionalism. The transformation also underlines that the nobility – or at least significant parts of it – was not inherently resistant to change. Its former 'feudal' service certainly had been redefined, with the mounted knight becoming an officer in infantry or cavalry regiments. The nobility, and particularly the numerically preponderant lesser nobility, had become a service caste, acting as officers in the state's permanent forces, their main military virtue being obedience. But a fundamentally personal relationship between ruler and elite remained central to this service.[52]

For individual nobles in most continental countries, the army was a good option and not – as has been claimed for eighteenth-century

[52] Lynch, *Bourbon Spain*, pp. 391–3; Best, *War and Society*, pp. 26–7; Scott, *Response of the Royal Army*, pp. 190–1; G. Chaussinand-Nogaret, *La Noblesse au XVIII^e siècle: de la féodalité aux Lumières* (Paris, 1976). But we should not ignore the role of enlightened noble-soldiers throughout Europe. Cf. details of subscribers to the *Berliner Monatschrift* in the later eighteenth century, in T.C.W. Blanning, 'Frederick the Great and Enlightened Absolutism', in Scott, *Enlightened Absolutism*, p. 286. Cf. Anderson, *War and Society*, pp. 119–20.

England – a career only for the stupidest cadets who could not find alternative employment. Military service also represented one of the ways in which nobles sought to counter the threat of declining political power, since their monopoly of the officer corps, and their role in other parts of the military establishment, meant that they effectively controlled the new instruments of coercion developed by the state. This success offers an alternative model to that proposed by historians a generation ago who linked a crisis of the nobility with the loss of its military function and ethos in the early modern era. Not the least important aspect of their success was the extent to which a nobility newly imbued with more refined notions of behaviour (gentility) set the tone of the officer corps everywhere, such that – for generations – officer and gentleman (and all they implied) have been virtually synonymous.[53]

The new situation also had important implications for the state and for the nobility's relationship with it. Although the nobility played a crucial part in facilitating the important military-political changes that were at the heart of the Military Revolution and in the organization and leadership of the armed forces, the new relationship established thereby between nobles and state also contributed to the supremacy of the latter. In the eighteenth century, after decades of opposition, the nobles of many countries allowed themselves to become the mainstay of the state, identifying their interests with it and abandoning the spirit of Estates-based separatism: this evolution was particularly apparent in Prussia. A new loyalty to the state developed, even if this continued to be expressed in the traditional terms of personal fealty to the king as supreme military commander. The extent of the integration between nobility, army, and state was by no means the same everywhere. But by redefining themselves, and accepting redefinition, as a military service elite, nobles, and overwhelmingly the lesser nobility, were integrated to an ever greater degree within the developing state.[54] These links were strengthened by the long wars against Revolutionary and Napoleonic France, and they would endure at least until the First World War.

[53] Adamson, 'The Baronial Context', p. 120; cf. on nobles as 'mediators' of power in early modern states: C. Mozzarelli, *Lo stato gonzaghesco: Mantova dal 1382 al 1707*, in (Utet) *Storia d'Italia* XVII (Turin, 1979); Marchisio, 'Ideologia e problemi', pp. 128 ff.

[54] Cf. Donati, 'Esercito', on concept of 'statizzazione'; Berdahl, *Politics of the Prussian Nobility*, p. 92. Cf. also the loyalties of Bohemian nobles in 1740s, analysed by E. Hassenpflug-Elzholz, *Böhmen und die böhmischen Stände in der Zeit des beginnenden Zentralismus*, 'Veröffentlichungen des Collegium Carolinum', XXX (Munich and Vienna, 1982), and summarized by Dickson, *Finance and Government* I, p. 90: of 351 nobles holding central government office (including army commissions), 302 declared for Maria Theresa. In contrast, 114 of 132 nobles holding local office declared for Charles Albert of Bavaria.

## *Acknowledgements*

This article results from a research project on 'The European Nobility 1600–1800', funded by the Leverhulme Trust. We are grateful to the Trust for its generous financial support. We also thank Dr Derek McKay of the London School of Economics and the editors of this journal for their helpful and constructive comments on an earlier version of this article.

*University of Dundee*
*and the University of St Andrews*

# [2]

# German Women and War, 1500–1800

*Peter H. Wilson*

Recent research has only just begun to scratch the surface of the history of women in early modern European warfare. The picture that is emerging indicates that women both formed a normal part of early modern armies and played a vital role in sustaining their operations. They were removed from armies by the militarization of the support services and subsequently 'written out' of military history by nineteenth-century male historians.[1] The nature of women's relationship to war and their role within it are still only partly understood. In particular, there has been a tendency to focus on those women who were involved in actual combat or worked in the logistical support services. At worst this produces a simple inversion, replacing tales of bloodthirsty male warriors with those of aggressive heroines.[2] At best, the far larger group of women affected by conflict and militarization are still ignored in favour of a minority of highly interesting but exceptional cases. An Anglocentric bias predominates, with little coverage of continental Europe beyond the Atlantic seaboard of France and Holland.[3]

This study seeks to widen the parameters by exploring the relationship of German women to war, and their role in the armed forces of the various states that made up the Holy Roman Empire. It will exclude those general aspects of the impact of war which differed little from those affecting male civilians, in favour of investigating the position of women who were involved by direct contact with the military establishment. It will also question the prevailing view that the exclusion of women from the armed forces came with the militarization of the support services in

I would like to thank Jeremy Black for his helpful comments on a draft of this paper.

1 See the valuable survey by B.C. Hacker, 'Women and Military Institutions in Early Modern Europe: A Reconnaissance', *Signs: Journal of Women in Culture and Society* VI (1980–1), pp. 643–71.

2 R. Miles, *The Women's History of the World* (London, Paladin, 1989), pp. 50–2, 173–9.

3 F.C.G. Page, *Following the Drum: Women in Wellington's Wars* (London, Deutsch, 1986); E. Ewing, *Women in Uniform Through the Ages* (Totowa, NJ, Rowman & Littlefield, 1975); L.G. De Pauw, 'Women in Combat: The Revolutionary War Experience', *Armed Forces and Society* VII (1981), pp. 209–26; R. Dekker and L.C. van der Pol, 'Republican Heroines: Cross-Dressing Women in the French Revolutionary Armies', *History of European Ideas* X (1989), pp. 353–63; M.T. Lacau-Mougenot, 'Des femmes dans l'armée aux sous-officiers', *Revue Historique des Armées* II (1986), pp. 100–7.

the later eighteenth century, arguing instead that this occurred earlier and was influenced by wider changes in social and moral outlook beyond purely military concerns.

## I

Examination of women's legal status reveals both changes in their role in military life and a significant shift in official attitudes to it. From the start of professional mercenary armies in the late fifteenth century, the authorities tried to regulate female contact with soldiers. These attempts need to be seen as part of a general tendency to control soldier's behaviour by the imposition of codes of martial law called 'articles of war'.[4] This in turn must be viewed within the wider context of the process of social disciplining by which post-Reformation church and state sought to turn people into diligent, obedient and pious subjects.[5] These areas are linked by a common shift from an emphasis on discipline to one of moral control. As the military authorities moved from efforts to contain insubordination to attempts to control soldiers' personal lives, the civil authorities switched attention from church discipline to moral policing. This shift is noticeable in both spheres after about 1650, and is a reflection of the growing confidence of church and state after the upheavals of the Reformation and the Thirty Years War. It was paralleled by a move away from legislation designed to control women associated with the army and towards efforts to exclude them from involvement altogether. Women were transformed from a recognized part of the military establishment to the status of civilians, albeit still often under martial law. This process was accompanied by a general decline in their status in the eyes of both civil and military elites and 'respectable' society.

The roots of these developments were already present in the sixteenth century. Early articles of war were already characterized by the basic principle of bringing those deemed useful to the army under martial law and excluding those who were not. Initially, the former category included a large number of women associated with the baggage train who provided logistical support and sexual favours and

[4] W. Erben, 'Ursprung und Entwicklung der deutschen Kriegsartikel', *Mitteilungen des Instituts für österreichische Geschichtsforschung* VI (1901), pp. 473–529; H.-M. Möller, *Das Regiment der Landsknechte* (Wiesbaden, Steiner, 1976), pp. 31–40; M. Nell, *Die Landsknechte* (Berlin, 1914); S. Fiedler, *Kriegswesen und Kriegführung im Zeitalter der Landsknechte* (Coblenz, Bernard & Graefe, 1985), pp. 77–8, 92, 166; E.v. Frauenholz, *Das Heerwesen in der Zeit des freien Söldnertums*, (Munich, Beck, 1937); R. Baumann, *Das Söldnerwesen im 16. Jahrhundert im bayerischen und schwäbischen Beispiel* (Munich, Wölfle, 1978), pp. 102–12, and his *Landsknechte* (Munich, 1994), pp. 48–53, 79–86.

[5] G. Oestreich, *Neostoicism and the Early Modern State* (Cambridge, Cambridge Univ. Press, 1982); W. Schulze, 'Gerhard Oestreichs Begriff "Sozialdisziplinierung" in der Frühen Neuzeit', *Zeitschrift für historische Forschung* XIV (1987), pp. 265–302; R. Po-Chia Hsia, *Social Discipline in the Reformation: Central Europe 1550–1750* (London, Routledge, 1989).

acted as entrenchment workers. Such women fell under the jurisdiction of the same articles of war that governed the conduct of both male baggage personnel and combatants, even if they were not formally sworn in. These codes were intended to enforce behavioural norms and a hierarchical structure to enable the few in command to control the mass. They are indicative of the authorities' fear of the collective action of both male and female personnel. The disciplinary measures were directed at containing not only the pay strikes and mutinies of male soldiers but also the not infrequent refusal of the baggage women to undertake entrenchment work. By the 1540s these measures had been supplemented by a policy of issuing passes to legitimize certain male and female members of the train and to exclude those who were unwanted.[6]

This policy continued into the eighteenth century, but increasingly it was only those women who were legally married to soldiers who were given a recognized status in martial law. Other women were excluded and classed as civilians. A prisoner-of-war exchange cartel negotiated between imperial and French generals in 1692 stipulated that captured women were to be returned without payment, whereas male sutlers and other non-combatant personnel were to be regarded as privates.[7] By the mid-eighteenth century, regulations governing the baggage train assumed that all personnel were male.[8] The special clauses in the articles of war covering the treatment of women by soldiers also tended to disappear. Early articles included strong exhortations that young mothers, pregnant women, and virgins were not to be harmed.[9] These were either removed entirely in later editions or replaced by more general rules covering all civilians. For example, while the Württemberg articles of 1705 and 1727 included the traditional clauses, those of 1758 and 1769 only contained rules governing soldiers' marriages.[10] The Bavarian articles of 1717 merely included women in a general category of civilians to be spared during war.[11]

Meanwhile, soldiers' wives increasingly became a legally distinct group of women remaining under martial law. Saxony had developed the practice by the 1680s of placing officers' families under martial law as long as the marriage lasted, while those of NCOs and men fell under its jurisdiction if they were with them in the field. By the eighteenth

6 Baumann, *Landsknechte*, pp. 151–4; Baumann, *Söldnerwesen*, pp. 150–1; Möller, *Regiment*, pp. 42, 152–63.

7 B. Sicken, *Das Wehrwesen des fränkischen Reichskreises: Aufbau und Struktur (1681–1714)* (2 vols., Nuremberg, Spindler, 1967) I, pp. 306–7. A Franco–Dutch agreement of 1673 contained similar arrangements.

8 e.g. the Austrian regulations of 1759 in Hauptstaatsarchiv Stuttgart, C14: Bü. 77. Unless indicated otherwise, all subsequent documents referred to are in this archive.

9 Imperial articles of 1508 (Art. 14) in Frauenholz, *Söldnertums*, pp. 180–3.

10 A30c: Bü. 2, 7; A202: Bü.2302; A.L. Reyscher (ed.), *Vollständige, historisch und kritisch bearbeitete Sammlung der Württembergischen Gesetze* (19 vols., Stuttgart/Tübingen, Cotta, 1828–50), XIX 1, Nos. 252, 278, 338, 425, 443, 450, 461.

11 E. v. Frauenholz, *Das Heerwesen in der Zeit des Absolutismus* (Munich, Beck, 1940), pp. 411–20 at p. 413.

century, most soldiers' wives were under military discipline as long as they remained in the garrison towns.[12] Civilian women were only brought under military jurisdiction when they did something detrimental to military efficiency. The Palatinate, like many other territories, adopted the provision of the imperial duel mandate of 1668, which set out stiff punishments for women who failed to prevent or even encouraged their husbands coming to blows. Women who encouraged desertion or assisted illegal recruitment by other powers could find themselves handed over to the military authorities for punishment.[13]

The low importance attached to women in early German population statistics is a further indication of the minor role they now played in the military calculations of the state. By the mid-eighteenth century several smaller territories introduced annual surveys in an effort to maximize the military potential of their populations through some limited form of conscription. In Württemberg an annual census was begun in 1757. While officials were required to provide a detailed breakdown of the male population to assist recruitment, women only appeared in the overall totals. A similar preoccupation with males characterized the Hessen-Kassel census demanded by the 1762 conscription decree.[14]

Changes in women's legal status both reflected and were a product of a change in official attitudes. While these remained ambivalent throughout, it is possible to discern a move towards a more negative view. From the start there was a tendency to use derogatory terms to describe women in the army: *Hure* (whore) or even *Beischlaf* (German legalese for sexual intercourse) were the most common in the early sixteenth century. However, it has been suggested that these labels did not necessarily have the same level of odium attached to them in contemporary civil society or later within the military establishment.[15] Certainly, the legal position of such women was not unfavourable. The articles of war accorded female partners, including *Beischlaf*, full rights of inheritance and even gave concubines present in the camp precedence over any wife at home.[16] Moreover, much of the moral condemnation that so characterized later thinking was lacking. Michael Ott and Jacob Preiß went as far as advocating institutionalizing prosti-

[12] W. Thenius, *Die Anfänge des stehenden Heerwesens in Kursachsen unter Johann Georg III und Johann Georg IV* (Leipzig, Quelle & Meyer, 1912), p. 124. After 1752 Prussian army wives who were not present with the regiments fell under civil jurisdiction: Frauenholz, *Absolutismus*, pp. 276–7.

[13] A202: Bü.2299, 21 Apr. 1751, case of Agatha Raischlin; F. Munich, *Geschichte der Entwicklung der bayerischen Armee seit zwei Jahrhunderten* (Munich, Lindauer'sche Buchhandlung, 1864), p. 123.

[14] A15: Bü.218; Reyscher (ed.), *Gesetze* XIV, pp. 527–9; M. Schaab, 'Die Anfänge einer Landesstatistik im Herzogtum Württemberg, in den Badischen Markgrafschaften und in der Kurpfalz', *Zeitschrift für Württembergischen Landesgeschichte* XXVI (1967), pp. 89–112; P.K. Taylor, 'The Household's Most Expendable People: The Draft and Peasant Society in 18th Century Hessen-Kassel' (Ph.D., Univ. of Iowa, 1987), pp. 401–3.

[15] Baumann, *Landsknechte*, pp. 154–6, 161–2.

[16] Op. cit., p. 201.

tution in their treatise on war of 1524. In addition to women for sewing and nursing, they recommended that each garrison have 'two or three women who are every man's wife', who were to be given regular pay contracts and the personal protection of the commander.[17] This view began to change in the mid-sixteenth century. Whereas Emperor Maximilian's articles of war of 1508 had made no mention of women in the camp, Charles V already prohibited his artillery-men from 'whoring'. Comprehensive imperial articles issued in 1570 went further by drawing a distinction between 'indecent women' (*unzüchtige Weiber*), who were prohibited from accompanying the army, and 'unsuspicious women' (*unverdächtige Weiber*), who were needed to care for the sick, for washing, and 'other innocent things'.[18]

As indicated above, this latter category of women had largely disappeared from official regulations by the mid-seventeenth century, while the former was increasingly excluded from army life. While the Brandenburg code of 1656 stated that if soldiers wished to keep a 'whore' they had to marry her first, later laws excluded women altogether. The imperial code of 1668 banned 'mistresses and concubines' from the army, while the supply regulations issued the same year made no allowance for the provisioning and accommodation of women.[19] These rules were tightened up in 1682 and were widely copied in the articles issued by the various territorial armies.[20]

The result was a tendency to equate any woman connected with the army with 'whore'. This already characterized civilian attitudes: by 1600 venereal disease was known in Swabia as *Landsknecht* (mercenary soldier).[21] A Württemberg decree of 1700 termed all unmarried partners of soldiers *gaile Dirnen* (lascivious whores), and *Dirne* was generally used to label women accused of encouraging desertion.[22] Such views were widespread by the early eighteenth century and included prejudice towards men as well as women. The Würzburg city council objected to the proposed construction of new barracks in 1721 on the grounds that soldiers spread disease and were associated with large numbers of poor women and children. Village authorities often tried to deny soldiers poor relief on the grounds that they were individuals of ill repute. Such prejudice was in part motivated by self-interest: the Würzburg council wanted to preserve prime building land, while the village headmen wanted to retain assistance for their own clientele.[23]

Other aspects of official policy encouraged such prejudice. Despite

17 Op. cit., p. 156.
18 Printed in Frauenholz, *Söldnertums*, pp. 180–3, 221–5, 256–300.
19 Frauenholz, *Absolutismus*, pp. 131–43, 363–74.
20 Op. cit., pp. 380–98, 426–30 (Saxony 1700), 411–20 (Bavaria 1717).
21 Baumann, *Söldnerwesen*, p. 154.
22 L6.22.5.83; A6: Bü. 63; A202: Bü. 2299. The same was true in Hessen-Darmstadt; see the decree against desertion 20 Mar. 1739 in Staatsarchiv Darmstadt, E8B 107/16.
23 W. Kopp, *Würzburger Wehr. Eine Chronik zur Wehrgeschichte Würzburgs.* (Würzburg, Freunde Mainfränkischer Kunst & Geschichte, 1979), p. 75; Taylor, 'Draft and Peasant Society', pp. 219–25.

the numerous prohibitions of sexual licence in the military codes, soldiers were often exempt from the normal fines for fornication. The military authorities themselves made frequent use of women in the very roles they condemned. For example, women were often employed to entice soldiers to desert and enlist in other armies. Recruiting stations maintained by the large territorial states in the imperial cities were generally lodged in inns where women, along with music and alcohol, were used to attract potential recruits. The building used to lodge conscripts in late eighteenth-century Potsdam offered a dance floor and girls to keep the men happy and discourage desertion before they were assigned to their units.[24]

While the spread of syphilis in the sixteenth century was a contributory factor, it is important to see this change in attitude both within the context of a shift in wider moral perspectives beyond purely military considerations and as a development affecting men as well as women. While the move to limit or prevent the presence of women in the army was rationalized as the need to restrict the size of the baggage train and facilitate greater strategic mobility, it was also part of a general change in moral attitudes associated with the Reformation and the rise of the territorial state. Sentences for prostitution, adultery, bigamy, infanticide, and homosexuality all became more severe in the sixteenth century.[25] The articles of war were profoundly affected by these changes and, like most territorial civil legal codes, often adopted the barbaric punishments of Charles V's *Carolina* of 1532, regardless of the confession of the issuing authority.[26] Both Protestant teaching and the state's fiscal needs led to legislation reinforcing paternalism and the patriarchal family. Although detailed examination of the dynamics of family life reveals that women retained considerable autonomy, their legal status often declined appreciably.[27] This was paralleled by their loss of individual status in martial law and reduction to that of 'dependants' of male personnel. It is also significant that the efforts to exclude 'loose women' from army life occurred at the same time that church and civil courts increasingly turned their attention to cases of sexual misconduct.[28]

This hardening of moral attitudes affected the punishment of men for sexual offences in the military as well as the civil sphere. It is a

[24] O. Ulbricht, 'Infanticide in Eighteenth-Century Germany', in R.J. Evans (ed.), *The German Underworld* (London, Routledge, 1988), pp. 108–41 at p. 127; D. Kotsch, *Potsdam: die preußische Garnisonstadt* (Brunswick, Westermann, 1992), p. 96. See also the discussion of women's role in recruitment below.

[25] Hsia, *Social Discipline*, pp. 144–5.

[26] Examples include Swabian Circle articles, 21 Nov. 1710 (A30c: Bü. 2), Württemberg articles, 9 May 1705 (Reyscher (ed.), *Gesetze* XIX/1, pp. 384–94) and 25 June 1727 (A30c: Bü. 2). See also Frauenholz, *Söldnertums*, pp. 256–300, and *Absolutismus*, pp. 363–7, 380–98.

[27] D.W. Sabean, *Property, Production and Family in Neckarhausen 1700–1870* (Cambridge, Cambridge Univ. Press, 1990), esp. pp. 166–74. E. Cameron, *The European Reformation* (Oxford, Clarendon Press, 1991), pp. 401–5.

[28] Hsia, *Social Discipline*, pp. 124–9, 144–6.

popular misconception to see late seventeenth- and eighteenth-century armies as havens for criminals and the 'dregs of society'.[29] This was simply not the case. Only in dire emergencies, and usually only then when they knew the units would be serving outside territorial boundaries, did early modern German governments recruit large numbers of criminals. A good number of men did join up to escape marital strife, illegitimate children, or amorous difficulties.[30] Nonetheless, the authorities' attitude to known sex offenders was normally severe. Early military codes generally specified the death penalty for rape, attempted rape, and adultery, and while these punishments were moderated in the later eighteenth century under the influence of the Enlightenment, the rules also became more sophisticated and comprehensive.[31] Civilians attempting to escape punishment by enlisting were not normally recruited. Those caught doing so in the Duchy of Württemberg were to have their sentence increased. An investigation was ordered in 1714 to root out those who had joined up to avoid keeping a promise of marriage or the responsibilities of fatherhood. These rules coincided with ducal efforts to enforce the ideal of responsible male housekeeping (*Haushaltung*) in the civil sphere, and were motivated by fiscal and moral criteria.[32] Men who deserted their wives, committed adultery or another sexual offence, and then joined up were regularly handed over to the civil authorities for punishment.[33] Württemberg law also permitted abandoned wives to petition the War Council to send wayward husbands to appear before the marriage court, though the army insisted that two officers be present at the trial.[34] Even foreign governments were permitted to pursue sex offenders who tried to shelter in the ranks.[35]

Nonetheless, the army's insatiable desire for additional manpower was allowed to override both the law and women's interests when the state deemed it necessary. This tended to be when all or part of the army had to mobilize quickly or when prolonged conflict made recruitment difficult. The authorities had the least scruple when they knew the regiments would be serving elsewhere; for example the Württemberg units transferred to Austrian and Prussian service,[36] or the Ansbach infantry hired to Britain in 1777, which included a number

[29] e.g. M. Kitchen, *A Military History of Germany from the Eighteenth Century to the Present Day* (London, Weidenfeld & Nicolson, 1975), p. 23; W. Doyle, *The Old European Order 1660–1800*, 2nd edn (Oxford, Oxford Univ. Press, 1992), p. 243.

[30] Examples in W. Schüssler, 'Das Werbewesen in der Reichsstadt Heilbronn vornehmlich im 18. Jahrhundert', (Ph.D., Univ. of Tübingen, 1951), p. 261; R. Atwood, *The Hessians: Mercenaries from Hessen-Kassel in the American Revolution* (Cambridge, Cambridge Univ. Press, 1980), p. 211.

[31] See the codes printed in Frauenholz, *Söldnertums* and *Absolutismus*.

[32] L6.22.6.1 6 and 20 Aug. 1714; Sabean, *Neckarhausen*, pp. 101–15.

[33] Examples in A202: Bü. 2262 (1745); Bü. 2263 (3 Jan. 1739); Bü. 2266 (9 June 1741); Bü. 2278 (28 May 1756).

[34] A202: Bü. 2266 (6 Oct. 1738); Bü. 2278 (25 Nov. 1746).

[35] A202: Bü. 2260 (24 July 1750), case involving an adulterer from Hessen-Darmstadt.

[36] A202: Bü. 2109-14, 2254-5; 2298 (22 Aug. 1737).

of 'fornicators' serving in place of punishment.[37] The mania for particularly tall soldiers that swept several German states in the 1720s and 1730s also enabled a number of men to escape punishment.[38] While these examples do reveal the authorities' double standards in this area, they also indicate how closely women's involvement with war was shaped by moral and fiscal impulses that went beyond purely military considerations.

## II

This analysis is borne out by an examination of the official policy towards soldiers' marriages, which remained the main area of martial law dealing with women after the mid-seventeenth century. Early military codes were little concerned with soldiers' legal spouses. As late as 1656, Brandenburg regulations permitted any soldier to marry and be accompanied by his wife.[39] Increasingly, however, the authorities sought to restrict the number of married personnel. As indicated above, this was only partly a result of military considerations. Indeed, much of the desire to reduce the size of the train derived from the view that women were not only non-essential personnel but inherently a threat to discipline. In addition, the evolution of permanent armies after 1650 altered the economic basis for soldiers' marriages. This coincided with the new conception of marriage as the cornerstone of state and society which emerged after the Reformation. Together, these developments produced a radically different policy toward servicemen's marriages from that which had predominated before the mid-seventeenth century.

Prior to the retention of permanent cadres in peacetime after 1648, most German soldiers served on temporary contracts which often expired when either winter or lack of funds halted operations. Evidence for early soldiers' marriages is patchy, though most seem to have been so-called *Maienehen* – semi-official liaisons forged in May when the campaigning season began and the living was relatively easy, and breaking up in winter when life became more difficult.[40] The one surviving serviceman's diary from the Thirty Years War does indicate that long-term marriages and even careful provision for children's schooling were possible, despite an itinerant existence and consecutive service in different armies.[41]

[37] E. Städter, *Die Ansbach-Bayreuther Truppen im Amerikanischen Unabhängigkeitskrieg 1777–1783* (Neustadt/Aisch, Egge, 1955), p. 31. For another example see F.K. Erbprinz zu Hohenlohe-Waldenburg, 'Über hohenlohisches Militärwesen', *Württembergisch Franken*, NF XL (1966), pp. 212–41 at p. 215.

[38] A6: Bü. 32, 26 July 1732.

[39] Frauenholz, *Absolutismus*, p. 137.

[40] Baumann, *Landsknechte*, pp. 157–9.

[41] J. Peters (ed.), *Ein Söldnerleben im Dreißigjährigen Krieg* (Berlin, Akademie Verlag, 1993).

Nonetheless, it was only the growing permanence of armies after 1648 that created a more settled material basis for marriage. Unfortunately, this coincided with a serious decline in soldiers' wages as states struggled to finance permanent forces and cope with the legacy of the Thirty Years War. While mercenaries' wages were often irregular between 1500 and 1650, they were substantially better than those of later regular soldiers. When paid, sixteenth-century soldiers had received considerably more than most civilian workers, while personnel during the Thirty Years War had at least been on par with journeymen-craftsmen. Pay rates after 1650 were low and were further eroded by inflation, so that by the eighteenth century most soldiers' wages were in line with those of day labourers. Only officers' pay held up reasonably well, though most subalterns were hardly wealthy.[42] Thus, while soldiers could now offer a prospective partner a more settled existence, they were scarcely able to provide a financially secure one. As well as being a key factor behind the growing civilian prejudice towards military personnel, this also motivated official efforts to restrict soldiers' marriages. Far from simply being the result of 'long-standing concerns that wife and child might distract the soldier from his duties',[43] the authorities were also afraid that men would simply be unable to support their families. Although regarding marriages as useful for limiting desertion, the Saxon government decided to restrict them for this reason in 1693.[44]

The political and moral factors associated with social disciplining were also important. Marriage assumed a central importance in the strategies of social control of the post-Reformation church and state. It was crucial to their efforts to enforce codes of behaviour and exploit the resources of subject households through the growing fiscal apparatus. Moreover, the Protestant view of marriage shifted the focus of consent away from potential partners and reinforced that of the household and community by insisting on parental consent. This process greatly increased official intolerance of traditional German marriage customs after the early seventeenth century, in favour of recognizing only those that had received the blessing of church and state. By condemning premarital sex, the authorities sought to eradicate those liaisons which lacked official sanction. In doing so they saw promiscuity where it had not previously existed: sex between unmarried couples was traditionally and popularly regarded as premarital, and even in the mid-eighteenth century illegitimate births rarely accounted for more

[42] Baumann, *Landsknechte*, pp. 86–91, 131–45; *Söldnerwesen*, pp. 112–24; F. Redlich, *The German Military Enterpriser and His Workforce* (2 vols., Wiesbaden, Steiner, 1964–5) I, pp. 54–104, 122–34; II, pp. 30–46, 231–67.

[43] Hacker, 'Women and Military Institutions', p. 659.

[44] Thensius, *Anfänge*, pp. 124–5.

than 10 per cent of the total, while many were retrospectively sanctioned by marriage.[45]

These wider trends made themselves felt in the policy towards soldiers' marriages in the later seventeenth century. Like civilians, soldiers and their prospective partners found that the decision to marry was taken out of their hands. The imperial articles of 1682 specified that soldiers had to try and obtain the consent of their parents or guardians before permission would be granted.[46] This was intended to prevent bigamy. Given that German armies remained relatively heterogeneous throughout the eighteenth century, with between 10 and 30 per cent of personnel being recruited from other (largely German) territories, the prospect of inadvertently sanctioning a bigamous or otherwise illegal marriage remained a constant fear of the authorities. Indeed, it was generally impractical to insist on parental consent, which is why most regulations substituted the permission of the company commander instead. Hessen-Kassel required this as early as 1682 and most other states followed suit by 1700.[47] A similar policy was adopted in France at about the same time.[48] Quotas were often introduced to restrict the number of wives per company. Simultaneously, severe punishments were imposed on couples marrying without permission; by the mid-eighteenth century most states had adopted the rule that men had to run the gauntlet of 200 soldiers between 12 and 24 times, while women were imprisoned in the workhouse for at least a year.

These rules were an important factor in the growing separation of soldiers and civilians which accompanied the development of the standing armies. The criteria for granting permission were different from those used in civilian life. The woman's material position, rather than that of the man, was the deciding factor. Indeed, the regulations discouraged the marriage of the higher-paid NCOs and officers, granting permission only when poor men 'could make their fortune' by marrying a richer partner. Some regulations even expressly excluded married men from holding NCO rank. In contrast, privates could gen-

[45] Hsia, *Social Discipline*, pp. 143–51; Ulbricht, 'Infanticide', p. 116; C. Dipper, *Deutsche Geschichte 1648–1789* (Frankfurt/Main, Suhrkamp, 1991), pp. 46–7; T. Robisheaux, *Rural Society and the Search for Order in Early Modern Germany* (Cambridge, Cambridge Univ. Press, 1989), pp. 95–120. Roper, *The Holy household: Women and Morals in Reformation Augsburg* (Oxford, Clarendon Press, 1989). For illegitimacy rates see S.C. Ogilvie, 'Coming of Age in a Corporate Society: Capitalism, Pietism and Family Authority in Rural Württemberg'. *Continuity and Change* 1 (1986), pp. 279–331 at 288–91, and R. Pröve, *Stehendes Heer und städtische Gesellschaft im 18. Jahrhundert. Göttingen und seine Militärbevölkerung 1713–1756* (Munich, Oldenbourg, 1995), p. 114.

[46] Frauenholz, *Absolutismus*, pp. 380–98.

[47] H.G. Böhme, *Die Wehrverfassung in Hessen-Kassel im 18. Jahrhundert bis zum siebenjährigen Kriege* (Kassel, Bärenreiter, 1954), pp. 31–2; *Reglement vor die Preußische Infanterie 1743* (repr. Osnabrück, Biblio, 1976), pp. 601–2; Städter, *Ansbach-Bayreuther Truppen*, pp. 39; Frauenholz, *Absolutismus*, pp. 165–6, 220, 344; Reyscher (ed.), *Gesetze* XIX/1, pp. 260–1 (30 Apr. 1687).

[48] I. Woloch, 'War Widows' Pensions: Social Policy in Revolutionary and Napoleonic France', *Societas* VI (1976), pp. 235–54 at pp. 236–7. C. Jones. 'The Welfare of the French Footsoldier'. *History* LXV (1980), pp. 193–213 at p. 208.

erally marry provided the prospective bride was not 'extremely poor'. Officers were also empowered to reject women who were not considered 'honest' or 'morally upright'. Unlike civilian marriages, the army took no account of premarital pregnancies: all unsanctioned liaisons were declared null and void.[49]

These criteria also reflected the distinction between officers and men which emerged after 1700. Whereas previously all military personnel had been subjected to the same articles of war, officers were now treated differently. This coincided with the gradual replacement of non-nobles by nobles in most officer corps, especially in the more senior ranks.[50] In contrast to ordinary soldiers, officers had to apply directly to the territorial ruler for permission.[51] This reflected the longstanding connection between the prince and his personal warrior servants, but also represented an attempt by the emergent absolutist state to subordinate the officer corps to the ruler's authority. Officially, officers were discouraged from marrying and increasingly obstacles were placed in their path. The Prussian regulations of 1743 stated flatly that the king preferred that 'an officer should remain single'. After 1763 it was very rare for Frederick II to grant permission to younger officers and he even refused it to senior ones, especially when the prospective bride was not from the nobility.[52] The same occurred in states like Württemberg which used Frederican regulations as the basis of their military codes. Other territories adopted the practice of placing financial hurdles to discourage marriages. After 1778 Würzburg compelled senior officers to pay a high deposit before being granted permission. Bamberg and Bavaria followed suit in 1779.[53] Officers who married without permission were cashiered.

Fiscal and economic motives were the key factors behind this practice. In Prussia, Frederick Wilhelm I had begun the practice of discour-

49 *Reglement vor die Preußische Infanterie 1743*, pp. 600–2; Württemberg *Militär-Reglement* (15 Dec. 1740) and *Reglement* (1 Jan. 1754), printed in Reyscher (ed.), *Gesetze*, XIX/1, Nos. 425 and 443. P. Löw, *Der preußische Unteroffizier im stehenden Heer des Absolutismus bis 1806* (Konstanz, Hartung-Gorre, 1989), pp. 308–9; J. Kraus, *Das Militärwesen der Reichsstadt Augsburg 1548 bis 1806* (Augsburg, Mühlberger, 1980), pp. 208–9; I. Kracauer, 'Das Militärwesen der Reichsstadt Frankfurt im 18. Jahrhundert', *Archiv für Frankfurts Geschichte und Kunst.* NF XII (1920), pp. 1–180 at pp. 79–82; Pröve, *Stehendes Heer*, pp. 102–3, 121. There was no difference between imperial cities and princely territories in this respect.

50 K. Demeter, *Das deutsche Offizierkorps in Gesellschaft und Staat 1650–1945*, 4th edn (Frankfurt/M., Bernard & Graefe, 1965); Redlich, *Military Enterpriser* II, pp. 112–69.

51 Thensius, *Anfänge*, pp. 124–5; O. Schuster and F.A. Franke, *Geschichte der sächsischen Armee* (3 vols., Leipzig, Duncker & Humblot, 1885) I, p. 189; Redlich, *Military Enterpriser* II, pp. 168–9; Böhme, *Wehrverfassung*, pp. 31–2. In Bavaria this prerogative was delegated to the Court War Council: Munich, *Bayerischen Armee*, p. 72.

52 *Reglement vor die Preußische Infanterie*, p. 600; C. v. Jany, *Geschichte der Preußischen Armee* (4 vols., Berlin, Siegismund, 1928–9) III, pp. 37–8.

53 E. Hagen, 'Die fürstlich würzburgische Hausinfanterie vom Jahre 1757 bis zur Einverleibung des Fürstbistums in Bayern 1803', *Darstellungen aus der bayerischen Kriegs- und Heeresgeschichte* XX (1911), pp. 1–142 at p. 47; J. Güssregen, *Die Wehrverfassung der Hochstiftes Bamberg im 18. Jahrhundert* (Bamberg, St Otto, 1936), p. 42 n. 121; Munich, *Bayerischen Armee*, p. 176.

aging non-noble brides for officers in the belief that commoners should keep their dowries within the civilian economy. While aristocratic prejudice prompted Frederick II to continue this, he was also keen that the state should not be burdened by demands from impoverished widows.[54] The system of deposits introduced by the south German states was intended to provide money to support widows and orphans. Governments were aware that such funds were likely to be inadequate, and took steps to reduce their own liabilities. Already in 1774 Würzburg officers had been permitted to marry provided they signed statements renouncing any entitlement to state welfare. All Bavarian officers and military administrators were told in March 1789 that they also had to sign away claims to a pension if they wanted to marry. This practice was extended to the rank and file. Prospective brides in Ansbach were warned not to expect automatic assistance if their husbands were sent to the front. A Bavarian order of 1778 restricting the number of married privates to four per company stated that exceptions would be made only if the prospective couples paid a 300-florin deposit.[55]

Military professionalism was only secondary to these economic and fiscal concerns. It was most pronounced in Prussia, where Frederick II believed that women and property dampened aggressive enthusiasm, remarking to General Zieten that good officers 'made their fortune not by marriage, but by the sabre'.[56]

The desire to limit marriages quickly affected recruiting practices and extended through these to interfere with civilian marriage arrangements. As early as 1700 Palatine officers were told not to recruit married men. Generally, all states preferred single men provided they could be obtained in sufficient numbers.[57] Where possible married soldiers were discharged and replaced by single men.[58] Wartime manpower requirements compelled governments to relax these rules and accept married volunteers.

Insufficient volunteers first became a serious problem in the 1680s, during the prolonged conflict with France and the Ottoman Turks. Many states resorted to some form of conscription by adapting their militia systems based on a division of the able-bodied male population into two or more categories.[59] Militiamen were taken from one or more

[54] Redlich, *Military Enterpriser* II, pp. 168–9.

[55] Hagen, 'Hausinfanterie', p. 47; Städter, *Ansbach-Bayreuther Truppen*, p. 77; Munich, *Bayerischen Armee*, pp. 182–4. For similar policies elsewhere see A30: Bü. 111; F. Mürmann, 'Das Militärwesen des ehemaligen Hochstiftes Paderborn seit dem Ausgange des Dreißigjährigen Krieges', *Westfälische Zeitschrift* XCV (1939), pp. 3–78 at p. 29.

[56] Quoted in Jany, *Preußischen Armee*, III, p. 38. Hanoverian senior officers held similar attitudes: see Pröve, *Stehendes Heer*, p. 103.

[57] Munich, *Bayerischen Armee*, p. 127; A6: Bü. 32, 34, 51, A8: Bü. 59; A30a: Bü. 105; A202: Bü. 2005–7; L6.22.7.4a; L6.22.8.1.

[58] For an example in Württemberg: A202 Bü. 2278 2 Nov, 1737; Reyscher (ed.), *Gesetze* XIX/1, pp. 620–1. For Hanover see Pröve, *Stehendes Heer*, pp. 104–5.

[59] H. Schnitter, *Volk und Landesdefension* (Berlin, Militärverlag der DDR, 1977).

category, depending on the scale of the emergency. Normally, only the younger, single, and economically dispensable males of the first category were called out. The methods of conscription introduced in many territories from the 1690s were intended to draw men from this category directly into the regular army.[60] To prevent a reduction of the reserves of single men, the authorities attempted to enforce a minimum age for civilian males ranging from 20 (Hessen-Kassel after 1762) to 25 (Prussia, Württemberg). Sometimes this was combined with a requirement to complete a period of service in the militia before marriage. Others, like Mainz, merely insisted on compulsory militia service without specifying a minimum age. As in Ansbach, the agreement of the army was generally necessary before civilian males could marry.[61]

Although evidence is patchy, these measures undoubtedly affected civilian marriage strategies, especially where they resulted in a substantial level of recruitment over a long period. Women were adversely affected by the introduction of conscription in Hessen-Kassel, where families sacrificed their daughters' marriage prospects in efforts to secure exemptions for their sons. Family assets were devolved to male offspring, to give them the property qualifications necessary for exemption. This left little over for daughters' dowries, compelling them to marry below their status, or not at all. The reduction of daughters' marriages provided families with female substitute labour if sons were drafted. Daughters were also married to men from outside the district and even in neighbouring territories, to provide wider kin networks which could be used to shelter draft-dodging relatives. This represented a radical change in traditional customs, whereby parents favoured local boys as partners for their daughters. It has been suggested that fairy stories functioned to condition girls to accept their self-sacrifice and to avoid liaisons with soldiers.[62] It is likely that, though Hessen represents an extreme case, these trends were present elsewhere.

There was a significant shift in attitudes in the larger territories, especially Prussia, around the middle of the eighteenth century, leading to increased tolerance of soldiers' marriages and a slightly more favourable view of women. Although wives were still considered the enemy of 'a free heart' for officers, they were now seen as a stabilizing

60 Taylor, 'Draft and Peasant Society', pp. 47–125; R. Frhr. v. Schroetter, 'Die Ergänzung des preußischen Heeres unter dem ersten Könige', *Forschungen zur Brandenburgischen und preußische Geschichte* XXIII (1910), pp. 81–145; C. v. Jany, 'Die Kantonsverfassung Friedrich Wilhelms I', ibid XLVIII (1926), pp. 225–72. The literature on the Prussian canton system has tended to obscure the fact that many other territories used similar methods.

61 Taylor, 'Draft and Peasant Society', p. 400; Frauenholz, *Absolutismus*, p. 251; Städter, *Ansbach–Bayreuther Truppen*, p. 27; R. Harms, 'Landmiliz und stehendes Heer in Kurmainz namentlich im 18. Jahrhundert', *Archiv für hessische Geschichte und Altertumskunde*, NF VI (1909), pp. 359–430 at pp. 378–85.

62 Taylor, 'Draft and Peasant Society', pp. 238–333; P.K. Taylor and H. Rebel, 'Hessian Peasant Women, Their Families and the Draft: A Social-Historical Interpretation of Four Tales from the Grimm Collection', *Journal of Family History* VI (1981), pp. 347–78.

influence on the rank and file and useful for the cameralist objectives of state policy.[63] Foreign recruits had traditionally been encouraged to marry local girls to tie them to Prussia and discourage desertion.[64] Prussian conscripts were prevented until 1743, when Frederick II loosened restrictions and abolished the fees for marriage licences. The aim was 'to populate the country and to preserve the stock, which is so admirable'.[65]

Behind the rhetoric of Prussian population policy lay a third factor which was common to much of early modern German legislation: the sheer impossibility of enforcing all the rules. This is clear when we examine the policies in practice. The proportion of married men was often far higher than that specified in the regulations, while many of the unmarried men maintained long-standing relationships which were tolerated and sometimes even recognized by the officers.

The Prussian limit of one-third of total strength was already generous compared with smaller territories like Bavaria and Württemberg which tried to restrict the number of wives to two to five per company, or under 5 per cent of establishment strength.[66] Tables 1–5 indicate that these targets were rarely achieved in practice, though there was considerable variation between different armies and types of unit.

The general pattern was for front-line combat formations to have fewer wives than garrison or bodyguard units which were not expected to take the field. For example, between two-thirds and three-quarters of the garrison of the Hohentwiel fortress in Württemberg were married (Table 1, nos. 1, 14, 19, 21, 25), except in wartime, when the proportion was still over 40 per cent (nos. 4, 26, 27). The proportion was also higher in the ducal Garde du Corps (nos. 17, 20), which enjoyed better pay. Wartime formations contained proportionately fewer married men than those in peacetime. Between 16 and 37 per cent of men in combat units were married in peacetime compared to 6 and 11 per cent in mobilized formations (nos. 12, 13, 24).[67] Units which had just returned from the front had similarly low proportions (nos. 3, 5).

These figures reflect official attitudes towards women's relationship to the military establishment: combat formations did not need women. Recruitment targeted single men, and mobilization often resulted in

[63] C. Duffy, *The Military Experience in the Age of Reason* (London, Routledge, 1987), p. 87.

[64] K. Schwieger, 'Militär und Bürgertum. Zur gesellschaftlichen Prägekraft des preußischen Militärsystems im 18. Jahrhundert', in D. Blasius (ed.), *Preußen in der deutschen Geschichte* (Königsstein, Neue Wissenschaftliche Bibliothek, 1980), pp. 179–200 at p. 186; Jany, 'Kantonsverfassung', p. 266. The fact that those who did sign up had to do so for an unlimited period of service was a considerable disincentive.

[65] Jany, *Preußischen Armee* II, p. 251; Political Testament of 1768, quoted in C. Duffy, *The Army of Frederick the Great* (Newton Abbot, David & Charles, 1974), p. 60.

[66] A202: Bü. 1871 (31 Aug. 1737); Bü. 2278 (9 Dec. 1741); Munich, *Bayerischen Armee*, pp. 183–4. A Frankfurt decree of 1729 ordering all women to avoid any sexual relations with ordinary soldiers in the civic forces was hopelessly unrealistic but not untypical: Kracauer, 'Frankfurt', p. 79.

[67] Other Württemberg evidence corroborates this and indicates that only 6–7% of the 6 000–15 000 strong field corps serving in the Seven Years War was married.

**Table 1.** Proportion of married soldiers in Würtemburg, 1678–1800

| *Code no.* | *Unit* | *Date* | *Men* | *Married* | *Proportion (%)* | *Children* | *Average per family* |
|---|---|---|---|---|---|---|---|
| 1 | Hohentwiel garrison | 1678 | 125 | 95 | 76.0 | 135 | 1.4 |
| 2 | 2 inf. companies | 1678 | 116 | 29 | 25.0 | 28 | 1.0 |
| 3 | Inf. rgt Bils | 1690 | 120 | 12 | 10.0 | 10 | 0.9 |
| 4 | Hohentwiel garrison | 1692 | 273 | 141 | 42.0 | 237 | 1.7 |
| 5 | Inf. rgt Alt-Württemberg | 1720 | 1 472 | 173 | 11.8 | 54 | 0.3 |
| 6 | 2 inf. companies | 1726 | 73 | 16 | 21.9 | 32 | 2.0 |
| 7 | Dragoon detachment | 1726 | 19 | 4 | 21.1 | 9 | 2.3 |
| 8 | Inf. rgt Garde-Fusilière | 1728 | 567 | 93 | 16.4 | 163 | 1.8 |
| 9 | Inf. rgt Leib | 1728 | 574 | 128 | 22.3 | 182 | 1.4 |
| 10 | Leib Dragoons | 1728 | 270 | 78 | 28.9 | 112 | 1.4 |
| 11 | Württ. Kreis cavalry | 1729 | 158 | 56 | 35.4 | 106 | 1.9 |
| 12 | Inf. company | 1734 | 143 | 8 | 5.6 | 11 | 1.4 |
| 13 | Württ. Kreis inf. | 1741 | 1 401 | 155 | 11.1 | 146 | 0.9 |
| 14 | Hohentwiel garrison | 1748/9 | *c.* 115 | 88 | 76.5 | ? | ? |
| 15 | Hussar squadron | 1751 | 99 | 37 | 37.4 | ? | ? |
| 16 | Inf. in Stuttgart | 1752 | 1 076 | 90 | 8.4 | ? | ? |
| 17 | Garde du Corps | 1753 | 110 | 60 | 54.5 | ? | ? |
| 18 | Hohentweil garrison | 1755 | 92 | ? | ? | 66 | ? |
| 19 | Hohentweil garrison | 1758 | 85 | 53 | 62.4 | 85 | 1.6 |
| 20 | Garde du Corps | 1764 | 201 | 79 | 39.3 | 89 | 1.1 |
| 21 | Hohentweil garrison | 1765 | 126 | 87 | 69.1 | 136 | 1.6 |
| 22 | Entire army | 1789 | *c.* 3 700 | 1 358 | 36.7 | 2 074 | 1.5 |
| 23 | Hussar rgt. | 1789 | 144 | 44 | 30.6 | 35 | 0.8 |
| 24 | Württ. Kries inf. | 1793 | 1 059 | 97 | 9.2 | 45 | 0.5 |
| 25 | Hohentweil garrison | 1794 | 84 | 55 | 65.5 | ? | ? |
| 26 | Hohentweil garrison | 1796 | 111 | 50 | 45.0 | 104 | 2.1 |
| 27 | Hohentweil garrison | 1800 | 132 | 54 | 40.9 | 126 | 2.3 |

*Sources*: A6: Bü. 17, 27–30; A8: Bü 251; A14a: Bü. 137; C14: Bü. 338; L5: Tom. 157, fo. 249; Tom. 159, Fo. 213; L6.22.7.28; Kolb, 'Feldprediger', p. 133; Andler, 'Regimenter in Griechenland', p. 249; Martens, *Hohentwiel*, pp. 143, 147, 177, 191–2, 200.

the discharge of older, usually married men, or their transfer to garrison units.[68] Würzburg, which generally had an army of approximately similar size to that of Württemberg, displayed similar characteristics (Table 2) with the general staff, bodyguards, fortress artillery, and garrison troops all having a higher proportion of married men than the field regiments. The same was true of Mecklenburg, where over half of the Dömitz garrison were married but only 8–15 per cent of front-line units were.[69] In the Imperial City of Frankfurt only 16 per cent of

[68] None of the 491 recruits inducted into the Württemberg Kreis Infantry in 1741 was married. The proportion of married men was higher in the grenadier companies, which contained most of the veterans. C14: Bü. 338, 28 Aug. 1741.

[69] G. Tessin, *Mecklenburgischen Militär in Türken- und Franzosenkriegen 1648–1718* (Cologne/Graz, Bählau, 1966), p. 177, figures for the period 1697–1712.

**Table 2.** Proportion of married soldiers in Würzburg, 1789

| *Unit* | *Men* | *Married* | *Proportion (%)* | *Widowers* | *Children* | *Average per family* |
|---|---|---|---|---|---|---|
| General staff | 42 | 31 | 73.8 | 1 | 99 | 3.2 |
| Garde du Corps | 50 | 21 | 42.0 | 2 | 19 | 0.9 |
| Hussars | 82 | 13 | 15.9 | 1 | 22 | 1.7 |
| Fortress artillery | 69 | 14 | 20.3 | – | 26 | 1.9 |
| Königshofen garrison | 214 | 37 | 17.3 | – | 64 | 1.7 |
| Guttenberg dragoons | 465 | 47 | 10.1 | 2 | 68 | 1.5 |
| Ambotten inf. rgt | 628 | 62 | 9.9 | 7 | 112 | 1.8 |
| Drachsdorf inf. rgt | 685 | 81 | 11.8 | 8 | 130 | 1.6 |
| Stetten inf. rgt | 616 | 82 | 13.3 | 1 | 136 | 1.7 |
| | 2 851 | 388 | 10.1 | 22 | 676 | 1.7 |

*Source*: Sicken, 'Streitkräfte', tables 1–5.

the field (*Kreis*) soldiers were married, compared with 58 per cent of the garrison infantry in 1733.[70]

The smaller territories had greater difficulty in enforcing regulations than larger states. The contingents of the petty Swabian territories all tended to have a higher number of wives than the Württemberg regiments (Table 3). The same seems to have been true of the collective forces of the Franconian states, where none of the larger Nuremberg contingent was married, compared to nearly half of the grenadiers pro-

**Table 3.** Proportion of married soldiers in the smaller Swabian contigents, 1729–1756

| *Unit* | *Date* | *Men* | *Married* | *Proportion (%)* | *Children* | *Average per family* |
|---|---|---|---|---|---|---|
| Cavalry rgt Württemberg* | 1729 | 102 | 53 | 52.0 | 90 | 1.7 |
| Nördlingen inf. | 1736 | 76 | 26 | 34.2 | ? | ? |
| Lindau, Ravensburg, and Ulm dragoons | 1741 | 63 | 9 | 14.3 | 16 | 1.8 |
| Inf. rgt Württemberg* | 1741 | 197 | 59 | 29.9 | 105 | 1.8 |
| Inf. rgt Württemberg* | 1756 | *c.* 100 | 50 | 50.0 | ? | ? |
| Other 3 inf. rgts | 1756 | 2 204 | 518 | 23.5 | ? | ? |

* Contingents provided by smaller Swabian territories which were combined with Württemberg soldiers to form joint units. See also Table 1, nos. 11 and 13.

*Sources*: A6: Bü. 17; C14: Bü. 338, 713.

[70] Kracauer, 'Frankfurt', p. 79. The proportion amongst the garrison artillery was even higher, at 80%. The situation in Augsburg was similar: see Kraus, *Augsburg*, p. 208. The proportion in Electoral Cologne and Hanoverian field regiments in the first half of the eighteenth century fluctuated between 20% and 45%: Pröve, *Stehendes Heer*, pp. 100–1; E. Herter, *Geschichte der Kurkölnischen Truppen in der Zeit vom Badener Frieden bis zum Beginn des siebenjährigen Krieges* (Bonn, Rhenania, 1914), pp. 18, 36.

vided by Hohenlohe. A muster of the Upper Rhine Hessen-Darmstadt foot regiment in 1725 provides a similar picture. Two-thirds of the company provided by the Imperial Cities of Speyer and Worms were married, compared to under a quarter of the men in the eight Darmstadt companies (Table 4). This was one of the reasons why contemporaries often considered the forces of the smaller states of low military value.[71]

Comparing the material over time, it is possible to detect a general upward trend in the proportion of married soldiers. Whereas just over one-fifth of the Württemberg army had been married in the 1720s, well over a third was by 1789. While only 7 per cent of Holstein-Gottorp's soldiers were married in 1690, a year after the foundation of the army, the total had risen to 34 per cent by 1711. In Frankfurt the overall average rose from under a third in 1733 to nearly two-thirds twenty years later.[72] Scattered evidence from other states seems to indicate similar trends (Table 4), though the overall proportion for Würzburg at least remained comparatively low. The long peace from the end of the Seven Years War (1763) to the outbreak of the French Revolutionary Wars (1792) was responsible for this trend. Most small and medium states reduced their armies after 1763 and drastically cut

**Table 4.** Proportion of married soldiers in other German armies

| *Unit* | *Date* | *Men* | *Married* | *Proportion (%)* | *Children* | *Average per family* |
|---|---|---|---|---|---|---|
| Münster inf. | 1660 | 918 | 335 | 36.5 | 373 | 1.1 |
| Brunswick army | 1671 | 3,293 | 850 | 38.7 | ? | ? |
| Hessen-Darmstadt inf. | 1725 | 489 | 109 | 22.3 | 174 | 1.6 |
| Speyer and Worms inf. | 1725 | 73 | 48 | 65.8 | 82 | 1.7 |
| Franconian inf. | 1725 | *c.* 500 | 49 | 9.8 | 67 | 1.4 |
| Six Brunswick rgts. | 1748 | 4,680 | 1 374 | 29.4 | ? | ? |
| Hanoverian invalids | 1750s | 240 | 80 | 30.0 | 120 | 1.5 |
| Four Münster rgts. | 1760 | 808 | 156 | 19.3 | 175 | 1.1 |
| Hanoverian dragoons | 1785 | 332 | 132 | 39.8 | 320 | 2.4 |
| 1 Hessian inf. rgt. | 1790 | 705 | 120 | 17.0 | 135 | 1.1 |
| Saxon army | 1806 | *c.* 30000 | 7 379 | 24.6 | 12 378 | 1.7 |

*Sources*: Staatsarchiv Darmstadt, E8B 208/2–4; H. Helmes, 'Kurze Geschichte der fränkischen Kreistruppen 1714–1756', *Darstellungen aus der bayerischen Kriegs- und Heeresgeschichte* XVI (1907), p. 10; Elster, *Braunschweig-Wolfenbüttel* II p. 121; J. Niemeyer and G. Ortenburg, *Die hannoversche Armee 1780–1803* (Beckum, 1981), p. 13; Taylor, 'Draft and Peasant Society', p. 347; Schuster and Franke, *Sächsichen Armee* II, p. 232; Redlich, *Military Enterpriser* II, p. 209; H. Querfurth, *Die Unterwerfung der Stadt Braunschweig im Jahre 1671* (Brunswick, 1951), p. 267; Pröve, *Stehendes Heer*, p. 162.

[71] B. Sicken, 'Die Streitkräfte des Hochsstifts Würzburg gegen Ende des Ancien Régime', *Zeitschrift für bayerische Landesgeschichte* XLVII (1984), pp. 691–744 at p. 730.

[72] G. Knüppel, *Das Heerwesen des Fürstentums Schleswig-Holstein-Gottorf 1600–1715* (Neumünster, Wachholz, 1972), p. 163; Kracauer, 'Frankfurt', p. 79.

**Table 5.** Proportion of married soldiers in Prussia, 1751–1784

| *Unit* | *Date* | *Men* | *Married* | *Proportion (%)* | *Children* | *Average per family* |
|---|---|---|---|---|---|---|
| Inf. rgt Knobloch | 1751 | 1 360 | 1 077 | 79.2 | 1 925 | 1.8 |
| Units in Berlin | 1752 | 16 220 | 3 620 | 22.3 | 4 696 | 1.3 |
| Inf. rgt Saldern | 1771 | 1 654 | 800 | 48.4 | ? | ? |
| Units in Berlin | 1776 | 18 052 | 5 633 | 31.2 | 6 816 | 1.2 |
| Units in Berlin | 1777 | | | | | |
| (a) present | | 18 055 | 5 763 | 31.9 | 7 050 | 1.2 |
| (b) on leave | | 9 280 | 5 538 | 59.7 | 7 284 | 1.3 |
| Inf. rgt Wunsch | 1778 | 1 672 | 1 132* | 67.7 | 1 446 | 1.3 |
| Inf. rgt Prinz Ferdinand | 1778 | 1 672 | 953** | 57.0 | 1 181 | 1.2 |
| Hussar rgt Belling | 1782 | 1 160 | 632 | 54.3 | 918 | 1.5 |
| Cav. rgt Backhoff | 1784 | 817 | 412 | 50.4 | 748 | 1.8 |

* including 580 men with 781 children on leave.
** including 506 men with 566 children on leave.

*Sources*: Jany, *Preußischen Armee* II, p. 251, III, p. 62; Hanne (ed.), *Rangirrolle*.

recruitment. To save money, many governments now preferred to allow existing soldiers to marry and remain with the colours rather than discharge them and incur the cost of finding a replacement. Although Prussia did not embark on this course after 1763, the proportion of married men none the less rose significantly as restrictions on army marriages were lifted. Altogether, the average seems to have risen from about one-quarter in the 1750s to half or more by the later 1770s, and remained at this level till the end of the century (Table 5).[73]

These overall proportions mask a considerable discrepancy between the different military ranks. Apart from in Prussia and contrary to the prevailing official attitude, the higher a soldier's rank the more likely he was to be married (Table 6). The difference could be extreme:

**Table 6.** Marital status and military rank

| *Unit* | *Date* | *Proportion married by rank (%)* | | |
|---|---|---|---|---|
| | | *Officers* | *NCOs* | *Privates* |
| Hohentwiel garrison | 1678 | 100.0 | 100.0 | 68.1 |
| Württ. Kreis inf. | 1741 | 62.5 | 9.6 | 9.6 |
| Württ. Hussars | 1751 | ? | 85.7 | 24.4 |
| Inf. in Stuttgart | 1752 | 47.9 | 6.5 | 6.5 |
| Hanoverian dragoons | 1785 | ? | 80.0 | 34.3 |
| Franconian units | 1793 | 48.0 | 54.0 | 15.0 |

*Sources*: As Tables 1–4.

[73] In 1802, when the total strength of the army was somewhat over 200 000 men, there were 95 761 wives and 130 056 children: Jany, *Preußischen Armee* III, p. 448.

while only 3 per cent of privates in two Würzburg regiments were married in 1789, nearly half the officers were.[74] The better pay and more advanced age of those in the higher ranks provide the explanation for this discrepancy.

The openly hostile attitude of the monarch to officers' marriages did keep the proportion lower in Prussia, but even here there was a tendency for a large number of the higher ranks to be married. Although the seven Berlin infantry regiments only had 43 married officers between them in 1772, or about an eighth of the total, nearly a sixth of the officers stationed in the city were married in 1776. Almost half of Infantry Regiment Hacke's 52 officers were married in 1783. Moreover, 75 per cent of the NCOs in Infantry Regiment Saldern were married in 1771, compared with 47 per cent of the privates.[75] What is remarkable about those figures is not the relatively low proportion of married officers, which has attracted attention in the past, but the high number of married privates. This is undoubtedly a consequence of the high degree of militarization of Prussian society, which would have made it impossible to enforce the low proportion called for in other territories, where soldiers formed a far smaller section of the population. It is also interesting to note that Prussia recognized the need to adapt official policy towards soldiers' marriages, whereas Hessen-Kassel, which militarized to a similar extent after 1762, failed to do so and apparently experienced greater disruption to civil marriages and a higher level of desertion.

Though it proved impossible to enforce the regulations to the letter, between 50 and 95 per cent of soldiers were prevented from marrying, creating considerable problems including desertion, illegitimacy, and secret marriages. Women were often blamed for causing desertion. Captain Hoyer in Paderborn complained in 1784 that if he refused permission to young men who had reached marriage age, they simply ran after their sweethearts.[76] A Württemberg decree of 1700 accused 'roving foreign wenches' (*vagirende fremde Weibsbilder*) and 'foreign whores' (*fremde Dirne*) of causing ill discipline, theft, and desertion. The punishments for marrying without permission were stiffened in 1727, expressly because there were 'various easygoing whores in our duchy who tempt the soldiers into fornication in the hope of marrying them or even persuading them to desert, as has indeed happened'.[77] The heavy desertion from a Würzburg infantry regiment marching to Hungary in 1739 was blamed on hordes of women following the unit.[78]

Blaming women and stigmatizing those involved as 'whores' were

74 Sicken, 'Streitkräfte', pp. 719–24; Löw, *Unteroffizier*, pp. 266–7.

75 Jany, *Preußischen Armee*, III, pp. 38, 62; W. Hanne (ed.), *Rangirrolle, Listen und Extracts ... von Saldern Infanterie Regiment Anno 1771* (Osnabrück, Biblio, 1986).

76 Mürmann, 'Militärwesen', pp. 27–8.

77 A30c: Bü. 2; Reyscher (ed.), *Gesetze* XIX/1, pp. 371–4 (1700), 518 (1727).

78 H. Helmes, 'Das Regiment Würzburg im Türkenkriege des Jahres 1739', *Darstellungen aus der bayerischen Kriegs- und Heeresgeschichte* XIII (1904), pp. 60–93 at pp. 77–8.

part of the official process of discouraging contact between soldiers and women and criminalizing unsanctioned liaisons. The fact that women were often employed by recruiting agents to entice soldiers to join another army added conviction to official arguments. However, examination of individual cases reveals the 'easygoing whore' to be fiction of the regulations. Occasionally men left units at the front to see wives and loved ones left behind.[79] However, most who deserted in connection with women did so either to avoid the consequences of an unplanned pregnancy or to evade restrictions on marriage. Many did not intend to desert completely, but merely to cross into neighbouring territory to marry and then return. Unfortunately, this was often impossible, as the authorities elsewhere were reluctant to marry such couples for fear of sanctioning bigamy.[80] Some were compelled to enlist in another army as a last resort. One Württemberg grenadier returned to his regiment having gone as far as Hungary to marry.[81] Christina Egin and Private Michael Schmidt were less fortunate. Having failed to get permission despite an illegitimate child, a three-year relationship, and Schmidt's ten years of service, the couple went to Schmidt's home village to marry. The pastor refused because they lacked a birth certificate for the child. They then roamed south Germany for six weeks in a vain attempt to marry elsewhere. Having already refused an offer to enlist in the Spanish army, Schmidt finally agreed to join Prussian service in return for a promise that marriage could be arranged in Nördlingen.[82]

An investigation of illegitimacy reveals a similar picture. Women were blamed for a problem caused largely by official restrictions on marriage and the inability of German governments to pay soldiers adequate wages to support a family. Württemberg army chaplains complained that the women following the regiments refused to let them baptize their illegitimate offspring, preferring instead to go across the frontier to foreign priests. This was allegedly to enable them to name innocent men as the father, either to protect the identity of the real father, or in the hope of extracting property or money.[83] However, it is unlikely that the majority of women were as 'shameless' as the outraged chaplains believed. While there was a higher incidence of illegitimacy

[79] Examples in Tessin, *Mecklenburgisches Militär*, p. 189; G. Eisentraut, 'Der Briefwechsel zwischen dem Landgrafen Wilhelm VIII von Hessen und seinem Generaladjutanten Generalmajor Freiherr v. Fürstenberg in den Jahren 1756/57', *Zeitschrift des Vereins für hessische Geschichte und Landeskunde* XL (1907), pp. 72–138 at p. 79. On reasons and level of desertion from German armies see P.H. Wilson, 'Violence and the Rejection of Authority in Eighteenth Century Germany', *German History* XII (1994), pp. 1–26. Most deserters were unmarried: Pröve, *Stehendes Heer*, p. 104.

[80] See cases in A6: Bü. 63; A202: Bü. 2299. Schüssler, 'Werbewesen', pp. 150–1.

[81] A6: Bü; 63, 23 Aug. 1729.

[82] A202: Bü. 2299, Dec. 1743–Jan. 1744. The couple were arrested by Württemberg soldiers. Schmidt escaped and Egin was eventually released after interrogation.

[83] Von Kolb, 'Feldprediger in Altwürttemberg', *Blätter für Württembergische Kirchengeschichte* IX (1905), pp. 70–85, 95–124 at p. 81, relating to 1762. Hanoverian officers thought the same; Pröve, *Stehendes Heer*, pp. 110–11.

around garrison towns, the situation of most of those involved was generally desperate. It is not surprising that a large number of women convicted of infanticide had been involved with soldiers.[84]

Given these circumstances, it is understandable that some men deserted when they could find a wealthy partner. The commander of the Trier regiment in the imperial army complained (with some exaggeration) in 1759 that 'if we don't leave Saxony soon, the entire imperial army will marry Saxon women, especially as men are rare in this area and can often get considerable farms through a woman. Privates can get 1400 to 1500 Thaler with a girl.'[85]

Illicit liaisons were a further consequence of the marriage restrictions and a sign that they could not be fully enforced. Many officers were happy to tolerate such liaisons or even give them semi-legal status. There were often considerable inducements for them to do so. Regulations frequently specified that soldiers wishing to marry had to pay a fee to their company commander. Many men were prepared to pay far more to obtain permission, and trafficking in marriage licences became an additional means by which officers could profit from the 'company economy'.[86] The introduction of conscription in Prussia enabled officers to extend the practice into the civil sphere despite efforts to prevent this. Long after Frederick II abolished fees in 1743 the saying 'you can get a wife for 1 Thaler 14 Groschen' remained current in the army.[87]

Although such practices were open to widespread abuse, they are indicative that official policy was not totally inflexible, and may even have had a liberating effect for some of those involved. Liaisons with soldiers could offer an escape from parental control, especially for girls from poor families. Evidence from Hessen-Kassel suggests that women could become independent without entering domestic service by attaching themselves to soldiers on furlough in their village. Such women would acquire a cow, a few goats, and some chickens and graze them illegally on common land. The presence of their partner in the village for up to ten months a year protected them from the customary punishments. Villagers were frightened to take them to court because the soldier's comrades would intimidate them by smashing their windows. Similar complaints in contemporary Prussia of the scarcity of

84 C.W. Ingrao, *The Hessian Mercenary State* (Cambridge, Cambridge Univ. Press, 1987), p. 135; Ulbricht, 'Infanticide', p. 127. Over 70% of illegitimate children born in Göttingen 1721–51 were fathered by soldiers: Pröve, *Stehendes Heer*, p. 114.

85 H. v. Eicken, 'Die Reichsarmee im siebenjährigen Krieg dargestellt am Kurtrierischen Regiment', *Preußische Jahrbücher* XLI (1879), pp. 1–14, 113–35, 248–67 at p. 117.

86 A202: Bü; 2278, 22 Apr. 1741. See Redlich, *Military Enterpriser*, II, pp. 14–76, on the company economy.

87 Frauenholz, *Absolutismus*, pp. 243–4, 251, 293; Jany, 'Kantonverfassung', pp. 245–7; O. Büsch, *Militärsystem und Sozialleben im alten Preußen 1713–1807*, 2nd edn (Frankfurt/M., 1981), p. 39.

women willing to become servants indicates that this may have been a fairly common phenomenon.[88]

Moreover, permission granted by company commanders overrode parental objections, enabling some couples to marry who would otherwise have been prevented. Indeed, some men turned up in the hope of obtaining permission in return for enlisting. Even if full permission was denied, officers would often connive in unofficial liaisons by allowing men to cross the frontier to marry elsewhere or protecting them from the civil authorities. Württemberg chaplains complained that officers granted 'regimental consent' enabling couples to live together that the chaplains had refused to marry.[89] Prussian officers often tolerated 'concubines', and those in the guards even issued 'lovers' certificates' (*Liebstenscheine*) to soldiers with pregnant partners to protect them from police action.[90] Nonetheless, such practices generally worked to the women's disadvantage. Soldiers already seem to have been unreliable partners, with those in eighteenth-century Berlin deserting their wives more frequently than civilian husbands. Men in unofficial liaisons were free to end the relationship with no fear of punishment. The female partner had no legal rights and, as a civilian, stood under an entirely different jurisdiction. Furthermore, in the event of the death or disablement of her partner, a woman had no right to official welfare, as even pensions for legal widows remained a matter for the ruler's discretion (*Gnadensache*). Such women fell through the gaps in corporate society and were quickly labelled 'whores' by the community.[91]

The patchy evidence on marital relations further emphasizes the discrepancy between official attitudes and actual conditions. The official consensus was that only irresponsible or poor women would want to marry a soldier. General Warnery believed that any sensible girl who could earn her own living would need a lot of persuading. Ansbach and Württemberg decrees implied that only 'easygoing whores' would want to make such a marriage. Pastor's son Friedrich Christian Laukhard, who served in the Prussian army, believed that soldiers' wives were 'largely from the lowest class . . . of the worst character – generally soldiers' daughters.'[92] Certainly, the most prized catch – a rich heiress – was a rarity.[93] However, army wives were far from being especially debauched, and generally came from the same social background as

88 Taylor, 'Draft and Peasant Society', p. 255; Büsch, *Militärsystem*, pp. 53–4.

89 A6: Bü. 34, 4 Feb. 1734; Kolb, 'Feldprediger', pp. 80–2; Pröve, *Stehendes Heer*, pp. 107–9. See Sabean, *Neckarhausen*, pp. 329–34 for parental pressure in marriage choice.

90 Kotsch, *Potsdam*, p. 48; Jany, *Preußischen Armee*, III, p. 62.

91 H. Schultz, 'Social Differences in Mortality in the Eighteenth Century: An Analysis of Berlin Church Registers', *International Review of Social History* XXXVI (1991), pp. 232–48 at p. 238; Pröve, *Stehendes Heer*, pp. 108–11.

92 C.E. Warnery, *Das Herrn Generalmajor von Warnery sämtliche Schriften* (9 vols., Hanover, 1785–91) II, p. 28; Städter, *Ansbach-Bayreuther Truppen*, p. 39; Reyscher (ed.), *Gesetze* XIX/1, p. 371; F.C. Laukhard, *Leben und Schicksale* (2 vols., Stuttgart, Schramm, 1930).

93 Taylor, 'Draft and Peasant Society', pp. 378–9.

the soldiers themselves. Ralf Pröve's detailed analysis of marriage patterns amongst soldiers stationed in Göttingen 1713–56 suggests a fairly close correlation between civilian women's social status and their husband's military rank. Women from the lower sections of the town's population without the official status of resident citizen (*Bürger*) generally married privates. Citizens' daughters married NCOs, while those of councillors (*Ratsherren*) and university professors married officers. Towns with permanent garrisons tended to experience a fair degree of intermarriage between their civil and military populations, partly because of the official policy of discouraging soldiers' ties to out-of-town women in order to reduce desertion. Over two-thirds of Augsburg's civic defence force had married local women in 1775, compared with only 6 per cent who had married 'foreigners'.[94] The major exception to these patterns were marriages involving officers. As most territorial officer corps became more aristocratic in composition and more professional in ethos after 1700, they also became more exclusive in their marital choices. Already discouraged by official regulations, many Prussian officers felt little compulsion to marry, knowing that other family members would carry on their line. The poor pay and social status of subalterns hindered marriages into prestigious or wealthy families. While senior officers did marry, the average age at which they did so rose from 31.8 years before 1675 to 36.3 after 1700. Families tended to intermarry at senior rank, with the result that the range of prospective partners for generals' and colonels' daughters tended to be limited to mature military men. Evidence from Schaumburg-Lippe and elsewhere also indicates that non-noble officers with aristocratic wives were a rarity.[95]

Initially, wives lived with their husbands in peacetime. Until the early eighteenth century most German armies lacked barracks. Apart from small garrisons lodged in antiquated castles, most soldiers were quartered on the civilian population, with the units periodically moving between districts to spread the burden. Even when barracks began to be built there were often no separate quarters for married personnel until the mid-eighteenth century. As late as 1781 the bishop of Würzburg was horrified to discover that married couples lived together with other soldiers. Unreliable men were still quartered with married NCOs in Prussia and women were given free access to the Viennese barracks at the end of the century.[96] However, the practice of giving extended

[94] Pröve, *Stehendes Heer*, pp. 276–82; Kraus, *Augsburg*, p. 209. Of the Augsburg force, 21% were single.

[95] P.-M. Hahn, 'Aristokratisierung und Professionalisierung. Der Aufstieg der Obristen zu einer militärischen und höfischen Elite in Brandenburg-Preußen von 1650–1720', *Forschungen zur Brandenburgischen und preußischen Geschichte*, NF 1 (1991), pp. 161–208, esp. pp. 203–4; C.U. Frhr. v. Ulmenstein, *Die Offiziere des Schaumburg-Lippischen Truppenkorps 1648–1867* (Berlin, Verlag für Standesamtwesen, 1940).

[96] Hagen, 'Hausinfanterie', p. 50; Reyscher (ed.), *Gesetze* XIX/1, pp. 712–16; Hanne (ed.), *Rangirrolle*, pp. 35–6; P. Lahnstein (ed.), *Report einer 'guten alten Zeit'. Zeugnisse und Berichte 1750–1805* (Stuttgart, Kohlhammer, 1970), pp. 525–7.

leave to substantial parts of the army, begun in Prussia in the 1720s and copied elsewhere from the 1740s, resulted in large numbers of married soldiers living in family homes for most of the year.[97] About half of the married servicemen in Prussia lived away from their regiment by the 1750s (Table 5).

Women were discouraged from following their menfolk on campaign. When the 5,765 strong Brunswick corps marched to serve in Holland in 1748, only 258 women were allowed to go with it, although nearly a third of the total strength was married. The German regiments hired by Britain to fight in the American War of Independence followed British regulations and restricted the number of wives to six per company.[98] These figures indicate a reduction in the number permitted to go earlier in the century, reflecting the growing prejudice towards women.[99]

Contemporaries were often struck by the affecting scenes when regiments left for the front. Private Ulrich Bräker recalled his regiment's departure from Berlin in 1756: 'Then the drums struck up; tears from civilians, tarts, pros, etc., were flowing in torrents. Those warriors, too, who were natives of the place and leaving behind wives and children, were really cut up, broken-hearted they were.'[100] Not surprisingly, desertion was often worst immediately after mobilization. Although this tended to confirm official suspicions that women were responsible for desertion, the authorities were not totally insensitive to such concerns. Several German armies ran field postal services by the mid-eighteenth century, which, though expensive, were surprisingly reliable.[101] A few letters survive, though none from women to men. They indicate that garrisons were close-knit communities, though couples also desired privacy. Letters from the front were clearly passed around families eager for news. Some soldiers declined to name comrades who had been killed or wounded in action for fear of alarming relations back home. Prussian trooper Nicholas Binn told his wife to buy sealing wax to send him private letters rather than have him 'open notes that others have already read ten times before I get them'. Men answered complaints from wives struggling to make ends meet at home by sending money or saying that things were much worse at the front. Most expressed concern or asked after their sweethearts. Binn promised to build his wife a nice cottage if he returned alive. In a revealing insight

97 M. Lehmann, 'Werbung, Wehrpflicht und Beurlaubung im Heere Friedrich Wilhelm I', *Historische Zeitschrift*, LXXVII (1891), pp. 254–89.

98 O Elster, *Geschichte der stehenden Truppen im Herzogtum Braunschweig-Wolfenbüttel* (2 vols., Leipzig, Heinsius, 1899–1901) II, pp. 115, 121; Atwood, *Hessians*, p. 52.

99 See A6: Bü. 30; E. Hagen, 'Die fürstlich würzburgische Hausinfanterie von ihren Anfängen bis zum Beginne des Siebenjährigen Krieges 1636–1756', *Darstellungen aus der bayerischen Kriegs- und Heeresgeschichte* XIX (1910), pp. 69–203 at pp. 130–1.

100 U. Bräker, *The Life Story and Real Adventures of the Poor Man of Toggenburg* (Edinburgh, Edinburgh Univ. Press, 1970), p. 132. See also Duffy, *Military Experience*, pp. 156–7; Page, *Following the Drum*, pp. 1–2, 17–22.

101 Elster, *Braunschweig-Wolfenbüttel* II, p. 123 gives a good description of such a service.

into the division of labour within soldiers' families, many men bombarded their partners with instructions to look after the children, to see that they were wrapped up warmly and went to school.[102]

Family life was precarious even when the men were not at the front. Contemporaries noted that soldiers' children had a very limited chance of survival. General Warnery commented 'that I have known a German company for 30 years which has never had fewer than 40 women. This number has been renewed at least once during this time, but altogether they have not had 40 children, of whom none has lived beyond 11 years.' While this picture seems especially black, Tables 1–5 confirm that soldiers' families were considerably smaller than the average. In the century after 1648 most German women bore four to five children, of whom half survived into adulthood. That soldiers' families were around 40 per cent smaller was due to the restrictions on the marriage of younger soldiers and the general impoverishment of military personnel.[103] Infant mortality was higher than average: servicemen's families were the worst-affected group in eighteenth-century Berlin. This can only be partly explained by soldiers' poor material conditions. It is true that Hanoverian couples waited nearly twice as long before having children if the husband was a private rather than a better-paid NCO. Soldiers were also more likely to marry and start a family if they had been recently promoted to NCO rank. However, adult soldiers had a higher than average life expectancy in peacetime, as regular pay, rations, and health care guaranteed a minimum existence. As Helga Schultz has suggested, part of the blame must therefore fall on the official attitude to wives and children as 'tiresome ballast'. Restrictions on marriage encouraged a larger number of illegitimate children who were more likely to succumb to epidemics and malnutrition than those born to stable civilian families.[104]

Officers' relations with women differed somewhat, indicating the growing divide between officers and men. Most officers' aristocratic origins and greater material wealth equipped them with notions of 'gallantry' which permitted more varied relations and possibly greater promiscuity. Bräker reports his captain enjoying a great time with the girls while detached as a recruiting officer in south Germany. General Haack used his authority as governor of Berlin to instruct the sentries to report the arrival of any 'distinguished ladies' in the city. Colonel Pritz thought it natural that his young nephew, Ensign Lemcke, should take an interest in the local girls, and even encouraged him to evade a

[102] H. Bleckwenn (ed.), *Preußische Soldatenbriefe* (Osnabrück, Biblio, 1982); Jakob Walter, *The Diary of a Napoleonic Foot Soldier*, ed. M. Raeff (Moreton-in-Marsh, Windrush, 1991), pp. 137–51, with letters of German soldiers serving in Napoleon's Russian campaign of 1812.

[103] Warner, *Sämtliche Schriften* II, p. 27; Dipper, *Deutsche Geschichte*, pp. 45–9; Pröve, *Stehendes Heer*, pp. 116–18.

[104] Schultz, 'Social Differences', pp. 237–8, 242; Pröve, *Stehendes Heer*, pp. 115–16, 133–4. NCOs also tended to have larger families than privates: Staatsarchiv Darmstadt, E 8 B 208/2–4, muster-roll of Inf. Rgt. Hessen-Darmstadt; Löw, *Unteroffizier*, p. 310.

mother's observation of her attractive daughter. Lemcke's subsequent spurning of her once he had been promoted and was on active service indicates that at least some officers followed Frederick II's dictum that they should place their career before personal interests.[105]

# III

Up until now discussion of women's roles within early modern armed forces has focused predominantly on their activities as combatants and in the support services. In fact, women were rarely involved in combat. While cross-dressing female soldiers have attracted considerable attention, their experience was hardly typical. An extensive trawl through the Stuttgart archives yielded only one case of a woman serving as a soldier in seventeenth- and eighteenth-century Württemberg. In 1749 the War Treasury granted an annual pension of 10 florins to Anna Maria Christmännin, 'who had served as a soldier in the former Leibregiment in Hungary for 1½ years' in 1716–18. This was paid punctually until her death on 2 March 1761. Beyond this, nothing is known about her, and little is available for the few other identifiable cases.[106] Only 16 women are known to have served in the British army over this period, between 30 and 50 served in the forces of revolutionary France, and 119 cases have been identified in Holland for 1550–1840. The total numbers in Germany were probably as small, and certainly lower than in America, where at least 400 women posed as soldiers during the Civil War.[107]

Male officers and administrators were often surprisingly ambivalent towards such cross-dressing women, and tolerated their deception even after it had been discovered.[108] Nonetheless, such cases were extremely rare, and it must be doubted that all involved the intention to assume

[105] Bräker, *Life Story*, pp. 110–14; A.v.Witzleben, *Aus alten Parolebüchern der Berliner Garnison zur Zeit Friedrichs des Großen* (Berlin, Mittler, 1851), pp. 63–4; R. Waltz (ed.), Kriegs- und Friedensbilder aus den Jahren 1754–1759 nach dem Tagebuch des Leutnants Jakob Friedrich v. Lemcke 1738–1810', *Jahrbüchern für preußische Geschichte* CXXXVIII (1909), pp. 20–43. See also Duffy, *Military Experience*, p. 87.

[106] L5: Tom. 157 fo. 245; A32: Bd. 4 fo. 160b. For a case in Dortmund in 1701 see K. Rübel, 'Kriegs- und Werbwesen in Dortmund in der ersten Hälfte des 18. Jahrhunderts', *Beiträge zur Geschichte Dortmunds und der Grafschaft Mark* VII (1896), pp. 106–58 at pp. 107–14.

[107] Ewing, *Women in Uniform*, pp. 28–9; Dekker and Pol, 'Republican Heroines', pp. 355, 358; De Pauw, 'Women in Combat', pp. 217–19; R. Dekker/L. v. d. Pol, *The Tradition of Female Transvestism in Early Modern Europe: Women Living as Men in the Dutch Republic* (Basingstoke, Macmillan, 1989). For a contemporary account of a Dutch example see the *Memoirs of Peter Henry Bruce, Esq.* (Dublin, 1783, repr. London, Cass, 1970), pp. 8–11.

[108] This is obvious from the memoirs of Nadezhda Durova, who served as a Russian cavalry officer in the Napoleonic Wars: M.F. Zirin (ed.), *The Cavalry-Maiden* (Bloomington, Indiana Univ. Press, 1990). See also comments in Dekker and Pol, 'Republican Heroines', p. 359, and the reference by an army doctor to a female soldier in a German regiment in Danish service in J. Dietz, *Memoirs of a Mercenary: Being the Memoirs of Master Johann Dietz. . .* (London, Folio Society, 1987), pp. 75–6.

a male identity and role. Officers were known to disguise their mistresses as soldiers or servants to circumvent the prohibitions of women accompanying the regiment. The Duke of Brunswick's secretary reported seeing Major Plotho's wife 'who had followed her husband in male attire' in the thick of the fighting at the battle of Lobositz in 1756, where she felt safer than staying with the baggage and risking attack from enemy irregulars.[109]

The reduction in the number of women permitted to accompany the field army also lessened the likelihood of female involvement in combat. Apart from women out foraging for supplies, those most likely to become involved were the female inhabitants of cities under siege. Although contemporaries sometimes compared besieged towns to maidens whose virtue was under attack, women were generally not expected to help in the defence except in dire emergencies. By the eighteenth century most important towns were fortified with self-contained citadels for prolonged resistance once the civilian area had surrendered. Women were excluded, and often ran the risk of being designated 'useless mouths' and expelled from the city by governors worried about dwindling supplies.[110] There was more chance of women being involved in defending small settlements or those without modern fortifications. However, unlike the women of Spain, few German women appear to have participated in actual fighting. Incidents such as the defence of a south German town by the 'women of Schorndorf' in 1688 were often greatly exaggerated by contemporary publicists. Their actual role was restricted to seizing the male officials to prevent them from opening the gates to a French raiding party.[111] The action of the wives of the German garrison of Bonn, who dragged their husbands from their posts during the futile defence against the Dutch and imperialists in November 1673, is probably more common than instances of women copying conventional male heroism.[112]

There is also a danger of exaggerating women's work for the support services. It is misleading to believe that European 'camp followers were part of an army's logistical support apparatus and their activities were encouraged'.[113] The official attitude to army women already indicates

[109] Bleckwenn (ed.), *Soldatenbriefe*, pt. 1, p. 8.

[110] C. Duffy, *Siege Warfare: The Fortress in the Early Modern World 1494–1660* (London, Routledge & Kegan Paul, 1979), pp. 249–64. See also the plans to send the women to safety if the French besieged the Hohentwiel fortress: K. v. Martens, *Geschichte von Hohentwiel* (Stuttgart, Metzer, 1857), pp. 194–200. J.W. Wright, 'Sieges and customs of war at the opening of the eighteenth century', *American Historical Review* XXXIX (1933/4), pp. 629–44.

[111] Duffy, *Siege Warfare*, p. 251; R. Rudorff, *War to the Death: The Sieges of Saragossa 1808–1809* (London, Hamish Hamilton, 1974); R. Krauß, 'Die Weiber von Schorndorff. Ein Beitrag zur Württembergischen Geschichte des Jahres 1688', *Württembergische Vierteljahreshefte zur Landesgeschichte*, NF XXX (1921), pp. 90–115.

[112] C.J. Ekberg, *The Failure of Louis XIV's Dutch War* (Chapel Hill, Univ. of North Carolina Press, 1979), p. 137.

[113] De Pauw, 'Women in Combat', pp. 210–11; also Hacker, 'Women and Military Institutions', pp. 643–6.

that the authorities did not regard them as performing essential services. Most of women's work for the army was necessitated by their material survival, rather than a military need for their labour.

The work of army women can be divided into six categories: food provisioning (including the roles of sutler, cook, and scavenger), medical (including nurse and midwife), general ancillary (cleaner, washerwoman, servant, seamstress), prostitution, industrial production, and military recruitment. Food provisioning was initially important, as sixteenth and early seventeenth century German armies lacked formal logistical support. Not only did women play a vital role in procuring and cooking food, but their activities as scavengers were often essential to soldiers' material survival. The anonymous diary from the Thirty Years War indicates that husband and wife operated as an efficient scavenging unit, with the woman braving the flames during the sack of Magdeburg in 1631 to seize bedding and valuables from burning houses.[114]

Such activities had always been illegal, but had been tolerated in the absence of any efficient mechanism for supplying and paying troops. After 1648 German states sought to solve this through a combination of organized logistical support, direct purchasing and requisitioning from the local populations. By 1700 most supply arrangements were in the hands of official contractors who provided basic rations. Soldiers still bought additional food from civilian traders, some of whom were women and some of whom would have depended on the army for custom. However, most of these sutlers were men and even their activities began to be severely restricted. Conscious of the need to boost the civilian economy and eradicate evasion of excise duty, many governments tried to cut out sutlers and encouraged soldiers to buy what they needed directly from civilians.[115] Meanwhile, the system of state magazines and depots established by Prussia and some of the larger territories further reduced the size of the baggage train by dispensing with civilian traders accompanying the regiments. Though 'canteen women' and other sutlers continued to supply food into the later eighteenth century, most army mess arrangements centred on the purchasing and preparation of food by the soldiers themselves in squads of four or more men who pooled their resources and shared tasks.[116] Thus, the professionalization and militarization of support services which began in the mid-eighteenth century and was completed after 1800 involved the replacement, not of women by male soldiers, but of civilian contractors by permanent military logistics units.[117]

[114] Peters (ed.), *Ein Söldnerleben*, esp. p. 138.

[115] A202: Bü. 2278, 8 Oct. 1739; Frauenholz, *Absolutismus*, pp. 274–6 (order of 21 Oct. 1749).

[116] Bräker, *Life Story*, pp. 121–32, 135–6; S.C. Brown (ed.), *Collected Works of Count Rumford* (5 vols., Cambridge, Mass., Harvard Univ. Press, 1968–70) v, pp. 208–11.

[117] A6: Bü. 7; A202: Bü. 2277; M. van Creveld, *Supplying War: Logistics from Wallenstein to Patton* (Cambridge, Cambridge Univ. Press, 1977); Peter Broucek and Paul Hainsius in *Vorträge zur Militärgeschichte* VII: *Die Bedeutung der Logistik für die militärische Führung*

Similar development occurred in the area of medical work. From being regarded as valuable assistants, women were officially excluded from the care of sick and injured soldiers after 1648. Though in practice many were still called to act as nurses and hospital orderlies,[118] the situation was in complete contrast to that in Britain, where almost all army nurses were female in 1750 and women were not excluded until the later professionalization of the medical services.[119]

The gradual exclusion of women from military life also reduced their role as providers of general ancillary services. Officers' servants were normally male, which was of value to those who wanted to pass them off as soldiers in order to pocket additional pay. Peacetime garrison life provided some women with work washing unmarried soldiers' clothes and linen from the barracks.[120] A few were allowed to accompany the regiments in the field in this capacity.[121] However, there was usually little such work available. In the mid-eighteenth century the Württemberg army, which then varied from 4 000 to 16 000 men, employed only two women to clean the war council offices once a week and wash the windows of the guardhouse. A further four women were paid to distribute fresh straw, move furniture, and mend mattresses in the barracks. From the amounts paid to these women it is clear they would have been unable to support themselves from such wages alone.[122] Individual soldiers were usually too poor to pay for such services. Army wives working as hucksters in Prussian garrison towns had to rely on additional civilian customers. Most soldiers did their own washing and mending or expected their female partners to do it as a household chore. The authorities also expected women to do a variety of unpaid tasks by virtue of their connection with soldiers. Saxon instructions of 1694 specified that wives of soldiers quartered on civilians had to assist in making the fire, while in Württemberg they were told to sweep the barracks.[123] This type of work was very similar

*von der Antike bis in die neueste Zeit* (Herford/Bonn, Mittler, 1986); H. de Nanteuil, 'Logistische Probleme der napoleonischen Kriegführung', in W. Groote and K.-J. Müller (eds.), *Napoleon I und das Militärwesen seiner Zeit* (Freiburg, Rombach, 1968), pp. 65–77; F. Redlich, 'Contributions in the Thirty Years War', *Economic History Review* XII (1959/60), pp. 247–54; and 'De Praeda Militari: Looting and Booty 1500–1800', *Vierteljahrschrift für Sozial- und Wirtschaftsgeschichte*, XXXIX (Wiesbaden, 1956), pp. 1–76.

[118] See J. Steininger, *Leben und Abenteuer des Johann Steininger* . . . (ed. G. Diezel, Stuttgart, 1841), p. 41.

[119] Thensius, *Anfänge*, pp. 126–30; Sicken, *Wehrwesen* I, pp. 297–304; Munich, *Bayerischen Armee*, pp. 184–5; Reyscher (ed.), *Gesetze*, XIX/1, pp. 580–2; P.E. Kopperman, 'Medical Services in the British Army 1742–1783', *Journal of the History of Medicine and Allied Sciences* XXXIV (1979), pp. 428–55 at pp. 436–43.

[120] A32: Bd. 226–55; Steininger, *Leben und Abenteuer*, p. 18; Kotsch, *Potsdam*, p. 25.

[121] Each of the two 800-man Würzburg infantry regiments was allowed to take four to five washerwomen with them when they marched to Holland in 1747: Hagen, 'Hausinfanterie . . . 1636–1756', p. 194.

[122] A32: Bd. 1, fo. 27b; Bd. 247, fo. 216b; Bd. 248, fo. 289.

[123] Thensius, *Anfänge*, p. 124; Reyscher (ed.), *Gesetze*, XIX/1, pp. 712–16; Jany, 'Kantonverfassung', p. 266.

to that performed by civilian women and, like it, went largely unrecognized and unrewarded.

Though the records are almost entirely silent on this area, there is a tendency in modern writing to assume that women accompanying the army worked as full- or part-time prostitutes.[124] While the wording of contemporary decrees implied this, and chaplains protested about hordes of 'shameless camp whores', these statements need to be treated with some caution. Some units refused to tolerate prostitutes, and whipped and expelled those who were caught. Poverty did drive some army women to resort to prostitution: Berlin police raids netted many soldiers' wives and daughters in 1711, 1718, and 1783. Prostitution did increase in Göttingen after the establishment of a permanent garrison. However, the general decline in soldiers' income after the sixteenth century would have greatly reduced the opportunities for professional prostitutes.[125]

Altogether there is little evidence that women associated with the army were engaged in some kind of autonomous 'female economy'. The male-dominated corporate structure of German society already curtailed female economic independence. Restrictions designed to protect civilian (largely male) employment often prevented army women from undertaking any legal commercial activity, especially in the imperial cities.[126] It seems that what income a woman obtained was only supplementary to that of her partner. Although the authorities tried to insist that soldiers only married brides who were materially independent, it is clear that most women were unable to support themselves when the regiments marched to war. The situation was especially critical because soldiers' wages were paid to the men in the field, leaving wives dependent on what their husbands were able, or chose, to send them through the post. In the 1680s governments were already compelled to provide financial assistance to women left behind. By the mid-eighteenth century this had often become a means-tested system of welfare payments, supplemented by free lodgings in the vacated barracks.[127] Though female income could still make a major difference in a family's finances, the material position of soldiers' partners was

[124] P. Englund, *The Battle of Poltava* (London, Gollancz, 1992), pp. 57–8; F.W. Seidler, *Frauen zu den Waffen? Marketenderinnen, Helferinnen, Soldatinnen* (Bonn, Wehr & Wissen, 1979), pp. 24–5.

[125] Kolb, 'Feldprediger', pp. 81–3; L. and M. Frey, *Frederick I: The Man and His Times* (Boulder, CO., East European Monographs, 1984), p. 142; W. Ribbe (ed.), *Geschichte Berlins* (2 vols., Munich, Beck, 1988), pp. 384–5; Baumann, *Landsknechte*, pp. 162–5.

[126] S.C. Ogilvie, 'Women and Proto-Industrialization in a Corporate Society: Württemberg Woollen Weaving 1590–1760', in P. Hudson and W.R. Lee (eds.), *Women's Work and the Family Economy in Historical Perspective* (Manchester, Manchester Univ. Press, 1990), pp. 76–103; Kracauer, 'Frankfurt', p. 81.

[127] A202: Bü. 2006; L6.22.8.1; L6.22.8.2; R. v. Andler, 'Die württembergischen Regimenter in Griechenland 1687–89', *Württembergische Vierteljahrshelfte für Landesgeschichte* XXXI (1922/4), pp. 217–79 at p. 268; Munich, *Bayerischen Armee*, p. 72; Elster, *Braunschweig-Wolfenbüttel*, I 208; Jany, *Preußischen Armee* II, p. 252, III, p. 62–3; Städter, *Ansbach-Bayreuther Truppen*, p. 77.

greatly reduced by the decline in army wages between 1600 and 1800. Wives were frequently among those caught stealing vegetables from the gardens outside eighteenth-century Berlin.[128] Furthermore, women were affected by changes in the military establishment beyond their control. Reductions in strength at the end of hostilities resulting in the discharge of married men, and a further loss of pay for those still in the ranks were often followed by repressive legislation against begging by soldiers' wives and children.[129]

Another indication of this is provided by the growing number of schemes designed to provide employment for soldiers' dependants, mostly in the textile industry. Some were put into practice; many wives of Württemberg soldiers found work in the Ludwigsburg silk factory after 1735 until it went bankrupt twenty years later.[130] Fired by the spirit of enlightened utilitarianism, reformers believed that such work would improve both the moral and material position of those concerned. A wool spinnery was established for this reason in the Hohentwiel fortress in 1795, while army wives were employed as cooks in the Munich military workhouse established by Count Rumford 'for putting an End to Mendacity, and introducing Order and useful Industry among the more Indigent Inhabitants of Bavaria'.[131]

However, welfare was not the only motive. The female dependants of soldiers represented cheap labour for the state. In 1761 the Württemberg government ordered soldiers' wives and children to work as unpaid spinners in the cotton industry in return for their free accommodation in army barracks. Only the six most industrious families were to receive a reward of 15 florins a year.[132] This form of economic exploitation of female labour needs to be seen in its wider context. German governments looked on army personnel as a pool of potential labour, already receiving pay and docile under military discipline. From sorting out books in the Landgrave of Hessen-Kassel's library to rebuilding a workhouse for the bishop of Würzburg, soldiers were accustomed to being made to work on state projects.[133] The exploitation of their female dependants derived from these women's connection to the army. That soldiers' families were employed in the same

[128] Witzleben (ed.), *Parolebücher*, pp. 25–7.

[129] For an example in Würzburg, see Hagen, 'Hausinfanterie . . . 1636–1756', p. 169; Kopp, *Würzburger Wehr*, p. 78.

[130] A. Schott, 'Wirtschaftliches Leben', in *Herzog Karl Eugen und seiner Zeit* (issued by the Württembergischer Geschichts- und Altertumsverein, 2 vols., Esslingen, 1907–9) I, pp. 313–60 at p. 352).

[131] Martens, *Hohentwiel*, p. 194; Brown (ed.), *Collected Works* V, pp. 1–98.

[132] G. Krauter, 'Die Manufakturen des Herzogtums Württemberg in der zweiten Hälfte des 18. Jahrhunderts', *Jahrbücher für Statistik und Landeskunde von Baden-Württemberg* I (1954/5), pp. 260–77 at p. 269.

[133] Ingrao, *Hessian Mercenary State*, pp. 168, 175; Kopp, *Würzburger Wehr*, p. 99. Prussian manufacturers often recruited their workers exclusively from military personnel and their dependants with the co-operation of the unit commanders: Löw, *Unteroffizier*, pp. 299–300. Widows accommodated in the invalids' hospital established in Darmstadt in 1772 were expected to work in the cloth factory and look after soldiers' orphans: Staatsarchiv Darmstadt, E8B 115/1–7.

institutions reserved for criminals, vagrants, and other 'idle poor' is also indicative of how low their status had sunk in many territories.

Gender stereotypes did influence government policy towards the work and education of soldiers' children and orphans. State provision was generally better for boys: the Potsdam orphanage catered for between twice and ten times the number of boys than girls, though there was a gradual change in favour of the latter. While both sexes were taught the same basic skills, boys were trained as apprentices or expected to become soldiers, while girls entered domestic service.[134]

The recruitment of soldiers formed an important area of women's work which has largely escaped attention. Even states which had adopted conscription relied heavily on volunteers to fill the ranks. The mania for especially tall soldiers in the 1720s and 1730s put a premium on suitable recruits and compelled governments to develop ever more elaborate means to entice men into the army. Most states sought to exclude recruiters from other territories in order to conserve their manpower. This compelled many to operate clandestinely, often from posts in the imperial cities where the more powerful princes claimed the right to recruit. While officers remained in the safety of the city, trusted NCOs or civilian agents were sent out to contact potential recruits in the neighbouring territories. The Prussians were particularly adept at this and became skilled in the art of *debauchieren*, or enticing trained soldiers of other armies to desert directly into Prussian service.

Women feature prominently in documented and contemporary fictional cases. The female relations of potential recruits were frequently used to contact and persuade men to enlist or desert. Occasionally recruiters used their own wives, but most other intermediaries came from the same 'bent society' (*kocheme Gesellschaft*) of prostitutes and vagrants that military regulations condemned. Both recruiting parties and intermediaries also relied on the deception, disguises, and practices of such society. Women were used to entice prospective recruits onto unfamiliar territory where they could be seized, or ply them with drink till they volunteered.[135] The risks were considerable and the rewards small. The details are sketchy, but most women seem to have been given only fancy clothes or small sums of money, usually far less than the value of the recruitment bounty. Those who were caught were sentenced to up to two years in the workhouse or expelled from the territory, effectively condemning them to join 'bent society' if they

[134] Kotsch, *Potsdam*, pp. 28–9, 90–3; Jany, *Preußischen Armee*, I 720–1, II 252; Brown (ed.), *Collected Works* v, pp. 5–6; Munich, *Bayerischen Armee*, pp. 176–7; R. Uhland, *Geschichte der Hohen Karlsschule in Stuttgart* (Stuttgart, Kohlhammer, 1953).

[135] A6: Bü. 54; A202: Bü. 2299; Anon., *List- und Lustige Begebenheiten derer Herren Offiziers auf Werbungen* (1741, repr. Osnabrück, Biblio, 1971); Schüssler, 'Werbewesen', pp. 35, 290–4; Lahnstein, *Report*, pp. 509–13; E. Schubert, *Arme Leute, Bettler und Gauner in Franken des 18. Jahrhunderts* (Neustadt/Aisch, Degener, 1983); C. Küther, *Menschen auf der Straße. Vagierende Unterschichten in Bayern, Franken und Schwaben in der zweiten Hälfte des 18. Jahrhunderts* (Göttingen, Vandenhoeck & Ruprecht, 1983).

were not already part of it.[136] Male clandestine recruiters were rarely caught and were usually protected by their superiors; one Prussian lieutenant was even sprung from Ulm gaol by five hussars sent in disguise by Frederick II.[137]

## IV

The development of standing armies, the growth of social disciplining, and the accompanying shift in attitudes displaced women from their traditional role within military affairs, propelling many into civil society and compelling the rest to redefine their relationship and seek alternative means of support. The authorities meanwhile moved from legislation designed to control women in the army to efforts to exclude them altogether. This was already well under way by the late sixteenth century, though full implementation was delayed by the Thirty Years War. While practical military considerations were behind this, the moral and political concerns of post-Reformation church and state were as important.

As women were excluded on moral and disciplinary grounds, the status of those still involved with soldiers declined appreciably. This continued after 1648, when the regularization of supply arrangements removed the need for many female workers. The inability of governments to pay soldiers adequate wages provided a further incentive for official efforts to limit their contact with women whom they could not afford to support. Restrictions were placed on soldiers' marriages by the 1680s, while all other women were removed from military jurisdiction and classed as civilians. Simultaneously, the development of limited forms of conscription led to military interference in civil marriages in an effort to preserve reserves of single males as potential recruits. Traditional marriage strategies were disrupted, with daughters suffering in extreme cases.

Meanwhile, the material position of soldiers' wives declined with the erosion of their husbands' pay and the loss of employment opportunities within the support services. From the 1680s states developed welfare measures to assist such women when armies took the field. This compounded women's dependent status, as already defined by official regulations. Employment in the textile industry and other state enterprises was both an extension of these welfare measures and indicative of women's low status in the eyes of the authorities and 'respectable' society.

However, the sheer impossibility of enforcing official regulations created limited opportunities for poorer women to escape parental control and achieve some material autonomy through semi-official liaisons with soldiers. Moreover, women continued to play an active and

[136] See A202: Bü. 2299, and Schüssler, 'Werbewesen', p. 308, for example sentences.
[137] Jany, *Preußischen Armee* II, pp. 246–7.

important role in illicit recruitment well into the eighteenth century, even if this was fraught with risks and poorly rewarded. Overall, if women's involvement in early modern warfare emerges as less bloodthirsty and vital to military efficiency than the current historiography implies, it also appears as more varied and no less important to the wider social and political development of Germany.

*University of Newcastle upon Tyne*

# [3]

# LOUIS XIV, ARISTOCRATIC POWER AND THE ELITE UNITS OF THE FRENCH ARMY

GUY ROWLANDS*

The traditional 'statist' interpretation of the French 'absolute' monarchy under Louis XIV depicted a progressive centralization of power by a bureaucratic and authoritarian régime, but in recent years this portrayal has attracted heavy criticism. The most notable challenges to the old orthodoxy appeared in the wor[illegible]iam Beik and Sharon Kettering, who, starting from different research bases and pursuing different agendas, have both posited an alternative model of a society in which the crown and the elites co-operated for mutual benefit. Yet both historians relied for their arguments upon evidence garnered from outlying southern provinces, and both largely confined their study to provincial administration and power relationships in the period before 1685.[1] The new model of a limited 'absolutism', which depended upon the elites for the preservation of order and peace, and which was characterized by repeated compromises to satisfy the interests of numerous interested parties, has not received universal support. In particular, the army and navy continue to hold out as the last bastions of traditional interpretations of Louis XIV's reign.

The belief that the period 1661–1715 saw greater 'control, centralization and bureaucratization' in the sphere of the armed forces has in recent months received a considerable boost with the publication of John Lynn's monumental survey of the army during the *Grand Siècle*.[2] One of Lynn's most important messages is that 'seen from the perspective of the army, the now much-debated term *absolutism* still makes sense in describing a new level of control exerted by the monarch'.[3] Lynn's case relies heavily on the development, during the period 1635–88, of a ministerial administrative infrastructure which boosted the authority of the *secrétaire d'état de la guerre* at the expense of the power of the *grande noblesse*, and which extracted greater obedience from the French officer corps. In essence, there is little different here from the

* The author is a Lecturer in the Department of History at University of Durham. He would like to thank Exeter College and the British Academy for their support during the writing of this article, and Miranda Stewart and Philip Carter for their valuable comments on an earlier draft. The author dedicates this article to David Parrott of New College, Oxford, with thanks for all his inspiring guidance and friendship over the last seven years.

[1] W. Beik, *Absolutism and society in seventeenth-century France: state power and provincial aristocracy in Languedoc* (Cambridge, 1985); S. Kettering, *Patrons, brokers and clients in seventeenth-century France* (Oxford, 1986).

[2] J. A. Lynn, *Giant of the Grand Siècle: the French army, 1610–1715* (Cambridge, 1997), p. 31.

[3] Ibid. p. 599.

traditional depictions of the seventeenth-century royal army in the classic works of Camille Rousset, Louis André and, more recently, André Corvisier.[4]

These studies of the army have a great deal to commend them, and certainly serve as a warning to 'revisionists' who may be tempted to deny the notion of Louis Quatorzian centralization. After all, it would be difficult to deny altogether that the French forces operating in the Nine Years War were better organized in almost every way than the armies of the period 1635-59. Undoubtedly the War Ministry deserves some credit for this, even if its role has been exaggerated. Moreover, the army is unquestionably of crucial relevance to the debate over the relationship between crown and people in seventeenth-century France, as Lynn rightly argues. Nevertheless, a number of caveats to traditionalist arguments need to be entered. Roger Mettam has already warned of the need for scepticism about the ability of the French crown to exact compliance from its subjects in the years after 1672.[5] Lynn's own forays into the French archives has also gradually alerted him to the fact that the full implementation of royal regulations and policies in the army was not possible. For example, duelling persisted and regiments remained below full strength, even if they were less depleted than in the era before 1659.[6]

The most problematic aspect of Lynn's work, like earlier French books, is that it unquestioningly presumes that the power of the crown could only increase through an ever-strengthening War Ministry, and at the expense both of the authority of the high aristocracy and the autonomy of the officers. Implicit within this approach is the assumption that the *grands* and the most senior military officers, who were drawn principally from the upper echelons of the *noblesse d'épée*, were progressively deprived of any real power and left with only its form in the shape of prestigious sinecures and commands where they were subject to ministerial domination. This view cannot be sustained when the military and court records and private papers of Louis XIV's reign are subjected to detailed scrutiny. If the personal rule of Louis XIV saw the assertion of an ideology exalting the power of the sovereign, this was also accompanied within the elites by a shift in noble attitudes which led them enthusiastically to embrace notions of obedience and commitment to the monarchy. This could partly be said to stem from the Fronde and repulsion at Condé's determination to persist with rebellion until he was offered terms commensurate with his rank and sense of honour.[7] By the second half of the seventeenth century the upper tiers of the nobility recognized that the surest way to advancement or to security of status was

[4] C. Rousset, *Histoire de Louvois et de son administration politique et militaire* (4 vols., 1862-4); L. André, *Michel Le Tellier et l'organisation de l'armée monarchique* (1906); idem., *Michel Le Tellier et Louvois* (1943); A. Corvisier, *Louvois* (1983); idem., *L'armée française de la fin du xvii^e siècle au ministère de Choiseul: le soldat* (2 vols., 1964).

[5] R. Mettam, *Power and faction in Louis XIV's France* (Oxford, 1988).

[6] Lynn's earlier articles did not acknowledge the limits of royal authority to the same degree as his *magnum opus*.

[7] See, for example, M. Bannister, 'Crescit ut aspicitur: Condé and the reinterpretation of heroism, 1650-1662', *Ethics and politics in seventeenth-century France: essays in honour of Derek A. Watts*, ed. K. Cameron and E. Woodrough (Exeter, 1996), pp. 119-28.

devoted service to the crown, as long as the crown at least partially satisfied their needs. The maintenance of a standing army and the domination of the period 1672–1715 by war provided sufficient opportunities for these principles to be put into practice. Contests for authority and power were consequently fought out within the state, and most notably at court and in the armies. Competition for favour and position in royal service if anything intensified after 1661.[8]

Nevertheless, the current orthodoxy on the armed forces still accepts as truth the notion that ministerial power, under the king's direction, exercised an ever-tightening grip on the army during Louis XIV's 'personal rule' at the expense of the military and social elites. It is certainly true that the ministers had emerged as the most important administrative figures by 1688, but, in practice, they had to contend with the power and influence of a number of officers who outranked them socially and who, on the whole, enjoyed the highest degree of royal confidence. Such posts included the *Colonels-généraux* of the cavalry, the dragoons and the Swiss forces, the *Grand Maître de l'Artillerie* and the *Grand Amiral de France*, several of which were filled by royal bastards. These offices have never received the attention they merit.[9]

The position of the most prestigious parts of the French military structure was even more complicated. The elite units of the army consisted of the *Maison du Roi* (also known as the *Maison militaire*), the *Gendarmerie de France*, the régiment des Gardes Françaises and the régiment du Roi infanterie. Though the Gardes Françaises and the régiment du Roi remained outside the *Maison militaire*, which was almost entirely a mounted corps,[10] they were nonetheless the two elite French regiments of foot, occupying a privileged position in the military structure and enjoying a special relationship with the crown.[11] The roles and composition of these forces, and the mechanisms for controlling them, receive negligible treatment in Lynn's book, and they have never been examined for what they might reveal about the power and ethos of the French monarchy. The rest of this article will look at the relationship between Louis XIV and the most illustrious units of his armed forces in order to illuminate the importance of the military and social elites, and to lay out the reasons why Louis allowed an ever-widening gap to open up between the nobles serving in the elite forces and those other, generally poorer, members of the second estate who eked out a humbler military existence in the ordinary regiments.

[8] See the author's recent thesis for a full expounding of this argument: G. Rowlands, 'Power, authority and army administration under Louis XIV: the French crown and the military elites in the era of the Nine Years War', unpub. D.Phil. thesis (Oxford University, 1997).

[9] For a full discussion of most of these positions see chapter one of my thesis: Rowlands, 'Power, authority and army administration under Louis XIV', pp. 30–81. By contrast, Lynn dismisses these positions as having little relevance under Louis XIV: *Giant of the Grand Siècle*, pp. 97–104.

[10] G. Daniel, *Histoire de la milice françoise* . . . (2 vols., 1721), ii. 115, 231, 236; G. Marie, 'La maison militaire du roi de France sous Louis XIV (de 1686 à 1715)', *Mémoires de l'Académie des sciences, inscriptions et belles-lettres de Toulouse*, 129 (1967), 162–3, 169.

[11] The Gardes Suisses, because of its foreign status, will not form part of this picture. This regiment also guarded the royal palaces, but it was subject to the authority of the *Colonel-général des Suisses et Grisons*.

I

The *Maison militaire du Roi* was essentially a creation of the reign of Louis XIV. Before 1660 there had been a number of Household companies which were regarded as a collection of guards rather than a military corps. In 1659 the four companies of the king's Gardes du corps consisted of a hundred men each, only a quarter of the size they were to become by 1676,[12] and there was only one company of Mousquetaires du Roi (the other was Mazarin's private company until 1660). On a par with the Gardes du corps was the one hundred-strong company of Cent-Suisses de la Garde, the only foot unit in the *Maison militaire*. The two companies of Gendarmes and Chevaux-légers de la Garde dated from Henri IV's reign. The guard units in 1660 lacked the high status which Louis XIV was determined they should acquire. The first step towards the pre-eminence of these assorted units was taken in 1664 with a royal *ordonnance* of 30 September reorganizing the companies of the Gardes du corps. This was followed by the emergence of the term *Maison militaire du Roi* in 1671, and it was crowned in September 1691 when the corps, acting as a separate body rather than as an appendix of the cavalry, distinguished itself at the battle of Leuze.[13]

The *Maison militaire* enjoyed a complicated and semi-independent relationship with the royal ministries. To begin with, it was not technically under the jurisdiction of the *secrétaire d'état de la guerre*, a post which was held between 1643 and 1701 by three successive generations of the Le Tellier family.[14] Actual jurisdiction was the preserve of the *secrétaires d'état de la maison du Roi*, who were emphatically neither clients nor allies of the Le Telliers: Henri de Guénégaud (1643–69), Jean-Baptiste Colbert (1669–83), Jean-Baptiste Colbert, marquis de Seignelay (1683–90), Louis Phélypeaux, comte de Pontchartrain (1690–9) and Jérôme Phélypeaux, comte de Maurepas (1699–1715).

The 1664 *ordonnance* concerning the Gardes du corps is quite clear on the jurisdiction that the *secrétaire de la maison du Roi* possessed: Guénégaud (and not Le Tellier) was responsible for delivering commissions to the officers and provisions to the guards of these companies on the king's behalf, and later archival evidence, including the minutes of the *expéditions* of the *Maison du Roi*, confirms the continued role of this ministry in the *Maison militaire*.[15] In wartime and on campaign, however, the situation seems to have been

[12] The four companies had been reduced to 360 men each by the end of the reign: see B[ibliothèque] N[ationale] MS fr[ançais] 8006 fo. 45$^r$.

[13] Daniel, *Milice françoise*, ii. 114; Corvisier, *Louvois*, p. 182.

[14] Father, son and grandson, with their dates in office as *secrétaire de la guerre*, were respectively Michel Le Tellier (1643–77), François-Michel Le Tellier, marquis de Louvois (1662–91) and Louis-François-Marie Le Tellier, marquis de Barbézieux (1691–1701).

[15] BN MS fr. 8006 fo. 2$^r$, ordonnance of 30 Sept. 1664; for examples see BN Clair[ambault] 683 fos. 81, 336, 750, 979, 992; S[ervice] H[istorique de l']A[rmée de] T[erre, château de Vincennes] Ya 262, n[o] p[agination], *ordonnance du roi* (copy), 3 Oct. 1689; ibid., 'Rolle de la Compagnie des deux cent Chevau legers de la garde ord$^{re}$ du Roy . . .', 10 Nov. 1689. See also, for the 1670s, Daniel, *Milice françoise*, ii. 139–43.

particularly complicated, giving rise to all sorts of organizational headaches. First, though commissions were ultimately delivered by the *secrétaire de la maison du Roi*, there seems to have been no clear ministerial channel involved with the process of nominating candidates to positions in the *Maison militaire*, and certainly at least in the Mousquetaires du Roi.[16] There is an obvious blurring of ministerial responsibility. Secondly, on campaign the units of the *Maison militaire* formed a corps separate from the cavalry, but it was unclear whether they were under the authority of the senior cavalry commander in each army.[17] After command difficulties arose in the army of Germany in 1690, Louis decided to issue a definitive *règlement* on 15 July for the service of the cavalry: 'Mes Gardes doivent être sous les ordres du commandant de la cavalerie, tel qu'il soit pour le service ordinaire, & pour la garde à cheval de ma Maison, ou de celle de mon fils. Il n'y a que pour le guet que l'on doit detacher sans en rendre compte a personne.'[18]

The *Maison militaire* remained in an anomalous position *vis-à-vis* the War Ministry. Louis XIV even seems to have been determined to prevent the *secrétaire de la guerre* exercising serious control over it through either his civilian or his military agents. In January 1689 the duc de Noailles, captain of one of the Gardes du corps companies, wrote to de Lignerie: 'Ce n'est pas l'intention du Roy que ledit sieur de Quinson [an inspector] ny aucun autre inspecteur ait rien a voir sur ses gardes, et jamais sa Maj$^{té}$ ne l'a entendu.'[19] No evidence has been forthcoming to suggest that ministerial inspectors operating under War Ministry control ever gained jurisdiction over the *Maison militaire*. On the other hand, military necessity meant that the *secrétaire de la guerre* had to involve himself in the administration of these units when they were in the field, especially when logistical problems arose, such as over horses.[20] What this all strongly suggests is that Louis XIV's reign saw a redefinition of the status and position of the *Maison militaire du Roi* in relation to the other forces, but that there was no serious attempt to determine and mark out its relationship with the War Ministry. The result seems to have been muddle and confusion both at court and in the field. The companies of this corps were not wholly answerable either to the *secrétaire de la guerre* or to the *secrétaire de la maison du Roi*; nor were they clearly designated as either independent of or an integral part of the cavalry. This vacuum of ministerial responsibility was

[16] See, for example, SHAT A$^1$ 1137, n.p., Barbézieux to Pontchartrain, 30 May 1692.

[17] SHAT Ya 307, n.p., *Recueil de plusieurs Reglemens du Roy* . . ., 'reglement ecrit de la main de sa Majesté', 15 July 1690. The last time these units were mixed in with the cavalry in the field had been during the War of Devolution in 1667.

[18] SHAT A$^1$ 975 piece 35, Saint-Pouenges to Louvois, 11 July 1690; piece 58bis, Louvois to Saint-Pouenges, 'Extrait du Reglement pour le service de la brigade de la Maison du Roy, dont l'original a été envoyé a Monseigneur', 19 July 1690; Ya 307, n.p., *Recueil de plusieurs Reglemens du Roy*. . ., 'reglement ecrit de la main de sa Majesté', 15 July 1690.

[19] SHAT Ya 307, n.p., *Recueil de plusieurs Reglemens du Roy* . . ., copy of letter of duc de Noailles to Lignerie, 28 Jan. 1689.

[20] BN MS fr. 7995 fo.150, Barbézieux to Dudoyers, 11 Nov. 1692.

filled by the king himself and by those men who directly ran the units of the *Maison militaire*.

The key to royal control over the *Maison militaire du Roi* were the officers who commanded its companies, appointed by Louis in reward for loyal and steadfast service. The most important units in the *Maison militaire* were the four companies of the Gardes du corps, each headed by a captain. In September 1664 the captains were deprived of their proprietorial rights over all officer and lower-rank appointments within their companies in return for an annual indemnity of 14,000 *livres* which was still being paid in the 1740s. In spite of the appointment in 1666 of a major and four *aides-majors* to oversee and co-ordinate the administration of the four companies, the four captains continued to occupy an exceedingly important place in the court hierarchy and the running of their units.[21] When they were serving their tour of duty about the king (*en quartier*) they were provided with a set of rooms on the ground floor of the inner courtyard at Versailles, in the wing to the north of the king's bedchamber. In peacetime they would serve for three months each year at the head of the Gardes du corps, but during the Nine Years War and the War of the Spanish Succession they were usually employed as commanders of field armies, so one captain would remain in attendance on the king for the duration of the campaign season. These men controlled access to the monarch and were as powerful as the *premiers gentilshommes de la chambre du Roi* though, in this case, their influence deriving specifically from their office stretched well beyond the bounds of the court. When the king left his private apartments the captain followed immediately behind him, and nobody could speak to the king without his permission. The captain *en quartier* never left the king when he was outside his *chambre*, whether the king was at court or not. The captain and lieutenant of the Compagnie Écossoise (the captain was the duc de Noailles) were even allowed to attend permanently on the king when they were not *en quartier* owing to the company's seniority. However, in a neat example of Louis's determination to preserve an atmosphere of pluralistic court politics and to prevent a monopoly of access to his person by a particular faction, the captain *en quartier* always served with lieutenants and *enseignes* of different companies, and even the guards of the four companies found themselves mixed together.[22]

Louis XIV himself took nominal charge of all selection for the companies in 1664, and the captains, it is widely held, found themselves reduced to a largely ceremonial and court role. But as an extension of their positions as men who already enjoyed the highest royal trust and favour and were (or subsequently became) either *ducs* or *maréchaux de France*, they actually wielded great influence over the administration of their companies and over the royal

[21] SHAT A[1] 1179 fo.47, 'Mémoire de Mr. le Vasseur', *c.* 1740; BN MS fr. 8006 fo. 2[r], ordonnance of 30 Sept. 1664; Marie, 'La maison militaire', pp. 170–1; Rousset, *Louvois*, i. 217; Daniel, *Milice françoise*, ii. 143.

[22] Daniel, *Milice françoise*, ii. 161; BN MS fr. 22756 fos. 1[v]–2[r].

patronage machine. First, the captains of the Gardes du corps did not at any time have to suffer inspection by ministerial agents. Secondly, they exercised considerable influence over the composition of their companies, both in the officer and the lower ranks, and did so in a manner suggesting the importance they attached to the possession of such units. By convention the posts of *enseigne* were filled alternately from two pools: from the *maréchal des logis* of the company or from cavalry *mestres de camp*. This, however, no more restricted the captains in their wishes than it did the king in his final choice of candidate. On 3 September 1688 Luxembourg persuaded the king to provide his third son with the position of *exempt* of his Gardes du corps company. Luxembourg's nephew the chevalier de Valençay also became an *exempt* in his company in 1691.[23] Gardes du corps captains also sought to advance their subordinates to positions outside their companies, thereby building up their affinities.[24]

When it came to recruitment of the rank and file of the four companies, the king was utterly dependent upon the upper nobility for suggestions. Before 1664 the position of a *garde du corps* was in the gift of the captains and was sold (often to sons of the bourgeoisie), with the result that there was massive absenteeism and trafficking in salaries. But the September *ordonnance* of that year proscribed venality for the four companies. Minimum specifications were laid down for the recruits, and some requirements did not change (such as Catholic faith), though others, such as the stipulation of nobility, were dropped at various times during the reign. During the Dutch War the crown depended upon provincial governors to supply recruits during the campaign season,[25] but the four captains also had a great deal of freedom to select men of their choice when it was convenient for them to do so. Circular letters from Barbézieux (*secrétaire de la guerre*, 1691–1701) in the Nine Years War continued to testify to the importance of governors in recruitment.[26] By the end of the Nine Years War there was still no satisfactory resolution to the problem of recruitment to the four companies, for the task remained split between the captains, the cavalry *mestres de camp* and provincial governors and *intendants*.[27] Only in the War of the Spanish Succession does the crown seem to have turned more towards the cavalry *mestres de camp* and dragoon

[23] Daniel, *Milice françoise*, ii. 221; *Mémoires du marquis de Sourches sur le règne de Louis XIV* (13 vols., 1882–93), ii. 221–2, 3 Sept. 1688; iii. 342, 2 Jan. 1691. See also Sourches, *Mémoires*, iii. 79, 25 Apr. 1689, for evidence that Louis gave his captains a great deal of free rein in filling vacancies.

[24] SHAT A[1] 1209 piece 1, Luxembourg to Louis, 1 Oct. 1693.

[25] BN MS fr. 7996 fo. 269, Louvois to duc de Chaulnes, 17 Aug. 1674.

[26] Rousset, *Louvois*, i. 217–18; L. Tuetey, *Les officiers sous l'ancien régime – nobles et roturiers* (1908), pp. 107–8; for an example of one of these letters, see SHAT A[1] 1270 piece 182, circular letter from Barbézieux to provincial governors, *commandants* and *intendants*, 9 Nov. 1694. The fact that it was Barbézieux and not Pontchartrain is further evidence of anomalies in the *Maison militaire*'s administration.

[27] Dangeau, *Journal du marquis de Dangeau . . . avec les additions inédites du duc de Saint-Simon* (19 vols., 1854–60), iii. 428, 8 Nov. 1691; Tuetey, *Les officiers*, pp. 107–8, 111–15; SHAT A[1] 1140, n.p., Luxembourg to Louis, 4 Sept. 1692; A[1] 1138, n.p., Louis to Luxembourg, 22 Sept. 1692.

colonels to supply recruits from their regiments for the Gardes du corps companies.[28]

However, this did not by any means eradicate the influence of the four captains over their units and over the king. If, after 1664, the final choice of officers and men fell to the king, the captains were on the whole able to surround themselves with members of their affinity, and they could at least ensure that candidates inimical to their interests were not selected. Except for the reforms in the 1664 *ordonnance*, administrative changes which apparently took power from the captains were not carried through because a despotic crown voraciously sought to centralize control. On the contrary, reform decisions were taken primarily on grounds of practicality during wartime and after consultation with the captains.[29]

Owing to the power of the Gardes du corps officers, it was therefore important to the king and to the *secrétaires de la maison du Roi* and *de la guerre* that a balance of influence among the captains was achieved and that Louis installed the right men in these posts (see Table 1). In 1672, for example, the Le Telliers and the Colberts joined forces to persuade Louis to remove the comte de Charost from one of the captaincies. Charost's son was married to the daughter of the disgraced and imprisoned former *surintendant des finances* Nicolas Fouquet, who had been brought down largely by the two great ministerial clans and the possibility of whose release from prison they did not welcome.[30] It was not until 1711 that Charost's grandson was restored to a captaincy. When the maréchal-duc de Luxembourg died in January 1695 there was a scramble to replace him as captain of the first company.[31] The king's eye fell upon his favourite François de Neufville, duc de Villeroy and *maréchal de France*, a decision which delighted Barbézieux, who now at last had a firm Le Tellier ally as a captain in the Gardes du corps. The Le Telliers even provided some of the financial backing to allow Villeroy to acquire this post.[32]

Space precludes discussion of the Cent-Suisses de la Garde, the Grenadiers à cheval (created in 1676) and the two companies of Mousquetaires du Roi (none of which was owned by *grands*),[33] but in other units of the *Maison militaire*, aside from the Gardes du corps, the influence of the *grands* continued to hold sway, certainly beyond the reach of the *secrétaire de la*

[28] BN MS fr. 7995 fo. 164, circular letter from Chamillart to cavalry *mestres de camp* and dragoon colonels, 10 Jan. 1707. It should not be forgotten, however, that many of these *mestres de camp* were *grands* or senior *épée* nobles themselves.

[29] SHAT A[1] 1138, n.p., Louis to Luxembourg, 22 Sept. 1692.

[30] Dangeau, *Journal*, iii. 184–5, 3 Aug. 1690, with annotations by Saint-Simon; F. de La Chesnaye des Bois et Badier, *Dictionnaire de la noblesse* (19 vols., 1863–76), iii. 121–2. The Charosts drove a hard bargain with the king for their resignations, wresting two *duchés*, a *brevet d'entrée* for continued unimpeded access to the king, and the written promise of a *pairie* from Louis (fulfilled in 1690).

[31] SHAT A[1] 1330 piece 6, Tessé to Barbézieux, 14 Jan. 1695.

[32] SHAT A[1] 1326 fo. 58, Barbézieux to Tessé, 31 Jan. 1695; Sourches, *Mémoires*, iv. 419, 9 Jan. 1695.

[33] For an analysis of the situation in these units see chapter 2 of Rowlands, 'Power, authority and army administration', pp. 95–8.

Table 1 Captains of the Gardes du corps, 1661-1715[a]

| *1st Company* | *2nd Company* |
|---|---|
| **René Potier**, duc de Tresmes, 1649-69 | **Louis de Béthune**, comte de Charost, 1634-72 |
| **Antoine-Nompar de Caumont**, comte de Lauzun, 1669-73 | **Jacques-Henri de Durfort**, comte later duc de Duras (1689), *maréchal de France* (1675), 1672-1704 |
| **François-Henri de Montmorency-Bouteville**, duc de Piney-Luxembourg, *maréchal de France, 1673-95* | **Louis-François, duc de Boufflers**, *maréchal de France*, 1704-11 |
| **François de Neufville**, duc de Villeroy, *maréchal de France*, 1695- | **Armand de Béthune**, duc de Charost, 1711- |
| *3rd Company* | *Compagnie Écossoise* |
| **Louis-Marie-Victor d'Aumont**, marquis de Villequier, later duc d'Aumont (1667), 1652-69 | **Anne, duc de Noailles**, 1643-78 |
| **Henri d'Aloigny**, marquis de Rochefort, *maréchal de France* (1675), 1669-76 | **Anne-Jules, duc de Noailles**, *maréchal de France* (1693), 1678-1707 |
| **Guy-Aldonce de Durfort**, comte later duc de Lorge (1691), *maréchal de France* (1676), 1676-1702 | **Adrien-Maurice, comte d'Ayen**, then duc de Noailles (1708), 1707- |
| **Henri, duc d'Harcourt**, *maréchal de France* (1703), 1703- | |

[a] I have given the dates of their social advancement only if they came during their tenure of a captaincy. Lauzun became a *duc* only in 1692.

*guerre*. This was particularly the case in the two companies of Gendarmes de la Garde and Chevaux-légers de la Garde, each 200 men strong. The captain-lieutenance of the Chevaux-légers de la Garde was presented to Charles-Honoré d'Albert, duc de Chevreuse, in 1670 and remained in the possession of him and his sons until well into Louis XV's reign.[34] This elite company, which enjoyed the king as its titular captain, was organized independently of the War Ministry, and administered directly from the hôtel de Luynes, the Parisian seat in the faubourg Saint-Germain of the Albert family, with Chevreuse's own private secretary du Guet as *secrétaire* of the company.[35] Chevreuse and the king were the sole participants in the decisions surrounding admittance to and dismissal from the company, and the captain-lieutenant accounted for its administration only to the king in person. If the king agreed to accept someone as a *chevau-léger*, Chevreuse would expedite a *brevet* in his own name to the recruit authorizing him to be received into the company.[36] The king's personal approval was still necessary for admission, in spite of Chevreuse's autonomy, and the captain-lieutenant was scrupulous in ensuring that Louis was fully consulted.[37]

Chevreuse was an active administrator of the company. A letter from the *duc*, undated except for 'Vendredy' and '1688', seems to be addressed to his secretary du Guet. In it he alludes to the unspecified problems posed for the

[34] SHAT Ya 262, n.p., 'Rolle de la Compagnie des deux cent Chevau legers de la garde ordre du Roy . . .', 10 Nov. 1689; La Chesnaye, *Dictionnaire*, i. 237.

[35] La Chesnaye, *Dictionnaire*, i. 236; SHAT Ya 262, n.p., d'Arvaraux to du Guet, 15 Feb. 1689.

[36] Daniel, *Milice françoise*, ii. 200, 209.

[37] SHAT Ya 262, n.p., draft certificate for sieur Laurens Antoine, 2 Mar. 1689.

financing of the unit; he goes on to discuss the need to replace a particular horse which has died, and the management of certain members of the company. He was also concerned to ensure speedy delivery of woollen cloth and lace for the men's uniforms and girths for the horses, which on Chevreuse's behalf Louvois was having made by a man called Titon.[38] Chevreuse also appears to have had a considerable hold over the *commissaire à la conduite* responsible for the Chevaux-légers de la Garde, who supervised the musters and the payment of the company.[39] Clearly, Chevreuse did not treat his post as a sinecure.

Ultimately, however, what mattered to the French nobility was patronage, which provided them with social and career advancement, greater incomes (and often greater outlays at the same time) and more influence. As well as getting men into his company, Chevreuse, like the captains of the Gardes du corps, could also secure advancement for them, and here too he assiduously sought to influence the king. Louis even appears to have given the captain-lieutenant prescriptive rights to name men from his company to be lieutenants in cavalry regiments, a concession strongly suggested by one of Chevreuse's letters of 1688.[40] This patronage is the real measure of the level of influence held by certain *grands*, with which the *secrétaire d'état de la guerre* was confronted under Louis XIV.

Unfortunately, though original papers survive for the Chevaux-légers de la Garde, none appears to have been preserved for its sister company, the Gendarmes de la Garde; it seems, however, that much of the authority enjoyed by Chevreuse was replicated with the captain-lieutenant of the Gendarmes.[41] After 1672 this position was in the hands of François-Armand de Rohan, prince de Soubise, who passed it in 1703 to his son Hercule-Mériadec, duc de Rohan-Rohan. François-Armand was a lieutenant-general after 1677 and saw active service in the Dutch and Nine Years Wars in this capacity. He was also shown considerable favour by the king, who may have had amorous intentions towards his wife in the early 1680s.[42] In March 1681 Louis provided Soubise with considerable financial assistance towards the purchase of the *gouvernement* of Berry by altering the officerships of the Gendarmes de la Garde: 'le roi crea en sa faveur une nouvelle charge d'Enseigne et une nouvelle de Guidon, qu'il vendit 50m[ille] ecus, pour lui aider à payer le prix de ce Gouvernement'.[43] This is clear evidence of the crown manipulating the composition of its military units in order to give financial aid to *grands*.

[38] SHAT Ya 262, n.p., Chevreuse to du Guet?, n[o] d[ate] 1688.

[39] SHAT $A^1$ 3780 piece 312, 'Memoire des droits et fonctions du Commissaire tirés des ordonnances du Roy', n.d. [*c.* 1689–1704].

[40] SHAT Ya 262, n.p., Chevreuse to du Guet?, n.d. 1688.

[41] The earliest material at Vincennes is found in SHAT Yb 67, a register from the 1740s listing some of the *gendarmes* of that decade who had served since the 1680s. The rather sparse records of the *Maison du Roi* for the reign of Louis XIV reveal little more about the Gendarmes de la Garde, though a few lists of the personnel in this period can be found in BN Clair 820 fos. 263–331.

[42] G. B. Primi Visconti, *Mémoires sur la cour de Louis XIV, 1673–1681* (1988), p. 170.

[43] BN MS fr. 22622 fo. 307.

Extremely strong familial links between the Rohans and the Luynes bound these two companies of Gendarmes and Chevaux-légers even more firmly together. Chevreuse was Soubise's great-nephew via his grandmother Marie de Rohan, and simultaneously his step-nephew via his stepmother Anne.[44] The personnel of the two companies also found themselves involved in the Rohan-Luynes affinity: Charles-Antoine, marquis de Heilly, an *enseigne* of the Gendarmes de la Garde and later a *maréchal de camp*, even married into the clan in 1694.[45] Chevreuse and Soubise worked together on aspects of the financing of their two companies,[46] and Soubise seems to have been as diligent in some matters as his great-nephew.

Before 1672 the captain-lieutenant and the other officers of the Gendarmes de la Garde had a number of places in the company at their gift, depending on their rank. Until the new incumbent Soubise pointed it out to him, Louis was unaware that this venality, which he had abolished eight years earlier in the Gardes du corps, still existed in the Gendarmes company. Immediate abolition of this system followed but, as with the Gardes du corps captains, Louis compensated the officers for their loss of earnings by granting an extra 26,000 *livres* per annum of *appointements* between them.[47] Soubise's motives for informing the king must remain a matter of conjecture, but they may have been twofold: concern that the junior officers of the company should channel all their presentations for vacancies through the captain-lieutenant, coupled with a desire to monopolize, like Chevreuse, the presentation of recruits directly to the king. If the captain-lieutenant also lost the right to fill vacancies on his own authority, he may have been confident that almost all, if not the entirety, of his recommendations would be accepted by the king, as they were with Chevreuse in the Chevaux-légers de la Garde. Soubise certainly continued to win patronage for his officers and men, for in February 1690 the marquis de Dangeau recorded that Clérembault sold the *gouvernement* of Toul to l'Hôpital for 45,000 *écus*: 'Le gouvernement vaut 12,000 livres de rente; c'est M. de Soubise qui a obtenu l'agrément pour M. de l'Hôpital, qui a été longtemps dans les gendarmes du roi.'[48]

Limited as our information is on Soubise's management of the company of Gendarmes de la Garde, it does speak volumes about the attitude of the French high aristocracy towards the king after 1661. It highlights particularly their determination to work within the system that Louis XIV was constructing where all patronage flowed from the crown. If Soubise and others played the game judiciously they could hope to profit far more than if they set themselves up as somehow outside the system, or even against it. Within this political structure, however, factional battles were central, and both the Gendarmes and

[44] La Chesnaye, *Dictionnaire*, xvii. 507–8, 518–20, i. 233–6.
[45] Ibid. ix. 510, i. 234–6.
[46] SHAT Ya 262, n.p., Chevreuse to du Guet?, n.d. 1688.
[47] Daniel, *Milice françoise*, ii. 192. 'Appointements' were salary.
[48] Dangeau, *Journal*, iii. 62, 3 Feb. 1692.

Chevaux-légers de la Garde were dominated by *grands* whose family ties and personal interests put them far closer to the Colberts and other great *épée* families than to the Le Tellier war ministers and their successors, Chamillart (1701–9) and Voysin (1709–15). It is also worth noting that between 1676 and 1695 the Gardes du corps were in the hands of Luxembourg, Noailles, and the brothers Duras and Lorge (of the La Tour d'Auvergne clan), none of whom was on good terms with the war ministers Louvois (1662–91) or Barbézieux (1691–1701). Taking the Gendarmes and Chevaux-légers de la Garde together with the Gardes du corps, and taking into account the juridical authority and influence over the *Maison militaire* wielded by the *secrétaire d'état de la maison du Roi*, one can safely conclude that the power of the War Ministry was fairly negligible over this most elevated corps of the king's armies. Though Louis himself took a stronger interest in the *Maison militaire* than in most of his forces, he left the direct supervision of these units largely to those senior figures who commanded them. It was a system characterized by unusually harmonious co-operation between a sovereign and his greatest subjects, and it depended heavily on reciprocal understanding of the interests, aspirations and political attitudes of both parties.

## II

The elite cavalry and infantry forces outside the *Maison militaire du Roi* were also either in the grip of princes or of their captains or colonels, with little visible War Ministry control. The *Gendarmerie de France* had evolved over the course of the sixteenth and seventeenth centuries into an elite cavalry force, the mounted shock troops of the armies, as was seen at the battle of La Marsaglia in 1693. The companies of *gendarmes* and *chevaux-légers* which made up the corps formed part of the *Maison militaire du Roi*, but only when serving with the armies in the field.[49] Jurisdiction over them was anomalous and confusing. Each company was commanded by a captain-lieutenant, but whereas the captain-lieutenants of the *chevaux-légers* were under the authority of the *Colonel-général de la cavalerie*, those of the *gendarmes* did not need to obtain the *Colonel-général*'s letters of endorsement. When serving with an army they were, like the rest of the *Maison militaire*, under the authority of the senior cavalry commander.

In 1660 the king disbanded almost all companies of the traditional *Gendarmerie*, recasting and retaining only those of the royal family, which were supplemented as the royal family grew over the following thirty years.[50]

[49] Lynn thought they were always a part of the *Maison du Roi*: Lynn, *Giant of the Grand Siècle*, p. 490.

[50] By 1690 they numbered: Gendarmes écossois (1660); Gendarmes anglois (1667); Gendarmes bourguignons (1668 and 1674); Gendarmes de Flandre (1673); Gendarmes de la Reine (1660); Chevaux-légers de la Reine (1660); Gendarmes Dauphins (1666); Chevaux-légers Dauphins (1667); Gendarmes de Bourgogne (1690); Chevaux-légers de Bourgogne (1690); Gendarmes d'Anjou (1669); Chevaux-légers d'Anjou (1689); Gendarmes de Berry (1690); Chevaux-légers de Berry (1690); Gendarmes d'Orléans (1647); Chevaux-légers d'Orléans (1647?). Daniel, *Milice françoise*, ii. 231–3, 246–54; BN MS fr. 22760 fo. 49$^{v}$.

The Gendarmes and Chevaux-légers d'Orléans, not part of the *Gendarmerie* until 1677–8, were unaffected by the 1660 reorganization. After 1679 all companies stood at fifty *maîtres* each and by 1694 the *Gendarmerie* companies had been raised to a hundred men each, though there were significant variations. The Gendarmes Dauphins stood at 200 men and the Gendarmes d'Orléans at 150. There were six officers in each company except for the Gendarmes d'Orléans (eight), and the Chevaux-légers Dauphins and d'Orléans (five each).[51] In 1692 the marquis de Dangeau had also reported of the *Gendarmerie* that there were fifty supernumeraries in each company, volunteers either supporting themselves or dependent on the officers.[52]

Adult members of the royal family were allowed considerable input into the administration of their units. From some point in the 1680s the Grand Dauphin ('Monseigneur') was given free rein to manage the Gendarmes and Chevaux-légers Dauphins. When the marquis de La Trousse sold the Gendarmes Dauphins to the chevalier de Saucourt, Monseigneur gave Saucourt 'les entrées chez lui', a sign that he had chosen the new captain-lieutenant. In December 1688 he nominated the marquis de Villarceaux *fils*, captain of the Chevaux-légers Dauphins, as a *chevalier du Saint-Esprit*.[53] The control exercised by Louis XIV's brother, Philippe I, duc d'Orléans ('Monsieur'), over his *Gendarmerie* companies was even more extensive. Before the battle of Cassel in 1677 these units had been deemed part of the 'Maison de Monsieur', holding rank with his personal company of Gardes du corps. They accompanied only Monsieur to the armies on campaign and were in attendance about his person and other members of his family. After Cassel, they were united to the other companies of the *Gendarmerie de France* but this did not mean they were fully integrated into its structure. Until 1716 the officer corps of the Orléans companies was kept separate from that of the other *Gendarmerie* companies, and Monsieur, and then his son Philippe II, duc d'Orléans, maintained family control throughout the period over the men who staffed their units, some of whom also held office in the Orléans court.[54]

The other companies of the *Gendarmerie de France* were controlled by the king through the *état-major*, created by Louis in 1690 to give some administrative co-ordination to this expanding corps. It was composed of a major and several *aides-majors*.[55] The major's role was to report to the king on the administration of the companies and, according to Père Daniel, 'lui proposer les sujets les plus dignes de remplir les Charges vacantes, & les personnes qui se presenteroient pour acheter celles qui seroient à vendre,

[51] BN MS fr. 22765 fo. 7, 'Maison du Roi: Gendarmerie, 1694'.

[52] Dangeau, *Journal*, iv. 60, 15 Apr. 1692.

[53] Dangeau, *Journal*, iii. 119, 8 May 1690; Sourches, *Mémoires*, ii. 292, 2 Dec. 1688.

[54] Daniel, *Milice françoise*, ii. 253–4; BN MS fr. 22760 fos. 92$^{v}$, 93$^{v}$, 94$^{v}$, 99$^{v}$, 153$^{v}$; BN Clair 1168 fo. 91, placet to Louis XIV of Charles d'Estampes, marquis d'Estampes, n.d. [1713]; Dangeau, *Journal*, iii. 285, 12 Feb. 1691; iv. 482, 24 Apr. 1694; vi. 107, 22 Apr. 1697; La Chesnaye, *Dictionnaire*, ii. 752–3.

[55] Dangeau, *Journal*, iii. 189–90, 11 Aug. 1690.

après avoir examiné s'ils étoient d'assez grande naissance pour en obtenir l'agrément'. An *état-major* may have been created because of the Dauphin's three under-age sons who were the titular proprietors of six companies.[56] Such captains could not be expected to run their companies as the Dauphin and Monsieur did, although for the companies de Bourgogne, d'Anjou and de Berry it seems that Louis took into account Monseigneur's wishes, as he did over the administration and personnel of the three princes' households.[57] Clearly the authority of princes remained potent in the *Gendarmerie de France* throughout the period 1661–1715.

## III

The *Maison militaire* and the *Gendarmerie* provided the elite mounted forces of the king's armies and the guard for the king, the Dauphin and particular princes at court and in the field. But two other French units outside these structures also enjoyed enormous prestige and privileged relationships with the crown: the régiment des Gardes Françaises and the régiment du Roi, both part of the infantry. While both were line and garrison units, the Gardes Françaises also played an important role at court, guarding the king while he was *en dehors* of his palaces. By 1689 it was over 4,000 men strong.[58] Historians have generally supposed that this regiment came under greater ministerial control under Louvois, but the evidence for this is weak.

In 1672 the retirement of the colonel of the Gardes Françaises, the duc de Gramont, prompted Louis to choose as his replacement François d'Aubusson, duc de La Feuillade, who became a *maréchal de France* in 1675. However, La Feuillade was not yet wealthy, so the king himself paid 440,000 *livres* to Gramont while La Feuillade contributed only 60,000 *livres*. This was an exceptionally large investment by the king in a senior officer's career, and was repeated on this scale by Louis XIV only for his bastards. The level of the king's generosity is a measure of his confidence and trust in La Feuillade. He continued to support La Feuillade financially by creating posts in the regiment specifically for the colonel to sell for his own profit.[59] Posts in the *compagnie colonelle* remained at the colonel's disposal, for in 1689, 1690 and 1693, when the second and third lieutenances of the colonel's company became vacant, the new officers dealt directly with La Feuillade or his successor Boufflers, who gained financially from the sale of these posts. The colonel of the Gardes Françaises therefore had real and lucrative proprietorial rights over his own

[56] Marie, 'La maison militaire', p. 177. The three princes were the Grand Dauphin's sons the ducs de Bourgogne, Anjou and Berry.

[57] SHAT $A^1$ 1212 fos. $245^{r-v}$, Louis to Monseigneur, 2 Sept. 1693. See also BN MS fr. 32770 fos. $142^r$–$143^v$ for evidence that men moved between direct military service to the Dauphin and service in his three sons' companies.

[58] L. Susane, *Histoire de l'infanterie française* (5 vols., 1876), ii. 73; BN MS fr. 22748 fos.$19^{r-v}$, $42^r$, $53^r$, $59^v$, $64^v$–$316^v$.

[59] BN MS fr. 22748 fos. $14^r$, $40^v$.

company in the regiment, which were not even shared by the Gardes du corps captains.

From the outset of Louis's personal rule, La Feuillade's predecessor Gramont had already been deprived of the power of direct presentation to the company officerships and the most important members of the *état-major*: the major and *aides-majors*.[60] The only power over the regiment La Feuillade appears to have lost during his period in office was the power of patronage over the rest of the *état-major*, for in July 1678 the king reserved for himself the nomination to all remaining *charges* in this body, which, in practice, were of fairly minor social or political significance.[61] However, the evidence from the filling of officerships in the regiment makes clear that the king almost always worked through the colonel: the colonel, like so many other *grands*, could no longer dispose of military offices without reference to the crown but he still had extensive opportunities to bend the king to his will and to manipulate the appointments system.[62] The colonel won handsome compensation for the loss of prescriptive rights of appointment: during his tenure as colonel La Feuillade received 10,000 *livres* per annum in *appointements* and an 8,000 *livres* pension from Louis; but in 1678, when he lost control over the last nominations left to him in the *état-major*, Louis gave him the right to levy *aumônes* on the pay of both officers and men, which brought in another 35,000 *livres* per annum. In all, La Feuillade legally drew 53,000 *livres* income each year from his post.[63] One of his chief priorities remained the making of as much money as possible out of his position, some of which helped to finance the construction of the Place des Victoires in Paris.

In spite of losing the last vestiges of prescriptive control over appointments in the regiment, La Feuillade's ability to control the internal administration was undimmed. It seems that the supreme decisions were often taken by La Feuillade alone and sometimes jointly with the king. There was little or no input from the *secrétaire de la guerre*. In 1677 the chevalier d'Harbonnières described La Feuillade as 'absolument le maistre' of the regiment.[64] Six years later, in 1683, La Feuillade decided to rid himself of the burden of organizing the clothing of the regiment, with which he had been charged since 1680. His proposal that the task be delegated to the captains was accepted by the king. He had even suggested the money for clothing be retained in the hands of the *trésoriers des Gardes Françaises et Gardes Suisses* until after the uniforms had been checked, in order to avoid the suspicion of fraud. But Louis trusted La

[60] BN MS fr. 22748 fo. 11v.

[61] BN MS fr. 22748 fos. 15, 84; Dangeau, *Journal*, ii. 424, 6 July 1689.

[62] A. Etienne-Gallois (ed.), *Lettres inédites de Feuquières tirées des papiers de famille de Madame la duchesse Decazes* (5 vols., 1845-6), iv. 122, chevalier d'Harbonnières to marquis de Feuquières, 11 May 1677.

[63] A[rchives] N[ationales] KK 538 fo. 17, 'Creation du Regiment des Gardes Françoises avec une Partie des changements qui y ont été faits en differens Tems'; J. Robert, 'Les Gardes-Françaises sous Louis XIV', *XVIIe siècle*, 68 (1965), 8, 15.

[64] Gallois, *Lettres de Feuquières*, iv. 123, chevalier d'Harbonnières to marquis de Feuquières, 11 May 1677.

Feuillade and his Gardes officers so much that he was happy to allow them access to the money in advance.[65] This financial leeway and administrative autonomy was not something Louvois or his son Barbézieux tolerated for ordinary regiments.

The internal administration of the régiment des Gardes Françaises was so much of a mystery to the crown and the War Ministry that Louis used the opportunity of La Feuillade's death on 19 September 1691 to suspend the colonelcy and give himself time to get acquainted with the ways of the regiment. The marquis de Dangeau hinted at no small degree of royal concern over the administration of this unit, for a large number of complaints had reached the king that La Feuillade had extracted, through corruption and extortion, more than 50,000 *écus* from the regiment's lodgings in the Paris faubourgs.[66] Louis summoned the *prévôt des marchands* of Paris, who explained that La Feuillade, in order to grease the city wheels and ease the lodging of his troops, allowed the *prévôt* and the *échevins* to take 16,000 *livres* per annum in 'kickbacks' from the system, though La Feuillade had not personally profited from it. In what seems to have been a thinly disguised warning, Louis then suggested to the *prévôt* that if the faubourgs were prepared to shoulder the burden of expenditure for building barracks, the bourgeoisie would find that their overall burden lightened over the long term. The result of this discussion was a royal order for the *prévôt des marchands* to construct barracks for the Gardes Françaises and Suisses, and work was under way by January 1692 though it continued sporadically in the decades to come.[67] Once Louis had satisfied his curiosity about the running of the Gardes Françaises he installed Louis-François, marquis de Boufflers, as the new colonel on 4 February 1692. Boufflers had forged a close relationship with the king while he had been *Colonel-général des dragons* from 1678 and he had become one of Louis's favourites.[68]

The surviving documents from Boufflers's tenure as colonel between 1692 and 1704, when the regiment was returned to the Gramont family, reveal more about the workings of the appointments system to the regiment than about the daily administration. La Feuillade had closely guarded the officer positions in the regiment, even forcing the king to back down on occasions,[69] and Boufflers too was highly assertive. In his efforts to secure patronage for those whom he chose to favour, Boufflers religiously followed a procedure preferred by the

[65] BN MS fr. 22748 fos. 17$^{v}$–18$^{r}$.

[66] Dangeau, *Journal*, iii. 400, 19 Sept. 1691; iii. 410, 30 Sept. 1691.

[67] BN MS fr. 22748 fos. 20$^{v}$–21$^{r}$; SHAT Ordonnances Militaires 17 (1692–94), 'Arrest du Conseil d'Etat du Roy, qui Ordonne qu'à la diligence des sieurs Prevost des Marchands et Echevins, il sera construit des Cazernes pour le logement des soldats des Gardes françoises et suisses de sa Majesté, au soulagement des Bourgeois, Propriétaires, et Locataires des maisons de la Ville et Faubourgs de Paris, sujettes aux logements desdits Soldats', 14 Jan. 1692; Dangeau, *Journal*, iv. 10, 17 Jan. 1692; Robert, 'Les Gardes-Françaises', p. 32.

[68] SHAT A$^{1}$ 1138, n.p., Louis to Boufflers, 12 Aug. 1692. He was also related to Louis through a fifteenth-century marriage.

[69] E. de Broglie, *Catinat: l'homme et la vie, 1637–1712* (1902), pp. 13–14.

king and which was later outlined by the duc du Maine with regard to the Swiss regiments:

> Il est la pluspart du temps inutile de proposer pour une compagnie plus de quatre ou cinq personnes. Il faut marquer tres scrupuleusement tout ce qu'on sçait sur leur sujet; apres quoy l'on peut exposer son opinion. Le Roy veut qu'on en use ainsi, pour luy faciliter un détail qu'il ne sçauroit avoir dans la teste comme celuy qui en est particulierement chargé, et qui roûsle sur des officiers qui n'ont guésres l'honneur d'estre connus de S.M. [Sa Majesté]. Dailleurs cela le met en estat de juger sur l'exposition des faits si l'opinion qu'on a formée est judicieuse, si les consequences sont bien tirées, et si les conclusions sont raisonnables.

This was Louis's preferred method of working and it allowed his most senior subjects a great deal of influence in military patronage.[70]

One *mémoire* of recommendations for officerships in the Gardes Françaises has survived from Boufflers's time, dating from late 1693. For the vacant captaincies, lieutenances, *sous-lieutenances* and *aides-majorités*, Boufflers gave each of the several candidates a *résumé* of about fifty words, and for *enseigne* candidates about half that. A typical example would be the sieur de Pontac, who was appointed to the captaincy of the 14th company: 'Il est le second lieutenant du regimt tres galant homme tres bon officier tres brave et tres estimé. Il a esté blessé l'année passée au combat de Steinkerque faisant tres bien son debvoir, et est d'une famille des meilleures et des plus distinguées du parlement de Bordeaux.' The only real challenge to Boufflers's authority over the regiment during the Nine Years War seems to have come from the lieutenant-colonel, the marquis de Rubentel, who held the post between 1681 and 1696 when his resignation was forced.[71]

Boufflers was in turn succeeded as the regiment's colonel in 1704 by Antoine de Gramont, duc de Guiche, the eldest son of the duc de Gramont, governor and viceroy of Béarn and Basse-Navarre, who was one of Louis XIV's most trusted *intimes*. Guiche's control of the regiment was as firm as Boufflers's had been, and this was to be of no small consequence as the end of the reign approached. Guiche was the brother-in-law of Adrien-Maurice, duc de Noailles, who was a captain of the Gardes du corps from 1707, and the two families operated together as an unusually united bloc, linked closely to Boufflers as well. As death claimed ever more members of the royal family from 1711, Philippe, duc d'Orléans manoeuvred for the likely regency and engineered a

[70] SHAT A[3] A 76 fo. 246, 'Mémoire instructif que j'ay fait pour mon fils le Prince de Dombes en novembre mil sept cent dix, pour luy donner les notions qui sont necessaire au Colonel General des Suisses'; A[1] 1138, n.p., Louis to Boufflers, 12 Aug. 1692.

[71] SHAT Ya 284, n.p., 'Memoire des officiers que M[r]. le Mar[al]. de Boufflers croit les plus propres pour remplir les charges vaccantes du regiment des gardes françoises', n.d. [Aug. 1693]; *Mémoires du duc de Saint-Simon*, ed. A. de Boislisle (40 vols., 1879–1928), iii. 322–5; Sourches, *Mémoires*, v. 225, 25 Dec. 1696.

*rapprochement* with both Noailles and Guiche, with whom he had been on bad terms in the 1700s. By 2 September 1715, the day after Louis XIV's death, Orléans had sufficient faith in the Noailles-Gramont axis to organize, with Guiche, the deployment of the Gardes Françaises around the Ile de la Cité for the crucial *séance* of the *Parlement* of Paris, which would overturn the provisions of the late king's will and endow Orléans with full powers as regent. Guiche himself, in full dress uniform and carrying his colonel's baton, ostentatiously stationed himself in one of the open boxes overhanging the *Grand' Chambre* of the *Parlement*.[72]

The Gardes Françaises' rival for the accolade of most prestigious infantry regiment was the régiment du Roi infanterie, created by Louis XIV in 1663 with the explicit purpose of training junior officers to become colonels of infantry regiments. By December 1691 the regiment could boast four *bataillons de campagne* in addition to its *compagnies de garnison* (that is, fifty-two *compagnies de campagne* and 109 *de garnison*), a strength of around 9,600 men. Like the Gardes Françaises, the régiment du Roi effectively operated outside the established structure of ministerial administration. In the late 1670s the marquis de Dangeau, its first colonel-lieutenant (the king being colonel), had tried to have the regiment treated as fully independent of the War Ministry by granting it the same hazy notion of loose attachment to the *Maison du Roi* as was enjoyed by the Gardes Françaises and Suisses. Louvois's opposition prevented Dangeau from succeeding in his design.[73]

Dangeau's successor as colonel-lieutenant was Gaston-Jean-Baptiste de Mornay, comte de Montchevreuil. The Mornay family was closely tied to the royal bastard interest. Gaston-Jean-Baptiste's brother Henri, marquis de Montchevreuil had been governor of both the comte de Vermandois and the duc du Maine and was especially close to Madame de Maintenon, Louis's morganatic wife. On 15 March 1692 Henri was appointed governor of Maine's household at the *duc*'s request. The Mornay de Montchevreuil family was not in the remotest sense allied to the Le Telliers, yet held such a strong place in the king's heart that Henri, marquis de Montchevreuil had been one of the few to witness Louis's secret marriage to Madame de Maintenon, along with Louvois.[74] In the spring of 1693 the comte de Montchevreuil gave up the colonel-lieutenance of the regiment, but on 25 March the king appointed another member of the royal bastards' affinity in his stead, Louis-Charles d'Hautefort, marquis de Surville, the son-in-law of the maréchal d'Humières and colonel-lieutenant of the régiment de Toulouse, owned by the comte de Toulouse.[75] He remained in post until 1706. Some time during the winter of

[72] H. Leclercq, *Histoire de la Régence pendant la minorité de Louis XV* (3 vols., 1922), i. 101–2; J.-C. Petitfils, *Le Régent* (1986), p. 237.

[73] V. Belhomme, *Histoire de l'infanterie en France* (5 vols., 1893–1902), ii. 270, 281, 303; Daniel, *Milice françoise*, ii. 397–8.

[74] Susane, *Histoire de l'infanterie*, iii. 204, 262; La Chesnaye, *Dictionnaire*, xiv. 597–9, vi. 5; Dangeau, *Journal*, iv. 45, 15 Mar. 1692; BN MS fr. 22753 fo. 226; Corvisier, *Louvois*, pp. 318–19.

[75] Dangeau, *Journal*, iv. 250, 25 Mar. 1693; Susane, *Histoire de l'infanterie*, iii. 204.

1692–3, Montchevreuil and Surville had the satisfaction of seeing the king emancipate the régiment du Roi definitively from the War Ministry. As Père Daniel described it, Louis ordered that the regiment would no longer be subject to inspectors, nor to the *secrétaire de la guerre* for the disposal of officerships, thereby putting it on the same footing as the Gardes Françaises and the *Maison militaire*.[76]

The king was clearly adamant that the influence of the War Ministry over his own regiment would not grow. This seems all the more peculiar when the central place of the régiment du Roi in the French infantry is contemplated. If it was regarded as a finishing school for moulding young officers, why was the king obstructing ministerial inspection, curtailing ministerial patronage power and installing as colonel-lieutenants men who were not close to the Le Telliers? The reasons are not altogether clear, but personal interest and vanity on Louis's part may have been a major factor. The little ministerial authority which the forceful Louvois had managed to exercise over the regiment evaporated after his death in July 1691; yet the régiment du Roi continued to provide an abnormally high number of colonels from the ranks of its captains and lieutenants, men who owed their advancement largely to their superior officers and to the king directly, not to the *secrétaire de la guerre*. It was a regiment which, along with the Gardes Françaises, set the tone for the entire French infantry.

## IV

Hand-in-hand with the strengthening of the power of *grands seigneurs* in the *Maison militaire*, the *Gendarmerie de France*, the Gardes Françaises and the régiment du Roi, was the gradual monopolization of officer posts in these units by an elite within the nobility. For example, in the Gendarmes de la Garde not only did Soubise secure the succession as captain-lieutenant for his second son, he also installed his fourth son Henri-Louis, chevalier de Rohan, and his sixth son Maximilien-Gaston-Guy-Benjamin as *enseignes*. The ratchetting process, by which the officer positions in the *Maison militaire*, the *Gendarmerie de France* and the elite regiments went increasingly to the rich nobility and to those with powerful relatives, patrons and creditors, began in earnest during the 1680s.[77]

The most convincing evidence for the idea of a restriction of access to the officer ranks of the elite units comes from the Gardes Françaises. The maréchal de Boufflers's list of recommendations for posts in the regiment in late 1693 is striking in that all the candidates for the posts of captain, lieutenant, *aide-major* and *sous-aide-major* were already serving officers in the regiment. Of

[76] Daniel, *Milice françoise*, ii. 402: Daniel said Surville was colonel-lieutenant at this time but it was probably still the comte de Montchevreuil. Maine and Toulouse were Louis's two illegitimate sons by the marquise de Montespan.

[77] For supporting detail on the Chevaux-légers de la Garde, see chapter 2 of Rowlands, 'Power, authority and army administration', pp. 120–1.

the candidates to be *sous-lieutenants*, five were *enseignes* in the regiment, one was a captain in the régiment des Cuirassiers cavalerie, one a captain in the régiment Royal infanterie, one a captain in the régiment Colonel-général des dragons, and one a captain of a naval *compagnie franche*. Of the candidates for *enseigne*, four were *mousquetaires du Roi*, one was in the cadet companies, one was an infantry captain and one had not served before. Boufflers took the advice of two of the battalion commanders, who gave him references on fifteen of the thirty-eight candidates on the list. Boufflers himself, as the previous dragoon *Colonel-général*, would have been familiar with the comte de Laur, who was second captain of the régiment Colonel-général des dragons and seeking a *sous-lieutenance* in the Gardes Françaises. The sieur de Lordat, candidate for an *enseigne* position, came highly recommended by Jacques-Louis de Beringhen, *premier écuyer du Roi*, for Lordat had been *premier page du Roi* in the *Petite Ecurie* and had advanced from there into the Mousquetaires du Roi. Boufflers had commented alongside the name of the only surviving son of the comte de Caravas: 'Le fils de Mr le comte de Caravas n'a pas encores servi mais il peut entrer dans les mousquetaires pour y servir tel temps que Sa Majesté jugera apropos avant que d'exercer la charge d'enseigne aux gardes.' As well as *mousquetaires* seeking *enseigne* positions, the sieur d'Entragues, himself also an *enseigne* seeking a *sous-lieutenance*, had been a *page du Roi* for three years and then a *mousquetaire* for four years. Pontac, the lieutenant of the 20th company, came from a rich *parlementaire* family in Bordeaux, and the chevalier de Montgon, a captain in the régiment des Cuirassiers seeking the post of *sous-lieutenant*, was brother to another chevalier de Montgon, a brigadier in the armies. Three candidates were the brothers of officers who had been killed while serving in the Gardes Françaises and one was the brother of a serving lieutenant in the regiment. All three brothers of the deceased officers were seeking to enter the regiment from outside in order to take up their siblings' old *charges*.[78]

A similar pattern of selecting from a narrow elite pool of the court, of senior *robin* families and of families with existing connections to the Gardes Françaises can be seen in a list of September 1692 detailing the appointment of officers to vacancies in the regiment. In January 1694 the position of *enseigne* in the 7th company was filled by Cressy, who was not only an officer in the régiment de Boufflers but also the son of the captain of Boufflers's personal company of guards. Boufflers would also occasionally suggest a single candidate for a vacancy, a particular sign of favour: in July 1694 he wrote to Louis on behalf of the chevalier d'Entragues (brother to the *sieur*), asking he be made lieutenant of the 10th company, a request which was granted.[79]

[78] SHAT Ya 284, n.p., 'Memoire des officiers que M^r^. le Mar^al^. de Boufflers croit les plus propres pour remplir les charges vaccantes du regiment des gardes françoises', n.d. [Aug. 1693].

[79] SHAT Ya 284, n.p., 'Memoire des officiers que le Roy a choisis pour remplir les charges vacantes de son regiment des gardes tant par mort que par ceux que Sa Majesté a fait monter', n.d. [Sept. 1692]; BN MS fr. 22748 fo. 131; SHAT A[1] 1261 fo. 211[v], Louis to Boufflers, 11 July 1694.

There is some further information about the officers who served in the Gardes Françaises during the Nine Years War (of which there were 271 in total), in addition to that proffered above. It only confirms that a creeping monopolization of officerships in the Gardes Françaises by the court nobility, their entourages and senior *robin* families progressed alongside the emergence of a self-perpetuating oligarchy in the regiment in the later seventeenth century.[80] Worthy of particular note is the presence of scions of the senior *noblesse de robe* among the officers of the Gardes Françaises. Not only did they seek positions in the army and navy in order to secure and improve the social acceptability of their families to the *noblesse d'épée*, but their interest in service was welcomed by the king because it expanded his pool of potential officers and imbued the *robe* with traditional martial values. This in turn brought the *robe* and the *épée* closer together as a more cohesive second estate.[81]

The surviving material on the Gardes Françaises also provides some evidence as to why the pool of potential officers was narrowing under Louis XIV. The most important factor was the growing financial burden on officers in units which served both at court and in the field. It is clear that this was making it increasingly difficult for many nobles to contemplate commissions in these units. There were still entry and exit charges for officers taking up positions or being promoted in the Gardes Françaises until Louis suppressed them in 1686 at the request of La Feuillade, who could see the detrimental effect they were having on officers.[82] Such financial burdens were upsetting existing officers and disturbing the composition of the officer ranks in the Gardes Françaises, so they were abolished;[83] but the rising tide of financial pressure on Gardes Françaises officers and aspirants did not recede.

The huge price increases for posts in the period *c.*1672-1704 can be ascribed to a number of factors, some associated with prestige, others with the rising cost of warfare. The régiment des Gardes Françaises already possessed seniority over all other infantry regiments. Of more importance, the duc de La Feuillade was keen to protect the status and position of his officers and even to improve it. The distinguished performance of the Gardes Françaises at the siege of Mons gave La Feuillade the opportunity to press Louis about the rank of his captains. On 26 March 1691 the king promulgated an *ordonnance* under which captains and lieutenant-colonels of the Gardes Françaises and Suisses would have the status of infantry colonel, in effect the right of command over all infantry colonels and

[80] A fairly complete list of officers in the regiment at this time can be found in BN MS fr. 22748 fos. 81ᵛ-316ᵛ; see also E. Forster (ed.), *A woman's life in the court of the Sun King: letters of Liselotte von der Pfalz, 1652-1722* (1984), p. 81, Madame to Sophia, 28 June 1693. For a full list of people identified as possessing excellent connections, see chapter 2 of Rowlands, 'Power, authority and army administration', pp. 125-6.

[81] For a full elaboration of this argument: G. Rowlands, 'The ethos of blood and changing values? *Robe*, *épée* and the French armies, 1661 to 1715', *Sevent-Cent Fr Stud*, 19 (1997), 95-108.

[82] BN MS fr. 22748 fo. 19.

[83] Gallois, *Lettres de Feuquières*, iv. 123, chevalier d'Harbonnières to marquis de Feuquières, 11 May 1677.

brigadiers when in the field.[84] On 4 February 1692, the day Boufflers took the oath as the new colonel, Louis issued another *ordonnance* which gave lieutenants of the Gardes Françaises the power to command over all infantry captains (except lieutenant-colonels) and the *enseignes* and *sous-lieutenants* the power to command over all infantry lieutenants: 'Ce fût M[r] le Marquis de Boufflers Colonel du regiment qui obtint cette ordonnance du Roy' (Dangeau). Louis had earlier refused this upgrading when approached on the matter by La Feuillade. Finally, at the end of 1692, and as a further reward for the regiment's performance at the battle of Steinkerque, the king retrospectively fixed all its captains with the permanent rank of infantry colonel from the date of the March 1691 *ordonnance*. These were all moves that had been consistently opposed by Louvois because they would inflate the price of posts.[85] The consequence was that money was channelled into the purchase of prestigious Gardes Françaises companies bringing the status of colonel, rather than into the ownership of whole regiments which automatically brought that rank.

A comparison of the prices of Gardes Françaises companies with those of full regiments is instructive. By February 1693, when two companies in the Gardes Françaises were bought for 80,000 *livres* each, cavalry regiments had a crown-imposed price ceiling of 24,500 *livres*;[86] but cavalry regiments consisted of 600 men, five times as many as in a Gardes Françaises company. From the perspective of the War Ministry this was an extremely inefficient use of the nobility's resources in the king's service. The crown finally set a ceiling on the price of Gardes Françaises companies in January 1694 but held it at what had become roughly the market rate, of 25,000 *écus* (or 77,500 *livres*).[87]

To compound the problem, officers of the elite forces were expected to invest large sums of their own money in the upkeep of their companies. The marquis de Dangeau estimated in 1690 that a man needed at least 1,000 *pistoles* a year just to maintain a brigade (half a company) of Gendarmes or Chevaux-légers, and this was with significant royal subsidies.[88] This pushed the selling price of units ever higher. The awesome prospect of maintaining the standards of one exceptional company in the Gardes Françaises, the property of the recently deceased sieur de Cailhavel, was too much for two officers. Instead of bidding for this company, as their seniority entitled them to do, Lage and Le Conclaye preferred to take two other vacant companies in February 1689, 'craignant l'un et l'autre de ne la pouvoir soutenir dans le bon état où elle est'.[89]

[84] SHAT Ordonnances Militaires 16 (1690–1), 'Ordonnance du Roy, concernant le Rang que sa Majesté veut que tiennent les Officiers de ses Regimens des Gardes Françoises & Suisses, qui se trouveront commander lesdits Regimens entiers, ou par détachemens, & dans les tranchées, avec les Officiers des autres Regimens d'Infanterie', 26 Mar. 1691.

[85] Daniel, *Milice françoise*, ii. 269; Dangeau, *Journal*, iv. 19, 4 Feb. 1692; BN MS fr. 22748 fos. 21[v], 42[v]; Rousset, *Louvois*, iii. 316.

[86] Dangeau, *Journal*, iv. 238, 21 Feb. 1693; BN MS fr. 22748 fo. 164; BN MS fr. 22767 fo. 121[v]; Dangeau, *Journal*, ii. 350, 10 Mar. 1689.

[87] Dangeau, *Journal*, iv. 442, 25 Jan. 1694.

[88] Ibid. iii. 263, 20 Dec. 1690. 1,000 *pistoles* were roughly 12,000 *livres*.

[89] Ibid. ii. 322, 1 Feb. 1689; ii. 330, 14 Feb. 1689.

By way of compensation for these huge outlays of capital and subsequent expenses, officers benefited from royal *largesse*: the Gardes Françaises took a share of the royal military pensions and gratifications disproportionate to the size of their ranks; officers who remained within the king's service when they left the regiment often moved on immediately to be governors of *places*, or colonels of other regiments; and captains were sometimes presented with a 6,000 *livres* pension for retirement.[90] To justify the rising prices, throughout his reign Louis accorded to the officers a large number of prerogatives, ranks and privileges, including those of *committimus* and exemption from mounting guard in the king's absence.[91] Ironically, though, this may have helped feed demand for posts in the regiment, thereby driving prices even higher. After the battle of Blenheim in 1704, Louis pledged he would henceforth replace all baggage, transport and arms lost in actions by the four Gardes du corps companies, thus making these units even more attractive to aspiring officers and contributing to even greater competition for them, much as with positions in the Gardes Françaises.[92]

The rising cost of service was also a problem in the *Gendarmerie de France*. In May 1690 the market price for a normal captain-lieutenance was about 100,000 *livres*, but exactly three years later Dromesnil bought the Chevaux-légers Dauphins from d'Urfé for 40,000 *écus* (128,000 *livres*); in August 1693 the marquis de Lanmarie bought the captain-lieutenance of the Gendarmes de la Reine for 136,000 *livres*. The prices in the Gendarmes écossois were the highest.[93] The price rises stemmed from an increase in the size of some units, but principally from a rise in demand owing to the status such illustrious corps were coming to possess. To ensure the right men were installed as captain-lieutenants, the king was forced to intervene and buck the market. When the Chevaux-légers d'Anjou were set up in January 1689, Louis was determined to present the captain-lieutenance to Rozamel, who was *sous-lieutenant* of the Gendarmes de Flandre. But Rozamel was unable to bear the financial burden of raising the new company alone, even with the usual royal support, so Louis was forced to provide additional financial aid. He gave Rozamel the post of *cornette* of the new company to sell on, 'pour lui donner moyen de lever la compagnie'.[94] Two months later the captain-lieutenance of the Gendarmes anglois became vacant on the retirement of La Guette. The king forced on him a maximum selling price of 82,000 *livres* and presented the post to Cralei, the *sous-lieutenant*, who sold his own post for 77,000 *livres*. Louis's anxiety to

[90] BN MS fr. 22734 (ii) fos. 215-71, 'Rolle de plusieurs parties et sommes de Deniers . . .', 'Deniers payez par ordonnances' [gratifications], Jan. to Dec. 1696; BN MS fr. 22748 fos. 180, 195ᵛ; BM MS fr. 22761 fo. 200ᵛ.

[91] Robert, 'Les Gardes-Françaises', pp. 16–17.

[92] BN MS fr. 8006 fo. 20.

[93] Dangeau, *Journal*, iii. 119, 8 May 1690; iv. 279, 5 May 1693; BN MS fr. 22760 fos. 10ᵛ, 11ᵛ, 32ᵛ. In May 1690 the Gendarmes Dauphins, which was double the size of the other companies, was sold for 195,000 francs (*livres*).

[94] Dangeau, *Journal*, ii. 294, 8 Jan. 1689.

promote Cralei from within the company led him to pay La Guette the difference of 5,000 *livres* himself. The demand for the post had been enormous and La Guette lost out heavily by the king's decision to impose a price ceiling on his *charge*, for some people had offered him up to 150,000 *livres*.[95]

Nevertheless, such a policy of trying to ease *sous-lieutenants* of the Gendarmerie into captain-lieutenant vacancies and of holding the prices down could not be sustained for very long. Four years later, when the Gendarmes de la Reine, which had nearly doubled in size, was put on the market in April 1693, it proved impossible to find any *sous-lieutenants* within the *Gendarmerie* who could afford to fill the vacancy with its asking price of 136,000 *livres*.[96] The financial cost of advancement was beginning to bite into the French nobility at a lower level in the military hierarchy than before. By 1689 the asking price for the junior position of *guidon* in the Gendarmes anglois was 10,000 *francs* (*livres*).[97] All this reflects the more general problem of the French officer corps which was emerging in the second half of Louis XIV's reign: a glass ceiling was already under construction which was excluding the poorer provincial nobility from service as officers in the elite units, and consequently disadvantaging them in the search for further advancement.

This was particularly true with the régiment du Roi, whose very existence and *raison d'être* made it more difficult for captains in less prestigious regiments to acquire colonelcies.[98] While it is true that the officer ranks of the régiment du Roi were not monopolized by an inner noble elite, nevertheless those men in the regiment who were being appointed to colonelcies elsewhere were predominantly captains and also possessed some social standing. Between 1663 and 1715 the régiment du Roi exported large numbers of its officers to other regiments. For example, in November and December 1695 fifty new infantry regiments were created from *bataillons de garnison* belonging to other regiments. The colonelcies of ten of these new regiments were given to captains in the régiment du Roi. In 1684–5, thirty-three infantry regiments were created: out of fifty-seven colonels who headed them at one point during the Nine Years War, nineteen had been captains in the régiment du Roi. Moreover, these figures do not include those colonels who may have been subalterns in the regiment, as this data is barely recorded.[99] Though not wholly reliable, these figures give a firm impression of the overrepresentation of ex-captains of the régiment du Roi amongst the infantry colonels of 1688–

[95] Ibid. ii. 356, 19 Mar. 1689; ii. 386, 2 May 1689.

[96] Ibid. iv. 263, 11 Apr. 1693.

[97] Ibid. ii. 308, 23 Jan. 1689.

[98] The two companies of Mousquetaires du Roi were also geared to the training of young nobles for a fast-track career in the regular regiments and the other elite units: Rowlands, 'Power, authority and army administration', pp. 132–3.

[99] BN MS fr. 22749 (i) fos. 107–32; BN MS fr. 22753 fos. 214–78. Some colonels had only been lieutenants in the regiment, though this data is sparsely recorded: for an example of one, see BN MS fr. 22754 fo. 26ᵛ.

97. Had the regiment supplied colonels in proportion to its share of the infantry captaincies in the whole officer corps, it would have provided only about 4.5 per cent of the infantry colonels of the Nine Years War rather than the approximately 15 per cent it did.

Of those captains who were given regiments in 1663-1715, many enjoyed prestigious connections, even at the highest levels in the court. The backgrounds of all fifty colonels of the new regiments of 1695 are worth closer consideration. Of the forty who were *not* drawn from the régiment du Roi, four were officers of the Gardes Françaises and eleven others had connections with the court or with the affinities of princes and *grands*. Of the total number of new colonels in November-December 1695, therefore, 50 per cent were officers of the military elite, were in the service of the *grands* or were closely connected with them.[100] This is conclusive evidence that patronage and advancement were more easily secured by those men already advantaged by their existing positions. The crown seems to have become sensitive about these problems. When Louis appointed four new captains on 4 September 1689, a public statement he made suggested that he was anxious people should realize these men were being promoted on merit and not as a result of their social station or wealth.[101] But Louis's utterances could not mask the fact that officers in the most prestigious units and with the most powerful social and political connections were getting a disproportionately large share of the patronage spoils.

The idea of a progressive exclusion of the lesser nobility from the most prestigious and lucrative positions in the French armies was common currency in mid-eighteenth-century France. However, historians have yet to explain how and when it began. The superficially attractive assumption that the regency of the duc d'Orléans began an aristocratic backlash, which led to the domination of the upper ranks of the French armies by an increasingly degenerate *haute noblesse* by 1756, seems an inadequate explanation. Without doubt, the gradual monopolization by a privileged and restrictive elite within the nobility of posts in the *Maison militaire* and the other great units, and of colonelcies of infantry, cavalry and dragoon regiments, caused massive resentment in France amongst the lesser nobility, particularly from 1748.[102] Contemporaries, including the king himself, also perceived a decline in discipline during the first half of Louis XV's reign in the units of the *Maison militaire du Roi*.[103] While the growing anger over the performance and composition of the elite units by the 1740s does not appear to have yet been articulated during the late seventeenth or very early eighteenth centuries, this does not mean that the

[100] BN MS fr. 22753 fos. 218-68; BN MS fr. 22749 (i) fos. 107-32.

[101] Dangeau, *Journal*, ii. 464, 4 Sept. 1689.

[102] For example, captain Jacques Mercoyrol de Beaulieu, *Campagnes, 1743-63*, ed. marquis de Vogüé and A. Le Sourd (1915), cited in L. Kennett, *The French armies in the Seven Years War* (Durham, N.C., 1967), p. 57.

[103] J. Chagniot, 'Une panique: les Gardes Françaises à Dettingen (27 juin 1743)', *Rev Hist M*, 24 (1977), 84-5, 91.

process, by which an oligarchy within the nobility got a hold on much of the army, had not begun under Louis XIV. Already by 1690 the officer ranks of the *Gendarmerie de France* were dominated by men with the titles of *comte* and *marquis*, and this was before such titles had been completely devalued.[104]

Evidence from the *Maison militaire*, the *Gendarmerie*, the Gardes Françaises and the régiment du Roi suggests strongly that recruitment into the middling and senior ranks of the officer corps was from an increasingly narrow base within the nobility after 1661, and this trend accelerated under the pressure of an inflationary war effort after 1688. This can be seen at its starkest in the growing number of appointments of under-age but well-connected colonels during the War of the Spanish Succession, as suitable candidates with sufficient resources dwindled.[105] Access to the officer positions of the most important 'feeder' units, which were also the most prestigious, was progressively restricted by crown policies over the course of Louis XIV's reign. The move to Versailles, and the increasing concentration of a larger court there after 1682, led to a rise in the cost of living and of attendance on the king. The increase in the size and status of the companies of the Gardes du corps, the *Gendarmerie* and the Gardes Françaises pushed the price of officerships in them beyond the reach of all but the rich, the powerful and the well-connected, and even they found themselves burdened by mounting personal debt. The determination of the king to give his elite forces an increase in status *vis-à-vis* the rest of his army, and his wish to put them on a pedestal, meant that demand for posts in these corps soared. Finally, this demand was boosted further by knowledge that officers in these units, and in the régiment du Roi, stood a very high chance of greater advancement. If Louis was to be successful in firmly binding the elite forces to the crown for now and the future, in a context where service in close proximity to the monarch was increasingly expensive, he had no choice but to give up all thoughts of intervening to ensure the prices of officerships in these units were low. It was left to his successors to cope with the corrosive social and political effects which his policies began.

## V

In the *Maison militaire* and the *Gendarmerie*, and in the régiments des Gardes Françaises and du Roi, the influence of the *grands* and the unit commanders remained strong. The war ministers made insignificant inroads into the power of the social elites in these forces, and these illustrious corps remained far more autonomous than ordinary regiments. While the high aristocracy lost the last scraps of prescriptive authority still remaining to them early in Louis's

[104] BN MS fr. 22756 fo. 52. Of the sixteen men in each rank, fourteen of the captain-lieutenants, ten of the *sous-lieutenants*, nine of the *enseignes/premiers cornettes* (plus a member of the Janson family) and eight of the *guidons/seconds cornettes* were titled.

[105] See, for example, régiment de Gondrin, BN MS fr. 22749 (i) fo. 20v; régiment d'Agenois, MS fr. 22753 (i) fo. 363.

'personal rule', if not as early as the 1650s, in practice they retained their influence over patronage and much of the administration, and continued to manipulate the king in their own interests. As a whole, the court aristocracy can actually be said to have had rather more control over the crown's elite forces by 1697 than they possessed in 1661, particularly because these units had been redefined and now acted as a magnet for those courtiers seeking military positions for themselves or their affinities. Perhaps this would not have mattered so much had these forces been cocooned from the rest of the army, but they supplied a hefty proportion of the French officer corps who went on to achieve the rank of colonel and above. They also set the tone not only for the entire French army but also for the elite forces of other European sovereigns. The highly visible presence of the *Maison militaire* and the Gardes Françaises at the French court was an integral part of the projection of the Bourbon image across France and Europe. What is more, André Corvisier has estimated that in 1691 about 3,000 nobles were serving in the *Maison du Roi* and the *Gendarmerie* alone, more than 10 per cent of the total number of nobles serving in the whole French army at this time.[106] Even this may be an underestimate and the true figure may be nearer to 4,500, or at least 18 per cent.

Established ministerial control would have allowed responsibility for these units to be easily transferred into the hands of the *conseil de la guerre* in 1715 on the death of Louis XIV and the accession of the child Louis XV. The absence of ministerial authority and the persistent power of the *grands* in these forces meant that it was imperative for the duc d'Orléans to take the troops of the *Maison du Roi* into his full control at the start of the regency. Just over a year before his death, anticipating the succession of a minor and determined to prevent Orléans wielding full power, the old king made his final will and testament. Not only did it divide responsibility for Louis XV's upbringing and education between Orléans and Louis's own bastard, the duc du Maine, it also gave Maine full control over the *Maison militaire du Roi* except when these troops were serving on campaign. The threat this posed for the stability of the realm was so strong that in the *séance* of the *Parlement* of Paris on 2 September 1715, the day after Louis XIV's death, Orléans had the provisions of the will overturned, and he became full regent. Maine, himself sensing the potential for significant future strife, did not demur. Orléans gained control over all the armed forces, which would be administered by two councils for the army and the navy, with the *Maison militaire du Roi* under his own direct authority.[107] In achieving this outcome he was aided by the officers of the *Maison militaire* and the Gardes Françaises themselves. For the *séance* of 2 September, Orléans staged a display of military might using units who were

[106] Corvisier, *Louvois*, p. 343.

[107] Dangeau, *Journal*, xv. 139, 4 May 1714; Testament of Louis XIV, 2 Aug. 1714, reproduced in Leclercq, *Régence*, i. 108–9, 119–23; [Président Aligre], 'Relation de ce qui se passa au Parlement de Paris à la mort de Louis XIV (août et septembre 1715)', *Revue Rétrospective* , ser. 2, 6 (1836), 16–18.

factionally loyal to him, notably the Gardes Françaises which swamped the Île de la Cité fully armed so as to deter Maine, the *Colonel-général des Suisses*, from trying any counter-demonstration of force using the régiment des Gardes Suisses.[108] But, more importantly, the officers of the *Maison militaire* insisted that they could take orders from nobody but the king, or, failing that, a regent.[109] This was nothing less than the first of several posthumous setbacks for Louis XIV's efforts to elevate the status and power of his bastards. Ironically the disciplined loyalism towards the king and the regent exhibited by the *Maison militaire* officers owed a great deal to Louis XIV's ability to meet the demands and expectations of the upper echelons of the French nobility.

Historians must be wary of attributing too many modern notions of governmental and military efficiency to Louis XIV's management of his armies, for if efficiency were the principal criterion for administration then some of Louis's actions were clearly counter-productive. In fact, Louis was always principally concerned with the future of the dynasty, which ultimately required the support of the *grands*. Accordingly, the king himself was prepared to sacrifice much 'rational' and centralized efficiency in order to satisfy the aspirations of the senior *noblesse* and to enhance his own *gloire*, and thereby to safeguard the future of the monarchy through the careful nurturing of loyal and contented sentiment. The princes of the royal family and other trusted *grands* were allowed to surround themselves with men who would add lustre to their units and thus uphold the status not only of the leading families of the realm but also the prestige of the Bourbon dynasty. Unfortunately for many provincial nobles, this cost money which they did not and could never hope to possess. They found themselves gradually excluded from service as officers in the most prestigious parts of the French armed forces, principally because of the emergence of an elite within the nobility and the increasing cost of service in the most illustrious units.

Louis XIV's approach of encouraging attachment to the crown and the dynasty was facilitated in great measure by compromise with elite interests, and this applied equally to the command of armies, the ownership and raising of regiments, and the maintenance of traditional offices in the land and sea forces where they did not overtly hamper war efforts or restrict the king's personal authority. But Louis's overriding general dynastic concerns, which were the dominant factors behind royal policy towards the state machinery and the nobility, were most keenly on display with the elite military units. Success and political stability, not to mention loyalty to the main Bourbon line, required the encouragement of strong feelings of attachment amongst the nobility, even and most especially in the armed forces. During Louis's own lifetime he was spectacularly successful at binding the second estate to the crown. He strengthened the Bourbon dynasty's links with the military elites, and

[108] Aligre, 'Relation', p. 21; Petitfils, *Le Régent*, p. 237. Both regiments were garrisoned in and around Paris.

[109] Aligre, 'Relation', p. 18; Leclercq, *Régence*, i. 120.

entrenched those elites in prestigious positions of authority. Louis XV, however, would later face the consequences of continuing his great-grandfather's policies towards the most illustrious units of the French army. The resultant discontent amongst the provincial nobles ultimately helped to weaken both the monarchy and the *ancien régime*.

# [4]

# Army Provisioning, Logistics and Strategy in the Second Half of the 17th Century

By

G. PERJÉS

## The Growth of Army Manpower in the Second Half of the 17th Century

The most decisive phenomenon in the warfare of the second half of the 17th century was the enormous growth of manpower in the armies.[1]

During the Thirty Years' War, the effective strength of the armies of opposing parties varied from 100 000 to 120 000 men; in the War of the Spanish Succession, as many as 450 000—500 000 soldiers were fighting on both sides.[2]

Naturally, these considerable forces did not operate together in the same theatres of war, but were divided into several "camps", i.e. several independent armies.[3] At the time of the Thirty Years' War the strength of the belligerent armies involved in pitched battle was usually 30 to 40 000 combatants on both sides; by the time of the War of the Spanish Succession this number had risen to 60—80 000, sometimes even to 100 000 men.

All this took place at a time when the growth of Europe's population was not rapid at all; in France, for example, the population even decreased by the end of that period.[4] Except for England and the Netherlands, there was no change in the level of agricultural production, nor in that of transportation facilities. So it happened that, given substantially unchanged population num-

[1] General references: X. AUDOUIN: *Histoire de l'administration de la guerre.* I—IV. Paris 1831. II. p. 261. — G. HANOTAUX: *Histoire de la nation française.* Tome VIII. *Histoire militaire et navale.* Vol.I. — J. COLIN: *Der origines aux croisades.* — FR. REBOUL: *Des croisades à la révolution.* Paris 1925. p. 427. — E. FRAUENHOLZ: *Das Heerwesen in der Zeit des Absolutismus.* München 1940. p. 35. — *Feldzüge des Prinzen Eugen von Savoyen.* Vols I—XIII. Wien 1876—1886. Vol. III. p. 21., IV. p. 630. — SCHMOLLER: *Preußische Verfassungs-, Verwaltungs- und Finanzgeschichte.* Berlin 1921. p. 110. — LAVISSE—RAMBAUD: *Louis XIV. 1643—1715. (Histoire générale VI.)* Paris 1912. p. 711.

[2] It seems almost incredible how small the forces were in the Thirty Years' War that entailed so great consequences. Wallenstein's army consisted of 120 000 men in 1627, Gustavus Adolphus had 100 000 men in 1632. —E. FRAUENHOLZ: *Das Söldnertum in der Zeit des dreißigjährigen Krieges.* München 1938. p. 36.

[3] As for the interpretation of the "camps" see my introduction to Zrinyi's "Tábori kis trakta" (Short Treatise on Camps). In *Zrinyi Miklós hadtudományi munkái* (Works on Military Science). Budapest 1957. p. 97.

[4] W. WILLCOX: *Increase in the Population of the Earth and the Continents since 1650.* New York 1931. p. 71. — M. REINHARDT: *Histoire de la population mondiale de 1700 à 1948.* Paris n.d. p. 56. — HUBER—BUNLE—BOVERET: *La population de la France.* 3rd edition, Paris 1948. p. 21. — The population of France amounted to 21.1 millions in 1700, whereas only to 18 millions in 1715; M. LEVASSEUR: *La population française.* I—III. Paris 1888—1892. Vol. III. p. 206.

bers and no agricultural progress, food had to be provided for armies three to four times as big as before; considerable quantities of amassed food had to be transported behind the armies on roads that were not a bit better, and with transport facilities of no greater capacity than in the past.

The problems involved in the provisioning of bigger armies had a decisive influence on strategy.[5] The essence of the strategic problem lay in the fact that it was impossible to procure on the spot the great quantities of food required for the armies; food had to be collected in magazines well before campaigns were launched, had to be processed, and then transported behind armies operating in the field. All this resulted in command difficulties never experienced before, and affected the warfare of the age as a whole.

It was for this reason that the experts of the time usually wished to set limits to army manpower, and established an uppermost limit, an optimal strength, at which an army was still sufficiently combat-worthy, but not too big to render provisioning and command impossible. Zrínyi has set such strength at 48 000, Montecuccoli and Turenne at 50 000 men.[6] Yet the warnings of the military experts were of no use. Manpower grew unavoidably, and it is easy to see why this was so. It was not the military and technical factors that were decisive in the last analysis, rather it was social and political laws that acted towards increasing the effective strength of armies. In any event, the misgivings of the military experts were not without foundation, and difficulties of command arising from the growth of manpower proved to be ever less surmountable. Even in the second half of the 18th century, Guibert, the famous French military expert, saw the principal reason of the "decline of the art of war" in the fact that Louis XIV and Louvois had "imprudently" inflated the manpower of armies, as a result of which they became clumsy, unmanageable masses.[7]

[5] H. Delbrück: *Geschichte der Kriegskunst.* Vol. IV. Berlin 1920. p. 343.

[6] Zrinyi M.: *Tábori kis trakta.* — Montecuccoli: *Della Guerra col Turco in Ungheria.* Operi di —. 2. ed. I—II. Milano 1831. Lib. III/XXVI. — Audouin: op. cit. II. p. 244.

[7] Guibert: *Essai générale de tactique.* Vol. I—II. London 1772. II. p. 6. As we have already seen Guibert explained only with accidental causes the increase of manpower in the armies and was not able to perceive its social and economic causes. At the same time historiography later imputed the reluctance of contemporary military experts to armies with too many men to some erroneous view, or even to some superstitions. Clausewitz, for example, wrote as follows: "Ein anderer Beweis liegt in einer wunderbaren Idee, welche in den Köpfen mancher kritischen Schriftsteller spuckte, nach der es eine gewisse Größe eines Heeres gab, welche die beste war, eine Normalgröße, über die hinaus die überschießenden Streitkräfte mehr lästig als nützlich waren." *Vom Kriege.* 9. Aufl. Berlin 1915. III. Buch, 8. Kapitel, p. 132. — Jähns, one of the greatest figure of the German military historiography, shares entirely Clausewitz' opinion: "Dieser Aberglaube, daß ein Heer'zu groß' sein könnte, hat lange geherrscht; erst die neue Zeit hat ihn vernichtet." M. Jähns: *Geschichte der Kriegswissenschaften.* I—III. Leipzig 1889—1891. I. p. 466. All this was, however, entirely false. The contemporary experts did not refuse the too numerous armies because of some erroneous opinion, but as we have already seen because of the difficulties of supply. They recognized very clearly the importance of the numerical supremacy and strove, of course, to attain it, nevertheless they could restrict

What actually happened therefore was that, owing to the aggressive intentions of that age, the numerical growth of armies far exceeded progress in the means of production, and surpassed the limits at which armies still could have been provisioned and led properly considering the existing potentialities of supply, transport and techniques of command. This advance of politics beyond military factors was a natural consequence of the world-wide struggle for hegemony in Europe, for the monopolization of world trade and the colonies; but that such advance could take place at all was made possible by a growing absolutistic centralization, by an improvement in the means and methods of state administration, whereby it became possible to mobilize, equip and marshal more and more men.[8]

## An Estimation of the Support Capacity of 17-Century Theatres of War

Granted that the provisioning of armies encountered extraordinary difficulties, the question presents itself logically: what was the support capacity of the various theatres of war in the 17th century? To answer this question directly, i.e., on the basis of available historical sources, is not possible because statistical surveys of this kind had not yet been made. And the estimation procedures applied to armies were confined to generalities — apart from the fact that they usually only referred to fodder reserves — so that their returns cannot be used for our purpose.[9]

It was not until the beginning of the 19th century that statistics were able to provide a certain basis for military command concerning the resources of given theatres of war.[10] On the one hand, the ever increasing number and improving quality of descriptive statistical reports, and, on the other, more accurate censuses and land-surveys, making possible population density calculations, provided an opportunity for a regional division of Europe with respect to military operations. The theoretical basis of this method was the

their demands within sober limits by reason of the very difficulties in the supply itself. One has to read only Montecuccoli's argumentation, and it is obvious what a considerable importance was attributed to the numerical superiority by the contemporary experts. — *Ausgewählte Schriften des Raimund Fürsten Montecuccoli.* Edited by A. Veltzé. I—IV. Wien 1899—1904. I. pp. 73—74. MONTECUCCOLI: *Della Guerra.* Lib. III/XXV.

[8] I. Hajnal wrote: "Formerly war was rather the king's affair, now all social resources are thrown into it. The administrative state may dispose more and more directly of the whole strength of society." I. HAJNAL: *Az újkor története* (Modern History). (Egyetemes történet 3.) Budapest 1936. p. 444.

[9] Such contemporary estimations are to be found in PUYSÉGUR: *Art de la guerre par principes et par règles.* I—II. Paris 1749. One has to remark that his book based on the experiences of wars in the decades of the turn of the 17—18th century, was written in the 1720s and was published well after his death.

[10] See in greater detail in my article "*Statisztika és hadtudomány a 19. század elején*" (Statistics and military science at the beginning of the 19th century.) (In manuscript.)

realization that there exists a close correlation between the population density and the resources of a given area, whereby an army could count on more food in a densely populated region than in a thinly populated one. Beginning with this assumption, it was possible to calculate on the basis of certain empirical data what amount of food might be found by an army in a given area. The results of these calculations were then verified on the basis of the data of descriptive statistics — an approach was leading to the aforementioned regional division method.

Of the works known to us, the most thorough-going and most practicable is "Über die Militärökonomie im Frieden und Krieg, und ihr Wechselverhältnis zu den Operationen", a book by Kancrin, the Russian army commissary, published in St. Petersburg in 1823. The author shows that an army can operate without magazines set up beforehand only in areas whose population density is over 35 persons per square kilometre.[11]

Granting that prior to the general use of railways and steamships that could carry great masses of grain, most regions of Europe were self-supporting, i.e. grew their bread-grain themselves; granting further that the rotation of crops was employed in the 17th century just as in the early 19th century, we must also conclude, that in the 17th century it took 35 inhabitants per square kilometre to provision an army without magazines. Relying on the data of historiodemographic research, the trends of population density in various European countries showed the following picture in the 17th and 18th centuries:

| | |
|---|---|
| Turkey (1700) | 5 |
| Hungary (1700) | |
| *a)* the former royal Hungary | 16—18 |
| *b)* the former Turkish regions | 5— 6 |
| Russia | 6 |
| Poland | 8 |
| Pomerania (1720) | 9 |
| Prussia (1700) | 15 |
| Spain (1700) | 16 |
| Württemberg (1660) | 24 |
| Hessen (1669) | 25 |
| Saxony (1700) | 31 |
| Silesia (1740) | 31 |
| Austria (1754) | 34 |
| England, Wales (1700) | 34 |
| France (1700) | 39 |
| Rhineland (1768) | 39 |
| Belgium (1700) | 50 |
| Westphalia (1707) | 52 |
| Lombardy (1700) | 55 |

[11] The author expressed population density in square miles. We converted them into Prussian square miles, which resulted in 56.7 sq. km. I.e. 2000/sq.m. = 35/sq. km. Essentially the same facts were used by Clausewitz, who stated that a given area could supply an army three of four times larger than its own population, for a few days. For example an area of 44 square miles could supply an army of 30 000 men, as far as the army was in continuous advance. Op. cit. p. 311.

It appears from these data that in the period under investigation population density was over 35 per square kilometre only in France, in the Rhineland, in Belgium, Westphalia and Lombardy.[12]

## Army Bread Requirements Compared with Stocks of Grain to be Found in Theatres of War

Although we have no reason to casting doubt upon the approximate correctness of the data in Kancrin's book, there are certain circumstances that induce us to take closer look at the support capacity of theatres of war, and to compare it with army requirements. On the one hand, we do know that wars were never waged without magazines even in regions with a population density over 35/sq.kilometre; on the other hand, a true realization of the tremendous difficulties of army provisioning — to be described later on — is only possible with the knowledge of certain numerical data.

Let us start with the bread requirements of the armies.[13] The daily bread ration per man was about 1 kg in all European armies. Let us consider the war time-strength of an operating army — the "camp" mentioned previously — to be 60 000 men. Hence the daily bread requirements of the army proper were 60 000 rations, but the wagon drivers, craftsmen, workers, etc. also had to be victualled, and those of higher rank were given bigger rations. The mass of people to be fed was therefore much larger than the combatant force proper. The difference usually amounted to half the effective force, which means that in our case the army consumed not 60 000, but 90 000 bread rations per day.[14]

Given a baking ratio of 3 : 4, 0.75 kg of flour were required for producing 1 kg of bread, and this flour was obtained from the same amount of grain at an extraction rate of 100 per cent. Calculating on this basis, the army's bread and flour (grain) requirement for one day, one month, and six months — the duration of the campaign — are shown in round figures as follows:

[12] Principal sources: RANDA: *Handbuch der Weltgeschichte.* Freiburg 1956. — J. CONRAD: *Die Geschichte und Theorie der Statistik. Die Bevölkerungsstatistik.* 4.ed. Jena 1918. — M. REINHARDT: *Histoire de la population mondiale de 1700 à 1948.* Paris n.d. — E. LEVASSEUR: op. cit. — M. MÓRICZ: *Kétszáz év Magyarország népesedése történetéből* (Two centuries of the history of the demography of Hungary) (Manuscript) Budapest 1954. — HÄPKE: *Die Bevölkerung des Mittelalters und der neueren Zeit bis Ende des 18. Jahrhunderts in Europa.* (Handwörterbuch der Staatswissenschaften, Bd. II. Jena 1924.) — V. GOEHLERT: *Die Ergebnisse der in Österreich in vorigen Jahrhundert ausgeführten Volkszählungen.* Wien 1954.

[13] As for the following facts see: my *Mezőgazdasági termelés, népesség, hadseregélelmezés és stratégia a 17. század második felében. (1650—1715).* (Agrarian production, population, army supply and strategy in the second half of the 17th century.) Budapest 1963.

[14] Puységur calculates for 120 000 soldiers 180 000 rations of bread. Op. cit. II. p. 62. Dupré d'Aulnay, calculating merely the surplus rations of the general staff, felt necessary a daily ration of bread, one third greater than the effective strength of the army. — DUPRÉ D'AULNAY: *Traité générale des subsistances militaires.* Paris 1744. p. 116.

| | Bread, q | Grain or flour, q |
|---|---|---|
| 1 day | 900 | 675 |
| 1 month | 27 000 | 20 250 |
| 6 months | 160 000 | 121 500 |

How did the bread requirement of the army compare with the stocks of the theatre of war? Considering that the annual per capita bread-grain requirement amounted to 3.5 q at that time,[15] and given a theatre of war of 10 000 square kilometres with different population densities, the stocks of grain immediately after the harvest and six months later were as follows:[16]

| | 5 | 10 | 20 | 30 | 40 | 50 |
|---|---|---|---|---|---|---|
| | population density per sq. km | | | | | |
| Number of inhabitants (1000) in 10 000 sq. km area | 50 | 100 | 200 | 300 | 400 | 500 |
| Quantity of harvested grain in million q | 0.175 | 0.35 | 0.70 | 1.05 | 1.4 | 1.75 |
| Grain quantity six months after harvest, in million q | 0.09 | 0.18 | 0.35 | 0.52 | 0.70 | 0.90 |

Comparing these figures with the data of the previous table it appears that the 121 500 q grain meeting the army's half-yearly requirement could be obtained from the theatre of war immediately after the harvest even in case of the lowest population density; and that six months after, it was only at density 5 that the stocks of grain prove insufficient.

Yet historical data show that the inevitable devastation of war, arson carried out for strategical purposes, pillaging soldiers and corrupt officers who ruined the population, very soon exhausted the theatres of war, as a result of which the latter were no longer able to support the armies. All this was aggravated by certain technical problems which may now be discussed.

[15] The average yearly consumption of 3.5 q grain was calculated by way of some physiological and alimentation-historical considerations in my book cited above. On a discussion upon my book in the Institute of Historical Science of the Hungarian Academy of Sciences the opinions were divided, some accepted this number, others rejected it. A resumé of this discussion see: in Agrártörténelmi Szemle 1964. No 3—4.

[16] It is not necessary to estimate the quantity of cereals being at the disposal of the army in the second half of the year, i.e. from autumn to spring, for the campaigns took place in the summer half of the year as a rule.

## The Technical Problems of Baking, Milling and Transportation

*Theatres of war in a "wider" and "stricter" sense.* So far we have calculated with the stocks of a 10 000 square-kilometre theatre of war. It is obvious, however, that an operating (marching, fighting, or resting) army could not directly draw on all reserves of a theatre of war, but was reduced to those of immediate access. An operating army was not supposed to expand without restriction over the entire territory of a theatre of war; on the contrary, it had to be kept in rather right formation for the sake of security and to preserve its striking-power.

Suppose that an area to be utilized directly by an army represents a sphere with a 10—15 km radius, comprising 300 to 700 square kilometres. Let us take an average of 500 square kilometres. This only amounts to 5 per cent of a 10 000 square-kilometre theatre of war, which means that the army is able to avail itself directly of not more than one twentieth of the stocks calculated in the foregoing. Let us call this area of 500 square kilometres the theatre of war in the stricter sense.

*Baking.* The stocks of grain in such a theatre of war would have been more than sufficient for an army.

Counting a population density of twenty, the stocks of bread-grain to be found in the area may have been 35 000 q immediately after the harvest, while the daily requirement of the army only amounted to 675 q. But grain is not yet bread, and stocks of grain proper were of no use to an army. The grain reserves of any region could serve an army only in the form of bread. Yet to obtain immediately 900 q of bread in a theatre of war of this size was out of the question.

In such circumstances an army could not rely on being supplied with bread by the population, and had to take its own steps for baking. But baking for an army that consumed 900 q of bread per day was no easy task, as will be shown by the following data.

It appears from a description by Montecuccoli that it was possible to bake two bags of flour (about 1.5 q) by utilizing an oven of 1.8 by 1.2 by 0.3 m size. Counting six hours for the first, and four hours for each successive baking, 10 bags of flour could be baked on five successive occasions per day; counting 1.5 pounds of bread per capita, this sufficed for 1333 men.[17]

There were usually three-day baking runs, and bread rations for four days were baked in one run. This scheme was partly determined by the economical use of the ovens, partly by the circumstance that to carry away bread, and, especially, to issue it for the troops, was no easy task. Consequently the number of days on which bread was issued had to be reduced as much as

[17] *Ausgewählte Schriften* I. p. 205.

possible. On the other hand, to give more than four days' ration at once was not feasible because this would have been too great a load for the men. In the case of our army, four days' bread supply amounted to 360 000 rations. Given three-day baking runs, 120 000 rations had to be baked on one day. Counting 2000 rations per oven — Montecuccoli counted with 1333, the French with 2000 to 2500 rations per oven — at least 60 ovens were required, and they had to be operated by a total of 240 bakers. It took about 500 bricks, or an equivalent quantity of stone, to build an oven, and thus the total requirement was 30 000 bricks. Calculating 2 kg weight per brick, and 500 bricks per cart, 60 carts were needed for the transportation of the building material. And it took at least 15 days to build such a bakery and the necessary magazines.[18]

The amount of firewood used for baking was not small either, and procuring it was very trouble some.[19] Half a Viennese cord (1.4 cubic metres) of wood was reckoned for 10 Viennese quintals (5.6 q) of flour. Since 800 bread rations were baked from 10 quintals of flour, it took 225 cords, i.e. 315 cubic metres of wood to bake the 360 000 rations of a three-day baking run. Taking the weight of one cubic metre of wood as 6 q, and figuring 10 q per cart, the firewood requirement of one baking run was 189 carts; 7.5 baking runs per month required 1400 carts, which meant 17 000 carts of firewood in a year. Today this quantity of wood would amount to 1500—1700 wagonloads. According to all indications, it must not have been easy to obtain such quantities. During the Turkish wars wood was supplied for the Imperial armies from Austria. During Rákóczi's War of Independence the shortage of firewood, especially in the Hungarian Plain, created great difficulties for the Imperial armies, but also for the Kuruts.[20]

*Milling.* The milling of grain involved even greater difficulties. At that time the capacity of the mills, operated by water, wind, animals or men, was very limited. While in our days a smaller mill satisfying the requirements of one village is able to grind 100 to 150 q in 24 hours, one capable of grinding 25 to 30 q per day was regarded a big mill at that time; and the capacity of most mills was not above daily 5 q.[21]

[18] *Encyclopédie Méthodique.* Paris 1784. Art Militaire, entry: "Subsistances". Though these facts were from the second half of the 18th century, they must not have differed fundamentally in the period under consideration.

[19] *Feldzüge* I. p. 687. — According to French calculation to bake 100 bags of flour 5 cords of firewood were needed. 1 bag of flour = 96 kg, 1 cord = 3.9 cu. m. Compared with the data of Vienna, about 1.1 cu. m. of firewood was needed for baking 5.6 q of flour. — Dupré d'Aulnay, op. cit. p. 145.

[20] S. Takáts: *A dunai hajózás a XIV. és a XVII. században.* (The Danubian navigation in the 14th and 17th century) Magyar Gazdaságtörténeti Szemle 1900. pp. 168., 217. — *Feldzüge* II. suppl. H. p. 66. — *Archivum Rákóczianum* I. p. 464. III. p. 236.

[21] K. Lambrecht: *A magyar malmok könyve.* (The book of Hungarian mills) Budapest n.d. — I. Pekár: *Földünk búzája és lisztje* (Wheat and flour of our Earth) Budapest 1886. —

At a 5 q milling rate per day, the 675 q grain requirement of the army should have been satisfied by 135 mills. But was such a number of mills to be found by an army in a theatre of war? Given a daily milling capacity of 5 q and 200 working days in a year,[22] the annual production of one mill was 1000 q. This means that in the 10 000 square kilometres of the theatre of war in the wider sense, an even 175 mills were needed for grinding the yearly grain requirement of the population with a density of five; for a population density of ten, the number of mills was 350, and 1050 mills were needed with a population density of thirty. Thus it appears that with a population density of five as many as three-fourths, and with a population density of ten, about two-fifths of the mills in the area of operations ought to have been used for grinding one daily grain requirement of the army. This, however, was out of the question in any event, because the army only could have used the mills to be found in the 500 square kilometres of the smaller area of war; and, assuming even a population density of fifty, the maximum number of mills to be reckoned with in this area was 90.

It was precisely the small number and limited capacity of the mills that rendered them important strategically; and this was manifest in the fact that they became the principal targets of incendiary operations.

Because the army could rely on the mills of the theatre of war only to so slight an extent, it used querns for grinding the grain issued from the magazines or found on the spot. There were very many types of querns.[23] Some were only suitable for coarse grinding. With others it was possible to produce finer flour, but only for higher-ranking officers, to be sure. The querns were carried on carts, and their weight varied from 50 to 250 kg. Their capacity was relatively high. It was possible to grind with them as much as 2.5 to 5 q grain in a day. Their great disadvantage was that grinding was very difficult and that they wore out very soon.[24] And it seems that the quality of grinding was not too perfect either, because Rákóczi wrote that in 1705 an epidemic due to flour ground in querns broke out in Herbeville's army.[25]

O. Zsemley: *A magyar sütő-, cukrász és mézeskalács-ipar története* (The history of Hungarian baking confectionary and honey cake making ) Budapest 1940. — J. Frecskay: *Mesterségek szótára* (A dictionary of artisanships) Budapest 1912. — Burchard—Bélaváry: *Malomipar* (Milling industry) (Magyarország közgazdasági és közművelési állapotai. VIII.) Budapest 1898. — G. Luther: *Die technische und wirtschaftliche Entwicklung des deutschen Mühlengewerbes.* Leipzig 1909. — Krünitz: *Ökonomisch-technologische Encyclopaedie.* Berlin, entries "Brod", "Mühle" and "Mehl". — *Encyclopédie ou dictionnaire raisonné des sciences, des arts et des métiers.* Publ. par Diderot et d'Alambert. 3rd ed. Livorno 1773. Entries "Farine" and "Froment". — *Révai Lexikon*, entry "Malom" (Mill). *Annuaire International Statistique Agricole.* Rome 1917.

[22] I.e. the mills did not work all the year owing to drought, frost and calm.

[23] *Dictionnaire militaire.* Par M. E. Nuovelle éd. Dresden 1751. — Krünitz, op. cit. entry "Mühle". — *Zrínyi Miklós hadtudományi munkái* p. 460.

[24] *Feldzüge* VII. p. 452. — VIII.p. 447.

[25] *II. Rákóczi Ferenc emlékiratai* (Memoirs of —) Budapest 1951. p. 131.

To sum up, the flour supply of an army was satisfactory only if the grain needed for the period of the campaign was milled beforehand and stored in magazines; or if mills were erected in the magazines proper, or in their immediate vicinity; or if the magazines were located in places where high-capacity mills were available. We know for instance that, owing to the shortage of mills in Hungary, the Imperial high command had to set up water-mills along the Danube and the Vág between 1670 and 1680.[26]

*Transportation.* An average load of 10 q could be calculated for each cart at the time in question.[27]

Since we have seen that the army could not rely on the reserves to be found on the spot, and was therefore in need of magazines (which restricted its movements considerably), it might be asked why the army did not carry with it larger stocks of provision, sufficient, say, for one month. Why did Zrínyi write: "And there is no way for one man to carry with him food for one or two months in camp."[28] Let us calculate how many carts and draught animals would have been needed by our army to carry stocks of provision for one month.

Suppose that our army carries one half of its monthly bread requirement as flour, one quarter as bread, and one quarter as biscuit. The bread requirement for 15 days is 13 500 q, and it takes 10 000 q of flour to bake it. Consequently 1000 carts are needed for transportation. Bread rations for seven days amount to 6300 q, and if we calculate only 5 q per cart — because in the case of bread, loading space cannot be utilized economically — this requires 1260 carts. Counting 500 q of biscuit for one day, the ration for eight days is 4000 q which can be carried by 400 carts. Thus the transportation of bread for one month would have required 2660 carts.

Fodder was obtained almost exclusively on the spot. But the usual practice was to have certain reserves in order to allow for unexpected difficulties. This was corn fodder, because rough fodder was not practicable owing to its large bulk. Counting 2 kg of oats per day, the monthly requirement amounted to 24 000 q, whose transportation required 2400 carts. Add 2 to 4000 carts for carrying rough fodder gathered every four days. Let us take 3000, which means that, reckoning with rations for 90 000 men and 40 000 animals, 8000 carts would have been needed for carrying the army provisions of one month. But the daily rations for 90 000 men and 40 000 horses would have sufficed only for the fighting strength of the army, and for the men and draught animals of the train that carried one or two days' food for the army, ammunition, technical and artillery equipment. It was by no means sufficient

[26] Takáts, op. cit. p. 246.
[27] After Puységur, Montecuccoli, Zrínyi and other sources.
[28] Zrinyi, op. cit. p. 119.

for meeting the requirements of the men and draught animals of a train that had risen to 8000 carts. Thus we also have to compute this new requirement. Making a careful calculation, we see that the increase is 5000 carts when compared to the original number; and we must likewise account for 10 000 drivers and helpers, as well as 30 000 draught animals. To carry 30 days' bread requirement for 10 000 men, an even 300 carts, to carry fodder for 30 000 animals, another 2200 carts, 5000 additional men and 15 000 draught animals would have been needed. And food for these 15 000 animals and 5000 men would to have been carried by an additional 900 carts — and so we could keep calculating endlessly. Summing up what has been said so far, we see that transportation of food for one month would have required 11 000 carts, 22 000 drivers and helpers, as well as 50—70 000 draught animals.

Yet to provide and maintain such an immense vehicle park would have been utterly impractical on financial grounds. In the 1700s the cost price of 11 000 horse-drawn carts amounted to 5—6 million florins in Austria, and to about 17 million livres in France. By comparison, in 1703 Austria's total military budget amounted to only 30 million florins, and the total revenue of the French state in 1700 to 160 million livres.[29]

To keep a train of such magnitude moving would have been impossible as well. Calculating a length of 12 metres for one cart with horses, and a distance of 6 metres between carts, the overall length of a train made up of 11 000 carts would have been 198 kilometres.[30] What the moving of such a monster would have meant with respect to command and marching technique may be seen from the following data: given a marching performance of 25 kilometres per day, the rear of the column would have followed the head at a distance of eight marching-days. The commanding officer could only have been informed of events at the rear — e.g. a raid by the enemy — in no less than two days even with excellent dispatch-riders. Moreover, tactical coverage for most of this column would have been quite impossible. Considering further that this immense mass of draught animals ought to have been provided grass, rough fodder and water in the immediate surroundings of the march route every day, it is obvious that transportation of food for thirty days was out of the question.

### Insufficient Nourishment and Epidemics

In the era under discussion feeding the troops was rather simple, especially on campaign when only bread, biscuit, salt and some kind of beverage were regarded as "absolutely necessary" provisions. Basically, the men's fare

[29] *Feldzüge* I. pp. 266., 665. and V. p. 63. — DUPRÉ D'AULNAY, op. cit. p. 198., p. 204. — H. SÉE: *Histoire économique de la France.* I—II. Paris 1948—1951. I. p. 161.

[30] DE VAULT—PELET: *Mémoires militaires relatifs à la succession d'Espagne sous Louis XIV.* Paris 1835. V. p. 791.

included fresh or salted meat, butter, cheese, bacon, tobacco, dry fish and vegetables, but these rations were seldom issued. Not that the governments did not realize the necessity of giving more substantial and varied food to the soldiers; rather the scarcity of resources, the difficulties involved in the supply services, and the inadequacy of preserving procedures prevented any improvement. Moreover, it appears from available data that, compared to the time of the Thirty Years' War, military victualing deteriorated, which evidently resulted from the fact that agricultural production and transportation techniques were substantially unchanged whereas the requirements of the armies had grown immensely at the same time.[31]

At any rate, tremendous efforts were made to furnish, in addition to bread, at least the daily rations of meat. Even if the nutritive power of the various foodstuffs was not known accurately — caloric and protein value calculations were unknown then — it was known by experience that meat was not only savoury and appealing as food, but maintained the fitness of the men better than did bread alone.[32] For the specific purpose of solving this problem many experiments were undertaken. The efforts of Louvois, who even conducted experiments in processing meat, are especially noteworthy in this respect. But his endeavours were of no avail, and it was not possible to secure a steady meat supply in the French army, which otherwise was the most advanced with respect to contemporary administration.[33]

All this was the natural consequence of the circumstance that livestock was them scarce and of poor quality.

Let us now calculate the nutritive power of a soldier's food in this period. Let us take at an average 1 kg bread and 300 g meat per day. Today the caloric value of 1 kg of wheat-bread is 2350, that of 1 kg rye-bread is 2200. Let us reckon 2300 calories in view of the fact that bread was produced from a mixture of both in most cases. But we know also that the flour of ration bread contained a full quota of shorts, hence 20 to 25 per cent of this bread had no nutritive value at all. In this way the soldier's daily bread ration contained 1700 calories at best. Today one kg of wheat-bread contains 75 g, one kg of rye-bread contains 55 g protein. Reckoning with 65 g, and subtracting the

[31] H. Spigl: *Die Besoldung, Verpflegung und Bekleidung des kaiserlichen Kriegsvolkes im dreißigjährigen Kriege.* (Mitth. d. Kriegsarchivs 1882.) p. 460. — *Die Ernährung und Leistungsfähigkeit der k. k. Truppen im Felde, von der Zeit des dreißigjährigen Krieges bis zur Gegenwart* (Mitth. d. Kriegsarchivs 1885.) p. 288. — Audouin, op. cit. II. p. 248.

[32] The General Chamley wrote in 1703: "On a vu des troupes vivre de la seule viande, sans pain, sans riz, et souffrir peu." De Vault—Pelet, op. cit.

[33] Rousset: *Histoire de Louvois.* 6e éd. Paris 1879. I. pp. 300., 451., II. p. 322. — «M. Feu de Louvois voulut, à l'exemple des Orientaux, faire distribuer aux Troupes de la poudre de viande. Comme dans ces pays chauds, c'est le Soleil qui faite cette poudre, ce qui ne pourroit pas se pratiquer dans ces climats. M. de Louvois avoit fait faire de grands fours de cuivre capables de contenir huit boeufs, ou il en avoit fait faire des essais. Sa mort a interrompu cette entreprise.» *Dictionnaire Militaire*, entry "Viande".

non-nutrient proportion, this is an even 40 g. The caloric value of 300 g of beef is 600, the protein value 60 g. Consequently a soldier's daily food contained 2500 calories and 100—110 g protein at best. Compared to the rations of modern armies it appears that the nutritive power of the soldiers' food of that time was very low, especially as concerns caloricity. Prior to World War I, and between the two wars, 3200 to 3500 calories and 100—120 g protein were calculated for men on garrison duty. While on major manoeuvres and in war-time the amount was raised to 3800 calories and 140—160 g protein. The weekly menu consisted of 15 to 20 different dishes, in the U.S. army even more.[34]

However, the nutritive power we have calculated for the period under survey should be regarded as the optimum, for we know that the problem of meat supply could not always be solved. Thus it happened that the men marched, worked and fought on 1700 calories and 40 g protein for a considerable time. No wonder, then, that the men grew weak, that their physical and psychic resistance broke. This was partly manifested by the fact that they were incapable of a higher level of performance. Characteristically, their average daily marching performance was 20 kilometres, whereas it is 35 to 40 km in our days. Even worse, their afeebled organisms were an easy prey to all kinds of infection, and this gave rise to raging epidemics. It is easy to see that even in the best case, when the men were also given meat, nourishment was completely one-sided and was altogether void of those foodstuffs, rich in vitamins and containing prophylactic substances (milk, eggs, vegetables, fruit, potatoes, cheese), which are so highly important in the diet of modern man. And when they had not meat at all the loss in caloric power as well as the complete absence of animal protein which affords protection against infections and diseases, entailed disastrous consequences.

This was the reason why destructive epidemics befell armies, especially at the end of summer and early in autumn. Military experts and commanders reckoned with these epidemics, and the loss of strength due to diseases and resulting deaths was taken into account in the initial plans of operations.[35] Owing to the privations of the campaign, inferior flour, a deficiency of vitamins and possibly of salt, the resistance of the men was minimal. All this was aggravated by the greatest single peril, one which an enfeebled organism was not

[34] J. Madzsar: *A táplálkozás reformja.* (The reform of alimentation). Századok 1911. p. 3. — L. Nagy: *Élelmezés kézikönyve.* (Manual of alimentation) I—II. Budapest 1930. I. p. 52. — *Le problème de l'alimentation.* I—IV. Genève 1936. III. p. 140.

[35] Montecuccoli thought September to be the less healthy month. A. Schempp: *Der Feldzug 1664 in Ungarn.* Stuttgart 1909. p. 212. — On 31 August 1702, the Marshall Vendôme wrote from Italy: "J'attends avec grande patience que la saison des maladies se passe". Cit. by Saint-Simon: *Mémoires.* Éd. par Boislisle. Paris 1879—1905. VII. p. 493. — The General Vaudemont wrote on 14 June 1703 also from Italy, that he must speed up the campaigns, because "la fin du mois de juillet est la saison dangereuse pour les maladies dans nos armées, ce qui les diminuit". Cit. by De Vault—Pelet, op. cit. III. p. 208.

able to fight off: namely the hungry soldiers, having grown disgusted with monotonous food, greedily fell upon unwashed, unripe fruit and grapes. The result was an epidemic of dysentery and typhoid which decimated the army.[36]

## Foraging

*Fodder requirements in general.* With a ratio of 2 : 1, an army 60 000 strong usually comprised 40 000 infantrymen and 20 000 mounted men.[37] However, in addition to the saddle-horses of the cavalry proper, the army had large numbers of draught-horses for the artillery, for the carts carrying camping tools and equipment, as well as draught-horses and oxen for the supply train. Thus the number of horse rations was higher than that of the riding horses, and, — besides, — higher ranks were given larger horse-rations, just as in the case of bread. Generally speaking, twice as many horse-rations were needed as the number of the cavalry horses proper, and hence the number of horse-rations for an army with 20 000 mounted men may be put at 40 000.[38]

Fodder was provided in an extremely complex manner. Supply through transporting the tremendous amounts of fodder was not possible, and requisitioning on the spot was made difficult by the limited fodder reserves of agriculture at that time. Even to make up the food and the rations for the horses was a complicated affair. While in modern times the horses are fed in much the same manner both in winter and summer, the daily portions were entirely determined by the season in the past.

Different sorts of fodder were given in different mixtures and quantities according to the season. First of all the fodder rations given during a campaign and in winter-quarters were different. It followed as a matter of course that in winter the horses were only given dry fodder, while on campaign green forage served as the basis of supply for the most part. But the principal difference lay in the fact that during a campaign rough fodder was never transported behind the army, and that solid feed was carried only exceptionally;

[36] In 1664, the experts expected the end of the epidemics in the imperial army, only when grapes out, after which the soldiers would be fed merely by the supply. A. Schempp, op. cit. p. 216. — In 1597 Geizkoffer also referred to the maladies caused by the consumption of fruits. Cit by A. Heischmann: *Die Anfänge des stehenden Heeres in Österreich.* Wien 1926. p. 103. — Rákóczi wrote of the campaign of Rabutin in 1706: "All this happened in the month of October, and I let the enemy vintage in the vineyards of Tokaj, as the young wine, the sweet grapes, the cold nights and the river Tisza were fighting the enemy more successfully than my forays did." *Emlékiratok,* p. 156.

[37] Zrínyi calculated a ration of 2 : 1 "in spacious terrain" and of 3 : 1 "in hilly, down, watered and gully terrain". Op. cit. p. 109.

[38] Zrínyi calculated 13 600 horses to an army consisting of 18 000 infantry and 6 000 cavalry. Op. cit. p. 117. Puységur calculated 80 000 horses for 120 000 fighters. Op. cit. II. p. 64.

thus fodder supply was substantially based on requisitions made on the spot. Furthermore, as contrasted to modern practice in which feed is considered indispensable, at that time it was regarded as quite natural that horses should live on rough fodder alone. It was a rule for every army to issue oats from the central magazines only in the first and in the last month of the campaign, at a time when there was not yet any hay, or when it was no longer available.[39]

*The foraging periods.* Broadly speaking, four foraging periods could be distinguished. The first period were the three winter months, which will not be discussed here. The second was the time of "pasturing" in the spring months. The third were the 6—8 weeks prior to the harvest when the standing, unripe crop was given as fresh fodder. The fourth period lasted from harvest to the end of the campaign time, during which the animals were given dry fodder first of all, and fresh fodder to a limited extent only.

Although the pasturing period usually preceded the campaign, we must speak of it in some detail. Taking the horses to spring pastures was justified mainly by considerations of health. It was a thousand-year-old experience that grazing on the first grass "purified" and refreshed the animals. What was involved here was not known to the people of the past: it is the extremely important biological effect of vitamin-rich spring grass which restores the vitality of the animals that had been kept on meagre winter-food of usually very poor quality. This is expressed by Bálint Balassi, the great Hungarian poet of the 16th century, in his salute of unequalled beauty to Pentecost: "Those brave swift horses only rejoice in thee, For thou givest them strengthened limbs after fatigue, Tallowing them with fine dewy grass, Building with new strength their sinews for chasing." This purifying, refreshing effect of grassing was known to the Turks, to the Imperials, the French and the Kuruts alike.[40]

[39] As for the Austrian army see: H. MEYNERT: *Geschichte der k. k. österreichischen Armee.* I—IV. Wien 1852—1854. III. p. 166. — *Feldzüge* I. p. 279. — As for the French army see: PUYSÉGUR, op. cit. II. p. 63. — DE VAULT—PELET, op. cit. II. p. 757. and V. p. 553. — In the Rákóczi insurrection the reglements of the Hungarian army stated very explicitly that in the time of campaign there was no central supply of oats: "In the months of Summer neither the commons, nor the Estate of the Officials shall by any means claim fodder for their horses . . .". *Regulamentum universale* II. p. 5. — The budget for 1708 calculated oats only for the six winter month. *Archivum Rákóczianum* V. p. 618.

[40] With the Turks horses were "purifies" on the meadows for two weeks in May before the beginning of the campaign. MONTECUCCOLI: *Della Guerra.* Lib. III./XLVI — According to Feuquières it is necessary to graze the horses on spring herbage, in order to "faire perdre la mauvaise nourriture qu'ils peuvent avoire prise pendant l'hiver, et les refraichire . . ." FEUQUIÈRES: *Mémoires sur la guerre.* Amsterdam 1734. — According to the Hungarian Tessedik in springtime cattle ought to be fed with clower, "damit es sich von dem im Winter gesammelten Unreinigkeiten, Seuchen-Material auspurgiere." L. HANZO: *Tessedik néhány kiadatlan gazdasági írása* (Some Unpublished Economic Writings of Tessedik). Agrártörténeti Szemle 1961. No 2. p. 252. — In April 1710 Rákóczi wrote: Nothing can be done "before grass" because "the army horses are depressed and look down on the ground". *Archivum Rákóczianum* I. p. 229.

But "grassing" was also needed because on roads that had become soft and muddy in late winter and early spring it was not possible to carry supplies to armies lying in winter-quarters or "postierungen". The fodder reserves of the population hardly sufficed for feeding their own animals. Thus it was only the pástures that could support the horses.[41] Grassing was considered absolutely indispensable, and campaings were not launched as a rule until the horses had been on the pasture for some weeks. Thus the commencement of campaigns was determined by the growth of grass.[42] The Kuruts also attached extraordinary importance to "grassing camps". Turning to any year's correspondence during Rákóczi's War of Independence, we are confronted at every turn with the problems of grassing in springtime.

The third foraging period was during the first half of the campaign. To obtain grain fodder in the theatre of war at this time was out of the question, and to carry the immense mass of fodder behind the army was impossible. Although the yield of the pastures and meadows in the area of operations might have met requirements, grazing or mowing in such a large area was unfeasible for technical reasons. Consequently the armies simply had the standing crop of the area grazed or mowed.[43] This manner of foraging was the most devastating one for the region concerned. Namely on account of the high water content usually twice as much was needed of green fodder, i.e. standing crops, as of dry feed.

During the fourth foraging period, which lasted from harvest till the end of the campaign period, the animals consumed the region's harvested crop in the form of corn (rye, wheat) and straw as dry fodder; green fodder was given to them only in negligible quantities.

*Fodder rations.* 25 kg of green forage were calculated for one horse per day; this quantity could be grown in an area of one *toise-carrée* put under corn. 1 *toise-carrée* is the equivalent of about 76 square metres, i.e. 0.76 ares. One are therefore sufficed for keeping 1.3 horses, one hectare for keeping 130, and one cadastral acre for keeping 74. I.e. 300 hectares were needed for keeping 40 000 animals. But the troops did not much care about sparing the peasants' crops;

[41] By spring fodder reserves became so exhausted that sometimes thatched roofs were also fed up by the horses. *Archivum Rákóczianum* XII. p. 361. — DEVAULT—PELET, op. cit. III. p. 927. — L. HANZÓ, op. cit. p. 262.

[42] ROUSSET, op. cit. I. p. 144. — *Feldzüge* IV. Suppl. H. p. 118. — DE VAULT—PELET, op. cit. II. p. 313. — Before wars exhausted France, one of the reasons of her military supremacy was the fact that she might start the campaign earlier than her enemies, for she could feed her horses with oats from her magazines, whereas her enemies had to wait for the sprouting out of the grass and the green crops. Therefore the French supply-system was admired all over Europe. — ROUSSET, op. cit. II. p. 309. — In the spring of 1676 grass was sprouting very early, so the enemies of France might go warring at the same time as her. Indignantly referred to this Louis XIV: "Il seroit fâcheux, que ceux qui n'ont pas de magazine, pussent se mettre en campagne peu de temps après moi." Ibid. pp. 214—215.

[43] DE VAULT—PELET, op. cit. IV. p. 405. — MÁRKI: *II. Rákóczi Ferenc.* Budapest 1907—1910. II. p. 268.

they trampled them down, destroyed them for the most part, and Puységur therefore only reckoned with half of the available supplies. Consequently one hectare was sufficient not for 130, but only for 70 horses, and for keeping all the horses of the army, not 300, but 600 hectares were required.[44] About 300 men were needed for mowing the crop of 600 hectares.[45] And the daily fresh forage rations for 40 000 horses made up 1000 cartloads.

During the four months from harvest to the end of the campaign period, the horses were mostly given dry fodder. One horse ration of dry fodder may have consisted of the following: 7—8 kg hay and 2—3 kg straw; or 2—3 kg oats, 4—5 kg hay and 2—3 kg straw; or 9—10 kg hay only.[46] Let us calculate with 2 kg oats, 5 kg hay, and 3 kg straw for a day. In this case the dry fodder requirement of the army's 40 000 horses is as follows:

| | Oats q | Hay q | Straw q |
|---|---|---|---|
| 1 day | 800 | 2 000 | 1 200 |
| 1 month | 24 000 | 60 000 | 36 000 |
| 4 months | 96 000 | 240 000 | 144 000 |

## Technical and Tactical Problems of Foraging[47]

The term "foraging" had a stricter and a broader sense. In the stricter sense it was understood as action taken for obtaining food for the horses, in the broader sense it included also food for the men.[48]

One of the most difficult tasks to be shouldered by an army was foraging. This is easy to understand if we only consider the technical difficulties. As we have seen, the daily fodder requirement of our army amounted to 10 000 q at the time of fresh feed, and to 4—6000 q at the time of solid feed. To carry this amount of fodder, 400 to 1000 carts were needed, and, depending on the time available, 4000 to 10 000 men were required for mowing standing crops.

[44] PUYSÉGUR, op. cit. II. p. 64.

[45] Chevennières thought necessary for reaping a "fauche prée" (559 square fathoms = 21 ares) a man in the first half of the 18th century. This meant 5 men for one hectare and 3 men for one cadastral acre. CHEVENNIÈRES: *Détails militaires.* I—II. Paris 1750. I. p. 76.

[46] MONTECUCCOLI: *Ausgewählte Schriften.* II. p. 248. — PUYSÉGUR, op. cit. II. p. 63. — *Regulamentum universale* IV. p. 2. — J. S. GRUBERN: *Die heutige neue vollkommene Kriegs-disziplin.* Leipzig 1702. p. 139.

[47] All contemporary military books dealt with the problem of forage. Our work is based primarily on the boks of Montecuccoli and Puységur, as well as the corresponding entries of the *Dictionnaire Militaire.*

[48] MONTECUCCOLI: *Della Guerra.* Lib. I./XLII. — CHARLES ARCHDUKE: *Beiträge zum praktischen Unterrichte im Felde.* Wien 1893. p. 190.

All this was very hard to manage, even if foraging was carried out under undisturbed circumstances, far from the enemy. Yet this was feasible in exceptional cases only. Fodder had to be procured at the very place where the army was momentarily located, i.e. in the immediate vicinity of the enemy in most cases. And the enemy, of course, made every effort to prevent foraging, or at least to make it difficult, thus grave tactical difficulties were involved in addition to the technical ones. When selecting an area that could serve for foraging, tactical circumstances had to be taken into account as well as crop and pasture conditions. In this way the organization of foraging required much technical knowledge (estimation of the fodder reserves of the area in question, organization of mowing, gathering and transport, etc.), and clear military judgment, and thorough tactical organization. It is for this reason that contemporary books on military subjects emphasize the importance of expert knowledge in the matters of foraging. An essential element in the qualification of a commander of that time was his expertise in foraging.

The period of time at which foraging became necessary was a decisive factor. As we have seen, a double amount of fodder was needed at the time of fresh feed, and this presented considerable difficulties with respect to mowing and transport them. Fresh feed nevertheless afforded greater safety with regard to supply, because dry fodder was easier for the enemy to set on fire or carry away.

The first thing to do when organizing forage was to reconnoitre the area in question. Reconnaissance included estimation of stocks and examination of tactical aspects. The boundaries of the area to be used for foraging were marked out on the basis of estimating the supply expected to be encountered. Estimation of the likely quantities of fodder was made by staff officers, quartermasters and commissaries on the basis of the norms presented in the foregoing. In the fresh feed season, trial mowings were made over some square metres, and the extent of the area to be used was determined by converting these results. In the dry fodder season, estimates were made of the harvested grain, straw and hay stored in barn-yards, sheds, or pits.

Marking out the area to be used for foraging was followed by tactical reconnaissance. Keeping in mind the strength, distance and enterprising spirit of the enemy, the line of covering units, the posting of the advanced guards and of the reserves were marked in accordance with the terrain. Great attention was given to places where the terrain could be used by the enemy for ambushing or for raids on foraging troops and transports.

Foraging practically never took place without fighting. Work connected with mowing, gathering and transportation, temporary decentralization of the army's force, were instances of weakness, and the opposing parties took mutual advantage of this circumstance. In some cases such engagements did not go beyond the scope of simple skirmishes *(escarmouches, Scharmützel)*.

but sometimes they grew into regular actions, even into battles that engaged the entire military forces of the opposing parties. The number of troops deployed for covering the foragers was determined by the general tactical situation; in some cases the strength of the covering troops hardly amounted more than to a few battalions and cavalry companies, sometimes as many as two-thirds of the army had to cover them. Actually, however, foraging work affected the army as a whole because even the men left in the camp had to be in constantly prepare to help the deployed covering units if necessary.

Whether foraging was transposing in front of the army, at its flank or to its rear, also meant a great deal. The general principle was to use first of all the supplies of more distant areas, and of areas in advance of the army, and to hold in reserve for more critical times the supplies in areas behind the army. This was so because foraging involved the greatest difficulties when carried on in front of the army as these areas were nearest to the enemy. Foraging on the flanks was less dangerous, but to deploy the bulk of the army here in case of emergency was much more difficult, because from its original posting it was able to engage in combat only after complex flanking, swerving and changes of formation.

To maintain the order and discipline of foraging presented a special problem. The men sent out for requisitioning were inclined to rapine, looting, wasting supplies, to crossing the marked-out boundaries, and foraging usually offered good opportunities for desertion. It was for this reason that the duty of the troops deployed for covering consisted not only in holding off the enemy, but also in keeping a check on their own men. A gaoler and a few hangmen were detailed to every foraging party, and they were authorized to execute the violators of regulations on the spot.

The general rule was to gather supplies for four to five days in each occasion. To collect more was not practicable, partly because fresh feed kept longer than that would perish, partly because the storage, and particularly the transportation of a greater supply would have encountered insurmountable difficulties. It appears from all this that, just as in the case of baking runs, foraging too imposed a certain periodicity on army life; and to depart from these rules was not possible — even if strategical circumstances called for entirely different steps — without running the risk of losing all the army's horses.

## Provisioning from Magazines

*Magazine-provisioning and military historiography.* As we have seen from the foregoing, in the period under survey and with the given agricultural and demographic conditions, the armies could not rely upon the supplies in the theatres of war; nor could they afford to carry with them great quantities of food supplies. So they had no choice but to amass food required for the campaigns in magazines, and to feed the armies from them. All this is an altogether natural consequence, deriving from the logic of things. The reason why we nevertheless wish to devote some space to proving the necessity of provisioning from magazines is that quite a number of military historians refuse to admit such necessity. If this were simply a material error, we certainly should not deal with this subject, for we believe that what we have said so far disproves this contention sufficiently. But much more than that is involved here: it is the fundamental methodological question of military historiography, and it is exactly for this reason that we want elucidate this problem from the viewpoint of principle.

What one has to ask first is: how did it happen that a considerable number of researchers in military history did not, or did not want to realize the necessity of provisioning from magazines, this extremely striking fact that emerges from the sources at every turn? In an attempt to answer this question, we must go back to the decades of the French Revolution and the Napoleonic wars. The tremendous military successes of the young French republic, then of the Empire, filled contemporaries with profound admiration; and, as usual, some explained them in this way, some in another. Of the many explanations the one held most widely, and also the most important in relation to our problem, was that the French revolutionary army, and Napoleon who elevated its practice to still higher standards, broke with provisioning from magazines that had impeded army movements so badly, and replaced it by procurement on the spot. This was presented as an innovation of which only the republican army, fired by revolutionary enthusiasm and overthrowing radically the former methods of warfare and military science, and then Napoleon's genius were capable. Yet this belief has two fundamental flaws. On the one hand, it altogether neglects the agricultural and demographic changes that took place in contrast to the *ancien régime*, changes which facilitated acquiring supplies on the spot, in certain regions of Europa at least. And in the first period of the French Revolution, wars were waged in Europe's most densely populated and agriculturally most advanced regions, and that with armies whose effective strength was not much greater than that of the armies operating during the ancien régime. On the other hand, the advocates of this view forget that when under Napoleon the strength of the armies rose to several hundreds of thousands, magazines were just as indispensable as before. And when these armies left Central Europe's civilized and densely populated regions, and found themselves amid practically 17—18-century conditions, not even magazines were of help any longer. Only think of the campaigns in Spain, Poland, and — above all — Russia. Considering all this, we cannot share the opinion of those who have drawn a sharp dividing line between the supply systems of "old" and "new" warfare. And in theory, we regard it altogether wrong that the advocates of this view, failing to realize that the necessity of magazine provisioning arose from existing economic and social conditions, considered it a mistake that could have been avoided with prudence, boldness and a more refined comprehension of military science. It was from this error that the contempt and depreciation of 17—18-century warfare followed, and that practically all military specialists shared this view in the first half of the 19th century.

We read in the *Militärokönomie* — which has been quoted above and may be regarded as excellent in many a respect — that the reason of 17—18-century magazine provisioning was the over-caution of the strategists, the narrow-minded war-aims, and the "school-bookish" rules of warfare.[49] The writers of the *Militär-Conversations Lexicon*, published in 1841, only spoke of magazine provisioning in the tone of profound disapproval because it was expensive, was tying the hands of the strategists, and "paralyzed the energies of war".[50] In his work *Theorie des grossen Krieges*, published in 1840, Willisen, one of the outstanding figures of 19-century German military literature, wrote that Frederick the Great had put on himself the shackles of magazine provisioning without any compelling reason, and that he was fortunate only in that his enemies got entangeld in this system even more deeply; "But he could have got rid of these shackles at any moment, for the region could have supported his small armies much better than the big ones later on" — so Willisen concluded his train of thought from which it is quite clear that time had stopped for him, and that he saw no difference whatsoever between an 18-century Europe and the one hundred years after.[51]

Yet this opinion owed its survival and firm integration into the military science of a later period not because of these writers. To be able to survive, it had to have the stamp of a much greater name. The person in mind is Clausewitz, whose thought had a tremendous influence on military science. And the prestige of Clausewitz, the philosophical profoundity and methodical nature of his work, his treatment of the problems of war on so high a theoretical level as to be unknown before his time, not only ensured eternal life to his "truths", but also enveloped his errors with a protective casing whose rupture would not only be difficult, but a thankless task at the same time. And few of his errors have left so deep an impression as his particular opinion conceiving the differences between "old" and "new" warfare, including the question of provisioning. He rejected magazine provisioning, the "artificial clockwork" of an obsolete supply service, altogether. In his opinion this was applicable only to wars in which the internal expansive force, a far-reaching political aim was absent, and which did not even approximate the "absolute concept" of

[49] Ibid. p. 62.
[50] Ibid. p. 391.
[51] Cit. by CAEMERER: *Die Entwicklung der strategischen Wissenschaft im 19. Jahrhundert.* Berlin 1904. p. 105.

war taken in the philosophical sense. To examine how Clausewitz, who in many respects grasped the social and political roots of war so unerringly, commuted such an error would lead us too far; here we must be content with concluding that the reading of some of his statements conveys the impression that it had not even occurred to him that the old system of provisioning necessarily resulted from demographic and agricultural conditions, and that the choice of one or another system was not principally a matter of discretion and recognition. This is best characterized by his remark on the poor provisioning of 18-century armies: Frederick the Great has accomplished great things with his underfed soldiers, but this cannot serve as a yardstick "for we do not know how much greater a performance they would have been capable of had he provided for them in the manner of Napoleon (i.e. requisitioning on the spot, G. P.)".[52]

This opinion survived especially in German and Austrian literature on military science. At every moment we are confronted with statements like this: Montecuccoli, Turenne and Condé missed many a great opportunity because they attached too much importance to magazines "although magazines would have been dispensable in many cases because a relatively small army could have subsisted from the resources to be found on the spot", wrote the authors who were obviously not too well-versed in economic history.[53] According to the writer of the *Feldzüge*, the commanders of that age endeavoured to secure provisions from magazines, and increasingly abandoned the practice of war supporting war; since in any event wars had lost the character of seeking for a decision, whereas the importance of magazine provisioning had grown, the "art of manoeuvring" aimed at the protection of supply lines emerged.[54] Jähns, one of the finest representatives of German military historiography, distinguishes between the old and the new system of requisitioning; he sees the specific feature of the former in the prior collection of food in magazines, while in the new system requisitioned food was accessible to the troops at once. He condemned Bülow, an interesting figure of military science in the late 18th century, for still regarding magazines as the requisite of provisioning, whereas it was precisely at his time (i.e. in the first years of the French revolution) that magazines could no longer serve as the basis of supply.[55] The German chiefs of staff published their work on the history of provisioning in 1913. The authors of this book condemned the "cumbersome" and "overmethodical" management of war and system of provisioning of the second half of the 17th century: "Requisitioning the resources of the theatres of war was practically unknown because the troops were fed from magazines. From this it followed that the movements of armies were determined by the place and

[52] Clausewitz, op. cit. p. 310.
[53] Obauer—Gutenberg: *Das Train-Communications- und Verpflegswesen.* Wien 1871. pp. 380—381.
[54] *Feldzüge*, I. p. 586.
[55] Jähns, op. cit. III. p. 2144.

the number of magazines. Consequently the problems involved in the transportation of food restricted military operations to a much greater degree, even in rich regions, than would have been justified and practical otherwise."[56]

Yet all this is a gross error. One cannot help but point out that these researchers of military history spoke of, and looked at, something that was altogether different from the substance of things, and failed to realize that the warfare of any age is basically determined by economic and social circumstances. It may be considered excessive that in this context we expect military experts to possess profound socio-historical erudition; it may even seem quite unfair to demand of them accomplishments uncharacteristic even of historical specialists of the time, especially as concerns agricultural production and demographic trends. Yet to become aware of the necessity of magazines would not have required such a profound knowledge at all, for it was precisely the sources of military history in the strict sense that offered obvious evidence in this respect, let alone the contemporary books on military science which all emphasized the extreme importance and inevitability of magazine provisioning. To disregard all this was possible for the researchers only by starting from certain false theoretical presuppositions, and by accepting as a fact that the experts and commanders of that age were stricken with blindness, and that their sober thinking and correct judgment had been confused by the principles of some baseless, artificial and nonsensical theory of military science.[57]

*Eugene of Savoy and magazine provisioning.* It would lead us too far to show the necessity of magazine provisioning by affording examples from the wars of that time. On the other hand, we are simply unable to resist the temptation of demonstrating the indispensability of magazines by means of the exploits and writings of Eugene of Savoy. For according to the researchers of history and military history — chiefly the Austrians — he was the very commander who, recognizing the "eternal regularities" of war, was ahead of his age, broke with the cumbersome warfare of the 17th century, and, naturally, also with magazine provisioning.[58]

As commander of the imperial army operating in the Italian theatre of war in 1701/02, he regarded it as indispensable to erect magazines in Tyrol and Friaulia; and when he handed over command to Starhemberg, he mentioned in his instructions the erection of magazines as the "principal point". In 1705 he was informed that intrigues had been concreted against him at court, rumours had been launched that he was not conducting the operations in Italy energetically enough. He complained to Stahremberg asking him

[56] *Heeresverpflegung.* Berlin *A "methodizmus"* 1913. p. 2.

[57] See my article *A „methodizmus" és a Zrínyi—Montecuccoli vita* (The so-called methodicalness and the controverse between Zrínyi and Montecuccoli). Századok 1961. No 4—5. 1962. No 1—2.

[58] *Feldzüge* I. pp. 586—587. VIII. p. 355. — O. Redlich: *Österreichs Großmachtbildung.* Gotha 1921. p. 45.

to judge as a general, who was familiar with the region and knew all the ins and outs of warfare, whether he, Eugene of Savoy, could have possibly undertaken more daring operations when, owing to the impotence of the Viennese Court, no magazines could be established.

In 1708, after the battle of Oudenarde, it seemed, in pursuing the defeated French army, that the allies could have advanced as far as Paris. But the fact that in this case they would have to have left Lille Castle behind them spoke against this plan: the French garrison troops of the fortress might have disturbed, possibly cut off altogether, the supply lines of the advancing army. At the Allied war council, Marlborough was for pursuit, whereas Eugene of Savoy regarded it as indispensable to secure a firm basis of supply first by capturing Lille where magazines could have been established. Eugene of Savoy's stand prevailed at the war council, and this was the beginning of that expensive, very protracted siege, lasting late into the winter, during which the menace of the invasion of France passed, and the opportunity of taking Paris was last once and for all. English historians and researchers of military history put the blame for all this upon Eugene of Savoy. Yet with regard the conditions of the time, and especially the problems of provisioning, truth was certainly on his side, and Marlborough's plan contained many risky elements as a result of which such a campaign would probably have ended in disaster.

In 1709, after Marlborough's position had become shaky, the allies wanted to make Eugene of Savoy commander-in-chief of the war theatre in the Netherlands. Eugene of Savoy, although at that time the most intransingent advocate of a showdown with the French, attached certain conditions to his assuming supreme command. The most important was to speed up replenishment of the magazines so that they could ensure provisioning of the army at the beginning of the campaign.[59]

It was actually from generalization of one single instance that researchers drew the conclusion that Eugene of Savoy had emancipated himself altogether from magazines. This instance was the splendid campaign of Piedmont in 1706 when, in an operation of extreme audacity, he abandoned his magazines in Tyrol, swept past the French positions, joined forces with the Duke of Savoy, with whom he then relieved Turin. Yet it is a known fact that he ventured upon this campaign with no little anxiety, and that it was successful only by a hair's breadth; he found but little food in the region, and he was able to provision his army only with the food sent to him by the Duke of Savoy. One year after he wrote in retrospect of this campaign: "Anybody who knows even a little about war must be astonished how this campaign could succeed without a single magazine."[60]

[59] *Feldzüge* III. Suppl. H. p. 13.; IV. pp. 44., 696., Suppl. H. p. 230., IX. Suppl. H. p. 35. — G. M. Trevelyan: *England under Queen Anne.* I—III. London 1930—1934. II. p. 367.
[60] *Feldzüge* IX. Suppl. H. p. 37.

*Magazine provisioning of Rákóczi's army.* The magazines were also of decisive importance in Rákóczi's War of Independence. Rákóczi writes in his memoirs that whenever a fortress had been captured, and the army had been divided into organizational units, the Hungarians erected magazines. But this statement is not quite accurate because we know that they had established magazines well before they captured the fortresses held by the Imperials — in which, incidentally, they never succeeded completely — and it would even seem that erecting magazines was an activity of high priority in the organization of the Kuruts army. As early as during the first two years of the War of Independence, i.e. at the time when the Kuruts army was actually being organized, the erection of magazines was under way, and more and more magazines were established, or provision made for the storage of grain, in the territories occupied by the army.

Major importance was attached to magazines, and it was a firmly established principle that they must be kept in good working order. It was for this reason that whenever a magazine was exhausted, it was immediately replenished. The *Regulamentum Universale* strictly ordered the commissaries to transport food to empty magazines without delay. It appears from available data that this command was carried out.

Magazines were indispensable not only to the success of operations, but also in order to spare the troops and the population, and to maintain discipline. When, for lack of magazines, the troops directly requisitioned the supplies of the population, the work involved in accumulating grain and any other food was a great burden upon men and horses alike. Abuses and violent acts, unavoidable in such cases, corrupted military discipline, inflicted heavy damage on the population at the same time, and, in general, upset the pre-determined scheme of distribution and levying. All this eventually led to severe administrative disorder.

## The Problems of Logistics and Conduct Technique

*The concept of logistics.*[61] The Greek word logistica means the art of calculation. In the system of the military science of the Greeks and Byzantines, logistics represented the third aspect of war management, in addition to strategy and tactics. It comprised the material supply, and — generally speaking — all operations based on quantitative calculation in connection with the

[61] *Kaisers Leo des Philosophen Strategie und Taktik.* Übers. u. kommentiert v. Bourscheid. I–IV. Wien 1777–1780. — A. H. JOMINI: *Précis de l'art de la guerre.* Nouv. éd. Paris 1855. — JÄHNS, op. cit. I. p. 161., III. p. 1798. — CAEMERER, op. cit. p. 35. — *Military Dictionary.* Ottawa 1945. — HATTON: *The Influence of Logistics on Military Strategy.* (In The Army Quarterly. 1956. No 2. p. 173.) — *Encyclopaedia Britannica.* London 1960. See the entry "Logistics".

movements, equipment, organization and fighting of an army. The concept was still used by Leo the Wise, but after his time it vanished together with strategy and tactics from military terminology not to emerge again until the second half of the 18th century.[62] By that time the scope of the concept had narrowed, and it only denoted that part of general staff services the function of which was to co-ordinate the requirements of strategy and supply services, and to organize the movements of the army. Consequently the task of logistics is not the performance of quantitative mathematical operations connected with all activities of an army, nor does it mean the entirety of supply as in the ancient world. It only comprises that part of general staff services which arranges marches, and gets the necessary materials in the required condition to the correct places at the proper time. This is a leadership task par excellence. As such it is not concerned with procuring material, or with the technology of material processing, nor with the administration of material handling. It is concerned with the movements of material, fit for consumption or use, in accordance with operational requirements. Hence logistics, as a service calculating and organizing the harmony between operational movements, transportation and distribution, supplies the dynamics of the quantitative data of a war or a campaign, but simultaneously places such dynamics within a framework and decisively influences its trends. In the following we shall use the concept of logistics in this calculating-planning, quantitative and dynamical sense.

## The Special Mechanism of the "Army Plant" and the Shuttle-Service

Surveying the highly complex processes of storing, milling, baking, foraging and transportation, we may conclude that fighting was only one of the army's activities, and that another connected activity, i.e. the supply of men and horses with food, was by no means less important than the former. Moreover, if we keep in mind that during a campaign actual fighting took place on a few occasions only while food had to be provided every day, it is easy to see that the tasks involved in provisioning surpassed by far the activities connected with fighting in respect to duration, extent and continuity. Having recourse to an analogy, we may say that an army was not only a war machine, but an immense milling, baking, foraging and transportation device at the same time, a device with a particular mechanism that operated according to rules all its own. It was very difficult to integrate the self-movements of this

[62] The opinion, establishing itself under the influence of Jomini, that found the origins of the word "logistics" in the French "major général des logis" was therefore wrong. — JOMINI, op. cit. II. p. 146. — And it is also erroneous that the word is of unknown origin and was used only in the 18th century for the first time, as Leighton assumes in the Encyclopaedia Britannica (in the entry on "Logistics".)

mechanism into the framework of requirements arising from the given war situation, into the range of strategy in the strict sense; consequently the co-ordination of the requirements of supply and strategy was only possible with certain concessions made by the latter. In judging situations, in reaching decisions and planning, the strategists had to reckon with the mechanism of the "army plant",[63] had to consider what operations an army could possibly undertake, when and where it was to pitch a camp, how long it was supposed to stay there, and whether it was to engage in hostilities with the enemy or should avoid them. The requirements of storing, baking, foraging and transportation played a decisive role in all this. In the last analysis, the dynamism of a campaign determined by operations was interwoven with another dynamism arising from the army mechanism, and the trends and rhythm of the latter were determined by the cyclic recurrence of baking and foraging. Consequently a commander had to shoulder also a task of rhythm-compensation the essence of which was to co-ordinate the work-rhythm of a combat machinery and an army organization. Yet in addition to this rhythm-compensation, it was also necessary to co-ordinate the movements of the army with those of the transportation facilities. Let us have a look at the tasks which arise in this connection.

As we have seen, provisioning of armies was based on magazines, completely with respect to bread supply, partially with respect to fodder supply. The stocks of the magazines were usually transported to the troops in carts. Since, however, transportation facilities were available only to a limited extent only, the carts, after unloading food, had to return to the magazines for loading food for the next 4—5 days. Consequently a shuttle-service had to be set up, and not between two stationary points, but between one stationary and one moving point; the baking runs and the days of foraging likevise had to be co-ordinated. To organize all this without a hitch would have required a mathematical apparatus much superior to the attainments of practical experts of that age; thus, in practice, all co-ordination was carried out by the "trial and error" method.[64]

Shuttle-services assumed their classical form in the so-called "five-march system" (Fünfmarschsystem) of the mid 18th century. The essence of this system was that an advancing army established bakeries at a five-day march distance from the magazines. Flour was carried from the magazines to the bakeries by the army-train in shuttle-service, and bread was carried to the

[63] In connection with the plan of a raid General Tesse wrote in 1707: "Tout cela sur le papier est bien plus facile à démontrer qu'à exécuter, et le mécanique des subsistances, les transports, les dépôts . . . nous peuvent déranger." Cit. by De Vault—Pelet, op. cit. VII. p. 7.

[64] One might arrive at the solution only by using a graphic method. Although the system of co-ordinates was already known owing to Descartes' discovery, but it was used only in analytical geometry on the level of Newton and Leibniz.

troops by the troop-train also in shuttle-service. In this way the vehicles of the army performed not one, but two shuttle-services: one in the "line of communications area", the other in the "zone of action", to use two modern terms. Since, owing to troop-train capacity, it was impossible to move farther away the bakeries than 2—3 days' distance, it is easy to calculate that an army could not proceed farther from its magazines than 7—8 daily marches. Consequently the "radius of action" of an army was 7—8 marches, i.e. about 140—160 kilometres. When this limit was reached, the magazines had to be located farther ahead in some way — usually by water — after which everything had to be started anew.

As we have said, the five-march system was developed only in the middle of the 18th century. In the period we are considering here, people were unable to solve — either theoretically or practically — the shuttle-service system, even if they realized its necessity. It is very important to emphasize this, because we are very often confronted with the view that the five-march system developed as early as the second half of the 17th century.[65] Yet this is by no means the case. The necessity of shuttle-services was realized only by a few experts, and the number of those who gave a clear formulation of the problem was even smaller.

Of the experts of that age known to us, it was Zrínyi who most sharply defined the necessity and substance of shuttle-services. His conclusions made in this connexion deserve to be quoted in full: "Prepared food has to be carried by men, and this can be accomplished either by water or overland . . . And there is no possibility of the men simultaneously carrying food for one or two months in camp. For, as we have written in the preceding part, food for only five days can be loaded on those 205 carts (i.e. the carts of an army 24 000 men strong taken as the basis by Zrínyi, G.P.). Hence these carts must only keep *coming and going* (italics mine, G.P.) back and forth between the latest town under your control, to which one must carry grain in sufficient time, as much as is deemed necessary; and having baked there, bread must be carried to the camp uninterruptedly. If such a place is very far away, a fortification must be established at some suitable, halfway point, and bakeries must be set up there."[66]

Montecuccoli's description is not so explicit, though he doubtless hints at the necessity of shuttle-services: "Magazines must be placed near the army in several fortresses, and these must be in favourable places with respect to transportation by water, carts or pack-animals; but the latter (i.e. the transportation facilities, G.P.) must be available in double quantity in order that

[65] H. Delbrück: *Ueber die Verschiedenheit der Strategie Friedrichs und Napoleons.* (Historische und politische Aufsätze) Berlin 1887. p. 30.

[66] Zrinyi, op. cit. p. 119.

while a portion of them is marching to the camp, the other should be able to start from there to fetch the new load."[67]

In one passage the *Dictionnaire Militaire* quotes Montecuccoli word for word, but neither does it tell substantially more elsewhere: bread for four days should always be with the men and on the transportation facilities, and the supplies "keep coming and going because the troops get bread every four days".[68]

To show how immature the supply system was at that time, and how wrong the assertion was that Eugene of Savoy owed his successes to his bold breaking away from magazine provisioning and the five-march system (which of course did not exist in that age) — we quote its lines, which he wrote in Italy in 1705: "Without a train . . . I am unable to advance further, especially when the army is going from one region to another, and the magazine located here or there is too far away, and it takes several days to establish a magazine in the new place, and to put the bakeries into operation. And meanwhile the army is in need of bread and if we cannot take bread with us, how should I help myself?" Shortly afterwards there was again trouble with the organization of supplies: "I have dispatched all sutler vehicles to the infantry, but cannot move freely even so because I have to wait until they return (i.e. from the magazines)". And because he could not hold bread in reserve, nor take it along, it was not possible to issue rations of bread for the two days during which the carts went back and forth between the magazines and the troops.[69] All this shows that not even the shuttle-service, let alone the five-march system, was fully developed in the Austrian army at that time.

Marshal Puységur, the greatest supply specialist of the age and, in fact, the founder of modern logistics, did not consider at all the shuttle-service system for solving the supply problem in one of his operational examples serving for purpose of instruction. He sent farth an army 120 000 men strong with eight days' food supply, and when this had run out, supplying was possible, in his opinion, only with conveyance by water.[70]

## The Crisis of Logistics and Leadership Techniques, and the Emergence of Crisis-Awareness

The co-ordination of supply and strategic requirements of armies, which had expanded into immense baking, foraging and transporting apparatus as a result of a sudden increase in manpower, raised considerable problems that remained momentanly insoluble. As a result logistics and leadership techniques experienced a real crisis. This crisis was felt rather intensely by the people of

[67] MONTECUCCOLI: *Della Guerra.* Lib. I./XLII.
[68] *Dictionnaire Militaire,* see the entries "Magasin" "Munitionnaire" and "Convoi".
[69] *Feldzüge.* VIII. Suppl. H. pp. 305., 375.
[70] PUYSÉGUR, op. cit. II. p. 61.

the time, and even if they misinterpreted its nature, and, above all its causes, the fact itself was accurately recorded. We have the good fortune to possess a picture of this crisis, or, more exactly, its image in people's minds from a description by a figure no less distinguished than Saint-Simon. Although Saint-Simon did not gather too many laurels during his own military career, and can hardly be regarded a military expert, he was excellently informed of everything as a result of his many appearances at court, and his close contacts with the highest-ranking civil and military functionaries. So we may attach much importance to his opinion.

At any rate we must at least know that he was an extreme conservative, a stubborn fighter for the privileges of the aristocracy, who regarded the repression of his class by the new administration, the shackling of feudal lords by absolutist centralization, as a national disaster. He saw the essence of change in the passing of the great men of glorious old days, in the extinction of righteous characters and talents. Naturally, he also looked at the crisis in the conduct of war in this manner. He often mentions in his memoirs the good old days when generals were equally adept in commanding troops and pitching camps, in manoeuvring and building fortifications, in foraging and planning marches — yet there came a new generation, the generation of the unworthy sons of brave fathers, which was no longer competent in all these things. He was shocked at the ignorance and shallowness of young people: "Being unable to speak of subjects which they do not comprehend, the men of our days only keep babbling of cards and women. Take the men of the past! They talked only of transportation and foraging." The days had gone when young people listened raptly to the war time adventures of older persons, and learned from their experience. He especially castigated their lack of aquaintance with the goals of logistics. In his recollections about Marshal de Lorge, his father-in-law who was a prominent figure of the old generation, he emphasizes among other things than the former was extremely skilled in co-ordinating various aspects provisioning with the movements of the army. On the other hand, of General Villars whom he detested, he wrote as follows: "He had no idea of the details of provisioning, transportation, foraging and marching, and left these problems to generals who were willing to take all the necessary pains."[71] It appears, then, that the diagnosis of Saint-Simon was substantially correct even if he misinterpreted the causes behind the symptoms: The commanders are no good at logistics, and it is this element which has evoked a crisis in military management.[72]

[71] SAINT-SIMON: *Mémoires.* XIII. pp. 344—354., X. pp. 311., 353.

[72] The French military historian, Reboul also drew attention to the crisis of the art of war resulting from the difficulties of logistics. G. HANOTAUX: *Histoire de la nation française.* Tome VIII. *Histoire militaire et navale.* Premiere vol. — J. COLIN: *Des origines aux croisades.* FR. REBOUL: *Des croisades à la révolution.* Paris 1925. p. 466. Also Guibert attributes the "retrogression" of the art of war to this. GUIBERT: *Essai général de tactique.*

It would seem, however, that the situation was no better in the Austrian army either. Eugene of Savoy complained that, although there was no shortage of courageous and brave generals, "the army has recently deteriorated to such an extent that practically none of them is of any use for a higher assignment". On another occasion he wrote "it is a recognised fact that we are not too well supplied with generals". At the time of the War of the Spanish Succession, for practical purposes only Guido Stahremberg and Rabutin besides Eugene himself, were fit for duty as independent commanders-in-chief, and there were not as many generals of superior qualification as there were theatres of war. It was for this reason that Heister had to be tolerated in Hungary, although everybody knew that he was unfit for an independent post. And when in 1710 Stahremberg was taken ill, the Court encountered great troubles in finding somebody to appoint in his stead as commander-in-chief of the Imperial armies in Spain.[73] It may be assumed that, just as in the French army, it was not the generals who were of poorer quality, but that the tasks had multiplied, and had become more complex when compared to former times, in view of the novel logistical problems.

## The Lack of Supervision over Logistics Functions, and Their Devolvement on Quartermasters

The confusion surrounding logistics resulted not only from the novel nature of the difficulties that arose but also from the circumstance that within an army there was actually nobody in charge of logistic functions. It was thus that the problem of logistics comported as many as three aspects. The first was the quantitative and material factor: how could one to supply the suddenly expanded armies in view of substantially unchanged resources and means? The second was qualitative, a feature of war management par excellence: how was it possible to co-ordinate operational requirements with the mechanism of an army supply apparatus which was tending towards independence? The third aspect was organizational: who should be the person to create this harmony, and what organization should be at his disposal for dealing with this task?

To understand this latter problem, we must take a cursory glance at the organization of logistics in modern times and in the period under survey. Nowadays[74] the co-ordination of operational and supply functions is the responsibility of the chief of staff (staff commander, quartermaster). Two persons or

[73] *Feldzüge.* XIII. Suppl. H. p. 91., VIII. Suppl. H. p. 7., VII. Suppl. H. p. 126. Arneth: *Prinz Eugen von Savoyen.* I—III. Wien 1858. II. p. 479.

[74] Having had no possibility to take into consideration the changes following the Second World War, the above mentiones facts refer only to the period between the two World Wars.

staffs are at his disposal for this purpose: the staff officer in charge of operational planning in the strict sense, and his operational staff; and the staff officer in charge of supply planning with his staff and his subordinate organs such as the quartermaster general's department, ammunition department. weapons department, fuel department, train, etc.[75] Thus in a modern table of organization the tasks are precisely circumscribed, duties are defined clearly, co-ordination of operational and material requirements is ensured because all strings are in the hands of a person endowed with unchallengeable authority, in the hands of the chief of staff. He himself, his commander, his subalterns and co-workers are experts trained in uniform methods on the basis of uniform principles, men who hold the same views and act according to the same practice.

In the time preceding our period during the Thirty Years' War, the organization of logistics was not yet centralized to such a degree; there actually existed two machineries which operated in parallel fashion and which took the necessary measures independent of each other, or in very loose correlation at best. Operational planning and action in the strict sense was the responsibility of the commander-in-chief, who was assisted by a few aids. Matters of supply were the responsibility of an intendant or commissary who was responsible directly to the government and was not subordinate to the commander. Yet this loose organization was still able to ensure the continuity of logistics, the co-ordination of operational and supply requirements, because the provisioning of small armies was by no means such a difficult task, required no major apparatus or machinery that tended to follow its own rules, might have decisively influenced the conduct of war. Thus, essentially, there existed a situation in which the commander had more freedom of action, could concern himself more readily with stuctly military viewpoints and aims without meeting as many obstacles, could proceed with less interference. And the intendant or commissary in charge of supply was able to fulfill the demands of the commander more easily. In such circumstances the intendant or commissary was in no need of special military qualifications, and the commander himself could also get by without profound, specialized knowledge of supply techniques.

All this changed practically overnight in the period after the Thirty Years' War. This separation, this parallelism of functions could not be maintained any longer. Co-ordination of these two functions, development of unified logistical planning, became an urgent necessity. A new position had to be created for this purpose, or the scope of duties of some existing position had to be expanded to include logistical functions.

The latter was done. Logistical tasks were turned over to the quartermaster general (called *campmaster general* by Zrínyi, *maréchal général des logis* by the French, and *Generalquartiermeister* by the Germans). The position of

[75] NYITRAY: *Anyagi szolgálat.* (Supply Services) Budapest 1944. — J. D. HITTLE: *The Military Staff.* Harrisburg 1949.

quartermaster had existed as early as the 16th century; it owed its existence to the nature of warfare of that time, i.e. to the fact that camps were of extreme importance in the life of any army. Originally, the duty of the quartermaster consisted of selecting and marking out the camp site. Yet as time passed, a number of other jobs were added. In order to look for a camp site, the quartermaster had to precede the army, and hence reconnaisance was also made his responsibility. Reconnaisance, in turn, involved inspection of the terrain, and protection of the site selected raised the problems of fortification. Thus the quartermaster soon found scouting a part of his duties, became the chief expert in cartography, even attended to military engineering tasks if necessary.[76] And because it was he who knew the terrain best, he was likewise consulted in planning the march, and after some time the dispatching of marching columns was made his responsibility entirely. March planning, on the other hand, meant as a matter of course that the quartermaster should have a decisive say in the direction of trains. In this way the cartmaster became his special functionary and directed the train according to the quartermaster's intentions.[77] But all this was the result of a rather slow process, and in the period with which we are concerned the quartermaster's sphere of duties was not yet so broad, and logistic functions were not definitely his obligation.[78] From the descriptions of Puységur we have accurate information concerning how the logistic functions had become the quartermaster's duties. As a young, ambitious officer, Puységur thought that the position of a quartermaster was a key post in the army, and so he accepted it, although others despised such assignment. He wrote: "This function is considered inferior to the others, from which I can only judge that people are ignorant; the tasks entrusted to me can be broadened if a person has the necessary talent." He had relatively rich experiences as a quartermaster when in the nineties he was made quartermaster general in the army of Marshal Luxembourg. By that time he saw clearly upon what lines his scope of duties should be expanded. To be sure, at the beginning of his service in Luxembourg's army his task consisted of nothing more than to put the Marshal's plans and orders in writing and to forward them to the troops. This was the custom of the time, because, apart from a few, exceptionally gifted commanders, there was no one who would have been skilled in comprehensive operational planning, let alone logistics. But Puységur surpassed all his predecessors in attainments, and, besides, always had precise information owing to his close contact with the troops and his many visits

[76] JÄHNS, op. cit. II. p. 264.

[77] GRUBERN, op. cit. pp. 123—124.

[78] According to Hittle the organization of supply belonged from outset to the quartermaster's tasks. But this is not so. Neither Zrínyi nor Montecuccoli give any facts proving this. ZRINYI, op. cit. p. 462. — MONTECUCCOLI: *Ausgewählte Schriften.* I. p. 206. — For further references see JÄHNS, op. cit. I. p. 758., *Feldzüge* I. p. 303. — *Dictionnaire Militaire* the entry "Maréchal Général des Logis".

upon the terrain. He thus caught Luxembourg's attention, and was gradually entrusted with the entire organization of marches and transports. In this way he became the first logistical expert of the Frenchy army, and the adviser of Louis XIV. The King then dispatched him, according to need, either to this or that army for the purpose of directing logistics, which shows that at that time logistics were not yet the routine responsibility of army quartermasters. On the other hand, the circumstance that such an itinerant logistical expert was needed indicates how very little this sphere of duties was known.[79]

*Provisioning by Stages (Étapes).* It often became necessary to shift persons, troops or complete armies from one part of the country to another, or to redistribute forces between theatres of war. In such cases supply was based on "étapes", i.e. provisioning by stages or relays. Food was supplied to the stations set up for this purpose in various ways. The simplest method was when the civil authorities provided persons or troops with food and horses in return for cash payment or upon presentation of an official statement.[80] Yet this method of supply gave rise to much abuse and confusion. Nor was it always possible to supply larger masses of persons in this way. The State therefore established magazines along the military roads which could be used either under its own direction or by means of contractors.[81]

Considering what has been said so far, it might seem that the organization of relay provisioning was mostly an administrative task and that it involved only a few dynamic, logistical element. More precisely, that particular logistic function of organizing transportation for an army moving away from the magazines, and of establishing a cart shuttle-service was altogether absent because the armies marched from magazine to magazine. The reason why we discuss it here, in connection with logistics, is that marches executed in the interior of the country, far from the theatres of war, were also of strategical importance, because it was in this way that redeployment became possible. This was of major significance especially in the case of France because, considering the wars of that age as a whole, fighting was always going on along an interior line. But even in the case of Austria, where operations on an interior line could only be considered in relation to the theatres of war in Northern Italy, on the Rhine and in Hungary, it was very important that the armies should reach their destinations as soon as possible, and with the least possible exertion, via the provisioning stations kept in readiness.

[79] PUYSÉGUR, op. cit. II. pp. 84., 155. — CHEVENNIÈRES complained that the function of supply and strategy was separated. Op. cit. I. p. 11.

[80] *Dictionnaire Militaire*, the entry "Etappes". — *Feldzüge* III. pp. 76., 409. 442. — In Hungary the étape-supply for the Imperial Army was regulated by an Imperial patent issued in 1695. J. HORNYIK: *Kecskemét város története.* (History of the town Kecskemét) I—IV. Kecskemét 1860—1866. II. p. 432. — During the Rákóczi Insurrection the "stations" i.e. the étapes were partly set up by the counties.

[81] *Dictionnaire Militaire*, the entry "Étapier, ou entrepreneur des vivres".

Provisioning by stages was also of great importance in cases where redeployment took place by flanking movement, i.e. at right angles to the axis of operations. In such cases the troops marched via the magazines located behind the front-lines, or within the national boundary, and did not have to carry food with them, and this facilitated their movements considerably. The north-eastern and eastern network of fortifications, and the magazines located in them, provided the French excellent opportunities for carrying out such redeployment. It was these magazines that made possible the redeployment of armies in the theatres of the Netherlands, at the Moselle and in Alsace, which was a considerable advantage to France with respect to the "économie des forces".

Provisioning by stages gave rise to specific logistic problems in cases where fortress and magazines were found over the entire theatre of war. By making use of them, the army was able to supply itself with food by relay even in areas controlled, or at least menaced, by the enemy. During Rákóczi's War of Independence food was supplied in Hungary by this method of provisioning. Victualing was generally handled by the Kuruts army in this way, and by the Imperial army frequently.

## The Crisis of Strategy

In what sense can we speak of a crisis in 17 and 18-century strategy? It is a generally accepted view in the literature of military history that in the period from the second half of the 17th century, and lasting to the French revolution, strategy was somewhat different from that of other ages. Regarding the essence of this difference, the views of researchers diverge, and they also interpret the causal factors in various ways. Some of them see the chief characteristic of that strategy in the fact that, owing to the petty nature of the differences that lay behind political objectives and wars, military conflicts had lost their inherent character, namely the annihilation of the enemy and the occupation of his country. Wars had became mitigated, had been "humanized", had developed into a parlour game of kings. In their view, all wars were "cabinet wars" waged only for dynastic interests. This view found general acceptance in the literature on military history especially under the influence of Clausewitz. The interpretation which attributed the decline of strategy to a false theory of military science, namely, excessive methodicalness, had the same origin.[82] Though it had few advocates, a third view deserves mention. According to it, the crisis resulted from the fact that the armies fighting along drawn-out lines moved clumsily. Regrouping of marching formations into

[82] See my article *A "methodizmus" és a Zrínyi—Montecuccoli vita.* Századok 1961. No 4—5. and 1962. No 1—2.

battle-formations, and vice versa, took too much time. As a result, it was very difficult to force the enemy to fight, and it was practically impossible to continue a succesful battle by pursuing and annihilating the enemy.[83] Finally, let us mention Delbrück who, practically speaking, saw no crisis at all, but held that of two types of strategy (which he called "crushing" and "attrition"), only the latter could be employed due to the given economic and social conditions.[84] In his opinion, the strategy of that age fully corresponded to the potentialities of the time, consequently — and this is our contribution to Delbrück's train of thought — there was no discrepancy between war aims and the strategy employed, which also means that there was no crisis.

Considering all this, we may ask what was the truth. Was there a crisis in 17—18-century strategy, or was there none? In our opinion, there was. Yet, in contrast to Clausewitz and his followers, we by no means see the reason for this crisis in the circumstance that, owing to petty war aims, a striving for annihilation was absent from warfare. Anybody who is even modestly familiar with the history of that age must know that issues of great consequence were involved, especially in the second half of the 17th century. And we have nowhere found any indication that there was some false, mistaken theory of military science that would have obstructed, or entirely frustrated efforts to achieve a though decision.

As concerns the third view which asserts the existence of a crisis — and in effect as we have seen explains it on tactical grounds, we are of the opinion that the growth of armies in the 19th century gave rise to still graver problems of marching and deployment, but, after all did not result in a crisis.

We believe that this crisis lay essentially in the fact that there was a discrepancy between the political objectives of wars and the only kind of strategy that could be employed in the given circumstances; and that strategy was no longer able to meet the requirements of politics. We should like to elucidate our ideas through Clausewitz's theoretical analysis of the aims and substance of wars, without, however, agreeing in the slightest with his particular opinion of 17-century strategy.[85]

According to Clausewitz, there can be two sorts of war. One is aimed at defeating the enemy in order to compel him to defer to one's own will.

[83] R. Mousnier: *Les XVI^e et XVII^e siècles.* 2. ed. (Histoire Générale des Civilisations· IV.) Paris 1956. p. 287.

[84] H. Delbrück: *Ueber die Verschiedenheit der Strategie Friedrichs und Napoleons.* (Historische u. politische Aufsätze.) Berlin 1887. — *Die Strategie des Perikles.* Berlin 1890. and the *Geschichte der Kriegskunst.* Berlin 1920. Vol. 4. Chapter "Der Strategie-Streit."

[85] The following parts of the "*Vom Kriege*" were used principally: "Nachricht", Book 1. Chapters I—II; Book 4, Chapters X, XI; Book 7, Chapters I, II, VI; Book 8, Chapters I, IV, V. Concerning Clausewitz's scientific method I posed some problems in my above cited article, and my other article, entitled: *Élelemellátás, logisztika és stratégia a vasutak elterjedése előtti kétszáz esztendőben.* (Supply of food, logistics and strategy in the two centuries before the general use of railvays.) (Hadtörténelmi Közlemények 1963. No 1.).

The defeat of the enemy may consist in complete military annihilation, but also in making him incapable of further defence. The other sort of war is aimed not at crushing the enemy, but only at the occupying certain territories, usually frontier provinces. This is called the "war of limited aims".

If we now consider the wars of that age from this point of view, we conclude that, apart from a few exceptions, they all belonged to the first type. There were but few wars where the aim was solely the occupation of certain provinces; much more far-reaching goals were involved, and even if certain wars ended in apparently nothing but the annexation of this or that province, the result was — particularly if we regard the wars of that time in their entirety — a complete rearrangement of Europe's balance of power and political structure. We need only keep in mind that the period between 1660 and 1715 saw the disintegration of the Spanish world empire, the growth of England, Austria and Russie into European big powers, the economic and political decline of the Netherlands, the vanishing of French hegemony, and the collapse of Turkish dominion in Hungary. And because all these wars belonged to the first type, it was obviously the aim of the belligerent parties to force their will upon one another, to defeat, even to annihilate even another. This was definitely the aim of the French when they were at war with the Dutch in 1672, and it was practically always the objective of the wars between the Turks and the western powers.

Nor were these wars void of the criteria which Clausewitz regarded as so essential for annihilating, or rendering defenceless, the enemy: to annihilate the enemy's forces, to occupy its country, and to crush its war potential. One or another of these criteria, explicitly or implicitly, were included in the operational plans of that age, and even if they could not be realized in most cases, this was not because the commanders had given up these aims in principle, or had failed to recognize their necessity; it followed simply from the fact that the means of strategy were inadequate, and this very fact indicates the crisis of strategy. For we certainly could not speak of the crisis of strategy if the wars had been waged for limited aims. In this case, namely even inadequate strategical means would have sufficed fully for achieving limited war aims. And, obviously, there would have been no crisis either if strategy had been adequate in every respect for achieving the completely destructive, "will-imposing" aims of the wars.

The substance of what we want to say is this: It is justifiable to speak of a 17-century crisis of strategy, but not because attempts at annihilation should not have been included in political and immediate war aims as Clausewitz maintained; and not because the governments and commanders of that age, realizing the inadequacy of means, should have renounced from the outset a strategy aiming an annihilation, and should have followed ab ovo the principles and practice of an "attrition" strategy as Delbrück asserts. Rather we speak of a crisis merely because of the fact that the annihilation of the enemy's armed forces, the occupation of his country, and the crushing of his will formed the basis of plans, but, owing to the inadequacy of the means of strategy, all this could not be accomplished.

*The experts and the crisis of strategy.* To support our conclusions, let us quote the opinion of certain contemporary experts. It appears from all of these authorities that the commanders of that time were inspired by the example of Gustavus Adolphus, who started from a remote corner of Europe, conquered a major portion of the continent, annihilated armies, and crushed the will of his opponents.

In 1697, Marshal Choiseul, the commander-in-chief of the French army operating in the upper Rhine region, made apologies for his failures to Louis XIV. As he writes, he was not able to achieve decisive success because he could not find sufficient food in the region, and this paralyzed his operations. Some blamed him saying that Turenne was able to subsist with his army in the same region; but the advocates of this view forget that Turenne's army was only 20 000 strong, and also that the crop was better that year. In any event he remarks — the German theatre of war differs from any other, because it is much more difficult to find food here than elsewhere.[86]

In 1704, when Marlborough was marching from the lower Rhine to the Danube to join forces with the *Reich* German and Austrian armies, the French supreme command entertained the idea of launching an attack in the Neckar region to prevent the jonction of the Allies. But the fundamental obstacle to this plan was the circumstance that it was impossible to manage the food supply of the army. General Chamlay, one of the best military experts of that time, writes as follows: "In Germany it is very difficult to ensure supply for the armies without magazines. Prior to the Peace of Münster, all Protestant princes and towns were on the side of the French, and the French armies were by no means so numerous as the ones now at the Rhine, so it was much easier for them to support themselves."[87]

Puységur, studying the strategic problems of his time, also departed from the Thirty Years' War. At that time nothing hindered the small armies in going on long expeditions, while in the second half of the century the numerically increased armies were no longer able to break away from their magazines, and could only fight "frontier wars" and "it is precisely these frontier wars that are the most difficult and most scholarly of all".[88]

This problem still existed in the second half of the 18th century. Tempelhoff writes: "It is easier to invade the enemy's country with ten, fifteen or

[86] SAINT-SIMON: *Mémoires.* IV. pp. 386—487.

[87] *Campagne de M. le Maréchal de Tallard en Allemagne. 1704.* I—II. Amsterdam 1762. I. p. 264. — For further references see my article: *A höchstädti csata* (The Battle of Blenheim). (Hadtörténelmi Közlemények 1958. No 3—4.).

[88] PUYSÉGUR, op. cit. II. pp. 151—152.

twenty thousand men, than with fifty, sixty or hundred thousand men. This is why it was easy to overrun Germany at the time of the Thirty Years' War."[89] And Guibert says that "at the time of the Thirty Years' War it was possible to make great conquests even with small armies," but ever since the effective force of the armies had grown, and since provisioning difficulties had developed, commanders despaired of movement and wars consist of nothing but sieges.[90]

All this supports our previous conclusion: strategy had reached a crisis indeed by the second half of the 17th century; and this crisis arose from the circumstance that the means of strategy were insufficient to carry out military operations of a decisive nature, even if the governments and commanders made efforts to this end, and emphasized the good sense and the absolute expediency of such objectives. But something else, too, emerges from the foregoing: the inadequacy of strategy resulted first and foremost, and conclusively, from the difficulties involved in the provisioning of numerically increased armies. All this tallies completely with what we have said so far in our treatise. What still remains to be done is to summarize how provisioning difficulties paralyzed the strategy of that age.

We shall discuss the *dénouement* of provisioning difficulties from two different approaches. First, we shall examine the question of how provisioning determined the conduct of war in the strict sense. Than, we shall consider how state administration was effected. Such a separation of consequences is rather arbitrary because they developed reciprocally, amplified each other and then reacted mutually upon provisioning proper. Our reason for separating them despite their interrelationship is the desire, justifiable we trust, to achieve clarity of expression.

*The effects of difficulties in provisioning on the proper conduct of war.* In studying this consequence we base ourselves on the three criteria which Clausewitz regarded as fundamental for defeating the enemy. As we have seen, these three criteria were: annihilation of the enemy's armed forces, occupation of his country, and crushing the will of the opponent. Let us now consider how provisioning was instrumental in so far as these criteria could never be met simultaneously, and only in rare cases successively.

If we take the first criterion, we must scrutinize the problem of fighting or avoiding a decisive battle. As is known, the researchers of military history see the essence of the difference between "old" and "new" warfare — i.e. the warfare of the ancien régime and that of the time following the French revolution — principally in the dissimilar manner in which decisive battles took place during these two periods. With the new type of warfare, from the very launching of the campaign, every thread, every event, the entire logic of things,

[89] Lloyd—Tempelhoff: p. 190.
[90] Guibert, op. cit. "Discours" and II. p. 61.

led toward the decisive battle, which was by no means the case with the old kind of warfare. Yet there was a difference also in the consequences of such a battle: in the time of the old warfare, a decisive battle itself resulted in a real decision only in exceptional cases, while in the new type of warfare it was usually a decisive battle, or a series of decisive battles, that led to strategic victory. What was the role of provisioning in the fact that the nature of a "decisive" or open battle was so different in the two types of warfare?

First of all, we must examine the already discussed logistical problems more closely. A sufficient comprehension and appraisal of these difficulties is a rather laborious task for the modern researcher, because in modern wars the problems of provisioning are by no means so important in operational planning as they were in the past. This difference lies in the circumstance that in our days problems of provisioning arise on another level, to another degree, and in altogether different relationhips. Nowadays procurement of food is the question least military in nature. The combatant army is usually supplied by the home-country, and even if the army requisitions the stocks found in the theatre of war as a matter of course, to find, inventary, collect and distribute them is the responsibility of civil organs appointed by the government. This is to say that today the problem of food procurement emerges only on the governmental level, i.e., as a problem of higher strategy comprising all economic, political and military aspects of a war. As we have seen, this was quite different in the past. Fodder, representing a considerable part of the entire food requirement, was always procured by the fighting army itself, and so was bread in some cases. Thus the problem of food procurement appeared on a much lower level, on the level of military strategy, of operational command in the strict sense.

It follows from this, too, that in modern wars the problem of provisioning is present in the conduct of war proper to a different degree. Today the commander is only concerned with the logistical aspect of supply, and is not engaged in its procurement, technological and administrative facets. In the past, on the other hand, the operations of the combat apparatus had to be adjusted to the working of the "army plant", and the technical problems of food procurement, processing and transportation affected operational planning directly.

The relationship between food procurement and the conduct of war is different, too. In our days, food supply is only one among the many items of operational planning, while it was the most decisive item in the past, was often the aim itself. The commander of our days decides what he wants to do, and simply informs the commissariat department how much food it is to procure. In the past, by contrast, a commander usually had to start with the consideration of how long available food supplies would last, how far away he could move from his magazines, where he could possibly find fodder. Moreover, the attempt to find a region which would be able to sustain the army was the chief element of the entire campaign plan in many a case.

All this would constitute a considerable difference even if in the past estimation of needs and supplies, processing and transportation of food, could have been based on rational calculation, and the persons making these calculations had been fully aware of what they had to do.[91] Yet this was by no means the case. As we have seen, no concrete, rational numerical data on possible resources were available to governments and commanders, given the standards of contemporary statistics. In any case all preliminary calculations were rendered illusory by the circumstance that fodder, i.e. the major part of requirements, was provided by the theatre of war, the capacity of which was determined by the altogether incalculable and unforeseeable events of the war. Not only estimation of available food, but also its processing and transportation to the troops were decided by the actions of numerous incalculable factors. That is to say, milling, baking, the transportation of bread and fodder, were determined by natural, organic and biological factors which were, for the most part, uncontrollable and incalculable by human effort. Whether or not the water and wind conditions permitted the operation of mills, whether the roads would be turned into seas of mud by rain, whether the condition of the draught animals would make transportation possible — on all this man had very little influence, or none at all, nor could the trends of any these factors be forecast. In our time, given the means of a mechanized methodology, which has largely liberated itself from natural and organic restrictions, the functioning of an army supply apparatus can be calculated, foreseen and planned. The difficulties of the past were aggravated by the circumstance that — as we have seen — people were at a loss what to do in the face of novel problems arising from the growth of army manpower and moreover, that, specifically logistical functions were assigned to no one in particular.

All this means that in the wars of the past the unexpected, incalculable elements, "luck", which Zrínyi so often pondered, played a much greater role. According to Zrínyi, only a fractional portion of military events can be calculated; the rest must be left to chance, for man has no control whatsoever over the events of war. Even the best of commanders can do not more than to narrow down the boundaries of fortune's empire. He is not able to eliminate fate altogether. All this follows from the very nature of war, from the obstacles that stand in the way of war machinery's functioning, from the "frictions" to use Clausewitz's term. And among the factors producing frictions in the past, one of the most important was the aforesaid uncertain, unforeseeable

[91] Dupré d'Aulnay wrote: "Mon objet a été de développer, d'éclaircir et de simplifier des matiers d'autant plus intéressantes aujourd'hui, que les opérations militaires semblent être devenues asujetties et subordonnées aux Subsistances, par la confusion et l'obscurité qu'on affecte de mettre ou d'entretenir dans le service de celles-ci." DUPRÉ—D'AULNAY, op. cit. pp. III–IV.

functioning of the supply apparatus, influenced by organic and natural factors.

It follows from this particular relationship of provisioning and the conduct of war that in the past the dynamics of warfare were entirely different from those of our days, and that the order of events did not necessarily lead to a battle, it rather led away from it. On the one hand, the mechanism of the army did not always permit a battle; let us consider, for instance, that the men and the horses could not be left without food, that both side had to bake, forage and transport food, whereby time and place of a clash was by no means determined purely by the war situation. On the other hand, the survival of an army depended decisively on food supply, hence annihilation or incapacitation of the enemy's army was possible not only through a battle, but also by making food supply difficult, or altogether impossible. This was all the more likely because the supply lines of the army were much more vulnerable than today. This resulted from the disadvantageous proportion of supply lines and battle lines; supply lines were very long, battle lines were narrow, as a result of which the army had difficulties in covering its supply lines, and was scarcely able to repel the enemy's attacks against these lines. And the vulnerability of supply lines offered ample opportunity for all kinds of enclosing movements directed against these lines. This is why — in addition to other reasons — manoeuvres, or to be quite accurate, "manoeuvring", played such an important role in the strategy of that age.

Difficulties of provisioning could determine not only the occurrence or non-occurrence of a battle; they also had an influence on the exploitation of battles that actually had taken place. As is commonly known, both the winning and losing side suffer more or less the same casualties in a battle, unless the winner has succeeded in encircling his opponent completely. However, envelopment battles like that of Cannae, ending in annihilation of the enemy's armed forces, are rare in military history. The real loss is suffered by the loser when he leaves the battlefield, i.e. during his retreat, when his battle-alignement is dissolved, when the men become panick, abandon their arms and equipment, and only think of fleeing. Thus, normally, the winning party inflicts the heaviest casualties on his opponent not in the battle proper, but in the subsequent pursuit, casualties which may eventually lead to the complete annihilation of the enemy. Now, in the age we are considering, pursuit was in most cases made impossible by the difficulties of food supply because to adjust the cumbersome mechanism of the supply apparatus to the rapid speed of pursuit was clearly impossible — and pursuit must be quick, or else it has no effect. When the pursuit could be started as soon as the battle was over, provisioning presented no special problem because the men, drunk with success, were able to endure hunger for possibly several days, and if the horses did not get their rations for one or two days, this was no particular calamity either.

Consequently, if it was possible to annihilate the fleeing enemy completely within the limits of an army's biological endurance, i.e. practically within one or two days, the victory could have become decisive. But the difficulty behind all this was that — owing to the tactical reasons we have mentioned, i.e. the fact that changing of battle- and marching-formations took much time — the retreating side could easily slow down the advance of the pursuer by rear-guard action which forced him to engage in time-consuming redeployment during which interval the bulk of the pursued army could find an escape match. In this way the pursuit turned into a slow backtracking movement in the course of which the pursuer gradually fell behind, and eventually last the opportunity of dealing a coup de grace to the defeated enemy. This was the case even if the fleeing enemy did not devastate the land behind it — and there was small probability of its not having done so — because the mere fact that two armies followed each other on the same marching route had the result of leaving hardly any supplies on the spot for the second, the first having consumed practically everything. In this way the winning side was able to find fodder — for it was fodder that mattered above all — only in villages and surroundings farther away from the marching route, which however, involved a considerable loss of time. As a consequence of all this, the pursuit slackened automatically. In any case, the retreating party was in a much better position with respect to supplies because it was coming ever closer to its supply basis, whereas the pursuer was moving away from his. We conclude therefore that the particular position and function of the "decisive", pitched battle of the old type of warfare was determined and affected by food supply as shown above.

What about the second criterion, the occupation of the enemy's country? How did difficulties of food supply matter in this respect? Suppose that the first presupposition of occupying the enemy's country, i.e. the annihilation of its armed forces, has been fulfilled. If, after this, the winning side advances steadily, there is nothing to prevent it from occupying the enemy's country. Since movement is a temporal function, we must examine the time element.

The time of campaign and the time of winter-quartering were sharply distinct in that era. The principal reason for doing so was that supplying of larger field armies was practically impossible between autumn and spring. Mass transportation on poor roads was virtually out of the question in that season. Bread supply of advancing armies could not be guaranted for the same reason. And the fodder supply of horses could not be managed either, because, as we have seen, the winter reserves of the population were so scanty that they had great difficulties in wintering their own animals, let alone maintaining the animals of an army. Transportation of fodder was even less feasible than that of bread, since the quantities required were four to five times larger than those of bread.

But not even the six months suitable for a campaign could be utilized by an army for uninterrupted advance. This was because the pitched battle, which hopefully would end in victory, and which was regarded as the purpose of such an advance, could be fought only in exceptional cases immediately after the beginning of the campaign, owing to the difficulties we have outlined in connection with the starting of such a battle. It usually took several months until the situation was ripe for a battle. Thus it was not more than three to four months, i.e. hundred days on the average, that were available for continuous advance. But even from these hundred days we must deduct the time spent on foraging, issue of bread, rest, and the pushing forward of magazines. If we calculate the issuence of bread and foraging every four days, we have used up 25 days of the time available for advancing. Resting every six days takes an additional 16 days. Thus there are only 59 marching-days left. If we calculate that magazines are pushed forward every 6 to 8 days, and if we calculate — cautiously — 4 days for one relocation, we have to deduct an even 30 days from the number of marching-days. Hence all that is left for advancing is a mere 30 days. Counting a 20-kilometre march for each day, the army could cover no more than 600 kilometres. This was not enough at that time for any belligerent state to occupy the country of any of its opponents, but was too much for covering the supply line extended to an immense length. To be sure, there were no such marching performances in any of the theatres of war in Central or West Europe. Marlborough's 1704 march from the lower Rhine to the Danube was considered a very great achievement at the time, and created a sensation: Yet the distance covered only amounted to 450 kilometres, lay entirely on Allied territory, the troops were provisioned at relay stations, and no interference by the enemy had to be anticipated. Another famous march of the same year was the advance of the French army from Strasbourg to Bavaria. Yet the marching distance was only 200—250 kilometres, and the route led for the most part through territories under French and Bavarian control. In 1707, at the time of the Toulon expedition of the Allies, the troops advanced only on enemy territory, but the distance was not more than 150 kilometres, and food was supplied to the army on most of the route by the English Mediterranean fleet. To sum up, occupation of the enemy's country was thwarted by lack of time.

Limits of space, resulting from the requirements of food supply, also cast difficulties in the way of advance. The free movements of armies were obstructed by dependence upon magazines first of all. As we have seen, to move further away from magazines than 6—8 marching-days was impossible. Greater freedom of movement was possible only by using waterways, but in this was the direction of the current determined the direction of operations from the outset. Operations were also restricted in space by the scarcity and poor condition of roads. And the geographical features of a theatre of war, terrains difficulties, restricted movement to a much greater degree than in our days; relatively low mountains, forests and rivers often became impassable barriers for clumsy carts carrying food and lots of other war material.

Military operations were also greatly restricted in space by fortresses. Those impaired offensive movement by blocking the routes of advance. The question may be raised: why did the attacker not bypass the fortress? The additional distance he would have to frame travelled to out of the range of the fortresses guns would have amounted to a few kilometres only. Yet the matter was not as simple as that. For if the army detoured around the fortress, and thus left the latter on its rear, it would have run the risk of allowing the enemy to cut off its supplies. But fortresses also restricted offensive advance by covering the magazines which had to be established for supplying major campaigns of an offensive nature. Thus the attacking side was restricted in its movements not only by the enemy, but also by his fortresses. In view of the fact that the delaying power of fortified positions was so great at that time, the problems of supply must have played a fairly considerable role. This, then, was the reason why the wars of that age became "frontier wars" as described by Puységur, and why they did not as a rule move away from the area of fortresses and fortification networks built along the national boundaries of the belligerent parties. It was these conquests in limited areas that caught the attention of researchers of military history, and it was on this basis that they formed their opinion: the wars of that age were waged for petty aims, only for the conquest of a few frontier provinces.

Limits of time and space, as well as obstacles to fighting and exploiting the decisive battle, made it impossible for campaigns to end decisively. Even campaigns which started with the prospect of success, and had the promise of greatest accomplishments, had to be discontinued in autumn when the campaign season was over. Consequently the achievments of a campaign time were of no great use, for they did not lead to the annihilation of the enemy's armed forces, nor to the occupation of his country; and to carry over profits to the next year, as in boǫk-keeping was of course impossible. During the inevitable winter rest the enemy recovered from the losses suffered, was able to regather his strength, and could open the campaign year in spring with a well-equipped, combat-worthy army that had overcome the crisis of morale resulting from defeat. We need merely recall what tremendous victories the allies gained in the battles of Blenheim-Höchstaedt, Ramillies, Turin and Oudenarde in the War of the Spanish Succession: And what was the result? The next spring they were confronted with a French army that was even stronger than in the preceding year. Thus it is evident that it was not possible to force a decision during one campaign, and it took several campaigns to conclude a war. But in this way the wars became terribly protracted. This, in turn, meant that the theatres of war — whose constant character has been discussed — because increasingly exhausted, the problems of supporting the army proliferated, operational possibilities were further restricted — in short, the crisis of strategy became even more serious. At the same time protraction of the war thoroughly exhausted the belligerent states, administration had to shoulder growing burdens, and all this impaired the supply of armies and, as a result, strategy, too. But this will be discussed in connection with our second approach to the examination of the consequences of provisioning difficulties.

All this combined had the effect of making Clausewitz's third criterion, i.e. crushing the enemy's will to resist, hard, to fulfil. Since the most efficient way to do this, i.e. to annihilate the enemy's armed forces, was seldom feasible, and to occupy the enemy's country was even less possible, the idea of crushing the enemy's will to resist indirectly, i.e. through attrition was increasingly accepted. And the protraction of wars offered very good opportunities for accomplishing this. The war aim now was to avoid decision more than before, to protract the war even more, to exhaust the enemy as much possible, and to put him in a position where he had no choice but to sue for peace.

In summary, with respect to leadership in the strict sense, provisioning difficulties reduced strategic possibilities of forcing a decision; and the more the possibility of a decision was reduced, the more the war became protracted. This, in turn, increased the difficulties of provisioning, and the crisis of strategy became ever more serious as a consequence.

*Chain reaction and the failure of conventional means of State Administration.* The initial trouble, the inadequacy of strategy arising from difficulties of provisioning, was followed by many other troubles. They all began to interact, they amplified one another, and in combination made the basic problems can worse. As we have said, the circumstance that the armies were not able to advance quickly and continuously meant that they were a nuisance to certain regions for longer periods, and so it happened that even richer and more densely populated regions were not able to support an army. All this resulted in further restriction of the dimensions of campaigning in the manner we have described, and led to the protraction of wars. The protraction of a war gave rise to financial difficulties and to a general economic depression, which decreased the efficiency of state administration — which was not too great anyway — and made procurement of means for conducting the war extremely difficult. Thus a chain reaction was set off, which began with provisioning, spread through the sectors of strategy, state finances and state administration, was amplified by intermediate factors, then returned to the causal element where it received new impulse, and eventually reverberated on an ever increasing scale in the entire field of state and economic life.

Let us now depart from the realm of metaphors and examine in a concrete manner what effects provisioning difficulties had upon state administration and finances. At the time of the Thirty Years' War, states procured food for their armies through forced contributions or by means of state purchases. In the period we are considering, both methods failed. The essence of the state purchasing system was that the government levied taxes in money, and used these sums for buying grain and fodder through its agents. The advantage of this system was that it freed the state apparatus, but mainly the armies, from the considerable trouble of amassing food, made it possible to effect purchases in accordance with market trends at the most suitable places and times, which facilitated a more even distribution of burdens and a better reserve economy; finally — and this was the most important advantage — food thus entered the economic process of trade in the form of a commodity, speeded up the circulation of money, ameliorated monetary difficulties arising from the shortage of means of payment — which was more or less a general feature of the age — and had an animating effect on economic life as a rule. Zrínyi thought very highly of this method, regarded it as the most expedient from the military, humane and economic points of view. Writing of this, he forthwith replies to the possible objection that to procure food with government money is very expensive. First — he says — expensive or not, the soldier "must eat"; second, there is nothing more expensive than when the soldier himself "carries away bread from the poor man's house . . . and makes a bargain with the poor man war-axe in hand". However inexpensive it might seem if the state did not actually pay with money for food, "our country's money is thoroughly wasted if the poor man leads a wretched life and lingers in misery". And from the economic point of view he considers it definitely useful if the money of the state reaches the artisans and peasants enabling them to pay taxes, because in this way the money spent on food flows back to the treasury. He concludes his train of thoughts as follows: "Thus they can pay taxes again, and all the money returns to the republic, whence it will again flow out in the future. And this circulation is so necessary and so useful to our country in every respect that it is easier to admire its great usefulness than to describe it."[92]

All the same, this procedure could no longer lead to success in the period under survey. Owing to the numerical increase of effective forces, it was not the 26—48 000 men of the "armada" envisaged by Zrínyi that had to be provided for; it was the 200—500 000 fighters of an army. And even if the governments, struggling with permanent financial difficulties, had actually the money required for purchasing those immense quantities of food — and this money was available to them in very rare cases only — the utterly corrupt civil servants and agents, inexperienced in business life, ignorant of market

[92] *Zrínyi Miklós hadtudományi munkái.* p. 120. — The recognition of the importance of the circulation speed of money and beyond that the recognition of the fact that the very riches of the state lies in the welfare of the subjects, and the projection of all this from the section of military supply into the whole economic and social life of the state is unique in contemporary military science.

and credit conditions and working with clumsy, bureaucratic methods, would not have been able to cope with this task. So it happened that the food that got to the soldiers was expensive, tardy and of poor quality, and in many a case it did not get there at all. Austrian food supply was then the poorest of all beyond any question, and this was mainly so because food was procured by state purchases as a rule.[93]

Another method of food procurement at the time of the Thirty Years' War was contribution, i.e. food tax levied in kind. In the period we are considering this method was no longer suitable to secure food to the armies; to support numerically increased armies, immense amounts of food were required, and even in the cases which it was possible to collect them on the basis of taxation in kind, sending them from the home-country to the fighting armies met with tremendous difficulties of transportation. This was the case especially in Austria, where the central power was weak, the administration was disorderly; it often happened that food gathered in certain provinces could not be sent to the theatre of war. Generally speaking, the tasks involved in the levying, collecting and transporting large quantities of food were well beyond the means and potentialities of the administration of that time. Owing to the unreliability of contemporary "statistical work", the governments were misinformed about the actual situation. The civil servants were corrupt. Taxes levied in kind burdened the various regions disproportionately. All this led to very poor management of the country's resources.[94] The problematic character of contribution in kind is best demonstrated by Rákóczi's War of Independence. As we know, food for the Kuruts army was taken for the most part from the tax in kind paid by the serfs. Quite apart from the fact that smooth supply could no longer be ensured in this way during the second half

[93] To prove our statement that the Austrian system of supply was the poorest in Europe at that time, we are citing four experts. Marlborough wrote from Bavaria in 1704: "Our greatest difficulty is that of making our bread follows us; for the troops that I have the honour to command, cannot subsist without it, and the Germans (I.e. the Austrian and Imperial troops — G.P.) *that are used to starve* (my italics — G. P.) cannot advance without us." Cit by G. M. TREVELYAN: *England under Queen Anne.* I—III. London, 1930—1934. I. pp. 366—367. — The Marshal Villars wrote from Strassbourg in 1705: "Et à la dureté que nous voyons aux ennemis sur toutes les pertes, il semble qu'ils comptent rien les hommes et les chevaux. Leurs troupes manquent souvent de pain, sont très mal payées, et rien n'étonne tant nos ennemis que de voir toutes celles de votre majesté depuis le premier officier jusqu'au dernier soldat, entièrement payées, le pain de munition régiulier, et les équipages de vivres et d'artillerie plus complets et en meilleur état qu'ils n'ont jamais été." Cit. by DE VAULT—PELET, op. cit. V. p. 545. — The Marshal Vendôme wrote from Italy in 1702, that this task was much aggravated by the fact that he had to take a much greater care to the supply, than his adversaries: "... car je serais fâché d'avoir à disputer de subsistance avec une armée aussi *gourmande* que celle-ci, contre une aussi *sobre* que la leur." (my italics — G. P.) — Ibid. II pp. 218—219. — Let us see Eugene of Savoy himself; in 1710 he wrote from Flanders: "Wann die Auxiliares wie die Kaiserlichen Hunger zu leiden gewohnt wären, würde ich mich des Brodes halber so sehr nixht (sic!) sorgen ... aber ... die Auxiliares wann das Brod nur einen Tag ausbleiben würde, keinen Schritt marschieren würden." *Feldzüge*, VIII. Suppl. H. p. 212

[94] Dupré d'Aulnay referred to several abuses in the collecting of the tax in kind. DUPRÉ D'AULNAY, op. cit. XI. p. 1.

of the war, there are indications that this system made the financial crisis even more serious by withdrawing from trade a great volume of commodities which exceeded in value and quantity all others, and reduced the country practically to the standards of a natural exchange and barter economy.[95]

*The role of contractors in provisioning.* Since contribution and procurement through state purchases were insufficient owing to the great quantities of food involved and the inadequacies of the administration apparatus, the governments turned to contractors. A contractor had all the qualities that civil servants lacked; he was quick and versatile, was familiar with market conditions and the secrets of business life, had money, and, still more important, enjoyed practically unlimited credit through connections often extending over entire Europe. A contractor was able to conjure up with his money all the hidden reserves which people were concealing from the abuses of state agents. Co-operation of the contractor, of the army-broker in the maintenance of armies was not a new feature. What was new here was the form of this co-operation. Up to that time, businessmen were only accustomed to put credit at the disposal of a government; but now the contractor became directly involved with the working of the supply apparatus, was managing it on a quasi lease basis. This had doubtlessly harmful consequences, but not those so often mentioned by the contemporaries and then by historians, namely that the contractors defrauded the state and pocketed tremendous profits. These accusations were basically exaggerated and arose from the hatred of contractors feel by the people of that time. The medieval attitude, according to which "Homo mercator vix aut numquam potest Deo placere", was still alive, and people condemned the methods of the capitalist businessman who made profits well above the "iustum pretium". In addition to these objections of ethical origin, fundamental class differences were also instrumental in giving rise to hatred of contractors. It was the jealousy of the feudal aristocracy, interested in business life, toward businessmen of middle-class extraction. But even the state apparatus was hostile to contractors, for their activities put an end to state purchases by which the officials had profited so much. Be that as it may, however many supposed or real, justified or unjustified, arguments were voiced against contractors, the governments kept turning to them, because whenever a contractor undertook delivery, the soldiers would surely

[95] The question is very complicated, and its enlightenment would be of fundamental importance. At any rate there are indications that the tax in kind, which Rákóczi insisted on for social and political reasons, had the contrary effect, for it aggravated the situation of the serfs. Of course, the question, how the fundamental difficulty, the lack of the means of payment, was to be cured, is hard to be answered. The same evils manifested themselves all over Europe in this age, and England was the only country that could overcome them by the help of the banknotes issued by the Bank of England. It is a fact, however, that in order to set the much discussed "copper coin circulation" in motion, goods were needed first of all. which, as a rule always the best remedy against all inflational trouble. Well, the tax in kind took the very merchandises out of circulation.

receive their food, while in case of contribution or state procurement just the opposite happened as a rule.[96]

It was not only because of the inadequate functioning of the state organs that contractors had to be called in; there were financial reasons, too. Involved in permanent financial difficulties, governments were often unable to raise the considerable sums required for procuring food. The costs of army provisioning often amounted to 10—20 per cent of all state revenues, and to 25—50 per cent of war expenses.[97] Loans granted by a contractor, or deliveries effected on terms of subsequent payment were a tremendous relief to the government; moreover, this was sometimes the only possibility of continuing the war. No wonder that, in such circumstances, the contractor exploited the straits of the government and charged prices for his performance far above normal prices.[98] But this attitude was to a certain extent intended as a defence, a guarantee for the contractor, who had to deal with governments that were utterly irresponsible with respect to finances, fulfilled their obligations to pay reluctantly, and often cancelled the contractors' rightful claims with a stroke of the pen. Innumerable are the contractors who went bankrupt in their transactions with the governments of that time.

Even if we regard the co-operation of contractors in the provisioning of armies as a positive, and, moreover, a necessary activity, it cannot be denied that this co-operation had also harmful consequences. Through his tremendous services rendered to the state, the contractor claimed, and acquired, the right of exerting an influence upon the conduct of war. This was practically manifest in the fact that the contractor was allowed to attend councils of war and to place a veto on operational plans that jeopardized his business interests directly.

[96] In 1697 the Imperial Court made contract with the contractors Oppenheimer and Wertheimer in order to cover the requirement of the Army in Hungary. Kollonich arranged the collection of the contract, in the firm belief of saving at least a half million gulden by means of state purchase. In five days the impracticability of this plan came to light; the troops demanded food, therefore the Court was forced to turn again to the contractors. These, on the other hand, demanded considerably higher prices this time, referring to the fact that Kollonich's action caused serious damage to them. The Treasury had no choice but to accept the new conditions and it was only a poor consolation for them, that they complained to the Emperor against Kollonich for his unauthorized interference. — *Feldzüge* I. p. 41.

[97] According to our calculation which cannot be discussed in detail here, the yearly costs of food of the French Army amounted to 24 millions livres, when in the 1700s the entire national income was 160 millions livres. This would mean 15%, but the price of cereals grew by about 80%, between 1705—1711, thus the share became 25%. In Austria the military budget amounted to 6.4 million gulden in 1706, of which the food cost 2 millions. — *Feldzüge* VIII. p. 57. — In Rákóczi's army the costs of food amounted to 30—40% of the entire military budget. See J. TAKÁCS: *Közteherviselés II. Rákóczi Ferenc korában* (General Sharing in Taxation at the time of Ferenc Rákóczi II.). Zalaegerszeg 1941. pp. 9 ff. — In Zrínyi's calculation the cost of food amounted to 10% of the war expenditure. — Op. cit. pp. 118—120.

[98] In France in 1709 the contractors sold a bag of grain for 50 livres to the state, when its market price was only 30 livres. AUDOUIN, op. cit. I. p. 388. — In 1703 in South Germany a quintal of flour cost 2.8 gulden, 50 pound oats cost 1.3 guldens, and the contractors sold them for 6 and 2.5 guldens respectively. Oppenheimer demanded 67 guldens for a pair of oxen in 1701, when their market price was only 40—50 guldens. — *Feldzüge* V. p. 109., III. pp. 69—70.

So it happened that at a time when there was an urgent need for disposing of the various competencies active in matters of supply and strategy, and for the unification of logistics, there emerged a new competence, that of the contractor.[99]

*Final conclusion.* We have made but a cursory survey of the effects of provisioning difficulties as they rebounded through state administration and finances. Numerous aspects of this problem would deserve thorough investigation, because this might enrich with numerous data and viewpoints the image we have formed of the process of absolutistic centralization, and could elucidate many details of the process of initial capital accumulation through the examination of the contractor's role. In any case, what has been said here may perhaps give an idea of the extraordinary interest and importance of this problem.

We must here be content with emphasizing that our chain reaction problem complex, arising from provisioning difficulties, penetrated into the various sectors of state life and constituted an incessant alternating process which, reverting to the causal element, intensified the latter; and, in the last analysis, exaggerated the seriousness of the crisis. For if the efficiency of strategy was already impaired by the initial trouble, difficulties arising from the low standards of food supply and agrarian techniques, low population density and the backwardness of transportation methods, how much greater was the gulf between the political aims of war and the strategy destined to realize them since the inadequacy of state administration and financial difficulties themselves were instrumental in widening this gap. The edge of the "flashing sword of reprisal", was blunted by all this, and the working of war machineries that replaced politics was rendered increasingly difficult — in short: the crisis of strategy was thus intensified!

Г. ПЕРЬЕШ

## Снабжение армии продуктами питания, логистика и стратегия во второй половине XVII века

Резюме

Во второй половине XVII. в. укрепление абсолютистских монархий влекло за собой повышение эффективности государственной администрации, вследствие чего оказалось возможным вооружать и доставить на поле сражения значительно больше количество людей, нежели в предыдущие времена. Оперирующие на отдельных участках войны армии, значит, количественно значительно возрасли, однако, без того, чтобы экономсческие возможности снабжения и средства связи улучшились бы. Все это повлияло на стратегиче-

[99] As for the contractors, for further references see: M. Weber: *Wirtschaftsgeschichte.* Leipzig 1924. — Gebhardt: *Handbuch der deutschen Geschichte.* Bd. 2. Stuttgart 1955. — The works of Dupré d'Aulnay and of Audouin, as well as the pertinent entries of the *Dictionnaire Militaire.*

ское руководство весьма отрицательно и принуждало к тому, чтобы оно согласовало свои цели и методы с действительными возможностями армии, прежде всего с возможностями снабжения продуктами питания: полководец не мог сделать то, что было бы наиболее правильным с точки зрения тактики и стратегии, а лишь то, что позволяло снабжение армии прежде всего продуктами питания.

В первой части статьи автор показывает результаты исторической статистики относительно производства и потребления продуктов питания того времени. Данные указывают на то, что теоретически было произведено столько пшеницы и ячменя — несмотря на небольшую цифру плотности населения, которое было бы довольно для снабжения армии в 60 000—80 000 человек, однако на деле нельзя было обеспечить должным образом снабжение, так как находившиеся вблизи полей сражения продукты питания не были в таком виде, в каком можно было бы употреблять в силу плохого обстояния собрания, молотьбы, приготовления, перевоза продуктов.

Поэтому стало необходимым создавать склады проуктов питания, которые так значительно приковывали возможность передвижения войск и решения полководцев. На этом пункте автор вступает в дискуссию с тем мнением, будто полководцы старого режима всячески цеплялись за склады просто по привычке; представители подобных взглядов не видят детерминацию данного вида снабжения армии продуктами питания экономическими и общественными моментами.

В дальнейшем автор ищет ответ на вопрос о том, каким образом повлияли на стратегию и логистику меры по снабжению армии продуктами питания. Вопрос имеет три аспекта. Один — это доставание самого продукта питания. Другой — вопрос организации, состоявшийся в том, что не было специалистов логистики вплоть до тех пор, пока позиция «марешал до ложи» не была введена в армию. А что касается третьего аспекта, тут вопрос заключался в том, чтобы приспособить нужды армии как «завода» — потребителя к «заводу молотьбы, выпечения, прикармливания и доставщика», что оказалось не малой задачей.

Нечего удивляться, что стратегия в данный период пришла в стадию упадка. Автор показывает на основе переписки государственных деятелей и полководцев кризис и его отражение в сознании людей. Кризис этот по сути состоял в том, что стратегия не в силах была отвечать своим задачам и не могла претворить в жизнь свои решения. В самом деле конец войнам данного периода положили не оружия, а взаимное истощение. Кризис углублялся тем, что государства могли отвечать требованиям войны все в меньшей степени в смысле финансов и организации и поэтому пришлось сдавать в аренду отдельным предпринимателям задачи по снабжению, а это привело к тому, что предприниматели ставили на первое место свои интересы даже в ущерб интересам армии.

Импотенция стратегии, вызванная трудностями снабжения продуктами питания, вызвала в виде как бы цепной реакции такое влияние в государственной жизни, в ее отдельных секторах, где эти влияния получили новый стимул и укрепившись повлияли еще более отрицательно на исходную точку — на кризис стратегии.

# [5]

# Social Militarization in Eighteenth-Century Germany*

Peter H. Wilson (*University of Sunderland*)

Grand concepts have long been a forte of German historians. In particular, writing on the early modern period has been especially rich in conceptualization, with such terms as 'confessionalization', 'social disciplining' and 'territorialization' long dominating the debates. A serious omission from these discussions has been the idea of 'social militarization'. This is only now coming under serious review, despite the fact that the arguments implicit within it have profoundly shaped the general view of German history well beyond the eighteenth century. The event of the recent publication of a fine English translation of the original work on this idea seems an appropriate opportunity to reflect on its historiographical impact and reconsider its value as an analytical tool in the light of previously neglected evidence.[1] As I intend to show, the original concept lacks firm substance and distorts our understanding of the relationship between army, society, politics and economics by overemphasizing certain factors, most notably Prussia's alleged uniqueness and that of its system of military recruitment in particular.

The term 'social militarization' was coined by Otto Büsch in his 1953 doctoral thesis to describe the process by which army and society became interrelated in eighteenth-century Prussia. The importance of the army to Prussia's emergence as a European power had, of course, long been recognized, even glorified, within German historiography, as had its impact on social and political institutions. The novelty of Büsch's approach was his argument that the nature of Prussia's military expansion strengthened the socio-economic position of the landowning Junkers and assisted their political survival into the nineteenth century. The key mechanism in this process was the famous canton system (*Kantonverfassung*) of recruitment, introduced by 1733 and retained,

* I would like to thank Chris Storrs and the participants in the History Seminar at Dundee University (Nov. 1997), where I presented an earlier version of this paper, along with three anonymous readers who commented on the first draft, and also David Moon and Andy Nicol for stimulating discussions on Russian peasants and conscription.

[1] Otto Büsch, *Militärsystem und Sozialleben im alten Preußen 1713–1807. Die Anfänge der sozialen Militarisierung der preußisch-deutschen Gesellschaft* (Berlin, 1962); translated by J. G. Gagliardo as *Military System and Social Life in Old Regime Prussia 1713–1807. The Beginnings of the Social Militarization of Prusso-German Society* (Atlantic Highlands, N.J., 1997). What purports to be the introduction to the English edition is in fact a translation of the introduction to the 1981 German edition. See note 4 below.

with modifications, until 1814. By tailoring the state's demand for manpower to the Junkers' labour requirements, the canton system encouraged a convergence of interest between monarchy and aristocracy with the result that militarization and serfdom became mutually reinforcing systems.

This interpretation met with a hostile reaction in Germany, which delayed its publication by nearly a decade despite the force and sophistication of its argumentation. By indicating that later German problems might have their origins as early as the eighteenth century, Büsch was decidedly out of step with the historical establishment of the 1950s. Most sided with Gerhard Ritter whose four-volume work, *Staatskunst und Kriegshandwerk*, regarded German militarism as a twentieth-century aberration associated with a few dangerous individuals like Ludendorff and Hitler.[2] It is highly significant for the later reception of Büsch's thesis that when the debate opened up in the 1960s, it did so in the light of research on the post-1871 regime in Germany. Like Büsch's, Fritz Fischer's hugely influential book on Germany's aims in the First World War related militarism not to Ritter's sphere of high politics, but to broader socio-economic structures.[3] The subsequent controversy in the Federal Republic produced a rich variety of further studies, critical of the conservative view of Prussian history. However, with the partial exception of the work of Hanna Schissler, to be discussed below, these did not move the timeframe back to the area originally covered by Büsch. Matters were not improved by Büsch's own decision to concentrate on later Prussian history, leaving his original thesis unrevised, despite an ostensible 'second edition' in 1981.[4]

Instead, perhaps rather understandably, his interpretation was simply woven into the broader account of what was now becoming the *Sonderweg*, or belief that German development had deviated from a liberal western European norm, and followed its own 'special path' of aristocratic reaction and belligerent militarism. Exemplifying this trend is Hans-Ulrich Wehler's influential *Gesellschaftsgeschichte* which, in addition to offering by far the most sophisticated and careful account of German development in these terms, endorses social militarization almost without reference to other views.[5]

Büsch's concept also struck a chord with historians elsewhere who produced work similar to, or incorporating, the social militarization thesis. Though written without reference to Büsch, Gordon Craig's study of the Prussian army

[2] G. Ritter, *Staatskunst und Kriegshandwerk. Das Problem des 'Militarismus' in Deutschland* (4 vols., Munich, 1954–63). Ritter's few critics also concentrated on the later period: W. Sauer, 'Die politische Geschichte der deutschen Armee und das Problem des Militarismus', *Politische Vierteljahresschrift*, 6 (1965), 341–53. For an analysis of the debate, see V. Berghahn, *Militarism. The History of an International Debate 1861–1979* (Leamington Spa, 1981).

[3] Fritz Fischer, *Griff nach der Weltmacht* (Düsseldorf, 1961). The controversy is summarized in G. Martel (ed.), *Modern Germany Reconsidered 1870–1945* (London, 1992).

[4] Published under the original title in Frankfurt. Apart from a new introduction and bibliographical appendix, it is identical to the first edition. All future references are to the 1981 edition.

[5] H.-U. Wehler, *Deutsche Gesellschaftsgeschichte* (3 vols., Munich, 1987–95), vol. I, pp. 244–54. For the reception of this work, see the extended reviews in *German History*, 9 (1991), 211–30 and *German Historical Institute Bulletin*, 28 (1996), 27–34.

emphasized that its political influence stemmed from the integration of both Junkers and peasants into the monarchy's military system.[6] Subsequent Anglophone writers have drawn, largely uncritically, on both Büsch and Craig for their studies of the German army in its wider context. Like much of the work produced within the Federal Republic, these British and American works rarely returned to original sources for verification of the period prior to 1806 and almost always interpret the whole of German military development through the Prussian experience.[7] A possible explanation for this trend may be found in the work of German émigré historians working in the United States, whose conclusions on old-regime Prussia often seem to confirm Büsch's interpretation.[8] A similarly regrettable reluctance to return to the archives often characterized those historians in the German Democratic Republic who examined the social and political position of the Prussian army. Marxist historiography did raise some important conceptual challenges to elements of the social militarization thesis, as we shall see later. However, the general tendency was to criticize Büsch simply as a representative of a 'bourgeois' viewpoint, without actually saying anything very different.[9]

Now an established part of the historical mainstream,[10] social militarization is only just coming under critical review from a new generation of scholars in the reunified Germany. A welcome aspect of this reappraisal is its basis in fresh archival research, testing stale clichés and opening up new issues. Mention should be made here both of Hartmut Harnisch's work on landlord–peasant relations in Brandenburg and of Jürgen Kloosterhuis's examination of the canton system in Prussian Westphalia.[11] It is my intention to take this debate for-

[6] G. A. Craig, *The Politics of the Prussian Army 1640–1945* (London, 1955).

[7] For a variety of perspectives with similar conclusions see M. Kitchen, *A Military History of Germany* (London, 1975); J. M. Kolkey, *Germany on the March. A Reinterpretation of War and Domestic Politics* (Lanham, Mass., 1995); B. M. Downing, *The Military Revolution and Political Change in Early Modern Europe* (Princeton, N.J., 1991); E. Willems, *A Way of Life and Death. Three Centuries of Prussian–German Militarism. An Anthropological Approach* (Nashville, Tenn., 1986).

[8] See especially H. Rosenberg, *Bureaucracy, Autocracy and Aristocracy. The Prussian Experience 1660–1815* (Cambridge, Mass., 1966). Also important in this context is E. Kehr, *Der Primat der Innenpolitik* (Berlin, 1970) which influenced both the émigré historians and the new generation writing in the 1960s.

[9] H. Schnitter, 'Zur Funktion und Stellung des Heeres im feudalabsolutistischen Militarismus in Brandenburg-Preußen (17./18. Jahrhundert)', *Zeitschrift für Militärgeschichte*, 10 (1971), 306–14; H. Schnitter and T. Schmidt, *Absolutismus und Heer* (Berlin, 1987); P. Bachmann and K. Zeisler, *Der deutsche Militarismus* (2nd edition, Cologne, 1986); I. Mittenzwei and E. Herzfeld, *Brandenburg-Preußen 1648–1789* (Cologne, 1987), esp. pp. 197–225.

[10] For recent examples see S. Ogilvie and B. Scribner (eds.), *Germany. A New Social and Economic History* (2 vols., London, 1996), vol. II, pp. 254–5 and M. Erbe, *Deutsche Geschichte 1713–1790* (Stuttgart, 1985), pp. 155–6.

[11] For the most accessible introductions to their work see H. Harnisch, 'Preußisches Kantonsystem und ländliche Gesellschaft' and J. Kloosterhuis, 'Zwischen Aufruhr und Akzeptanz: Zur Ausformung und Einbettung des Kantonsystems in die Wirtschafts- und Sozialstrukturen des preußischen Westfalen', both in B. R. Kroener and R. Pröve (eds.), *Krieg und Frieden. Militär und Gesellschaft in der Frühen Neuzeit* (Paderborn, 1996). Further discussion, together with documents, is provided by J. Kloosterhuis (ed.), *Bauern, Bürger und Soldaten. Quellen zur*

ward in two ways. On the one hand, the once important but now neglected question of the canton system's origins needs to be addressed, including not only its complex relationship to both militia recruitment and voluntary enlistment, but also the deceptively simple issue of why it was introduced. On the other, the focus needs to be widened beyond Prussia to include a comparison with other German territories and the major European powers. First, however, Büsch's original concept needs to be examined in detail, beginning with the canton system itself. Only then can we reappraise the key elements of social militarization and evaluate its utility as an analytical concept.

## I: The Canton System

What has come to be known as the canton system was a form of limited conscription introduced by King Frederick William I into Brandenburg, Pomerania and East Prussia between 1713 and 1733.[12] It was extended to the Westphalian provinces in 1735 and introduced into newly conquered Silesia eight years later by Frederick the Great. West Prussia, acquired in the First Partition of Poland 1772, was also incorporated, as were Ansbach and Bayreuth four years after their reversion to the Prussian Hohenzollern line in 1792. However, the system was never uniform nor comprehensive in its application. Some regions, particularly industrial and urban areas, were exempt, as were certain individuals and social groups. These exemptions were widened steadily after 1733, while political sensitivity prevented the full extension of the cantons to East Frisia, acquired in 1744, and more significantly, to the additional Polish territory annexed after 1793.

These variations aside, the basic application remained the same. Each regiment was assigned a recruiting area (canton), subdivided (until 1763) into company districts. In a practice known as enrolling (*Enrollierung*), lists were kept of all eligible men from the age of religious confirmation. The regiment took an annual quota from the list to keep it up to strength and, subject to royal sanction, could draw additional recruits in the event of heavy casualties. Company commanders were in charge of selection until 1763/4, when this was entrusted to regional civilian committees under relatively indirect monitoring

*Sozialisation des Militärsystems im preußischen Westfalen 1713–1803* (Veröffentlichungen der staatlichen Archiven des Landes Nordrhein-Westfalen, Reihe C) (2 vols., Münster, 1992). Other examples of these new approaches can be found in R. Pröve (ed.), *Klio in Uniform? Probleme und Perspektiven einer modernen Militärgeschichte der Frühen Neuzeit* (Cologne and Vienna, 1997).

[12] The most comprehensive overview in English is provided by W. O. Shanahan, *Prussian Military Reforms 1786–1813* (New York, 1945), pp. 35–60. See also C. v. Jany, 'Die Kantonverfassung Friedrich Wilhelms I', *Forschungen zur Brandenburgischen und Preußischen Geschichte*, 38 (1926), 225–72 and the discussions by contemporaries: v. Arnim, *Über die Canton-Verfassung in den preußichen Staaten* (Frankfurt and Leipzig, 1788); F. F. Wilke, *Handbuch zur Kenntnis des preußischen Cantonwesens* (Stettin, 1802), and J. W. v. Archenholz, *Gemälde der preußischen Armee vor und in dem Siebenjährigen Kriege* (Berlin, 1791), esp. pp. 10–11, 29–30.

by the army's provincial 'general inspectors'. Conscripts generally received between twelve and eighteen months' basic training before being granted leave (furloughed, or *beurlaubt*) for about ten months of each subsequent year. During this time they worked in the civilian economy, but remained under partial military jurisdiction and were obliged to report for the annual exercise period, as well as any wartime mobilization. Service was for an unspecified term until 1792 when a limit of twenty years was stipulated. In practice, men were often discharged earlier, especially if they were considered too short by their officers. Approximately half the army continued to be recruited from volunteers, often, but not necessarily, foreigners.[13] Though the army preferred men to sign on for unlimited contracts, many were recruited on fixed, or renewable agreements (*Capitulationen*). They served throughout the year, but already under Frederick William a sizeable proportion were granted exemption from watch duty to work in the civil economy of their garrison town as *Freiwächter*.

## II: The Militarization of State and Society

It is the alleged consequences rather than the mechanics of this system that have caused the controversy. Many historians point to a three-fold militarization of state and society. First, the 'precedence of the military over the civil authority ... [became] ... a state maxim' as society and economy were geared towards supporting a disproportionately large army.[14] A frequently cited example of this is the extension of military jurisdiction into previously civilian spheres such as the power of the army to regulate civil marriages.[15]

A second aspect is the diffusion of military ways of thinking and acting throughout Prussian society. The high proportion of serving and former personnel within the population is believed to have encouraged the general adoption, or at least acceptance, of military attitudes, behaviour and, in particular, patterns of subordination and deference to authority. Labelled 'militarism', this mentality is generally judged as passive, in the sense that the bulk of the population came to accept the heavy military burdens without necessarily supporting or approving of them. The chief beneficiaries of this system, the Junkers, are identified as the true, active militarists.[16]

Thirdly, Prussia and its inhabitants became outwardly more military in

[13] The term *Ausländer* was applied by the Prussian army to any recruit drawn from outside a unit's canton. Up to half the so-called 'foreigners' could be from other Hohenzollern lands and most of the rest were recruited from within the Reich. For non-German recruits see E. Lukinich, 'Preußische Werbung in Ungarn 1722–40', *Ungarische Jahrbücher*, 6 (1927), 20–38.

[14] A. Corvisier, *Armies and Societies in Europe 1494–1789* (Bloomington, Ind., 1976), p. 81. See also pp. 58–9.

[15] These powers were eased after 1743.

[16] For examples of this view: Downing, *Military Revolution*, pp. 98–101; Willems, *Way of Life and Death*, pp. 19–48; A. H. F. Vagts, *A History of Militarism* (London, 1938), esp. pp. 63–7. For contemporary evidence of how retired officers and men still thought and acted like soldiers see C. Duffy, *The Military Experience in the Age of Reason* (London, 1987), p. 310.

appearance, heightening the contemporary perception of the country as an armed camp. Not only were soldiers a highly visible element of virtually every town, but the practice of enrolling involved the numbering of peasant homes by the military authorities. Furloughed soldiers were obliged to wear military insignia and Frederick William's practice of issuing new uniforms each year fuelled a second-hand market in surplus clothing with the result that the blue army coat became 'normal male costume' (*Volkestracht der Männer*).[17]

## III: Socio-Political Reaction

Militarization is regarded in the longer term as promoting the forces of German socio-political reaction by extending what is known as the Historic Compromise between the Hohenzollern dynasty and the feudal aristocracy. The first agreement in this long process was the 1653 Recess of the Brandenburg territorial estates (*Stände*). In return for crown support for their social pre-eminence and economic predominance, the Junker-dominated estates relinquished political power to the emergent absolutist state.[18] Though the opposition of many Junkers to the growth of a standing army is widely recognized, the 'triple alliance between monarch, officer corps, and Junker nobility' (Willems) was allegedly consolidated by the canton system.

The limited conscription introduced by Frederick William enabled the army to meet its manpower requirements without seriously disrupting the agrarian economy. Not only were conscripts discharged back into the domain or estate economy (*Gutswirtschaft*), but the Junkers benefited from being encouraged to monopolize the officer corps. Firstly, this resulted in a symbiosis of company commander and estate owner so the serf–conscript was 'often literally' under the authority of the same individual.[19] Military jurisdiction supposedly reinforced feudal jurisdiction, for the estate owner, as company selector, could choose whom to conscript, while fugitive serfs, as potential recruits, automatically became deserters hunted by the army. Moreover, the expansion of the

[17] H. Bleckwenn, *Unter dem Preußen-Adler. Das Brandenburgisch-Preußische Heer 1640–1807* (Munich, 1978), p. 60. See also Büsch, *Militärsystem*, pp. 29–30 and K. P. Merta, *Die Uniformierung*, vol. II of *Das Heerwesen in Brandenburg und Preußen von 1640 bis 1806* (Berlin, 1991).

[18] Classic formulations in Kitchen, *Military History*, pp. 6–21; Willems, *Way of Life and Death*, pp. 19–23; Vagts, *Militarism*, p. 47. An English translation of the Recess is printed in C. A. Macartney (ed.), *The Habsburg and Hohenzollern Dynasties in the Seventeenth and Eighteenth Centuries* (London, 1970), pp. 229–42. The standard formulation of the Compromise has been challenged effectively by W. W. Hagen, 'Seventeenth-century Crisis in Brandenburg. The Thirty Years War, the Destabilization of Serfdom and the Rise of Absolutism', *American Historical Review*, 94 (1989), 302–35. The implications of this are discussed below on pp. 27–8.

[19] There is almost universal agreement on this crucial point: Büsch, *Militärsystem*, p. 72: 'Der Kompaniechef im Regiment war Gutsherr Zuhaus'; Willems, *Way of Life and Death*, pp. 36–8; E. Sagarra, *A Social History of Germany 1648–1914* (London, 1977), p. 137; D. E. Showalter, *The Wars of Frederick the Great* (London, 1996), p. 22. R. M. Berdahl, *The Politics of the Prussian Nobility. The Development of a Conservative Ideology 1770–1848* (Princeton, N.J., 1988), pp. 92–4 also follows Büsch in his discussion of the nobles and the army.

army functioned as a form of 'aristocratic protection' (*Adelsschütz*), conserving the Junkers by providing employment and additional income to supplement their agrarian profits.[20] Control of the 'company economy' permitted officers from captain and above to supplement their salaries by manipulating the administrative and logistical arrangements of their unit.[21]

However, this was not all one sided, for the state and army gained too. Serfdom helped to precondition cantonists as disciplined potential recruits, while the Junkers also carried out crucial administrative tasks and served in the state bureaucracy.[22] The Compromise was self-reinforcing with the military system duplicating the social structure: the Junkers served as officers, the remaining free peasants acted as NCOs and the serfs were conscripted as privates. The fortunes of Junkers and state were tied together, both equally wary of anything that threatened their mutual benefits. Co-operation became habitual and was at the expense of not only the peasantry, but also the bourgeoisie who were largely excluded from social, economic and political opportunities. The long-term development of not only German democracy, but also the Prussian state, was impaired, as the Compromise left only limited room for modernizing reforms. Prussia's relative backwardness was already apparent by 1806 when it was decisively defeated by Napoleonic France, and later crises were only managed by a series of ultimately fatal strategies adopted during the Bismarckian and Wilhelmine eras.

These arguments root social militarization within the standard chronology of Prussian history, a timeline that has remained unchanged since the patriotic historians of the mid-nineteenth century, despite widely diverging interpretations of it subsequently. The belief that state and society rigidified as the eighteenth century progressed is associated with the concept of military decay after the Seven Years War (1756–63).[23] Not only did Prussia lose out to more advanced societies elsewhere, but its system was undermined from within by the penetration of the agrarian economy by the small entrepreneurial bourgeoisie. By 1806, in the words of one historian, 'this feudal ruin was propped up and preserved by the army and thus the state could hardly be reformed or modernized without the defeat or destruction of the army'.[24] Underpinning all

[20] Phrase from Büsch, *Militärsytem*, p. 105. See also Vagts, *Militarism*, p. 49 for a similar interpretation.

[21] Büsch, *Militärsytem*, pp. 89–134; also M. Messerschmidt, 'Preußens Militär in seinen gesellschaftlichen Umfeld', *Geschichte und Gesellschaft*, 6 (1980), 43–88, at 45–7. These aspects particularly attracted the attention of Marxist historians; for example, O. Groehler, *Die Kriege Friedrichs II.* (6th edition, Berlin, 1990), pp. 170–1. For a detailed analysis of the company economy see F. Redlich, *The German Military Enterpriser and his Workforce*, vol. II (Wiesbaden, 1965).

[22] Büsch, *Militärsytem*, pp. 43, 49.

[23] For example, Schnitter and Schmidt, *Absolutismus und Heer*, pp. 42–4. For a critical discussion of this issue see D. E. Showalter, 'Hubertusberg to Auerstädt: The Prussian Army in Decline', *German History*, 12 (1994), 308–33. For further material on the Prussian army after 1763 see the sources in n. 32 below.

[24] Kitchen, *Military History*, p. 6; see also pp. 364–5 and Büsch, *Militärsystem*, pp. 145–70.

such statements is an assumption characteristic of much German historiography: namely that political and military structures are fundamentally related.[25]

However, it is important to note that these views are far from monolithic. At least two variants emerged from Büsch's debate with his Marxist critics. Büsch accords some autonomy to the crown as a force for change, arguing that what gave Prussia its strength, but also its rigidity, was the interweaving of the interests of dynasty, state and aristocracy.[26] Marxist historians disputed this, partly because it threatened to make the Hohenzollerns unique amongst what were regarded as east European 'late feudal monarchies'. Absolutism, in this interpretation, is a projection of the nobles' power with the state 'captured' and ruling predominantly in their interest. The standing army served not the monarchy, but the 'feudal reaction', reinforcing the Junkers' control by intimidating the bourgeois and disciplining the serfs.[27] Though the theoretical differences are important, in practice there is little to distinguish those who have followed Büsch from those who arrive at social militarization from a more ideological approach. Most tend towards a version of what Hanna Schissler terms the 'military–agrarian complex' where state policy was shaped to suit the interests of army and Junkers.[28]

## IV: Unique to Prussia

A further common theme is the belief that social militarization is peculiar to Prussia and spread from there to the rest of Germany along with Hohenzollern rule in the nineteenth century. Again, the key is the canton system which is interpreted as fundamentally different from anything elsewhere, though it is recognized as influencing the introduction of conscription into Hesse-Kassel in 1762 and the Habsburg monarchy after 1771.[29] The reason for this Prusso-

[25] F. Gilbert (ed.), *The Historical Essays of Otto Hintze* (Oxford, 1975), pp. 159–215; H. Schmidt, 'Staat und Armee im Zeitalter des "miles perpetuus"', in J. Kunisch (ed.), *Staatsverfassung und Heeresverfassung* (Berlin, 1986), pp. 213–48.

[26] Büsch, *Militärsystem*, pp. vii–viii.

[27] In addition to the works cited in n. 9 above, see O. Rocholl, 'Das stehende Heer als Stütze der feudalen Reaktion', *Wissenschaftliche Zeitschrift der Karl-Marx-Unversität Leipzig, Gesellschafts- und staatswissenschaftliche Reihe*, 1 (1952/3), 449–510 and P. Anderson, *Lineages of the Absolutist State* (London, 1974), pp. 236–78.

[28] H. Schissler, 'The Social and Political Power of the Prussian Junkers', in R. Gibson and M. Blinkhorn (eds.), *Landownership and Power in Modern Europe* (London, 1991), pp. 99–110, at 103. For a recent challenge to this with respect to policy-making, see B. Simms, *The Impact of Napoleon. Prussian High Politics, Foreign Policy and the Crisis of the Executive, 1797–1806* (Cambridge, 1997).

[29] Examples of those who regard it as unique to Prussia include: Harnisch, 'Preußisches Kantonsystem', p. 139; Shanahan, *Prussian Military Reforms*, pp. 17, 43 and H. Schilling, *Höfe und Allianzen. Deutschland 1648–1763* (Berlin, 1989), p. 431. For Hesse-Kassel see C. Ingrao, *The Hessian Mercenary State. Ideas, Institutions and Reform under Frederick II 1760–1785* (Cambridge, 1987) and P. K. Taylor, *Indentured to Liberty. Peasant Life and the Hessian Military State 1688–1815* (Ithaca, N.Y., 1994). For Austria see O. Heinl, *Heereswesen und Volksbewaffnung in Vorderösterreich im Zeitalter Josefs II. und die Revolutionskriege* (Freiburg i.Br., 1941) and J. Zimmermann, *Militärverwaltung und Heeresaufbringung in Österreich bis 1806* (Munich, 1983).

centric perspective is the central importance attached to East Elbian serfdom: canton recruitment is regarded as dependent on the system of estate farming predominant in Brandenburg-Prussia. In turn, it is often related to the stock east–west division of European history, variously manifest in Cold War historiography, Whiggish liberalism and Marxist models of absolutism. The canton system typified the monarchical despotism, subordination of the civil to the military and general lack of freedom held as characteristic of eastern Europe and contrasted with the western traditions exemplified by English, and to a lesser extent French, history.[30]

## V: A Practical Problem

As will be clear by now, social militarization—like its historical relation, the *Sonderweg* thesis—is generally expressed in the language of social engagement and political commitment. Pervading the discussion is a sense of moral outrage at the suffering caused by the Junkers' cruelty and dangerous militarism. While these sentiments are entirely laudable and generally do not detract from what is often very fine scholarship, they do make it hard to engage with the concept without sounding like an apologist for absolutism or the Hohenzollern state. This has certainly dogged some of those who tried earlier, of whom the late Hans Bleckwenn is the most prominent representative. Noteworthy as a genuine attempt to verify the detail of Büsch's arguments against further evidence, Bleckwenn's work was nonetheless reminiscent of the older, patriotic Prussian school. The ills of the army and its system are blamed on foreign recruits whom Bleckwenn nevertheless believed to constitute only a tenth of the establishment, while conditions are portrayed as being much worse in places like Saxony.[31]

In the light of these difficulties, two considerations appear helpful. First, we should not interpret military or socio-political systems as inefficient, defective or inevitably doomed merely because we find them morally reprehensible. A great deal of the opposition to military reform in late-eighteenth-century Prussia stemmed not from a conscious desire within a declining elite to cling to power, but from the simple conviction that change was unnecessary and the existing military system did not require modification.[32] Secondly, it is time to question

[30] For example, Downing, *Military Revolution*, *passim*, and Corvisier, *Armies and Societies*, pp. 82, 197. It should be stressed that this interpretation has a long heritage since it often served earlier political agendas; for example eighteenth-century champions of English 'liberties' expressed similar views. See M. Schlenke, *England und das friderianische Preußen 1740–1763* (Munich, 1963), pp. 88–90, 273–94.

[31] H. Bleckwenn, 'Bauernfreiheit durch Wehrpflicht—ein neues Bild der altpreußischen Armee?', in *Die Bewaffnung und Ausrüstung der Armee Friedrichs des Großen* (Exhibition catalogue, Rastatt, 1986), pp. 1–14, and his *Unter dem Preußen-Adler.*

[32] For the reform debate see Shanahan, *Prussian Military Reforms*, pp. 61–87; C. E. White, *The Enlightened Soldier: Scharnhorst and the 'Militärische Gesellschaft' in Berlin 1801–1805* (New York, 1989) and P. Paret, *Yorck and the Era of Prussian Reform 1807–1815* (Princeton, N.J., 1966). A feature of these works is their focus on the reformers' perspective and they give insufficient consideration to the widespread reluctance to adopt what were often unproven innovations. The fact that the short and successful Dutch campaign of 1787 failed to reveal

the underlying assumption that government and military structures are automatically related and to examine recruitment in a social as well as political context.

## VI: German Recruitment Methods

Contrary to the prevailing view, Prussia did not develop a unique solution to the problems of military recruitment, but was forced, like other German territories, to use a variety of methods that look rational and planned only in retrospect. Moreover, though its army eventually grew far larger than even those of powerful electorates like Bavaria or Saxony, the difficulty it faced in finding suitable recruits in sufficient numbers was one common throughout Germany. Other territories maintained smaller forces, but they also had far fewer inhabitants and were often less likely to attract the foreign subsidies or enjoy the administrative economies of scale that could ease recruiting problems in larger states. To understand whether methods like the canton system could militarize society, we need to investigate how German armies acquired their manpower.

In what has been labelled the 'Military Revolution', changes in weapons technology fused with political and economic developments to alter the way in which armies were recruited and sustained by the early sixteenth century.[33] Germany lacked a single national monopoly of military power as the Holy Roman Empire (*Reich*) was already evolving along lines very different to those of France, England, or Spain.[34] Nonetheless, its constituent territories participated fully in the broader military developments, establishing recruiting practices that continued into the eighteenth century.

One standard form was voluntary enlistment (*freie Werbung*) whereby a recruit signed on for a cash bounty and a contract specifying length and terms of service. Such soldiers were mercenaries in the strictest sense of the word in that they served for pay, though the majority of them were recruited within the territory of their warlord (*Kriegsherr*) and were bound to him by obligations other than the purely contractual.

The small size of many territories, combined with the desire to preserve a large pool of taxpayers, induced many German princes to recruit outside their own domains. The emperor tried unsuccessfully to monopolize such rights, but

serious defects within the army also encouraged retention of the existing structure: P. H. Wilson, *German Armies: War and German Politics 1648–1806* (London, 1998), p. 292. Useful examples of contemporary criticism of the army in the later eighteenth century can be found in C. v. Massenbach, *Memoiren zur Geschichte des preußischen Staates unter der Regierung Friedrich Wilhelm II und Friedrich Wilhelm III* (3 vols., Amsterdam, 1809).

[33] On the differing interpretations see C. J. Rogers (ed.), *The Military Revolution Debate* (Boulder, Colo., 1995), and B. S. Hall, *Weapons and Warfare in Renaissance Europe* (Baltimore, Md., 1997).

[34] H. Neuhaus, *Das Reich in der Frühen Neuzeit* (Munich, 1997) and P. H. Wilson, *The Holy Roman Empire 1495–1806* (London, 1999) provide the latest overviews of the now substantial literature.

nonetheless retained considerable influence in the eighteenth century, particularly amongst the smaller territories.[35] The electors and more powerful princes gradually usurped former imperial privileges, arguing that their territorial armies were serving the common good by defending the Reich against the French and the Turks. The most effective way to secure such additional manpower was 'public recruitment' (*öffentliche Werbung*) with the permission of the relevant territorial authorities and the use of music, martial display and other advertisements. Failing that, soldiers could be found through 'silent recruitment' (*stille Werbung*) with permission, but without the public commotion that might arouse unwelcome suspicion among neighbouring states. If either local or imperial permission was unforthcoming, officers could proceed 'covertly' (*unter der Hand*) using disguise, deception, intermediaries and other illegal practices.[36] It is this latter method that has left the greatest literary legacy and coloured the general picture of mercenary recruitment.[37] Again, Prussia features prominently and not without reason since Frederick William's insistence on exceptionally tall recruits compelled officers to go to extraordinary lengths.[38]

These problems, combined with the associated expense, prompted recourse to militia systems as a second form of raising an army. Under these, civilians received periodic training, turning out in force during emergencies in response to a varying mix of legal and customary obligations to defend the territory and serve the ruler. In the popular view of military history, these part-time soldiers invariably proved inferior to the paid professionals who dominated the battlefield until the French Revolution and universal conscription opened up new ways of exploiting manpower.[39] This scheme glosses over what was in fact a much more complicated process and it is altogether better to regard militias and voluntary enlistment as ideal theoretical models never entirely reproduced in practice. This extends beyond the obvious fact that many volunteers did not

[35] For evidence of imperial recruiting efforts see Staatsarchiv Darmstadt (hereafter StAD), E8 B 9/8–9, 13, 16; B 10/1–2 4–5, 8–11, 18, 21, 23, 25–6, 29, 30; B 11/4–19 covering imperial requests to recruit within Hesse-Darmstadt. For similar evidence relating to Württemberg and the Swabian *Kreis* (Circle) see Hauptstaatsarchiv Stuttgart (hereafter HSAS), A6 Bü.55; A202 Bü.1161; C14 Bü.307, 586a.

[36] W. Schüssler, 'Das Werbewesen in der Reichsstadt Heilbronn, vornehmlich im 18. Jahrhundert', Ph.D. Thesis, Tübingen, 1951, esp. pp. 269–72; I. Kraucauer, 'Das Militärwesen der Reichsstadt Frankfurt am Main im XVIII. Jahrhundert', *Archiv für Frankfurts Geschichte und Kunst*, 3rd series, 12 (1920), 1–180, at 20–8. For recruitment methods see also J. Kraus, *Das Militärwesen der Reichstadt Augsburg 1548–1806* (Augsburg, 1980), pp. 186–91, 284–6; P.-C. Storm, *Der Schwäbische Kreis als Feldherr* (Berlin, 1974), pp. 275–95.

[37] Anon., *List- und lustige Begebenheiten dere Herren Offiziers auf Werbungen* (1741; reprint, Osnabrück, 1971); U. Bräker, *The Life Story and Real Adventures of the Poor Man of Toggenburg*, ed. D. Bowman (Edinburgh, 1970), esp. pp. 103–19.

[38] Examples in HSAS, A6 Bü.54, 63; A202 Bü.2226, 2299; C14 Bü.597; B. Sicken, 'Die preußische Werbung in Franken', in H. Duchhardt (ed.), *Friedrich der Große, Franken und das Reich* (Cologne, 1986), pp. 121–56; K. Zeisler, *Die 'Langen Kerls'. Geschichte des Leib- und Garderegiments Friedrich Wilhelms I* (Frankfurt/Main, 1993).

[39] For example, G. Best, *War and Society in Revolutionary Europe 1770–1870* (London, 1982); M. Howard, *War in European History* (Oxford, 1976).

enter service entirely of their own free will to the more fundamental point that no German army ever relied entirely on a single form of recruitment.

In addition to the variations in voluntary enlistment discussed above, German princes could hire (under subsidy) or transfer (purchase) serving soldiers or even entire units from other armies. These methods played a significant role in the expansion of the Prussian army under Frederick William who once famously acquired 600 cavalrymen from the elector of Saxony in return for a porcelain dinner service.[40] The practice was extended under Frederick the Great who not only relied on it to provide the cadre of virtually all the new regiments added to the army in 1740–4, but used it as the basis of his agreements with which he tied lesser German rulers to Prussian policy.[41]

Militia recruitment also assumed a variety of forms. Already in the late sixteenth century even the largest German territories were finding it difficult to raise the numbers they required from paid professionals alone. Starting in the Rhineland in the 1570s, many began reviving traditional militia structures to provide a cheap form of permanent defence. Trained in the use of the latest weaponry and tactics, these Territorial Defence Militias (*Landesdefensionen*) were expected to mobilize at short notice to confront internal disorder and external threats. However, they were never intended to replace mercenaries for major operations, serving instead as reserve or garrison troops when open warfare began. Far from disappearing in the course of the Thirty Years War, many militias were revived as the Reich became involved in further protracted conflict against the Turks and French from the 1660s.[42]

The reasons for this were not only military, but also social and demographic. Demobilization and the end of the Thirty Years War left a pool of potential recruits only partially diminished by the reintegration of former soldiers into the civil economy. These manpower reserves were drawn upon by Venice, Sweden, Spain and France which were still engaged in conflicts outside the Reich.[43] However, few princes appear to have found it difficult to find sufficient recruits provided they could pay the necessary bounties. Though the demographic recovery from the mid-seventeenth century provided a new generation of potential recruits, it proved harder to recruit these as they came of age in the 1670s. By this stage most territorial governments had implemented protectionist measures intended to preserve and nurture their limited human and

[40] C. v. Jany, *Geschichte der Preußische Armee vom 15. Jahrhundert bis 1914* (4 vols., Berlin, 1928–9, reprint Osnabrück, 1967), vol. I, pp. 651–2.

[41] See Wilson, *German Armies*, pp. 247–8.

[42] H. Schnitter, *Volk und Landesdefension* (Berlin, 1977), and his 'Die überlieferte Defensionspflicht. Vorformen der allgemeinen Wehrpflicht in Deutschland', in R. G. Foerster (ed.), *Die Wehrpflicht* (Munich, 1994), pp. 29–37; also W. Schulze, 'Die deutschen Landesdefensionen im 16. und 17. Jahrhundert', in Kunisch (ed.), *Staatsverfassung und Heeresverfassung*, pp. 129–49; H. Ehlert, 'Ursprünge des modernen Militärwesens. Die nassau-oranischen Heeresreformen', *Militärgeschichtliche Mitteilungen*, 38 (1985), 27–56.

[43] M. S. Anderson, *War and Society in Europe of the Old Regime 1618–1789* (London, 1988), p. 52.

material resources after decades of violent depletion. Integral to these policies were streams of decrees against enlistment in foreign armies.[44] Reclamation of abandoned farms and a revival of trade also discouraged many men from venturing on a military career. Declining supply met escalating demand as ambitious princes began a more active involvement in European conflict precisely when other continental armies were expanding to match the growth in French forces.[45] Though the demand for soldiers often gave access to foreign subsidies, most rulers found it difficult to pay for the size of army they believed necessary.[46]

In many cases the actual cost was less important than the means of collecting and administering the army's finances. In the case of regular regiments of professional soldiers, the central authorities amassed the money from domainal income, taxation, subsidies and loans whilst disbursing it through officers and private contractors for pay and supplies. This system was open to corruption and often broke down in cash-flow crises.[47] Militia structures offered a way out of these problems, not only securing native manpower, but providing the central administration with a mechanism to off-load responsibility for paying, feeding, clothing and arming the soldiers onto the local authorities who recruited them. It is certainly significant that the consolidation of permanent forces after the Dutch War (1672–9) was often accompanied by a revival and re-organization of the decayed militias.[48]

Some territories regarded these in the now traditional manner as a supplementary force alongside regular troops. This was the case in Bavaria and Hesse-Darmstadt, for example, where the militias continued to be periodically re-organized up to the late eighteenth century and provided mobilized or

[44] An overview of the demographic recovery and the economic measures is given in C. Dipper, *Deutsche Geschichte 1648–1789* (Frankfurt/Main, 1991), pp. 42–75. For examples of the numerous bans on enlisting see J. C. Lünig (ed.), *Corpus iuris militaris des Heilligen Römischen Reiches* (2 vols., Leipzig, 1723) and A. L. Reyscher (ed.), *Vollständige, historisch und kritisch bearbeitete Sammlung der Württembergischen Gesetze* (29 vols., Stuttgart and Tübingen, 1828–51), vol. XIII. These political and demographic factors are generally overlooked by those who explain mercenary recruitment and the subsequent shift to more coercive manpower policies in purely economic terms: Redlich, *Military enterprizer*, esp. vol. II, pp. 170–85; J. E. Thomson, *Mercenaries, Pirates and Sovereigns. State-building and Extraterritorial Violence in Early Modern Europe* (Princeton, N.J., 1994), pp. 10–11, 19, 26–32.

[45] Wilson, *German Armies*, pp. 44–100. For French strengths see J. A. Lynn, *Giant of the* Grand Siècle. *The French Army 1610–1715* (Cambridge, 1997).

[46] For the controversy over subsidies see P. H. Wilson, 'The German "Soldiertrade" of the Seventeenth and Eighteenth Centuries: A Reassessment', *International History Review*, 18 (1996), 757–92.

[47] R. Bonney (ed.), *Economic Systems and State Finance* (Oxford, 1995); P. T. Hoffman and K. Norberg (eds.), *Fiscal Crises, Liberty and Representative Government* (Stanford, Calif., 1994); A. de Maddalena and H. Kellenbenz (eds.), *Finanzen und Staatsräson in Italien und Deutschland in der Frühen Neuzeit* (Berlin, 1992). For an analysis of military costs including comparison with Prussia, see P. H. Wilson, *War, State and Society in Württemberg, 1677–1793* (Cambridge, 1995), pp. 37–42.

[48] For example in Saxony in 1684: W. Thensius, *Die Anfänge des stehenden Heerwesens in Kursachsen unter Johann Georg III. und Johann Georg IV.* (Leipzig, 1912), pp. 62–4.

'embodied' units in wartime.[49] However, there was already a tendency to adapt them as a recruitment pool for regular units. Embodied units could find themselves becoming part of the permanent army once mobilized, as was the case with a regiment from Celle in 1674, or even the entire Württemberg militia in 1690.[50] More usually, the mechanisms for drafting men into the militia were customized to provide recruits for the regular army. This could take one of two forms, both of which are important for understanding the evolution of the canton system. Using the militia as a depot involved inducting men from the parish rolls directly into the permanent regiments on a temporary or permanent basis. This became standard procedure in many medium-sized and smaller territories with the growth of a formalized system of imperial collective security after the 1681–2 reforms.[51] Men would be selected from the militia lists to make up the contingent required by imperial law for the common *Reichsarmee* and would usually be discharged once hostilities had ceased.[52] Frequently, the legislation was used as a cover to recruit men into regiments intended for subsidy service, or other arrangements more specifically tailored to princely political objectives. This occurred in Münster from the 1660s, Eisenach in 1702, Mecklenburg in 1709–11, and Hanover during the Seven Years War and Revolutionary Wars, to cite just a few examples.[53] Either way, the method had the advantage of utilizing an established structure and drew on men who had often already undergone some basic training. Even when this was not so, the system could be used to induct recruits into a special depot, or training company, attached to each regiment as, for example, in the case of Hanover during the Seven Years War.

In contrast to the depot system, which fed fresh recruits into the regular army, the use of reserves enabled the authorities to retain control over experienced former soldiers when they were discharged into civil society. This was a very old practice dating back to the early sixteenth century when the nascent territorial state struggled to assert itself over society in general and war-making in particular. Difficulties in financing war brought several campaigns to an abrupt end and frequently forced the reduction or disbandment of mercenary units. For the men concerned, this period of *Garden*, or 'time without pay' threatened their material survival and many engaged in violence and extortion,

[49] K. Staudinger, *Geschichte des Kurbayerischen Heeres* (5 vols., Munich, 1901–9). See also StAD, E8 B 138–57 covering the Hesse-Darmstadt militia from 1665.

[50] F. Schirmer, *Nec aspera terrent! Eine Heereskunde der Hannoverschen Armee von 1631 bis 1803* (Hanover, 1929), pp. 18–19; Wilson, *War, State and Society*, pp. 115–19 and the sources cited there.

[51] For this system see Wilson, *German Armies*, esp. pp. 62–7.

[52] For example, in Bamberg 1676–9, 1688, 1691–2: H. Caspary, *Staat, Finanzen, Wirtschaft und Heerwesen im Hochstift Bamberg (1672–1693)* (Bamberg, 1976), pp. 321–2.

[53] T. Verspohl, *Das Heerwesen des münsterischen Fürstbischofs Christoph Bernhard von Galen* (Hildesheim, 1909), pp. 26, 62–73; H. Patze and W. Schlesinger (eds.), *Geschichte Thüringens*, vol. V (Cologne and Vienna, 1982), p. 357; G. Tessin, *Mecklenburgisches Militär in Türken- und Franzõsenkriegen 1648–1718* (Cologne and Graz, 1966), pp. 154–6; Schirmer, *Nec aspera*, pp. 64–5, 102, 149–50.

or enlisted in the armies of rival powers like France. Such behaviour only heightened the general suspicion of a group whose appearance and lifestyle placed them outside the bounds of stable society and encouraged attempts to monitor and control them.[54] Official anxiety grew in the wake of the German Peasants' War (1524–6), in which many former mercenaries had participated, and resulted in a series of imperial, as well as territorial, legislation. In particular, two imperial police ordinances (*Reichspolizeiordnungen*) of 1530 and 1548 sanctioned and formalized measures already being developed by several territorial governments. In addition to the retainers (*Wartgeld*) paid by richer towns and princes to secure the services of former soldiers, discharged mercenaries were now given passports (*Laufzettel*) on the understanding they would return to their former employer when required.[55] The passports, which the bearer was obliged to show to all civil officials, provided some protection against arrest on vagrancy charges whilst extending state surveillance over a militarily significant section of the population.

The larger, permanent forces maintained by many German principalities after 1648 continued to rely on these measures to ease both mobilization and peacetime reductions. For example, the men discharged by Frederick William, the Great Elector, at the termination of hostilities in 1666 and 1679 were told to remain within Brandenburg-Prussia. Many were recalled to the colours at the outbreak of the Nine Years War in 1688. Increasingly, the practice was formalized and Elector Frederick III intended to incorporate those discharged in 1697 into a militia. Though this was not implemented, Prussian mobilization and army expansion in 1701–3 relied essentially on recalling men released on passports in 1697.[56] Increasingly, the passport system was extended as an integral structural feature of the permanent forces, particularly those maintained by the smaller, poorer territories. As early as the 1650s the bishop of Münster reduced each company in peacetime, releasing the native soldiers on half pay and rations for unspecified leave.[57] Other territories introduced similar measures after the Dutch War (1672–9), not only issuing passports to men formally discharged in the post-war reduction, but now granting some of the remaining soldiers regular leave. For example, 15 per cent of the Bavarian establishment

[54] R. Baumann, *Das Söldnerwesen im 16. Jahrhundert im bayerischen und süddeutschen Beispiel* (Munich, 1978), pp. 171–84 and his *Die Landsknechte* (Munich, 1994), pp. 131–45; P. Burschel, *Söldner im Nordwestdeutschland des 16. und 17. Jahrhunderts* (Göttingen, 1994), pp. 277–86.

[55] The legislation is printed in J. J. Schmauss and H. C. Senckenberg (eds.), *Neue und vollständige Sammlung der Reichsabschiede* (4 vols., Frankfurt/Main, 1747), vol. II, pp. 332–45, 487–606. B. Bei der Wieden, 'Niederdeutsche Söldner vor dem Dreißigjährigen Krieg: Geistige und mentale Grenzen eines sozialen Raums', in Kroener and Pröve (eds.), *Krieg und Frieden*, pp. 85–108, believes some rulers may have encouraged 'garden' to be sure of a manpower reserve.

[56] R. Frhr. v. Schrötter, 'Die Ergänzung des Preußischen Heeres unter dem ersten Könige', *Forschungen zur Brandenburgischen und Preußischen Geschichte*, 23 (1910), 81–145 at 106; Jany, *Preußische Armee*, vol. I, pp. 428, 569. For an attempt to implement this in Württemberg, see HSAS, L6.22.8.1, 6 June 1758.

[57] Verspohl, *Heerwesen*, pp. 64–5.

was furloughed each autumn and winter, the proportion rising to a quarter at harvest time. Trier adopted the measure around 1680, as did Holstein-Gottorp, Cologne and other small and medium-sized territories by the early eighteenth century.[58]

Prussia, far from unique in this respect, also introduced limited leave in April 1681 and followed the same general pattern of development, switching from paid to unpaid leave, whilst increasing the proportion who received it. Frederick William I extended the furlough to 25 per cent of company strength in 1714, permitting up to 40 per cent in harvest time, and raising that in other months for the infantry to 44 per cent and about half that for the cavalry in 1732. These norms were often exceeded in practice and well over half the army was on leave outside the spring exercise months under his successor.[59] The leave system was thus a structural element of all German standing armies and had very little to do with the canton system as such which it in any case predated. It emerged in response to a social demand from soldiers as they adapted to the greater permanence of territorial forces. Since much desertion was simply unauthorized leave, regularizing the practice assisted in the maintenance of discipline, as well as saving the state treasury and the officers' company economy valuable funds. Finally, it met the needs of a largely agrarian economy by releasing able-bodied manpower to help with the harvest. In short, the growth of permanent German forces was only possible by absorbing essential characteristics of a militia system within the new standing armies.

In addition to variations on voluntary and militia enlistment, most German governments had recourse to conscription, either in the form of impressment (*Aushebung*), or a quota system (*Auswahl* or *Landrekrutierung*), or both. In the former, the authorities targeted those they deemed socially undesirable or expendable who were obliged to enlist, often under threat of arrest for vagrancy or as commutation of a criminal sentence. Though such men generally received a bounty and so were technically volunteers, the coercive element made this a form of conscription.[60] The second method involved the imposition of manpower quotas on the district authorities who were often given a relatively free hand as to how they filled them. In Trier in 1742 and in Württemberg throughout the eighteenth century, men enrolled on the militia lists were required to muster before the local magistrates and an officer seconded from the army. If

[58] T. Fuchs, *Geschichte des europäischen Kriegswesens* (3 vols., Munich, 1972–6), vol. II, p. 113; Oberleutnant Möllmann, 'Zur Geschichte des Kurtrierischen Militärs', *Trierisches Archiv*, supplement 1 (1901), 60–87 at 64, 74, 76; G. Knüppel, *Das Heerwesen des Fürstentums Schleswig-Holstein-Gottorf, 1600–1715* (Neumünster, 1972), p. 193; E. Herter, *Geschichte der Kurkölnischen Truppen in der Zeit vom Badener Frieden bis zum Beginn des Siebenjährigen Krieges* (Bonn, 1914), pp. 37, 39.

[59] Schrötter, 'Ergänzung', pp. 98–9; Jany, 'Kantonverfassung', pp. 232, 261–3; Jany, *Preußische Armee*, vol. II, pp. 249–50; M. Lehmann, 'Werbung, Wehrpflicht und Beurlaubung im Heere Friedrich Wilhelm I', *Historische Zeitschrift*, 67 (1891), 254–89.

[60] For an example of its use in Saxony in 1696 see W. Thum, *Die Rekrutierung der Sächsichen Armee unter August dem Starken (1694–1733)* (Leipzig, 1912), pp. 11–12.

insufficient volunteers came forward to fill the quota, the remainder would draw lots or throw dice to determine who would serve.[61] In this case, conscription was based on the militia as depot system. Frequently, such formal mechanisms broke down, not least because those liable took to the woods or fled the country, forcing the authorities to use coercion to make up the shortfall. Such problems were predicted, encouraging the authorities to conceal their intentions. In Würzburg, which made periodic use of impressment after 1688, the district officials were required to submit detailed lists of those who, by their lifestyle, behaviour or inclination, might be enlisted from their area. After consideration of the likely repercussions for the local community, the central authorities would endorse the conscription of specific individuals and order the officials to proceed.[62]

Conscription was invariably seen as a last resort and it is important to note that the methods described here were rarely implemented in isolation. Instead, German recruitment generally operated on a sliding scale: the authorities preferred volunteers, but moved through escalating degrees of compulsion if these could not be found in sufficient number. Typically, a recruitment decree would sanction a variety of systems each to be adopted only if the preceding one failed to produce satisfactory results. Naturally, the order reflected the priorities of the territorial state, but these were devised to take some account of pressure from below. The set of measures sanctioned by Trier in December 1744 provides a good example. Local officials were instructed to seek volunteers, but if this failed to meet their quotas they were to impress beggars and those whose poverty or lifestyle made them a burden on the community. Any further shortfall was to be made good by conscripting unmarried men from large families drawn from those with four, three, or two sons in that order. If single sons had to be chosen, those available were to draw lots. At all stages, substitution was permitted if the man selected paid the cost of recruiting a volunteer

[61] Möllmann, 'Kurtrierischen Militärs', p. 69. For Württemberg see P. H. Wilson, 'Violence and the Rejection of Authority in Eighteenth Century Germany: The Case of the Swabian Mutinies 1757', *German History*, 12 (1994), 1–26 at 17–19. A variant of this system was used in Saxony 1702–6, 1711, 1729, 1775–8, 1796–8: Thum, *Rekrutierung*, pp. 19–72, 82–5; J. Hofmann, *Die Kursächsiche Armee 1769 bis zum Beginn des Bayerischen Erbfolgekrieges* (Leipzig, 1914), pp. 30–83; R. Mielsch, 'Die Kursächsiche Armee im Bayerischen Erbfolgekriege', *Neues Archiv für Sächsiche Geschichte*, 53 (1932), 70–103 at 71–2; O. Rudert, *Die Reorganisation der Kursächsichen Armee 1763–69* (Leipzig, 1911), pp. 89–105.

[62] W. Kopp, *Würzburger Wehr* (Würzburg, 1979), pp. 61–2, 103–10; E. Hagen, 'Die fürstlich Würzburgische Hausinfanterie von ihren Anfängen bis zum Beginne des Siebenjährigen Krieges 1636–1756', *Darstellungen aus der Bayerischen Kriegs- und Heeresgeschichte*, 19 (1910), 69–203 at 94–6, 101–2, 108, and his 'Die fürstlich Würzburgische Hausinfanterie vom Jahre 1757 bis zur Einverleibung des Fürstentums in Bayern', in *ibid.*, 20 (1911), 1–142 at 77–8; B. Sicken, 'Die Streitkräfte des Hochstifts Würzburg gegen Ende des Ancien Regime', *Zeitschrift für Bayerische Landesgeschichte*, 47 (184), 691–744 at 698–705, and his 'Müßiggänger und liederliche Burschen. Beobachtungen zur militärischen Aushebung ländlicher Außenseiter im Hochstift Würzburg Mitte des 18. Jahrhunderts', in P. Leidinger and D. Metzler (eds.), *Geschichte und Geschichtsbewußtsein* (Münster, 1990), pp. 269–307. For a similar case elsewhere, see K. Pfaff, *Geschichte des Militärwesens in Württemberg* (Stuttgart, 1842), pp. 66–7.

replacement.[63] Similarly, most armies specified height, age and marital status in their search for volunteers, bur relaxed these requirements if the initial target was not achieved.[64]

A prominent feature in all these systems was the preference for the devolution of responsibility and readiness to co-opt or adapt existing practices and administration structures. No territory before the late eighteenth century centralized recruitment or placed it entirely in the hands of the army. Even where officers were principally responsible, recruitment was still devolved to company or at the most regimental level. Civil officials were almost invariably involved, if only in the monitoring and surveillance procedures required for the passport and furlough system. Often they played a prominent part in the actual recruitment process since both state and army were keen to utilize their expertise, often extending to direct personal knowledge of potential recruits. Such expertise did not serve purely military objectives since all recruitment measures were related to the state's wider demographic, moral and economic objectives. Moreover, the variety of different systems and the manner in which one method frequently incorporated elements of another alerts us to a further general point: the German territorial state avoided imposing a rigid, uniform structure on what was an extremely diverse and multifaceted society. The quota system was an expression of this, attempting both to compensate for the inadequate reach of the central administration and ensure a measure of fairness and efficiency. Every community was expected to provide its share of recruits, but was left largely to its own devices as to how to do it. The state merely specified general guidelines and stipulated minimum requirements regarding height, age, fitness, marital status and so on. Here we see clearly the limits of state power since the method was adopted not only to off-load the technical and financial burden onto the local communities, but to avoid stirring their resistance. By entrusting recruitment to district officials and village headmen, the state ensured it was done by those who had a place within the community concerned, forestalling the possibility of united opposition if the task was handled by complete outsiders, such as army officers.[65]

## VII: Levels of Impact

It is time now to examine the impact of these recruitment methods on German society. The Büsch thesis maintains that this was most profound in Prussia, but in practice implementation of the canton system varied throughout the Hohenzollern territories. Brandenburg had an especially heavy concentration

[63] Möllmann, 'Kurtrierischen Militärs', pp. 69–70.

[64] For example, in Würzburg in 1793: Sicken, 'Streitkräfte', p. 698; and Bavaria in 1780: F. Munich, *Geschichte der Entwicklung der Bayerischen Armee* (Munich, 1864), p. 184.

[65] Bob Scribner's discussion of insiders and outsiders in early modern communities is highly instructive in this context: 'Communities and the Nature of Power', in Scribner and Ogilvie (eds.), *Germany*, vol. I, pp. 291–326.

of troops, even before the eighteenth century when ninety-six towns had permanent garrisons compared to forty-six in East Prussia.[66] Brandenburg cantons were also smaller than those elsewhere resulting in a heavier burden since regiment size was standard throughout the monarchy. A canton's size was measured by the number of 'hearths' or households within its boundaries, with 3,000 being the average in the 1730s for an infantry regiment based in Brandenburg compared with 8,700 for one in Westphalia.[67] Though the army more than doubled its size between 1740 and 1786 through the addition of new units and the augmentation of existing ones, the expansion of Prussian territory permitted an enlargement of many cantons. By the 1790s most infantry cantons appear to have been over 10,000 hearths, rather than under 5,000, with some as large as 15,000.[68]

Calculating the precise demographic impact is difficult in the absence of comprehensive and reliable population figures. It has been estimated that by 1800 1.17 million inhabitants were exempt from conscription through living in privileged regions whilst a further 530,000 had personal exemptions on the ground of wealth, occupation or status. Given that political sensitivity prevented full implementation of the system in the newly acquired Polish areas, a further 2.2 million had *de facto* exemption, leaving perhaps 2 million men liable out of a total population of between 8.7 and 11 million.[69] Comparatively few were taken in any one year: of the 2,156,812 cantonists enrolled in 1802, only 9,287 were drafted.[70] When the system was introduced into Silesia in 1743–4, the annual intake was fixed initially at 1,490 out of a total population of 1.2 million.[71] Nonetheless, implementation of canton conscription clearly increased the burden on such newly acquired provinces. After the extension of the system to Ansbach and Bayreuth in 1796, 106,190 males were enrolled by 1805, representing nearly a quarter of the total population, while the two margraviates

[66] W. Rohr, 'Märkische Garnisonen im 18. Jahrhundert', *Brandenburgische Jahrbücher*, 2 (1936), 110–20; W. Grosse, 'Kleine ostpreußische Garnisonen vor 250 Jahren', *Der redliche Ostpreuße*, 17 (1966), 80–5.

[67] Jany, 'Kantonverfassung', pp. 244–5. The strength of an average infantry regiment rose from 1,553 officers and men in 1739 to 1,858 in 1787. Cavalry regiments were generally half that size and their cantons correspondingly smaller. Each infantry company reqired an average of four to eight native recruits annually, representing a total intake per canton of forty-eight to ninety-six each year.

[68] A. Skalweit, 'Die Eingliederung des friderizianischen Heeres in den Volks- und Wirtschaftskörper', *Jahrbuch für Nationalökonomie und Statistik*, 160 (1944), 194–220 at 203. The canton of Inf. Rgt. Saldern (Nr. 5) based near Magdeburg had 10,343 hearths in 1771: W. Hanne (ed.), *Rangirrolle, Listen und Extracte...von Saldern Infanterie Regiment Anno 1771* (Osnabrück, 1986), p. 8. For the size of the Pomeranian cantons see B. Schulze, 'Die Kantone Pommerns 1733–1786', *Baltische Studien*, NF38 (1936), 265–316.

[69] Skalweit, 'Eingliederung', p. 208 n.; Shanahan, *Prussian Military Reforms*, pp. 58–9; R. Wohlfeil, *Vom stehenden Heer des Absolutismus zur allgemeinen Wehrpflicht (1789–1814)* (Frankfurt/Main, 1983), pp. 86–7.

[70] Jany, *Preußische Armee*, vol. III, pp. 443–4.

[71] *Ibid.*, vol. II, pp. 74–9.

were now supporting a garrison of about 6,000, or more than twice the military establishment of the previous regime.[72]

Within these broad variations we can detect further inequalities in distribution. Though at just under 23 per cent of total population the proportion enrolled in Brandenburg was roughly the same as that in Ansbach and Bayreuth, levels in the countryside were between 5 and 15 per cent above those in the towns.[73] Moreover, the army always took the tallest men first, so that those whose stature failed to reach the minimum of 5 feet 5 Prussian inches (171 cm) were effectively exempt, despite being recorded in the cantonal rolls. These gave an inflated picture of total manpower since the army enrolled all eligible males at the age of confirmation. Only 312,826 men, or about a seventh of those enrolled in 1802, were actually 5 feet or over. Of these only 22,338 reached the minimum height. An exemplary, if perhaps extreme, illustration of these problems is provided by Infantry Regiment Anhalt-Bernberg stationed in Halle. Though with 13,963 hearths its canton was larger than most and had 20,737 men enrolled in 1773, only 124 of these reached the minimum of 5 feet 5 inches, with a solitary individual standing at the preferred height of 5 feet 7. In such cases, the army took shorter men, discharging them when taller recruits became available. Not surprisingly, mothers warned naughty children not to grow 'or the recruiting sergeant will take you'.[74]

Overall, we can see that though the army made up between 3 and 4 per cent of the total population after the 1730s, conscription was concentrated on a specific section of society. Tall adult males living in rural areas bore the brunt of the burden, particularly in the Brandenburg heartlands where 7 per cent of all rural cantonists were called up.[75] Mobilization and wartime losses both raised these proportions and extended the recruiting net to shorter men who were drafted as baggage attendants and, as their taller comrades fell in battle, even into the front ranks. As is well known, several regiments lost the equivalent of two or even three times their entire establishment during the Seven Years War and overall, Helmut Harnisch estimates that 10 per cent of all cantonists were called up during the conflict.[76] Though extremely heavy, these manpower demands were not unique to Prussia since a number of smaller German territories raised forces proportionately greater than those of the Hohenzollerns. The tiny principality of Schaumburg-Lippe mustered the equivalent of no less

[72] O. Bezzel, *Die Haustruppen des letzten Markgrafen von Ansbach-Bayreuth unter preußischer Herrschaft* (Munich, 1939); Jany, *Preußische Armee*, vol. III, pp. 232–5. It is worth noting that the annual intake would have been relatively low, whilst the 1792 canton laws were modified in Ansbach-Bayreuth, reducing the maximum period of service to sixteen years.

[73] Harnisch, 'Preußisches Kantonsystem', p. 151 table 2.

[74] Skalweit, 'Eingliederung', pp. 210–11. The fact that the Anhalt-Bernberg regiment had an additional third battalion must have exacerbated its recruiting difficulties.

[75] Harnisch, 'Preußisches Kantonsystem', p. 152. This compares with a figure of 6% of Westphalian cantonists: Kloosterhuis, 'Zwischen Aufruhr und Akzeptanz', p. 190. These figures are considerably above estimates cited elsewhere—for example, only one cantonist in every 200: W. Hubatsch, *Frederick the Great. Absolutism and Administration* (London, 1975), p. 132.

[76] Jany, *Preußische Armee*, vol. II, pp. 665–8; Harnisch, 'Preußisches Kantonsystem', p. 138. See also Büsch, *Militärsystem*, p. 32.

than 8.8 per cent of its population under arms in 1760, whilst Hesse-Kassel and even the comparatively pacific archbishopric of Mainz made demands broadly comparable to those in Prussia during the same conflict.[77]

## VIII: Social Militarization or Social Disciplining?

Opinion differs as to the wider social consequences of these demands. There is an inherent contradiction in the social militarization argument which, on the one hand, argues that society was transformed by the canton system, yet, on the other, maintains that the army remained an isolated, alien body standing apart from the rest of the population. It is in this context that the stock references to the still high proportion of foreigners appear and the general civil–military divide is held to be a major factor in Prussia's collapse in 1806.[78]

One solution to this apparent paradox is suggested by Jürgen Kloosterhuis who stands the Büsch thesis on its head substituting the 'socialization of the military' for social militarization. Canton conscription adapted the army to the needs of society rather than the other way round and, particularly through the furlough system, partly civilianized it. While this highlights a neglected consequence of the canton system, it takes revision of Büsch too far by concentrating on one aspect of it. Soldiers, including men on furlough, were indeed a distinct group in Prussia, as were their equivalents in other territories, but they were also simply one group among many in what was already a segmented society. Furthermore, these segments overlapped, binding as well as dividing society so that an individual's place within it was determined by a complex matrix of relationships: legal, filial, economic, religious, political, linguistic and so on. These relationships could alter even in what is customarily regarded as a fairly rigid social order. The canton system provides a good case in point. Frederick William failed to specify a maximum length of service and though a limit of twenty years was imposed in 1792, the army's preference for retaining mature, experienced soldiers is widely regarded as resulting in cantonists serving for life. In fact, as we have seen, many were discharged much earlier, though wartime mobilization could result in their recall. Nonetheless, military service remained only one aspect of a man's life, particularly if he was a volunteer serving on a contractual basis.[79]

An alternative to militarization is to see 'social disciplining' as the conse-

[77] H. H. Klein, *Wilhelm zu Schaumburg-Lippe* (Osnabrück, 1982), pp. 35–41; R. Harms, 'Landmiliz und stehendes Heer in Kurmainz, namentlich im 18. Jahrhundert', *Archiv für hessische Geschichte und Altertumskunde*, NF6 (1909), 359–430 at 378–9; Taylor, *Indentured to Liberty*, *passim*; Wilson, *German Armies*, p. 278.

[78] For example, Downing, *Military Revolution*, pp. 106–12. Messerschmidt, 'Preußens Militär', p. 52 also argues that the officer corps especially became increasingly isolated from the rest of society after 1763.

[79] Further discussion in R. Pröve, *Stehendes Heer und städtische Gesellschaft im 18. Jahrhundert. Göttingen und seine Militärbevölkerung 1713–1756* (Munich, 1995), pp. 88–94, and B. R. Kroener, '"Das Schwungrad an der Staatsmaschine"? Die Bedeutung der bewaffneten Macht in der europäische Geschichte der Frühen Neuzeit', in Kroener and Pröve (eds.), *Krieg und Frieden*, pp. 1–24 at 12–18.

quence of the growth of German armies.[80] The idea that the canton system helped instil a sense of obedience and subordination is already integral to the Büsch thesis and indeed drew comment before.[81] There is certainly ample evidence to suggest that the Prussian system and similar measures elsewhere did extend the reach of state surveillance into previously largely private spheres of life. The apparatus of military recruitment reinforced monitoring procedures often already developed by the church and the fisc, particularly through additional record keeping and census data. For example, the Austrian version of canton recruitment, introduced after 1780, required a massive statistical survey of the entire monarchy begun in 1771 and involving a detailed census, the numbering of houses and the introduction of internal civilian passports.[82] Soldiers were employed in this process with those on leave being required to remain vigilant and report anything suspicious to their superiors.[83]

These developments should be seen in the general context of early modern *Polizei* rather than as militarization of society. The idea of the well-ordered police state (*Polizeistaat*) required an interlocking web of surveillance and regulatory systems that integrated military and civil spheres: the furloughed soldiers were themselves monitored by civil and military officials to whom they had to report and show their passes.

Moreover, as the critics of social disciplining have pointed out, it must be questioned whether these measures were entirely effective, particularly as they frequently had to be re-issued.[84] Certainly, the older image of crushed or docile German peasants has been extensively revised. Though there was no repeat of the nationwide Peasants' War of the early sixteenth century, the German territorial state continued to meet not just passive but active resistance. This took increasingly sophisticated forms as German peasants and artisans exploited the post-1648 juridification of imperial politics to utilize the formal structures of territorial and imperial justice to press their opinions.[85] Attempts by the Great

[80] As suggested by Kloosterhuis, 'Zwischen Aufruhr und Akzeptanz', esp. p. 190. For the debate on social disciplining, see W. Schulze, 'Gerhard Oestreichs Begriff "Sozialdisziplinierung in der Frühen Neuzeit"', *Zeitschrift für historische Forschung*, 14 (1987), 265–302 and J. Nowosadtko, 'Ordnungselement oder Störrfaktor? Zur Rolle der stehenden Heere innerhalb der frühneuzeitlichen Gesellschaft', in Pröve (ed.), *Klio in Uniform?*, pp. 5–34.

[81] N. Elias, *The Civilising Process* (2 vols. in 1; 1st published 1939; Oxford, 1994). See also M. Foucault, *Discipline and Punish* (Harmondsworth, 1979), pp. 135–69 arriving at broadly similar conclusions from French evidence.

[82] See n. 29 above.

[83] Instructions for men on furlough 31 Oct. 1779, HSAS, A30c Bü.12.

[84] In addition to the literature cited in n. 80 above, see the model study by P. Nitschke, *Verbrechensbekämpfung und Verwaltung. Die Entstehung der Polizei in der Grafschaft Lippe 1700–1814* (Münster, 1990).

[85] The literature in this area is now extensive. For recent contributions see B. Diestelkamp, *Rechtsfälle aus dem alten Reich. Denkwürdige Prozesse vor dem Reichskammergericht* (Munich, 1995), and his (ed.), *Das Reichskammergericht in der deutschen Geschichte* (Cologne and Vienna, 1990); W. Troßbach, *Soziale Bewegung und politische Erfahrung. Bäuerlicher Protest in hessischen Territorien 1648–1806* (Weingarten, 1987); and the illuminating case study by H. Gabel, *Widerstand und Kooperation. Studien zur politischen Kultur rheinischer und maasländischer Kleinterritorien (1648–1794)* (Tübingen, 1995).

Elector and his successors to close these opportunities to their subjects proved only partially successful for, as William Hagen has shown, Brandenburg peasants still utilized the Hohenzollern legal system to challenge their landlords effectively.[86]

A particular weakness of all German territorial states was their inability to fully harmonize their civil and military disciplinary measures. These often remained at cross-purposes, particularly as the development of a distinct code of martial law created a separate jurisdiction open to exploitation by soldiers seeking to avoid civil punishment. For example, though some governments permitted the civil courts to pursue sexual offenders sheltering in the ranks, most extended *de facto* exemption to serving personnel for all but the most serious crimes. Conversely, the sheer impossibility of imposing formal restrictions on soldiers' marriages encouraged many officers to tun a blind eye to long-term illicit liaisons.[87] The ambiguous legal status of furloughed soldiers was a particular source of problems. Experience of military service clearly gave some men the confidence to defy local officials, parents and employers when they returned home on leave. Ducal officials in Württemberg complained that furloughed soldiers failed to show the customary respect when asked for their passes, and caused trouble by poaching, gambling, stealing firewood and even physical assault.[88]

## IX: The Junker–Officer Symbiosis

The relationship of the army to the nobility requires particular attention and involves both the question of whether the company commanders were the canton's landlords and the broader issue of the Junkers' role in the Prussian officer corps. The first can be answered fairly quickly in the negative. The widespread assumption, discussed above, that company officers recruited their own serfs is not borne out by the evidence. Though half of the captains in regiments

[86] See W. W. Hagen, 'The Junkers' Faithless Servants: Peasant Insubordination and the Breakdown of Serfdom in Brandenburg-Prussia 1763–1811', in R. J. Evans and W. R. Lee (eds.), *The German Peasantry* (London, 1986), pp. 77–86 in contrast to Büsch, *Militärsystem*, pp. 67–71. For further evidence, see H. Kaak, 'Vermittelte, selbsttätige und maternale Herrschaft. Formen gutsherrlicher Durchsetzung, Behauptung und Gestaltung in Quilitz-Friedland (Lebus/Oberbarnim) im 18. Jahrhundert', in J. Peters (ed.), *Konflikt und Kontrolle* (Munich, 1995), pp. 54–117.

[87] Further discussion in P. H. Wilson, 'German Women and War, 1500–1800', *War in History*, 3 (1996), 127–60, and I. V. Hull, *Sexuality, State and Civil Society in Germany 1700–1815* (Ithaca, N.Y., 1996), pp. 101–2, 109–10.

[88] HSAS, A202 Bü.2248, 2276, 2278; A211 Bü.484; L6.22.8.15 covering cases from 1746 to 1749. Far from upholding the soldiers' right to leave as a civil liberty, the Württemberg estates urged the duke to keep them safely confined to barracks: L5 Tom.160 fol.394b-5, 402 from Dec.1752. For similar problems in Hesse-Kassel and Prussia, see Taylor, *Indentured to Liberty*, pp. 103–4, 187; Kaak, 'Herrschaft', p. 72, and Büsch, *Militärsystem*, pp. 53–4. With regard to the on-going debate on the concept of communualism (cf. Scribner's contribution in n. 65 above), it would be worth pursuing whether conscription and military service increased the differentiation within peasant communities, rather than reinforcing solidarity against external oppression.

stationed in East Prussia actually came from that province, this did not mean they necessarily held estates within their unit's canton. The proportion in other areas was much lower with only one-sixth of captains stationed in the central provinces coming from local families. Moreover, many nobles entering military and government service had no land at all, for nearly a third of those from the Kurmark had no estates and the proportion of landless aristocrats was often higher elsewhere.[89] Indeed, tying officer appointments to men with estates in specific areas would have rendered any careers and promotions structure completely impossible. On the contrary, the king encouraged the appointment of officers to regiments stationed far from their estates to compel them to concentrate on their military duties, while the periodic reorganization and expansion of the army resulted in numerous transfers from one unit to another.[90]

Even where the company commander was the local landlord, the period when he could act as a petty tyrant[91] was both relatively brief and an unintended by-product of Frederick William's style of government. It depended on the subdivision of the regimental canton into company districts where the local captain had the final say in selection and exercised military jurisdiction over potential recruits. This had been introduced in 1733 and though extended by Silesia ten years later, was abolished there in 1747 and completely throughout the monarchy in 1763 when selection was entrusted to regional management boards. Already prior to this date, the formal powers of the company commanders had been steadily curtailed.

This process was a direct result of the manner in which the canton system had been introduced. Frederick William had been concerned with the broad outline of manpower policy rather than the detail and his customary bluff style

[89] Figures from the period 1733–40: H. Bleckwenn, 'Altpreußischer Militär und Landadel. Zur Frage ihre angeblichen Interressengemeinschaft im Kantonwesen', *Zeitschrift für Heereskunde*, 320/1 (1985), 93–5. Only sixty of the 392 officers in the seven regiments of the Magdeburg Infantry Inspection serving in 1771 came from the same area as their canton, including only nine company commanders, or roughly 10% of the total: calculated from Hanne (ed.), *Rangirrolle.* Similarly, only 14% of Westphalian company commanders came from the area of their canton: Kloosterhuis (ed.), *Bauern, Bürger und Soldaten*, vol. I, p. xxxii. On the proportion of landless nobles, see Berdahl, *Politics of the Prussian Nobility*, pp. 21–3. Having peaked during the Seven Years War, the proportion of landowning Brandenburg nobles serving as officers declined over the rest of the eighteenth century: see F. Göse, 'Zwischen Garnison und Rittergut. Aspekte der Verknüpfung von Adelsforschung und Militärgeschichte am Beispiel Brandenburg-Preußens', in Pröve (ed.), *Klio in Uniform?*, pp. 109–42. Göse is highly critical of Büsch's failure to substantiate his claim for a symbiosis between Junker estate owners and company commanders.

[90] Lists of officers transferring between regiments are included in the unofficial contemporary unit histories reprinted as vols. X–XIV of *Altpreußischer Kommiss* (44 vols., Osnabrück, 1971ff, published under the general direction of H. Bleckwenn). See also the generals' biographies in K. v. Priesdorf, *Soldatisches Führertum* (10 vols., Hamburg, 1936–41). The relationship between many serving officers and their estates may have been fairly distant. It is clear from studies of individual Junker families that one male family member often administered the property, leaving the others free to pursue military careers.

[91] See Büsch, *Militärsystem*, pp. 33, 37–48; Jany, 'Kantonverfassung', pp. 246–7. As Göse, 'Zwischen Garnison und Rittergut', pp. 122–3 observes, a Junker's control over his serfs was often undermined by long absences serving with his regiment.

was clearly exacerbated by his failing health after 1734. Nonetheless, practical difficulties arising from ambiguities in the system forced him to issue more precise instructions.[92] These clearly failed to eliminate the abuses, to judge from the flood of complaints reaching his successor, Frederick the Great, in 1740.[93] The fundamental flaw was the captain's lack of accountability, a matter tackled immediately by Frederick in 1740 when he entrusted central oversight of selection to the regimental commander. These powers were strengthened in 1748, and the 1763 reform effectively made selection a civil matter. As contemporary discussions of the system often noted, many officers simply exploited their powers to supplement their salaries by selling exemptions, or otherwise left recruitment to subordinates who had no knowledge of the area. Though the tendency here is to moderate the Büsch thesis by emphasizing the erosion of the company commander's powers, it is worth remembering that both they and the senior NCOs retained considerable informal influence throughout. It was always wise for a furloughed soldier to return from leave with presents of food, money or cloth for the sergeant (*Feldwebel*) and captain.[94]

The wider relationship between the Junkers and the officer corps is more complex. As Büsch acknowledges, while most officers were noble, not all nobles were officers.[95] The aristocratic composition of the officer corps was neither unique within Germany nor had it always been the case in Prussia. Far from regarding military expansion as a benefit, many indigenous nobles opposed it throughout the later seventeenth century.[96] The Brandenburg nobility eventually accommodated itself with the army, as with other aspects of Hohenzollern absolutism, and was even prepared to serve in the infantry as well as the cavalry, unlike its Swedish counterpart which thought service on foot beneath it. This relatively flexible approach was forced upon the Brandenburg Junkers by their worsening economic position, inducing many to accept military service as an alternative to estate management.[97] Nonetheless, many East Prussians continued to refuse military service even into Frederick William I's reign, forcing his two predecessors to rely heavily on 'foreigners' as they established the army as a permanent institution (1655–1713). Many of these were

[92] See the orders printed in E. v. Frauenholz (ed.), *Das Heerwesen in der Zeit des Absolutismus* (Munich, 1940), esp. pp. 251–4.

[93] Skalweit, 'Eingliederung', pp. 203–4.

[94] Arnim, *Über die Canton-Verfassung*, esp. pp. 13–20; G. Schreiber, *Der badische Wehrstand seit dem 17. Jahrhundert bis zu Ende der französischen Revolutionskriege* (Karlsruhe, 1849), p. 163.

[95] Büsch, *Militärsystem*, pp. 97–8.

[96] J. Kunisch, *Fürst—Gesellschaft—Krieg* (Cologne, 1992), pp. 11–12.

[97] P.-M. Hahn, 'Landesstaat und Ständetum im Kurfürstentum Brandenburg während des 16. und 17. Jahrhunderts', in P. Baumgart (ed.), *Ständetum und Staatsbildung in Brandenburg-Preußen* (Berlin, 1983), pp. 41–79; E. Melton, 'The Prussian Junkers 1600–1786', in H. M. Scott (ed.), *The European Nobilities of the Seventeenth and Eighteenth Centuries* (2 vols., London, 1995), pp. 71–109 at 82–3.

outsiders, like the French Huguenot refugees, who formed 31 per cent of all officers in 1688,[98] but others came from the imperial nobility (*Reichsadel*), including families in the newly acquired Westphalian provinces. Both the Great Elector and Frederick I depended on such individuals not only to reduce their dependence on the more recalcitrant easterners, but also as part of their wider objective of cultivating a clientele within the Reich. It is still not clear whether Frederick William reversed these policies, but his successor certainly used the recruitment of officers and men as a way to extend Prussian influence into other territories.[99]

The rapid expansion of the army helped to reconcile the Junkers to the concept of state service. Here the sheer size of the army was important, providing 1,030 officer posts in 1688 composed with only 300 senior civil government positions. This figure had risen to 1,359 in 1717 and then accelerated to 3,116 by 1740, reaching 7,121 in 1806.[100] By 1713 the officer corps was being recruited from those families which had attached themselves politically to the Hohenzollern dynasty, or had an established tradition of state service. The substantial expansion under Frederick William created new opportunities for those indigenous nobles who had previously refused service or failed to gain access. However, many still remained outside as the officer corps became partly self-recruiting. Only 40 per cent of senior officers serving 1730–1813 were scions of feudal landowners (*Gutsherrnfamilien*), compared with 25 per cent whose fathers were already officers and 15 per cent from civil service families.[101] The expansion of the Hohenzollern state into Silesia and later West Prussia greatly increased the potential competition for places since the nobility of these provinces was far larger than that of the existing heartlands. Compared with 3,000 noble families in Brandenburg, Pomerania and East Prussia in 1800, there were 17,000 in the newly acquired regions and it has been estimated that at least two-thirds of all Junkers had no prospect of a civil or military appointment.[102]

Given these figures, we must question the assumption inherent in the concept

[98] R. Frhr. v. Schrötter, 'Das preußische Offizierskorps unter dem ersten Könige von Preußen', *Forschungen zur Brandenburgischen und Preußischen Geschichte*, 26 (1913), 429–95 and 27 (1914), 97–167 at (1914), pp. 110–14. This proportion declined to 12% by 1713. According to P.-M. Hahn, 'Aristokratisierung und Professionalisierung. Der Aufstieg der Obristen zu einer militärischen und höfischen Elite in Brandenburg-Preußen von 1650–1720', *Forschungen zur Brandenburgischen und Preußischen Geschichte*, NF1 (1991), 161–208 at 193, half of all native senior officers came from Brandenburg, compared with of 25% from East Prussia. Natives predominated in the senior ranks, holding 65% of all positions from colonel and above, compared with 25% from the Reich and 12% from France and elsewhere.

[99] Melton, 'Prussian Junkers', pp. 82–95.

[100] Hahn, 'Aristokratisierung', p. 192; Schrötter, 'Das preußische Offizierskorps', at (1914) p. 114. The total for 1786 was 5,511.

[101] E. Stockinger, 'Vorbildung, Herkunft und Werdegang militärischer Führer in Deutschland von 1730–1813', *Wehrkunde*, 24 (1975), 592–7 at 593 based on the biographies of 986 Prussian generals. The remaining 20% came from other backgrounds.

[102] Melton, 'Prussian Junkers', p. 108; Hagen, 'Seventeenth-century Crisis', p. 334.

of 'social militarization' that all Junkers were automatically militarists and that noble predominance throughout the civil administration can serve as evidence for the 'militarization of civil rule'.[103] There is certainly no direct link between the canton system and the presence of officers at the Prussian court since many military men had held court and government posts during the reign of the Great Elector. The court orders of ranks (*Rangordnungen*) issued in 1688 and 1713 already gave precedence to military personnel, but this itself was neither unique to Prussia nor evidence of militarization. Instead, these measures were intended to improve the army's social standing, integrate its officers into the state hierarchy and subordinate them to princely authority. Frederick William's personal obsession with all things military[104] certainly exaggerated the martial character of the Prussian court, but given the importance of the army to all absolutist regimes, most rulers were obliged to take a close interest in their armed forces. Despite being, in the words of one biography, 'totally indifferent' to his army, Elector Carl Theodor of the Palatinate nonetheless signed 20,000 military orders 1742–77, representing one-sixth of all government decrees that passed through his hands.[105] Finally, we must remember that, like many rank and file, officers frequently moved between civil and military occupations and often played a significant role in institutions of countries not normally associated with military rule; for instance, a large number of serving and retired officers sat as MPs in the eighteenth century English parliament.[106]

Far from consolidating Junker power, the canton system represented a further victory in the crown's long struggle for political control.[107] As in the other stages of the Historic Compromise, the state secured important advantages which are often overlooked. For instance, no new concessions were made to the nobility in the famous Brandenburg Recess of 1653 which merely confirmed or restored ones already granted in the previous century. On the contrary, the crown secured a major advantage in its right to tax the Junkers' peasants. This right was consolidated not merely by force of circumstance during the Northern War (1655–60), but by the Great Elector's success in securing confirmation through imperial legislation. Brandenburg led the way in forcing through Paragraph 180 of the Last Imperial Recess at the Regensburg *Reichstag* of 1654

[103] Phrase from Schissler, 'Social and Political Power', p. 104.

[104] Hahn, 'Aristokratisierung', pp. 184–7. K. R. and K. Spillmann, 'Friedrich Wilhelm I und die preußische Armee. Versuch einer psychohistorischen Deutung', *Historische Zeitschrift*, 246 (1988), 549–89.

[105] S. Mörz, *Aufgeklärter Absolutismus in der Kurpfalz während der Mannheimer Regierungszeit des Kurfürsten Karl Theodor (1742–1777)* (Stuttgart, 1991), pp. 25, 137. For the close relationship between monarchs and their armies see P. Mansel, *Pillars of Monarchy. An Outline of the Political and Social History of Royal Guards 1400–1984* (London, 1984).

[106] J. H. Broomfield, 'Some Hundred Unreasonable Parliament Men. A Study in Military Representation in the Eighteenth-century British Parliament', *Journal of the Society for Army Historical Research*, 39 (1961), 91–107.

[107] Here I follow Harnisch, 'Preußisches Kantonsystem', pp. 147–8.

which specified that all subjects of German territorial rulers were obliged to contribute towards military taxation.[108]

This is not the place to explore how the crown subsequently wore down opposition to its fiscal demands, as this is already covered elsewhere.[109] However, special mention needs to be made of Frederick William's defeat in 1717 of the Junkers' claims that military service should be based on the traditional feudal obligations of *ius sequelae*. Despite their appeals to the imperial courts, he established a direct claim to recruit their peasants, complementing the fiscal rights secured in 1653. However, it is highly significant that this victory did indeed include an element of compromise. Though the Junkers could no longer oppose the introduction of conscription, the king nonetheless protected their core interests by endorsing their continued feudal jurisdiction over their peasants, whether enrolled or not, until these were actually called up.[110] Since he had no intention of either freeing the peasants or alienating the nobles, Frederick William did not need to go further. Though it contained further safeguards for landlords' rights, the canton system had consolidated this arrangement by 1733. The state had intruded significantly into the Junkers' preserve, not displacing them, nor joining them as a partner, but emerging instead as a competitor for peasant labour. Though the Junkers gradually secured further recognition of their continued influence, they could no longer exclude the state or re-establish an exclusive monopoly over their dependent workers.[111]

In short, while the nobles were given preferential treatment within the Prussian military system, it was only on terms set by the crown. Further, it must be doubted whether the arrangements worked to the Junkers' long-term advantage. Battle casualties among officers were high, not only during the Seven Years War when over 1,500 died, but throughout the period as a whole.[112] More importantly, perhaps, the canton system inhibited the introduction of the new forms of economic management necessary to maximize profits. Certainly,

[108] Schmauss and Senckenberg (eds.), *Reichsabschiede*, vol. III, pp. 640–92. Further coverage in A. Müller, *Der Regensburger Reichstag von 1653/54* (Frankfurt/Main, 1992). For the socio-economic context, see Hagen, 'Seventeenth-century Crisis'.

[109] F. L. Carsten, *The Origins of Prussia* (Oxford, 1954), pp. 179–277 provides a good overview.

[110] Harnisch, 'Preußisches Kantonsystem', p. 148. This arrangement was not explicitly confirmed by Frederick William until 1739: see Büsch, *Militärsystem*, p. 55. The changes forced through in 1717 were linked to the crown's endorsement of the allodialization of noble estates; see Berdahl, *Politics of the Prussian Nobility*, pp. 23–5.

[111] 1792 Kantonreglement Para. 111, printed in Frauenholz (ed.), *Heerwesen*, pp. 309–36. Paragraphs 434–8 of the Prussian Allgemeines Landrecht of 1794 also confirmed that military service only temporarily interrupted a peasant's obligations to his landlord. Further evidence of the state's intrusion into the rural world is presented in the collection of essays, Peters (ed.), *Konflikt und Kontrolle*.

[112] Jany, *Preußische Armee*, vol. II, p. 668. Thirty-nine of the 253 officers who served in Inf. Rgt. Saldern (Nr. 5) 1708–71 were killed in action or died of their wounds: Hanne (ed.), *Rangirrolle*. Military service could also be very expensive and while some officers made profitable careers, many others failed and quit the service: Göse, 'Zwischen Garnison und Rittergut', pp. 129–34.

recent studies of agrarian developments east of the Elbe indicate a shift towards wage labour after 1763 that was increasingly at odds with the continued restrictions on peasant movement placed by the dictates of army and state.[113]

## X: Serfs and Soldiers

The Büsch thesis seems equally one-sided when we re-examine the position of the peasantry. That they suffered from the burdens of conscription is beyond question. Even with the numerous social and regional exemptions, military service still fell on a broad section of the male population while all were affected by the taxes required to sustain Prussia's inflated establishment. Nonetheless, as the canton system rationalized recruitment, it also made its demands more measurable, predictable and, therefore, easier to bear.

Moreover, as both Harnisch and Kloosterhuis have argued, the system adapted itself to the structures of peasant society. Its two fundamental institutions, the community (*Gemeinde*) and hearth (*Feuerstelle*), determined the shape and much of the internal administration of the cantons.[114] The constant widening of the exemptions, which began as early as 1714 and was still under way in 1800, suggests that the crown remained responsive to the interests of the mass of its subjects.[115] The furlough system permitted the conscript to maintain a firm relationship with his family; the situation was very different for Russian conscripts, who rarely saw their villages again.[116] Indeed, it remained possible for the Prussian conscript to lead a relatively 'normal' life, including marriage, which was also not always possible elsewhere. In contrast to most other German states, the Prussian army was far more likely to sanction soldiers' marriages and though these still depended on the Junkers' agreement, at least a third of all personnel were married in 1777,[117] a factor recognized by contemporaries as giving the canton system considerable stability.[118] Though this still awaits fuller investigation, it seems that the practice of

[113] Hagen, 'Junkers' Faithless Servants', and H. Harnisch, 'Peasants and Markets. The Background to the Agrarian Reforms in Feudal Prussia East of the Elbe, 1760–1807', in Evans and Lee (eds.), *German Peasantry*, pp. 37–70.

[114] For the structure of Brandenburg communities, see L. Enders, 'Die Landgemeinde in Brandenburg. Grundzüge ihrer Funktion und Wirkungsweise vom 13. bis zum 18. Jahrhundert', *Blätter für deutsche Landesgeschichte*, NF129 (1993), 195–256.

[115] The exemptions are discussed by Wilke, *Handbuch*, pp. 162–271; Kloosterhuis, 'Zwischen Aufruhr und Akzeptanz', pp. 180, 187–9; Skalweit, 'Eingliederung', pp. 205–8. Numerous examples are printed in Frauenholz (ed.), *Heerwesen*, pp. 225–351, and Kloosterhuis (ed.), *Bauern, Bürger und Soldaten*, vol. I. The 1792 Kantonreglement increased the number with personal exemptions on the grounds of religion, estate, profession or property by 230,000.

[116] J. H. L. Keep, *Soldiers of the Tsar. Army and Society in Russia 1462–1874* (Oxford, 1985), pp. 95–117.

[117] Figures from Skalweit, 'Eingliederung', p. 218. For examples and further discussion see Kloosterhuis (ed.), *Bauern, Bürger und Soldaten*, vol. I, docs. 287–97 and Wilson, 'German Women and War', pp. 134–52.

[118] W. A. v. Kaunitz, *Votum über das Militare 1762*, printed in H. Bleckwenn (ed.), *Zeitgenössische Studien über die altpreußische Armee* (Osnabrück, 1974), at p. 31.

discharging many conscripts prior to senility or disability permitted an element of retirement and allowed former soldiers to re-enter civil society, often in minor administrative posts.

Military demands, though harsh, could be accommodated within a peasant's reasonable expectations. As the system became measurable, it also became malleable, allowing limited possibilities for manipulation from below. Demographic structure ensured that most hearths had sufficient able-bodied men enrolled enabling the army to honour its promise in most cases not to draft single sons. Marriage strategies could be adapted to secure further exemptions and though bribery offered another route to avoiding the draft, Harnisch notes that wealth was no guarantee of success. Like the Junkers, the army also relied on the local patriarchs to keep order and ensure compliance with its demands.[119] Sanctions such as penalties for desertion endangered the entire family and its place in the community so that parental pressure often reinforced the formal ties binding a man to the army. Such compliance came at a price and the army had to show some respect towards local feelings.[120]

There is little evidence to support the central tenet of the Büsch thesis that serfdom was a vital prerequisite for the canton system.[121] Not only was this form of recruitment implemented in areas without formal serfdom, but similar methods were adopted in other German territories with very different socio-economic structures. We have already seen that key features of canton recruitment like the furlough system were well established elsewhere. Many territories went beyond this, also adapting militia organization to provide a flow of recruits into the regular army. This occurred in Ansbach in the 1720s, followed by in Württemberg 1733–7, Weimar in 1743–4, Neuwied after 1745, Schaumburg-Lippe in 1749–77, Hesse-Kassel from 1762, Münster in 1766–84, Austria from 1771, Baden from 1780 and Mainz throughout the eighteenth century, especially from 1773.[122] In some cases, particularly Neuwied, Weimar, Austria

[119] On the importance of these figures to the establishment of German and Habsburg absolutism, see H. Rebel, *Peasant Classes. The Bureaucratization of Property and Family Relations under Early Habsburg Administration 1511–1636* (Princeton, N.J., 1983). Bribery to gain exemption was also a feature of similar systems elsewhere, for example, Hesse-Kassel where local officials were not above misusing public funds to free their sons from the draft: Taylor, *Indentured to Liberty*, pp. 105, 138–9.

[120] Harnisch, 'Preußisches Kantonsystem', esp. pp. 151–7; Lehmann, 'Werbung', pp. 271–2. Taylor, *Indentured to Liberty*, pp. 113–256 detects similar strategies in Hesse-Kassel, but draws more negative conclusions. Berdahl, *Politics of the Prussian Nobility*, pp. 37–43 also argues that landlord–peasant relations were characterized by a limited flexibility.

[121] Büsch, *Militärsystem*, p. 73.

[122] Wilson, *War, State and Society*, pp. 176–82; Patze and Schlesinger (eds.), *Geschichte Thüringens*, vol. V, pp. 362, 370; V. Müller, 'Das alte Wiedische Militärwesen', *Heimatkalender des Landkreises Neuwied* (1970), 41–4; C. U. Frhr. v. Ulmenstein, *Die Offiziere des Schaumburg-Lippischen Truppenkorps 1648–1867* (Berlin, 1940), pp. 22–3; W. Kohl (ed.), *Westfälische Geschichte* , vol. I (Düsseldorf, 1983), pp. 646–9; F. Schülin, 'Die Werbeplätze für fremde Herren in der Grenzecke des Markgräflerlandes in der 2. Hälfte des 18. Jahrhunderts', *Das Markgraflerland*, NF4 (1973), 196–201; Harms, 'Landmiliz', *passim*. Würzburg also contemplated a similar system in 1741.

and Baden, Prussia was the direct inspiration for the changes; elsewhere the authorities appear to have reached them through their own process of experimentation with different forms.

Significantly, the authorities of these territories often pursued policies towards their rural inhabitants very different from the Hohenzollern practice of 'peasant protection' (*Bauernschutz*). This has been seen as a key link between the military and socio-political systems in Prussia and has been discussed at length by Büsch who regards it as serving state, not peasant, interests.[123] The policy involved safeguarding peasant holdings rather than individual liberties and was intended to restrict further expansion of Junker estates. Serfdom was thus regulated, not undermined. Büsch's argument is that this was essential for the canton system to function, because without some form of bondage, people would simply escape the draft by emigrating to exempt areas or outside the country altogether. There is ample evidence that contemporaries genuinely believed this and certainly the dismantling of serfdom after 1807 was accompanied by the extension of conscription to previously exempt groups and regions.

Nonetheless, the link was far from simple. The existence of serfdom undoubtedly did assist the army to monitor its potential recruits, but as the earlier discussion of the nobility's role has shown, the connection between cantons and estate management was scarcely direct. Moreover, other territories which lacked serfdom and permitted emigration still resorted to similar methods of recruitment. This is particularly true of Hesse-Kassel which, after 1762, made proportionately far heavier demands on its rural population than experienced in Prussia. The point here is that, while some system of surveillance was necessary to facilitate recruiting, serfdom was neither the only form, nor necessarily the most effective. For instance, revisions to peasant inheritance law undertaken in Hesse-Kassel to enforce primogeniture also enabled the authorities to preserve a pool of disinherited younger sons from which to recruit.[124]

Büsch's assertion that the canton system reinforced serfdom where this already existed is more problematic.[125] Certainly peasant emancipation was not an intention behind its adoption, though the association between freedom and military service was well established. There appears to have been a link between the revival of the Prussian militia after 1701 and a civil service proposal to abolish labour service in favour of cash rents paid to landlords. The

[123] Büsch, *Militärsystem*, pp. 56–61, 156–61.

[124] Ingrao, *Hessian* mercenary state, pp. 117–21; Taylor, *Indentured to Liberty*, pp. 70–4. Harnisch, 'Preußisches Kantonsystem' p. 146 concludes there was 'keinen funktionalen Zusammenhang zwischen Gutsherrschaft und Kantonsystem'.

[125] Büsch, *Militärsystem*, esp. pp. 51–66. A major problem with this argument is that it regards domain economy and lordship as relatively monolithic, whereas recent research stresses the complex and differentiated nature of East Elbian communities: see in addition to Peters (ed.), *Konflikt und Kontrolle*, the collection, also edited by Jan Peters, *Gutsherrschaft als soziales Modell. Vergleichende Betrachtungen zur Funktionsweise frühneuzeitlicher Agrargesellschaften* (HZ-Beiheft 18, Berlin, 1995).

idea that those who volunteered for duty should receive social benefits was also favoured within influential Pietist circles before 1713.[126] Though these benefits were still conceived in terms of old-regime privileges, the idea of extending personal freedoms in return for military service beyond the narrow circle of the nobility was potentially revolutionary. Significantly, these proposals were not enacted in Prussia and elsewhere there are examples of military manpower policy reinforcing serfdom such as in Mecklenburg, where the duke agreed with Sweden to exchange runaway serfs along with army deserters in 1715.[127] However, this was far from universal and the count of Schaumburg-Lippe freed any serf who volunteered for service after 1734.[128] Equally, both Baden and Austria introduced variants on the canton system precisely when their rulers were attempting to reduce serfdom.

It is difficult to draw general conclusions from these findings, but what does seem clear is that the ratio of military to civil manpower demands was often more important than the socio-economic structure of a given territory. Modest recruitment could generally be accommodated relatively easily, but sudden or prolonged demands placed all agrarian systems under strain since both agriculture and military service were labour intensive. Moreover, any compulsory service represented an intrusion into daily life and was liable to be resented as such, regardless of whether the man in question was a serf, free peasant or urban artisan. Evidence from Hesse-Kassel suggests that the army's manpower demands reinforced the power of peasant proprietors over their day labourers and servants who depended on continued employment to avoid military service. However, as recruitment increased, especially during the American War of 1776–83, labour relations were disrupted as employers were unable to provide the customary protection from the draft to which their own sons were often now being called. Similarly, the decision of the duke of Württemberg to double the size of his army at the start of the Seven Years War overloaded traditional militia selection methods and led to an influx of numerous unwilling conscripts who mutinied in June 1757.[129] Finally, the well-known failure of Joseph II's reforms in the Habsburg monarchy only partially bears out Büsch's assertion that social change could not be affected without undermining army and state. Canton-style recruitment was forced through, like the rest of Joseph's measures, at great speed compared to the Prussian system which emerged after the monarch had worn down much of the nobles' opposition and, crucially, established

[126] Schrötter, 'Ergänzung', pp. 104–6; C. Hinrichs, *Preußentum und Pietismus* (Göttingen, 1971), pp. 129–31.

[127] P. Wick, *Versuche zur Errichtung des Absolutismus in Mecklenburg in der ersten Hälfte des 18. Jahrhunderts* (Berlin, 1964), p. 49.

[128] Klein, *Wilhelm zu Schaumberg-Lippe*, p. 35. For similar examples elsewhere, see: Tessin, *Mecklenburgisches Militär*, p. 155; Sicken, 'Streitkräfte', pp. 700–5; Müller, 'Wiedisches Militärwesen', pp. 41–2.

[129] Taylor, *Indentured to Liberty*, pp. 129, 145–8; Wilson, 'Violence'.

mechanisms to recruit men without involving the old provincial estates.[130] In particular, sensitivity to peasants' core interests and the co-option of their key institutions ensured the Prussian crown enjoyed a broader and more stable basis upon which to force through its policies.

These conclusions suggest a new model for East Elbian absolutism, one that is closer to forms elsewhere in Europe, where the crown acted as power broker bargaining with key groups throughout society to secure their support and acquiescence.[131] Of course, this did not mean that the Hohenzollern state remained disinterested, or stood above society benevolently administering to the needs of all its members. On the contrary, it pursued its own objectives, defined largely by the wider European interests of the monarchy, and sought to sustain the internal balance upon which the maintenance of its own power and prestige was perceived to depend.

## XI: The International Dimension

Regardless of perspective, most commentators are convinced that the canton system assisted Prussia's rise to great power status. Opinions differ as to whether it did this by making the army qualitatively or merely quantitatively superior. Tying regimental recruitment to specific areas did give units the internal coherence and sense of common identity recognized as one of the Prussian army's chief strengths even by those otherwise highly critical of the system.[132] Most argue that it also provided the numbers required by Frederick William's military expansion, compensating for what is seen as the failure of voluntary, especially foreign, enlistment.[133] The compromises present in the system were thus an inevitable consequence of the need to reconcile increased manpower demands with the need to safeguard the state's social base.[134]

Nonetheless, foreign recruitment continued and was, as we have seen, even stepped up under Frederick the Great. It has been argued recently that canton conscription was adopted to reduce costs and so free funds to find tall recruits abroad to satisfy Frederick William's 'obsession with height requirements'.[135] While this may have been a secondary consideration, there is little to suggest that it was the driving force, especially as tall men continued to be sought within Prussia as well. Foreigners remained an integral element of every

[130] F. A. J. Szabo, *Kaunitz and Enlightened Absolutism 1753–1780* (Cambridge, 1994), esp. pp. 154–208, 278–95.

[131] For arguments in this direction, see Kaak, 'Herrschaft', esp. pp. 107–8.

[132] Schnitter and Schmidt, *Absolutismus und Heer*, pp. 54–5.

[133] Craig, *Politics of the Prussian Army*, pp. 8–12; Redlich, *Military Enterprizer*, vol. II, pp. 180–2; H. Rosinski, *The German Army* (London, 1966), pp. 17–18; H. W. Koch, *A History of Prussia* (London, 1978), pp. 87–9.

[134] Büsch, *Militärsystem*, pp. 11–20. This was already the line taken by Jany in 1926: 'Kantonverfassung'.

[135] W. R. Fann, 'Foreigners in the Prussian Army 1713–1756: Some Statistical and Interpretative Problems', *Central European History*, 23 (1990), 76–85.

regiment even if many of them were in fact Hohenzollern subjects recruited outside its canton. The customary distinction between reliable cantonists and untrustworthy foreigners should not be stretched too far, however.[136] A primary reason for preferring native recruits was they were easier to trace if they deserted, rather than their being necessarily more motivated.[137] Moreover, canton boundaries were subject to change over time, thus varying the regional intake of recruits. Some units were transferred to entirely different regions like Dragoon Regiment no. 2 which gave its Pomeranian canton to the newly raised Infantry Regiment no. 36 in 1740, eventually receiving a replacement area in Silesia two years later. The former Württemberg Dragoon Regiment taken into Prussian service in 1742 also received a Pomeranian canton, though interestingly, like an infantry unit purchased the previous year, it continued to draw additional recruits from the duchy for sometime thereafter.[138]

If long-standing connections with a locality did encourage solidarity in the ranks, the system's chief advantage was, in Frederick's own words, that it 'made the army immortal by providing it with a secure recruiting ground by which it has unceasingly regenerated ever since'.[139] This explains why he continued to recruit abroad since the cantonists were regarded as a reserve to be drawn upon sparingly when other manpower sources became unavailable.

None of this, however, accounts for Prussia's move to domestic coercive recruitment relatively late compared with many other German territories, not adopting the canton system until after 1713. Clearly no socio-economic developments were the driving force behind the change and for an explanation we need to examine the one area noticeably absent from the Büsch thesis: foreign policy. Prussia's international position did change after 1713 and directly affected Frederick William's desire for larger forces. To understand this we need to see how Prussia's military and foreign policy were related over the longer term. Prussia was already a significant military power within the Reich by the 1670s, but sustained its position by drawing on foreign resources. These included not only the French, Dutch and Spanish subsidies which have attracted attention before, but also the monetary and manpower benefits derived from the elector's influence in imperial politics. In the absence of a single national army, defence of the Reich devolved on the individual territories subject to varying degrees of co-ordination through imperial institutions. Many weaker territories remained unwilling or unable to contribute forces of their own and so lost the chief means of influencing policy. These 'unarmed estates' (*nicht*

[136] This is featured prominently in older, more conservative works, such as those by Jany and Bleckwenn.

[137] This was also the case in Hesse-Kassel: H. G. Böhme, *Die Wehrverfassung in Hessen-Kassel im 18. Jahrhundert* (Kassel, 1954), pp. 19–20.

[138] Schulze, 'Kantone Pommerns', p. 269; HSAS, A202 Bü.1207, 1210, 2113–14.

[139] Political Testament of 1752, printed in R. Dietrich (ed.), *Die politischen Testamente der Hohenzollern* (Cologne, 1986), at p. 411. Frederick expressed similar comments in his 1768 Military Testament: J. Luvaas (ed.), *Frederick the Great on the Art of War* (New York, 1966), pp. 75–6.

*armierten*) fell prey to their armed neighbours who, by fielding the missing contingents, gained a hold over their resources. The Great Elector and his immediate successor proved adept at extracting far more from these contributory territories than it cost to provide the substitute forces, which in any case frequently failed to appear with the official imperial army.

These opportunities were lost when the almost continuous warfare in western and central Europe ceased with the Utrecht–Rastatt peace settlement of 1713–14. Not only did Prussia's allies stop their subsidies, but the lesser German territories also refused to contribute and attempted to close their borders to further recruitment. Their new assertiveness received the emperor's backing, particularly as the exclusion of Prussia furthered Austrian access to the same recruiting grounds.[140] This coincided with a significant shift in the balance of power to the north and east as Sweden's decline permitted Russian penetration of Polish and imperial politics by 1716. Prussia now had to deal directly with the Tsar who had far greater reserves of men than the Swedes had ever possessed. Finally, the new royal title acquired in 1700 and recognized internationally in 1713 required an appropriate military establishment if it was to retain its value as a passport to great power politics. Though suffering considerable material losses, Saxony, Prussia's immediate German neighbour and longstanding rival, had retained possession of the Polish crown since 1697 and began rebuilding its forces after 1717. The international situation remained uncertain well into the 1720s, while Frederick William's efforts to reach an understanding with Russia proved unsatisfactory. Disillusionment with unreliable allies strengthened his desire for autarky and meant Prussia had to find its own means to sustain its expanding army.

Attempts to meet the increased manpower demand from voluntary enlistment were clearly failing by 1720, exacerbated by the king's mania for tall recruits. The army fell back on existing precedents, combining them in the hybrid that had become the canton system by 1733. Recruiting districts had been assigned to regiments as early as 1693 and though these were subsequently altered, it is clear that the local authorities were continually co-opted to impress additional men in their districts. A militia had also existed in the years 1654–79 and after long discussions from 1692 was partially revived in the period 1701–13. Finally, the furlough system had been developed since 1681 and was fully established by 1714, well before enrolling had been implemented. Foreign examples were also important, not least the Danish militia organization of

[140] For an overview, see Wilson, *German Armies*, pp. 44–149. For a detailed example, see K. Hüsgen, 'Die militärische Vertretung des Stiftes Essen durch Brandenburg-Preußen im 17. und 18. Jahrhundert', *Beiträge zur Geschichte von Stadt und Stift Essen*, 30 (1909), 1–92. Ulrike Müller-Weil has also argued that international pressure and the Hohenzollerns' desire to conduct a foreign policy free of domestic restraint lay behind their internal measures: *Absolutismus und Außenpolitik in Preußen. Ein Beitrag zur Strukturgeschichte des preußischen Absolutismus* (Stuttgart, 1992), esp. pp. 29–127.

1701—which later developed along lines similar to the canton system—and the Swedish method of provincial recruitment which was revised after 1719.[141]

Frederick William's measures institutionalized these procedures in a way that enhanced the surveillance powers of the central state without endangering its relations with any vital group in society. His decision to abolish the militia on 7 March 1713 signalled not so much a preference for a regular army, but a determination to rely only on centrally controlled institutions.[142] The militia as depot and as reserve returned as forms of recruitment. The former was introduced in 1716 with the practice of attaching unarmed recruits as supernumeraries (*Überkompletten*) to each regiment who served only during the spring exercise months, but marched with the others in wartime to step into the shoes of any fallen comrades. There were already 10,340 supernumeraries attached to the army by 1726 and their numbers were doubled in 1740/1 and again in 1755.[143]

A militia as reserve was established in 1729 with the formation of four 'Land' or New Garrison Regiments totalling initially 5,600 men.[144] These received supernumeraries and former soldiers discharged from regular units and acted as an emergency supplementary force in wartime. In that at least some regiments had reserves of trained but discharged cantonists, this aspect of manpower policy was in existence throughout other parts of the army.[145] Further units, formally designated 'Provincial Militia', were raised during the Seven Years War by drawing on reservists, cantonists and special groups like gamekeepers. These acted as a depot for the frontline units feeding recruits to them after basic training and preliminary experience in the defensive operations in Pomerania against the Swedes.[146] Finally, impressment continued alongside voluntary enlistment and foreign recruiting as an additional way of obtaining manpower in wartime. This was conducted ruthlessly into occupied territories like Saxony, Anhalt and Mecklenburg while foreign deserters and prisoners of war were also encouraged to enlist.[147] Such practices extended the arm of

[141] Jany, *Preußische Armee*, vol. I, pp. 568–75; Schrötter, 'Ergänzung', pp. 104–24; A. D. Ferguson, 'The Russian Military Settlements, 1810–1866', (Ph.D.Thesis, Yale, 1953), pp. 21–9 (covering Swedish conscription methods); J. Holmgaard, *Uden at landet besvaeres. Studier over Frederik 4.s landmilits* (Norrejylland, 1999) (on Danish measures). My thanks to Dr Michael Bregnsbo of Odense University for drawing my attention to this work.

[142] The order is printed in Frauenholz (ed.), *Heerwesen*, p. 194. Interestingly, the king did not abolish the local gun clubs (*Schützengilden*) until 1727. The nobility had already opposed Frederick I's attempts to reintroduce the militia after 1701, because they feared it would establish a direct link between monarch and peasant.

[143] The initial quota was twenty per battalion: Jany, 'Kantonverfassung', pp. 240–1, and his *Preußische Armee*, vol. II, p. 243.

[144] *Ibid.*, vol. I, pp. 646–7.

[145] See *ibid.*, vol. II, p. 242 for an example.

[146] *Ibid.*, vol. II, pp. 465–70.

[147] *Ibid.*, vol. II, esp. pp. 247–8, 666–7; Kloosterhuis (ed.), *Bauern, Bürger und Soldaten*, vol. I, esp. docs. 60–2, 185–96; W. v. Schultz, *Die preußischen Werbungen unter Friedrich Wilhelm I und Friedrich dem Großen bis zum Beginn des Siebenjährigen Krieges* (Schwerin, 1887); F. Wernitz, *Die preußischen Freitruppen im Siebenjährigne Krieg 1756–1763* (Wölfersheim-

Prussian recruiters back into those areas which had contributed before 1713 and, together with additional recruits secured by the king's influence in the smaller courts, compensated for the loss of the earlier advantages derived from the crumbling system of imperial collective security.

However, just as they helped to bring the canton system into being, external pressures also hastened its demise and it was already clear prior to the defeat at Jena in 1806 that this manpower policy could not be continued indefinitely. The territorial reorganization under way in central Europe since 1793 shifted Prussia eastwards into Poland which could not be easily absorbed into the canton system. Simultaneously, the Westphalian provinces were lost, followed by the other recruiting grounds in the Reich by 1802. The incorporation of the imperial cities into the surviving principalities deprived recruiting officers of their chief operational bases, while the administrative reforms in the remaining expanded states closed the frontiers more effectively than in the past.

## XII: Conclusions

Otto Büsch's concept of social militarization has remained highly influential and still shapes the general view of German and especially Prussian history today. As this paper has demonstrated, the new, differentiated view of the estate economy, together with comparisons with military–civil relations in other German territories, has made the original idea untenable. In its classic formulation, social militarization is tied to a specific version of 'Prussian militarism' that is at once both too narrow and too broad to be viable as an analytical tool. It is too narrow because by viewing Prussia as *the* archetypal military state it elevates it to the measuring stick for all militarisms.[148] Simultaneously, however, it is too broad because it defines militarism as the subordination of all aspects of society to military needs and considers militarization to be 'militarism viewed as a process'.[149] The problems raised by such an interpretation are amply demonstrated by recent studies of countries equalling or exceeding Prussia's level of military effort and success without reproducing its military or socio-political systems.[150] Militarization, if it is to retain value as a concept, needs to be redefined.

There has been a lively debate within the social sciences on the nature of militarization, but unfortunately, this has neither considered the Büsch thesis nor has it been taken account of by historians of old regime Prussia. As it stands, however, those historians who have engaged with this other militariz-

Berstadt, 1994); C. W. v. Prittwitz, *'Ich bin ein Preuße…' Jügend und Kriegsleben eines preußischen Offiziers im Siebenjährigen Krieg* (Paderborn, 1989), pp. 84–5, 112–13.

[148] This tendency has already been criticized by Berghahn, *Militarism.*

[149] Willems, *Way of Life and Death*, p. 6.

[150] J. Brewer, *The Sinews of Power. War, Money and the English State 1688–1783* (New York, 1989); M. t'Hart, *The Making of a Bourgeois State. War, Politics and Finance during the Dutch Revolt* (Manchester, 1993).

ation debate have been entirely preoccupied with late-nineteenth- and twentieth-century issues and so, like the social scientists, relate militarization exclusively with industrialization.[151] It would be fruitful to look beyond these time-specific interpretations, which are often linked to ill-grounded characterizations of old regime 'limited warfare', and to consider militarization as a multifaceted concept embracing economic, cultural and technical dimensions, as well as political and social factors.

Limitations on space prohibit such a project here but some brief comparisons can be drawn for seventeenth- and eighteenth-century Europe to place the German experience in its wider context. There do indeed appear to be two predominant forms of military organization in Europe but these are not those postulated by the old thesis of an east–west divide, contrasting absolutism and autocracy with liberal, parliamentary politics. On the one hand there are the permanent, paid, professional armed forces of the rich, commercializing and taxing states which could satisfy their defence requirements with only minimal recourse to coercive domestic measures. These included not only republics like Venice and the Dutch United Provinces, as well as England's limited monarchy, but also the archetypal absolute monarchy of France. All of these were highly militarized by the mid- to late seventeenth century in the sense that they had accumulated the means to maintain and project organized military force on both land and sea. All relied predominantly on voluntary enlistment, adopting impressment and forms of conscription either only partially or not at all and generally later and on a more limited scale than in the German states.[152] As a consequence their manpower levels fluctuated considerably between war and peace, particularly as they tended to rely on additional foreign auxiliaries hired for specific conflicts.[153] Apart from some limited schemes adopted for the French navy, little attempt was made to maintain a call on soldiers discharged back into civilian life, while militias generally remained distinct from the regular armies. Despite considerable difficulties and cash-flow problems, manpower requirements were nonetheless met thanks to relatively flexible labour markets and relatively large, or rising, populations.

By contrast, the Scandinavian and German states relied on more coercive forms of recruitment which, paradoxically, partly civilianized their large military establishments by integrating militia characteristics within a system of

[151] For recent contributions in this field, see P. M. Regan, *Organizing Societies for War. The Process and Consequences of Societal Militarization* (Westport, Conn., 1994); J. R. Gillis (ed.), *The Militarization of the Western World* (New Brunswick, N.J., 1989); M. Edmonds, *Armed Services and Society* (Leicester, 1988).

[152] For examples, see S. F. Graddish, *The Manning of the British Navy during the Seven Years War* (London, 1980); Lynn, *Giant of the* Grand Siècle, pp. 371–93; G. Hanlon, *The Twilight of a Military Tradition. Italian Aristocrats and European Conflicts 1560–1800* (London, 1998), p. 176.

[153] Examples of fluctuating manpower levels can be found in L. D. Schwarz, *London in an Age of Industrialization* (Cambridge, 1992) pp. 97–9 (for Britain 1701–1815), and Kroener and Pröve (eds.), *Krieg und Frieden*, p. 9 with details for France supplementing the figures in Lynn, *Giant of the* Grand Siècle, pp. 32–64.

permanent defence.[154] Regardless of whether they were monarchies like Prussia or civic republics like Frankfurt, these states generally lacked the means to raise large forces exclusively from paid volunteers. Labour was relatively scarce and inflexible while the state, despite intensifying its fiscal efforts since the sixteenth century, often had to contend with a limited tax base and an undercommercialized economy. In tailoring their military needs to social and economic reality, such states were not simply compromising with entrenched aristocratic interests, but turning their disadvantage into assets. Their manpower policy, combining a relatively high degree of coercion with an extended leave system, stood more chance of success given the small size of most German territories and the face-to-face nature of rural society.[155] These characteristics reduced social anonymity and the distance from political centre to periphery, easing the administrative problems and extending the reach of state surveillance. Co-option of village patriarchs, together with some sensitivity towards popular as well as elite interests, strengthened the system by giving it stability, but also reduced its ability to respond to military as well as socio-economic change. The absence of some of these elements in Poland, the Ottoman Balkans and not least Russia, suggests these cannot be grouped together with the German states in a monolithic 'eastern Europe' militarization schema, but instead need to be viewed as distinct forms in their own right. How these systems responded to the pressures of revolution and industrialization must await another study.

[154] For the Scandinavian monarchies, see L. Jespersen, 'The *Machtstaat* in Seventeenth-century Denmark', and J. Lindegren, 'The Swedish "Military State", 1560–1720', both in *Scandinavian Journal of History*, 10 (1985), 271–336.

[155] Even large urban centres in western Europe were far from anonymous, as demonstrated by A. Farge, *Fragile Lives. Violence, Power and Solidarity in Eighteenth-century Paris* (Cambridge, 1993). However, the level of state surveillance appears to have been much lower in these communities.

# Part II
# The Balkans

# [6]

# New Perspectives on the Historical Significance of the "Year of the Turk"*

The complex of events linked to the second Turkish siege of Vienna in 1683 often has been characterized as a turning point in East Central, indeed even European history, an argument which probably can be disputed only on semantic or philosophical grounds. For example, the late Hugo Hantsch once stated in private conversation that he firmly believed that the abortive Ottoman assault upon Austria's capital fundamentally determined the future of the Habsburg empire. Assuming that this judgment is valid, the purpose here is to refine, extend—and correct a bit—certain conclusions drawn in two earlier books, one in English and the other in German, concerning the subject in question. These observations are occasioned by the avalanche of writings evoked by the tercentennial celebration of the sieges in Vienna and elsewhere and by personal discussions of the author with the Hungarian historians, László Benczédi and Géza Perjes.[1] It is convenient to treat the topic under three headings: the antecedents of the Ottoman offensive, the significance of the events per se, including the delicate question of Polish participation, and the consequences of the allied victory and the subsequent campaigns in Hungary.

[1]Thomas M. Barker, *Double Eagle and Crescent: Vienna's Second Turkish Siege and Its Historical Background* (Albany: State University of New York Press, 1967); *Doppeladler und Halbmond—Das Entscheidungsjahr 1683* (Graz: Verlag Styria, 1982). The out-of-print American edition should be compared with the German version. Although the latter contains many improvements, some materials of the original had to be omitted. Most of the other new publications have a popular, antiquarian, local-historical or pedagogical character. The strictly scholarly contributions seek to clarify secondary issues and have not produced much that is novel with respect to either data or interpretation. The chief positive result of the many books, articles and professional gatherings has been largely an effort, albeit not entirely successful, to transcend narrow, religiously, dynastically and nationally based ideologies of the past. This holds true especially for Germanophone Austrian historiography. See the judiciously balanced critique of the literature by Karl Vocelka, "1683:1983. Ein Jubiläum? Fortschritt oder Stagnation der historiographischen Aufbereitung der zweiten Wiener Türkenbelagerung," *Mitteilungen des Instituts für österreichische Geschichtsforschung*, XCII (1984), 165-194. The more significant new studies will be cited in this article.

*The first draft of this article was read as a paper on June 9, 1983, in Vienna at the International Congress of Military History organized by the Austrian Commission for Military History. It was presented in substantially revised form on October 19, 1983, in Bloomington at a colloquium entitled "The Ottoman and Habsburg Empires During the Second Half of the Seventeenth Century" (sponsored by the Hungarian Chair of the Department of Ural and Altaic Studies of Indiana University and by the Center for Austrian Studies of the University of Minnesota). This final version has profited from the reactions of colleagues who participated in both meetings. The author is most grateful to Peter Broucek and Gunther Rothenberg for bibliographical data and other counsel.

The American edition of *Double Eagle and Crescent* offers four probable causes of the decision by Kara Mustafa and his master, Sultan Mehmed IV, to reopen hostilities with Austria: a) the inherently bellicose character of the Turkish state; b) the grand vezir's desperate need for money and the prestige of martial success in order to maintain his grip on domestic power; c) the rebellion in Hungary led by Imre Thököly; and d) the French diplomatic presence in Istanbul.[2] A footnote alluded to a fifth, possible factor, namely, the cabals of other foreign agents in the Porte's proximity.[3] In an earlier chapter there was also reference to the seignorial or, as Marxian historians would put it, feudal structure of Ottoman society.[4]

What might have been brought out more clearly, and what it is now possible to recognize beyond reasonable doubt as the result of a brilliant analysis by the Leipzig investigator, Ernst Werner, is the reciprocal relationship between the new provincial ruling class, the Ayanliks or, to use an alternate term, the Askeri, and the military adventurism of the central government.[5] The simplistic Leninist tenet that imperialism—a vague concept definable in many different, often contradictory ways—will inevitably lead to war deserves ready dismissal, but surely there is a plethora of examples throughout the course of time showing that the material and power interests of dominant elites may lead to armed conflict.

Of the five causes I was able to discern I stressed most heavily Kara Mustafa's character and putative subjective motivations.[6] I did this, I am virtually certain, because my neophyte historical vision, reflecting the conventions of graduate training thirty years ago, was conservative, circumscribed and not very imaginative—what was then called the "great man" approach and what is now commonly referred to as evenemential history, or *Ereignisgeschichte*.[7] Today most scholars view the past as a kaleidoscope of interacting factors and realize that historical causation is immensely more complex than previously suspected. To be sure, I have not changed my image of the Turkish potentate's personality. In this connection it may be noted that the eminent Polish Osmanist, Zygmunt Abrahamowicz, has meanwhile produced a solid, source-based biographical sketch of the grand vezir. It is grat-

[2]Barker, *Double Eagle,* pp. 149-151; Barker, *Doppeladler,* pp. 151-153.

[3]Barker, *Double Eagle,* note 90, p. 403; Barker, *Doppeladler,* note 74, p. 382.

[4]Barker, *Double Eagle,* pp. 55-63; Barker, *Doppeladler,* pp. 64-73.

[5]Ernst Werner, "Das Osmanenreich im 17. Jahrhundert—Systemverfall und Systemstabilisierungsversuche," in Robert Waissenberger, ed., *Die Türken vor Wien—Europa und die Entscheidung an der Donau 1683* (Salzburg: Residenz Verlag, 1982). Like most *Sammelwerke,* this volume is a mishmash of serious studies based upon original ideas and fresh research as well as less useful, entirely derivative pieces. The chronological table contains gross errors. Printed on glossy paper by a trade publisher, the book also reproduces seventeenth-century illustrations.

[6]Barker, *Double Eagle,* pp. 68-72; Barker, *Doppeladler,* pp. 79-81.

[7]Barker, *Double Eagle,* p. viii.

ifying that this work confirms my original thesis about Kara Mustafa's pecuniary and power-political dilemma.[8]

Nevertheless, were I to rewrite *Double Eagle*, I would surely downplay the historical autonomy of individual protagonists and would highlight the extent to which decisions are colored and probably, on occasion, determined by the economic, fiscal and socio-political ambience. Another element one would wish to emphasize would be the interplay of the rational and the affective in human existence, i. e., the role of psychology, whether of individuals or of groups (what French historiography nowadays refers to as mentalities). A related, equally important tack to pursue would be ideology as defined by contemporary social science, taking into account the fact that the political doctrines which have arisen since the eighteenth century were preceded by religious ones, Christian, Islamic or otherwise.[9]

It should be stressed here that Abrahamowicz, although persuaded that the ultimate cause of the 1683 campaign lay in the workings of Kara Mustafa's mind, does not overlook the existence of sociopsychological phenomena. The Polish researcher draws attention to the influence of an Ottoman anti-Infidel religious perspective, a kind of latent, Third-Rome outlook (my term, not his) in which the Viennese emperor is held to be a usurper, and to the conception of Austria—expressed so well by the writer Evliyâ Çelebi—as the enticing realm of the "Red Apple."[10] In all events, it is a prime obligation of historians to try to demonstrate how the actions of individual men are conditioned both by the quirks of their personalities and by the collective attitudes and beliefs of their immediate environments. From a theoretical stance, at least, all these cognitive tools can be profitably employed in further studies of the actions of Kara Mustafa and his compatriots.

In the English version of my book I also suggested that there was something morbid about the grand vezir's psyche. I would add now that his cruelty possibly exceeded the norms of a culture marked by a relatively high level of tolerance for violence, certainly, as indicated in *Double Eagle*, by no means the only example of its kind.[11] It is of course a great pity that the Ottoman

[8]Zygmunt Abrahamowicz, "Kara Mustafa Pascha," in Waissenberger, ed., *Die Türken vor Wien*, pp. 241-250.

[9]For a good working definition of ideology, see Lawrence Delbert Cress, *Citizens in Arms: The Army and the Militia in American Society to the War of 1812* (Chapel Hill: University of North Carolina Press, 1982), p. xii.

[10]Zygmunt Abrahamowicz, "Der politische und ökonomische Hintergrund des Wiener Feldzuges von Kara Mustafa," *Studia Austro-Polonica*, III (Warsaw: Państwowe Wydawnictwo Naukowe, 1983), 7-44, and *passim*.

[11]Barker, *Double Eagle*, p. 70. Clearly, most cultures tolerate violence and indeed legitimize it (armies). However, on occasion the degree of acceptance is especially marked. What is of fundamental interest to the historian is how, over time, the level is reduced. Cf. Norbert Elias, *Über den Prozeß der Zivilisation* (Frankfurt: Suhrkamp, 1977).

sources which have been discovered up to now do not provide the plenitude of background information that we would need in order to be able to make more tenable judgments about men, their behavior, decisions, and the course of events. Although we will probably be disappointed, we all live in the hope that further data will emerge from the Turkish archives.[12]

The possibility that Turkish historians may still be able to enhance our knowledge of what happened in their country in the late 1670s and early 1680s would be welcome from yet another, analytic perspective. It would enable us to test Géza Perjés' working hypothesis about the rational component of decisions concerning war and peace. Perjés has developed a grand theoretical framework for grasping the historical relationship between Hungary and the Ottoman empire, basing himself upon his intimate acquaintance with the thought of Clausewitz and with recent theoretical advances in the social sciences. He proposes that a constant objective of Istanbul's policy was to stabilize the empire's northwestern and northern frontiers by fostering the creation of subservient Hungarian political entities, buffer states or a kind of *cordon sanitaire*.[13] Whoever is a devotee of ancient history will be struck by the parallel with the client polities of the Roman Empire with its highly sophisticated system of strategic defense.[14] Admittedly, this is an inductive methodology bound to raise hackles. Indeed, Perjés has already caused something of a scholarly tempest within Hungary, particularly in light of criticisms by Ferencz Szakály and Domokos Kosáry. Nevertheless, his suggestions deserve to be discussed further, if only because the insurgent leader, Thököly, whether he wished to or not, could have become a new Turkish minion had the Porte not suffered disaster at the gates of Austria's capital.

We may next consider the siege and the culminating Battle of the Kahlenberg. Regarding the siege, let me refer to what one may call the "Leitsch

[12]Abrahamowicz, the best-informed Western researcher, has gleaned what are possibly the last kernels of new knowledge. Cf. "Islamische Quellen zur Geschichte des Türkenjahres 1683," typescript photocopy, International Congress of Military History, Vienna, 1983. (On file, Heeresgeschichtliches Museum Wien). It should be noted that the Turkish sources utilized in Barker, *Double Eagle,* are now available, expanded and emended with regard to details, in a single volume reflecting a well-coordinated international scholarly effort: Richard Kreutel and Karl Teply, *Kara Mustafa vor Wien: 1683 aus der Sicht türkischer Quellen* (Graz: Verlag Styria, 1982).

[13]Géza Perjés, "Die Türkenbelagerung Wiens im Jahre 1683—Arbeitshypothese zum Verständnis der Motivierung der osmanischen Staatsführung," typescript. See also *Mohács* (Budapest: Magvetö, 1979) and "The Battle of Mohács and the Disintegration of Medieval Hungary," *East European Quarterly,* XV (1981), 153-162. Perjés has held to his conception for some fifteen years. See "Az országut szélére vetett ország" [A Country Cast upon the Periphery of History], *Kortárs,* nos. 11 and 12, 1971, and no. 1, 1972.

[14]Cf. Edward N. Luttwak, *The Grand Strategy of the Roman Empire: From the First Century A.D. to the Third* (Baltimore: Johns Hopkins, 1970).

thesis," the argument in question having been proposed by the Viennese investigator, Walter Leitsch, who normally writes about political and diplomatic problems rather than military topics. The Austrian professor, who cites seventeenth-century observers—largely civilians, it appears, and including among the Westerners the well-known Romanian, Demetrius Cantemir—opines that Kara Mustafa deliberately restrained the offensive fervor of his troops. Leitsch emphasizes the undoubted fact that the grand vezir mounted a slow, methodical attack by means of approach trenches, artillery bombardment and mining and did not attempt a so-called general assault—a mass lunge or charge undertaken simultaneously from various directions. This, Leitsch hypothesizes, was because the Turkish leader wished to force the garrison to capitulate formally, which would have deprived the Porte's soldiers of their venerable right to rapine and would have meant that the vast riches erroneously thought to lie within the circumvallation, would have fallen entirely into his own hands.[15]

This interpretation cannot be upheld in light of the actual circumstances of the siege. It reflects, rather, unfamiliarity with military science—or the military art if one prefers—and the regrettable tendency of many historians not to concern themselves with essential technical data when they first venture upon the terrain of war and society. Although there are indeed a few examples of successful general assaults in the history of siege warfare,[16] such an outcome was simply not feasible in July and August of 1683. Three basic reasons may be adduced for this. The first is that the defensive works, albeit with little time to spare, had been placed more or less in a state of readiness—the subject is too esoteric to dwell upon here—and were manned by an adequate number of hardy, regular troops, some eleven thousand men as opposed to perhaps ninety thousand of the foe (a figure to be analyzed a bit further on). The tactically decisive factor of surprise—admittedly applicable to a siege only in a relative sense—was missing.

The second reason was that while Vienna was not designed as a fortress—in contrast to the ingenious geometric complexes Vauban was then building with clear strategic vision along France's eastern frontier—but was an old city to which fairly good modern works had been attached, its ramparts were massive and the moat very deep. A comparison may be made with Iraklion

[15]Walter Leitsch, "Warum wollte Kara Mustafa Wien erobern?", *Jahrbuch für Geschichte Osteuropas*, XXIX (1981), 494-515, esp. 511-512. The virtues of Leitsch's exhaustively annotated treatise are that it underlines the Ottoman perception of Habsburg weakness as a cause of hostilities and provides a new source-reference confirming domestic military pressures upon the Porte. Its main flaw—apart from the idea of a general assault—is a basically contradictory thesis (cf. pp. 449 and 511). Leitsch's citations of *Double Eagle* (pp. 502, 510) also suggest that he misunderstood the English text.

[16]They derive from the Thirty Years War but vary greatly from the situation about to be described.

(Candia) in Crete, where a similar, late sixteenth-, early seventeenth-century bastioned trace has survived more or less intact. To behold a colossus like this gives one pause to think. It would have been physically impossible to storm Vienna's walls, similar in magnitude and circumference, without further ado. Such an enterprise would have been extremely difficult even had there been adequate stocks of scaling equipment. For this there is no evidence in the sources. Indeed, all specialists, drawing upon both Christian and Ottoman accounts, underline the Turks' poor logistical preparations.[17] In practice, then, there was no alternative to the inherently gradual process of laying the groundwork for an assault by effecting breaches through gunpowder explosions, whether—primarily—by mining or—secondarily—by cannonry (the chief purpose of bombardment being to force the defenders to stay under cover).

The third reason for rejecting Leitsch's view is the nature of the combat that accompanied the siege. Close study of the operations demonstrates that both sides exerted themselves to the maximum possible extent. Moreover, only one part of the Ottoman host—the Janissary infantry with a strength of perhaps twenty thousand men—was suited for executing the tactics which a beleaguerment mandated. Moreover, these storm troops—the term derives not from the Nazi era but from the 1918 spring offense against the Allies in France—could be employed solely in the relatively constricted sector of the front selected for the attack, nowadays the park stretching from the Hoftheater to the new wing of the Hofburg. There was in fact no other utilizable site. A goodly portion of the moat was either under water or swampy, another segment of the bulwarks faced the Danube Arm, and on the south the walls were paralleled by the then unregulated *Wienfluß,* which in the case of heavy rain could suddenly swell into a torrent. Although the defenders were at the point of collapse by September 13, the numerical odds were not, for the reasons mentioned, as disparate as the ratio 90 to 11 might lead one to infer.

In support of this judgment, made initially in the English edition of my book,[18] I may cite the views of two internationally recognized authorities in the abstruse field of fortifications, the Sandhurst scholar, Christopher Duffy, and the now-retired specialist of the Vienna Municipal Museum, Walter Hummelberger. Duffy and I have personally discussed the Leitsch thesis and agree that it cannot be substantiated.[19] Hummelberger, for his part, has recently published two highly pertinent monographs. The title of the first

[17]Fahrı Çeliker, "Zweite Türkenbelagerung Wiens und Ursachen der Misserfolge" *(sic),* typescript photocopy, International Congress of Military History, Vienna, 1983, *passim.*

[18]Barker, *Double Eagle,* note 78, pp. 419-420.

[19]Cf. Christopher Duffy, *Fire and Stone: The Science of Fortress Warfare, 1660-1860* (Newton Abbot: David and Charles, 1975).

piece, "Totale Verteidigung Wiens," states the author's case incisively.[20] The contents of the second article, "Bemerkungen zur Taktik und Bewaffnung der Verteidiger Wiens 1683," elaborate his theme of maximal effort on both sides. Referring to the same eye-witness account that I used in researching *Double Eagle,* Hummelberger concludes that the resistance in the area of the Palace Bastion *(Burgbastei)* was bitter and that the actions of the opposing forces occurred within a tightly confined tactical milieu. He adds:.

> Bei den Verteidigern kam es stets darauf an, nach Überwindung des Explosionsschocks die Bresche gegen die sogleich einsetzenden und bei etwaigem Mißerfolg wiederholten Infanterieangriffe der Belagerer abzuriegeln. Tatsächlich konnten die Türken eine Erstürmung nur mit ihrer infanteristischen Elitetruppe, den Janitscharen, versuchen, deren Unterstützung durch die Artillerie zwar heftig aber doch nie ausreichend war.[21]

To sum up, the only way in which a general assault could have succeeded would have been for the Ottoman host to have arrived two weeks—or even a week—earlier than it did and to have made adequate logistical preparations for the task at hand.[22]

A technically more complex and hence more easily disputable topic is the relief operation on the heights of the *Wienerwald* and in the vineyards just below. For many years I have debated by letter and in personal meetings with my good friend, the distinguished Warsaw historian and connoisseur of the Year of the Turk, Colonel Jan Wimmer, certain aspects of Poland's formidable military efforts. As far as the number of Polish soldiers is concerned, we are finally in accord. The results of Colonel Wimmer's meticulous archival labors are quite convincing. It is now certain that 21,000 odd men or about 31% of the total relief force came from beyond the Carpathians.[23] The significance of this fact is another matter, however. To argue or to imply that Duke Charles of Lorraine could not have rescued Vienna without the Polish contingent really amounts to speculation. No matter how much most scholars enjoy doing it, reasoning based upon "ifs" can never be a fully

[20]In (no author), *Bedrohung und Befreiung Wiens: Materialien zum Vertragszyklus 1683* (Vienna: Gesellschaft für österreichische Heereskunde [Heeresgeschichtliches Museum Wien], 1983), pp. 33-46.

[21]In *Studia Austro-Polonica,* III, 81-110 (quotation, p. 96). See also Jan Wimmer, *Wiedeń 1683: dzieje kampanii i bitwy* (Warsaw: Wydawnictwo Ministerstwa Obrony Narodowej, 1983), p. 270. The volume is also available in a condensed German version (which lacks the fine maps and the scholarly apparatus of the original) as *Der Entsatz von Wien 1683* (Warsaw: Verlag Interpress, 1983). Cf. pp. 152-153.

[22]For technical military questions, especially regarding fortifications, the most up-to-date survey is Peter Broucek, Erich Hillbrand and Fritz Vesely, *Historischer Atlas zur zweiten Türkenbelagerung Wiens* (Vienna: Deuticke, 1983).

[23]Jan Wimmer, "Le déblocage de Vienne en 1683 et la part que les Polonais y prirent," *Revue Internationale d'Histoire Militaire,* LII (1982), 63.

satisfying intellectual exercise. One can go no further than to say that, while military engagements have been won and sieges lifted by armies with numbers inferior to their enemies,[24] the advent of the battle-steeled Polish warriors was probably essential to the success of the undertaking. In short, the historian is free only to *suspect* that the additional numbers and the improvement of morale that the impending Polish help appears to have brought about were decisive.

A second issue that Colonel Wimmer and I have differed over is Sobieski's role as commander-in-chief. Rereading what I have written on this problem, I am not certain whether Colonel Wimmer has correctly interpreted my position, something that is not necessarily his fault.[25] In any case, it has never been my intention to imply that Poland's king was only nominally in charge of the allied host and that he performed a merely decorative function. John III assuredly did not play Hindenburg to Charles of Lorraine's Ludendorff or Max Hoffmann. What struck me originally in trying to reconstruct the Battle of the Kahlenberg with its vast and difficult range of terrain and what has impressed me in examining other military encounters since then is that close tactical control is sometimes impossible—even if it becomes more feasible with the perfection of the *armée machine* in the eighteenth century—and that in practice the commanders of individual sectors may demonstrate much initiative and independence. I have likewise become more cognizant of the fortuity of battle, a factor heavily stressed by the most perceptive seventeenth-century military writer, Raimondo Montecuccoli.

In any case, it now seems that Colonel Wimmer and I have narrowed the gap between us on one central issue, to wit, the significance of the action on the left wing and of the Austrians' determination to reach the gates of the city as rapidly as possible.[26] However, we would still not agree, I imagine, as to which of various turning points in the battle was most crucial.[27] Accepting the military scientific maxim that "der Ansatz zur Schlacht entscheidet über ihren Ausgang," at least as a general rule, I see the start of the encounter in the decision of the Duke of Lorraine to seize the Kahlenberg and the Leopoldsberg and the commencement of combat in that sector. We are also greatly indebted to Colonel Wimmer for the most complete account of the Polish thrust on the right flank and for ascertaining that Sobieski's prime goal, though he failed to achieve it, was to cut off and shatter the Ottoman

[24]Dr. Broucek suggests the following examples: Gradisca in 1617 (Wallenstein), Nördlingen in 1634 (Gallas and the Cardinal Infante), Thionville in 1637 (Piccolomini) and Rocroi in 1643 (Condé).

[25]Barker, *Double Eagle*, pp. 322-324; Barker, *Doppeladler*, pp. 304-305.

[26]Wimmer "Le déblocage de Vienne en 1683," pp. 82, 92. Cf. Günter Düriegel, *Wien 1683—die zweite Türkenbelagerung* (Vienna: Böhlau, 1981), pp. 113-114.

[27]Wimmer, *Wiedeń 1683*, pp. 336-338, and *Der Entsatz*, p. 208.

army.[28] This is further affirmation of the king's outstanding strategic talents. After all, annihilation of the foe, that is, destruction of the capacity to resist further, is the classical objective of combat.

It is evident that the figure of the Polish monarch and Poland's participation in the relief of Vienna remain sensitive subjects for Poles, Austrians, and, to a presumably lesser degree, for Germans. Let me try—my American origins may afford me a modicum of impartiality as Colonel Wimmer has been so generous as to concede[29]—to be as precise as possible about this subject. First, it is axiomatic that critical remarks concerning the national heroes or observations about the perceptible common psychological traits of other peoples cannot be automatically equated with prejudice. Rather it behooves historians to judge the many facets of the past as dispassionately as they can and to be aware at least of the influence their own value-systems exert upon them. Thereby, naturally, one always runs the risk of being mistaken on an individual question. On the whole, Poland's monarch seems an attractive, indeed inspiring personage. Yet has there ever been a champion who was not somehow flawed? Sobieski did manifest, I think, a few less appealing personality-traits, some owing no doubt to political necessity and to the decidedly adverse social and constitutional circumstances in his native land.

Regarding the Battle of the Kahlenberg, there is now a consensus that the allies' triumph was a joint accomplishment and that no party's share in it—let us not forget, for that matter, the exertions of *volontieri* from outside the Holy Roman Empire and Poland—should be denigrated. However, it is impossible to concede that Sobieski's role was "the greatest,"[30] that he was "the father of the victory" or that "to him must be ascribed the main credit [for the outcome] regardless of what the majority . . . [of non-Polish] historians have had to say about the subject."[31] The truth is that the engagement constitutes a laudable, historically uncommon example of cooperation and harmony between upper staff echelons and multinational forces. The fact that Sobieski served as supreme commander—in an inherently haphazard, loosely coordinated operation at that—is insufficient reason to regard his contribution as more deserving than that of Charles of Lorraine and his asso-

[28]Wimmer "Le déblocage de Vienne en 1683," p. 82. Abrahamowicz ("Islamische Quellen," p. 6) stresses that the Ottoman sources all credit the Poles as having contributed "decisively" to the Kahlenberg victory and to the subsequent successes along the Danube in western Hungary. However, the statement is of a rather general character and might be construed as exculpatory. Admittedly, the case is stronger with regard to the Danubian campaign.

[29]*Ibid.*, p. 57

[30]*Ibid.*, p. 83.

[31]Zbigniew Wojcík, "Johann III. Sobieski—ein polnischer Staatsmann," in Waissenberger, ed., *Die Türken vor Wien*, p. 183.

ciates with whom the king dealt prior to the engagement as peers in every respect save the protocol of social rank. The most rational and just conclusion is that the laurel leaves should be apportioned *equally* among the dedicated military professionals in question.[32]

One final thought may be offered about the importance of Poland's participation in the relief of Vienna. Even if in the last analysis Sobieski's decision to help Austria was not a revelation of unadulterated altruism but rather of enlightened personal and national self-interest, it nonetheless serves to symbolize the fact that Poland was and is a part and parcel of the Western world. The monarch's personal attachment to and understanding of Christianity can probably also be considered an expression of this reality. The gifted and spirited Polish people, who have had to suffer so much and so long (and indeed are still suffering) from an exposed geopolitical situation, weaker numbers and resources, and hence from the constant intervention of powerful and thoroughly ruthless neighbors, merit a generous portion of historiographical sympathy.

The third theme established at the outset of these observations—the consequences of the reverses suffered by the Ottoman empire on September 12, 1683, and in the succeeding War of the Holy League—can be addressed but briefly in the present context. In my book, apart from the admittedly crucial topic of coffee and coffee houses, I paid no attention to the cultural facets of the confrontation between cross and crescent. While it is a commonplace of anthropology that cultural receptivity characterizes all human collectivities to a greater or lesser degree and while there were quite intriguing effects upon some aspects of life in the West, especially in the culinary and artistical realms, historians must discriminate between greater and lesser extraneous impulses. It is impossible to detect in the conflict between Turkey and Austria the presence of any major stimuli to the development of Western civilization. This stands in sharp contrast, of course, to conditions in Medieval Spain, the sanguinary *reconquista* having been accompanied by pronounced Islamic influence upon the esthetic and intellectual growth of the Christian world. In other words, one should guard against overemphasizing the results of more pacific contacts between the Austrian occident and the Ottoman orient. The cultural achievements of the Habsburg empire must be seen primarily within the confines of European development, the balance of the

[32]Colonel Wimmer's assertion that the "chief" share of (personal?) glory should go to Sobieski conflicts with his willingness, in another place, to divide credit equally ("Le déblocage de Vienne en 1683," pp. 90-91, *Der Entsatz*, pp. 289-290). However, he is undoubtedly correct in stressing the symbolical importance of Sobieski's achievement for later generations of Poles (*ibid.*, p. 290).

exchange between Turkey and the West over the past three centuries tilting strongly in the latter direction.[33]

We may next inquire whether the military events under discussion caused any substantial alteration of economic and social conditions. Certainly the imposition of one's will upon an adversary through the use of force can evoke radical transformations of this kind. The Soviet October Revolution is perhaps the most trenchant instance. To my mind, however, Kara Mustafa's defeat and later Ottoman setbacks in Hungary and the Balkans had only a modest effect upon the infrastructures of either Turkey or Austria, though the results for the Habsburg monarchy in a strictly economic sense were more than marginal. Turkey did not begin to change appreciably until the latter part of the nineteenth century,[34] whereas there was no readily perceptible acceleration of evolution in Austria until the time of Maria Theresa and Joseph II.

The chief result of the great war between 1684 and 1699, named after the "holy League" of Christian states, was political—whether with regard to Austria's gains in the Pannonian basin or, as Professor İnalcik has so lucidly demonstrated,[35] with respect to Turkey's reverses north of the Black Sea. I have commented upon this aspect, as far as the France of Louis XIV is concerned, in my book, and Jean Bérenger has recently thrown important new light upon the topic.[36] In any case, speaking from a strictly European perspective, the significance of the victory was almost certainly greater for the Habsburgs and for the Kingdom of Hungary than for others. Although the

[33]See Anton C. Schaendlinger, "Die Entdeckung des Abendlandes als Vorbild: ein Vorschlag zur Umgestaltung des Heerwesens und der Außenpolitik des osmanischen Reiches zu Beginn des 18. Jahrhunderts," in Gernot Heiss and Grete Klingenstein, eds., *Das osmanische Reich und Europa 1683 bis 1789: Konflikt, Entspannung und Austausch,* in *Wiener Beiträge zur Geschichte der Neuzeit,* X (Vienna: Verlag für Geschichte und Politik, 1983), 89-112. Also in the same publication: Filiz Yenişehirlioğlu, "Western Influence on the Ottoman Architecture in the 18th Century" *(sic),* pp. 153-178; Michaila Stajnova, "Neue Richtungen im künstlerisch-literarischen Schaffen der osmanischen Türkei zu Beginn des 18. Jahrhunderts," pp. 179-193. See also Vojtech Kopčan, "Die tschechoslowakische Literatur zu den Türkenkriegen," in *Die Türkenkriege in der historischen Forschung* (Vienna: Franz Deuticke, 1983), pp. 79-97, esp. 92-94. The title of another joint study, (no author), *Die Türkenbelagerung Wiens 1683 und ihre Auswirkungen für die politische, kulturelle und geistige Entwicklung der Balkanvölker,* in *Mitteilungen des bulgarischen Forschungsinstitutes in Österreich,* vol. II (Vienna:. Bulgarisches Forschungsinstitut, 1983),is, unfortunately, a misnomer. The articles all deal not with the consequences of the siege but rather with a variety of earlier, general Eastern European themes. One piece does address the antecedents of the subject.

[34]The ultimate consequence of the defeat at Vienna and later reverses was acceleration of the process of decline in the central government's authority. See İlber Ortayli, "Die gesellschaftlichen und wirtschaftlichen Folgen der zweiten Belagerung Wiens für das osmanische Reich," *Studia Austro-Polonica,* III, 199-206.

[35]Halil İnalcik, "The Northern Front 1683-1700." Paper delivered at the 1983 Indiana University colloquium.

[36]Jean Bérenger, "Ludwig XIV. und Frankreichs Streben nach der Vormachtstellung in Europa," in Waissenberger, ed., *Die Türken vor Wien,* pp. 37-45.

origins of the dynasty's gradual withdrawal from the affairs of German empire may be traced back to the first third of the sixteenth century, there can be little doubt that the fifteen-year struggle on Europe's southeastern periphery was a major watershed. It was the centerpiece of an era which witnessed the formation of a great power, "das Werden einer Großmacht," to use Oswald Redlich's perspicacious phrase and which has loomed large in public consciousness ever since.[37]

In conclusion—disregarding for the nonce my earlier stricture about historical "ifs"—it may be argued, as I did in *Double Eagle* and as Aulic Councillor Dr. Allmayer-Beck has affirmed in an address to members of the Austrian Commission for Military History, that we now have a much clearer understanding of the fundamental meaning of the 1683 drama and its sequel.[38] Western civilization was not saved on the slopes of the Kahlenberg. Had the Turks managed to seize Vienna, their advantage would have been fleeting at best. They could not have maintained themselves there for long. They were, to borrow an heuristically useful concept from Marxian historiography, the representatives of a polity characterized by "retarded" socioeconomic circumstances; the Ottoman state did not follow the upward curve of "historical progress." Turkey was not only at the end of its logistical tether. It also lacked the basic internal sources of strength for further conquests. It could no longer maintain its venerable tradition of military expansion. The fact that the grand vezir had reached the end of his rope too must thus be regarded as emblematic.[39]

*State University of New York, Albany* THOMAS M. BARKER

[37]Oswald Redlich, *Das Werden einer Großmacht: Österreich in der Zeit von 1700 bis 1740*, 4th ed. (Vienna: R. M. Rohrer, 1962). The tercentennary celebration, with its spate of special museum exhibits, especially in Austria, was indicative of a long-standing popular fascination with the topic. The most spectacular show of the "Türkenrummel" was organized in Vienna's *Künstlerhaus* by the Municipal Historical Museum but, unfortunately, was marred by serious Turcological blunders and the use—in only slightly modified form—of published historical maps without attribution.

[38]Johann Christoph Allmayer-Beck, "Bedrohung und Befreiung Wiens 1683: eine weltgeschichtliche Einführung," in (no author), *Bedrohung und Befreiung Wiens 1683*, pp. 1-12.

[39]Although not within the immediate purview of this article, mention should be made of the work of the Czech archivist Jaroslav Macek, who has unearthed the only fresh source materials for the events of 1683. The data show, *inter alia*, that the Vienna garrison was probably able to communicate with the Austrian field army on a regular basis notwithstanding the siege. Jaroslav Macek, "Kaspar Zdenko Kaplíř von Sullowitz und seine Bedeutung für die Verteidigung der Stadt Wien—ein Beitrag zum Türkenjahr 1683," *Österreich in Geschichte und Literatur* XXVII (1983), 203-224. Czech depositories may yet provide other illuminating factual details. Cf. Macek, "Böhmische und mährische Archivalien zur Geschichte des Jahres 1683," *Scrinum: Zeitschrift des Verbandes österreichischer Archivare*, XXI-XXX (1979-1984), 431-444.

# [7]

# *Infantry Battlefield Tactics in the Seventeenth and Eighteenth Centuries on the European and Turkish Theatres of War: the Austrian Response to Different Conditions*

**Alexander Balisch**

This paper intends to give an overview of the changes in military tactics during the 17th and 18th centuries with special reference to the developments in the Austrian army as they affected its wars against Turkey. By its nature the paper will have to resort to generalization and in parts even over-simplification and will deal exclusively with infantry battlefield tactics and only marginally refer to the tactics of artillery and cavalry. Neither could a discussion of the "small war" and of the problems of logistics be included.

All European armies were affected by the political and technical developments and their implications which were to lead to the creation of standing professional armies and the standardized and formalized 18th century line tactics. Contrary to other Western and Central European armies, however, the Austrian army had to develop alternate tactical and strategic concepts to combat successfully their *Erbfeind*, their traditional enemy, the Turks. This enemy differed drastically from all others in several aspects.

The Ottoman Empire was an enemy with a fanatically pursued mission: to conquer Christian Europe and bring it into the fold of Islam. This was not a threat which could be taken lightly. The Turks could easily put armies into the field against Austria which greatly outnumbered the forces the Habsburgs could muster. Furthermore, the tactics employed in the 18th century against the conventional armies of European nations proved ineffective against the Turks whose wild hordes did not adhere to the rules of formalized European warfare. Therefore, in addition to responding to the general European developments of tactics, the Austrians had to find different methods to combat successfully an unconventional military challenge.

In Europe, during the 17th and 18th centuries, tactical ideas and practices changed steadily as a result of changes and advances in weaponry and of practical experiences gleaned during the long wars of this period. As a result of this constant demand for change the whole system of warfare was in a state of flux.

Prior to the 14th century the main striking force of European armies had been the knightly cavalry. In the 15th century the appearance of disciplined infantry, particularly the Swiss pikemen and their copy, the German *Landsknechte,* had led to the decline of this knightly cavalry. Following the transformation of the cavalry in the 17th century into a recruited force, the cavalry partly regained its relative importance in the European armies. During the Thirty Years' War, cavalry formed at least half of a typical army.[1]

The usual battle order during the Thirty Years' War consisted of two or three lines of infantry squares, usually eight to ten deep, flanked by cavalry. Each infantry square consisted of a core of pikemen, flanked, and sometimes also fronted by ranks of musketeers. Loading and firing was slow and cumbersome and the firing method used was that of the *caracole.*[2] During the war a new method, the peloton fire,[3] was introduced, as improvements in musket development of faster firing muskets and shallower formation of infantry squares of six ranks were made possible and the use of musketeers increased. Gradually the battalion developed into a force armed for fire action as well as shock action.

The number of pikemen, which at the beginning of the 17th century had formed the majority of the infantry, drastically declined during this war. By 1670 the pikemen in the Austrian Field Marshal Montecuccoli's army formed only one third of the infantry.[4]

In spite of the now increased firepower, a result of the improved weapons, Field Marshal Montecuccoli still considered the pike important for the infantry—"the queen of weapons".[5] He did not believe that musketeers alone could withstand a cavalry attack, as the musketeers now formed their separate squares.[6] He therefore insisted that the front of musketeers between the pike squares be no wider than seventy to eighty men,[7] as otherwise cavalry could open a gap in the frontline. His argument seemed to have been a sound one, considering the conditions of the time. In 1674 the French Marshal Turenne, for example, protected his infantry against a German cavalry attack by forming a pike square with his musketeers in its center. The German cavalry did not dare to attempt penetration.[8]

Montecuccoli retained the formation of pikemen in six ranks. A shallower one he considered too vulnerable, a greater depth would have been worthless, as the pikes of the sixth rank reached only to the first rank.[9] The battle order, according to Montecuccoli, still consisted of the army arranged in two lines, the infantry in each line in six ranks, the cavalry in three ranks. The battalion was the tactical unit of the infantry with a suggested strength of 1280 men: 480 pikemen, 720 musketeers and 80 shieldbearers, whose task it was to 'sneak' between the attacking enemy cavalry.[10] He favoured alternating infantry battalions and cavalry squadrons, although the usual practice was (a practice which was retained into the eighteenth century) to place the cavalry on each wing of the battle order.

The last years of the 17th century saw an intensification of the rapidity of change in the development of weapons and tactics. The adoption of two innovations was responsible for the most consequential tactical changes: the development of a reliable, faster firing fusil and the invention of the bayonet. The faster firing fusil led to a further reduction of the number of ranks, first to four (introduced by the Austrians around 1700) and eventually to three ranks. This last reduction was only gradually adopted by the European armies. For example, the Prussians introduced the three-rank formation in 1718, whereas the Austrians retained the four-rank formation until 1757.

The ongoing argument about the value of pikes was finally settled by the introduction of the bayonet which gave the fusil the qualities of both fire and shock weapon. The experience of the Austrians with the Turkish cavalry, which had proven able to break pikes with their sabres, may explain why the Austrians became the first to abandon the pike in favour of the fusil with bayonet during the last years of the 17th century.[11] The other European armies followed the Austrian example within a decade. Although some military theoreticians (e.g. the Marshal de Saxe) deplored the abandonment of the pike, it had, to all intents and purposes, disappeared forever.

Two methods of firing emerged as the preferred ones: the peleton fire in which each platoon fired by ranks and the battalion by alternating platoons to keep up a continuous fire, became the most favoured method, followed in importance by the firing by ranks in succession. Keeping up a regular peleton fire during battle proved to be difficult; after two or three orderly discharges every man fired more or less at his own speed. Before the middle of the 18th century only the Prussian army, drilled and disciplined to a degree previously unknown, was to come closest to the ideal. Usually, an army advancing toward the enemy had to stop to fire. As it was difficult to get the men moving again, several generals advocated attack without firing. The Austrians tried this in the battle of Chotusitz in 1742, but suffered heavy losses through the accurate, regular fire of the Prussians.[12]

The possibilities of the bayonet as both offensive and defensive weapon were only slowly recognized. As, originally, the bayonet had to be inserted into the barrel of the fusil, one could not fire with bayonet mounted. Therefore, the bayonet could only be mounted in the last moments before actual contact with the enemy. The invention of the socket bayonet eliminated this problem. Yet, although firing with fixed bayonet was possible during the first decade of the 18th century, it was not practised until the Prussians introduced it in 1732.[13] It should be noted here that, as in the case of the pike, actual hand to hand combat with fixed bayonet rarely occurred.[14]

The European armies also were slow to realize the advantages and implications of the introduction of the thin line formation with its uniformly armed infantry and increased fire power. The Prussian army was the exception. The Prussian generals realized that to take full advantage of this new formation and its possibilities, extreme discipline and rigorous drill were required. They aimed at the greatest possible rate of fire at a time when all other armies still practiced a firing drill at slow, measured rate. Later in the century, when the Austrians, too, intensified drill and achieved a more rapid rate of fire, they continued to put more emphasis on aimed fire at a slower rate than the Prussians.

By 1740 the Prussian army had developed into the best drilled and best disciplined army of Europe. The Austrian army, however, had gone through a period of decline during the two decades before the accession of Maria Theresa to the Habsburg throne. Her father, Charles VI, had not shown the same interest in military matters as had his contemporary, Frederick William I of Prussia. Prince Eugene of Savoy, under whose leadership the Austrian army experienced the greatest successes in its history, had grown old and, to an extent, had lost his firm grip on the military establishment. Moreover, although a brilliant field commander and a born leader, he had contributed little to military thought nor had he founded a school of military theory.[15]

Whereas the Prussians had introduced their first drill manual to be adhered to by all infantry regiments in 1702, the different regiments of the Austrian army (both infantry and cavalry) each had their own drill manual until the middle of the 18th century when the first manuals for the whole army were issued. In several respects these regimental manuals showed great differences, especially in the execution of evolutions and in the wording of commands. In addition, drill and discipline were deplorably neglected.[16]

Such conditions naturally led to confusion, particularly when during the 1720's and 30's discipline in the Austrian army deteriorated. The Austrian War Council was aware of these shortcomings and, in 1714, ordered all regiments to submit their drill and duty manuals so that general regulations could be composed. In 1717 Field Marshal Duke Alexander of Württemberg, Prince von Bevern and other generals were ordered to prepare a manual for the imperial infantry. Prince Eugene approved the draft, but decided not to take any action as he did not want to introduce changes against the wishes of the regimental proprietor colonels, in order to preserve peace and unity in the army.[17] A military commission, established in 1737, finally did complete the task and the first infantry drill manual to be used by all regiments, was issued by the War Council. However, the Turkish Wars of 1737/9 and the Wars of the Austrian Succession, 1741/8, prevented the implementation of these uniform drill regulations. In her 'Political Testament', written in the 1750's, Maria Theresa complained that at the time of her accession to the throne no general regulations existed in her army, "everyone executed different evolutions during marches, drill—in everything; one used rapid fire, another slow fire; the same command words meant different things in different units."[18]

The military reverses during the above mentioned wars clearly showed the consequences of these deplorable conditions. It must be emphasized, however, that such conditions existed not only in the Austrian army. Whereas the Austrians suffered defeat in every battle against the Prussians during the wars of 1741/8, they were victorious in the major engagements against the French, Bavarian and Spanish armies.

Finally, in 1748, a military reform commission was set up to initiate reforms of the whole military establishment. One of the results of the deliberations of this commission was the introduction of drill and duty manuals for the whole Austrian army.[19] The new manuals did not contain any drastic changes of tactical concepts and practices; their role in greatly improving the quality of the Austrian army was due mainly to the strict implementation of the new regulations. During the Seven Years' War and the War of the Bavarian Succession, the Austrian army showed itself the equal of the Prussian army. The Austrian defeats in battles of the Seven Years' War could be blamed more on inferior generalship than on the Austrian army itself. Of course, these reforms were only part of the thorough reforms of the state under Maria Theresa and would not have been possible without the fairly successful centralization of government and the resulting decline of the power of the estates.[20] The manuals of 1749/51 remained in their main points unchanged until the introduction of Field Marshal Lacy's drill manual of 1769 which served the Austrians up to the last years of the century. One important change was introduced after the battle of Kolin in 1757: the reduction of the infantry formation to three ranks.

On the whole, the battle order to be employed during the late 18th century by the Austrian army on the Central European theatre of war remained relatively unchanged since the early years of the century with the above mentioned exception of a reduction of the infantry lines to three ranks. Warfare throughout Europe had become standardized and formalized. Armies were drawn up in two lines with a possible third line as reserve. Infantry formed the centre, cavalry was deployed on the flanks. The protection of the flanks rested therefore nearly entirely on the cavalry. This practice proved acceptable against armies which followed the same tactical principles. This, however, was not the case in the wars against the Turks. Against this enemy the above battle order proved too vulnerable.

The development of artillery and its tactical deployment in battle during the eighteenth century shall only be touched on here, as there was little difference in artillery tactics on the European and Turkish theatres of war.

During the reign of Charles VI, the Austrian artillery had suffered a decline in line with the general deterioration of the army. It was Wenzel Prince Liechtenstein who, in the course of the general reform of the Austrian military establishment during the reign of Maria Theresa, thoroughly reformed and built up the Austrian artillery. The tactical deployment of artillery was alike in all armies of the eighteenth century on the European theatre of war. The heavier field guns were deployed in batteries in front of the infantry and, where possible, behind or on higher ground on the flanks and in the rear of the battle order. The light guns, mostly three and six pounders, were positioned between the infantry battalions and used with them.

The superiority of the Turkish cavalry (see below) forced the Austrians to make a slight change in the deployment of their artillery in open battles against Turkish forces. The heavier field guns were placed in fortified positions to the rear and flanks of the battle order and protected by relatively strong infantry detachments, also in protected positions. The light regimental guns were placed on the corners of the infantry squares where they were effectively protected by the infantry. Equally, the Austrians seem to have been unable to use their light cavalry with the same effectiveness against the Turks as they did against European enemies. The Spahi formations in the field usually far outnumbered the units of Hussars the

Austrians had available. Therefore, detached Hussar units were far too vulnerable and their employment and successes in the Small War (Kleiner Krieg) were of lesser significance and effectiveness against the Turks.

II

The significant changes in warfare during the late 17th and early 18th centuries, particularly the development of the line tactics introduced and strictly adhered to by all European armies, were not paralleled by similar changes in the Turkish army. Thus the Austrian army was forced to develop tactical formations and principles to meet an enemy who did not adhere to the rules and tactical methods of the Christian European armies.

From the 16th to the late 18th century the Turks during their nearly incessant wars against the Habsburgs—amongst others—played an important role in the history of European warfare and posed an omnipresent threat to the Habsburg lands. Twice they appeared before the walls of Vienna, the only bulwark of consequence of Christian Europe against the East and even after the second siege of Vienna in 1683 they remained a menace. It was only with the decay of the Ottoman Empire in the 18th and early 19th centuries that this menace gradually disappeared. Thereafter not the danger of Turkish attack but the problems in the Balkans created by the breakup of the Ottoman Empire were to present difficulties to the Habsburg Monarchy.

The Turkish army of the 17th and 18th centuries presented in its organization, methods of warfare, armaments, discipline and spirit a picture drastically different from that of the European armies of the time. The spirit and drive of the Turkish armies was guided by the Islamic teaching which required the Moslems to spread Islam—if necessary—by the sword. Much of the religious fanaticism which inspired this mission was channeled toward the conquest of Europe through the Balkans. This obsession with their mission fired the Turks with their spirit of aggressiveness. Their treatment of enemies and prisoners—barbaric in Christian eyes—turned the Turks into the most feared enemy of the Habsburg armies. (More shall be said below about this psychological effect.)

The numerical strength of the Turkish armies was usually far greater than that of their enemies. Their cavalry forces particularly exceeded by far in numbers those the Habsburgs could muster. The Turks could easily field an army of 100,000 men for a major war. In most engagements they outnumbered the Austrians about two to one.

A comprehensive discussion of the highly complicated organization of the Turkish army would exceed the scope of this paper. A short sketch of the Sultans' forces will have to suffice here.

Two main divisions of the Turkish army can be discerned: the relatively small standing forces and a variety of forces which, to some extent, can be compared to the feudal levies, militias, etc. of the European states. The troops of the first category included the Spahis of the Porte, the sultan's elite cavalry, and the Janissaries, the crack infantry. Both, however, had lost much of their earlier effectiveness and discipline by the 18th century. The Janissaries, originally formed of Christians and confined to barrack life and discipline, had, since the later 17th century, been allowed to engage in trade and business, they had received permission to marry and a hereditary class of Janissaries had developed. Furthermore, the old child tax was abolished in 1685 and the inclusion of ethnic Turks destroyed the homogeneity of this force. Discipline and fighting spirit gradually declined. However, the Spahis of the Porte and the Janissaries still formed the backbone of the Turkish forces throughout the 18th century.

Much more numerous than these regular forces were the many varieties of levied troops which included contingents from all parts of the far flung Ottoman Empire, both Moslems and Christians. Amongst them were the feudal Spahis—not to be confused with the Spahis of the Porte. These feudal levies made up the bulk of the Turkish army. The quality and reliability of the various types of levies varied considerably and contemporary sources indicate that fighting spirit and discipline of all Turkish forces gradually declined during the late 17th and the 18th century. Field Marshal Montecuccoli, the victor of the battle of St. Gotthard in 1664, had considered the Turks "a model in warfare." He praised not only their wisdom to begin wars at times advantageous to them, but also the efficiency of their campaigning. Even after their serious defeat at St. Gotthard they had retreated in good order and had been able to mount a second offensive.[21] In later wars a marked deterioration of these qualities became increasingly noticeable. It was unfortunate for the Habsburgs that after Prince Eugene's successes during the early years of the 18th century, the quality of the Austrian army also declined so that the Turks, even after the wars of 1716/18 still posed a serious threat to the Austrians.

In a memorandum, dated 1769, to the Austrian War Council, Field Marshal Neipperg recognized the Janissaries and Spahis as formidable enemies and also credited the various levies from the Balkans with praiseworthy discipline. He stated that the latter in particular, usually retained good order even when retreating and he discouraged pursuit of the enemy for fear of counterattacks. On the other hand, Neippberg had little respect for the troops from Asia and "other faraway lands", who, once their attack had been repelled tended to retreat in wild flight.[22]

J.H. Hoyer, in his *Geschichte der Kriegskunst,* printed in 1799, had little praise for the performance of either the Austrian or the Turkish armies during the war of 1737/39: "One had to have Turks as the enemy so as not to lose more than one actually did."[23] The decline in the morale of the Austrian army which became evident in the war of 1737/39 seemed to have been coupled with a lack of outstanding generals. None of the commanders of this war was the equal of Montecuccoli or Prince Eugene. During Eugene's last years the control of the army seemed to have lacked a firm hand and a general decay seemed to have set in. Maria Theresa remarked in her *Political Testament* that it is no wonder that her father's armies—shortly before her accession to the throne—had always been beaten.[24] Of equal influence on the misfortunes of the Austrian army during this war may have been the tactics applied. In the wars against the Turks under Montecuccoli and Prince Eugene, the Austrian armies formed a long rectangle by closing the flanks between the two lines with ranks of infantry. During the war of 1737/39 this precaution was often neglected.[25]

By the 1730's the *ordre de bataille,* accepted as the standard formation on the European theatre of war—infantry in the center in four ranks, flanked by cavalry—the army usually deployed in two lines, proved unsuited against the Turks. Due to the numerical inferiority of the Austrian cavalry to the Turkish Spahis, the former could not provide adequate protection for the flanks of the Austrian battle order. In addition, the Turks never attacked on a broad front but launched instead separate and alternating attacks on various points of the front. They often attempted flank attacks or even attacks on the rear of the Austrian front. This made the line formation extremely vulnerable.

Throughout the 18th century, the Turks still did not employ a systematic *ordre de bataille.* In open terrain they usually deployed their troops in dense masses, infantry and cavalry arranged and alternating without any obvious plan.[26] Disciplined attacks in ordered formations were unknown to them. Contemporary Austrian generals referred to attacks by "wild hordes" and regarded the Turkish Spahis not only superior in numbers but also as more accomplished, faster and more agile horsemen than their Austrian counterparts.[27] The tremendous fervour and the lack of discipline in the European sense frequently led the most fanatic of the often drugged attackers to forge ahead of the main body, so that the attacking force took the shape of an advancing wedge. However, unlike the solid Roman *cuneus,* the Turkish wedge was weak at its point, as only the most ferocious formed this disorganized spearhead. Thus, a firm defender, firing steadily and, if possible, even advancing toward the attacker, could repel this spearhead. As a result, the retreating 'hotheads' would often bring the main attacking force into confusion and turn it into headlong flight. However, this retreat was often only over a short distance and pursuing cavalry could then easily be overpowered by the Turks in a counterattack.[28]

In the memoranda to the Austrian War Council in 1769, Field Marshals Sachse-Hildburghausen and Neippberg recommended that one should abstain from prolonged pursuit of the enemy[29] and that one should keep the army in close formation unless Hussar units, chasseurs or others volunteered to take the risk of pursuing the enemy.[30]

It was the Austrians' good fortune that the Turks refrained from war during the time when Maria Theresa had to defend her lands against European enemies in two long and exhausting wars. During the long lull in hostilities between Austria and Turkey, from 1739 to 1788, the Austrians were able to re-organize and to revitalize their military establishment, whereas no comparable improvements were made by Turkey. In 1769, when the possibility of renewed hostilities with the Porte was recognized by the Austrian War Council, two proposals were submitted to at least two Austrian field marshals for evaluation. These proposals presented two different plans for tactical formations to be employed against the Turks. Although this author was unable to find the actual proposals in the Austrian War Archives, the two lengthy memoirs evaluating them, submitted by Field Marshals Sachse-Hildburghausen and Neippberg allow a reconstruction of the proposals, especially the one which later, with modifications, was adopted.

This new tactical formation seemed to have been first introduced by the Russians who transformed the formation of one undivided long rectangle into several smaller ones, each comprising up to twelve battalions—still a rather clumsy formation. In 1774, Field Marshal Rumiantsev divided his army into even smaller squares—the largest of six, the smallest of one battalion—which could support each other. Rumiantsev even marched his army in this formation and formed these squares into a line, with grenadier and chasseur battalions on the wings. In this formation the Russians defeated the Turks at Schumla on 30 August 1774.[31] The march in such a formation was feasible in open country. In the Balkan theatre of war such terrain was rarely present. Thus the Austrians proposed to march in columns which could be quickly and easily formed into separate squares before contact with the enemy was made.

Field Marshal Sachse-Hildburghausen gave several examples from the 1737/39 war between Austria and Turkey to emphasize the need for new tactical methods to be applied against the Turks. He explained the initial reverses in the battle of Cornia (1739) as the result of the use of the traditional order of battle with cavalry on the flanks. Thus the numerically inferior Austrian cavalry was driven unto the lines of infantry, causing the collapse of the Austrian flank. On the other hand, a hastily formed oblong infantry square in the battle of Krozeka could repulse a ferocious Turkish attack.[32]

The 1769 proposal which both Sachse-Hildburghausen and Neippberg supported, still provided for large oblong squares with grenadiers on the corners and cavalry in the center of the square. Obviously, the positioning of the cavalry inside the square limited the usefulness of the cavalry. Much thought seemed to have been concentrated on further improving on this tactical formation. So far, I have been unable to locate documentary evidence of this process of study. However, the last war against the Turks in the 18th century—1788/89—shows the changes made since the proposal of 1769.

In the above mentioned memorandum, Field Marshal Sachse-Hildburghausen had supported the proposal of small infantry squares with cavalry behind them and between the two rows of squares. He also emphasized that under no circumstances should the flanks be protected by cavalry alone. This type of formation was used—with variations—in the campaigns of 1788 and '89. Aside from commenting on the proposed tactical changes, Sachse-Hildburghausen also pointed to a weakness in the Austrian army unrelated to tactical principles. He expressed the opinion that the Turkish army was only numerically superior to the Austrian army. With suitable tactical methods and firm morale, the Austrians should have nothing to fear of the Turkish 'hordes'. The Field Marshal admitted, however, that any Turkish attack, undertaken by superior forces, accompanied by the wild screaming of the Spahis and Janissaries could strike fear into the hearts of the defenders.

One of the principal causes for the Austrian reverses during the war of 1737/39 had been the belief in Turkish invincibility and the fear of Turkish atrocities. Sachse-Hildburghausen blamed many Austrian officers, even generals, for holding the belief that a determined Turkish attack could not be repulsed. Such fears had spread down into the ranks and the effect on morale had been disastrous. Similar 'fables' had been told about the superhuman courage of the Turks and their invincibility in individual combat. The Field Marshal rejected these beliefs as untrue. In his long experience in past wars against this enemy, he asserts, he had never seen Turks 'hack' through the *cheveaux de frises* and break into the Austrian lines, unless the defenders had broken rank and turned to flight before the Turks had even reached the Austrian positions. In examples from engagements in the campaigns of 1739 he showed that superior Turkish attacking forces had been repulsed by Austrian units which retained order, discipline and nerve. On the other hand, on sectors of the frontline where the Austrians, after only one general volley, lost nerve and turned to flight, the Turks naturally did break through, thus causing the collapse of the whole Austrian battle order.

The great length and detail in which Sachse-Hildburghausen discusses this problem illustrates the serious proportions which the decline of fighting spirit had reached before Maria Theresa's reforms. It would appear, however, that during the period between the wars with Turkey, the Austrian military leadership had been able to eliminate this problem. Only one incident is known from the campaign of 1788 during which Austrian troops panicked. This one incident did not even occur during an engagement but as a result of a false alarm during the night (at Karansebes on 21 September 1788). Even then, once order had been restored, consequent Turkish attacks were decisively repulsed.[33]

In 1788, when war broke out again between the Porte and Austria, the new ideas could be tested and improved on. Unfortunately, as had happened in earlier wars against the Turks, Austrian leadership initially, left much to be desired and during the campaign of 1788 it did not come to any open battles. The army, under the command of the elderly Field Marshal Lacy was strung out along the frontier in several corps, each too weak to undertake any decisive action. Luckily, the Turks, too, were not in the mood to undertake a large-scale offensive. Only the corps under Field Marshal Loudon in Croatia could book some small successes with the capture of the fortresses Dubitza and Novi and the occupation of part of Bosnia. Another corps, supported by Russian forces, could take Jassy and Choczim in Moldavia. Thus, as only minor siege operations took place, 1788 still provided no opportunity to test the new tactics.

The campaign of 1789 began under the command of the old and infirm Field Marshal Hadik who issued an interesting directive regarding the tactics to be employed against the Turks. The underlying principle of this directive was to avoid the cumbersome, immobile, large squares which contained the cavalry in their centres, thus preventing the cavalry from taking effective offensive action. Hadik proposed elongated infantry squares with cavalry in massed formations on both flanks in prolongation of the rear side of the infantry square. The outside flanks of the cavalry were to be protected by small squares of infantry.[34] Obviously, this was only a general guideline and individual corps commanders had discretionary powers to alter this formation to suit the occasion (Sachse-Hildburghausen had earlier in 1769 proposed encouraging generals to make independent decisions in emergencies). In the actual engagements during the campaign of 1789 the generals commanding the various corps preferred formations of several smaller squares, down to the one battalion square, interspersed by massed cavalry formations. Thus, each element could provide protection for its neighbouring square. Staggered formations of small squares or a checkerboard arrangement were the formations used throughout this campaign.[35] The placement of the artillery was such that its flanking fire could give added protection to the infantry and cavalry.

The greater part of the campaign of 1789 was fought under the command of Field Marshal Loudon who had replaced the ailing Hadik early in the year and now the Austrians finally fought under competent leadership. The battle of Mehadia (about 150 km east of Belgrade), on 23 August 1789, one of the few major engagements during that year, shall serve as a typical example of the application of the new Austrian tactics. (see map)

The Turkish force held strong positions, protected by artillery, across the valley and had posted their main force on a rise to the southwest. The Austrian corps under General Clerfayt took its main position in the valley north of the enemy and protected the flanking heights with five battalions of infantry, sharpshooters and artillery in fortified positions. The main force in the valley formed five infantry squares of one battalion each in checkerboard formation with 16 cavalry squadrons between them. Behind this formation three infantry battalions and 6 squadrons were stationed as reserve.

After an attack by Janissaries, supported by artillery, on the Austrian held heights west of the valley had been repulsed after three hours of fierce fighting, General Clerfayt gave the command

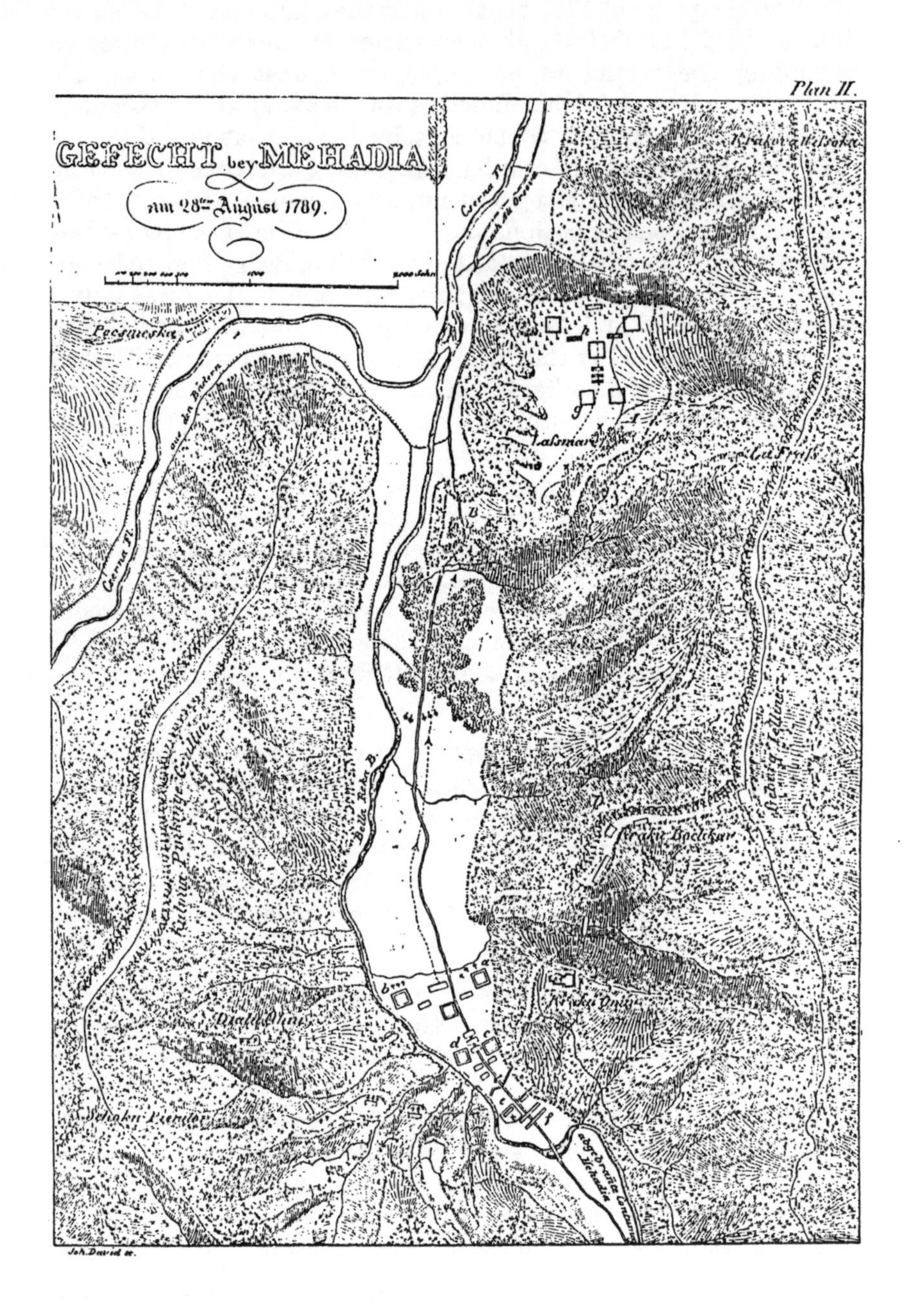
Plan II.
GEFECHT bey MEHADIA
am 28ten August 1789.
Czerna Fl.
Pecsenieska
Lasmiare
Kraku Boclikan
Kraku Onit
Czerna Fl.
Bella Reka B.
Kalinia Punkinye Grullu
Joh. David sc.

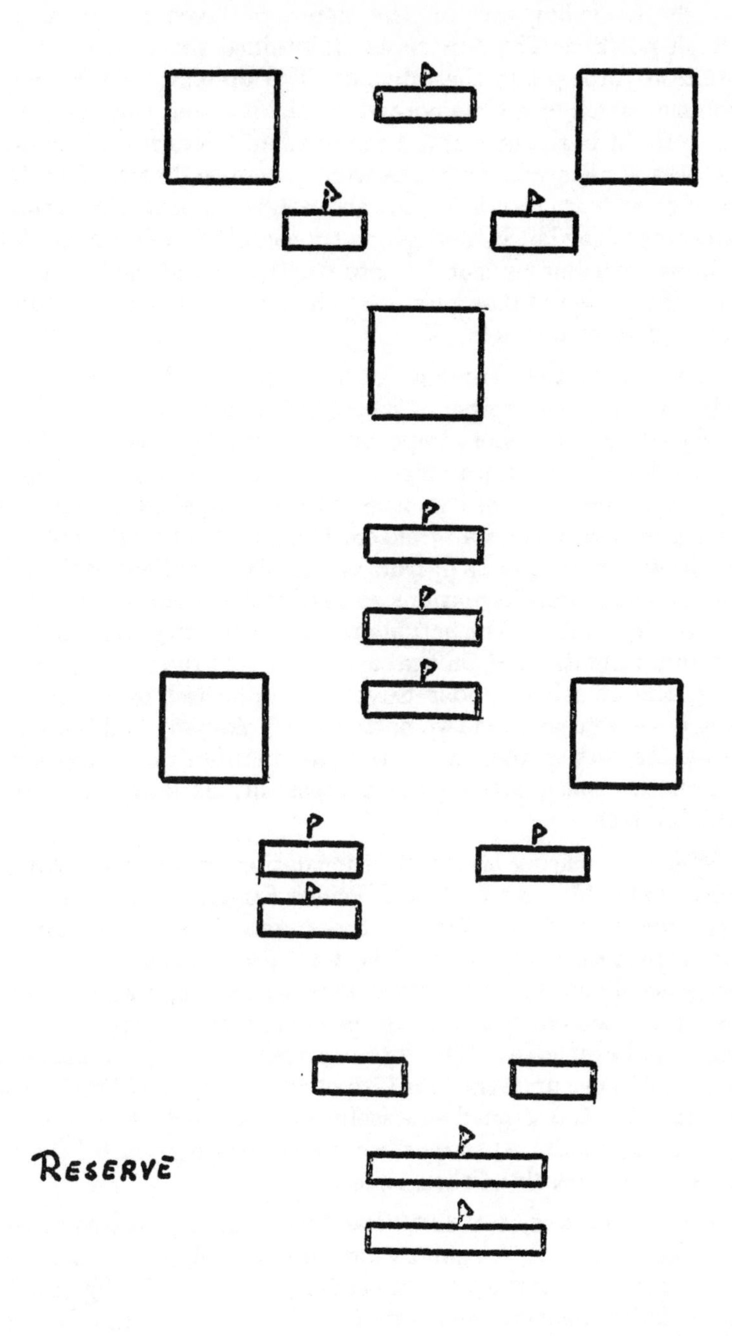
AUSTRIAN ORDRE DE BATAILLE
RESERVE

to the main force to attack the heights of Lassmare where the main Turkish body had begun to entrench itself. The Austrians advanced through the valley and up the slopes of Lassmare toward this Turkish position. The Austrians maintained the above mentioned formation throughout the advance. The opinion held by Sachse-Hildburghausen in his memorandum of 1769 that the Turks would turn to flight in the face of a disciplined and determined counterattack, was vindicated: the Turks were driven to disorganized flight, part of their force retreating toward Belgrade, part fleeing into the mountains. They left behind over a thousand of their number killed, five guns with ammunition fell into Austrian hands and 76 men and eight officers were taken prisoner. The Austrians lost only 38 men killed and 79 wounded.[36]

The rest of the campaign of 1789 consisted of several other engagements and a number of successful sieges of which the capture of Belgrade was the most important. During this siege, Field Marshal Loudon's army was divided into two corps: one, to carry out the actual siege operations, the other to guard against a relief army, which, however, never materialized. The infantry units of both corps were drawn up in squares of from one to six battalions each and the cavalry in squadron formations so that each segment could provide support for the next. The actual assault on the city was carried out in column formations.[37] On the eastern wing of the front against the Turks, the Russians under Suvorov, supported by an Austrian corps, were successful in two battles—at Fokshany and Martinishtje. In these battles, too, the battle order in infantry squares arranged in checkerboard pattern was successfully used against superior Turkish forces.

When comparing the tactical formations used by the Austrian armies under Montecuccoli and Prince Eugene, those used in the disastrous war of 1737/39 and the square formations applied in 1789, a pattern does evolve. The formations used in the time of Montecuccoli and Prince Eugene were still rather massive infantry formations ranged in two lines, protected on the open flanks by cavalry and grenadiers, thus forming a rudimentary oblong square. Pikes, still in use until the late 17th century, and the effective use of *cheveaux de frises* proved successful against Turkish attacks. During this period the Austrians were also capably led by the most outstanding generals of their time.

During the war of 1737/39 the Austrians lacked this excellent leadership and army organization and discipline had drastically deteriorated during the years preceding this war. The by then fully developed, formalized linear tactics did not prove suitable against the Turks. Furthermore, the development of the line tactics was not accompanied by a parallel development of standardization of drill. The more flexible square formations used in the campaign of 1789 provided in a much more sophisticated fashion the same quality of protection even against attacks from the flanks or rear as had the formations used by Montecuccoli and Eugene.

It is, of course, impossible to give sole credit to the new tactical formations used in 1789 for the Austrian successes against the Turks. Good military leadership, better drilled and disciplined troops accounted equally for these successes. Furthermore, the Ottoman Empire by then had long passed its zenith of power and these victories ended once and for all the Turkish menace to the Habsburg state.

FOOTNOTES

KA=Austrian War Archives, Vienna

1. Hans Delbrück, *Geschichte der Kriegskunst*, (Berlin: 1962), Vol. IV, p. 328.
2. In this maneuver the first line, after having fired, parted in the center and retreated behind the last rank to reload. The other ranks followed the same maneuver in sequence.
3. The peloton was a sub-division of the battalion. The number of pelotons per battalion varied.
4. Raimund Montecuccoli, *Besondere und geheime Kriegnachrichten*, (Leipzig: 1736), p. 24.
5. *Ibid.*, p. 12.
6. *Ibid.*, p. 14.
7. *Ibid.*, p. 20.
8. Hans Delbrück, *op. cit.*, p. 305.
9. Raimund Montecuccoli, *op. cit.*, p. 20.
10. *Ibid.*, p. 23 f.
11. Johann G. Hoyer, *Geschichte der Kriegskunst*, (Göttingen: 1799), Vol. II, p. 84.
12. *Ibid.*, p. 529.
13. *Ibid.*, p. 90.
14. Hans Delbrück, *op. cit.*, p. 309.
15. Max Braubach, *Prinz Eugen von Savoien*, (Munich: 1963), Vol. V, p. 346ff and 353.
16. Alexander Balisch, 'Die Entstehung des Exerzierreglements von 1749' in *Mitteilungen des österreichischen Staatsarchivs*, Vol. 27, 1974, p. 171 f.
17. *Ibid.* for detailed discussion of emergence of Austrian drill manuals.
18. Maria Theresa, *Maria Theresa's Politisches Testament*, Joseph Kallbrunner, ed. (Vienna: 1952), p. 72.
19. See Alexander Balisch, *op. cit.*, 171 f.
20. On these administrative reforms, their origins, implementation and results

see: H. Kretschmayr (ed.) *Die Österreichische Zentral Verwaltung* (Vienna, 1938); idem, *Die Theresianische Staatsreform von 1749* (Vienna, 1958) and the more recent, highly valuable studies by Franz Szabo, in particular "Kaunitz and the Reforms of the Co-Regency of Maria Theresa and Joseph II 1765-1780" (Ph.D. thesis, Alberta, 1976). This work is soon to be published.

21. Valentini, Frh. V., *Der Türkenkrieg,* (Berlin: 1822), p. 1.
22. KA, Mem 1-6, 1769.
23. Johann G. Hoyer, *op. cit.,* p. 15.
24. Maria Theresa, *op. cit.,* p. 72.
25. KA, Mem 1-8, 1769.
26. Valentini, *op. cit.,* p. 6 ff. See also the able summary by the Russian Military historian A.K. Baiov, *Russkaia armiia v tsarstvovanie Imperatristsy Anna Ioannovny* (St. Petersburg) 1906, I, II, 103-106.
27. Fieldmarshal Neippberg, memorandum to Austrian War Council, KA, Mem 1-6, 1769.
28. Fieldmarshal Sachse-Hildburghausen, memorandum to Austrian War Council, KA, Mem 1-8, 1769.
29. KA Mem 1-8, 1769.
30. KA Mem 1-6, 1769.
31. Valentini, *op. cit.,* p. 18. For the impact of the Turkish war on Russian tactical development see Bruce Menning, "G.A. Potemkin and A.I. Chernyshev: Two Dimensions of Reform and the Military Frontier in Imperial Russia," in D.G. Horward (ed.) *The Consortium on Revolutionary Europe, Proceedings, 1980* (Athens, GA. 1980), I.
32. KA, 1-8, 1769.
33. Gilbert Auger, *Geschichte der K.K. Armee,* (Vienna: 1887), Vol. II, p. 1066.
34. *Österreichische Militärische Zeitschrift,* 1825, Vol. I, p. 7. hereafter: *ÖMZ.*
35. *ÖMZ,* 1823, Vol. III, p. 191.
36. *ÖMZ,* 1825, Vol. I, p. 146 ff.
37. *ÖMZ,* 1825, Vol. II, p. 3 ff.

# Part III
# Russia and Eastern Europe

# [8]

RICHARD HELLIE

To the memory of
Oswald P. Backus,
1921-1972

## *The Petrine Army: Continuity, Change, and Impact*

The Petrine era is often portrayed as one of great reforms. This custom was initiated by Peter and particularly his contemporaries, and the idea remained in vogue for over a century, into the era of the Slavophile-Westernizer debates of the 1840's. Since that time much learned scholarship has been devoted to the Petrine reforms, first tending to confirm their magnitude, later often debunking them. These tendencies have continued to the present day, both within the Soviet Union and abroad. Somehow, particularly for the last half century or so, these studies have tended to overlook the army. Collections such as Marc Raeff's *Peter the Great: Reformer or Revolutionary?* and *Peter the Great Changes Russia* and the 1964 Soviet publication *Absoliutizm v Rossii* examine many issues, but ignore the army. This is indeed peculiar when one remembers that war was the central feature of Peter's reign, that Peter's overriding concern was with military affairs, that his long wars bankrupted the populace, and that perhaps the majority of the reforms had as one of their direct or indirect purposes the strengthening of the army's capacities.[1]

As is well known, the Petrine era witnessed a seemingly striking improvement in the fortune of Russian arms. Peter came to power partially because of dissatisfaction with the way his half-sister Sofiia's lover A. A. Golitsyn had bungled the Crimean campaigns of 1687 and 1689, which, as one historian put it, cried out for a reformer.[2] But Peter's initial ventures into the martial arena also had indifferent results: the Azov campaign of 1695 failed, and while that of 1696 was successful, it was immediately followed by the inglorious defeat of 1700 at Narva by Charles XII of Sweden. This was taken as a signal that not all was right. Reforms were undertaken, and Peter annihilated the Swedish army at Poltava in 1709. Two years later Peter blundered on the Pruth in an engagement with the Turks (with fateful consequences not only for Russia's designs on the Black Sea littoral, but also for the peoples of the Caucasus); after that a string of victories awarded Russia triumph in the Northern War (1700-1721) and the brief Persian campaign (1722-1723). Russia gained the reputation as the strongest power in Europe.

This essay will show what changes made such a reversal of military fortunes possible, while checking on the assertion by Prince Dolgorukii in 1717 that much of Peter's success was attributable to the restoration of "new formation regiments" of the old Muscovite army founded by Peter's father, Aleksei Mikhailovich, but allowed

1. John Perry, *The State of Russia Under the Present Czar* (London, 1716), pp. 19, 44, 164, 204-205, 251, 280; Vasili Klyuchevsky, *Peter the Great* (New York, 1958), pp. 77, 176; N. P. Mikhnevich, *Glavnyi shtab. Istoricheskii ocherk. Vooruzhennyia sily Rossii do tsarstvovaniia imperatora Aleksandra I*, in D. A. Skalon, ed., *Stoletie voennago ministerstva 1802-1902*, 13 vols. (St. Petersburg, 1902-1914), IV, pt. 1, bk. 1, sect. 1, p. 100.

2. A. G. Elchaninov, "Ocherk istorii voennago iskusstva do Petra Velikago," in *Istoriia russkoi armii i flota*, 15 vols. (Moscow, 1911-1915), I, 79.

to disintegrate after his time.[3] There will also be a check on the popular claim that Peter transformed the army "from an Asiatic horde into a professional force of the kind maintained by Sweden, France, or Prussia. The elite of the old army had been the *streltsi*. . . , composed of nobles. . . . Peter rebuilt the army from the ground up."[4] In addition to checking on Peter's role as a "reformer or revolutionary," this paper will discuss the consequences of Peter's actions in the military sphere and pose some questions which might be worthy of further study.

* * *

The putative break between Aleksei's army and that of his son claimed by Dolgorukii should be noted, but not accepted as totally true. Peter's contemporaries, both his friends and his enemies, had a known propensity to exaggerate. Some developments which Peter's contemporaries considered "innovations" were not. But the fact that these people assumed such measures were new would indicate that they must have gone out of use for at least a while. Later scholars have tended to perpetuate the legend of the revolutionary innovativeness of the Petrine military achievement by claiming, for example, that the basic armed force of Russia at the end of the seventeenth century was the gentry cavalry supported by service lands.[5]

At present I do not know the full extent of the break, nor its causes. One of these may have been the fact that Russia was not engaged in major conflict in the years immediately after 1689, so the expensive army of Aleksei, his new formation regiments discussed in my *Enserfment and Military Change in Muscovy*, may have been considered unnecessary and therefore were discharged. An equally probable cause may have been the fact that Peter, ironically, came to power in 1689 in a wave of reaction against Sofiia and Golitsyn, a solid "Westernizer," who had proved to be corrupt. A moral regeneration necessitated a discarding of corrupting practices–including the Western-style army instituted by Aleksei to wage the Thirteen Years War (1654-1667) for the recovery of the Ukraine, Belorussia, and other territory. The foreigners who commanded the new formation regiments were blamed for Russia's military defeats and were considered by some as agents of the devil.[6] The reaction may have precipitated some return to a reliance on the more traditional Muscovite middle service class cavalry and the obsolescent musketeers.

However, the extent of the reversion to the traditional forces of Muscovy must not be overestimated. Peter retained a number of foreign officers, his friends of the Northern-European Settlement (*Nemetskaia sloboda*). In the 1680's Peter began to create, on his father's example, the nucleus of his future army, but only formed a few regiments–the Preobrazhenskii, Semenovskii, Lefortovskii, and Gordonovskii. (They were named after their commanders, F. I. Lefort and P. I. Gordon, or their places of formation and quartering.) These regiments and their basically foreign officer corps

3. Klyuchevsky, p. 78.

4. R. R. Palmer, *A History of the Modern World* (New York, 1965), p. 214.

5. Iu. R. Klokman, "Severnaia voina 1700-1721 gg. Bor'ba Rossii za vykhod k Baltiiskomu moriu i vozvrashchenie russkikh zemel' v Pribaltike," in *Stranitsy boevogo proshlogo. Ocherki voennoi istorii Rossii* (Moscow, 1968), pp. 73-74.

6. P. O. Bobrovskii, *Perekhod Rossii k reguliarnoi armii* (St. Petersburg, 1885), pp. 119-120.

persisted through the 1690's.

In his campaigns of 1695 and 1696 to capture Azov and gain access to the Sea of Azov from the Don, Peter took an army of over 90,000, including about 28,000 infantry *soldaty*, 10,000 musketeers, and 6,000 middle service class cavalrymen.[7] These figures must be compared with the 110,000-plus forces of the Second Crimean Campaign of 1689, where there were 17,206 traditional Muscovite troops (cavalry members of the upper and middle service classes and the musketeers) and 78,652 of the semi-regular, semi-standing troops of foreign formation (nearly 30,000 cavalry *reitary*, almost 50,000 infantry *soldaty*).[8] The major change seems to be that in the Petrine campaigns the *reitary* were not present, that the landed elements were only in Sheremetev's corps. I do not know why the *reitary* were absent, but this may have made Peter's subsequent changes seem more important than I think they actually were.

Peter's military reforms began in 1699 after he had hurried home from his European tour to find the musketeers in revolt. He savagely suppressed the *strel'tsy*, and began to prepare the army for an attack on Sweden. He initiated the change from a semi-standing, semi-regular army to a standing, regular army by disbanding much of the Moscow garrison, converting 24,000 southern frontier infantry into taxpaying farmers, and ordering the raising of a new army of three divisions of nine regiments each. Attaining peace with Turkey on one day, he used his new army to attack Swedish possessions on the next. This opened the Northern War, the major impetus behind Peter's military innovations. Here I shall depart from a chronological approach in favor of a topical one.[9]

* * *

The Petrine era witnessed few military technological advances. The major one seems to have been the bayonet, introduced elsewhere in Europe at the end of the seventeenth century and in the Russian forces in the years just before Poltava.[10] Armed with flintlock muskets (in use for over half a century by this time) and bayonet, the Russian army was able to go on the offensive, to abandon the essentially conservative, defensive tactics of the past.[11] In 1708 infantry were armed with a .78 calibre, 14-pound smooth-bore, muzzle-loading musket with a range of 300 to 400 paces,

7. M. M. Bogoslovskii, *Petr I. Materialy dlia biografii*, 5 vols. (Moscow, 1940-1948), I, 283-284. The rest of the troops were Ukrainian and Don cossacks, Kalmyks, and others.

8. M. M. Denisova, "Pomestnaia konnitsa i ee vooruzhenie v XVI-XVII vv.," *Trudy gosudarstvennogo istoricheskogo muzeia*, 20 (1948), p. 44; Richard Hellie, *Enserfment and Military Change in Muscovy* (Chicago, 1971), p. 272.

9. The interested reader may find a superficial narrative account in English of Peter's military exploits in the article by Alexander M. Nikolaieff, "Peter the Great as a Military Leader," *The Army Quarterly and Defence Journal*, 80 (April and July 1960), pp. 76-86.

10. P. O. Bobrovskii, *Postoiannyia voiska i sostoianie voennago prava v Rossii v XVII stoletii po russkim i inostrannym pamiatnikam*" (Moscow, 1882), p. 21; A. R. Hall, "Military Technology," in *A History of Technology*, ed. by Charles Singer *et al.* 5 vols. (Oxford, 1954-1958), III, 348.

11. Klokman, p. 80. For a picture, see P. A. Rotmistrov, ed., *Istoriia voennogo iskusstva*, 2 vols. (Moscow, 1963), I, 105.

and fitted with a bayonet. Each man also had 50 live cartridges and 10 dummy cartridges, which facilitated more rapid firing; nevertheless, the average soldier could get off no more than 25 to 30 shots per battle, about double what had been possible with the earliest matchlocks used in sixteenth-century Muscovy. A sabre was added to infantry equipment after 1709.[12] (One hears little of armor in the Petrine army. The phasing out of armor was a pan-European phenomenon which had begun already in the seventeenth-century new formation regiments.[13])

One of Peter's tasks was to escape the dependence on imports of his father's time, and even in the first decade of the Northern War, when 25,000 weapons were brought in. A good start was made in the years 1700-1710, when 125,000 handguns were manufactured in Russian establishments.[14] With the development of a suitable metallurgical base, Russia was largely freed from reliance on imports. At the time of the Pruth debacle, Russia even had reserves of from twenty to thirty thousand guns.[15] These figures must be contrasted with those of the years 1647-1653, when over 35,000 muskets and carbines were made in Moscow, and in the following decade over seventy-five thousand muskets were imported.[16] Thus, roughly speaking, the ratio of domestic manufactures to imports were reversed in favor of the former by Peter as early as Poltava.

Military tactics in the Petrine era were inherited from the seventeenth century. Warfare was based on linear tactics, first introduced into Russia in the Time of Troubles (in 1605 at Dobrinichie) and extensively developed in the Thirteen Years War.

In the West, prior to the development of the bayonet, the slow-firing infantry arquibusiers and musketeers were protected from cavalry assault by pikemen. In Russia, pikemen were seldom used, and the infantry were protected by mobile fortifications (the *guliai gorod*) and the cavalry.[17] With the introduction of the bayonet, the use of cavalry changed. Under Peter, the cavalry used firearms much less frequently, and relied extensively on cold weapons. More will be said about this below.

During Peter's reign linear tactics were perfected in accord with the new technology. Optimally, the infantry were arranged in two lines in the center of the battle order, with the cavalry on either flank to correct the major weakness of linear tactics—the weakness of the flanks. (The square formation was not highly developed in Russia.)[18] The artillery was placed in a line in front of the battle order, in theory, but flexibility in the positioning and use of artillery was strongly recommended and prac-

12. Mikhnevich, p. 126. The cartridge had just been recently invented (Hall, III, 348). Rotmistrov, pp. 104-105; D. V. Pankov, ed., *Razvitie taktiki russkoi armii XVIII v.—nachalo XX v.* (Moscow, 1957), p. 6.

13. Hall, III, 353.

14. L. G. Beskrovnyi, "Strategiia i taktika russkoi armii v poltavskii period Severnoi voiny," in *Poltava. K 250-letiiu Poltavskogo srazheniia. Sbornik statei* (Moscow, 1959), p. 21; L. G. Beskrovnyi, *Russkaia armiia i flot v XVIII veke (Ocherki)* (Moscow, 1958), pp. 74-77.

15. Beskrovnyi, "Strategiia i taktika. . . ."

16. Hellie, p. 183. Chronologically parallel data for imports and manufactures are not available.

17. P. P. Epifanov, " 'Uchenie i khitrost' ratnogo stroeniia pekhotnykh liudei' (iz istorii russkoi armii XVII v.)," *Uchenye zapiski Moskovskogo gos. universiteta, kafedry istorii SSSR*, 167 (1954), p. 97.

18. Klokman, p. 106; Mikhnevich, pp. 130, 132.

ticed in fact. Firepower was preparatory for the bayonet kill. How battles should be fought was outlined in a number of manuals and instructions at the beginning of the eighteenth century, borrowed first from Austria and then Sweden, and finally produced domestically.[19] (Military regulations had also been published in the seventeenth century, but their use in practice was much less systematic.)[20] Under Peter, the Russians perfected the strategy of manoeuvre in linear formation, developed tactical ideas of active battle (moving from an active defense to the attack), and in decisive battles such as Poltava used bayonet attacks to exterminate the enemy. Moreover, they learned to pursue a fleeing enemy–in this way an additional seventeen thousand captives were taken by pursuing the Swedes after they had been routed on the battlefield in 1709.[21] This pursuit, which picked off nearly all of Charles XII's army and altered the balance of power in Europe, was a sign of the professionalization of the Petrine army. Pursuit was rare in the old Muscovite army because victorious troops did not want to leave the battlefield and thus miss the chance to loot the fallen enemy. Poltava thus reflected the changing goal of warfare, from an opportunity to accumulate booty to the destruction of an enemy for political ends. (This had not happened at Lesnaia, "the mother of the Poltava battle," in September, 1707, when half of the Swedes escaped because the Russians had failed to pursue them energetically after the battle.)[22]

Some historians have elevated Peter's own words and his success in annihilating the Swedish army at Poltava into a new Petrine strategy: rather than concentrating on the traditional late seventeenth-century warfare of position and maneuvre with its limited goals of disrupting an enemy's communications and seizing his fortresses (with their supply magazines) and occasionally his seat of government, Peter concentrated on the more risky annihilation of the opponent's army in field combat.[23] Peter may not have thought out this strategy prior to Poltava, but rather effectuated it in reality because of his youth, impetuous personality, and need to defeat the Swedes decisively to consolidate his Baltic conquests. Most of his more theoretical military writings post-date Pruth.[24]

* * *

Another of Peter's goals was to make his army into a standing, regular force. This necessitated issuing his troops standard uniforms. Standing forces with standard uniforms had existed since the time of the founding of the Moscow corps of arquibusiers by Ivan IV, but apparently they and their successors had made their own uniforms. Peter's efforts to regularize his troops was on a scale never before attempted. This necessitated large imports of cloth for the general issue until mills were set up in Moscow and Voronezh, giving a tremendous impetus to the development of a domestic

19. Beskrovnyi, "Strategiia i taktika . . .," pp. 22-26.
20. Hellie, pp. 161, 168, 175-176, 188, 199.
21. Klokman, pp. 101-102.
22. *Ibid.*, p. 93.
23. Mikhnevich, p. 133; Rotmistrov, p. 117. See also Hall, III, 349.
24. Beskrovnyi, *Russkaia armiia i flot*, p. 236; L. G. Beskrovnyi, *Khrestomatiia po russkoi voennoi istorii* (Moscow, 1947), pp. 150 *et seq.*

textile industry.[25]

Technological and tactical improvements were made in artillery. In the sixteenth century Russian artillery may have been the equal of any in the world, but in the seventeenth century others outstripped the Muscovites. The 181 field and siege weapons used (and lost to the Swedes) at Narva were old.[26] The remark of John Perry, the English naval engineer and hydrologist who served Peter at the beginning of the eighteenth century, that the Russians could not properly besiege any place indicates the extent of the decline of the Russian artillery prior to Peter's introduction of a regular artillery service branch in 1701.[27]

However, the seventeenth century provided a good base for Peter. Large orders were filled during the Thirteen Years War, and technological progress did not stop. Pieces could be made to order for specific calibres, and the parameters of each weapon were known. The Tula, Kashira, and Moscow factories continuously improved their output, gradually reducing the weight of weapons.[28] Contributions to the advancement of the artillery made during Peter's reign were the invention in 1697 of horse pack mortars, half a century before a similar piece appeared in Western Europe, and the creation in 1706 of a standing horse corps to pull artillery pieces which had 1986 horses and 1255 men in 1711—making the artillery more mobile.[29] The major innovation was of course the special artillery corps; prior to 1701 artillery had been assigned to each regiment. These changes made the artillery more effective, and at Poltava 1,471 round were fired in the process of defeating the Swedes.[30]

Peter's main objective was to make the Russian army a viable rival of Sweden's, which was among the best in Europe. As he could not introduce the new technology and inculcate well-disciplined linear tactics himself, he continued the practice of hiring foreign mercenary officers in large numbers to assist him. Foreigners had served in Russian armies for centuries, but only within the past century had Russians served under their command. This practice reached its peak in Aleksei's army, during the Thirteen Years War, when perhaps over eighty per cent of the command positions were held by non-Russians.[31] In 1696 there were 954 foreign officers in Russian service, of whom 723 were in the infantry and 213 in the cavalry, the lesser branch of service.[32] During his European embassy, Peter left behind in Moscow an army of twelve thousand men under the command of General Gordon and other mostly foreign offi-

25. P. G. Liubomirov, *Ocherki po istorii russkoi promyshlennosti* (Moscow, 1947), pp. 26, 37, *et passim*; E. I. Zaozerskaia, *Razvitie legkoi promyshlennosti v Moskve v pervoi chetverti XVIII v.* (Moscow, 1953), pp. 266-292.

26. Klokman, p. 78.

27. Perry, p. 277; Beskrovnyi, *Russkaia armiia i flot,* p. 43.

28. E. E. Kolosov, "Razvitie artilleriiskogo vooruzheniia v Rossii vo vtoroi polovine XVII v.," *Istoricheskie zapiski*, 71 (1962), pp. 260-268.

29. *Ibid.*, pp. 266-267; Klokman, p. 113; Beskrovnyi, "Strategiia i taktika . . .," p. 25.

30. Klokman, p. 59.

31. G. Forsten, "Snosheniia Shvetsii s Rossiei v tsarstvovanie Khristiny," *Zhurnal Ministerstva narodnago prosveshcheniia*, 434 pts. (St. Petersburg-Petrograd, 1834-1917), 275 (June 1891), 372; P. O. Bobrovskii, *Zachatki reform v voenno-ugolovnom zakonodatel'stve v Rossii* (St. Petersburg, 1882), p. 21; A. Z. Myshlaevskii, *Ofitserskii vopros v XVII veke. Ocherki iz istorii voennago dela v Rossii* (St. Petersburg, 1899), p. 44.

32. Myshlaevskii, pp. 37-38, 42; E. A. Razin, *Istoriia voennogo iskusstva*, 3 vols. (Moscow, 1955-61), III, 218.

cers to keep order.[33] Throughout Peter's reign at least one-third of all officers in every regiment had to be foreigners.[34] When foreign officers, including Huguenots driven out of France, reformers driven out of Hungary by Catholics, and Catholics driven out of England and Scotland, married Russian women, Peter attended the weddings.[35]

While Peter relied heavily on foreigners, some of his most important measures were undertaken to lessen Russia's dependence on them, which was costly militarily as well as financially. For example, during the 1695 siege of Azov a foreign artilleryman by the name of Jacob, who had not been paid and was being abused by his Russian officer, nailed up his cannon, deserted to the Turks, and advised them where successfully to attack the Muscovites.[36] At Narva the foreign officers, led by the artillery commander de Krua, sensing that the Russian forces were losing, went over to Charles XII.[37]

To lessen his dependence on foreigners, Peter established navigation, artillery and engineering schools which turned out three to four hundred officers per year.[38] Service, beginning at age 16, was for life. Decrees of 1714 and 1723 demanded that Russian members of the gentry becoming officers should know military affairs well.[39] Peter's measures to furnish his army with Russian officers proved to be successful, and may well have been his most important military contribution.[40]

We must not forget that major steps toward the professionalization of the officer corps had been initiated by Peter's predecessors. One such step was the seemingly trivial matter of adopting the names for the ranks, another the more important assignment of specific functions to each rank—something unknown in the traditional Muscovite cavalry.[41] The premise that the right to hold officer rank should depend not on birth, but on proved ability and experience, that the officer corps should be a meritocracy, was also established in the seventeenth century. Tsar Aleksei had intended that the foreign mercenaries would transfer their martial skills to the Russians, and in 1649 Western infantry regulations translated into Russian to aid in this aspect of the modernization of the army were published, the third civil book published in Muscovy. However, Aleksei had little success in establishing a native officer corps because both the Russians and the foreigners were reluctant to cooperate, Aleksei was not so adept at coercion, and the regulations were already out of date.

* * *

Another of Peter's concerns was army organization. His aspiration was to turn

33. Perry, pp. 156, 180.

34. A. K. Baiov, *Natsional'nye cherty russkago voennago iskusstva v Romanovskii period nashei istorii* (St. Petersburg, 1913), p. 8. This may have been as much for control as for strictly-military purposes.

35. Perry, p. 199; Bobrovskii, *Zachatki reform*, pp. 25-26.

36. Perry, p. 147. After the Russians captured Jacob in Azov in 1696, they tortured him to death, and made sure that the other foreigners knew about it.

37. Klokman, p. 79.

38. Beskrovnyi, "Strategiia i taktika," p. 23.

39. Mikhnevich, p. 101; Pankov, p. 5.

40. Perry, p. 274.

41. Georgius David, *Status Modernus Magnae Russiae Seu Moscoviae (1690)* (The Hague, 1965), p. 87.

the nation's forces into a regular standing army of proper balance between infantry and cavalry under a workable command structure. The reorganizations tending in that direction began in 1699/1700, with the establishment of three divisions (*general'stva*) comprising the field army, including the following regiments: two guards', twenty-seven infantry, and two dragoons'.[42] In 1704 the army was reorganized into the following regiments: two guards', forty-seven infantry, five grenadiers', thirty-three cavalry, and one artillery. This structure persisted through the years of Poltava (1708-1710).[43] These reorganization measures were a continuation of those carried out under Aleksei and Fedor.[44]

Because organization and command were so important, Peter made several attempts to rationalize the structure of the regiments. At first, two to five regiments were organized into a brigade, and three brigades into a division. Above this was the corps level. The brigade, division, and corps level were never standing, and in fact until roughly 1715 not all of the regiments were standing either.[45] As for the regiments themselves, various internal structural subdivisions were tried: in 1699-1704, infantry regiments consisted of two battalions of five companies each. In 1704, field regiments were to contain two battalions of eight fusilier companies and one grenadier company. Another reorganization was made in 1708, and reaffirmed in 1711, making the cavalry much like that of the infantry in 1699-1704 in its structure. In 1711, each regiment was to have 120 officers, 1367 men.[46]

As far as I can tell, these manipulations of the formal army structure constituted slight improvement over Aleksei's new formation regiments of the Thirteen Years War. At the time A. L. Ordin-Nashchokin had recommended that the army be made a standing one; neither the resources nor the will were then available, so the army remained only a semi-standing one.[47] The cost of making the change for Peter's generation will be discussed shortly.

Advance was made by Peter in instituting a unified military command, in abolishing the numerous separate Muscovite military chancelleries. In the second half of the seventeenth century there had been considerable confusion because there were essentially two armies trying to function simultaneously. In the old army, the Musketeers Chancellery directed its officers, the Military Chancellery its. In 1665 an attempt to subordinate partially the new army command, centered in the Foreign Officers Chancellery, to the Military Chancellery, was made, but confusion was limited thereby only slightly.[48] In the 1680's, there were eighteen military chancelleries.[49] In the years 1702-1707 these numerous Muscovite military chancelleries were closed, and the Chancellery of Military Affairs (*Prikaz voennykh del*) was created to run the armed forces.[50] In 1718, this was superseded by the Military College.

42. Beskrovnyi, "Strategiia i taktika," p. 23; Klokman, p. 78.
43. Beskrovnyi, "Strategiia i taktika," p. 23.
44. A. V. Chernov, *Vooruzhennye sily russkogo gosudarstva v XV-XVII vv.* (Moscow, 1954), pp. 156-160.
45. Bobrovskii, *Zachatki reform*, p. 33.
46. Beskrovnyi, "Strategiia i taktika," pp. 23-24.
47. Bobrovskii, *Perekhod Rossii*, p. 114.
48. Myshlaevskii, pp. 44-45.
49. Rotmistrov, I, 181.
50. Beskrovnyi, "Strategiia i taktika," p. 26.

Peter also introduced a general staff. The head of the army was the general field marshall, who convoked the advisory Military Council.[51] In the field, administration initially was by collegial military councils (*konsilii*), and one-man direction was introduced only gradually in the years 1710-1728.[52] The collegial system was inherited from Muscovite times, when, in reality field commanders seem to have had no discretion whatsoever, but were directed from Moscow by civilians who were often ignorant of the local conditions. The Petrine system can only have been an improvement, although reorganizations in the reign of Fedor Alekseevich were headed in the same direction. Efforts to centralize command were a pan-European phenomenon, an evolution away from the autonomy enjoyed by field commanders as recently as the Thirty Years War. In some respects Peter's moves in this direction were a parody of Westernization, for control by Moscow of battle conditions and the denial of autonomy to field officers had long been practiced. What was new for Russia in Peter's striving for rationality was the concentration of centralized direction from the capital in the Military College.

* * *

Earlier we have noted the Petrine concentration on the infantry for tactical reasons. This change from the traditional reliance on cavalry was initiated by Aleksei before the 1667 Truce of Andrusovo.[53] For reasons not entirely clear to me, the Englishman John Perry seems to have associated the introduction of the infantry (*soldaty*) with the elimination of the musketeers in 1699.[54] In fact, of course, *soldaty* had first been introduced during the Smolensk War (1632-1634), and most of the provincial musketeers had been converted into *soldaty* in the 1670's. The *soldaty* were active in the Azov campaigns, but Perry's remarks that they were a Petrine innovation would seem to indicate that they were not much in evidence when he came to Russia at the very end of the seventeenth century.

The gunpowder revolution relegated the cavalry to a secondary position in warfare. For years Tsar Aleksei had been trying to force the old cavalrymen, members of the middle service class-gentry, into the new army. He and his successors had had some success, but this must have been undone at least partially in the 1690's. After Narva, in the winter of 1700/1701, ten regiments of dragoons were created of these men.[55] Dragoons had been introduced during the Smolensk War, but were phased out in the early 1680's.

Peter's cavalry initially was made up entirely of members of the gentry who had served earlier as old-style cavalrymen, new-style cavalrymen (*reitary*), and as lancers. But after 1708, in view of the shortages of gentry, commoners were admitted into the dragoons, the intermediate status organization between the pure cavalry and the infantry.[56] (I do not know whether commoners were admitted to the cavalry.) A similar

51. Klyuchevsky, pp. 82-83; Pankov, p. 6.
52. Beskrovnyi, "Strategiia i taktika," p. 42.
53. Bobrovskii, *Zachatki reform*, p. 8.
54. Perry, pp. 184, 271.
55. Klokman, p. 79.
56. Pankov, p. 33.

evolution had been witnessed in Muscovy, when shortages of manpower of the appropriate social standing forced the government to recruit commoners into both the dragoons and the *reitary*; once the war was over, the non-landed elements were either discharged from the army or put into the infantry. I do not know whether such blatant class discrimination was practiced in the first quarter of the eighteenth century.

Because of technological change, the role of the cavalry was different in Peter's army than before. Prior to his time, the cavalry was crucial for protecting the infantry armed with hand guns, for, as already noted, pikemen were hardly used in Muscovy. The introduction of the bayonet allowed the infantry to protect itself, and the cavalry's task changed to scouting, sudden attack, and pursuit. Guns were used much less by the Petrine cavalrymen, who fought almost exclusively with cold weapons. In the early years of the eighteenth century the cavalry was nearly worthless, and only in 1709 did it become effective.[57] (Peter also restored the hussars, and a separate command for them was created in 1707.)

I suspect that the artillery was the prestige branch of land service in Peter's time. Aleksei had made notable attempts to raise the status of the infantry by making service compensation nearly equal to that for service in the cavalry.[58] This was particularly necessary because he was less willing than his son to use the knout to force change, in this case get the proud landowner off his horse onto the ground where militarily he was more effective. I do not know the extent to which Petrine cavalry service was more prestigious than infantry, and what precise measures the sovereign took to get the landed elements to serve effectively in the infantry.

To inculcate the necessary training in his troops, Peter introduced annual summer training camps.[59] This is reminiscent of his father's autumn month-long training putatively required of the troops of foreign formation.[60]

The Petrine garrison forces were also continuous with those of Muscovy. They were recruited, as in the past, largely from servicemen discharged from active field duty. However, true to Peter's striving for rationality, they had a more formal organization than their predecessors, and in 1711 fifty-eight thousand men were organized into thirty-two garrison regiments (thirty infantry, two dragoons.)[61]

* * *

One of the most striking things about the Petrine army is that it was roughly the same size as its predecessor. Obviously strength is not always measurable in numbers alone, as Ivashka Peresvetov recognized in the late 1540's or early 1550's, when he recommended that the cavalry numbers be drastically reduced in favor of a more effective infantry of lesser numbers but higher cost.[62] (Half of his recommendation was adopted: the *strel'tsy* were introduced but the cavalry kept on growing.) A century

57. Klokman, p. 113; Beskrovnyi, "Strategiia i taktika," pp. 59, 61.
58. Hellie, p. 191.
59. Pankov, p. 7.
60. D. O. Maslovskii doubted whether Aleksei's troops got this training (*Zapiski po istorii voennago iskusstva v Rossii*, 2 vols. in 3 pts. [St. Petersburg, 1891-94], I, 25).
61. Beskrovnyi, "Strategiia i taktika," p. 24.
62. I. S. Peresvetov, *Sochineniia* (Moscow-Leningrad, 1956), p. 175.

later, Aleksei seems to have planned his forces' numbers to equal what intelligence reports claimed his rivals had.[63] I have been unable to determine how Peter, verbally conscious of the problem, planned the size of his army, but after Poltava he reduced it in what seems to have been a conscious striving for quality rather than quantity. Toward the end of Peter's reign his standing regular army totalled 120-130,000 men.[64] This represented a 25 per cent increase over the size of his forces at the time of his disastrous fall into the hands of the Turks on the Pruth.[65] In addition, there were about 75-80,000 garrison troops.[66] Thus the Petrine land forces totalled 175-200,000 men. In addition, there were 20,000 cossacks; the navy numbered about 15,000 at the time of Pruth, 38,000 after the Northern War. The total establishment grew roughly from 210,000 to 265,000 men.[67] Subtracting for the navy, Peter's army was hardly any larger in the last years of his reign than it had been in 1681–about 215,000 men.[68] These facts are particularly noteworthy in light of such claims as that at the end of the seventeenth century the effective Russian army did not exceed 20,000 men, for such claims might convey the erroneous impression that it was only under Peter that, for the first time, Russia had an enormous military establishment.[69]

Notable in the Petrine period was a decline in the number of troops engaged in major campaigns. The Muscovites sent out over half of their total forces (over 100,000) in the 1660's-1680's,[70] whereas Peter sent far less: 34-45,000 to Narva,[71] 42,000 to Poltava,[72] 44,000 (32,000 infantry, 12,000 cavalry) to the Pruth,[73] and around 14-16,000 to Finland in 1713.[74] The lower Petrine figures probably represent the fact that Peter, in spite of his wishes, had to heed the cordon strategy of the day which dictated stationing men seemingly everywhere in the event of a surprise enemy attack, leaving less for concentrated, potentially decisive, offensive and defensive actions. The Petrine figures also may indicate a greater attention to quality and anticipated needs than earlier, but this by no means signifies that the armies sent out by

63. Hellie, p. 372 n. 31.

64. Perry, p. 277; *Polnoe sobranie zakonov Rossiiskoi Imperii*, 30 vols. (St. Petersburg, 1830), IV, no. 2319. In 1707 Peter's army was 145,000 (Klokman, p. 86). Kliuchevskii said 113,000 in 1709 (p. 81). This would represent more than parity with the 104,000 men at the disposal of Charles XII in late 1707; 54,000 in Saxony, 16,000 in the East Baltic, 14,000 in Finland, and 8,000 in Poland (Beskrovnyi, "Strategiia i taktika," p. 24), Mikhnevich gave the size of the Russian army in 1724 as 112,000 (70,000 infantry, 38,000 dragoons, and 4,000 artillerymen and engineers) (p. 126).

65. Beskrovnyi, *Khrestomatiia*, p. 143; E. Vinogradoff, "Growth of the Russian Military Establishment, 1700-1856" (unpublished ms.), p. 1.

66. Vinogradoff; Mikhnevich listed 68,000 garrison troops (p. 126).

67. Vinogradoff. Similar figures can be found in Pankov (p. 5), and slightly larger in Klyuchevsky (p. 81).

68. Bobrovskii, *Postoiannyia*, p. 32; Elchaninov, p. 71; Maslovskii, I, 50; Chernov, p. 189; Mikhnevich, p. 127; Hellie, p. 269.

69. Bobrovskii, *Perekhod Rossii*, p. 109.

70. N. P. Mikhnevich and P. A. Geisman, *Glavnyi shtab. Istoricheskii ocherk voznikoveniia i razvitiia v Rossii general'nago shtaba do kontsa tsarstvovaniia imperatora Aleksandra I vkliuchitel'no*, in Skalon, IV, pt. 1, no. 1, sect. 2, p. 69; Hellie, pp. 271-272.

71. Bobrovskii, *Perekhod Rossii*, p. 108 (the larger figure); Klokman, p. 78 (the lesser).

72. Klokman, p. 97. The Swedes had 30,000 troops, of whom 25-26,000 were in the battle (*ibid.*; Beskrovnyi, *Russkaia armiia i flot*, pp. 212, 214).

73. Beskrovnyi, *Russkaia armiia i flot*, p. 219. The Turks had 97,619 troops (*ibid.*).

74. Klokman, p. 105.

Aleksei, Fedor, and Sofiia were "hordes." the latter forces were as rationally organized and commanded for their day as Peter's were for his.[75]

In all probability, the cost of the Petrine army was greater than that of the Muscovite. For one thing, Peter had to discard reliance on booty as payment for his troops, partly because that form of compensation was becoming considered unprofessional, partly because in the first half of his reign most of the major operations were on Russian territory.[76] Peter had more success than did his father in making cash, rather than land, the basic reward for service.[77] In the process of completing the phaseout of the old Muscovite army, Peter's goal was to have the government pay the bills of the regular army. (In this, of course, he never succeeded entirely.) Kliuchevskii calculated that, in constant rubles, the cost of the army rose at least five-fold between 1680 and 1725.[78] According to other scholars, this figure is much too large.[79] No one questions that war costs were a scourge in the Petrine era, but only how bad it really was by comparison with what the earlier Muscovites had known. It would be interesting to try to calculate the comparative costs of Ivan IV's army in, say, 1583 (at the end of the Livonian War), Aleksei's army in 1667 (at the end of the Thirteen Years War), and Peter's army in 1721 (at the end of the Northern War), but no one, to my knowledge, has done so.

Another undisputed scourge was recruiting. Because Peter was at peace for only two years of his reign, and because of his considerable casualties, vast numbers of men were needed to fill the armed forces.[80] Ten recruiting levies between 1705 and 1713 drafted 337,196 men, a fair percentage of the roughly fifteen million Russians.[81] These levies, added to the taxes and official malfeasance, were the reasons for the discontent which Perry observed was so severe that if Peter had not won at Poltava, there would have been a general uprising in Russia.[82] The innovativeness of the recruiting itself is exaggerated. One frequently reads that something new occurred in 1699, when recruiting was "introduced," or in the years 1705-1709, when "a unified system of recruiting was introduced."[83] In fact, recruiting was solidly rooted in the seventeenth

75. Hellie, ch. xi.

76. Bobrovskii, *Perekhod Rossii*, p. 112.

77. A. V. Romanovich-Slavatinskii, *Dvorianstvo v Rossii ot nachala XVIII veka do otmeny krepostnago prava* (St. Petersburg, 1870), p. 153.

78. Klyuchevsky, pp. 83, 176-177.

79. P. N. Miliukov cut down Kliuchevskii's figures, and S. G. Strumilin reduced them even further ("K voprosu ob ekonomike petrovskoi epokhi," in *Poltava. K 250-letiiu Poltavskogo srazheniia*, p. 187).

80. Beskrovnyi, *Russkaia armiia i flot,* p. 113. Soviet authors always emphasize that Russian casualties were fewer than their enemies' (Klokman, p. 93 *et passim*). Vinogradoff lists 40,000 war deaths in the 1696-1725 period (p. 2).

81. Pankov, p. 5. Kliuchevskii gives the figure of 300,000 draftees for the years 1700-1709 (p. 81). Beskrovnyi says that only 131,319 were called up in these years. *Russkaia armiia i flot,* p. 23). For population statistics, see V. M. Kabuzan, *Izmeneniia v razmeshchenii-naseleniia Rossii v XVIII-pervoi polovine XIX v. (Po materialam revizii)* (Moscow, 1971), p. 10.

82. Perry, pp. 27-28. His friend, Ambassador Whitworth, had reported already in 1705 that Russia was exhausted (*Sbornik Imperatorskago Russkago istoricheskago obshchestva,* 148 vols. [St. Petersburg, Petrograd, 1867-1916], 39 [1884], p. 190).

83. Klokman, p. 93; Pankov, pp. 4-5; Beskrovnyi, *Russkaia armiia i flot,* pp. 24-29; Beskrovnyi, "Strategiia i taktika," p. 23.

century, and had simply been discontinued in the 1690's.[84] Mass recruiting had been initiated during the Smolensk War, and came of age during the Thirteen Years War, when over 56,000 were drafted in three systematic levies in the years 1658-1660, and over one hundred thousand were called during the entire war.[85] Both Aleksei's and Peter's draft calls were for one man per from 10 to 95-1/2 households—and began the change in living pattern from single family- to extended family-households.[86] Peter kept the commoners continuously under arms for much longer periods than was the practice in the new formation regiments. While this indubitably raised the level of discipline in the Russian army, the impact on the rest of the population has not, to my knowledge, been evaluated.

The recruiting had the virtue of making the Petrine army almost entirely national. In Aleksei's time, foreign officers brought entire companies of mercenaries with them. But Peter used only Russians as rank-and-file troops in his field army; other peoples were used in the garrison service and as irregulars.[87] (At the same time, the Prussian army, by comparison, was over half foreigners; the Swedish was largely national.) While Peter had to contend with desertion and discontent, he did not have the problem, as did his forebears, of troops who would readily go over to the enemy when losing. This factor certainly must have contributed to the success of Petrine arms.

* * *

The overall success of Petrine arms is indisputable. The reasons for this success are perhaps more controversial. As often occurs, the enemy's mistakes were worth at least as much as one's own actions. This was certainly true for Peter. The decision of his adversary, Charles XII, not to follow up his victory at Narva, but to campaign in Poland and Germany, gave Peter time to strengthen his own army and to annex an outlet to the Baltic. When Charles agains turned to Russia, in 1707, he was the victim of a combination of his own arrogance and his heretofore-successful methods of warfare. Charles was so sure that the Russians would fall before his onslaught that, while still in Saxony, he appointed a governor for Moscow, allotted specific houses in Moscow to his troops, and drafted a project to split Russia up into small principalities.[88] Much of this reminds us of the Mongols half a millennium earlier. Also like the Mongols, Charles used a blitzkrieg strategy, living off the land and moving by forced marches from one objective to another. This was successful elsewhere, but proved di-

84. Klyuchevsky, p. 79.

85. E. D. Stashevskii, "Smeta voennykh sil Moskovskago gosudarstva na 1632 god," *Voenno-istoricheskii vestnik*, 9-10 (1910), pp. 14-15; *Akty Moskovskago gosudarstva*, ed. N. A. Popov, 3 vols. (St. Petersburgh, 1890-1901), III, nos. 451, 504, 554, 582.

86. Beskrovnyi, *Russkaia armiia i flot*, pp. 25-28. Three generations crowded into one house to reduce the assessments for taxes and recruits, which were based on the household. Peter discovered what had happened, and at the end of his reign introduced a system based on male "souls."

87. Beskrovnyi, "Strategiia i taktika," p. 23.

88. Klokman, p. 83. One biographer of Charles XII, Ragnel M. Hatton, presents a different image of her subject's thoughts on the struggle with Russia: he realized it would be a difficult one. However, Hatton notes others who aver with good evidence that Charles was so contemptuous of the Russians that he and his Swedes assumed that very little effort would be needed to defeat Peter's army (*Charles XII of Sweden* [London, 1968], pp. 236, 238-239).

sastrous in Russia. Knowing the Swedish art of war, Peter ordered all supplies hidden, exported, or destroyed to deny Charles succor. In his arrogance Charles thought he could march straight to Moscow, but the Russians held him off, forced him into the Ukraine, and let the scorched earth strategy take its toll. This was followed by superb generalship and use of engineering works, and the result was the extermination of Charles XII's army at Poltava.[89] With no opposition, Peter could do as he wished while Charles spent five years in exile in Turkey after Poltava. The new Russian navy permitted Peter to carry the war to the enemy's heartland, the suburbs of Stockholm. These were the events which produced the Peace of Nystadt in 1721 and gave Russia the Kola and Karelian peninsulae, Lifland, Estland, and Ingria, the eastern shore of the Baltic from Riga to Vyborg.

Carelessness on Peter's part led to his disaster on the Pruth, and cost him Azov, Taganrog, and the success of his drive for the Black Sea. Only at the end of his reign did he have martial success in the south, on the Caspian, at the expense of Persia. By the terms of the Peace of St. Petersburg (1723), Russia acquired the southern and western Caspian coasts and other Persian territories, but returned them between 1729 and 1735 because they were too costly to keep.

* * *

Obviously factors other than the essentially extra-military ones of stupidity and luck also helped Peter thwart the Swedish drive on Moscow, annihilate its army, and then move on to further triumphs. Besides Peter's innovations (the use of the bayonet, the Baltic fleet, a woolens industry) and improvements (artillery, military organization, command, and training; the manufacturing and metallurgical base; making the army more national), note should be taken of improved revenue, supply, and provisioning. Some feel that the Petrine supply system was a great advance over its predecessors. The intention in 1699 with the creation of a regular army was for the treasury to provide weapons, food, and clothing for the troops in both peace and war. Ivan IV had tried to do this for his *strel'tsy*. The government tried to do no more for the new formation regiments than supply them during war time. Peter created a special office to provision the army on 18 February 1700.[90] A law of 18 February 1705 specified precisely the rations for each man.[91] However, the decrees represented only intentions, not necessarily reality. Professor Alexandre Bennigsen noted during the discussion at the Tercentenary Conference on Peter the Great and His Legacy that the Turks considered Golitsyn's Crimean campaigns of 1687 and 1689 to have been better provisioned than Peter's expedition to the Pruth in 1711. In fact, the Petrine commissary system seems to have advanced little beyond the sophistication and utility of Tsar Aleksei's Grain Chancellery (1663-1683) until, with a series of measures begun in

89. Klokman, p. 87. R. M. Hatton, while concentrating on "fate"—the alternating severe cold weather and Russian mud (as also have historians of Napoleon's and Hitler's misadventures into Russia), occasionally gives credit to the Russians' genuine martial merit in explaining Charles' debacle (compare her pp. 261-306, *passim*, with pp. 259, 266, 281).

90. F. P. Shelekhov, *Glavnoe intendantskoe upravlenie. Istoricheskii ocherk. Chast' I. Vvedenie v tsarstvovanie Imperatora Aleksandra I,* in Skalon, V, pt. 1, pp. 9-10.

91. *Ibid.*, p. 14.

1711, including the creation of the Commissariat of War, things began to improve.[92] Further major steps were taken in 1724 to improve provisioning.[93] It hardly can be claimed that the reforms of 1711 and 1724 played a major role in Petrine martial success, for by then the die had already been cast. As for the regularizing of the army, Peter himself noted in 1716 that this supposed major innovation had its origins in his father's activities as long ago as 1647.[94]

Important for Peter's military success was the fact that the tsar himself was a military man, could command, and developed a "Russian military school" consisting of himself, A. D. Menshikov, F. M. Apraksin, and B. P. Sheremetev—something his father never did or could have done.[95] Peter was willing to try to instill discipline in his troops, even to the extent of court martialing a general for failure and reducing him to a common foot soldier.[96] This stands in sharp contrast to Aleksei's remark that not all men are brave, so it is difficult to punish a man who is not.[97] Peter's army probably demanded leadership traits different from Aleksei's, but the materials essential to compose such comparative psychological portraits are not available.

I suspect why Peter seems to have a better military reputation than his father is due partly to the fact that Aleksei's troops (who actually conquered more, and perhaps more valuable, territory than did Peter's) were exhausted by repeated invasions of enemy territory and consequently were forced to retreat, as seen in the Treaty of Andrusovo. Peter, on the other hand, had the "good luck" to fight mostly on his home territory until he chanced to be able to annihilate his major enemy, and then went on to Nystadt. Peter's military reputation has also been enhanced by his direct, often highly theatrical, participation in his martial effort. In this regard, there can be no doubt that in matters of strategy and tactics Peter was a military leader who considered himself bound by no conventions or rules, whose goal was to win and who was willing to make innovations on the battlefield whenever it might be to his advantage.[98] He demanded that his troops "live according to the regulations, but act according to reason."[99] There can be no doubt that Peter certainly was one of the outstanding field commanders of his age. While a definitive work on the Petrine mystique has not been written, unquestionably the fact that Peter was nearly the sole male to rule Russia in the eighteenth century, that he took the title of emperor over 150 years after Russia had really become an empire, that he moved the capital from Moscow to St. Petersburg and thus opened Russia more directly to Western influence—all of these factors helped to reinforce his military reputation.

* * *

Most of the consequences of the Petrine army developments have been

92. *Ibid.*, pp. 16-19; Mikhnevich, pp. 119-120.
93. Shelekhov, pp. 24-26, 31-32.
94. Pankov, p. 4.
95. Klokman, p. 112.
96. *Ibid.* p. 89.
97. Samuel Collins, *The Present State of Russia* (London, 1671), p. 110.
98. Beskrovnyi, *Russkaia armiia i flot,* pp. 236-237.
99. Rotmistrov, I, 132.

mentioned—expansion on the Baltic and Caspian, the development of new industries, and exhaustion of the populace—and can be seen as part of a continuous development from the seventeenth century. The impact on society is also part of a generally continuous pattern.

Elsewhere I have discussed the impact of the military reforms of Aleksei and Peter on the peasantry and the development of serfdom.[100] Here I should like to present some thoughts about the impact on the middle and upper service classes, the provincial gentry and capital elite. Aleksei had, to a certain extent, sociologically dispossessed these people by turning the army command over to the foreign mercenaries he hired, by filling the ranks with draftees, and entrusting the government apparatus to bureaucrats and military discards. This allowed Aleksei to modernize the army and rule without any restraint other than that provided by oligarchic factionalism and hoi poloi inertia.

Peter undid this arrangement by putting the gentry back in harness and making state service the particular vocation, the only social function, of the former Muscovite privileged elements.[101] Moreover, with the introduction of the regular army, the character of service changed for these social elements. It was no longer for the sake of retaining a landed service estate (*pomest'e*), but as a member of an estate—the wellborn *shliakhetstvo*.[102] By the end of the eighteenth century this group almost became an indirect restraint of sorts on the oligarchic monarchy, sort of a later reincarnation of the middle service class of the years 1613-1649 which had dominated the Assembly of the Land and demanded the enserfment of the peasantry. Thus Peter almost created a defined social class capable of realizing independent strivings and thus nearly capable of restraining the autocracy which had created it.[103]

But Peter in his autocratic wisdom did not allow this to occur in his lifetime. He dissolved the old territorial militia organizations and sent the members of the gentry out of their native districts to join the regular regiments in remote areas. Thus, except for the elite guards regiments, no cadres were allowed to develop among the atomized *shliakhetstvo* which might have restrained the autocracy.

Peter continued the two-centuries-old development of the autocracy. He undermined the always meek church, exterminated the palace guard *strel'tsy*, allowed the leading merchant corporation (the *gosti*) to die out, and permitted the relatively new (since ca. 1649) Boiar Council and its members to expire.[104] The majority of the privileged landed elements were incorporated into service in such a way as to prevent their rapidly coalescing into a restraint on the autocrat. He failed to create a perfect autocracy because his guards regiments were not atomized, and for the century after his death were a central element in the "era of palace revolutions."

100. Hellie, ch. xiv.

101. Klyuchevsky, p. 90.

102. Romanovich-Slavatinskii, p. 117.

103. Sh. noted in 1887 that it was the general absence of such solid, defined social classes, not the Tatars or a seizure of power, which was the historical basis for the formation of the autocracy ("Dvorianstvo v Rossii. Istoricheskii i obshchestvennyi ocherk," *Vestnik Evropy*, 22, nos. 2-3 [March-June 1887], p. 559).

104. V. I. Sergeevich presented strong evidence indicating that the "Boiar Council" was not an "august institution," but largely a figment of the imaginations of N. P. Zagoskin and V. O. Kliuchevskii (*Drevnosti russkago prava*, 3 vols. [St. Petersburg, 1908], II, 380 *et seq.*).

Hopefully the preceding pages have provided food for thought about the claim by the distinguished nineteenth-century military historian A. Z. Myshlaevskii that there was no decisive step taken by Peter which was not prepared in some way by his predecessors.[105] It is my impression that this stress on the developmental continuity of fundamental military institutions between the Petrine era and the Muscovite period is an appropriate one. This is not to say, hypothetically, that the Petrine army in 1709 could not have routed Aleksei's army even more easily than it did Charles XII's: Petrine generalship and discipline, the bayonet and artillery, the ability and willingness to pursue and annihilate the enemy probably would have overwhelmed Aleksei's new formation regiments. Nevertheless, Dolgorukii was essentially correct: Aleksei sired not only Peter himself, but also the institutional base of Peter's army as well.[106]

*The University of Chicago*

105. Myshlaevskii, p. 6.
106. Mikhnevich, pp. 94-95.

# [9]

JOHN KEEP

# Feeding the Troops: Russian Army Supply Policies during the Seven Years War

Eighteenth-century Russia lagged behind other continental European powers in devising regular and effective means of provisioning her armies in the field. More advanced states, notably Prussia and France, set up networks of bases (magazines) in areas where military operations were expected. Ideally, troops should not have to march for more than five days before coming across a fresh source of food supply. This measure was designed to reduce the high rates of desertion which frequently ensued when troops were allowed or encouraged to live off the land.[1] Russia's military leaders, from Peter I onward, knew of these developments and sought to emulate them, but it was beyond the empire's capacity to do so in very systematic fashion. The main reason for this was economic underdevelopment: the vast distances made overland communication difficult; population density and crop yields were low; agricultural surpluses were uncertain and whole regions might be afflicted by famine, especially in the first half of the century.[2] In these circumstances it was hard to build up secure stocks of cereals, which constituted the main ingredient in the soldiers' diet. Second, the empire's administrative structure was still primitive. Officials saw themselves as servants of the autocrat rather than as state functionaries. They were prone to exploit their position for career advancement or for sheer personal gain instead of taking initiatives to improve the public weal—an attitude that changed but little before Catherine II's reforms.

The "pre-rational" (in the Weberian sense) ethos of civilian *chinovniki* was only slightly less manifest among servitors in the military, the branch most favoured by male members of the elite before 1762. The beginnings of an organized, centrally directed supply service go back to the Muscovite era,[3] but it was Peter I who established bureaucratic bodies on western lines to feed his sizeable new standing armed forces, which were required to

1. E. Robson, "The Armed Forces and the Art of War," *New Cambridge Modern History,* Vol. 7 (1957), p. 168.

2. A. Kahan, *The Plow, the Hammer and the Knout: An Economic History of Eighteenth-Century Russia* (Chicago and London, 1985), pp. 46-48.

3. P. P. Epifanov, "Voisko i voennaia organizatsiia," in A. V. Artsykhovskii (Ed.), *Ocherki russkoi kul'tury XVI v.: material'naia kul'tura* (Moscow, 1976), pp. 375-76.

operate abroad. Much of his reign was spent in a desperate quest for funds for military purposes, and the measures then adopted (notably the introduction of the poll tax) left a lasting imprint on the empire's institutional and social order. More particularly, the "tsar reformer" set up, within the War College bureaucracy, two offices with a quasi-autonomous status (or, to be more precise, senior officials with dependent staffs). One, the Glavnyi krigs-kommisariat (here GKK), was responsible for the troops' pay and for supplies of uniforms, equipment, weapons, munitions, and so on. The General-proviantmeister's chancellery (here GPK) was charged with "provisioning" in the narrower sense of obtaining foodstuffs and forage, and it is with this aspect of the supply problem that we shall be concerned here.

The GPK experienced several confusing changes of status during the politically volatile post-Petrine years. In 1726 the omnipotent Prince A. D. Menshikov successfully resisted an attempt by his rival A. P. Tolstoi to bring the commissariat under tighter central control,[4] but in 1737 Field-Marshal B. Ch. von Münnich, who managed military affairs under Anna Ivanovna (1730-40), placed provisioning, along with other support functions, under the authority of an enlarged and strengthened GKK. Its headquarters remained in Moscow, the chief centre of the grain market; a subordinate office in St. Petersburg looked after the needs of troops in the Baltic provinces, where most of them were normally stationed.[5] Münnich built up the magazine network along the empire's major roads and laid down detailed regulations governing their administration. As a check on corruption, the men in charge were to be posted elsewhere after a certain term. Depots were to measure 32 by 7 *sazhens* (*ca.* 900 m$^2$) in area and their wooden floors were to rest on brick supports "so that no mice shall get through."[6] A new "table" or schedule (1731) had reduced the maximum prices payable to foodstuffs suppliers; but provincial governors still had leeway to adjust them to local market conditions, which varied greatly from one region or season to another. Such decisions were probably made after consulting the most influential landowners in each province. The

4. F. P. Shelekhov, "Glavnoe intendantskoe pravlenie: istoricheskii ocherk," *Stoletie Voennogo ministerstva, 1802-1902,* Vol. 5 (St. Petersburg, 1903), pp. 37-38.

5. *Ibid.*, pp. 45-46; *Polnoe sobranie zakonov Rossiiskoi imperii* [hereafter cited as *PSZ*], 1st coll. (St. Petersburg, 1830), Vol. 9, nos. 6441-6.

6. Shelekhov, "Glavnoe indendantskoe pravlenie," p. 43; *PSZ,* Vol. 8, no. 5819. Rodents would long continue to plague Russian army quartermasters, however.

purchasing authorities preferred to deal directly with large suppliers rather than with merchants, who were suspected of profiteering. The duration and terms of such contracts are not known. Where advances (*zadatki*) were offered, these will have given suppliers an incentive to live up to their undertakings.[7]

When Elizabeth Petrovna (1741-61) came to the throne by the *coup d'état* of 25 November 1741, she sought to win legitimacy by ordering a general return to Petrine practices. As a result the army's food supply agency regained its autonomy, but nothing was done to raise standards of efficiency and the bureaucratic apparatus soon lapsed into slothful routine. The GPK was kept short of funds by the treasury and failed to meet all its debts to suppliers, some of whom retaliated in 1749 by refusing to deliver produce. At that time the GPK was running a deficit of 2.3 million roubles, equivalent to nearly half the army's budget.[8] This neglect seemed likely to result in crisis if the empire should become involved in a major European war. At first, wisely enough, Elizabeth concentrated on building up Russian armed strength along the southern border and avoided far-reaching commitments to her hard-pressed Austrian ally. But after the peace of Aix-la-Chapelle in 1748 Chancellor A. P. Bestuzhev-Riumin, more convinced than ever that Prussia represented a menace to the empire's interests, emerged as leader of a "war party," and the tsarina was easily converted to this viewpoint. In 1755-56 the army was gradually placed on a war footing. In the Baltic provinces a 30,000-man Observation Corps was set up under the energetic P. I. Shuvalov. The British, who initially undertook to subsidize this force, had expected it to be used to protect Hanover against the French, but the Russian court evidently saw its role as to put pressure on Frederick II of Prussia, and the "diplomatic revolution" of 1756 made this its sole conceivable purpose.[9]

---

7. Our knowledge of the supply system's workings comes almost entirely from the regulations of 9 January 1758 (*PSZ*, Vol. 15, no. 10788), which codified earlier practices. These rules were initially devised for the Observation Corps but later acquired general validity. They were evidently still normative more than sixty years later: *cf. Proviantskie reguly dlia uchrezhdennoi pri Observatsionnom korpuse komissii generala-proviantmeistera-leitenanta,* 3d ed. (St. Petersburg, 1821).

8. Shelekhov, "Glavnoe intendantskoe pravlenie," p. 51.

9. H. H. Kaplan, *Russia and the Outbreak of the Seven Years War* (Berkeley and Los Angeles, 1968), pp. 32, 38. For the Russian army's performance in the war see now C. Duffy, *Russia's Military Way to the West: Origins and Nature of Russian Military Power, 1700-1800* (London and Boston, 1981), pp. 59-124; *cf.* also J. L. H.

The officials responsible for the military preparations paid relatively scant attention to building up food supplies. Complacency and neglect of the human factor were attitudes ingrained in the military establishment. Manpower was cheap and there was little prestige to be acquired by showing solicitude for the troops' well-being. Tough-minded senior officers took the view that the men were used to hardships, and that they could be expected to look after themselves. Russia's military leaders may also have believed that her western neighbours, being more richly endowed by nature, had ample stocks of foodstuffs to spare, which the Russian forces would be able to buy or confiscate (requisition) when they moved west. The old idea of living off the land was generally accepted doctrine so far as enemy territory was concerned. The relative merits of each course of action may not even have been seriously discussed, for the authorities do not seem to have calculated with any rigour how much their expanded forces would require—or at least no such document has yet come to light.

There are many difficulties in trying to calculate what the Russian army's actual needs were. We do not have accurate data on their numerical strength; cereals were measured by volume in *chetverti* (quarters), which in the case of rye grain were equivalent to 130 kg. but differed for other grains or milled flour; and the men baked their own bread in their artels, using varying amounts of flour. The following discussion is therefore speculative and confined mainly to cereals.

As fixed by Peter I, the peacetime annual ration for men in the field forces consisted of 3 *chetverti* of rye flour and 1½ of groats (*krupa*), the basis of a gruel called *kasha.* In wartime they were to receive a daily ration of 2 *funty* (*ca.* 800 gr.) of bread—presumably in lieu of the flour, 1 *funt* of meat, 2 *charki* (¼ litres) of wine, and 1 *garnets* (3¼ litres!) of beer, as well as a monthly allowance of 1½ *garntsy* (= 7½ *funty* or *ca.* 600 gr) of groats and 2 *funty* of salt.[10] But these generous provisions were no longer kept to in the present conflict. Regulations issued in 1758 provided that each soldier was to receive per month 72½ *funty* of flour or 52½ of biscuit (*sukhari*) and 1 *garnets* of groats.[11] This was equivalent to 29.68 or 21.49

Keep, "The Russian Army in the Seven Years War," in B. Kroener (Ed.), *Krieg, Wirtschaft und Gesellschaft im Zeitalter Friedrich des Grossen* (Freiburg i. Br., forthcoming).

10. *PSZ,* Vol. 4, no. 2034 (1705); Vol. 4, no. 3003 (1716), ch. 68.

11. *PSZ,* Vol. 15, no. 10788 (1758), VII, 1; D. F. Maslovskii, *Russkaia armiia v Semiletniuiu voinu* (Moscow, 1886-91) [hereafter cited as *RASV*], ii(ii). 146. The German translation of this major study, by A. von Drygalski, *Der siebenjährige*

kg respectively, plus 2.05 kg of groats. Meat and other items, it was now assumed, would be obtained largely by unit authorities as and when they became available, with the aid of money provided for the purpose.

The 1731 magazine schedule laid down that stocks should be held (in magazines of all types) of 592,500 and 37,024 *cherverti* of flour and groats respectively,[12] which would have sufficed for one year's consumption by an army of *ca.* 200,000 men. In May 1757 the actual strength of the field forces was probably about 129,000, and of garrison forces about 63,000.[13] At that size the field forces would have needed 387,000 *chetverti* of cereals per annum, or 32,250 per month. The army's first commander-in-chief (C-in-C), Field-Marshal S. F. Apraksin, stated that he needed 20,000 *chetverti* of flour a month to give his men the 2-*funt* daily bread ration[14]—i.e., perhaps one-quarter to one-third more in terms of unmilled grain? Elsewhere D. F. Maslovskii estimates that a 40,000-man army in 1758 needed 14,000 *chetverti* of (unmilled) cereals for six weeks;[15] extrapolating, we may assess Apraksin's monthly requirements at 31,500 *chetverti,* which is consonant with the first figure.

How many vehicles would have been needed to transport such an amount? Unfortunately we have no data as to the capacity of either type of vehicle then in use: the *telega* or the *povozka.* However, we do know that a regiment (*ca.* 1,000 men) was supposed to have 102 *povozki,* of which 36, each with three horses, were assigned to the transport of 20 days' foodstuffs (the rest being carried by the men on their backs).[16] Supposing this load to have consisted entirely of cereals, and estimating the requirement per man at 30 kg per month, the regimental transport would have had to carry a combined total of 20,000 kg, or 555 kg per cart. In 1757 Apraksin's army is said to have had a train of 50,000 carts. Let us suppose that one-third of these were available to carry provisions, and that each bore some 500 kg of cereals. In that case they could have transported 9 million kg, or (in

---

*Krieg nach russischer Darstellung* (Berlin, 1893), is unhappily defective in several particulars.

12. D. P. Zhuravskii, "Statisticheskoe obozrenie raskhodov na voennye potrebnosti, 1711 po 1825 gg.," *Voennyi sbornik,* 9 (1859), p. 59; *cf. PSZ,* Vol. 43(i), no. 5819 (1731).

13. *RASV,* i(i). 68, i(ii). 102. Much higher figures are sometimes encountered for 1756, but are best ignored: see appendix to Keep, "The Russian Army."

14. *RASV,* i(ii). 228, n. 19.

15. *Ibid.*, ii(i). 339.

16. *Ibid.*, ii(ii). 11.

terms of rye capacity) *ca.* 7,000 *chetverti,* equivalent to only one-quarter of the army's needs. This shows that alternative means of transport were essential; but in default of a large central "transport park" the authorities had to turn to civilian sources.[17]

In 1756 the authorities acted to prohibit export of cereals from the Baltic provinces and began to construct several new magazines on the western Dvina and upper Dnieper, as well as smaller ones in Livland and along the Niemen[18]—this despite a poor harvest that year in the north-western region. By October 1756 stocks at seven depots in the Baltic were put at 244,000 *chetverti* of flour and over 22,000 of groats.[19] In January 1757 the C-in-C gave assurances that his army had enough food for three months in such depots alone.[20] But what would happen once his forces moved across the border? Agents were despatched to secure supplies from friendly magnates in the eastern half of the Polish-Lithuanian Commonwealth (which was formally neutral in the war), but the first results were disappointing.[21] The army's stock of no fewer than 92,000 horses needed massive amounts of fodder which for some reason—Maslovskii blames this on negligence by the General-proviantmeister, Major-General M. N. Volkonskii[22]—were not brought to the depots in Livland. This was one reason why the invasion was so long delayed: implausible as it sounds, Apraksin decided to wait until sufficient grass had grown for his animals to graze on. Such "soft" fodder was in any case a poor substitute for proper nourishment, and explains why so many of the wretched beasts collapsed later in the year. The C-in-C also seems to have grossly overestimated what could be obtained from occupied East Prussia in the way of foodstuffs and vehicles. Even more reprehensible was the official failure to put together a fleet of sea-going vessels to transport supplies to the forward areas. Although Russia had no merchant navy of her own, foreign ships could have been leased, as was belatedly done, on a limited scale, from 1760

17. For resort to civilian transport: *ibid.*, iii(ii). 12 (1759), 165 (1760).

18. *Ibid.*, i(i). 85.

19. *Ibid.*, i(ii). 227.

20. *Ibid.*, i(i). 93.

21. *Ibid., loc. cit.;* N. M. Korobkov (Ed.), *Semiletniaia voina: materialy o deistviiakh russkoi armii i flota v 1756-1762 gg.* (Moscow, 1948) [hereafter cited as *SLV*], pp. 62*ff.* This important compilation has relatively little to say about supply questions.

22. *RASV,* i(i). 86.

onward.[23] The problem of suitable harbours where goods could be landed[24] was also tackled indecisively. Lack of imagination was involved here as well as lack of funds.

For all these reasons the first drive into East Prussia, which began in May 1757, was a resounding failure. Signs of crisis were evident already in the first few weeks. The low water level in the Niemen (*Versommerung:* a natural feature affecting all river systems in the region[25]) hindered shipping during the summer months and it was discovered that Russian galleys drew too much water to enter the Kurisches Haff. The need for forage soon became desperate: one overland transport, which arrived on the eve of the major battle of the campaign, at Gross Jägersdorf, brought a derisory 63 *chetverti* of oats. Foragers were sent out, but often returned empty-handed. The Cossacks' depredations touched off a spontaneous peasant guerilla movement. The very areas that they laid waste were those from which the army expected to obtain supplies once it withdrew to the Niemen.[26] The decision to turn back, taken on 27 August, startled contemporaries in Russia and abroad. It dealt a major blow to Russian prestige, and a hunt was launched for scapegoats. Apraksin was arrested and placed under investigation. However significant the C-in-C's political misconduct may have been,[27] the decisive factor in bringing about the

---

23. On the marine side see N. M. Korobkov, *Russkii flot v Semiletnei voine* (Moscow, 1946) (1760: pp. 83*ff.*).

24. Danzig, the obvious first choice, was unavailable: the inhabitants favoured Prussia and an assault on the city, often contemplated, was ruled out as it would have alienated the Austrians and French: *cf.* E. von Fritsch, *Zur Geschichte der russischen Feldzüge im siebenjährigen Kriege...* (Heidelberg, 1919), ch. 6; W. Konopczyński, *Polska w dobie wojny siedmoletniej*, pt. 2 (Warsaw, 1913), pp. 24-25.

25. G. Köster-Arnswalde, "Die Entwicklung der nordostdeutschen Verkehrsstrassen bis 1800," *Forschungen zur Brandenburgischen und Preussischen Geschichte*, 48 (1936), p. 121.

26. *Zhizn' i prikliucheniia Andreia Bolotova opisannye samim im dlia svoikh potomkov, 1738-1793*, appendix to *Russkaia starina*, 1 (1870), cols. 490-2; A. W. von Hupel (Ed.), *Über den ersten Feldzug des russichen Kriegsheeres gegen die Preussen im Jahr 1757* (Riga, 1794) [deposition of von Weymarn, the Quartermaster-general], pp. 55-57; G. von Frantzius, *Die Okkupation Ostpreussens durch die Russen im siebenjährigen Kriege...*, diss., Berlin, 1916; A. Rogge (contrib.), "Der Schreibkalender des Erzpriesters Hahn," *Altpreussische Monatsschrift*, 20 (1883), pp. 644-51.

27. V. A. Bil'basov, "Semiletniaia voina po russkim istochnikam," in *idem*, *Istoricheskie monografii* (St. Petersburg, 1901), Vol. 5, pp. 244-47.

retreat had clearly been lack of supplies. In Livland stocks were abundant—an inventory dated 27 October 1757 lists more than 350,000 *chetverti* of flour and groats[28]—but they were not drawn on in time. This seems to have been due largely to the transport breakdown. A well-informed eye-witness describes demoralized, exhausted, and famished Russian soldiers hauling carts along sodden, muddy tracks because their horses, with only oak-leaves to eat, were collapsing by the hundred each day.[29]

The government does at least appear to have learned something from the disaster. In January 1758 the Russian forces, now under a new C-in-C, General V. V. Fermor, occupied Königsberg after a brisk and bloodless winter campaign. They then advanced to the Vistula, where new supply depots were built in readiness for action in the Oder valley. A cavalry force under Major-General P. A. Rumiantsev was sent into Pomerania, where it was to seize cattle and other livestock.[30] Meanwhile in occupied East Prussia the Russians at first acted gingerly. The rights of civic estates and corporations were officially confirmed, a relatively modest one-million-taler levy ("contribution") imposed, and a civil governor appointed in the person of Lieutenant-General (Baron) N. A. Korf[f]. Korf used his high-level connections to protect the inhabitants from arbitrary exactions by the military. He and others at court, notably the Vice-chancellor, M. I. Vorontsov, appreciated the impact which such moderation would make on local and international opinion.[31] St. Petersburg announced that the province was open to foreign traders. It evidently hoped for an economic boom that would redound to Russia's credit and make East Prussia a well-equipped base area for the armies in the field.

This was a sensible policy. Fermor complemented it by turning to civilian contractors, particularly in Poland-Lithuania, to satisfy the bulk of the troops' immediate needs. Already in January 1758 "an agreement was closed with one Salurgus, a [Königsberg] merchant, respecting the delivery of a quantity of rye, and every regiment was ordered to take 20

28. *RASV,* i(ii). 9 (Table 44). The accompanying note is self-contradictory; some of this may have been previously consumed! There is some doubt about the total quantity since the stock was measured partly in barrels.

29. Hupel, *Über den ersten Feldzug,* pp. 136-41, 167.

30. *SLV,* pp. 266-67.

31. *Arkhiv kniazia Vorontsova* [hereafter cited as *AKV*], Vol. 34 (Moscow, 1888), pp. 117-53; Frantzius, *Die Okkupation Ostpreussens,* pp. 40-50, 91.

lasts from him and to make a provision of biscuit for 14 days."[32] In Danzig (Gdańsk) the Russians dealt with a merchant banker named Werneck.[33] On 23 February the Quartermaster-general, Ch. F. von Stoffeln, published a manifesto informing Poles "that all those who were willing to deliver hay and grain to the Russian magazines, on condition of being immediately paid for the same, had only to announce themselves to him and they would receive a certain sum in advance."[34] The response, it appears, was moderately encouraging. In the Commonwealth the Russians' principal agents were two Jewish merchants, Baruch and Aaron Iakubovich (typically, official sources do not record Baruch's first name; both men are referred to by the derogatory term *zhid*). In August Fermor concluded an agreement with Baruch (whose principal base seems to have been Posen/Poznań) for 25,000 *chetverti* of cereals, which he was to collect in the Warta (Warthe) and Notec (Netze) valleys; "for greater security" he was to be accompanied by a Russian official named Kudriavtsev, who had 77,000 roubles at his disposal. The goods were apparently delivered,[35] although whether Baruch got all the money he was promised is unclear. Iakubovich was alleged to have disappeared with some of the 10,000 roubles assigned to him for the supply of Rumiantsev's forces, and was placed under arrest. Despite these problems a new contract was signed with Baruch in October 1758, when the latter reported that he had procured more than 41,000 *chetverti* of cereals[36]—perhaps only a fraction of the total. According to Fermor, most of this had to be left behind in the autumn, when the army once again retreated—but this time only to its new base area on the lower Vistula. This decision, taken on 11 September, was once again prompted by a supply crisis, especially in regard to fodder.[37] Fermor also noted that Baruch was still owed 46,000 roubles by the Russian authorities, and commented: "if this money is not paid, we may lose all our credit with the Poles, whose cries [= complaints] will reach Warsaw and Her Imperial Majesty's court;"

32. J. G. Tielke, *An Account of Some of the Most Remarkable Events of the War between the Prussians, Austrians and Russians, from 1756 to 1763...* [i.e. 1758], transl. C. and R. Crauford (London, 1787), Vol. 2, p. 21; *RASV*, ii(i). 101 (where he is called 'Saturgus').

33. *RASV*, ii(i). 104.

34. Tielke, *An Account*, p. 49.

35. *SLV*, pp. 375-76; *cf. RASV*, ii(ii). 181.

36. *RASV*, ii(i). 186, 340-1; ii(ii). 134-5.

37. Fritsch, *Geschichte*, pp. 86-87; *SLV*, pp. 349-50.

he put the total government deficit on such purchases at 4 million roubles.[38]

By this time the supply problem had become a matter of top-level debate in St. Petersburg. Fermor (and Vorontsov) had formidable critics in the "war party," who contended that they were showing excessive tenderness towards foreigners under Russian control and that purchases on contract were draining the treasury. Could not foodstuffs be obtained more cheaply from the Russian interior through official channels? A. I. Glebov, the chief procurator and a *protégé* of Shuvalov, informed the Senate that he could supply 2,000 9-*pud* barrels of flour at 1.60 roubles each, for which civil contractors "here" [Moscow?] were asking 2.05 roubles; the Senate ordered the GPK to accept the offer and in future to report regularly on the prices at which foodstuffs were bought by commercial contract, so that "Her Imperial Majesty's [financial] interests are safeguarded."[39] Glebov, whom Catherine II later dismissed from his post, calling him "a rogue and a cheat," built up a large fortune by business speculations.[40] It is plausible to see in this a political move by Shuvalov, who could turn the army's predicament in October 1758 to his advantage and win support for a hard-line bureaucratic approach to military supply problems. This was more than just political intrigue: the resort to the free market had indeed turned out to be something of a mixed blessing—although one could argue that the government, by holding back on appropriations, had not given this option a fair trial.

The wrangle contributed to the fall of Fermor, who was recalled to St. Petersburg in January 1759 where he faced charges (not only of squandering funds but also of fleeing from the battlefield at Zorndorf), and to personnel and institutional changes in the supply organization. Its first chief, Volkonskii, had previously left the capital for army headquarters, presumably at Fermor's request; the C-in-C set up a Field Proviant Chancellery which would be under his own control. The Senate approved this in October 1758, but with evident reluctance, cutting down on the size of the staff requested.[41] Supply officials, who were as a rule officers no longer fit for active service, were often reluctant to obey the orders of the field officers to whom they were nominally subordinate—partly, one may surmise, from a narrow sense of jurisdictional loyalty, but partly also

38. *RASV*, ii(ii). 310.

39. *PSZ*, Vol. 15, no. 10902 (2 December 1758).

40. J. L. H. Keep, *Soldiers of the Tsar: Russian Army and Society, 1462-1874* (Oxford, 1985), p. 187.

41. *PSZ*, Vol. 15, no. 10895 (28 October 1758).

because they considered their commands impractical or unwise. Conversely, field officers tended to look down haughtily on support personnel, suspecting them of laziness, corruption, and fondness for civilian ways.

Nevertheless under their direction the forward magazine network was taking shape. An inventory, drawn up in May 1758, of stocks in 14 depots situated mainly between the Niemen and the Vistula shows them holding some 145,000 *chetverti* of cereals fit for human consumption plus 30,000 of oats.[42] But transport remained a problem: how were these provisions to be brought rapidly to the front on the Oder and the long lines of communication secured against the risk of enemy attack? In practice combat troops were often obliged to detail personnel and to expend much effort on making up deficiencies. The complicated marches and countermarches which the army executed across the plains of western Poland and eastern Germany had to be interrupted for rest days, which the troops used mainly for the preparation of food. From 2 to 6 August 1758, for example, the army halted at Königswalde (south of Landsberg), where its main activity was "baking bread and acquiring provisions and forage."[43] Brigadier (later Major-General) T. Démicoud took a force of light cavalry to the borders of Pomerania and Neumark, "where he levied contributions and brought off all the cattle and horses he could find;" some of this booty was distributed among the troops on 30 June, when "each regiment received 60 head of the cattle and 150 of the sheep that were collected in Pomerania."[44] If villages refused to pay up, local officials would be seized as hostages.[45] Démicoud s operations amounted to plunder and transgressed the rules of war as then commonly understood. Fermor, concerned about the political consequences, had the commander arraigned, but he was able to exonerate himself by pleading that his men were beyond control.[46] There was something to this argument: the Cossacks and hussars stemmed from the empire's half-tamed southern border, and their autonomous semimilitary organization allowed them to maintain their own life-style and ethos, which differed from what was customary among the Great Russians

42. *RASV,* ii(ii). 137-8; Tielke, *An Account,* p. 60, gives the March figures, but only in barrels.

43. D. E. Bangert, *Die russisch-österreichische Zusammenarbeit im siebenjährigen Kriege in den Jahren 1758-1759* (Boppard a. Rh., 1971), p. 98; Tielke, *An Account,* pp. 105, 109, 127.

44. Tielke, *An Account,* pp. 67, 83.

45. *Ibid.*, p. 115; Konopczyński, *Polska w dobie wojny siedmoletniej,* p. 74.

46. Tielke, *An Account,* pp. 78-79n.; Duffy, *Russia's Way,* p. 85.

who constituted the bulk of the army, and even more so among Baltic Germans. Their example was infectious and other units, tempted by the lure of easy prey, were quick to emulate them unless the authorities intervened with severe counter-measures.

It is unfortunately impossible to quantify the proportion of the army's food consumption that was acquired from local sources as against that brought up from the rear—or to say how much of the stocks in the magazines were filled by contractors' deliveries as distinct from regular transfers from bases in the hinterland. All methods were used simultaneously and policy varied according to each commander's preferences and to the predicament of his troops.

In May 1759 Fermor was replaced by General P. S. Saltykov,[47] a native Russian who despite his age (60) and unimpressive physical appearance was a better commander-in-chief than either of his forerunners. But increased military efficiency meant greater hardship for civilians within the war zone. Under his command supply policy shifted towards stiffer exactions on the inhabitants. Contributions were levied on several towns: Frankfurt-on-Oder, captured in June, was required to pay 200,000 talers as a first instalment. Its magazines yielded unspecified quantities of "flour, rye, barley, oats and salt,"[48] which, however, had to be shared equally with the Austrians. The little town of Züllichau, 80 km south-east of Frankfurt, paid 3,000 talers to a certain Captain Kovacs, "who compelled the local inhabitants to give up as much grain and forage as could be found."[49] Krossen, asked for 100,000 talers, came up with only one-tenth of this amount;[50] a certain Captain Ozerov appropriated 500 talers for himself out of a subsequent levy and the town had to provide at once 80,000 soldiers' rations as well as 50,000 for their horses. In the surrounding countryside there was a "horrible devastation;" churches were broken into and the plate stolen; clergymen and schoolmasters were robbed and beaten.[51] Fermor had responded to the threat of demotion with an eloquent plea for regular supply methods, but his proposals for the 1759 campaign were as

47. *SLV*, pp. 410-11.

48. *Ibid.*, p. 445.

49. *Ibid.*, p. 458.

50. *Ibid.*, p. 472.

51. W. Bruchmüller, "Ein Beitrag zur Geschichte des Russeneinfalls in die Neumark im Jahre 1759," *Forschungen zur Brandenburgischen und Preussischen Geschichte*, 26 (1913), pp. 226-29.

makeshift as before.[52] Moreover, in instructions which he gave to a subordinate at that time he began to sing to the new tune: Stargard in Pomerania, he wrote, should be forced to yield 20,000 talers "under threat of destruction by fire and sword."[53] Although several commanders recommended that foragers should avoid oppressive measures, these suggestions cannot have been taken very seriously.[54]

At irregular intervals supply convoys would wend their way from the lower Vistula area via Poznań to the army's headquarters somewhere in the Oder valley. In a typical despatch to the empress two weeks before the great battle of Kunersdorf (1 August 1759) Saltykov complained that "Lieutenant-General [A. A.] Menshikov, residing in Poznań, is acting very dilatorily and wasting time in superfluous correspondence, as he is loath to subordinate himself to my command. It seems to me that, at a time when the army is energetically pursuing and fighting the enemy, he should not be making excuses . . . ."[55] A month later he was more cheerful: "Your Imperial Majesty's army is not now suffering any food shortage, thank God, for we have discovered some grain in the country and a few days ago some small convoys began to arrive from Menshikov."[56] Unfortunately the arrival of these columns was no easier to predict than the yield of local foraging parties. The primitively constructed wagons frequently broke down and civilian artisans had to be mobilized to assist the army's own mechanics. A design for a model cart was circulated but few unit commanders adopted it;[57] of 2,500 horses that arrived from Russia, fewer than one-quarter were fit for use.[58] Rivers had to be forded when they could not be bridged, and there were few boats to ply them; in any case only

52. *RASV,* ii(ii). 308-9.

53. *SLV,* p. 433; civilians were, however, not to be interrogated under torture or their dwellings set on fire.

54. As is suggested with regard to Rumiantsev by L. M. Leshchinskii, *Voennye pobedy i polkovodtsy russkogo naroda* (Moscow, 1959), pp. 31-32; a check on the source cited (*SLV,* p. 323) shows that the order in question was more concerned with protecting foragers' security from guerilla attacks than with any respect for civilians' rights.

55. *SLV,* p. 472 (18 July 1759); *cf.* p. 476. Menshikov took over as General-proviantmeister in May 1759. At first he was independent of Saltykov, which the C-in-C resented; later in the year he got this arrangement reversed. *RASV,* iii(i). 70, 73.

56. *SLV,* p. 495; *cf.* p. 501.

57. *RASV,* iii(i). 390n.

58. *Ibid.,* iii(i). 214.

the Notec and Warta flowed in an east-west direction. Polish and German roads were little if any better than those in Russia; the surface consisted "of crushed sand or of clay, which according to season was either stone hard or devoid of any foundation," and they rarely crossed the broad marshy meadows that flanked these gently-flowing streams.[59]

Apart from natural obstacles there was the ever-present risk of attack by enemy raiding parties or guerilla bands. A Swedish officer in Prussian service later recalled how, with a small body of troops, he surprised the 300-man garrison guarding the Russian supply base at Bydgoszcz (Bromberg), with its "great magazines of foodstuffs and baggage":

> I burned a number of boats laden with rye, which I could not carry, and allowed my men to help themselves to clothing, boots, shoes and stockings, so that each soldier acquired a complete portable wardrobe—a most pleasing sight. Whatever could not be carried off was burned, along with the carts, in the middle of a square outside the town, which filled the inhabitants with terror.[60]

Another, much larger force of Prussian raiders under General Wobersnow so alarmed the Russian high command that it ordered all goods likely to fall into enemy hands to be evacuated or destroyed.[61] Partly because of this risk, it was decided to leave food stocks that had been contracted for in the hands of their suppliers, rather than concentrated in magazines;[62] but the increased security was offset by the reduced degree of control.

For all these reasons Saltykov was in no position to establish his army's forward bases in the Oder valley, as had long been urged by Austrian representatives at headquarters and in the capital. An obvious alternative was for Russia's chief ally herself to supply the Russian troops with food. But Vienna showed little comprehension of the difficulties under which the Russian army laboured when it was operating at such distances from home, and Austrian officials were quick to suspect that

---

59. Köster-Arnswalde, "Die Entwicklung," p. 122.

60. Comte [J. L.] de Hordt [Hard], *Mémoires historiques, politiques et militaires,* ed. M. Borrelly (Paris, 1805), Vol. 2, pp. 26-27. *Cf. RASV,* iii(i). 76 for the Russian reaction to this raid.

61. Frantzius, *Die Okkupation Ostpreussens,* p. 58; *cf. SLV,* pp. 435, 447, and for further attacks in September and October 1759 *RASV* iii(i). 185-6. Local inhabitants joined in the depredations, sometimes allegedly dressed in Cossack uniforms.

62. *RASV, loc. cit.*

bureaucratic bumbling was but a pretext for egoistical political calculations. There were personal tensions, too: Field-Marshal (G. E.) Laudon, for instance, looked on Saltykov as "basically an evil man, who cannot be trusted in the slightest,"[63] and Saltykov's animus against the Habsburg generals was common knowledge. The root of the problem was that the two armies' logistical networks were too distant from each other for close cooperation to be feasible—as indeed the Austrian C-in-C, Field-Marshal (Count L. J.) Daun recognized in June 1759.[64]

In any case the political will for such collaboration was lacking: the allies' essential interests were too diverse, and so each pursued its own objectives. No joint body was set up to demarcate the regions within which each force might collect supplies; instead matters were discussed at various levels on an *ad hoc* basis, and usually in ignorance of the other's needs. Moreover, the Russian commanders were reluctant to reveal the actual extent of their food stocks (if indeed they were aware of them), lest this information be abused; often they passed on inaccurate or misleading information. They were instinctively afraid—perhaps with good reason—that, by becoming dependent on Austrian supplies, they would forfeit control over strategic decisions and be reduced to the humiliating role of auxiliaries. From the Russian viewpoint there was little to be gained by responding to allied pressure to cross the Oder, still less to fight in distant Saxony; both geography and politics made Pomerania and Brandenburg far more fitting theatres of operations.

Thus although the idea of Austrian supply aid was mooted by Vienna on several occasions in 1758 and early 1759, it was not until after the success at Kunersdorf that the Russians, having at last crossed the Oder, took up the matter. The Habsburg authorities collected stocks, mainly of forage, at various depots, but when the Russians arrived there it was food they needed most, and of this they found precious little. An order of 8 September (NS) releasing 20,000 centners of flour[65] does not seem to have been acted upon; a cash grant (of 60,000 guilders) was insufficient to tempt Saltykov to remain in the area; and after several weeks of inconclusive correspondence he ordered his forces to withdraw once again to winter

63. Bangert, *Die russisch-österreichische Zusammenarbeit*, p. 275. This thorough study offers an authoritative guide to this aspect of the problem; see especially the summary on pp. 370-76.

64. *Ibid.*, p. 196.

65. *Ibid.*, p. 265.

quarters (11/22 September).[66] At one moment in late September the Russians even had to supply an Austrian corps with five days' ration of bread.[67]

Inter-allied cooperation was no better in the following years, for reasons that have yet to be clarified in detail.[68] Disappointment on this score, whether merited or not, intensified the conviction among Russian policy-makers that they had to exploit more systematically food resources in the territories they controlled. From 1759 onward occupation policy in East Prussia became appreciably more severe. A contribution of 2 million talers—twice as large as the first—was levied, half on Königsberg and half on country areas.[69] This involved assessing the non-propertied elements for a poll tax; landowners were to pay according to the value of their estates. Since cash (specie) was in short supply, the authorities permitted payment to be made in kind, and then, in response to strong high-level representations, allowed supplies delivered to the army to be reckoned against the sum assessed. The rural areas provided so much that half their assessment was written off.[70] Governor Korf resisted a projected levy of recruits: "unused to living and eating in the Russian fashion, some will die and others, separated from their relatives and ignorant of the language, will desert, however closely they are guarded."[71] To these humanitarian arguments he added more persuasive economic ones: the province had already incurred a loss of nearly 8 million roubles,[72] and it would be more sensible to concentrate on providing foodstuffs and vehicles. Vorontsov seems to have persuaded the government to concur; at any rate it was not until 1761, after Korf had been replaced (by V. I. Suvorov, father of the famous generalissimo, who significantly was also the chief supply official), that a new contribution of 508,000 roubles was imposed in lieu of the projected recruits. This worked out at a poll tax of 2 roubles on the non-privileged, but it is not known how much of this was collected.[73] The requisitioning of horses and vehicles dealt a severe blow to the province's

66. *Ibid.*, p. 260-77, 373-74; *SLV*, pp. 506, 509; *RASV*, iii(ii). 107.

67. *Ibid.*, p. 275.

68. *Cf. AKV*, Vol. 6 (1873), pp. 387-88; but Maslovskii, *RASV*, iii(i). 456n., states that cooperation was good in August 1761.

69. *AKV*, Vol. 34 (1888), pp. 120-25.

70. Frantzius, *Die Okkupation Ostpreussens*, pp. 72-75.

71. Korf to Vorontsov, 9 January 1760, *AKV*, Vol. 6, pp. 441-42.

72. *Ibid.*, 26 January 1760, *AKV*, Vol. 34, pp. 178-87.

73. Frantzius, *Die Okkupation Ostpreussens*, p. 77.

agriculture and detracted from the authorities' otherwise quite successful efforts to encourage trade.

Suvorov was Saltykov's nominee for the chief supply job. His forerunner, Brigadier N. Khomutov, along with Menshikov and another supply official, T. von Dietz, had previously been called to St. Petersburg to account for their actions and their papers placed under seal.[74] Presumably they were suspected of malfeasance, but it is not known what action, if any, was taken against them. Suvorov inherited 77,000 *chetverti* of cereals in the Vistula magazines, but the army had now grown to about 98,000 men.[75] He set about expanding the depots in Poznań and elsewhere in the forward zone, but like his predecessors suffered from a lack of cash, particularly in foreign currencies, with which to pay suppliers.[76] Contracts with civilians were still concluded—for instance with Count Gurowski in July—but these apparently now required confirmation at the top level, and the prices offered (about 2 roubles for 1 *chetvert'* of flour) were apparently far below the market rate.[77] The Conference (the empire's chief policy-making body) adopted a typically hypocritical attitude: while commending Suvorov for his "exceptional assiduity" and stating that "contracts must be strictly (*sviato*) adhered to," it continued: "but since money cannot be sent to you very soon, although sizeable sums will be despatched shortly [sic!], we recommend that you observe the necessary economy, however that you ensure above all that no lack of provisions causes the army to be held up on campaign."[78]

What this really meant, but could not be stated openly, was that supplies might be commandeered whenever necessary. Since 1759 vouchers had been issued in lieu of cash, which could be exchanged only in St. Petersburg after they had been "verified."[79] Another expedient was to give soldiers 30 kopecks a day in lieu of rations which the supply authori-

---

74. *RASV,* iii(ii). 116, 135.

75. *SLV,* p. 597; *RASV,* iii(i). 378. In March 1759 the strength may have been around 84,000.

76. *AKV,* Vol. 6, p. 361. In June 1759 only one-third of the sums owed to contractors in Poland had been paid: *RASV,* iii(ii). 17-18; but later that year money sufficient to cover this debt appears to have been paid out: *ibid.,* iii(i). 298, 412; iii(ii). 134.

77. For price data see *RASV,* iii(i). 68, 403, 418n.; iii(ii). 17-18.

78. *SLV,* p. 613.

79. *RASV,* iii(i). 218; iii(ii). 131, paras. 2, 3, 5.

ties could not provide.[80] But if there was no money for contractors, where was this to come from? As it was, the men's pay lagged several months behind schedule. The Poles were so aggrieved at payment with vouchers of uncertain worth that the Sejm was prorogued to prevent their dissatisfaction receiving unwelcome publicity. Suvorov is said to have received a sum of money[81] to keep the critics quiet, but to have distributed it so sparingly that it had no marked effect. A joint Russo-Polish commission broke up in disagreement.[82]

By September 1760 the food shortage was again so acute that the army had to abandon its siege of Glogau, and soon afterwards it withdrew once more to the Vistula. The supply organization was still in a chaotic state, although the famous raid on Berlin in October 1760 netted sizeable amounts of foreign specie along with other booty.[83] Officials had to be instructed simply to take over stocks that had been purchased on contract but not yet paid for.[84] Passing through the rear bases on his way to take over as C-in-C, Saltykov's successor, Field-Marshal A. B. Buturlin, wrote privately to Vorontsov that "I find the supply administration in a parlous state."[85] Two months later he claimed that "utilization of enemy resources saved the army up to 400,000 roubles, not counting other advantages for the troops in regard to foodstuffs," such as an "abundant" distribution of meat,[86] but this was to depict matters in the most optimistic colours. There were further destructive enemy raids, notably by a force under General D. F. von Platten; grain expected from Pomerania failed to arrive, necessitating a hasty mobilization of regimental transport to collect cereals

80. *Ibid.*, iii(i). 218.

81. There is some doubt as to its size. *SLV,* p. 634: 100,000 roubles; *AKV,* Vol. 6, p. 374: 200,000; *RASV,* iii(i). 297: 400,000.

82. Konopczyński, *Polska w dobie wojny siedmoletniej,* pp. 73-75.

83. General Totleben's contribution levied on the Prussian capital amounted to 1½ million talers, excluding 200,000 paid in lieu of supplies in kind. Not all of this could be collected and there were arguments about disposition of the loot which led ultimately to Totleben's defection. See *AKV,* Vol. 6, pp. 458-77; *RASV,* iii(i). 342-5, iii(ii). 51-75, 152-61, 170-2; *SLV,* pp. 687-706, 717; J. E. Gotzkofsky, *Geschichte eines patriotischen Kaufmanns aus Berlin...* (Augsburg, 1789); E. Kessel, "Totlebens Verrat," *Forschungen zur Brandenburgischen und Preussischen Geschichte,* 49 (1937), pp. 371-78.

84. *RASV,* iii(i). 300.

85. Buturlin to Vorontsov, 6 October 1760, *AKV,* Vol. 6, p. 376.

86. *RASV,* iii(i). 409; Duffy, *Russia's Way,* p. 119, approves of the new hard line.

from the Poznań depot; 500 carts had to be hired in Danzig while at least 700 more were taken in East Prussia; and even in Königsberg troops were going short of food.[87]

Nevertheless on a long-term view the situation was not wholly bleak. Belatedly the authorities now made use of the sea link to build up the Vistula magazines, which were supposed to be able to supply 100,000 men with enough food for eight to ten months.[88] In the winter of 1760-61 they could not supply all the troops in winter quarters,[89] but by May 1761, 88,000 *chetverti* had arrived there.[90] Maslovskii exaggerates the degree of success achieved, but there does seem to have been a greater sense of urgency among the officials concerned, whose duties were assigned in more systematic fashion. Requisitioning in Poland was now carried through in such a way as to leave suppliers one-third of their stocks for their own needs.[91] The overland convoys (in columns of about 100 carts) were better guarded and organized, with officers detailed to supervise their movement—which still did not, however, preclude enemy attack.[92]

More significantly, Rumiantsev's forces in Pomerania were built up to a point where, after a lengthy and difficult siege, he was able to capture the key port of Kolberg (8 December 1761). This changed the strategic situation in Russia's favour, giving her direct access to a potential base in the forward area; but the victory came too late to be of any assistance in the Seven Years War. On the very day that the port's fall was announced in St. Petersburg, the empress Elizabeth died (25 December OS). She was succeeded by her nephew, the Grand Duke Peter, whose sympathies for Frederick of Prussia were well known. Within weeks the army was being readied for a campaign against Denmark in order to further the new ruler's dynastic interests, and on 5 May 1762 Russia and Prussia concluded peace on the basis of the status quo.

Thus all the bloodshed had been in vain. The army leaders' sense of humiliation created a mood in which the *coup d'état* of 28 June, which brought Catherine II to the throne, seemed to presage a return to rational-

87. *RASV,* iii(i). 379, 392-3; for the raids: *AKV,* Vol. 6, pp. 378, 450.

88. *RASV,* p. 399. From Korobkov, *Russkii flot,* it would appear that the navy confined its supply functions almost wholly to the littoral as far as Pillau and Königsberg.

89. *RASV,* iii(i). 359.

90. *Ibid.,* iii(i). 379, 402.

91. *Ibid.,* iii(i). 403.

92. *Ibid.,* iii(i). 463-4.

ity in foreign and military policy. The generals had not wanted war against Prussia, a power which posed no serious threat to the empire's basic interests, and had seldom pursued the struggle with vigour. Nevertheless it may have cost Russia as many as 120,000 lives.[93] It imposed a heavy burden on taxpayers and upset foreign trade.[94] Nationalistic historians have endeavoured unconvincingly to find redeeming features, for instance the emergence of experienced younger generals who would later achieve signal successes against the Turks;[95] (they would have derived even more valuable experience from harassing the Crimean Tatars).

Another such claim is that during the Seven Years War Russia learned to develop a regular supply system whereby goods were ferried from rear bases to provisional ones further forward, and also to exploit "the resources of enemy territory in a way that for the time was exemplary in the orderly and equitable distribution of obligations."[96] The facts as available at present do not support such a large claim.[97] Maslovskii favoured requisitioning on principle, even as a desirable measure in a forthcoming Russian-German war! The evidence suggests rather that the supply officials and their superiors remained unable to opt clearly between rival policies, or even to perceive that a choice had to be made. Nor were supply questions given due weight in military planning. Instead the Russian army was fed, even at the war's end, by a set of makeshift devices that did not readily complement each other. The resulting shortages had a crippling effect on operations. It is true that in 1761 Rumiantsev's forces were relatively plentifully supplied, but this achievement owed more to the skill of local (*Prussian!*) officials and to local resources than to efficient trans-

---

93. B. Ts. Urlanis, "Liudskie poteri vooruzhennykh sil v evropeiskikh voinakh," in *idem, Narodonaselenie: issledovaniia, publitsistika: sbornik statei* (Moscow, 1976), p. 156.

94. The number of ships leaving Russian Baltic ports (excluding those in Kurland) was 1,029 in 1754; in 1758 it dropped to 532 and did not surpass the earlier figure until 1769: Kahan, *The Plow,* p. 301 (Table 6.10); the decline was most obvious in iron and forest products, whereas exports of industrial crops increased during the late 1750s: *ibid.*, p. 191 (Tables 4.34, 4.35).

95. *RASV,* iii(i). 555; and numerous general works.

96. *Ibid.,* iii(i). 562.

97. Extensive study (notably of file 1669 in the Central State Archive of Military History [TsGVIA], Moscow) would be necessary to establish this point definitively.

port from the rear;[98] and the main army was still going short even at this late juncture.

Nor was the experience gained during the conflict made the object of considered reflection by the Military Commission which Catherine II set up in 1762. Thus even in later years, although depots continued to be set up or enlarged as the occasion required, soldiers would go hungry, particularly when they were fighting abroad—as happened in the campaigns against Napoleon and in the Crimean War. Not until after the latter conflict did the development of railroads make it possible to establish a modern network of military stores; and even so some Russian officers in the late Imperial era thought that armies should in part live "off the land" in the ancient manner.[99] It was only then that the authorities realized that fighting men required a balanced diet and that food could be more efficiently prepared by trained staff rather than by the men themselves—a step which, however, reduced still further the soldiers' minimal autonomy. Fortunately in 1756-62 the age of great military bureaucracies and scientific mechanized warfare still lay far ahead.

98. *RASV,* iii(i). 529-31.

99. F. A. Maksheev, *Voenno-administrativnoe ustroistvo tyla armii,* fasc. 1 (St. Petersburg, 1893), p. 111.

# [10]

# Russian Military Innovation in the Second Half of the Eighteenth Century

*Bruce W. Menning*

What were the sources of Russian military innovation in the second half of the eighteenth century? More than a century of serious speculation on the nature of the Imperial Army from Elizabeth Petrovna (1741-1761) to Catherine II (1762-1796) has shed far more light on the character of military change and its consequences than on its causes. The purpose of this study is to examine the issue of change in its institutional and operational context to determine what inspired Russian departure from the 'unalterable precedent' of European military practice. Of necessity this task involves a return to the concerns of traditional military history, the more recent proponents of which have included Dennis Showalter and Christopher Duffy.[1] In the current instance, the effort seems worthwhile, for it promises added insight into the forces favouring military innovation, including what contemporary Soviet observers would label the 'initiatives' which result in more advanced military technique.[2]

At issue are important departures in organization and tactical practice, the sum of which for the first time in nearly a century brought a return to decision on the battlefields of southeastern Europe. Far more than many observers have been willing to admit, the Imperial Russian Army of the 1750s and 1760s was a conventional continental military institution wedded through structure, armament, training, habit, and preference to prevalent European—even Prussian—notions of organization and tactics. However, by the 1790s the same army regularly demonstrated an unconventional penchant for organizational and operational flexibility, which many writers have argued thrust the Russians along with the French into the vanguard of revolutionary military change. To be sure, Russian developments often seemed either to anticipate or duplicate the French. They involved flexible formation, innovative tactics, the march to objectives over parallel routes, an emphasis on enthusiasm, and the tendency to employ large numbers of light forces relying on firepower and manoeuvre to screen and protect more cumbersome regular forces.[3] What observers of comparative military history have often failed to emphasize is the possibility that similar innovations could have both sprung from and remained appropriate to widely varying circumstance and experience.[4]

To describe mid-to-late eighteenth-century military change and its effects has traditionally been easier than to isolate its causes. In retrospect—despite oversimplification—the historian might cite at least three distinct patterns of military development, all of which supported a return to decisive engagement on European battlefields. The most obvious (and most conservative) was the pursuit of advantage through superior application of conventional technique and leadership. This is the departure best represented by Frederick II of Prussia, whose soldiers fired more often and marched more precisely than any others in Europe. Excellence of drill together with an uncharacteristic penchant to seek decision made Frederick the envy of his military contemporaries, especially those who sought perfection of system. Another departure, one born of desperation, was the concerted application of disparate innovations to seek a genuine breakthrough against the forces of military convention. This is the pattern most frequently identified with the military changes of the French Revolution. A third departure, one less frequently noted in historical literature, relied on institutional adaptation to accommodate within a conventional framework an unconventional foe in an environment conducive to experimentation and improvisation. With all its possibilities and limitations, this is probably the model of military development most appropriate to a discussion of Russian military innovation during the second half of the eighteenth century.[5]

Russian military historians have traditionally explained change by seizing on the first variant and parts of the third, dressing them respectively in Prussian and nativist clothing, then pitting them against one another in a Manichean-like struggle of opposites. Unfortunately this approach ignores nuance and obscures both the subtleties of development and the sources of military change. On the one hand, to reject the Frederician model as somehow foreign and inappropriate to Russia begs important issues of technological and institutional continuity. On the other hand, to emphasize selective innovation from within and above fails to account fully for the importance of external factors in prompting departures from tactical and organizational precedent. The appearance in Russia during the last quarter of the nineteenth century of rival nationalist and academic schools of military historiography only complicated the basic issue by redressing key aspects of contending views in positivist and chauvinist clothing. Subsequently, Soviet military historiography, while not ignoring the objective side of military operations, has consistently displayed a strong nativist bias. For the Soviets, innovation has sprung from native military genius operating within the larger and unique context of the Russian armed forces. Or, to put the argument briefly, it was the art of

Russian great captains leading a truly national army which thrust Russia along with the Revolutionary French into the vanguard of eighteenth-century military change.[6]

The Russian experience both before and after the Seven Years' War aptly illustrates the persistent influence of the Frederician model on Russian military development. Peter III, the Prussophile Tsar whose reign extended only six months, is generally credited with the first impulse since the 1730s to remodel the Russian Army in the Prussian image, but this is only partially correct. During the hectic half year before his abrupt overthrow on 28 June 1762, Peter introduced only a few changes, including the symbolic adoption of multi-coloured Prussian-style uniforms with their tight waistcoats, powdered wigs, and uncomfortable gaiters. He threatened more substantial dislocations ranging from alterations in regimental organization and designation to a reduction in status for the Guards regiments ('Janissaries', he called them), but these changes had little time in which to take effect before they helped provoke the predictable reaction in the form of a palace coup led by officers of the Guards.[7]

The accession of Catherine II, marked by proclamations of a return to the military traditions of Peter the Great, failed to eradicate Prussian influences within the Russian Army. True, the new Empress immediately halted her husband's organizational changes and restored the Guards to their pre-eminent position within the Russian military establishment. However, she left in effect legislation directing adoption of Prussian-style uniforms. More important, she entrusted imperial military affairs to officers whose ideas and policies, despite protestations to the contrary, remained strongly tinged by Prussian influences. These officers consciously or unconsciously helped perpetuate an institutional drift to Prussian forms, a departure which not only postdated but clearly antedated Peter III's short-lived attempts at transforming the army on the model of his beloved Frederick II.[8]

Catherine's Military Commission of 1762 represented an important element linking the military aspect of her reign to earlier flirtations with Prussian influences. On 5 November 1762, the Empress appointed the Commission to review in cooperation with the Military College 'not only the main establishment of Her Majesty's Army, but also the smallest details of service for every rank from lowest to highest.' In effect, Catherine entrusted the officers who made up the Commission with the task of reshaping the Russian Army both in the light of the recent experiences of the Seven Years' War and in anticipation of the Empire's future military needs.[9] What contemporary and later observers have failed to note was that a number of the Commission's members, including Petr Saltykov, Zakhar

Chernyshev, Petr Panin, and Grigorii Meshcherskii, had already been instrumental in introducing Prussian-related change into the army even before the onset of the Seven Years' War and the army's brief exposure to the reform measures of the unpopular Peter III.

These same officers had served in a similar organization, the Military Commission of 1754, which Peter III's immediate predecessor, Elizabeth Petrovna, had innocuously designated 'for the deliberation of affairs related to the Military College.' Elizabeth, like Catherine twenty years later, had ascended the throne in 1741 in the wake of a palace coup with strong anti-German, and even anti-Prussian, overtones. Like Catherine, Elizabeth had proclaimed a return to Petrine military virtue, which in matters of drill and field service meant adherence to the outmoded Military Regulation (*Voinskii ustav*) of 1716. Word went out from the Military College that 'in all regiments without distinction evolutions and drum beat are to be executed in accordance with former instructions, as during the lifetime of Peter the Great, without change, *and not in the Prussian Manner*.' So strongly was the question of military reform identified with advancing Prussianism that more than a decade elapsed before the Empress agreed to convoke the Commission of 1754 and then only to update the 1716 *ustav* in details of tactics and manoeuvre.[10]

In spite of its limited mandate, the Commission had proceeded to embark on a revision of regulations and a reorganization of structure, both of which drew critical fire for the way they embodied Prussian military elements. In particular, Zakhar Chernyshev's new drill regulation, *Opisanie pekhotnogo polkovogo stroia* (Description of Infantry Regimental Organization), known informally as the *ustav* of 1755, stressed the development of firepower over shock action to a degree which contemporaries and later observers considered a profound violation of the Petrine legacy. Andrei Bolotov, who on the eve of the Seven Years' War commanded a company of the Arkhangelogorodskii Regiment, commented in his memoirs that Chernyshev's regulation represented such a departure from Peter's *ustav* that 'veteran soldiers had to be completely retrained' in the new system.[11] A.I. Gippius, an official historian writing more than a century later, noted that the regulation drew so heavily from foreign models that its rendering in Russian was 'labored and in places frankly even incorrect.'[12] Among the more remarkable aspects of the *ustav* was that it provided for Prussian-style reliance on an infantry battle line three ranks deep, that is, a formation clearly favouring fire action over shock. In addition, the *ustav* made provision for the delivery of frontal, cross, and oblique fire from battalions arrayed for volley fire on command by rank, division, half-division, and even double file. The objective of these variations on the delivery of volleys was to confront the enemy with a solid line rippling with continuous and withering fire. Lest any Russian commander miss the point, chapter IV of the new regulation stated that 'the whole training of the soldier has in view loading and firing.' The soldier who proved inept or incompetent was to be treated 'with the strictest severity, and with punishment for failure . . . so that for every violation he receives a few blows of the stick.' The hapless soldier who so much as dropped a cartridge during loading exercises was 'to be beaten with rods before the regiment.'[13]

In addition to Chernyshev's *ustav*, Elizabeth's Military Commission in 1756 produced a new table of organization calling for an infantry arm approximately 150,000 strong to be distributed among three Guards, four grenadier, and forty-six musketeer (fusilier) regiments. Here the chief departure from tradition was a reorganization of the regiment from its previous complement of two battalions to one of three battalions. The third battalion was actually a depot battalion intended to serve a permanent recruiting and training function in garrison for the regiment's two remaining field battalions. The organizational table of 1756 also called for a mounted arm of more than 31,000 cavalrymen assigned to one Guards, six cuirassier, six mounted grenadier, and eighteen dragoon regiments. Cossacks and other irregular levies of uncertain quality contributed another 44,500 light cavalrymen whose primary functions included security and reconnaissance. The overall composition of the regular cavalry, calling for a curious mixture of heavy and medium formations, was strongly reminiscent of Field Marshal B. Kh. Münnich's Prussian-inspired innovations of the 1730s.[14]

The Seven Years' War did little to change either the army's organization or the way its leaders chose to write drill regulations. Perhaps the war revealed few significant shortcomings in the *ustav* of 1755, or perhaps the subject of military change was simply too volatile to admit a direct approach. Catherine II herself seemed to preclude any drastic alterations in regulations when shortly after her accession she issued orders 'to maintain in the future in both infantry and cavalry regiments the same drill manual and exercises which were published in the reign of the late Empress Elizabeth Petrovna.'[15] This directive, when coupled with the successes of the recent war and with the overlapping membership between the Military Commissions of 1754 and 1762 assured a high degree of continuity between the two Empress' reigns. Not surprisingly, the Military Commission of 1762's new regulation, the *ustav* of 1763 was, in the words of the military historian A.K. Baiov, 'almost indistinguishable from the regulations of the Elizabethan period.'[16] Except for a genuine effort to reduce the complexity and variety of tactical evolutions, the regulation of 1763 duplicated in unequivocal fashion the earlier Prussian-style emphasis on the development of firepower by tactical deployment of the three-rank line.[17]

The organizational continuities between the armies of Elizabeth and Catherine are just as striking. Between 1763 and 1765, the Commission of 1762 rewrote the army's table of organization to retain the commitment of 1756 to an infantry force of three Guards, four grenadier, and forty-six infantry regiments. The major difference between the organizational tables of 1756 and 1765 was a reversion to the two-battalion regiment, which on paper reduced the infantry to 100,000 men, but which in reality had negligible effects on field strength. In addition, the Commission also permitted limited experimentation with light infantry (*jäger*) troops by allocating several small formations to commands in Finland and pre-Baltica. Cavalry organization reflected the overall stress on continuity with one major difference: a growing emphasis on heavy formations of the Prussian type. Despite opposition by non-member P.A. Rumiantsev, the Commission chose to imitate the Prussian squadrons of F.W. Seydlitz by transforming nearly all the Russian dragoons into cavalry of the carabineer type. To compensate for the obvious loss in flexibility, the Commission added seven regiments of dragoons raised from former irregular formations of various types. However, difficulties in recruitment and equipment soon cancelled the expansion program. Consequently, the Commission's work left the Russians with twenty-five regiments of heavy and medium formations and about 50,000 Cossack and irregular auxiliaries.[18]

Thanks to the cumulative work of the Military Commissions of 1754 and 1762, the Russian Army of 1765 reflected a strong continental, if not Prussian, bias in its organization and drill regulations. This situation had resulted not from the capricious designs of any single monarch, but in large part from the studied opinion and organizational planning of high ranking officers, many of whom had first-hand knowledge on the receiving end of Frederick II's style of warfare. Although pre-revolutionary Russian and later Soviet historians have often chosen to stress the unique aspects of Russian military development, no amount of emphasis on such factors as the army's homogeneous ethnic composition can obscure the pronounced tendency in the 1760s and 1770s to seek a 'mirror image' of Frederick II's army. During Paul's reign some twenty years later A.V. Suvorov might dismiss the Prussians by exclaiming, 'We have always beaten the Prussians. Why imitate them now?' However, during the first years of Catherine's reign the Frederician model held indisputable sway, with the result that even officers such as P.A. Rumiantsev sometimes succumbed to the temptation to idealize the Prussian Army. Thus, although Rumiantsev seemed clearly aware of the system's defects, for a time, one of his aides,

L.N. Engel'gardt, describes him as 'enraptured by the Prussian Army, at that time the best in the world.'[19]

Institutional habit and stagnant technology reinforced the various threads of military continuity joining Catherine's reign with Elizabeth's. The entire existence of European professional armies was characterised by a systematic inertia that was hallowed by practice, ordained by technology, and blessed by the battlefield successes of Frederick II and his imitators. None of the various Russian military commissions which met periodically throughout the eighteenth century ever seriously considered departure from the two-to-one proportional emphasis accorded infantry over cavalry (including irregular) in formal organizational tables. Similarly, there were no substantial changes in the basic infantry weapon, the .78 calibre smoothbore musket modified to fit a socket bayonet. Because of the continuing emphasis on infantry and because of the necessity to generate maximum combat power, there seems to have been a natural gravitation in all European armies, including the Russian, to a more rigid adherence to drill and linear tactics as a means of facilitating the delivery of firepower. Perhaps the French Marshal J.F. de Puységur best summarized the rationale behind this development when he said, 'It is a fact known to everyone in war that the greater fire silences the other.'[20]

The problem was that not all observers, writers, and reformers agreed with de Puységur. As R.S. Quimby has pointed out, during the course of the eighteenth century a controversy raged within the French Army over the question of whether the musket joined to the bayonet was primarily a shock weapon or a fire weapon. Advocates of the former contention proposed exploitation of the bayonet's shock effect through the creation of tactical formations in depth (*ordre profond*), while advocates of the latter supported a continuation of the thin order (*ordre mince*) to permit development of maximum frontal firepower. Tactical practice during the wars of the French Revolution gradually led to a kind of rough compromise between the two extremes; however, few commentators except Quimby have noted that the compromise actually favored the views held by partisans of the thin order, that is, the advocates of firepower.[21]

Within the Russian context the basic debate was further complicated because the argument between proponents of shock and firepower rapidly assumed both political and cultural overtones. Opinion frequently divided between self-styled supporters of the Petrine tradition emphasizing cold steel in the attack and 'innovators', a term euphemistically applied to officers whose views and policies were perceived—correctly or incorrectly—to reflect Prussian influences. Historians have seen little reason to challenge the validity of these characterizations, with the result that literature on the Russian version of the shock-versus-firepower controversy usually pits nativists against Prussian imitators.[22]

The whole debate between nativists and Prussians has obscured both the subtleties of development and the sources of military change in Russia. In the west, historians generally concede that the French Revolution served to focus, catalyze, and enlarge upon a series of military innovations, many of which long antedated the upheaval, to produce a truly revolutionary change in the nature of warfare. In Russia, historians perceive an analogous spirit of military innovation, but they attribute the source of that innovation to individual genius operating within the larger and unique organizational context of the Russian armed forces. One of the dangers inherent in this approach is that it can easily degenerate into an exercise depicting military innovation as something which stems from disembodied calculation.[23] In reality, genius flowered in response to a set of unique military problems which the Russians faced during the last three decades of the eighteenth century. More than anything else, the nature of these problems and the pragmatic answers developed in response to them explain Russian departures from the more rigid European and even Prussian models of the period. In turn, these departures often either corresponded with or foreshadowed similar military changes identified in the west with the era of the French Revolution.

During Catherine II's two Turkish wars and subsidiary conflicts with border peoples, military operations in the south confronted Russian commanders with an especially formidable set of challenges. First, Russian forces were expected to operate persistently in thinly populated areas well in advance of normal quarters and forward bases. Second, while conducting offensive operations, the Russians had to provide both for the security of their own communications and for the security of an advancing line of settlement across wide areas of the south steppe. Finally, and perhaps most significantly, the Russians were expected to subdue enemies who refused to observe the rules of conventional warfare. Unlike the Russians, who had come to rely increasingly upon a continental, even Frederician-style professional military force, the Turks had placed only a portion of their troops on a regular footing. Their armies possessed a hard core of janissary infantry surrounded by the softer pulp of irregular foot soldiers and light cavalry. The latter in both its Turkish and Tatar variants had long imposed the ways of nomadic warfare on adversaries who expected to fight in the steppe. Turkish and Tatar horsemen travelled lightly, concentrated rapidly and struck unexpectedly in overwhelming numbers. Their chief operational virtues were mobility and surprise, and like the plains Indians of the North American West, they were superb individual fighters.[24]

Against these adversaries the best course was to rely upon the regular army's superior discipline, firepower, and staying power in sustained combat operations. However, as any modern commander would testify, to bring regular strength to bear against irregular weakness has not always been an easy task. Within the geographical context of the south steppe, the leisurely ways of a conventional eighteenth century army were even less likely to produce results than in western and northern Europe. Defeating the Turks and their steppe allies would require adjustments in tactics, organization, and indeed, the entire attitude governing the approach to operations. As early as 1737, Villim Fermor, a second generation Russian commander of English descent, had composed a set of instructions for Field Marshal Münnich which detailed the kinds of changes required to defeat the Turks. Fermor stressed the importance of taking the offensive to the enemy in a manner that would produce results in a general engagement. 'It is necessary to seek out battle to defeat the enemy', he wrote, while at the same time expressing a preference 'to conduct an offensive war by attempting to carry it to the enemy's territory'. Victory came through knowledge of the enemy's weaknesses and the ability to exploit those weaknesses by instilling 'a bold spirit in all ranks' and by training soldiers 'how to attack, fight, shoot, and defend'. Above all, the entire army had to be taught 'only that which it is necessary to do in battle.'[25] In many ways Fermor's prescriptions foreshadowed an emphasis on basics and a willingness to seek decision that later came to be associated with a new generation of generalship during the reign of Catherine II.[26]

Although both Fermor and Münnich evidently felt compelled to seek decision against the Turks, neither demonstrated consistent mastery of the techniques necessary to force decision in the field. Fermor wrote of the need to increase the army's mobility, but his superiors initially remained committed to fighting in the cumbersome and vulnerable linear formation even in the steppe. Only in 1739, during the Stavuchani campaign, did Münnich display willingness to depart from convention by forming his army into three large hollow squares which he directed in a ponderous but successful advance upon Turkish forces outside Khotin.[27]

The hollow square was an important element of tactical continuity spanning the period between the 1730s and the 1790s. While Münnich had experimented with an embryonic version of the square, Catherine II's ablest field commanders refined its usage until the square became one of the chief means assuring a return to decision against southern enemies. The square itself was not a novel formation. Since the disappearance of the pike formations of the previous century, infantrymen deployed in linear formation had learned to fold their flanks into a box-like formation affording complete perimeter defence against cavalry attack. Cannon and grenadiers guarded the corners, and since the infantry's normal practice was to fix bayonets, the entire array came to resemble a hedgehog with an empty centre and sides three or four ranks deep. The square was ideal for resisting the fury of the horde-like attacks of Turkish and Tatar light troops, the more so once the Russian infantry discovered that by 'maintaining their calm and presence of mind, it was sometimes even possible to ward off the enemy without firing a shot.'[28]

Crucial developments came during the course of Catherine's Turkish wars, when P.A. Rumiantsev and A.V. Suvorov refined the square to transform it into a credible offensive formation. G.A. Potemkin is said to have attracted Rumiantsev's attention to the advantages of the square early in 1770, when Potemkin successfully used it to escape annihilation by a vastly superior Tatar force.[29] Whatever the immediate source of renewed interest, Rumiantsev went on to adapt the square to his own tactical and operational requirements by multiplying the number of squares deployed and reducing their composition to a force ranging in size from two to eight battalions. Suvorov in turn reduced the composition of each square to either one or two battalions. In addition, he often cleverly deployed his squares in a checkerboard pattern of four lines with infantry occupying the first two and cavalry the third and fourth. Cossacks, hussars, and light infantry covered the flanks and rear. The hapless Turks and Tatars who mustered the courage to advance against such an array soon found themselves caught in a blistering crossfire from the infantry squares. Those enemy troops who managed to slip past the first two lines of infantry were then cut down by the Russian cavalry.[30]

In the hands of capable commanders the ability to deploy for battle by squares became a powerful offensive weapon. Although both Russian and Soviet military historians have described the virtues of the formation, they have generally neglected to state explicitly why the square now favoured the offensive. One reason was that the square permitted delivery of an articulated assault in which one or more squares advanced to conduct a pinning frontal attack while one or more others struck from the flank and rear. The chief merit of the articulated attack was that it permitted energetic commanders to seek hammer-and-anvil style engagements in which annihilation of enemy forces became a realistic objective. Rumiantsev's engagements at Larga and Kagul during the campaign of 1770 were classic examples of the infantry square being put to devastating use in the hands of a capable and energetic commander.[31]

A second advantage of the square was that it facilitated the development of operational mobility. The perception that the square made the Russians all but invulnerable to the most ferocious attack opened new possibilities in the realm of troop movement. Commanders could divide their field armies into separate marching columns to advance rapidly against a single objective over parallel or converging routes without fear of sudden attack and defeat in piecemeal while on the march. In the event of ambush or surprise attack, well-drilled soldiers moved with carefully rehearsed precision from march column to square formation, from which they might conduct a limited attack of their own or await reinforcement from nearby marching columns. Although there is evidence to demonstrate that the Russians used converging columns as early as the 1730s, again the classic example is the Larga-Kagul campaign which Rumiantsev launched by dividing his army into six separate marching columns, each of which was rigorously trained to form the square either on the march or at the objective. If the square made possible the articulated attack, it also made possible the articulated march.[32]

Less dramatic though no less important were other means adopted to improve mobility in the vast distances of the south. Fermor had earlier advised his fellow officers to reduce the size of the army's baggage train, but his prescription fell on deaf ears. Three decades later, Catherine's regimental commanders regularly insisted that their troops shoulder the burden of their own baggage and equipment plus four days' rations. Commanders also insisted on conditioning their soldiers to march longer distances at a quicker pace with fewer rest periods. Maurice de Saxe had written in his *Reveries* that 'all the secret of manoeuvres and combats is in the legs', and distances in the steppe no doubt encouraged his Russian students such as Potemkin to draw the same conclusion. Speed meant time, and with the conquest of time and distance came victory. Suvorov perhaps best exemplified the emphasis on speed when he asserted that 'one minute decides the outcome of a battle, one hour the success of a campaign, one day the fate of an empire . . . I operate not by hours but by minutes.'[33]

The composition and size of the army also reflected the need for additional mobility and the burden imposed by protracted southern conflict. The pace of recruitment rose during Catherine's reign to produce additional troops needed to meet the seemingly contradictory requirements of offensive concentration and defensive dispersion in the south while simultaneously maintaining credible forces in the north. Between 1767 and 1795, the table of organization for regular troops increased from a figure in excess of 185,000 to nearly 320,000. More revealing than numbers alone was the precise composition of those numbers. Between the beginning of the

First Turkish War and the conclusion of the Second Turkish War, the army's table of organization expanded to add more than 35,000 light infantry, while the number of light cavalry formations (with the addition of dragoons) showed an increase of more than 28,000. The need for speed and mobility generated a demand for special kinds of troops, light infantry and light cavalry, the presence of which improved the army's ability to close with, engage, and then pursue an elusive enemy across long distances.[34]

More outwardly noticeable were changes in uniforms and equipment which have come to be associated with the military administration of G.A. Potemkin, first as Vice President, then as President of the Military College (1774-1791). As a result of his own experience during the First Turkish War, he advocated a no-nonsense approach to questions of outfitting soldiers for combat. In place of the Prussian-style uniforms adopted in 1761, Potemkin in 1784 prescribed loose-fitting trousers, caftans, round-toed shoes, comfortable haircuts, and serviceable hats and capes. Potemkin believed that 'the beauty of military dress lay in uniformity and the way that articles corresponded with their use.' Any feature of uniform or toilet requiring an inordinate amount of upkeep he considered worthless. One of his favourite maxims was that 'as soon as a soldier gets up he should be ready to fight.' Another was that 'heavy cavalry was only heavy to itself.' Consequently his name became synonymous with repeated efforts to lighten the equipment and dress of the Russian cavalry, regardless of type. Eventually he and Rumiantsev were even able to get the cuirassiers to discard their cumbersome breastplates in the general quest for mobility and tactical flexibility.[35]

Potemkin's organizational activities also focused on widescale efforts aimed at military and civilian colonization of the south steppe. The twin requirements for security and mobility reinforced a trend to military settlement which had long been characteristic of southern expansion. When the Ukrainian *landmilitiia* and various experiments with foreign military settlements failed, military reformers turned increasingly to the Cossacks, former service and free types, to fill gaps in regular organization and to colonize vast expanses of the south. The continued existence and even expansion of the Cossack hosts seemed an ideal answer to the complex challenges of military operations along the southern frontier. The Cossacks were nearly self-supporting, and their settlements in the great river valleys of the south served as bulwarks against incursion from both the Caucasus and the Danube. Because they employed the tactics of the enemy and because they enjoyed the same mounted mobility, the Cossacks were invaluable auxiliaries to the more cumbersome regular cavalry.[36]

Logistics remained a major consideration behind various colonization projects, civil and military. In the south steppe beyond the line of friendly settlement there was often no local populace upon which an army could rely for quarters and provisions. To meet the challenges of sustained operations in areas of uncertain support, commanders mobilized smaller, more compact fighting forces which moved faster and were more easily supplied than larger forces from mobile magazines. Saxe had once argued that the optimum size for a field army was about 46,000; to exceed this limit was to court problems with supply and to invite manoeuvre difficulties. In addition, as Russian naval forces in the south grew in strength, thanks in large part to the indefatigable organizing activities of Potemkin, the Russians, like the Turks, used the river net and the Black Sea as highways to carry troops and supplies. The Russians also used a system of advanced bases and supply magazines which received provisions from the interior and from Poland. Finally, Russians carrying empty knapsacks often closed speedily with the enemy in hopes of reprovisioning from his captured baggage train. More than once Suvorov resupplied his famished men with provisions obtained from the looted train of a vanquished foe.[37]

A sustained emphasis on logistics, together with innovations of a tactical, operational, and organizational nature, enabled the Russians to project military power into the steppe on a predictable basis. Although the resolution to seek the offensive was not new, thanks to a combination of changes ranging from the addition of light formations to a new emphasis on mobility, the Russians were now able to support consistently the offensive resolve of their best commanders. Because commanders could forget preoccupations with the cumbersome battle line, they could concentrate on fielding compact forces of sufficient mobility to conduct powerful offensive operations across vast distances to engage enemies who had defied the Russians for more than a century. Unfettered by the dead hand of convention, the Russians were able to pursue a strategy of annihilation analogous to that adopted by the United States Army in the nineteenth century against the plains Indians of the American West: in the approach march use light formations for reconnaissance and security; once the enemy was located, preferably in camp, move rapidly to contact in parallel or converging march columns; for engagement deploy in small, flexible tactical formations capable of conducting simultaneous pinning and envelopment attacks; and finally, when the enemy broke, unleash light formations to seek total victory in the annihilation of shattered remnants. With variations on this general theme to accommodate circumstances, Russian field armies marched to victory after victory over their once intractable foes.

The problems of siege warfare were less amenable to satisfactory resolution. In part the continuing resilience of the Turks stemmed from their ability to maintain a network of strongholds around the periphery of the Black Sea which served both as rallying points and supply bases for large field forces. The dual threat posed by the fortresses and their covering armies forced the Russians to adopt a counter strategy calling for the existence of at least two active field armies, one to engage the Turks in the open and the other to invest the appropriate covering fortress. Because various solutions to logistical problems remained tenuous, the Russians never satisfactorily resolved the complex problems of siege warfare in the south. To engage in the classic Vauban-like reduction of fortresses such as Ochakov, Izmail, Bendery, and Khotin required copious amounts of time, troops, provisions, and a siege train, all of which were in short supply. Therefore, necessity usually forced the Russians to seek the *coup de main*, for there were but two ways to take a fortress: slowly and painfully or quickly and painfully.[38]

Russian victories in the pontic steppe during the First and Second Turkish Wars were predicated upon interlocking elements of tactics, operations, and logistics. Geography and enemy came together in a way that underscored mobility and flexibility. The Russian Army of the Seven Years' War, wedded as it was to conventional European models, was ill-suited to engage in the kind of far-flung and far-reaching operations that would produce military decision in the south. The advent of decision required significant departures from the northern European ideal, which in the 1760s and the early 1770s was embodied in the army of Frederick II of Prussia. While native Russian genius remained an important factor governing the evolution of Russian military art, warfare on the steppe frontier encouraged that genius to seek and apply innovation in ways that were either ignored (as in the case of the North American precedent), unknown, or embryonic in the west until the era of the French Revolution.[39]

The foregoing analysis underscores the importance of operational context in explaining military adaptation and innovation. In their own ways representatives of both the 'academic' and 'nationalist' schools of Russian military historiography were correct. The former justifiably emphasized the importance of constants in the evolution of military art, while the latter emphasized the uniqueness of environment and assets, both material, moral, and personal. What brings the two approaches together and endows them with significance is the operational aspect, the necessity to resolve identifiable problems of time, distance, and enemy with the materials at hand. The 'golden age of Russian arms' provides sufficient examples to justify—at least partially—either approach, and without recourse to full operational context, dialogue between the two schools degenerates into an inconclusive academic exercise.

At the same time the operational aspect underscores the importance of what is sometimes called 'drum and trumpets' history in explaining major institutional developments. Armies are something more than large bureaucracies which monopolize the instruments of violence. Unlike many other institutions of the modern state, military establishments generally remain subject to a rigorous accounting process in which institutional rigidities and failures to adapt produce mistakes which must be buried in single or multiple numbers. Theory and style sometimes explain how armies fight and change, but as Roger Beaumont has recently written, so do improvisation and flexibility. Indeed, contemporary Soviet military analysts are perhaps closer to the mark in perceiving the roots of tactical innovation when they dwell less on social context and more on the necessity to avoid stereotype (*Ne po shablonu* or 'not according to pattern,' they exhort).[40]

There remain the two related issues of persistence and transfer in the eighteenth century. Pre-revolutionary Russian and Soviet military historians, both of whom have often demonstrated an obsessive regard for Russia's relationship with the West, have made much of the advanced nature of Russian military art, especially in the age of Catherine II. Without doubt, the special circumstances of warfare in the south caused the Russians to adopt some of the same operational and tactical expediencies which the French would put into practice between 1792 and 1815. And without a doubt, some of the broader implications of fighting on the frontier, including the importance of speed and mobility, found their way into Russian practice outside the steppe and in another era. One might also argue in general terms that a whole generation of commanders (including notably M.I. Kutuzov, P.I. Bagration, and M.B. Barclay de Tolly) who would later face Napoleon and his marshals served their apprenticeship in the hard school of steppe warfare, often in light units. However, there seemed a natural reluctance, perhaps one which characterizes all regular officers serving in an unconventional environment, to extrapolate too much from their unconventional experiences. Suvorov himself demonstrated a tendency to see two distinct military worlds, each with its appropriate forms, when in 1778 he prescribed the following tactical formations to the Crimean and Kuban Corps: 'against regular forces the linear order as in the Prussian war; against irregulars as in the last Turkish war.'[41] At the same time the vastness of the Russian Empire and its wealth in military manpower seemed to preclude the kind of thoroughgoing social change wrought in France and later in Prussia by the perceived military needs of a revolutionary age. For a time only the Cossacks, who owed their continuing existence to changing perceptions of the need for light cavalry, seemed to reflect the persistent influence of war on Russian social institutions after the passing of the southern military frontier.

## Notes

An earlier version of this article with a different focus was read as a paper during the conference, 'Russia and the West in the Eighteenth Century,' held on 21-26 July 1981 at the University of East Anglia. For various kinds of research support the author gratefully acknowledges the Miami University Faculty Research Committee and the Russian and East European Centre at the University of Illinois. All dates are given according to the Julian calendar, which in the eighteenth century lagged behind the Gregorian by eleven days, and with only several exceptions the modified Library of Congress system of transliterating Cyrillic characters into their Latin equivalents has been observed. St. Petersburg and Moscow are abbreviated in the notes respectively as 'SPB' and 'M.'

1. Dennis E. Showalter, 'A Modest Plea for Drums and Trumpets', *Military Affairs*, 39 (April 1975), 71-4, and Christopher Duffy, *Russia's Military Way to the West* (London 1981), xii; for a broader perspective, see Walter Emil Kaegi, Jr., 'The Crisis in Military Historiography', *Armed Forces and Society*, 7 (Winter 1981), 299-316.
2. A thoughtful, recent Soviet treatment of this subject in the eighteenth century is A.A. Komarov, 'Razvitie takticheskoi mysli v russkoi armii v 60—90-kh godakh XVIII v.', *Vestnik Moskovskogo universiteta*, seriia 8, Istoriia, 3 (1982), especially 62-3; see also M.K. Gordienko and V.V. Khoroshcho, *Initsiativa i samostoiatel'nost' v boiu* (M 1970), 3-5.
3. Many of the changes are summarized in A.A. Strokov, *Istoriia voennogo iskusstva*, 2 vols. (M 1955, 1957), I, 624-5; on similarities between the Russians and the French, see, for example, P.A. Geisman, *Kratkii Kurs istorii voennogo iskusstva v srednie i novye veka*, 3 pts. (SPB 1893-1896), pt. 3, 308-9.
4. Two exceptions are P. Bobrovskii, 'Kubanskii Egerskii Korpus', *Voennyi sbornik*, No. 1 (January 1893), 9-10, and N.F. Dubrovin, *A.V. Suvorov sredi preobrazovatelei ekaterininskoi armii* (SPB 1885), 49-51.
5. These observations, especially as they relate to Russia, are from Bruce W. Menning, 'Russia and the West: The Problem of Eighteenth-Century Military Models', in A.G. Cross (ed.), *Russia and the West in the Eighteenth Century* (Newtonville, Mass. 1983), 284; on Frederick and the Frederician model, see Peter Paret, *Yorck and the Era of Prussian Reform 1807-1815* (Princeton 1966), especially 12-28, and Christopher Duffy, *The Army of Frederick the Great*, chapters V and VI; the changes engendered by the French

Revolution are ably summarized in Gunther E. Rothenberg, *The Art of Warfare in the Age of Napoleon* (Bloomington, In. 1978), chapter IV; on adaptation and improvisation, see Gunther E. Rothenberg, 'The Habsburg Army in the Napoleonic Wars', *Military Affairs*, 37 (February 1978), 1.

6. The development of rival 'academic and Russian' schools of historiography is surveyed in L.G. Beskrovnyi, *Ocherki voennoi istoriografii Rossii* (M 1962), 182-8, and in Peter Von Wahlde, 'A Pioneer of Russian Strategic Thought: G.A. Leer, 1829-1904', *Military Affairs*, 35 (December 1971), 148-52; for a sampling of the Soviet view, see N.M. Korobkov, 'Armii i strategiia epokhi Semiletnei voiny,' *Voenno-istoricheskii zhurnal*, 2 (April 1940), 86-7, A.I. Gotovtsev (ed.), *Istoriia voennogo iskusstva*, 2 vols. (M 1951), I, 407-20, and L.M. Leshchinskii, *Voennye pobedy i polkovodtsev russkogo naroda vtoroi poloviny XVIII veka* (M 1959), 24-5.
7. D.F. Maslovskii, *Zapiski po istorii voennogo iskusstva*, 2 vols. (SPB 1891, 1894), I, 342-3, and A.K. Puzyrevskii, 'Ocherki iz istorii pekhoty', *Voennyi sbornik*, No. 11 (November 1876), 49-53; see also Marc Raeff, 'The Domestic Policies of Peter III and His Overthrow', *American Historical Review*, 65 (June 1970), 1289-310.
8. *Polnoe sobranie zakonov rossiiskoi imperii* [hereafter *PSZ*], 1st series, 46 vols. (SPB 1830-39), XVI, nos. 11594, 11595 (both 5 July 1762), and 11668 (22 September 1762), 11 and 70-2; and A.V. Viskovatov, *Istoricheskoe opisanie odezhdy i vooruzheniia rossiiskikh voisk, s risumkami, sostavlennoe po Vysochaishemu poveleniiu*, 2nd ed., 19 pts. (SPB 1899-1902), pt. 3, plate 390 and pt. 4, plate 494.
9. *PSZ*, XVI, No. 11707 (11 November 1762), 109-10.
10. *PSZ*, XI, No. 8498 (15 January 1742), 558; L.G. Beskrovnyi, *Russkaia armiia i flot v XVIII veke* (M 1958), 154.
11. *Zapiski Andreia Timofeevicha Bolotova 1738-1795*, 4 vols. (SPB 1871-75), I, *pis'mo* 32, cols. 360-1.
12. A.I. Gippius (comp.), *Obrazovanie (obuchenie) voisk* in D.A. Skalon (ed.), *Stoletie Voennogo Ministerstva*, 48 pts. in 13 vols. (SPB 1902-14), IV, pt. 1, bk. 2, section 3, 52.
13. L.G. Beskrovnyi (comp.), *Khrestomatiia po russkoi voennoi istorii* (M 1947), 196-7; the regulation itself appears in *PSZ*, XIV, No. 10494a (15 December 1755), 76-130.
14. D.F. Maslovskii, *Stroevaia i polevaia sluzhba russkikh voisk vremen Imperatora Petra Velikogo i Imperatritsy Elizavety* (M 1883), 129-30, 160-1; Beskrovnyi, *Russkaia armiia i flot v XVIII veke*, 63-5; B.A. Shteifon, *Natsional'naia voennaia doktrina* (Tallin 1937), 120.
15. *PSZ*, XVI, No. 11668 (22 September 1762), 71.
16. A.K. Baiov, 'Ocherki voennogo iskusstva i sostoianie russkoi armii pri blizhaishikh preemnikakh Petra Velikogo', *Istoriia russkoi armii i flota*, 16 vols. (M 1911-13), II, 62.
17. *PSZ*, XVI, No. 11773a (12 March 1763), pp. 1-103, esp. 19-26; Gippius, *Obrazovanie (obuchenie) voisk*, 75.

18. Beskrovnyi, *Russkaia armiia i flot v XVIII veke*, 311-12, 316-18.
19. Suvorov is quoted in Philip Longworth, *The Art of Victory* (New York 1965), 226; on Rumiantsev, see *Zapiski L'va Nikolaevicha Engel'gardta 1766-1836* (M 1867), 21-2, and Duffy, *Russia's Military Way to the West*, 168-9.
20. The technological continuities are illustrated in N.I. Gnatskii and P.A. Shorin, *Istoriia razvitiia otechestvennogo strelkovogo oruzhiia* (M 1959), 24-9; on the various military commissions, see *Voennaia entsiklopediia* (1911-15 ed.), XIII, *s. v.* 'Komissii (Komitety) voinskiia vremennyia'; on the gravitation to firepower, see the treatment on Guibert in Robert S. Quimby, *The Background of Napoleonic Warfare* (New York 1957), 113-33; de Puységur is quoted by Quimby, 17.
21. Quimby, *The Background of Napoleonic Warfare*, 4-6.
22. A.N. Petrov (ed.), *Russkaia voennaia sila*, 2 vols. (M 1892), II, 177-93, and Iu. R. Klokman, *Fel'dmarshal Rumiantsev v period russko-turetskoi voiny 1768-1774 gg.* (M 1951), 23-5.
23. See for example, A.A. Gotovtsov (ed.), *Istoriia voennogo iskusstva*, 2 vols. (M 1951), I, 407-20; G.B. Karaev, *Suvorovskaia 'Nauka Pobezhdat" v svete peredovoi sovetskoi voennoi nauki* (Leningrad 1950), 3, 8-9; A.A. Strokov (ed.), *Istoriia voennogo iskusstva* (M 1966), 118-20; and N.N. Golovin, *Suvorov i ego 'Nauka Pobezhdat"* (Paris 1931), 53-83.
24. A.K. Baiov summarizes the characteristics of the Turkish forces and their allies in *Russkaia armiia v tsarstvovanie Imperatritsy Anny Ioannovny*, 2 vols. (SPB 1906), I, 103-5; see also David Chandler, *The Art of Warfare in the Age of Marlborough* (New York 1976), 14-15; on the general problems of frontier warfare, see Robin Higham, 'Military Frontiersmanship', International Commission of Military History, *ACTA No. 4.* [Ottawa 23-25 August 1978] (Ottawa 1979), 52-3.
25. M.G. Kriudener (ed.), 'Dispozitsiia boevogo poriadka i manevrov v general'noi batalii s turkami', in D.F. Maslovskii, N.F. Dubrovin, *et al.* (eds.), *Sbornik voenno-istoricheskikh materialov*, 16 vols. (SPB 1892-1904), XV, 56-7, 63.
26. For a treatment of the 'new' offensive strategy, see V. Ivanov, 'P.A. Rumiantsev—osnovopolozhnik reshitel'noi nastupatel'noi strategii reguliarnykh armii', *Voenno-istoricheskii zhurnal*, No. 1 (January 1980), 77-81.
27. Maslovskii, *Zapiski po istorii voennogo iskusstva*, I, 214-17.
28. The words are Fermor's in Kriudener, 'Dispozitsiia boevogo poriadka i manevrov v general'noi batalii s turkami', 66.
29. A.N. Petrov, 'Largo-Kagul'skaia operatsiia 1770 goda', *Voennyi sbornik*, No. 12 (1892), 99.
30. A.N. Kochetkov, 'Takticheskie vzgliady A.V. Suvorova', in D.V. Pankov (comp.), *Razvitie taktiki russkoi armii* (M 1957), 100-3; a recent discussion is Komarov, 'Razvitie takticheskoi myski v russkoi armii v 60—90-kh godakh XVIII v.', 60-1.
31. See, for example, Rumiantsev's plan of 6 July 1770 for an attack against enemy dispositions on the River Larga in P.K. Fortunatov and L.G. Beskrovnyi (eds.), *P.A. Rumiantsev. Dokumenty*, 3 vols. (M 1947, 1953, and

1959), II, 322-3; see also, Baiov, 'Ocherki voennogo iskusstva', 64-5.

32. See Rumiantsev's marching orders in Fortunatov and Beskrovnyi (eds.), *P.A. Rumiantsev*, II, 289-92; on the precedent of the 1730s, see C.H. Manstein, *Memoirs of Russia, Historical, Political, and Military* (London 1770), 100-1.
33. Quoted in I. Krupchenko, 'A.V. Suvorov i voennoe iskusstvo', *Voenno-istoricheskii zhurnal*, No. 10 (October 1980), 73; see also Longworth, *The Art of Victory*, 309-10.
34. Beskrovnyi, *Krestomatiia po russkoi voennoi istorii*, 202-3; on the need for light cavalry in the south, see especially A.A. Prozorovskii to P.A. Rumiantsev in N.F. Dubrovin (ed.), *Prisoedinenie Kryma k Rossii*, 4 vols. (SPB 1885-92), I, 87-8.
35. N.P. Mikhnevich, *Istoriia voennogo iskusstva s drevneishikh vremen do nachala deviatnadtsatogo stoletiia* (SPB 1895), 361; Viskovatov, *Istoricheskoe opisanie odezhdy i vooruzheniia rossiskikh voisk*, pt. 4, 67-74, 95, 100-108.
36. Maslovskii, *Zapiski po istorii russkogo voennogo iskusstva*, nn. on 28-31, and Bruce W. Menning, 'G.A. Potemkin and A.I. Chernyshev: Two Dimensions of Reform and the Military Frontier in Imperial Russia', in Donald G. Horward (ed.), *The Consortium on Revolutionary Europe Proceedings 1980*, 2 vols. (Athens, Ga. 1980), I, 238-43.
37. Longworth, *The Art of Victory*, 152-4. Little has been written about Suvorov's capacity to support his operations from an administrative and logistical point of view; see F.A. Maksheev, 'Voenno-administrativnyi oblik Suvorova', in *Suvorov v soobshcheniiakh professorov Nikolaevskoi Akademii General'nogo shtaba*, 2 vols. (SPB 1900), I, 197-213.
38. See, for example, G.A. Leer, *Obzor voin Rossii ot Petra Velikogo do nashikh dnei* (SPB 1893), 70-99.
39. On North America and the Europeans see Peter Paret, 'Colonial Experience and European Military Reform at the End of the Eighteenth Century', *Bulletin of the Institute of Historical Research*, 37 (1964), 47-59.
40. Roger A. Beaumont, 'The Field-Expedient Factor: Adaptation and Survival in the First Battle', *Military Review*, 60 (October 1980), 69-75, and Richard S. Kosevich, 'Ne po shablonu: Soviet Tactical Flexibility', *Military Review*, 62 (August 1982), 24-32.
41. Quoted in A. Petrushevskii, *Generalisimus Kniaz' Suvorov*, 3 vols. (SPB 1884), I, 475.

# [11]

# *Patriotism and Professionalism: The Polish Army in the Eighteenth Century*

**Daniel Stone**

The most immediate cause of the Polish Partitions was the failure to protect the borders against foreign invasion. The partitions put an end, some thought forever, to a Polish state which had lasted over 800 years and, at its height, had extended from the Baltic to the Black Sea since Polish armed forces had previously equalled or excelled those of her neighbors both in numbers and in technological development. Under the influence of military success, Polish culture took on a military orientation which subsequent failure did not dispell; indeed, the militarism of a beleaguered Poland may well have deepened as many Poles, particularly, although not exclusively, nobles, volunteered to fight to protect the national cause. As the partitions prove, patriotism failed to compensate for professional shortcomings but at least it provided the building materials for an eighteenth century revival that permitted a creditable last stand during the 1794 Insurrection and gave the military its reputation as guardian of the nation that Poles, including the government during the recent crisis, have used and abused ever since.

As in other countries, the roots of the Polish army reach into feudal levies and noble practices of the Middle Ages. As in other countries, too, Poles took advantage of technological developments in the sixteenth and seventeenth centuries by organizing musket and artillery regiments which helped them build their Eastern empire against Turkish, Tartar, Muscovite and Cossack resistance and also stand up to the powerful, westernized Swedish army for control of the Baltic Coast. However, continued technological progress required ever greater professionalization during the seventeenth century which the Polish state found increasingly difficult to supply. Political practices, not intellectual backwardness or pacifist inclination, interfered. The *liberum veto* and a host of other devices prevented the efficient tax collection required to create strong modern forces responsive to central authority. Furthermore, the unbalanced growth of the economy in the direction of plantation-style agriculture interfered with the development of local mechanical technology and the spread of serfdom inhibited recruiting from the ever-increasing area of noble estates.

Decline came slowly. Sweden's conquest of Poland in the mid-seventeenth century resulted more from political intrigue than military weakness as the rapid expulsion of the Swedes shows. Poles pretty much held their own militarily against Muscovites and Cossacks at the same time even if the birth of Cossack and Ukrainian national consciousness forced Poland to surrender half the Ukraine. And Sobieski's great charge against the Ottomans in 1683 raised the siege of Vienna. Nevertheless, problems loomed more and more ominously. A supreme effort during the Great Northern War at the beginning of the eighteenth century raised about 90,000 troops (70,000 for King August II and 20,000 for the pretender, Stanisław Leszczyńsky), a number which scarcely equalled the peacetime armies of Poland's powerful neighbors. As before, the government lacked the strength to impose adequate taxation for the nobles evaded the *kwarta*, a tax specifically designed to support the military; other military taxes (such as the *hiberna* for winter quartering and similar levies on nobles, clerics, and Jews) fared little better.[1]

Poland fell into abject military impotence after the conclusion of the Great Northern War. Military stores had been destroyed, civilians had been greatly impoverished, and great rents had opened in the political fabric, particularly when the noble Tarnogród Confederation rallied noble military support against the absolutist, but reform-minded, King August II. No effective government existed to repair the damage. The "Silent Diet" of 1717 enacted a few financial and military improvements without providing sufficient revenues to meet the goal of raising a tiny 24,000 man army. Political strife, enhanced by parliamentary practices such as the *liberum veto,* prevented any further reform for another half-century. The miniature Polish army might control peasant disorders but it could not protect the borders. Inefficiencies vitiated the functioning of even this tiny army. Too many generals collected high salaries without performing useful services so that too little money remained to bring the army up to strength or train the soldiers properly. In form the Polish army continued to separate the Foreign Contingent (consisting of mostly Polish soldiers and officers), whose training and weaponry resembled the Saxon army, from the National Contingent or National Cavalry, an ill-disciplined mounted force made up almost entirely of nobles without infantry or artillery support. Less than half the army consisted of infantry, far less than in the west, even if the figure represented an improvement over seventeenth century patterns. In short, the Polish army had become so small and poorly organized, that private armies of great magnates probably outnumbered the state forces and, in cases like the army of Count Stanislaw Radziwill, equalled them in training.[2]

The difficult task of rebuilding the army began in the reign of King Stanisław [August] Poniatowski, who came to the throne in 1764, but only slow progress ensued. The Czartoryski Party, of which Poniatowski was a junior member, aimed to raise tax revenues in order to bring the army up to its legal strength, rebuild fortresses, and cast artillery pieces; in addition, it intended to recruit volunteers from traditionally exempt noble estates with a promise of freedom from serfdom after ten years.[3] Most of these plans could not be realised but the young king personally established a cannon foundry and small arms factory which had a measurable, if small, impact on preparedness. The Diet set up Treasury Commissions to collect taxes more efficiently, and Military Commissions (separate for the Polish "Crown" provinces and for the Grand Duchy of Lithuania) which exercised logistical and political control over the military. The Commissioners reduced the number of officers, spent the savings on increasing the number of common soldiers, and generally regularized such routine but important procedures as leaves, promotions, and discipline, so the Polish army came to resemble other European armies in everything but size. They paid particular attention to military training as did the Diet itself through creation of a Royal Cadet School which offered a good general education with special military studies. A number of noted generals graduated from the school including Tadeusz Kościuszko, Jakub Jasínski, and Karol Kniaziewicz while other members of the country's young elite gained a general appreciation of military matters. The king's authority grew somewhat thanks to the establishment of Guards Regiments, partly at his own expense and partly from the public purse. Polish vocabulary gradually replaced German in the language of command.[4]

The outbreak of the War of the Bar Confederation in 1768 halted military reconstruction abruptly. Patriotic but generally reactionary, the Bar Confederates attempted to drive out the Russians who had greatly assisted the Czartoryskis in putting Poniatowski on the Polish throne and continued to dominate the country in a conflict that dragged on for four years and ended with the first Partition. The Polish army bloodily suppressed a Cossack and peasant uprising in the Uman district of eastern Galicia in 1768, but rarely fought against the Confederates, perhaps because the commanders feared for the loyalty of the troops. Nevertheless, the war affected the army drastically. Tax collecting suffered, pay became irregular, and many soldiers deserted; recruiting and logistical supplies also declined. By 1772, the regular army had fallen to about 10,000 men.

The work of building up the army resumed as the diets of 1775 and 1776 (confederated to allow decisions by majority rule instead of unamimity) established the Permanent Council as a more effective executive authority and, within it, the Military Department, which superseded, without abolishing, the Military Commissions. In fact, the King's Military Chancellery, headed by General Jan Komarzewski, who had trained in the Prussian army, did most of the work of recruiting, training, and equipping the troops within strict financial constraints. Under Komarzewski, fixed (and lower) stipends for remaining sinecure positions were established, the pay schedule for servicemen was regularized, and garrison duties were carefully described. More dramatically, the formal distinction between the so-called Foreign and National Contingents was abolished (although National Cavalry regiments remained unchanged in the combined command), new instructions were written for all branches, Polish weapons became more uniform, and so did clothing. In this fashion, the Polish army became a regular European army instead of a rag-tag rabble.

Nevertheless, the Diet could not affect the only reform which really counted—increasing the size of the army significantly—since the economy revived only slowly after the partition and noble opposition to taxation remained intense. Although the partitioning powers permitted Poland to increase its army to 30,000, the Poles failed to reach even 20,000 over more than a decade after the first Partition. The failure represented inadequate governmental revenues rather than neglect of the army. From 1768 to 1788, the Diet allocated and the government spent about 50% of its total revenues on the army. This figure compares favorably with Necker's 1781 budget which promised 25% of France's revenues to the military although it falls far short of Prussia's 75-80%.[5] Poniatowski hoped to tap new sources by joining in the Russo-Turkish War of 1787 in exchange for Russian subsidies while, for their part, his political opponents advocated the alternative approach of raising a Polish cavalry corps specifically for service in the Russian army.

Russia refused both rival plans to increase the army, but the Russo-Turkish War had an even more profound impact on Polish military development than their proponents could have designed. As the continuing hostilities distracted Russia, political changes occurred which reflected a radically altered national consciousness and removed many stumbling blocks to the creation of an effective army in Poland. Egged on by the Prussian ambassador, the Diet ignored the king and his Russian protectors and abolished, first, the Military Department, then the entire Permanent Council, before approving a plan to raise a 100,000 man army under its own control. Most amazingly, the deputies to the diet, all nobles, taxed themselves to pay for it. As a result, revenues more than doubled and expenditures on the army tripled so that the government was spending about 60% of its funds on the military.[6] Nevertheless, the Diet had to scale down its target. 57,000 men served in 1791, three times the number serving three years previous, and 65,000 in 1792 although cavalry still constituted about 45% of the total, in part because the National Cavalry cost less.

Promotion, recruitment of foreigners, and repatriation of Poles serving abroad supplied officers for the new army; common soldiers came from noble estates through voluntary recruitment as well as from national and royal estates, as before. Systematic ennoblement of non-noble army officers in 1790 demonstrated the respect with which society viewed the military.[7] Weapons proved a problem since Polish industry lacked the capacity to supply sufficient quantities, so the government bought foreign arms, mostly outmoded Prussian muskets, which worked poorly. Over-all the army of 1788-92 remained a somewhat unbalanced, inexperienced force despite the government's earnest efforts to solve problems of expansion, but it represented an enormous improvement over anything Poland had fielded in the previous seventy-five years and could seriously attempt to defend the borders.[8]

Russia put the young army to the test after finally defeating Turkey in 1792. Heavily outnumbered units commanded by Prince Józef Poniatowski and Tadeusz Kościuszko retreated slowly in good order while fighting a number of engagements on roughly even terms but some other units in other sectors retreated helplessly, stepped aside, or surrendered without a fight. In any event, the King and the leadership of the Diet considered military resistance futile and used the hostilities to gain time for fruitless diplomatic approaches to Petersburg (Poniatowski) and Berlin (Ignacy Potocki and Adam Czartoryski). The King capitulated after only two months of fighting, acceded to the puppet Targowica Confederation, and ordered the army to lay down its arms, which it did reluctantly. Poniatowski violated his pledge to fight to the finish and rejected plans to arm the burghers whose loyalty had been won by passage of progressive urban legislation. In this brief war, the Poles had shown themselves capable of building an army which might count for something on the scales of the European Balance of Power, but it was still at an early stage of development and the country could not protect itself by conventional means.

Appeal to Polish traditions of patriotic voluntary service presented an alternative, or at least a supplement, to professional eighteenth century warfare. While all European countries had used feudal levies during the Middle Ages before turning towards professional forces in early modern times, Poland's failure to develop a strong, centralized government caused it to rely on improvised forms, particularly against the mid-seventeenth century Swedish "Flood", which made central government collapse utterly. Provincial governments in unoccupied parts of the country raised armies on as high a professional level as possible to repel the invader, although the results often lagged far behind the intent. Large numbers of nobles also responded to patriotic appeals by local clergy and by the exiled king by flocking to Polish armies wherever they stood or by forming their own units with peasant support. A few all-peasant units even appeared and great nobles contributed their private armies which had been created originally in the East to fight against Turks, Tartars, Cossacks, Muscovites, and rebellious peasants. The success of these assorted forces in lifting the siege of Czestochowa and eventually expelling the Swedes established the legend of the nation-in-arms. Improvised units continued to appear in times of crisis for the next hundred years and more although they chiefly rallied against Polish kings who sought to extend their prerogatives or impose unwelcome reform.

The last eighteenth century War of the Bar Confederation represented such an impulse. For the most part, the Confederate armies consisted of small improvised groups although popular leaders like Kazimierz Pułaski could occasionally gather substantial numbers. However large or small, the Confederates attacked without logistical or technical support and failed to coordinate their efforts or take advantage of the widespread support among the lower classes that their passionate defence of Catholicism earned them.[9]

Despite these obvious inadequacies, the Bar Confederation fought on for four years over most of the country displaying particular strength in the two most populous provinces, Wielkopolska and Małopolska. Their struggle against a superior foe inspired popular songs, poems, and sermons which encouraged further sacrifice and lent some plausibility to arguments in favor of retaining the National Cavalry in the regular army to represent the martial spirit of the average Polish noble. Some politicians built political support on this sentiment during the inter-partition period by presenting at the 1786 Diet, for example, a bill prohibiting foreigners or naturalized Polish citizens from serving as officers and by preventing the imposition of stricter disciplinary measures on the National Cavalry.[10]

Opposition voices appealed to noble pride before the 1788 Diet and enjoyed partial responsibility for the course of that diet. Hetman Franciszek Branicki led the fight to maintain the high proportion of National Cavalry in the expanded army and succeeded, partly because it was easy and inexpensive to recruit noble cavalrymen as long as the terms of service remained light. Newly-created units filled up quickly. Lax discipline and active service on the eastern border watching the Russo-Turkish War demoralized the units, although the fault often lay with inexperienced commanders more than with anarchic lesser nobles. By 1792, volunteering had diminished and the army turned to commoners to fill the ranks of the National Cavalry.[11]

The experience of the American Revolution only a few years before and the contemporary events of the French Revolution provided additional support for the idea of a patriotic volunteer army, even if such forces had rarely performed well in Poland. In America, local militia had provided an invaluable supplement to regular troops on many occasions and had even won some victories on their own against British regulars. Poles had become thoroughly familiar with the lessons of the American Revolution through extensive coverage in the Polish and the imported press while many Poles could observe the rapid expansion of the French army in the revolutionary era, particularly since unreconciled losers of the 1792 War with Russia had gone west into exile.[12] Furthermore, one of the few heroes of the 1792 War, General Tadeusz Kościuszko, had served with distinction in America before returning to Poland and since his superior officer, Prince Józef Poniatowski, felt bound by his ties to his uncle, the King, not to join the exile movement even though he himself had left the country after laying down arms, Kościuszko succeeded to military leadership. Advising the emigre political leadership that a popular war could liberate Poland from the Russians, he expressed confidence that "freedom and independence would bring forth the willingness to sacrifice in the heart of every soldier here as it did there" and pointed to the American Revolution as "an example of making war for eight years without money". Specifically, Kościuszko proposed to correct the mistakes of 1792 by strengthening and expanding the army, by enlisting private noble armies, by summoning the noble *lévée en masse (pospolite ruszenie),* and by arming the cities.[13]

Kościuszko's observations offered hope to the exiles and ran parallel to the ideas of another insurrectionary, Hugo Kołłątaj, a priest and educator turned politician, who became known by the exaggerated sobriquet of the Polish Robespierre from his leading the movement for urban reform. As early as 1784, Kołłątaj proposed adding military instruction to the curriculum of regional high schools run by the National Education Commission throughout the country so that graduates would become trained to lead militia units composed of local peasants. Like Kościuszko, Kołłątaj appears to have been inspired in part by the success of improvised American forces against the British. A few years later, Kołłątaj unsuccessfully proposed to the 1788-92 Diet that villages raise one soldier for each 300 acres and that burghers form militia units.[14]

Kościuszko acted promptly to put these ideas into practice on a broad national basis as military commander of the 1794 Insurrection. He dictated the act of confederation issued on March 24 in Cracow which called "all citizens" to arms. Local authorities summoned all males between 18 and 40 years of age without class or estate distinction to report for military drill on Sundays with any weapons that they could procure—usually agricultural implements. Insurrectionary authorities throughout the country issued similar decrees.[15] The guilds took matters into their own hands in Warsaw and Wilno, spontaneously mobilizing, procuring arms from the arsenals, and joining regular detachments to expell the Russian garrisons after heavy fighting.[16] Kościuszko hastened to prepare a general decree for the country as a whole which placed additional emphasis on recruiting for the regular army. He hoped to get one soldier from every five households while the remaining males between 18 and 60 years of age would serve in local militias. The regular army would call upon local troops to supplement its strength while operating in the region. In order to encourage peasants to volunteer, he promised them freedom from serfdom.[14]

Throughout the insurrection, over 90,000 men served in local militias commanded by officers appointed by local authorities on Kościuszko's recommendation, chiefly in the Crown provinces. Of the 73,000 rural militiamen, by far the most famous were the 2,000 peasants from the Cracow district who won the battle of Racławice with an heroic charge against a Russian battery. Local units also performed valuable services by disrupting enemy communications, intercepting supplies, and hampering the freedom of enemy armies to move about the countryside. The formation of militia units behind Prussian lines relieved the first siege of Warsaw and doubled the lifespan of the Insurrection. Urban militias also contributed greatly. About 18,000 burghers played a prominent role in the battle of April 17-18 against the Russian garrison and during the siege of Warsaw. Jan Kiliński, a master cobbler, figured in conspiratorial preparations for the Insurrection and distinguished himself in action; he became a colonel in the militia. In Wilno, General Jakub Jasiński, a professional officer, led the guild militia against the Russian garrison but the Cracow militia provided little support for the Insurrection after Kościuszko's departure from the city because the guild elders and city government opposed the Insurrection.

The militia supplemented, but did not replace, the regular army to which Kościuszko devoted most of his attention. The Russians had ordered demobilization of part of the Polish army after the 1792 war and the Insurrection broke out in 1794, not because the time was somehow ripe, but because General Antoni Madaliński refused to break up his command. Emergency taxes and levies on all classes of Polish society provided the finances to increase the army to about 70,000 while a munitions industry was hastily and successfully improvised. Under his command, insurrectionary armies won the early battle of Racławice and withstood the first siege of Warsaw but later lost at Szczekociny and Maciejowice, where the wounded Kościuszko fell into Russian hands. The Insurrection ended after Suvorov stormed Praga on the east bank of the Vistula securing access to Warsaw and frightening the city population by ruthless treatment of the civilian population.

Poland's military achievement in withstanding the energetic efforts of two great powers, Prussia and Russia, for more than six months proved that Poland had emerged once again, if briefly, as a significant factor in European politics. Although the Insurrection failed, it forced the two powers to turn their attention towards Poland instead of Revolutionary France and, in a very real way, ensured France's victory on the Western Front. In the course of the Insurrection, the Poles raised more regular troops than at any time since the Great Northern War and, counting militia units, far more than at any time in Poland's modern history, an achievement possible only because the Insurrection appealed to burghers and peasants as well as nobles. This great effort also created a legend which inspired patriotic insurrections throughout the nineteenth and twentieth centuries.

The literature of the Enlightenment offers a further indication that military affairs had come to concern the Polish nation as a whole and not just the nobility. Two plays in particular stand out because of their treatment of the military as a backdrop for pressing social concerns. Although late eighteenth century theatre did not dwell on military matters, so many characters were set as soldiers and officers as to imply that the Polish army rivalled other European armies in size.

"The Deserter for Love of Family" is the polonized version of a German play prepared for the 1776 theatre season by an otherwise unknown author named Bernard. The play criticizes mistreatment of peasants by hard-hearted and grasping nobles through a portrayal of a village in which an army detachment is billeted. A soldier, long separated from this, his home village, finds that the family farm is about to be repossessed by the landlord. The captain, pleased by the son's character and military devotion, presents him with half the sum needed to pay off the family's debts but the family cannot raise the remainder until, in desperation, the hero pretends to desert in order to be "captured" by his uncle, who received a reward sufficient to pay the debt; the son willingly accepts harsh corporal punishment. The parents patriotically disown their son when they hear of his desertion but the situation resolves when the uncle reveals his secret. The parents are grateful, the officers amazed, and the King, who "happens" to visit the scene, makes the hero an officer granting him the title of nobility that his character warrants. The grasping noble who almost ruins the peasant family becomes the butt of public ridicule.[17]

As "The Deserter" speaks of peasants, "The Mayor of Poznan", based on Collet d'Herbois's "Le Paysan Magistrat" and performed in 1782 for the first time, explores the Polish burgher estate. The hero, Redlich, represents a burgher archetype: hard-working, loyal to the king, respectful of the warrior nobility, and proud of his own condition. Again, a new regiment arrives to take up quarters and he, as a prominent burgher, hosts the commanding general, with whom he becomes friendly despite their differing status. However, Redlich's daughter encounters a captain whom she had previously met in Warsaw and the two young people fall in love much to Redlich's annoyance since he opposes inter-marriage between estates. The captain abducts the daughter, whom Redlich has confined to the house, intending to marry her but he is caught, imprisoned, and brought to trial—before Redlich, who has just been elected mayor. Tension builds as Redlich threatens energetic prosecution and the army threatens reprisals but relents when it turns out that the captain is the son of Redlich's friend, the General, and the representatives of the two orders agree to the marriage; the General also grants an army commission to Redlich's son. Politically, the play portrays a reconciliation between the upper bourgeoisie and the nobility which foreshadows the actual events of 1789-91 when a coalition of the two groups passed an important law of urban reform and made it part of the Constitution of May 3, 1791.

Both plays express high regard for the army and for military service. The function of the nobility is clearly understood to be military leadership, if necessary at the cost of shedding blood. But the other estates are also capable of possessing a patriotism and nobility of soul which compells respect and which must be harnessed to the needs of the country. The plays illustrate the change in the perception of Polish life during the eighteenth century and in due course affected Polish life as well, including the military.

Poland started the century as a large and reasonably prosperous country but one which was incapable of building a strong army because political paralysis prevented it; its weakness made it dependent on foreign powers which deepened its political incapacities. Slowly, Poles came to understand the negative effects of clinging to traditional liberties like the *liberum veto*. A program of reform and regeneration won out at the end of the century, too late to permit victories over Poland's neighbors who feared the reemergence of another great power in the region. The partitions ended Polish statehood for many years but the struggle ensured the continuation of a Polish nation based on noble leadership and a martial mythology which assimilated the lower classes as well. The experience of other central and eastern European countries suggests that Poland would have re-emerged after World War I even without the insurrectionary tradition fostered in 1794 and continued over the next century. But Poland would have emerged far less pugnacious and her historical path would have changed beyond recognition had patriotism and professionalism not combined to foster Poland's eighteenth century military revival.

FOOTNOTES

1. Jan Wimmer, *Wojsko rzeczypospolitej w dobie wojny polnocnej* (Warsaw 1956), pp. 75-83.
2. *Zarys dziejow wojskowości polskiej do roku 1864* (Warsaw, 1966), II, 160.
3. Jerzy Michalski, ed., *Historia Polski 1764-1795; Wybor Tekstow* (Warsaw, 1954), p. 77.
4. Konstanty Gorski, *Historya Piechoty* (Warsaw, 1893), pp. 100-10; Gorski, *Historya Artilleryi Polskiey* (Warsaw, 1902), pp. 160-73.
5. Marian Drozdowski, *Podstawy finansowe działalności państwowej w Polsce, 1764-1793* (Warsaw, 1975), pp. 51-2, 104-6, 112-5, 197-8; see also André Cor-

visier, *Armies and Societies in Europe, 1494-1789* (Bloomington, Indiana, 1979), p. 112.

6. Drozdowski, pp. 144-5.
7. Daniel Stone, "Commoners in the Polish Officer Corps in 1790", *East-Central European Society and War in the Pre-Revolutionary Eighteenth Century,* ed. by Gunther Rothenberg, Bela K. Kiraly and Peter F. Sugar (Boulder, Colo.: Social Science Monographs, 1982), pp. 238-50. This volume and other volumes in the series, War and Society in East Central Europe, include a number of articles in English, mostly by leading Polish scholars, surveying the field.
8. See Leonard Ratajczyk, *Wojsko i obronność Rzeczypospolitej 1788-1792* (Warsaw, 1975).
9. Jozef Andrzej Gierowski, "The Polish-Lithuanian Armies in the Confederations and Insurrections of the Eighteenth Centuries", *East Central European Society and War in the Pre-Revolutionary Eighteenth Century,* especially pp. 233-6.
10. See Emanuel Rostworowski, *Sprawa Aukcji Wojska na tle Sytuacji Politycznej Przed Sejmem Czteroletnim* (Warsaw, 1957).
11. Ratajczyk, *Wojskoi obronność,* p. 142.
12. Irene Sokol, "The American Revolution and Poland: A Bibliographical Essay", *Polish Review,* XII:3 (Summer 1967), pp. 3-17.
13. Tadeusz Kościuszko, *Dwie Relacje o Kampanii Polsko-Rosyjskiej 1792 Roku,* ed. by Piotr Bankowski, (Warsaw 1964).
14. Hugo Kollataj, *Listy ánonimowe (Cracow, 1954), I, 212; Emanuel Rostworowski, "Hugo Kollataj wobec Zagadnienia Obywatelskiej Sily Zbrojnej"* *Przeglad Historyczny* XLII (1951), 330-64.
15. Jerzy Kowecki, *Pospolite Ruszenie w Insurekcji 1794 R.* (Warsaw 1963), pp. 79-80ff.
16. "Zbieg z Milosci ku Rodzinie", *Drama Mieszczanska* (Warsaw 1955).
17. "Burmistrz Poznanski", *Drama Mieszczanska.*

# Part IV
# Western and Central Europe

# [12]

# The Distinctiveness of Gaelic Warfare, 1400–1750

*James Michael Hill*

In studying the art of war in early modern Europe, military historians generally have overlooked Gaelic Scotland and Ireland. Such an omission is understandable when one considers that the Highland Scots and the Irish inhabited the physical as well as the cultural fringes of Western civilization. When Michael Roberts argued a generation ago that European warfare from 1560 to 1660 had undergone significant changes, he made no mention of the Scots and the Irish. Since then others have built upon Roberts's conclusions, and with few exceptions they, too, have not figured the Gaels into the equation.[1] That is why it is refreshing to see Geoffrey Parker and Jeremy Black in their recent works, *The Military Revolution: Military Innovation and the Rise of the West, 1500–1800* and *A Military Revolution? Military Change and European Society 1550–1800*, respectively, devote some attention to Irish and Scottish warfare.[2] While the major powers led the way in bringing about changes both in tactics and strategy, and in the scale and the societal impact of war from the fifteenth through the eighteenth centuries, the military system of the Highlanders and the Irish continued to develop outside the mainstream. Simply put, the Gaels based their warfare on a fundamental combination of speed, mobility and primal shock power, rejecting the tenets of modern, scientific technology- and logistics-orientated warfare embraced by most other European nation-states.

The purpose of this article is to demonstrate the distinctiveness of Gaelic warfare by comparing and contrasting it with more conventional forms of warfare during the early modern period and to show that at least one small corner of Europe did not experience a 'military revolution'.

After the Swiss pikemen's rout of the Burgundian heavy cavalry in the 1470s, footsoldiers came to dominate European battlefields. Knightly combat had been based on personal prowess involving small forces because of the obvious economic and social restraints limiting the number of combatants. By the late Middle Ages, notes Michael Howard, 'the single knight expanded into a "lance", a team of half a dozen men, like the crew of some enormous battle tank. The whole apparatus came very expensive indeed.' As early as the Welsh uprisings in the mid-thirteenth century, feudal cavalry had proved all but useless against nimble guerrilla forces operating across rugged terrain. In fact, it was from the Welsh and the Scots in the thirteenth and early fourteenth centuries (e.g. the battles of Lewes, 1264 and Bannockburn, 1314) that the English learned the value of the longbow in the hands of skilled footsoldiers. The importance of infantry troops against heavy cavalry became evident about the same time in central Europe when the Swiss pikemen and halberdiers routed the Austrian chivalry at Morgarten (1315), and later at Laupen (1339) and Sempach (1386).[3]

The diminished role of feudal cavalry and the corresponding rise of the infantry in the fourteenth century made possible a dramatic increase in the size of armies among the major powers and, of course, also brought about changes in weaponry and tactics. The defeat of the French cavalry by the English longbow at Crécy (1346) and the slaughter of Charles the Bold's knights by Swiss pikemen more than a century later heralded another age of European warfare. The longbow remained an important weapon, especially within the British Isles (where archers were not dropped from the standard company formation until after 1589), but it was the pike that became 'queen of the battlefield'. By the end of the fifteenth century masses of pikemen 'were a necessary part of every serious armed force'. It had been discovered that phalanxes of pikemen could not only stop a charge of heavy cavalry, but could also be employed successfully against one another. Whereas the longbow, a missile weapon, was better suited for defence, in the hands of a determined attacker the pike dominated offensive infantry tactics in Europe until the late fifteenth and early sixteenth century.[4]

The rise in importance of infantry and the corresponding potential increase in army size ushered in the '[c]ommercialization of organized violence'. Armies were now paid wages. Mercenaries gradually replaced communal militia in the Italian states and feudal levies in trans-Alpine Europe. This commercialization of violence gradually diminished the role of the soldier skilled in what Parker calls the 'actions' of war, while at the same time it increased the importance of the art and science of war. Thus on the eve of the 'gunpowder revolution', European warfare already reflected the dominance of infantry and non-landed forms of wealth – two factors that eventually resulted in an expansion of the scale, destructiveness and expense of military conflict.[5]

While footsoldiers began to supersede cavalry on the Continent during the late Middle Ages, infantry remained the predominant element in Gaelic armies. The most important Gaelic infantry were the *gallóglaigh* – west Highland and Hebridean mercenaries who settled in Ireland from the late thirteenth through to the fifteenth century. The term *gallóglaigh* (Anglicized as 'gallowglass' or 'galloglas') literally means 'foreign' (*gall*) 'warrior' (*óglaigh*). *Gallóglaigh* troops first appeared in the Irish annals in 1290, but they had been employed by Irish chiefs since mid-century. They were a fierce admixture of Gaelic and Norse blood, and under the leadership of Angus Oge of the Isles they introduced a style of war that revolutionized Ireland's military system. Whereas the native Irish chiefs traditionally had depended on a general levy, similar to the Anglo-Saxon 'fyrd', to raise armies, the arrival of the *gallóglaigh* provided them with a permanent force of professional soldiers.[6]

Ireland in the late Middle Ages had no permanent military establishment. As a result, the Irish fought few formal, pitched battles in the open; they preferred various forms of guerrilla tactics utilizing the nimble, lightly armed and accoutred *kerne*. When Edward Bruce invaded Ireland in the early fourteenth century, he discovered that the Irish chiefs favoured running skirmishes with missile weapons (mainly bows and spears) instead of set-piece battles that necessitated the use of close-quarter blade weapons. This type of combat resulted in fewer casualties and made it attractive to a chief whose main objective was the acquisition of tenants rather than the wanton destruction of life and property. Conversely, the unequivocal objective of the *gallóglaigh* was the destruction of enemy armies. If there was a 'military revolution' within the Gaelic world, it was precipitated in part by the flood of Scottish mercenary troops to Ireland from c. 1300 to c. 1500.[7]

Most of the *gallóglaigh* bands in Ireland were under command of a warrior-captain and received their pay in the form of land-grants and *buannadha*, a system similar to coyne and livery wherein troops were billeted upon the people of a lordship. Other bands roamed the countryside at will, living off the land and hiring themselves out to the highest bidder. Such a system undoubtedly contributed to increased chaos in Ireland; however, the services of Scottish mercenaries were crucial in driving out the formidable Norman men-at-arms.[8] John Dymmok described the *gallóglaigh* as

> . . . picked men, of great and mighty bodies, cruel, without compassion. The greatest force of the battle consisteth in them, choosing rather to die than to yield; so that when it cometh to hardy blows, they are quickly slain, or win the field. They are armed with a shirt of mail, a skul [helmet], and a skeine; the weapon they use most is a battle-axe or halbert, six feet long, the blade whereof is somewhat like a shoemaker's knife, and without a pike; the stroke whereof is deadly where it lighteth. And being thus armed, reckoning to him a man for his harness bearer, and a boy to carry his provisions, he is named a sparre, of his weapons so called, eighty of which sparres make a battle of Gallowglass.[9]

Contemporary descriptions of the *gallóglaigh* reveal that they adopted the weaponry of their Norse ancestors, with the important exception of the bow and arrow. Both Vikings and *gallóglaigh* employed a variety of swords for close-quarter offensive combat, but the weapon that distinguished them from other warriors of the day was the long-handled, broad-bladed battle-axe. The *galló-glaigh* (and their sixteenth-century 'redshank' cousins) were noted for their deadly use of the famed Lochaber axe. As for defensive accoutrements, both Norsemen and Scots carried shields or targets (restricted, however, to troops wielding smaller, single-handed swords), mail shirts and iron helmets.[10]

One of the most important differences between Viking and *gallóglaigh* tactics concerns the use of missile weapons, particularly the bow and arrow. Typical Norse tactics, at the battle of Stiklestad (1030) for instance, involved the employment of two distinct types of troops with different functions. One contingent was armed primarily with bows and spears and opened the battle by discharging volleys of missiles to disorder or break the enemy's front. After the impact of this 'artillery' barrage, the shock troops advanced. Lightly accoutred and armed with swords and battle-axes, they charged from a stand of high ground. As the attack unfolded, the bowmen and spear-bearers stood as a reserve that could be deployed either offensively or defensively, depending upon the outcome of the initial assault.[11]

*Gallóglaigh* tactics can best be understood by a study of the battle of Knockdoe (appropriately meaning 'hill of the axes') in 1504.[12] The battle occurred on open ground. The *gallóglaigh* deployed on both wings in order to take advantage of their superior mobility, and in the centre to profit from their ability to deliver or absorb a shock assault. Even at this relatively late date the tactics of the Scots mercenaries had changed little from the past two centuries. Unlike the Norse, the *gallóglaigh* made no distinction between missile-bearing and close-quarter combat troops. Each Scottish warrior, or more precisely each 'sparre', combined the functions of both. Since bows and arrows were not part of the *gallóglaigh* arsenal, the opening volley consisted of a discharge of light spears or javelins. In place of a heavy missile volley to begin the fighting, the Scots mercenaries concentrated on delivering a powerful shock assault. And since there is no evidence that a reserve was left behind, the Scots obviously gambled on carrying the enemy position with the first attack. Such tactics required that each man be resolute in pressing home the charge, because disaster befell the entire army if it was repulsed. The Irish Lord Deputy, Sir Anthony St Leger, informed Henry VIII in 1543 that the *gallóglaigh* swore an oath before each battle not to abandon the field; they therefore remained 'the one part of an Irish army that could be entrusted to stand its ground to the end'.[13]

The late G. A. Hayes-McCoy's study of the role of Scottish mercenaries in Ireland until 1603 did not attempt to compare *gallóglaigh* traditions with contemporaneous European military institutions. Before about 1500 only among the Italian *condottieri* and the roving 'Great Companies' and the Swiss were there similar professional military organizations. But the respective societies that nurtured the *gallóglaigh* and the *condottieri* could not have been more dissimilar, at least on the surface: the Gaelic world was among Europe's most rural, non-commercial regions, while northern Italy arguably was its most urban and economically advanced. Yet both areas witnessed the rise of small, professional standing forces of infantry as efficient as any in Europe until the end of the fifteenth century.[14]

Gaelic and most pre-1500 European infantry forces differed

mainly in weaponry, tactics and the role of the individual on the battlefield. The Scots and Irish had no chivalric tradition; thus, cavalry played only a minor part in their military systems. A lack of suitable mounts and terrain (except in parts of central Ireland) for massed cavalry tactics, among other factors, undoubtedly deterred the Gaels from becoming expert horsemen. Instead they learned to fight on foot in bog, mountain and glen. Many Scots and Irish 'irregulars' were highly accomplished with the bow, but (with occasional exception) after the advent of the *gallóglaigh* they relegated it to second place behind the sword or axe. Among the Gaels the individual footsoldier was fast becoming a self-contained combat unit. Armed with sword or axe and ever mindful of honour, he acted under the inducements of personal reputation rather than of firm discipline. On the Continent, conversely, an increased tactical use of the pike necessitated an emphasis on the disciplined collective body rather than on the individual warrior — men 'who would act as cogs in a machine. . .'. Standard European warfare, then, was on its way to becoming a science. In the Gaelic world it remained an art.[15]

Charles VIII's invasion of Italy in the last decade of the fifteenth century brought about further changes in European warfare. From Fornovo (1494) to Pavia (1525), combat was uncharacteristically bloody and decisive. More men were engaged and more casualties resulted because of the preponderance of infantry and the advent of gunpowder weapons. But these factors alone did not ensure that warfare would be extremely bloody during this quarter-century. Rather, combat became so destructive because tactics had not yet been adapted to new technologies. The shock power of the pikemen's charge, which had dominated assault tactics for over a generation, was no longer effective on a field increasingly planted with fortifications and swept by the fire of hand-guns and artillery. These defensively-orientated tactical innovations, largely the work of the great Spanish captain Gonzalo de Córdoba, reaped sizeable rewards for his own troops at Cerignola (1503), for the French at Marignano (1515), and for the Spanish again at Bicocca (1522). In all these contests, superior firepower from behind strong field entrenchments broke the surge of attacking infantry and cavalry. The decline in use of pikes as effective offensive weapons and the corresponding rise in use of firearms as weapons of defence heralded a period when mainstream European warfare would be dominated by defensive tactics.'[16]

Barring such contests as Mühlberg (1547), Zutphen (1586), White Mountain (1620), and the First and Second Polish–Swedish wars (1600–11 and 1617–29), the decisive battle all but disappeared from western and central European battlefields between Pavia (1525) and Breitenfeld (1631). Several general developments account for this: the defensive superiority of combining firearms and elaborate methods of field entrenchment; the development in certain regions of the *trace italienne* – a new type of fortification that rendered ineffective sieges predicated exclusively on the use of artillery; and the extension of military entrepreneurship from northern Italy beyond the Alps. Together with the increased expense of waging war resulting from the sixteenth-century price revolution, these factors caused kings and captains in most parts of western and central Europe to seek ways other than battle to attain their military objectives. In fact, battle, some said, now became the hallmark of the incompetent general.[17]

The tactical employment of the two primary infantry weapons – the pike and the hand-gun – caused the century between Pavia and Breitenfeld to be marked, with important exceptions of course, by the indecisive battle. The development of the Spanish *tercio* in the first half of the sixteenth century, 'so far from producing a fruitful collaboration between [shot and pikes] . . . , succeeded only in inhibiting the characteristic qualities of each.' Such complex tactics also made infantry frequently shun close combat in favour of long-range musketry duels, and made decisions on the battlefield much more difficult to obtain. That firearms alone usually proved indecisive was shown, for instance, during the initial stages of the battle of Ceresole (1544), where the French and Imperial armies spent most of the day engaged in a rather ineffectual exchange of fire.[18]

Hand-held firearms – the arquebus, caliver and matchlock musket – because of their slow rate of fire, short range, relative inaccuracy and cumbersome nature, proved inadequate for offensive warfare in the hands of most European troops. The musket, largest of the three pieces, was powerful enough to penetrate the heaviest armour, but could not be fired without a fork-rest, which precluded its use except for defensive purposes. In the sixteenth century, the proper offensive role of firearms was seen as to disorganize the enemy in preparation for a massed pike assault.

Perhaps this limited and passive role prompted J.R. Hale to contend that firearms 'raised problems of tactics, equipment, and supply . . . , but they had little effect on the fortunes of campaigns. . .'. Hale's assertion is correct, but only from an offensive standpoint. The problems of logistics and immobility precluded firearms' advantageous use as weapons of attack. Thus, as the number of musketeers increased relative to the number of pikemen in European armies, the roles of the weapons underwent drastic changes: firepower became the central responsibility of both foot and horse, the latter being 'transformed . . . from an instrument of shock into one of mobile firepower', while the pikeman now functioned to form a secure barrier behind which the shot could reload. With the exception of small numbers of mounted arquebusiers or pistoleers, Spanish sword and buckler troops, and German *landsknecht* pikemen, conventional European armies could muster little mobility or shock power during this century.[19]

Artillery also was virtually useless for offensive warfare during the sixteenth century. Charles VIII of France put the first mobile field artillery into action during his 1494 invasion of Italy. Fornovo (1494), where the French defeated the Italian allies, was the first battle in which artillery played a major role, but Ravenna (1512) was the first contest actually decided by artillery. There, a French train of over fifty guns pounded the Spaniards' fortified lines, forcing them into a desperate attack in which they were annihilated by superior French firepower. Attacking Swiss pikemen were routed by entrenched French field guns on the second day at Marignano (1515). At the end of the century lighter, more mobile field guns began to appear. Maurice of Nassau improved the Dutch artillery arm by standardizing types (twenty-four-, twelve-, and six-pounders) and by using limbers to increase mobility.[20] But once Maurice's guns were placed in their battlefield positions, it was difficult to move them to support an infantry advance. Before 1600 artillery in field operations, like the matchlock musket, was of little use except in softening up a position before an attack or in defending a position against an enemy assault.

The defensive employment of hand-held firearms and artillery by most Continental powers after 1500 stood in sharp contrast to the continued offensive use of blade weapons by the Gaels. Pikes and firearms, so important in Continental military developments, did not find favour with the Highland Scots and Irish until the late sixteenth and early seventeenth century. Even then, both pike and musket were of secondary importance when compared to the broadsword and target (a small, round shield similar to the Spanish buckler). Since their introduction, firearms had been condemned by some as the weapons of cowards; but, as we have seen, they were eventually accepted on the battlefield by the most chivalrous element of society. In the Gaelic world firearms were never given equal standing with the claymore or the broadsword and target, weapons that if properly wielded earned the much-sought praise of the bards. Tudor and early Stuart armies lagged behind most Continental armies, but even England's and Lowland Scotland's best-trained and -armed troops could not stand up to the Gaels' blade-dominated offensive tactics. In fact, until the development of a reliable bayonet in the late seventeenth century, the success of both offensive and defensive combat throughout Europe depended on the attacking infantryman's competence with the sword or other hand-held blade weapons and the defender's ability to counter with a combination of pike and shot.[21]

While the changing roles of gunpowder and the pike and the new art of military fortification caused a re-examination of battlefield tactics by many European commanders between Pavia and Breitenfeld, the Highland Scots, and especially the redshanks, continued to practice the traditional heavy infantry tactics of the *gallóglaigh*. Meanwhile the Irish Gaels began to develop a new type of warfare based on superior mobility, surprise, and the use of firearms in guerrilla-style ambuscades. The resulting blend of shock power and finesse, coupled with the individual prowess of their warriors, gave Gaelic commanders from about 1550 to 1640 an offensive capability unparalleled on the European continent, except perhaps by certain elements in the Spanish and Swedish armies, the latter under the military reformer Gustavus Adolphus.

Shane O'Neill proved the effectiveness of the new style of Gaelic warfare by driving the English out of Ulster in the early 1560s and then by defeating his erstwhile allies, the MacDonnells of Antrim, at Glentaisie (Glenshesk) in 1565. The Scottish redshank army under James and Sorley Boy MacDonnell fought at Glentaisie in the traditional *gallóglaigh* manner, drawn up in formal alignment and employing mainly the Lochaber axe and the two-handed claymore. Shane O'Neill's troops — both heavy infantry and light skirmishers (*kerne*) — combined blade weapons and firearms with mobility, the element of surprise and a judicious use of terrain, thus drawing together the best offensive tactical elements of the traditional and the new Gaelic warfare. There were numerous similarities between the weaponry and tactics of the two sides at Glentaisie, but there were enough differences to justify a claim that Shane O'Neill had begun to revamp the Gaelic military system. When he abandoned his new formula, he was soundly defeated by the O'Donnells at Farsetmore in 1567. Hugh Roe O'Neill, second earl of Tyrone, built on his uncle's success in the 1590s at Clontibret, Yellow Ford and the Moyry Pass against the best lieutenants England could field. He combined stealth, speed, formational flexibility, firepower and, above all, shock tactics. O'Neill met defeat only when he tried to fight the English at Kinsale (1601) on open terrain and under conventional circumstances. By attempting to form up his veteran Ulster troops into the unfamiliar Spanish *tercio*, O'Neill forfeited the offensive striking power of the Gaels and was routed by the combined cavalry and infantry of Charles Blount, Lord Mountjoy.[22]

Until the middle of the seventeenth century the Gaels had searched for the proper combination of weaponry and tactics to suit their military organization. In the three-and-a-half centuries since the advent of the *gallóglaigh*, their way of war had developed differently from that of the Continental powers: the Highland Scots and Irish basically resisted most of the ideas and technologies that constitute the foundations of Roberts's alleged 'military revolution'. Unlike some of their Continental counterparts, for instance, Gaelic armies did not increase in size and complexity as a result of Europe's general economic growth and expanded revenues. Neither did they redefine their military strategies based on these and other factors, such as the influential (though essentially defensive) innovations of Maurice of Nassau. There were, however, some definite changes in Gaelic tactics which resulted from an acceptance of new gunpowder technologies. When the Gaels finally did embrace gunpowder as an integral part of their battlefield tactics, it was in a manner peculiarly their own. Perhaps better than any of their contemporaries in Europe, the Scots and Irish solved what Roberts defines as the tactical problem 'of how to combine missile weapons with close-action; how to unite hitting-power, mobility and defensive strength'. Their use of hand-held firearms was not a sacrifice of offensive shock power and mobility in order to keep in step with modern, defensive- and siege-orientated military theory and practice; rather, it was an effective blending of old tactics with new technology, creating a type of warfare that for the next century was distinct from any other practised in western Europe.[23]

The military reforms of Maurice and Gustavus Adolphus in the final years of the sixteenth and the first one-third of the seventeenth century had little bearing on the development of warfare in the Scottish Highlands or Ireland. Though Maurice's introduction of a new infantry unit of more manageable size – the 550-man battalion – parälleled the traditional tactical organization of the clan regiment, this was one of few similarities between his style of modern military organization and that of the Gaels. While both drew up their forces in wide, shallow formations, the Maurician battle-line, according to Roberts, 'was essentially passive . . . [and] not apt for the offensive. . . . Of an offensive tactic he had little idea; of a campaign culminating in annihilating victory, none at all.' Since Gustavus Adolphus is his champion, Roberts thinks that Maurice fell short of solving the great military problems of the day, and left the great Swede 'to restore, both to horse and foot, the capacity for the battle-winning tactical offensive. . .'.[24]

Gustavus Adolphus increased the proportion of blade (pikes) to missile (musket) weapons among his infantry 'squadrons' (units comparable to Maurice's 'battalions') and introduced the salvo for more missile shock power. He increased the effectiveness of his infantry by introducing shorter and lighter matchlock muskets, but he did not introduce the more advanced wheel-lock or snaphance musket. Neither did he abolish the use of the cumbersome fork-rest. He initiated the use of mobile field artillery, two- and three-pounder 'leather guns', and restored the striking power of the cavalry arm, which by the early 1630s made up fully one-third of his army. The advance of Swedish musketeers, pikemen, and mobile leather guns firing pre-loaded cartridges of 'hail shot' (canister) was designed to give Gustavus Adolphus a 'fire-shock', which he intended to exploit with his pikemen (standing at a 2:3 ratio to muskets, as compared to the standard seventeenth-century ratio of 1:2 pikes to muskets), who were drilled to charge the enemy after a volley rather than to stand by passively and defend the shot. But hand-held firearms, including those carried by the cavalry, and artillery constituted his main capability. The concerted volleys of Gustavus Adolphus's musketeers alone, for instance, put out such a weight of fire at Breitenfeld that they broke the charge of the Imperial cavalry. When the regimental artillery was added, the Swedes enjoyed greater firepower than any previous army. Gustavus Adolphus's reforms did not lead to an increase in his infantry's speed, mobility and close-combat shock power; rather, they led to increased firepower, hardly an offensive revolution. His heavily-laden footsoldiers could not keep pace with the horse advancing at a trot. It was necessary, therefore, for the latter to move ahead very slowly, thus reducing mobility and shock. Nor could the leather guns, not to mention the heavier artillery, keep pace with the infantry except over ideal terrain for short distances. Roberts admits, then, that under Gustavus Adolphus 'the dilemma — speed or firepower — remained unresolved. . .'.[25]

To credit Maurice and Gustavus Adolphus completely with bringing back to European warfare organizational flexibility, offensive tactics and the decisive battle is to ignore contemporaneous developments in Gaelic warfare, however outside the mainstream such changes might have been. At the time of Gustavus Adolphus's death at Lützen (1632), the Gaels were about to begin a series of tactical innovations that would usher in what some have termed a 'Golden Age' (1644–1746) in their military development. David Stevenson believes the Highland charge was introduced in Ireland at the battle of the Laney (1642) by the military adventurer Alasdair MacColla. The Highland charge, as it evolved over the next century, was the centrepiece of Gaelic tactics. Primarily dependent on the broadsword and target, the charge involved the use of the musket (without the fork-rest) as an *offensive* weapon. Other European military systems would not begin to consider personal firearms as offensive weapons until the development of a reliable socket bayonet near the end of the century. Even then the musket–bayonet combination was more effective as a blade than as a missile weapon. Until the eighteenth century, hand-held firearms continued to be mainly defensive missile weaponry employed en masse by well-drilled soldiers arrayed in linear formations and lacking any sort of expertise in close-quarter combat. The Highland charge further distinguished itself from Continental tactics by emphasizing both the new linear and the old columnar attack formations, a flexibility that eluded most European tacticians until the eighteenth century.[26]

From 1644 to 1746, the Gaels won eight major battles by employing variations of the Highland charge, thereby disproving Roberts's assertion that after Gustavus Adolphus's death the 'careful combination of firepower and shock became rarer. . .'. Arrayed in line formation, ideally on a stand of high ground, they advanced rapidly toward the enemy with broadsword, target and musket. When somewhere between twenty to sixty yards distant, they fired a wild musket volley designed to confuse the defenders with lead and smoke. Muskets were then cast away, wedges or rough columns twelve to fifteen men wide hastily formed, and broadswords drawn for hand-to-hand combat. The musket volley, when followed quickly by the impact of the charge at several *Schwerpunkten* along the enemy line, usually routed numerically superior British armies that lacked defence in depth, expertise with blade weapons, and sufficient time to reload their pieces. The tactics of the Highland charge often resulted in the 'decisive battle', especially when the enemy attempted to fight without the benefits of field fortifications or well-served artillery.[27]

Gaelic warfare during the period 1644 to 1746 emphasized the frontal shock attack across rugged terrain, with the broadsword – not the musket – as the principal weapon. The combined use of blade and missile weapons in carrying out this type of offensive tactics set the Gaels apart from most other European armies as late as the mid-eighteenth century. Furthermore, while other armies were beginning to be weighed down by sheer size and complicated logistical requirements, the Highland Scots and Irish retained great freedom of manoeuvrability, speed and range. The Gaels were not restricted to siege warfare or frontal assaults because of a lack of mobility; rather, they enjoyed the tactical flexibility that allowed them to choose their method of attack – frontal or flank. Frontal attacks depended on shock power, flank attacks initially on superior mobility. Frequently, however, the Gaels combined the two capabilities, using mobility to enhance their shock power by forcing an enemy to turn 'front to flank', thus disrupting his formation and sowing confusion in his ranks. Highland armies indeed could be an effective combination of regular line troops and light 'rangers'. This sort of tactical combination was employed successfully at Auldearn (1645), Kilsyth (1645), Killiecrankie (1689) and Prestonpans (1745). In the remaining six major engagements during the period – Tippermuir (1644), Aberdeen (1644), Inverlochy (1645), Sheriffmuir (1715),

Falkirk (1746) and Culloden (1746) — the Gaels chose, for better or worse, the brutal frontal assault.[28]

Several eighteenth-century French captains — the Chevalier de Folard, the Comte de Guibert and Marshal de Saxe — understood that most ancien regime armies lacked the Gaels' mobility to force an enemy to give battle and their offensive shock power to defeat him. Folard was dissatisfied with the results of linear warfare and tried to 'devise tactical changes . . . to add flexibility and shock to the line's firepower'. He called for massive assault columns with half the troops armed with pikes.[29] Guibert advocated use of both line and column attack tactics, but realized that the column had limited shock power because it was made up of individual soldiers and hence was not a solid, cohesive mass.[30] Indeed, the massive columns envisioned by both Folard and Guibert were never widely accepted in the eighteenth century. They were judged deficient in firepower (which should not have been the *ultima ratio* for a column assault anyway), vulnerable to crossfire, and difficult to maintain in proper order once the assault was made. And in most cases, the formation and maintenance of attacking columns were matters of pure chance rather than of efficient leadership, as with the English at Fontenoy (1745).[31]

Saxe's views were more in line with Gaelic tactical doctrine and practice. He sought to enhance mobility, flexibility and shock power by first organizing mixed 'legions' of four or five regular and light regiments. Contrary to Folard's assault with massive columns, Saxe's attack would be initiated by light skirmishers, who would draw the enemy's fire, forcing them to reload in the face of a furious bayonet charge by regular troops. Saxe downplayed the effects of musketry against an attacking force except at extremely close range. Which army gains the victory, he asked, 'the one that gives its fire in advancing, or the other that reserves it? Men of any experience . . . give it in favour of the latter. . .'. He writes of having

> . . . seen whole vollies fired without even killing four men, . . . and if any single discharge was ever so violent as to disable an enemy from advancing afterward, to take ample revenge by pouring in his fire, and at the same instant rushing in with fixed bayonets, it is by this method only that numbers are to be destroyed and victories obtained.[32]

Saxe's tactics closely resemble the Highland charge; however, his dismissal of the horrible effects of musketry and grape- and canister-firing artillery levelled at an attacker within a range of thirty to fifty yards is foolhardy (as it was with the Jacobite high command at Culloden). Despite Saxe's call for the bayonet charge in the face of enemy fire, most evidence suggests that close-quarter combat with blade weapons and musket-butts was unusual in eighteenth-century European warfare. A contemporary British observer wrote that 'There is not probably an instance of modern troops being engaged in close combat; our tactics, produced by the introduction of firearms, are opposed to such a mode of action. . . .' A French authority maintained that 'firearms are the most destructive category of weapon, and now [1749] more than ever. If you need convincing, just go to the hospital and you will see how few men have been wounded by cold steel as opposed to firearms.'[33]

Gaelic warfare faced a crisis in the latter years of the seventeenth century that was brought on by tactical and technological improvements and changes on Europe's battlefields. The introduction of the socket bayonet gave the infantryman a close-quarters blade weapon for defence and eliminated the need for massed pike formations. Also, the coming of the lighter and more reliable flintlock musket allowed the infantry nearly to double its rate of fire. This development prompted a decrease in the number of firing ranks generally from five to three, meaning that more men could fire at once. Reinforced by light field artillery, which commonly was loaded with grape-shot or canister, the standard European infantry battalion by the beginning of the Nine Years' War (1688–97) possessed tremendous defensive capabilities. The increase in the effectiveness of their missile weapons tended to reinforce the infantry's role as a provider of static firepower. Hand-to-hand combat between footsoldiers remained unusual on European battlefields even during the large-scale campaigns of the War of the Spanish Succession (1702–14). David Chandler notes that during that conflict, despite the growing importance of infantry, 'most of the great engagements . . . were won, in the last analysis, by the cavalry, closely supported by the foot.'[34]

Since the Gaels most always took the tactical offensive on foot, and since a vastly improved British army had learned, especially after 1688, to combine effectively the infantry, cavalry, and artillery arms, the Highland charge no longer routed opposing armies with the ease that it had between 1644 and 1689. The battle of Killiecrankie (1689), though a convincing Gaelic tactical victory, cost the Highland army a stunning thirty per cent loss (600 of 1900 engaged). When compared with their lower casualty rate during the campaigns of Montrose and MacColla in Scotland in 1644–5 (e.g. at Inverlochy in 1645 the Royalist clans lost only 200 of 1500 men engaged), Gaelic losses at Killiecrankie give evidence that general improvements in defensive-orientated warfare could blunt (and eventually break) the fiercest offensive tactics.[35]

While most European infantry commanders between 1688 and 1750 continued to stress static firepower over the assault, a succession of Gaelic captains, along with Charles XII of Sweden, still preferred the attack. All, however, regularly faced much worse situations than that of John Graham, Viscount Dundee, at Killiecrankie: they attacked opponents who were armed with improved muskets, bayonets and artillery, and who practised disciplined methods of fire-control. Offensive infantry tactics similar to the Highland charge allowed Charles XII to defeat a much larger Russian force at Narva (1700), but he met defeat against static Russian firepower arrayed behind strong field fortifications at Poltava (1709). Fortunately for the Gaels, their British adversaries from 1689 to 1746 never once attempted to mimic the Russians by throwing up entrenchments to absorb the shock of the Highland charge. It remained, therefore, for the modernizing British army to devise another way of dealing with the Gaels' military strength.[36]

The relative indecisiveness of formal European combat stemmed from the growing complexities and ritualistic nature of eighteenth-century warfare. With the exception of conclusive contests such as Steenkerke (1692), Almanza (1707) and Malplaquet (1709), and the battles of the Gaels and the Swedes, warfare tended to be a slow, cautious and indecisive affair even under the most favourable circumstances. This can be demonstrated by examining the career of one of the most capable commanders of the era, John Churchill, Duke of Marlborough. Marlborough, unlike most of his contemporaries, disdained siege warfare and elaborate manoeuvre-for-manoeuvre's-sake, and sought to fight decisive battles whenever possible. Moreover, he frequently used mobile tactics on the flanks or wings of his enemy to achieve, or at least to set up, his victories. The coup de grace commonly came with a massed frontal cavalry assault, since infantry charges were difficult to execute (the attackers lacked hand-to-hand combat skills) and because any sort of fire control was nearly impossible to maintain. A British authority in 1727 wrote of this problem:

> In advancing towards the enemy, it is with great difficulty that the officers can prevent the men (but more particularly when they are fired at) from taking their arms, without orders, off from their shoulders, and firing at too great a distance. How much more difficult must it be to prevent their firing, when they have their arms in their hands already cocked, and their fingers on the triggers? I won't say it is impossible though I look upon it to be almost so.

In the early eighteenth century Marlborough favoured the use of superior mobility and infantry shock power, but frequently found that he could not escape the bonds of defensively orientated war.[37]

Like his Continental counterparts, Marlborough enjoyed the resources of the modern nation-state; he was plagued, too, by their very weight. According to Geoffrey Parker, the

> . . . foundation of the Bank of England, Parliament's guarantee of all government loans, and the organization of a sophisticated money market in London made it possible for a British army of unprecedented size — 90,000 men — to fight overseas for years [during the War of the Spanish Succession]. . . .[38]

But those abundant resources also made war a rather ponderous undertaking. A typical eighteenth-century infantryman carried well over sixty pounds of equipment (including weapons), which meant that he could carry almost no rations. Such a load limited a day's march to no more than fifteen miles over hospitable terrain. This, in turn, created the need for large numbers of transport vehicles which further slowed the advance, if for no other reason than by making it necessary to provide tons of forage for thousands of draught animals. If armies, replete with large contingents of cavalry and artillery, became too large to be supported by pack trains, logistics dictated either living directly from the land or establishing supply depots or magazines. The former alternative obviously was impracticable for large forces except for short periods in certain very productive areas such as the Netherlands, Picardy or northern Italy. The latter alternative certainly made more sense, but greatly reduced an army's range of operations. Warfare, then, with all of its trappings of modernity, was conducted 'with . . . deadening slowness and lack of decisiveness'. Only a Marlborough or a Frederick the Great 'proved occasionally capable of transcending these . . . limitations, and thus returned something of pace, colour and decisiveness to the conduct of warfare'.[39]

Where the Continental powers' ability to conduct warfare was impaired by the sheer size and complexity of their armies after 1700, the Gaels continued to fight much the same as always. Some similarities existed between the two military systems, but it must not be forgotten that even greater differences separated them. The Gaels did not have the modern nation-state from which to draw organizational, economic or technological benefits. These fundamental shortcomings precluded the development of any sort of effective, long-term strategies on the part of Gaelic chiefs or commanders. Thus, the Highland Scots and Irish concerned themselves more with the short-term tactical aspects of warfare, a factor that allowed them to win most of the battles and still lose the wars. When the Gaels did gain access to modern implements of war, such as firearms or artillery, they either relegated them to places of secondary importance (as in the Highland charge) or neglected them altogether. But by eschewing the engines and theories of modern war, they were able to field highly mobile, though small, armies usually commanded by men who led by example rather than from a secure position in the rear. Logistics, then, little concerned the Gaels, as they had need of but limited quantities of shot and powder, fodder, or other necessities and niceties so common among conventional armies. The resulting mobility permitted them to range far and wide in virtually any season, traversing the rugged, boggy terrain of their homeland and frequently surprising the slow-footed English and their allies. Because of their mobility and ability to surprise the enemy, the Gaels' battles usually were short, but decisive. At Prestonpans (1745), for example, the Highlanders took only about fifteen minutes to maul Sir John Cope's army. And because of the short duration of their battles, the Gaels, at least before 1689, suffered relatively light casualties. But perhaps most importantly, they enjoyed the option of choosing the type of battle they fought: flank attack or frontal assault.[40]

The British solution to the Highland charge arose from improvements in eighteenth-century warfare that hitherto had restricted the scope of offensive tactics and strategy on the Continent. In the end it took a force of well-trained, steady British regulars, armed with the socket bayonet and 'Brown Bess' musket, supported by mobile field artillery and cavalry, to break the shock power of the intrepid Gaelic offensive. The Gaels, however, contributed to their own undoing in no small manner. Despite superb mobility, rather primitive weaponry, and small armies, they chose variations of the frontal assault time after time against an enemy who already was quantitatively superior and quickly was becoming qualitatively competitive. Even under the best commanders, few eighteenth-century armies won victories with the frontal assault and close-quarter tactics.

Under such circumstances it is indeed remarkable that from 1689 to 1746 the Gaels usually won on the tactical level. But the headlong frontal assault was finally and completely broken on the open killing ground of Culloden Moor in 1746 by a combination of the Duke of Cumberland's infantry, cavalry and artillery fighting under conventional circumstances with methodical defensive tactics. Unlike at Falkirk some months earlier, the Highlanders at Culloden were not in possession of suitable ground over which to carry out their traditional attack tactics. But even at Falkirk, where they 'held almost every conceivable tactical advantage, . . . [the Gaels] did not destroy the enemy as their forebears had done in earlier campaigns'. The British army by mid-century could no longer be overwhelmed by the Highland charge. At Culloden, Lord George Murray, Prince Charles Edward Stuart's most able lieutenant, realized that if the Gaels were forced to fight on the open moor they would be slaughtered. Murray, a widely travelled professional soldier, knew that modern weaponry (the Brown Bess, socket or sleeve bayonet, and grape- and canister-firing field artillery) gave defensive tactics nearly every advantage over offensive tactics on a formal, conventional battlefield. Since the prince ignored Murray's pleas to move the Highland army from the open moor, the Jacobites were left to do the only thing they knew: attack, broadsword in hand. And the subsequent carnage testified to the superiority of hot lead and British discipline over cold steel and Gaelic impetuosity, at least for the time being.[41]

Developments in Gaelic warfare from 1400 to 1750 generally have been omitted from the writings of those who expound the theory of a 'military revolution' in early modern Europe. This is understandable, especially when one considers that most contemporary observers had little interest in the Scottish Highlands and Ireland. But the omission is unfortunate. The Gaelic system, because it did not fit the mould established by major Continental powers, offers a unique perspective for the study of the conduct of war in early modern Europe. The true distinctiveness of Gaelic tactical warfare until its demise at Culloden (and its resurrection as a part of post-1750 British tactics, especially in the French and Indian War in North America) lay in its stubborn insistence on offensive combat. Guibert might just as well have been thinking of the Highlanders and the dreadful effects of their attack when he wrote a generation after Culloden: 'The closer you approach the enemy the more fearsome you become, and a coward, who will fire at a brave man at one hundred paces, will not dare to so much as aim at him at close range.'[42] When attacking not 'cowards' but steady regulars, the Scots and Irish faced seemingly insurmountable defensive odds brought on by technological and organizational innovations that fundamentally altered the nature of European conflict until the age of Napoleon. And it took no less a figure than the Corsican to revitalize and reintroduce a style of tactical offensive warfare based on mobility, flexibility and shock power that the Gaels, in their simple manner, had never abandoned.

## Notes

1. Michael Roberts, *The Military Revolution, 1560–1660* (Belfast 1956), passim; Geoffrey Parker, 'The "Military Revolution", 1560–1660 — A Myth?', *Journal of Modern History*, Vol. 48 (June 1976), 195–214.

2. Geoffrey Parker, *The Military Revolution: Military Innovation and the Rise of the West, 1500–1800* (Cambridge 1988), 29–36, 51–2, 67–8, 152; Jeremy Black, *A Military Revolution? Military Change and European Society, 1550–1800* (London 1991), passim.

3. Michael Howard, *War in European History* (Oxford 1976), 3, 11, 15.

4. Sir Charles Oman, *The Art of War in the Middle Ages*, revised and edited by John H. Beeler (Ithaca and London 1953), 128–9; George Gush, *Renaissance Armies, 1480–1650*, 2nd edn (Cambridge 1982), 10; Howard, *War in European History*, 15; Parker, 'Myth?', 207.

5. Wiliam H. McNeill, *The Pursuit of Power: Technology, Armed Force, and Society since A.D. 1000* (Chicago 1982), 69; Michael Mallett, *Mercenaries and Their Masters: Warfare in Renaissance Italy* (Totowa NJ 1974), 2; Geoffrey Parker, *The Army of Flanders and the Spanish Road, 1567–1659* (Cambridge 1972), 13.

6. G.A. Hayes-McCoy, *Scots Mercenary Forces in Ireland, 1565–1603* (Dublin 1937), 5–8, 12–17; Andrew McKerral, 'West Highland Mercenaries in Ireland', *Scottish Historical Review*, Vol. 30 (April 1951), 1–14.

7. J.F. Lydon, 'The Bruce Invasion of Ireland', *Historical Studies*, Vol. 4

(1963), 111–25; Katherine Simms, 'Warfare in the Medieval Gaelic Lordships', *Irish Sword*, Vol. 12 (1975–6), 98–108.

8. G.A. Hayes-McCoy, *Irish Battles* (London 1969), 48–53; Hayes-McCoy, *Scots Mercenary Forces*, 23–5, 58, 73.

9. John Dymmok, *A Treatice of Ireland*, edited by Rev. Richard Butler (Dublin 1842), 7.

10. Johannes Brøndsted, *The Vikings*, translated by Kalle Skov (Harmondsworth 1965), 119–25; Gwyn Jones, *A History of the Vikings* (London and New York 1968), passim; Hayes-McCoy, *Scots Mercenary Forces*, 15–18; Edmund Spenser, *A View of the Present State of Ireland*, edited by W.L. Renwick (Oxford 1970), 117; Dymmok, *Treatice*, 7; Sir James Ware, *The Antiquities and History of Ireland*, 2 vols (London 1714), II: 161.

11. Brøndsted, *Vikings*, 103–4, 124; Jones, *Vikings*, 384.

12. Hayes-McCoy, *Irish Battles*, 48–67.

13. Hayes-McCoy, *Irish Battles*, 61–3; Dymmok, *Treatice*, 7; London, Public Record Office, State Papers, Ireland, St Leger to the King, 6 April 1543, SP 60/11/2 (hereafter cited as SP).

14. Hayes-McCoy, *Scots Mercenary Forces*, passim; Mallett, *Mercenaries*, 25–50; McNeill, *Pursuit of Power*, 77.

15. London, Lambeth Palace Library, Carew MSS, Sir Henry Sidney to Sir Francis Walsingham, 1 March 1583, Vol. 601, f. 89; Parker, 'Myth?', 196.

16. Sir Charles Oman, *A History of the Art of War in the Sixteenth Century* (New York 1937), 105–207; Howard, *War in European History*, 26–8, 33; Parker, 'Myth?', 207; J.R. Hale, *War and Society in Renaissance Europe, 1450–1620* (London and New York 1985), 46–74; Gerald de Gaury, *The Grand Captain, Gonzalo de Cordoba* (London 1955), 83–6.

17. Howard, *War in European History*, 26–7, 34, 37; J.R. Hale, 'The Early Development of the Bastion: An Italian Chronology, c. 1450–c. 1534', in J.R. Hale et al., eds, *Europe in the Late Middle Ages* (Evanston IN 1965), 466–94; Michael Roberts, 'Gustav Adolf and the Art of War', in Michael Roberts, ed., *Essays in Swedish History* (Minneapolis 1967), 56–81.

18. Roberts, 'Gustav Adolf', 59; Oman, *Art of War in the Sixteenth Century*, 229–43.

19. H.C.B. Rogers, *Weapons of the British Soldier* (London 1960), 45–53; Gush, *Renaissance Armies*, 11–12; J.R. Hale, 'Gunpowder and the Renaissance: An Essay in the History of Ideas', in C.H. Carter, ed., *From the Renaissance to the Counter-Reformation: Essays in Honor of Garrett Mattingly* (New York 1965), 114; Roberts, 'Gustav Adolf', 59; Howard, *War in European History*, 34; Theodore Ropp, *War in the Modern World* (New York 1962), 27.

20. Gush, *Renaissance Armies*, 109.

21. James Michael Hill, *Celtic Warfare, 1595–1763* (Edinburgh 1986), passim; Hale, 'Gunpowder', 120–1; C.G. Cruickshank, *Elizabeth's Army*, 2nd edn (Oxford 1966), 1.

22. Cyril Falls, *Elizabeth's Irish Wars* (London 1950; reprint edn, New York 1970), passim; Hayes-McCoy, *Irish Battles*, passim; Rev. George Hill, *An Historical Account of the MacDonnells of Antrim* (Belfast 1873), 132–40; Shane O'Neill to Lord Justice, 2 May 1565, SP 63/13/34; Sir William Fitzwilliam to Cecil, 16 May 1565, SP 63/13/38; Shane O'Neill to Sir Thomas Cusake, 22 May 1565, SP 63/13/48; Captain Power to Cecil, 27 December 1601, SP 63/210/260; Lord Mountjoy

and Council to Lord Chancellor and Council, 1 January 1602, SP 63/210/1,i; Captain Wynfield to Cecil, 25 December 1601, SP 63/209/255; Dublin, National Library of Ireland, MS 669, f. 11.

23. Parker, 'Myth?', 206–7; Michael Roberts, 'The Military Revolution, 1560–1660', in Roberts, ed., *Essays in Swedish History*, 196; Gush, *Renaissance Armies*, 106–10.

24. Parker, *Military Revolution*, 33–4; Roberts, 'Gustav Adolf', 52.

25. Roberts, 'Gustav Adolf', 60–2, 65–70; Parker, *Military Revolution*, 33–4; Gush, *Renaissance Armies*, 113; Theodore A. Dodge, *Great Captains, Gustavus Adolphus* (Boston and New York 1895), 42–4.

26. David Stevenson, *Alasdair MacColla and the Highland Problem in the Seventeenth Century* (Edinburgh 1980), passim; Roberts, 'Gustav Adolf', 74; David, Lord Elcho, *A Short History of the Affairs of Scotland in the Years 1744, 1745, 1746*, edited by Evan Charteris (Edinburgh 1907; reprint edn 1973), 460; Steven Ross, *From Flintlock to Rifle: Infantry Tactics, 1740–1866* (London 1979), 25; Christopher Duffy, *The Military Experience in the Age of Reason* (London and New York 1987), 99, writes that the 'strength of well-disciplined armies lay not in the motivation or prowess of individuals, but in the capacity for collective action'.

27. Roberts, 'Gustav Adolf', 75; Hill, *Celtic Warfare*, 45–150; Major-General Hugh MacKay, *Memoirs of the War Carried on in Scotland and Ireland, 1689–1691*, edited by Maitland Club (Edinburgh 1833), 51–2. A well-trained soldier in the mid-eighteenth century could carry out the complicated tasks of priming, loading and firing his flintlock musket two to three times a minute under optimum battlefield conditions. H.L. Blackmore, *British Military Firearms, 1650–1850* (London 1961), 277; H. Bland, *A Treatise of Military Discipline* (London 1727), 19–34.

28. Hill, *Celtic Warfare*, 45–150. A description of the brutal effectiveness of the Highland charge at Killiecrankie is found in Henry Jenner, ed., *Memoirs of the Lord Viscount Dundee, the Highland Clans, and the Massacre of Glenco, and etc.* (London 1908), 20: 'Many . . . officers and soldiers were cut down through the skull and neck, to the very breasts; others had skulls cut off above the ears. . . . Some had both their bodies and cross belts cut through at one blow; pikes and small swords were cut like willows. . . .' For the most recent study of the Scottish theatre during the War of the Three Kingdoms, see Stuart Reid, *The Campaigns of Montrose* (Edinburgh 1990).

29. Ross, *Flintlock to Rifle*, 33. For the Chevalier de Folard's ideas concerning columns, see J. Colin, *L' Infantrie au XVIII^e siècle: la tactique* (Paris 1907), 36–8.

30. J.A.H. Guibert, *Défense du systême de guerre moderne ou réfutation complette du systême de M. de M. . . . D. . . .* , 2 vols (Neuchâtel 1779), I: 169–71.

31. Duffy, *Military Experience in the Age of Reason*, 199.

32. Herman Maurice de Saxe, *Reveries or Memoirs upon the Art of War*, translated by W. Faucett (London 1757), quoted from Geoffrey Simcox, ed., *War, Diplomacy, and Imperialism 1618–1763* (New York and London 1973), 187–8.

33. W. Dalrymple, *Tacticks* (Dublin 1782), 113; translated from J.F. Puységur, *Art de guerre par principes et par règles*, 2 vols (Paris 1749), I: 227.

34. Roberts, 'Gustav Adolf', 75; B.P. Hughes, *Firepower: Weapons Effectiveness on the Battlefield, 1630–1850* (London 1974), 10–11; David Chandler, *The Art of Warfare in the Age of Marlborough* (New York 1976), 115. For a thorough examination of the development of the British army under William III, see John Childs, *The British Army of William III, 1689–1702* (Manchester 1987).

35. Hill, *Celtic Warfare*, 54, 64–79; Paul Hopkins, *Glencoe and the End of the Highland War* (Edinburgh 1986), 157–61; the Marchioness of Tullibardine, ed., *A Military History of Perthshire*, 2 vols (Perth 1908), I: 266; John Spalding, *Memorialls of the Trubles in Scotland and in England, A.D. 1624–A.D. 1645*, edited by Spalding Club, 2 vols (Aberdeen 1850–1), II: 444–5; George Wishart, *The Memoirs of James, Marquis of Montrose, 1639–1650*, edited by A.B. Murdoch and H.F.M. Simpson (London 1893), 85; Patrick Gordon, *A Short Abridgement of Britane's Distemper, from the yeare of God 1639 to 1649*, edited by Spalding Club (Aberdeen 1844), 101–2.

36. Chandler, *Art of Warfare*, 127–8; F.G. Bengtsson, *Charles XII* (London 1960), 85–90.

37. R. Ernest DuPuy and Trevor N. DuPuy, *The Encyclopedia of Military History from 3500 B.C. to the Present*, 2nd rev. edn (New York 1986), 608–12; David Chandler, *Marlborough as Military Commander* (New York 1973), passim; C.T. Atkinson, *Marlborough and the Rise of the British Army* (New York and London 1921), 222–36, 285–97, 339–44, 398–406; Bland, *Treatise of Military Discipline*, 80.

38. Parker, 'Myth?', 213.

39. Duffy, *Military Experience in the Age of Reason*, 168; M.S. Anderson, *War and Society in Europe of the Old Regime 1618–1789* (Leicester and New York 1988), 36–45; Ropp, *War in the Modern World*, 30–1; Chandler, *Art of Warfare*, 14–15.

40. Hill, *Celtic Warfare*, 2–4, 17, 22–44, 45–63, 64–79, 80–99, 127–56; Katherine Tomasson and Francis Buist, *Battles of the '45* (London 1962), 67–9.

41. Hughes, *Firepower*, 10–11, 26, 35–6, 81–5; Hill, *Celtic Warfare*, 140–50; Jeremy Black, *Culloden and the '45* (London and New York 1990), passim.

42. Translated from J.A.H. Guibert, *Essai général de tactique*, 2 vols (Paris 1772), I: 216.

*James Michael Hill*

is Associate Professor of History at Stillman College, Tuscaloosa, Alabama, and Visiting Associate Professor of History at the University of Alabama, Tuscaloosa. He is the author of *Celtic Warfare, 1595–1763* (Edinburgh 1986), and of several scholarly articles and book reviews in UK, Irish and US journals.

# [13]

# The Army of Lombardy and the Resilience of Spanish Power in Italy in the Reign of Carlos II (1665–1700) (Part I)

*Christopher Storrs*

## I

It is an extraordinary paradox that the later seventeenth century, an era in which historians have traditionally identified the Spanish Succession as crucial to European international relations, should still lack a basic account, far less a thorough scholarly assessment, of Spanish foreign policy concerns, methods and achievements. At many important points, even the basic details of Spanish policy in the reign of the last Habsburg, Carlos II (1665–1700), remain obscure. In part, this neglect of Spanish foreign policy in the later seventeenth century is merely symptomatic of a general neglect of that larger transitional epoch (1665–1746) which a leading English-speaking historian of Spain described a generation ago as the 'dark ages' of modern Spanish historiography.[1] It also reflects a widely held view that Spain – or more precisely the Spanish empire (or 'Monarchy' as it was known to contemporaries), of which peninsular Spain (i.e. the kingdoms of Castile and Aragon) was the hub – was in decline, a process hastened by the so-called mid-seventeenth-century 'Crisis' and symbolized by the supposed mental and physical degeneracy of the last Habsburg monarch. According to this view, in Carlos II's reign an exhausted Spain was eclipsed by an aggressive, expansionist France under Louis XIV, and only survived with the support of former enemies like England and the Dutch republic, who now saw Spain as too weak to represent a threat and in need of support against Louis.[2]

[1] H. Kamen, *The War of Succession in Spain 1700–1715* (London, Weidenfeld & Nicolson, 1969), p. xi.

[2] Cf. L. Ribot Garcia, *La Revuelta de Mesina, la guerra (1674–1678) y el poder hispanico en Sicilia* (Madrid, Fundacion Juan March, 1980), p. 27.

Superficially, at least, the period does present a strong contrast with the heroic century or more which began with the Catholic kings in the later fifteenth century and effectively ended in the reign of Philip IV (1621–65). Carlos II's reign did see some humiliating reverses and losses. In 1668 Madrid was obliged to recognize the independence of Portugal, while military defeat and territorial losses were also sustained in the Low Countries in 1667–8. Franche-Comté was lost to Louis XIV in the 1670s and Luxemburg in 1684. In Italy, too, Spain's position was seriously undermined in the 1680s as Louis secured the strategically crucial fortress of Casale in the Monferrato, close to Milan and astride its links with the wider Spanish Monarchy, and used his growing naval power to intimidate Spain's traditional allies in Italy, notably the republic of Genoa, to the further discomfiture of Spain's imperial communications in the Mediterranean. More broadly, Spain, the Monarchy, was increasingly an object of Great Power rivalry and international politics. Here is the origin and explanation of the paradox noted above.

Some historians have begun to challenge this picture of crisis and decline. Unfortunately the work of Henry Kamen, the leading revisionist writing in English, is concerned above all with peninsular Spain and largely ignores Spain's international preoccupations.[3] More pertinent in this respect is the work of Robert Stradling, who more than any other English-speaking historian has sought to show that there was life in the supranational Monarchy after the 1640s, and whose *Europe and the Decline of Spain* is the most accessible exception to the absence of a general study of Spanish policy in the later seventeenth century.[4] A number of Spanish historians have also begun to address aspects of foreign policy in this era.[5] However, even Stradling seems to believe that after 1678 that system was exhausted, and virtually impotent by the end of the 1690s; while most of the other, younger Spanish historians of foreign policy in Carlos II's reign also find little of interest after the so-called Dutch War (1672–8).[6] Typically, the revolt of the Sicilian city of Messina (1674–8) has attracted substantial attention, notably the copiously documented older

[3] H. Kamen, *Spain in the Later Seventeenth Century 1665–1700* (London, Longman, 1980). Kamen's earlier *War of Succession*, pp. 25ff., describes a decayed Spain in 1700.

[4] R. Stradling, 'Seventeenth Century Spain: Decline or Survival?', *European Studies Review* IX (1979), pp. 157–94; for Stradling's bleak view of the last decades of Habsburg Spain, see *Europe and the Decline of Spain* (London, George Allen & Unwin, pp. 189–90. Significantly, his chapter on the period 1678–1700 is entitled 'Pathology of a Power System'.

[5] J. Alcala Zamora, 'Razon de Estado y Geostrategia en la Politica Italiana de Carlos II: Florencia y los Presidios (1677–1681)', *Boletin de la Real Academia de la Historia* CLXXIII (1976), pp. 297–358.

[6] See A. Serrano de Haro, 'Espana y la Paz de Nimega', *Hispania* LII (2/81) (1992), pp. 559–84; D. Salinas, 'La diplomacia espanola en relacion con Holanda durante el reinado de Carlos II: una aproximacion a su estudio', *Hispania* XLIX (171) (1989), pp. 317–24; C. Sanz Ayan, *Los banqueros de Carlos II* (Valladolid, University of Valladolid, 1979) (details of remittances abroad in wartime); Sanz Ayan, 'Negociadores y capitales holandeses en los sistemas de abastecimientos de pertrechos navales de la monarquia hispanica durante el siglo XVII', *Hispania* LII (3/182) (1992), pp. 915–45.

study by E. Laloy, and more recently that by Luis Ribot, but not the subsequent two decades.[7] Not surprisingly, the observation, in D. McKay and H.M. Scott's textbook (1983) on international relations between 1648 and 1815, that Spanish foreign policy in this era remains largely unexplored remains broadly true.[8] For the reign of Carlos II, those seeking secondary accounts of Spanish policy must either use the Duque de Maura's dated general histories of the reign[9] or piece the story together from accounts of the policies of the other major powers.[10]

This is unsatisfactory, since it leaves a major gap in our understanding of international relations in the later seventeenth century. Spain remained throughout this era one of that small elite of leading contenders in international politics, which can be called Great Powers, who were using their own resources on a wide variety of fronts. Until the War of the Spanish Succession, Spain was a constant member of the alliances against Louis XIV. Although an independent Portugal obliged Spain to pay greater attention to its defences on that frontier, Portugal was much the weaker of the two peninsular powers and well aware of its own vulnerability.[11] Lesser princes and powers throughout Europe still looked to the king of Spain for subsidies and other material and less tangible rewards for supplying him with troops and other services.[12] Foreign diplomats recognized that a posting to Madrid was a more important and prestigious appointment than to most other capitals.[13] During the Nine Years War (1689–97) the King of Spain was clearly of greater dignity and

[7] E. Laloy, *La Révolte de Messine, l'expédition de Sicile et la politique française en Italie (1674–78)* (3 vols, Paris, 1929–31); L. Ribot Garcia, *La Revuelta antiespañola de Mesina. Causas y antecedents (1591–1674)* (Valladolid, University of Valladolid, 1982); Ribot Garcia, *La Revuelta de Mesina.* Ribot's most recent contribution to this subject, 'Las provincias italianas y la defensa de la monarquia', *Manuscrits* XIII (1995), pp. 97ff., a broad analysis of the way Spain's Italian dominions (and particularly Naples and Sicily) contributed to the defence of Spanish Italy as a whole, largely ignores the second half of the seventeenth century, in which (it is claimed) Spain's position in Italy essentially depended on the readiness of the Maritime Powers to come to the aid of Spain against France.

[8] D. McKay and H.M. Scott, *The Rise of the Great Powers 1648–1815* (Harlow, Longman, 1983), p. 348.

[9] Duque de Maura, *Vida y Reinado de Carlos II* (3 vols, Madrid, 1942; reissued in 1 vol. Madrid, 1990) (all references are to the later edn); and de Maura, *Carlos II y su corte. Ensayo de reconstruccion biografica* (2 vols, Madrid, 1911 and 1915). Henry Kamen's chapter on foreign policy in the reign of Carlos II, 'Espana en la Europa de Luis XIV', in P. Molas Ribalta, ed., *Historia de Espana Menendez Pidal* XXVIII, *La transicion del siglo XVII al XVIII. Entre la decadencia y la reconstruccion* (Madrid, Espasa Calpe, 1993) is useful but does not (for example) mention that Spain was fighting a major war in Italy in the 1690s.

[10] See P. Sonnino, *Louis XIV and the Origins of the Dutch War* (Cambridge, 1989).

[11] Nor was cooperation impossible. In 1695 the king of Portugal agreed to levy 1000 men for Ceuta, Spain's outpost in North Africa; Stanhope to Galway, 8 Sept. 1695, Madrid, Kent Record Office, U1590/015/4U.

[12] Carlos II's brother-in-law, the Elector Palatine, secured a substantial prize in being allowed to garrison Luxemburg following its recovery in 1697; Maura, *Vida y Reinado*, pp. 621–2.

[13] Alexander Stanhope to the Earl of Chesterfield [1689], British Library [BL] Additional Manuscripts [Add.]. 19253, fo. 170 (on Stanhope's appointment to Madrid: he had been destined for Florence).

power than many other members of the Grand Alliance against Louis XIV, for example the Duke of Savoy. In that war, the monarchy was fighting on a number of fronts on land – in Spain itself (Catalonia and Navarre), Flanders and Italy – besides North Africa and the Americas,[14] and made a not insignificant contribution to the allied war effort at sea. As one of the 'big four' allies (the others were England, the Dutch republic and the emperor), Spain's contribution and commitments were in a very different league from those of the Duke of Savoy or the Elector of Bavaria, to identify only two of the more substantial secondary princes in the Grand Alliance.[15] Like the Maritime Powers, Spain paid subsidies to its lesser allies. During the Nine Years War it also subsidized the costs of the English and Dutch fleets in the Mediterranean.[16] The fact that these were often in arrears, for example the subsidy given the Duke of Savoy, should be seen less as evidence that Spain was no longer a Great Power than as an indication that, like those of most other powers, Spain's resources were seriously tested by the efforts to wage major warfare.[17]

Spanish self-perception often irritated foreigners,[18] but was founded upon this persistence of wealth,[19] power and empire. Spanish ministers understandably resented any suggestion that their major contribution to the Nine Years War, and interest in it, were not properly valued. In August 1694 the Constable of Castile was indignant that the Duke of Savoy, Vittorio Amedeo II, had consulted the emperor about a proposed

[14] In the later 1680s, before the outbreak of the Nine Years War, the only conflict in which the monarchy was engaged was that in North Africa; see C. Fernandez Duro, *Armada española* (9 vols, Madrid, 1895–1903) v, pp. 215 ff. On the continuance of this conflict in the 1690s, see the Constable of Castile in the Council of State, 27 May 1690, in Archivo General de Simancas [AGS], Estado, legajo 3411/116; for Spanish diplomatic efforts to prevent the Moroccans purchasing arms in the Dutch republic, see *consulta* (of Council of State – unless otherwise indicated all *consultas* are of Council of State), 6 Sept. 1691, AGS Estado 3990.

[15] See the contribution of each allied power for the coming campaign, given in the conference of allied ministers at The Hague, AGS Estado 3989. For a contemporary (Spanish) reference to Spain as one of the 'big four', see G. Maura Gamazo, ed., *Correspondencia entre dos embajadores* (Madrid, Consejo Superior de Investigaciones Cientificas, 1952) II, p. 150, Don Pedro Ronquillo (Spanish minister in London) to the marquis of Cogolludo (Spanish minister in Rome), 29 Sept. 1690.

[16] Blathwayt to Shrewsbury, 2 Nov. 1694, Hague, BL Add. 37992, fo. 90; William III to Heinsius, 5 Oct. 1695, Loo, Add. 34504, fo. 187; Alexander Stanhope to Duke of Shrewsbury, 21 Sept. 1695, Madrid, SP 94/73, fo. 13, for Spanish agreement to pay the Dutch 50 000 crowns a month towards the cost of their Mediterranean squadron as during the Messina war in the 1670s.

[17] The subsidy paid by William III to the Duke of Savoy was 12 months in arrears when the latter abandoned his allies in the summer of 1696; see C. Storrs, 'Diplomatic Relations between William III and Victor Amadeus II 1690–96' (University of London PhD thesis, 1990), p. 280.

[18] See Blathwayt to Lexington, 14 Oct. 1695, Hague, Add. 46528A, fo. 190, commenting on the expulsion of William III's Dutch envoy from the Spanish court, seriously undermining Spain's relations with the Maritime Powers: 'tis wonderful what measures the Spaniards take every where thinking themselves no less considerable than they were in the reign of Charles ye 5th or Philip the 2nd'.

[19] For the still considerable wealth reaching peninsular Spain from its overseas colonies in the later seventeenth century, see J. Lynch, *Spain under the Habsburgs*, II*: Spain and America 1598–1700*, 2nd edn (Oxford, Blackwell, 1981), p. 209.

blockade of the French-garrisoned fortress of Casale but not the Spanish king, 'el que costea principalmente toda aquella Guerra'.[20] If Madrid's allies complained of Spain's apparent inability to campaign vigorously and to fulfil promises and obligations, the Spaniards had their own criticisms of the irresolution, sluggish execution of agreed plans and general inability to wage war effectively of those allies. In the summer of 1696, when Carlos II's ministers were forced to consider whether to fight on in north Italy, following the Duke of Savoy's conclusion of a separate peace with Louis XIV, they were critical both of the Emperor's inadequate efforts and of William III, whose failure to fulfil his own promises they believed had helped create their dilemma.[21] It was clear, too, that Spain's allies saw her as playing a leading role in certain theatres of war, not least Italy. Before the Duke of Savoy's defection, and in order to prevent it, discussions in Vienna concerning increased contributions to the war in Italy by the other major allies included proposals that Spain contribute much more (in cash and troops) than the Emperor and not much less than the Maritime Powers together.[22]

Not surprisingly, foreign policy issues were also a crucial factor in the turbulent domestic politics of Carlos II's reign, both during and after his minority.[23] Nor should we forget that the reign of Carlos II closed with the Spanish Monarchy largely intact. Indeed, that decrepit monarch's final decade witnessed something of a recovery by the Monarchy. Not only was Luxemburg regained, in 1697, but Louis XIV's troops were also forced out of their fortresses (Pinerolo and Casale) in north Italy. It was the new Bourbon dynasty, during the War of the Spanish Succession, not the declining Habsburg dynasty, which presided over the demise of the Spanish Monarchy in Europe. Finally, and above all if we are to understand fully the nature of international politics in the later seventeenth century, it is crucial that we restore the dimension of an independent, powerful Spanish Monarchy, pursuing its own policy objectives.

If we are to achieve this, the abundant Spanish archival sources must be used to clarify the role and functioning in the later seventeenth century of a number of crucial institutions and the attitudes that underpinned Spanish imperialism. These institutions include the Spanish diplomatic service and the various armies and fleets which were the instruments of Spanish power. The armies and fleets included the still

[20] AGS Estado 3420/20. Cf. Borgomanero's words to the conference of allied ministers in Vienna, 1695; Borgomanero to Count Kinsky, 8 Jan. 1695, Vienna, copy in KoninklijkHuisArchief [KHA], Hague XI/g/53.

[21] Borgomanero to Carlos II, Vienna, 19 Dec. 1693, AGS Estado 3937; same to Duke of Medinaceli, Vienna, 2 Oct. 1694, Archive of Dukes of Medinaceli, Casa Pilatos, Seville [CPS]. I should like to thank the Duchess of Medinaceli for allowing me access to this archive. For 1696, see *consulta*, 24 July 1696, AGS Estado 3423/85.

[22] Lexington to Blathwayt, 27 June 1696, Vienna, Add. 46528B, fos. 99–102; Lexington and Heemskerk to Blathwayt, 19 July 1696, Add. 46530A, fos. 150–52.

[23] This emerges clearly in Maura, *Vida y reinado.*

largely neglected (as Stradling has observed) army of Lombardy[24] and the Mediterranean galley fleets. These forces enjoyed their own distinctive roles, structures and routes, but have not received the same attention as that given the army of Flanders and its ancillary institutions in the classic study by Geoffrey Parker.[25] The present study seeks to locate the Spanish army of Lombardy, and the system surrounding it, within the larger framework of Madrid's concerns and policies, and to describe its structure and achievement in the final Habsburg decade. Spain's allies contributed in significant ways to Spanish resilience. They diverted French resources to other theatres and on occasion actively supplemented those of Spain in the face of French attack. This article, however, emphasizes that on the eve of the demise of Habsburg rule the Spanish Monarchy remained a relatively powerful, functioning military structure or 'system', a surprisingly integrated and coherent war machine. More strikingly, not only did it broadly succeed in achieving its objectives but it could also reverse the recent tide, recovering lost ground and strengthening Spain's position in Italy.

## II

Spain's Italian possessions in the later seventeenth century were still extensive and important. They comprised the kingdom of Naples and the island realms of Sicily and Sardinia in the south; the Tuscan *presidios* or garrisons in central Italy; Finale, an imperial fief on the Ligurian coast west of Genoa; and the duchy of Milan – also an Imperial fief – often known simply as the Milanese, or Lombardy. These territories were, moreover, undoubtedly more self-contained (i.e. concerned with their own defence) after 1665 than in the previous hundred years. This was the result both of the decision to recognize formally the independence of the Dutch republic in 1648 and of the subsequent losses to Louis XIV of Franche-Comté and Luxemburg. These developments undermined the *raison d'être* of the so-called 'Spanish Road' which linked Italy and Flanders and partly dismantled it, although Spain continued to maintain an army in the southern Netherlands throughout the later seventeenth century and simply

[24] R. Stradling, 'Domination and Dependence: Castile, Spain and the Spanish Monarchy', Review Article, *European History Quarterly* XIV (1980), p. 90. In fact, L. Ribot Garcia went some way towards opening up the subject in his article 'Milan, plaza de armas de la Monarquia', *Investigaciones Historicas* X (1990), pp. 203–38, although the scope of his survey is both wider and more general than that of the present article. In the main, Spain's armed forces (after 1650) have not attracted the attention of those historians seeking to assess the validity or otherwise of M. Roberts's 'Military Revolution'; cf. Roberts, *The Military Revolution 1560–1660* (Belfast, 1956), repr. in Roberts, *Essays in Swedish History* (London, Roberts, 1968); and, for a revisionist approach, J. Black, *A Military Revolution? Military Change and European Society 1550–1800* (London, Macmillan, 1991).

[25] G. Parker, *The Army of Flanders and the Spanish Road 1567–1659* (Cambridge, CUP, 1976). Even the army of Flanders is largely ignored by historians after 1659.

found new (maritime) routes to supply it from Spain.[26] The Habsburg military corridor along France's eastern border which had so alarmed earlier French policy-makers was by no means a thing of the past. The possibility of its reconstruction continued to concern Louis XIV and his ministers, while Spanish ministers as late as the 1690s toyed with the idea of sending troops from the Milanese to Franche-Comté, to exploit both Huguenot grievances and a supposed continuing loyalty to the Habsburgs. Some contemporaries in the late seventeenth century thought Spain had largely washed its hands of Flanders, effectively surrendering its defence to the Maritime Powers, and was becoming more Italian or even Mediterranean, a view echoed by some modern historians. This was not in fact the case, Flanders remaining a crucial focus of Spanish concern and efforts.[27] Generally speaking, for ministers in Madrid Lombardy was just one of the Monarchy's many remaining sources of prestige (or *reputacion*) and of power.[28] By the same token, Lombardy was also just one of its many continuing commitments and responsibilities, causing endless anxiety as ministers juggled scarce resources to meet urgent and changing needs in Italy, Flanders, Spain, North Africa and the Americas.

However, Italy was certainly pre-eminent for some;[29] and for the most part, under Carlos II, Spain's Italian possessions were less a source of troops for Spanish Flanders, as in the past, than a system providing for their own defence and that of Spain. In many respects, the early modern version of 'domino theory' strategic thinking, which underlay the pouring of men and money into the Low Countries from the 1560s, was simply applied to the Italian peninsula a century later: if Italy (beginning with any individual Spanish dominion) was lost, then it was believed that peninsular Spain would soon follow. In November 1690, following the defeat of a combined Spanish and Piedmontese force by a French army at Staffarda in Piedmont, the Council of State in Madrid (the chief policy-formulating body in the monarchy) feared that the defection of the Duke of Savoy would have fatal consequences for

[26] For the levy of men in Galicia and Asturias and their transport by sea to Flanders, during the wars against France of 1667–8 and 1683–4, see Stradling, *Europe and the Decline*, pp. 156–7, 181. For the same during the so-called Dutch War (1672–8), see A. Dominguez Ortiz, 'La crise intérieure de la monarchie des Habsburgs espagnols sous Charles II', in J.A.H. Bots, ed., *The Peace of Nijmegen 1676–78/79* (Amsterdam, 1980), pp. 157ff. For the transport of troops from Spain to Flanders by sea in the 1690s, see Stanhope to Nottingham, 20 Feb. 1692 and 11 Nov. 1693, Madrid, SP 94/73, fos. 55 and 234.

[27] Kamen, *Historia de Espana Meñendez Pidal*, argues that many Spanish policy-makers increasingly saw Flanders as a liability but his account shows that Madrid continued to make enormous efforts to defend and retain it. According to Stanhope to Nottingham, 9 May 1691, a *consulta* was held on surrendering the Low Countries to the Dutch, but this was vetoed by a junta of theologians; SP 94/73, fo. 31.

[28] For *reputacion*, see J.H. Elliott, 'A Question of Reputation?', Review Article, *Journal of Modern History* LX (1984), pp. 475–83.

[29] See Juan Alfonso Rodriguez de Lancina, *Comentarios politicos*, 1687, ed. J. Maravall (Madrid, 1945), p. 12. Lancina had served as auditor with the army in Italy; Ribot Garcia, *La Revuelta de Mesina*, p. 8.

Spain everywhere. Three years later, in November 1693, following another French victory in Piedmont, at Marsaglia, the Count of Frigiliana pointed out in the council of state that helping the Duke of Savoy would preserve not only Carlos II's Italian dominions but also Catalonia (by diverting Louis XIV's forces from the latter).[30] This greater readiness to use Italian resources for Italian defence may have contributed to a greater integration of the various parts of the Monarchy in Italy into the larger Monarchy and to what some historians have seen as a greater centralized control from Madrid.[31]

The Spanish system in Italy was largely geared towards the supply of the army of Lombardy. The effective functioning of that system depended above all upon two elements: sea power (to carry men, munitions and provisions from Naples, Sicily, peninsular Spain and to a lesser degree Sardinia to northern Italy via the Tuscan garrisons) and a secure route through the duchy of Monferrato, which was in the possession of the Gonzaga Dukes of Mantua and which lay between the territories of the Genoese republic, the Duke of Savoy and the duchy of Milan. To a lesser degree, Spanish security in northern Italy also depended upon the attitude both of the Duke of Savoy, whose territories lay between the Milanese and France (and commanded the exit into Italy from the passages through the Alps which any French force intended to invade the Milanese must pass), and of the Emperor, the suzerain of much of north Italy (*Reichsitalien*, including the Milanese, Finale and Monferrato) and who could also supply troops for the defence of Spanish Milan, as during the Thirty Years War. Finally, Spain's position in Italy generally, but particularly in north Italy, depended upon the goodwill of a host of lesser Italian princes and states, including the Duke of Mantua and the republic of Genoa, whose amity was ensured by a judicious mixture of favours (pensions, titles, marriages, offices and so on) and the threat of being on the receiving end of Spanish force which none of the other Italian powers could match.[32] Typically, Spain paid a subsidy to the Duke of Mantua after 1665 towards the costs of the garrison of Casale, the key to Monferrato and to communications between Milan and the rest of the Monarchy.[33]

The great threat to Spanish power in Italy came from outside the peninsula, and principally from France. In 1631 France had gained a foothold at Pinerolo in the Alps west of Turin, and during the 1640s

[30] *Consulta*, 23 Nov. 1690, AGS Estado 3654/14; *Consulta*, 13 Nov. 1693, AGS Estado 3655/85.

[31] A recent exponent of this view of a greater coherence and integration in this period, one which adopts a rather revisionist approach to the so-called 'neo-foralist' interpretation (which sees the period after the mid-century 'Crisis' as one of greater independence *vis-à-vis* Madrid or Castile), is L. Ribot Garcia in his contribution to *Historia de España Menendez Pidal* XVIII, esp. pp. 179ff. (Naples, Sardinia and Sicily).

[32] The Genoese republic could be coerced by threatening the extensive property of Genoese in the monarchy, particularly in Naples; Stanhope to Nottingham, 22 Oct. 1692, Madrid, SP 94/73, fo. 82. There is a useful map of north Italy in this period in C. Ingrao, *In Quest and Crisis* (Purdue, 1979), p. 81.

[33] L. Mazzoldi *et al.*, eds, *Mantova. La Storia* III (Mantova, 1963), p. 160.

and 1650s had unsuccessfully sought to seize both Monferrato and the Tuscan *presidios*, effectively dismantling Spain's Italian empire. From the 1660s Louis XIV, too, sought to undermine Spanish power in Italy, contributing to the preoccupation of Spain's Italian dominions with their own defence rather than that of Flanders. The first real threat posed by Louis came in the 1670s, when he supported the large-scale revolt of Messina against Spanish rule (1674–8). The revolt threatened the entire Spanish 'system' in Italy because – whether in French hands or independent, or simply (as with the Dutch from the 1570s) in permanent revolt – Sicily would no longer contribute to that 'system'. On the contrary, resources would have to be (as they were for the duration of the revolt of Messina) diverted from other parts of Italy and from Spain to suppress it. Naples and Sardinia would simply not have been able to supply Lombardy as hitherto.[34] The initial success of the French intervention on behalf of the Messina revolt owed a great deal to the deliberate creation by Louis and his ministers from the 1660s of a substantial naval force at Toulon and of a large galley fleet at Marseilles, which threatened Spain's maritime communications in the Mediterranean: as early as 1668 the viceroy of Naples had refused to send help to Milan on the grounds that a French assault was expected against Naples itself. Spain's success in ending the Messina revolt owed a great deal to Dutch naval support. However, the restoration of Spanish power in Sicily was followed by a renewal of the French threat at the other end of Italy, with the effective sale to Louis XIV, by the wayward Duke of Mantua, Fernando Carlo, of the fortress of Casale. The duke, whose Spanish pension was already in substantial arrears, had agreed to the sale as early as 1677. The Spanish minister in Turin, the Duke of Giovinazzo, underlining just how effective Spanish diplomacy could still be, soon learned of this deal and enabled the then governor of Milan, the Count of Melgar, to attempt the formation of an Italian league to oppose the cession. However, in the long run this proved impossible, and troops in Louis's pay entered Casale in 1681.[35]

The new situation in north Italy created by this French success was extremely menacing for Spain's position in the peninsula. It increased the French pressure on the duke of Savoy, who formally entered Louis XIV's camp. Caught between Pinerolo and Casale, Turin was a military ally, if not satellite, of Louis XIV after 1682. Long regarded as unreliable by Spanish ministers in Milan and Madrid, Savoy seemed definitely lost.[36] More importantly, the garrison of Casale could easily disrupt Milan's supply of men, *matériel* and money from other parts of

[34] For the Messina war, see Laloy, *La Révolte*, and Ribot Garcia, *La Revuelta*.

[35] Mazzoldi, *Mantova* III, pp. 159–60, and p. 184 for the stopping of Fernando Carlo's Spanish pension after the French occupation of Casale. Cf. Giovinazzo (Jovenazo)'s petition to Carlos II, 1691, detailing his services (largely diplomatic) in A. Valladares de Sotomayor, *Semanario erudito* (34 vols, Madrid, 1787–91) XXX, pp. 19ff.

[36] See G. Symcox, *Victor Amadeus II: Absolutism in the Savoyard State 1675–1730* (London, Thames & Hudson, 1983), pp. 89ff.

the Monarchy which were channelled through the Ligurian port of Finale and then overland across Monferrato.[37] French awareness of Casale's importance no doubt explains the massive fortifications built there in the 1680s. For the population of the Milanese, and for ministers there and in Madrid, the recovery and/or neutralization of the threat posed by Casale became an urgent new concern. This desire grew as the French position in north Italy strengthened in the 1680s. In 1684–5 Spain was again unable to form an Italian league to counter the French assault on Genoa, a testimony to the continued advance of French sea power in the Mediterranean. The Count of Melgar concluded a treaty of mutual aid with Genoa, and sent units of the army of Lombardy to the defence of the republic, but could not prevent a settlement between Genoa and Louis XIV which obliged the republic to end its traditional Spanish alliance and to deny harbour facilities to Spain's galleys.[38] Milan itself came under renewed pressure as the Duke of Mantua, subsidized by Louis XIV, built a major new fortification at Guastalla, 100 miles south-east of the city of Milan. By the end of the 1680s Guastalla had emerged as one of the strongest points in north Italy, and, with Casale, threatened to neutralize Milan (and worse) in the event of a major conflict.[39] The French naval threat intensified too. In 1689 a rumour that Louis XIV was seeking Porto Ferraio, the only non-Spanish base on the island of Elba (apart from the *presidios* complex) from its suzerain, the Grand Duke of Tuscany, rightly worried Carlos II's envoy in London, Don Pedro Ronquillo. With Porto Ferraio, the French could undermine the role of the *presidios* and effectively cut the route between Naples and Milan (see below for a fuller discussion of the *presidios* and their role in supplying the army of Lombardy).[40]

[37] The Marquis of los Balbases described Casale as 'la piedra del escandolo de Italia y particularmente del Estado de Milan', in the Council of State; *consulta*, Feb. 1694, AGS Estado 3419/43. In the summer of 1689, troops from Casale raided the Milanese; *London Gazette* no. 2358.

[38] Cf. AGS Simancas, 3620 and 3621.

[39] Mazzoldi, *Mantova* III, p. 162 and note. The Guastalla issue was related to important dynastic shifts within the Gonzaga family, which were typical of the way developments within the leading princely families both offered opportunities for the consolidation of but also created problems for Spanish power in Italy throughout the early modern era. Before 1678, when its Duke, Ferrante, died without heirs, the duchy of Guastalla (an imperial fief raised to ducal status in 1621) was ruled by the pro-Spanish Gonzaga di Guastalla. On Ferrante's death the fief was assigned, by imperial decree, to the Gonzaga di Mantua (i.e. to Duke Fernando Carlo). However, the fief was also claimed by Ferrante's cousin Vincenzo, who in 1679 married Ferrante's daughter to strengthen his own claims on Guastalla and who continued to press them throughout the 1680s. This dynastic dispute and Vincenzo's powerful Spanish connection (he had served as viceroy of Sicily and was a councillor of state and president of the council of the Indies in Madrid from 1680) may have contributed to Fernando Carlo's drift out of the Spanish orbit and into the French orbit. See Mazzoldi, *Storia* III, p. 184. I should like to thank the anonymous reader of this article for drawing this aspect of this issue to my attention.

[40] According to H. Richmond, *Statesmen and Sea Power* (Cambridge, CUP, 1953), pp. 60–1, the Dutch, recalling their experience during the Messina revolt, sought access to either Port Mahon (Minorca) or Porto Ferraio in the Nine Years War.

The French advance undermined Spanish prestige and power in Italy. Louis XIV's intrusion forced unwilling choices on the smaller Italian princes and republics. Spanish efforts to construct anti-French leagues, using the argument that Madrid should be helped in the effort to throw off the foreign yoke (the same argument that the French used in seeking allies in Italy against the Spaniards), was not rejected on the grounds that Spain herself was a foreign power, but because Spain was believed to be too weak to defend the Italian principalities against Louis XIV's resentment and possible reprisals. The Tuscan resident in London in 1689, Terriesi, surely spoke for all the Italian states when he told Ronquillo that they feared a weak Spain more than a strong one.[41] The 1680s had witnessed a major crisis of Spanish power and influence in Italy.

Therefore, following Louis XIV's declaration of war against Spain in the spring of 1689, and with Madrid ordering the governor of Milan, the count of Fuensalida, not to alienate the Duke of Savoy by an attack on Pinerolo,[42] the governor seized the opportunity to counter the most recent threat, that from Guastalla. A small armada, of more than 100 transports, carried men and munitions down the River Po to Casalmaggiore, near Guastalla, where 12 000 men encamped while troops from the western garrisons of the Milanese kept an eye on Casale. Faced with Fuensalida's threat to bombard Guastalla, and with little prospect of help from Louis XIV, who was preoccupied with a war in the Rhineland and Flanders in 1689, the Duke of Mantua was obliged to yield. Spanish troops entered Guastalla and were soon supervising the demolition of its fortifications.[43] The campaign of 1689 had demonstrated the potential effectiveness of the army of Lombardy, particularly against an Italian prince and when France was fighting on the Rhine and in Flanders. Not only did it restore Spanish prestige and power in the short term, it also encouraged the Duke of Savoy to break with Louis XIV and join Spain (and the Grand Alliance) in the summer of 1690, confident that he would be supported by a Spanish army (drawing on the resources of the monarchy) larger than anything he could field.[44] This in turn represented a major Spanish diplomatic success, Savoy reverting to what ministers in Madrid considered its proper role, a bulwark of the Milanese.[45] It also enabled the army of Lombardy to take further action against the Duke of Mantua. Fernando Carlo

[41] See Ronquillo to Fuensalida, 23 Dec. 1689, on the demolition of Guastalla releasing the Italian princes from the 'French yoke'; Maura, *Correspondencia*, p. 331; Terriesi to Grand Duke of Tuscany, 1689, Add. 25377.

[42] D. Maselli, 'Il glorioso rimpatrio nei documenti spagnoli', in A. de Lange, ed., *Dall Europa alle valli valdesi* (Turin, Claudiana, 1989), p. 192.

[43] Mazzoldi, *Storia* III, p. 162; 'Diario' of expedition, Add. 16483, fos. 116–17.

[44] See Storrs, 'Machiavelli Dethroned: Victor Amadeus II and the Making of the Anglo-Savoyard Alliance of 1690', *European History Quarterly* XXII (3) (1992), pp. 347–82; text of Spanish–Savoyard treaty in Solar de la Marguerite, *Traités publics de la maison de Savoie* (8 vols, Turin, 1836–61) II, pp. 121ff.

[45] Cf. Giovinazzo's petition, *Semanario Erudito*; Lancina, *Comentarios*, pp. 12ff., put it rather differently, but saw the Duke of Savoy as the key to Italy.

sought to compensate for the loss of Guastalla with new works further along the Po, at Gazzuolo and elsewhere, but in 1691 Spanish forces again invaded the duchy of Mantua, obliging the Duke to agree to the demolition of these and to his own neutrality in the struggle between the Grand Alliance and Louis XIV which had spread to Italy in 1690 with the breach between the Duke of Savoy and France. In 1691–2 Spanish and imperial troops (in Italy to support the Duke of Savoy) established winter quarters in the duchy of Mantua. Finally, in 1692, Spanish and imperial troops again intervened in Mantua, to enforce the Emperor's decision in the long-running dispute over Guastalla between the duke of Mantua and Vincenzo Gonzaga, in favour of the latter. As a trusted protégé and ally of the Monarchy, Vincenzo was allowed to refortify Guastalla under Spanish protection.[46]

Throughout the Nine Years War, a substantial detachment from the army of Lombardy campaigned each year in Piedmont; and in 1692 units of that force took part in the abortive invasion of Dauphiné, the allies' only incursion into France during that conflict. Frequent operations of this sort, whether offensive or defensive, provided the training and experience which produced the all-important veteran troops. The Marquis of Leganes (governor of Milan 1691–8) observed in 1692 that if the war continued Carlos II would soon have troops as good (i.e. experienced) as those of the emperor, and the best in Europe.[47] In 1692–3, Spanish ministers, fearing the consequences for Spain of the death of the Duke of Savoy (who had fallen ill during the invasion of Dauphiné), considered seizing power in Turin using their considerable military force.[48] This proved unnecessary. More importantly, in 1695 the governor of Milan's supply of men, *matériel* and money for the siege of Casale paid off, with the capture of this key fortress.[49]

On 26 June 1695 the siege of Casale (hitherto merely blockaded by the allies) began at last, after considerable preparations which had been greatly hindered by poor weather. The Spanish forces – more than 13 000 infantry and nearly 1400 cavalry – according to a review held just before the siege began, constituted the single largest element in the besieging allied force of about 22 000 which faced a defending force, commanded by the Marquis de Crenan, of about 3000. The Spaniards also made the single largest artillery contribution (including 30 pieces of heavy artillery and a considerable number of mortars). It was widely felt that, despite the strength of its fortifications, Casale

[46] See Mazzoldi, *Mantova* III, pp. 162ff.

[47] Leganes to Carlos II, 17 Aug. 1692, AGS Estado 3417/86.

[48] Cf. *consulta*, 5 Apr. 1693, AGS Estado 3418/71.

[49] For the enthusiasm of Leganes and other Spanish ministers for the 'empresa de Casal', see Leganes' correspondence with Borgomanero in Vienna, AGS Estado 3937. See Leganes to Medinaceli, 7 July 1694, Milan, CPS, for Spanish readiness to contribute artillery; Leganes to Medinaceli, 11 Mar. 1695, Milan, CPS, urging that troops and money be sent to him for a siege so advantageous to the King of Spain, and declaring that with the Anglo-Dutch fleet in the Mediterranean the seas were safe for the galleys (to carry these).

could not resist a siege. However, there was general surprise at Crenan's readiness to surrender after only 13 days of the siege, on 8 July, and at the speed with which a capitulation was agreed (11 July) between Crenan and the Duke of Savoy, the supreme commander of the allied forces. The capitulation provided for the demolition of the fortifications built at Casale in the 1680s and for Casale's subsequent return to the Duke of Mantua. In fact the capitulation had been agreed beforehand by Louis XIV, who was unable to spare troops from other fronts to fight their way across Piedmont to the relief of Casale, and who feared that the Emperor would retain Casale once it had fallen, and by Vittorio Amedeo II, who shared the latter concern. However, although the *empresa de Casale* in part succeeded because of a secret deal between Louis XIV and Vittorio Amedeo, that deal would not have been made if Casale had not looked like falling to a siege which the Spaniards had pressed for, to which they contributed enormously in terms of men and munitions and in which Spanish troops played a distinguished part.[50] The success of the *empresa de Casale*, and the demolition of its fortifications, revealed again just how effective the Spaniards could be, not least when they recognized that the project was fundamental to their strategic interests. It represented a major triumph, relieving the Milanese and the entire Spanish system in north Italy of a major threat. Spanish military potential also benefited in that Carlos II appropriated the largest share of the substantial quantity of artillery the departing French were obliged to leave at Casale. Not surprisingly, the news of Casale's surrender was greeted with celebrations in both Milan[51] and Madrid,[52] and with a flood of rewards for those who had contributed to its capture.[53]

The removal of the threat posed by Casale enabled Madrid to divert troops from the Milanese to the defence of Catalonia. However, Madrid had by no means abandoned hopes of using the army of Lombardy to further secure Spanish power in northern Italy, above all by finally ousting the French from Pinerolo as the Duke of Savoy desired. In the winter of 1695–6 Vittorio Amedeo pressed his allies to agree that this should be the object of their 1696 campaign in Italy, and to plan

[50] For a brief account of the siege, see M. Braubach, *Prinz Eugen* (5 vols, Vienna, 1963–5) I, pp. 217–18. It can be traced in greater detail in the reports of the Dutch commissary, van der Meer, from Turin in AlgemeenRijksArchief, Hague [ARAH], Staten Generaal [SG] 8644, esp. 180 ff. For the Spanish contingent, see AGS Estado 3422/46 and 47. There is a copy of the capitulation in Add. 46558A, fos. 243ff.

[51] In an act of rare generosity, the *congregazione* of the Milanese offered to increase its contribution to the cost of the army of Lombardy, although this turned out to be less generous in reality; Leganes to Carlos II, 27 July 1695, Camp at Casale, AGS Estado 3422/61.

[52] Stanhope to Lexington, 4 Aug. 1695, Madrid, Add. 46540, fo. 19; Stanhope to Galway, 11 Aug. 1695, Madrid, Kent Record Office, U1590/015/4.

[53] Cf. *consulta*, 30 Oct. 1695, AGS Estado 3422/103, for the Spanish desire to reward the marquis de Saint Thomas, chief minister of the Duke of Savoy, by finding a valuable ecclesiastical vacancy in the kingdom of Naples for his brother. The episode reveals the system of rewards and gratifications which helped sustain Spanish prestige and influence in the Italian courts.

accordingly. As in past campaigns, the Milanese was expected to supply 12 000 men and substantial quantities of powder, grenades and bombs. The Spaniards needed little convincing of the value of the project.[54] When it was discussed in the council of state, in February 1696, the Count of Frigiliana observed that the siege of Pinerolo was now the principal object of the war in Italy, for Spain at least, and would in the short term help divert the French from Catalonia.[55] The spring of 1696 therefore saw preparations in the Milanese for the army of Lombardy's participation in a siege which should expel the French from Italy at last. In fact, before the allies could launch their siege Louis XIV had taken the initiative, his forces invading Piedmont. In fact, Louis had already concluded another secret deal with Vittorio Amedeo, whereby the latter gained Pinerolo in return for having his erstwhile allies agree, using force against them if necessary, to end the war in Italy. More seriously for the Milanese, this secret deal resulted in Vittorio Amedeo's abandoning the Grand Alliance, and was followed by a Franco-Savoyard invasion of the Milanese and the siege there of the fortress of Valenza in the late summer of 1696. This was worse than the dark days of the 1680s. Austrian and Spanish Habsburg fears of a French conquest of the Milanese were undoubtedly the main explanation on the allied side for the conclusion with Louis XIV and Vittorio Amedeo II of the peace of Vigevano (October 1696), ending the war in Italy (although it continued in other theatres). In fact, however, the terms of that settlement confirmed the improved position of the monarchy in Italy which had emerged during the Nine Years War. The peace of Vigevano confirmed that Pinerolo, its fortifications demolished, should be returned to the Duke of Savoy. This meant that, for the first time in more than half a century, the French had no foothold in northern Italy. One of the consequences was that Vittorio Amedeo II, who understandably became suspect again in Milan and Madrid, was in fact no longer the French satellite of the 1680s. This situation may not have been the result of a successful siege of Pinerolo involving troops from the army of Lombardy. Nevertheless, the constant diversion of French troops in north Italy necessitated by an allied war effort in which the army of Lombardy played such an important part had undoubtedly convinced Louis XIV of the value of seeking to explode the coalition in Italy by sacrificing Pinerolo at last and agreeing to a neutralization of Italy which benefited Spain above all.[56]

Nor was the army of Lombardy inactive following the peace of 1696. In the winter of 1696–7 Leganes sent a detachment of 150 men to Mirandola (100 miles south of Milan), at the request of Princess Brigida Pico, guardian of the young Duke of Mirandola, whose uncles

[54] For Leganes' earlier preference for operations against Pinerolo, rather than an invasion of Dauphiné, see Leganes to Carlos II, Genoa, 12 Oct. 1692, AGS Estado 3417/106.

[55] *Consulta*, 11 Feb. 1696, AGS Estado 3939.

[56] See Symcox, *Victor Amadeus*, pp. 116–17; Braubach, *Prinz Eugen* I, pp. 223f.

sought to undermine the princess's position. The troops were only withdrawn in the summer of 1698. In 1699 units of the army of Lombardy intervened to restore the neighbouring Prince of Castiglione, following disturbances in his territories.[57] In many respects these episodes were typical of those policing operations in support of a friendly prince, which confirmed both the latter's inclination towards Madrid and Spain's prestige, influence and power (underpinned by its army) in the region. Italian princes and the Emperor also saw the army of Lombardy as the most obvious and effective instrument for enforcing the decisions of the Emperor and the Aulic court in Vienna (especially following the withdrawal of the Emperor's troops from north Italy in 1696) about the disposal of Imperial fiefs in north Italy.[58] All these factors helped ensure that the Spanish position in north Italy was better in Carlos II's last years than it had been for many decades.

## III

Spain's ability not only to stem the tide of French success in the 1690s but even to reverse it and take the offensive certainly owed something to the fact that Spain was part of a wide-ranging anti-French alliance, which both diverted French forces elsewhere and meant that Spain was not fighting alone in Italy. The Emperor sent substantial forces to Italy in the 1690s, while the Duke of Savoy acted as a buffer between France and Milan, as in the sixteenth century. From this point of view, the recovery of Spanish power in Italy must be set in the context of larger European developments, including the decision of the emperor (who had diverted his resources to the war in the east against the Turks in the 1680s) to give priority in the 1690s to the struggle against Louis XIV in the west and England's new European role after 1688. However, without wishing to ignore the importance of this larger perspective, account must be taken of Spain's own significant contribution to the allied military effort in all theatres, and especially in Piedmont. Generally speaking, Spain's contribution there in terms of men, *matériel* and money was greater than that of any of the other allies. Madrid's allies believed that the Spanish dominions in Italy could support a much larger military effort than Spain in fact made through the army of Lombardy, but they also recognized that without the contribution that was actually made, the allies could achieve very little in north Italy.[59]

The Spanish army of Lombardy, or Milan, effectively dated from Emperor Charles V's acquisition of the duchy in the 1530s and 1540s. The 3500 men he stationed there increased significantly, if erratically,

57 See AGS Estado 3425/97, *consulta* of 2 Apr. 1697; AG 3426/48 *consulta* of 5 June 1698; and AGS Estado 3442 on the army of Lombardy and Castiglione 1698–1700.

58 *Consulta* of 4 Nov. 1698, AGS Estado 3426/96.

59 Vittorio Amedeo II to Operti, 15 July 1691, Moncalieri, copy in Archivio di Stato, Turin [AST], Lettere Ministri, Olanda, mazzo 1.

thereafter. Of course, it must constantly be borne in mind that falsification (fraud), genuine loss and desertion (see below) mean that official figures for the total size of the army of Lombardy (as for most other European forces) cannot be taken at face value, and that even if they had some initial validity they very soon lost it. During the Thirty Years War the army of Lombardy had risen to as many as 35 000 (1640), and stood at between 15 000 and 20 000 for most of the 1640s and 1650s.[60] The peace of the Pyrenees (1659), however, was followed by the 'reform' of a number of regiments (i.e. their dissolution, or incorporation into other units),[61] in an attempt to cut costs and reduce the burden for the Milanese, Naples and Spain. The size of the army of Lombardy continued to fluctuate for the next 30 years, according to whether Spain was at war, or expecting it, or not. In 1675–6, during the Messina war, it totalled 15 000 men (114 infantry and 37 cavalry companies).[62] In 1689, a force of 8000 infantry and 4000 cavalry took part in the expedition against Guastalla.[63]

The prospect of the war on the Rhine and in Flanders spreading to Italy prompted new levies in 1690.[64] According to a review held in March 1690, the army of Lombardy totalled 15 277 infantry (including 2285 officers) and 3420 cavalry (including 345 officers) – a total of just under 18 700.[65] In the winter of 1690–91 the governor of Milan, the Count of Fuensalida, proposed that the army be increased to more than 30 000 (25 000 infantry, 6000 cavalry and 2000 dragons), a level not achieved during or since the Thirty Year War.[66] However, this proved far too ambitious, and a review of June 1691 revealed 15 416 infantry (including 1849 officers) and 3861 cavalry/dragoons (including 442 officers) – just over 19 000.[67] Fuensalida's plans were superseded by the new establishment drawn up in the summer of 1691 by his successor (1691–8) as governor, the Marquis of Leganes. This allowed for a more realistic total of between 21 000 (16 860 infantry and 4284 cavalry) and over 22 500 men (18 000 infantry and 4500 cavalry).[68] However, this took some time to achieve. At the end of the 1691 campaign, the army of Lombardy totalled just over 17 000 men (13 315 infantry and 3950 cavalry), and remained virtually unchanged

[60] Ribot Garcia, 'Milan, plaza de armas', pp. 203ff.; cf. review at Pavia, Nov. 1635, BL Add. 28453, fo. 188.

[61] Memoir of 'reformed' regiments 1659–1692, AGS Estado 3418/69.

[62] According to a complaint to Madrid from the representatives of the Milanese, Add. 14009, fos. 211ff.

[63] 'Diario', Add. 16483, fos. 116–17.

[64] *Consulta*, 26 June 1690, AGS Estado 3411/179.

[65] *Relacion* of review held on 20 Mar. 1690, AGS Estado 3411/83.

[66] *Consulta*, 9 Jan. 1691, on Fuensalida's proposed new establishment, AGS Estado 3414/17–19.

[67] Summary of review of 9 June 1691, AGS Estado 3415/28.

[68] *Consulta*, 3 Sept. 1691, on Leganes to Carlos II, 21 Sept. 1691, Staffarda, and accompanying documents AGS Estado 3415/89–102; *consulta*, 28 Jan. 1692, AGS Estado 3416/43.

by the spring of 1692;[69] and at the end of the 1692 campaign just under 20 000 men (15 525 infantry and 4338 cavalry).[70] In November 1693, following a campaign in which the army suffered substantial losses in Piedmont, it totalled just over 16 600 (10 831 infantry, 3996 cavalry and 1831 in garrison).[71] By the spring of 1694, following a 'reform', the army of Lombardy numbered just over 18 000 men (14 342 infantry and 4061 cavalry).[72] By the end of the 1694 campaign it totalled 20 000 (13 971 infantry, 4900 cavalry, 379 dismounted, and 1209 in garrison).[73] By the end of 1695, following another campaign and another reform, the army (infantry, cavalry and garrisons) totalled just over 20 500.[74] However, by the summer of 1696, the Milanese claimed to be supporting a force of 25 000 men. If the army of Lombardy stood at a much lower figure on Carlos II's death in 1700, this was due less to fundamental 'decline and decay' than to the normal process of budgetary cuts in military manpower at the end of a major conflict which affected all powers.[75]

Not surprisingly in view of these large numbers, the Milanese, which in the sixteenth century had boasted a significant armaments industry of its own, remained a significant arsenal (or could lay its hands on the necessary weaponry).[76] After the defeat at Staffarda in 1690, Leganes sought (through Spain's diplomatic network in Italy) to buy urgent military supplies from the neighbouring republics of Genoa and Venice.[77] At the end of the 1691 campaign, in a move suggesting that Spain's arms industry remained a vital source of weaponry and that Milan's armaments industry simply could not supply weapons on the required scale, Leganes requested 8000 Basque muskets, on the grounds that they were very appropriate in north Italy and far superior to the Italian arms carried by many of his Spanish troops.[78] In 1692 Leganes sent 150 wagons of ammunition to Piedmont for the invasion of Dauphiné. Whatever the shortages of artillery and munitions, for a lesser power like the duchy of Savoy the stores of powder and bombs,

69 *Consultas* on reviews (*muestras*), 23 Jan. 1692 and 22 April 1692, AGS Estado 3416/37, 129. (By way of comparison, the army of Flanders totalled 17 237 men, excluding garrisons, in February 1692.)

70 *Consulta*, 29 July 1692 on accompanying review certificates, AGS Estado 3417/51; *consulta* on *muestras*, 20 Dec. 1692, AGS Estado 3418/138–40.

71 *Consulta*, on reviews, 29 Dec. 1693, AGS Estado 3418/205–9.

72 *Consulta*, on reviews, 17 Apr. 1694, AGS Estado 3419/97.

73 *Consulta*, on reviews, 24 Dec. 1694, AGS Estado 3420/82–6.

74 *Consulta*, on reviews, 1 Dec. 1695, AGS Estado 3422/128.

75 Cf. the reports from Milan of the Dutch commissary, Albert van der Meer to Fagel, between Aug. 1696 and Feb. 1697, ARAH, SG, 8644/331–52. For a reduction in the size of the army of Lombardy in the later 1690s, see AGS Estado 3426, 3427.

76 Cf. accounts of arms, etc. which accompanied the army to Piedmont in 1690, AGS Estado 3412/108. In the spring of 1690, Fuensalida supplied arms to the Protestant irregulars, financed by the Maritime Powers and intended to open up a new front on France's south-eastern border; C. Storrs, 'Thomas Coxe and the Lindau Project', in de Lange, *Dall'Europa alle valli valdesi*, pp. 199ff. See also n. 201 below.

77 *Consulta*, 10 Sept. 1690, AGS Estado 3412/23.

78 *Consulta*, 28 Jan. 1692 on attached correspondence, AGS Estado 3416/47–59.

and the artillery train in the Milanese, was one of the attractions of having Spain as an ally.[79] Typically, in the spring of 1694, the duke of Savoy requested substantial supplies of munitions from the Milanese, which the governor did his best to satisfy.[80]

The prime purpose of the army of Lombardy was the defence of the Milanese (see below). A considerable proportion of that force might therefore be expected to be found in garrison in the many fortified places which were necessary to protect the rich but extremely vulnerable flat and open Milanese. These were a major source of concern to the council of state in Madrid and to the administration in Milan, which had strengthened them following Louis XIV's acquisition of Casale. According to the governor of the Milanese in 1678, requesting men and money from Madrid in view of an anticipated French attack, 5000 men were needed to garrison effectively all the fortresses of the Milanese. He was probably exaggerating. For most of this period, the number of troops in garrison in the Milanese and Finale (which was also garrisoned from the army of Lombardy) in peacetime totalled less than 2000. The review of March 1690 revealed just under 1700 infantry (officers and men) in 16 garrisons, the largest being Milan itself (over 400).[81] During the Nine Years War, with Savoy acting as buffer between Milan and France, the vast bulk of the army of Lombardy actually took the field during the campaigning season. In the summer of 1690 Fuensalida led 12 000 men, subsequently increased to more than 14 000, into Piedmont in fulfilment of the treaty recently concluded with the Duke of Savoy. The following year, Leganes also led 12 000 men (3000 cavalry and 9000 infantry) plus artillery into Piedmont; and in 1692 13 200 men.[82] However, the governor could not do without garrisons altogether and sometimes, particularly in wartime, had to increase them substantially, switching men as circumstances both dictated and allowed. At the end of April 1691, following a major (and successful) French offensive against the Duke of Savoy's inland and coastal territories, more than 11 000 troops (infantry and cavalry) were in garrison and as yet only 6000 (all infantry) in Piedmont.[83] The troops in garrison included nearly 3000 at the crucial Finale on the exposed Ligurian coast (see below), 1700 in Alessandria (20 miles south of Casale) and 300 at Gazzuolo, in the duchy of Mantua, supervising the demolition of the fortifications there. In 1692, while Leganes led his expeditionary force into France, nearly 6500 remained in garrisons throughout the Milanese, where the threat still posed by Casale could not be ignored.[84] Only the end of the French threat from Casale and that from Pinerolo in 1696 allowed a reduction of garrisons to the lower prewar levels,

[79] Landriani to Operti, 5 May 1691, Milan, AGS Estado 3654/76.
[80] *Consulta*, 29 Apr. 1694, AGS Estado 3419/112.
[81] *Relacion de la Muestra General*, 20 Mar. 1690, AGS Estado 3411/85.
[82] Leganes to Carlos II, Turin, 30 June 1692, AGS Estado 3417/48.
[83] *Consulta*, 29 May 1691 on attached documents, AGS Estado 3414/211–14.
[84] *Consulta*, 29 July 1692 on attached documents, AGS Estado 3417/51–6.

although the Franco-Savoyard invasion of the Milanese in 1696 inevitably obliged Leganes to switch more of his troops to garrison duty. Following this exposure of the vulnerability of the Milanese and its defences, Leganes planned a programme of improvements to those fortifications following the conclusion of the war in Italy in 1696.[85] The governor could only attempt to minimise the loss to the field army in assigning troops to garrison duty. In 1692 Leganes created three companies (subsequently reduced to two) of so-called *impedidos*, from among the aged, wounded and otherwise useless men on the army's strength, for garrisons.[86]

Since at least the establishment and rates of pay laid down by an earlier (the 1st) Marquis of Leganes in 1637, the organization of the army of Lombardy had approximated closely to that of the army of Flanders as described by Geoffrey Parker.[87] The whole was headed by the governor of Milan, as captain-general in Italy. Appointed by the King of Spain for three-year periods, as were all major officials in the monarchy, the governor was invariably (and for good reason, this being a military nerve centre of the Monarchy) an experienced and capable soldier. He was also generally a titled noble, often a grandee, originating in one of the realms of the Monarchy (but not always Castile): the Marquis of Leganes, for example, had been captain-general of artillery in Spain. The importance of the appointment inevitably made it a focus for the quarrels of the individuals and factions vying for power and influence in Madrid.[88] Precisely because he held such an important, responsible post, the governor had little scope for independent action, being subject to the king and council of state in Madrid, with whom he and his potential critics in the Milanese (below) maintained a frequent, regular and bulky correspondence.

Below the governor were the chiefs of the various arms: the artillery, cavalry, infantry and fortifications. The head of the infantry, the *maestre de campo general*, was second in command until 1678, when that position was assumed by the *gobernador de las armas*, a development which had occurred in Flanders 50 years earlier. The appointment in Milan was attributed to dissatisfaction with the governorship of the Prince de Ligne (1674-8), but was continued under his successors. Responsible to the *maestre de campo general* were the individual *maestres de campo*, or colonels of regiments or *tercios*. Responsible to the colonels were their regimental officers: company captains, chaplain, auditor, doctor, surgeon and so on. The captain headed the basic unit of the *tercio*, the company, with its official structure of *alferezes* and *sargentos*. Both *tercios*

85 Van der Meer to Fagel, [1696], Milan, ARAH/SG 8644/305.

86 Leganes to Carlos II, 4 May 1692, AGS Estado 3417/78.

87 Parker, *Army of Flanders*, pp. 106ff. and 274ff.

88 In Dec. 1685, according to the Duke of Montalto, the candidates for the governorship of Milan were the Marquis of Leganes, the Queen's candidate, and the Duke of Uceda, the candidate of the Count of Oropesa, the King's chief minister; *Coleccion de documentos ineditos para la historia de Espana* [CODOIN], LXXIX (Madrid, 1882), p. 337.

and companies varied considerably in size (and not just after the random losses of a campaign). In November 1695 the Spanish *tercios* in the Milanese each comprised 16 or 17 companies but varied from 700 to 1000 men in total. The Italian, German and Swiss regiments were generally smaller, and comprised fewer companies.[89]

Separate from the military organization was the pay office, or *oficio del sueldo,* responsible for pay and accounting. Regimental auditors were ultimately responsible to the chief accounting and pay officials, the *veedor general* and the *contador principal.* They administered, recorded and controlled the financial activities of the army, certifying the biannual reviews of the army of Lombardy, which ensured that there was no discrepancy between the pay-books in their office and the reality, and underlining the fact that the official figures cannot always be taken at face value.[90] The auditors also (along with the local Milanese administration) kept a watchful eye on the governor's expenditure. This is undoubtedly why in 1678 the governor sent the *contador principal* to Madrid to press his case for more men and money. A separate accounting branch for the artillery, originally established in 1646 and abolished in 1669 at a time of economies, was restored in 1692.[91] Such changes reveal a fluidity in the administrative structure of the army of Lombardy which contributed to the frequent clashes between the army officers, between civil and military officials and between the *veedor* and *contador.* By the end of the seventeenth century some of these offices were effectively hereditary. Diego Patiño, a mere *contador* in 1642, was *contador principal* by 1644 and *veedor general* by 1650. In 1692 Baltasar Patiño succeeded to the post of *veedor general* following the death of Don Diego Araciel, who had held the post as 'substitute' during Baltasar's 'minority'.[92] Occasionally special *visitadores* were sent from Madrid to investigate suspected fraud. A lengthy *visita* in Milan between 1678 and 1682 led to the arrest and trial of the governor of Finale. But this system was not always as effective as it should have been, and it is difficult to believe that fraud was eradicated. In 1691 Madrid had to remind the accounting officials in Milan that they must ensure that the proper procedures were followed in reviewing the troops, threatening dire consequences for officials found to be in breach of the guidelines.[93]

The representatives of the duchy of Milan at the Spanish court con-

89 *Consulta,* 1 Feb. 1696, on attached documents, AGS Estado 3423/6, 7.

90 The review of June 1691 revealed nearly 2000 men fewer than in the paybooks; AGS Estado 3415/27, 28.

91 *Consulta,* 20 June 1692, on related documents, AGS Estado 3416/153.

92 Cf. certificate of units of army of Lombardy lent to the Venetian Republic in 1686 for its war against the Turks, and terms, attested by D. Diego Gomez and D. Diego de Araciel, 'que por la menor edad de D. Baltasar Patiño situe de sustituto de Veedor General de dicho Estado y Exercito', 30 Jan. 1690, AGS Estado 3411/24. Leganes thought Baltasar Patiño incapable; *consulta,* 15 Apr. 1692, AGS Estado 3416/127.

93 Secretary of the *despacho universal* to Leganes, 6 Sept. 1691, AGS Estado 3415/136.

stantly complained to Spanish ministers of massive fraud in the army of Lombardy, and of a widespread misuse by the governor of his powers to spend. These claims must be treated with some scepticism as an indicator of the true scale (rather than of the main types) of fraud, but are a valuable insight into the complex system of payments which (as Parker has observed of the army of Flanders) could swell a soldier's basic salary, or *sueldo*. The main complaints of the Milanese in the 1690s echoed those of earlier decades: they claimed that large numbers of men were paid although absent, and asked for reductions both of the number of *ventajas* (bonuses) granted and of the number of officers allowed 'reformed' pay.[94] The essential problem was the large number of troops, each receiving the monthly *sueldo*.[95] However, there was also justifiable concern about sometimes real abuse of the complex system of allowances, basic costs being inflated by grants by the governor of *sobresueldos* (supplements) and one-off *ayudas de costa*,[96] sometimes without royal order.[97] In 1692 the council of state reiterated that the governor could bypass established procedures for emergency military expenditure, but not when granting *sueldos* and *ayudas de costa*.[98] But abuses and complaints continued. In 1693, the pay office complained that Leganes had ordered that Don Joseph Graelles receive the pay of a reformed captain which should (by order) only be enjoyed by those captains who had served in their present units for four years or who had been involved in a general 'reform'.[99] In 1695 the Milanese magistracy complained at Leganes' ordering the payment of arrears of *sobresueldo* to a number of colonels and captains.[100]

As in the army of Flanders, the costs of the army of Lombardy were swollen by a number of additional services provided for the troops by the administration. Lodging, or rather billeting, had long been a

[94] Cf. the appeal from the Milanese to Carlos II in 1676, another period of great activity and increased military expenditure, Add. 14009, fos. 211–14. The basic complaint in 1676 was that army numbers had increased, increasing the tax bill (the *ripartimento generale*) for the duchy as a whole.

[95] See L. Bulferetti, 'Documenti di storia Lombarda nei secoli XVI e XVII negli archivi di Spagna', *Archivio Storico Lombardo* VIII (5–6) (1956–7), VIII (5–6), for account of cost of army of Lombardy in 1678 taken from books of *contador principal* which gives an idea of the main expenditures and which would apply as late as 1700 (although, as with troop numbers, official costs cannot always be taken at face value).

[96] Fuensalida successfully requested an *ayuda de costa* for his return to Spain from his successor, Leganes; see *consulta*, 7 July 1691 on attached documents AGS Estado 3415/16–18.

[97] Cf. Carlos II's order to Leganes, 1695, to pay '8 scudos de ventaja al mes ademas de su plaza ordinario' to the *alferez* D. Pedro Gomez Serrano, after three years' service in the Milanese, Add. 15938, fo. 19.

[98] *Consulta*, 8 Aug. 1691, AGS Estado 3417/174, 175.

[99] Graelles had only been in the *tercio* of Naples four months before being allowed by Leganes to return to Spain; *consulta*, 12 Oct. 1693, AGS Estado 3418/58, 59.

[100] *Consulta*, 12 Feb. 1695, AGS Estado 3421/29. On this occasion the count of Frigiliana declared that if *sobresueldos* were not to be paid, they should not be granted in the first place, suggesting that some councillors (many of whom had personal experience of these problems – Frigiliana's brother, Don Jose Manrique, had served in Milan as general of the artillery from 1687) sympathized with governor and officers.

contentious issue in the Milanese (as it continued to be in many parts of Europe), until the sting was taken out of the issue with the introduction of taxation to replace billeting, with lodging becoming the responsibility of a contractor (the *remplazo* of 1662) by the then governor, Don Luis Ponce de Leon.[101] This solution of the problem was no doubt facilitated by the 30 years of peace in north Italy after 1659. The renewal of major warfare from 1689/90, perhaps inevitably, gave rise to renewed tension. The Guastalla campaign prompted complaints from the Milanese about its obligations (or freedom from them) to billet troops while the army was on campaign, reminiscent of similar ones in 1643 and 1676. Leganes was inclined to dispense with the *remplazo* and to billet his forces in the Milanese as in the past, but the council of state in Madrid advised against.[102]

Yet the administration was clearly assuming responsibility for many of the needs of its forces in Lombardy, as in Flanders. These services included field hospitals. In 1690, following the first campaign in Piedmont, the administrator of the hospitals of the army of Lombardy put their cost (including salaries and treatments) at 2000 (Milanese) *lire* a day.[103] But the most basic and impressive in scale was the supply of bread, or *pan de municion.* As in Flanders, this was done through a system of private contractors (*asentistas* or *impresarios*), who tendered for yearly contracts. In the summer of 1690 terms were agreed with Carlos Antonio Moltino for the supply of bread to the troops for the rest of the year, at different rates (depending on whether the army was in the Milanese or in Piedmont, where each ration would be more expensive).[104] Subsequent contracts conformed to this pattern, the only difference being the fluctuation in the price per ration, particularly as grain became more expensive with the dearth of the mid-1690s.[105] Contractors were also used to provide forage, campaign lodg-

[101] On the thorny question of billetting, among the heaviest burdens that the army of Lombardy represented for the population of the Milanese, and the administration's solutions to it, see M. Rizzo, 'Centro spagnolo e periferia lombarda nell'impero asburgico tra cinque e seicento', *Rivista Storica Italiana* CIV (1992), p. 342.

[102] *Consulta*, 3 Sept. 1691, AGS Estado 3415/89. See Leganes to Carlos II, Milan, 12 April 1697, for an account of agreement with contractor for *remplazo* for five years from 1697 (and reference to some of the problems of the war years); and, for comparison, Parker, *Army of Flanders*, pp. 166–7.

[103] Certificate, AGS Estado 3413/90. The cost of the field hospital was a constant, if minor, headache throughout the Nine Years War; see Leganes' memorial on costs and needs, considered in *consulta*, 23 Aug. 1696, AGS Estado 3423/163.

[104] *Consulta* (on *consulta* of council of Italy on the terms of the agreement), 12 Oct. 1690, AGS Estado 3413/27. For actual expenditure on *pan de municion*, see the account sent by Fuensalida at the end of the 1690 campaign, calculating the total of 6 *soldi*, 2 *dinero* multiplied by 13 000; AGS Estado, 3413/92.

[105] For the annual agreement, see Leganes to Carlos II, 30 Nov. 1692, AGS Estado 3417/152; same to same, 30 Nov. 1693, Milan, AGS Estado 3418/188; Consulta, 10 Feb. 1695, AGS Estado 3421/23; Leganes to Carlos II, 7 Nov. 1695, AGS Estado 3422/137.

ing[106] and the artillery train.[107] These contracts were established practice, and rarely provoked difficulties. However, when the governor had to act speedily to supply his troops extraordinarily, as in 1692, with 5000 pairs of shoes for the infantry destined for the difficult terrain of Dauphiné, his ordering the release of the necessary money without going through the usual channels prompted the Milanese magistracy to complain to the council of Italy (through its representative in Madrid), and the matter came before the council of state.[108]

Contractors were not always reliable, the forage contractor being ordered in 1678 not to give the men money in lieu. But, given that the remittances from the kingdom of Naples to pay the bread and other contractors (see below) were frequently in arrears,[109] it is by no means obvious that direct provision by the state would have been more effective. Indeed, by this time the debate between *administracion* and *asiento* examined by I.A.A. Thompson for an earlier period[110] had been decided largely in favour of the private sector; and it seems largely to have functioned well despite the financial (and, to a lesser degree, organizational) problems which plagued it, and which were exacerbated by 'foreign' campaigning in the 1690s. One indicator, perhaps, of the relative success of the system of providing for the army of Lombardy in the later seventeenth century is that, despite the fact that pay was often, as in the summer of 1696, in arrears, the army of Lombardy was not plagued by the sort of mutinies which undermined the effectiveness of the army of Flanders a century earlier. In 1691 some of the Grisons troops in Spanish service in Lombardy refused to march to Piedmont, claiming that they had not been paid. This delayed the start of the campaign by the allies,[111] but was rather unusual.

Since at least the 'reform' of 1659, the core of the army of Lombardy was represented by three Spanish *tercios* : *Saboya, Napoles* and *de la Mar de Napoles.* These constituted the 'establishment' of that force and could not, then or later, be considered for 'reform'.[112] During a

[106] Cf. Leganes' boasting of having agreed the *alojamiento* of the troops at a considerable saving; Leganes to Carlos II, Milan, 15 Nov. 1692, AGS Estado 3417/136.

[107] In the spring of 1692 Leganes agreed with the contractor who had supplied the artillery train in 1691 for the same in 1692 at reduced cost; Leganes to Carlos II, Milan, 19 Apr. 1692, AGS Estado 3416/146. See also *consulta,* 9 Oct. 1694, AGS Estado 3420/48.

[108] Leganes to Carlos II, Milan, 8 Aug. 1692, AGS Estado 3417/175.

[109] Leganes constantly complained of the delays in remitting from Naples the monthly sums agreed with the bread contractor. See Leganes to Carlos II, Milan, 3 Apr. 1693, AGS Estado 3418/96; and same to same, Milan, 6 March 1694 (*re* arrears owed the contractor for the artillery train), AGS Estado 3419/77.

[110] I.A.A. Thompson, *War and Government in Habsburg Spain* (London, Athlone Press, 1976).

[111] Vittorio Amedeo II to Fuensalida, 4 May 1691, AGS Estado 3654/73; Van der Meer to Fagel, 1696, ARA/SG 8644/315.

[112] *Memoria* of reformed units 1659–1692, AGS Estado 3418/66; untitled paper of 1693, AGS Estado 3418/229. An invaluable source for individual Spanish units is De Soto de Clonard, *Historia organica de las armas de infanteria y caballeria española desde la creacion del ejercito permanente hasta el dia* (16 vols, Madrid, 1851–62).

campaign the regular troops might be supplemented, or replaced, as garrisons by the rural and urban militias of the Milanese, despite the fact that Italians were generally suspected by the Spaniards of being inclined to capitulate to the enemy. Since the Milanese militias were obliged to serve in an emergency, they would also swell the ranks of the regulars when the Milanese was threatened with invasion – as in 1690 and 1693, following the allied defeats in Piedmont and in 1696, following the Franco-Savoyard invasion.

There was always a need for more troops, partly to make good losses. Desertion was a perennial problem. The authorities in Lombardy particularly feared desertion among those troops arriving from other parts of the monarchy.[113] Apart from better management of the troops and administration, particularly of pay, and agreements with Milan's neighbours (notably the duchy of Savoy, the duchy of Mantua, the republic of Genoa and the republic of Venice) to return deserters,[114] the authorities could only resort to severity. In 1688 a traveller passing through Finale recorded the execution of two soldiers, originally deserters from the French forces, who had been caught attempting to desert from Finale. The other main cause of wastage was the loss of men (prisoners, sick, wounded and dead) on campaign. The review following the Piedmontese campaign in 1690 revealed a fall in numbers totalling about 2000 and a substantial number (nearly 2500) of ill or wounded,[115] while Spanish losses at the battle of Marsaglia in 1693 were put as high as 4000.[116] Finally, besides making good losses, sometimes there was a need, as in 1689–90, to increase the army of Lombardy rapidly. These were the elements which explained the frantic efforts both to levy new forces and to complete existing ones in the winter months, a time-consuming and expensive process which occasionally obliged the governor of the Milanese to clash with the local Milanese administration as he sought to provide his recruiting captains and others with the necessary money.[117]

Spaniards were generally regarded as less likely to desert – or to refuse to fight, if not paid, than foreign troops – and were greatly esteemed for their fighting qualities. This no doubt explains why Span-

[113] Cf. *consulta*, 16 Aug. 1690, AGS Estado 3412/73.

[114] For Spanish preoccupation with desertion from the army of Lombardy to Genoa, and efforts to recover deserters who had entered Genoese service in 1680–81, see AGS Estado 3618/144, 145; 157–60; 211–12.

[115] *Relaciones*. See lists of casualties (and losses of horses, artillery and other equipment) sent to Madrid by Fuensalida, AGS Estado 3412/109, 110 and AGS Estado 3413/22, Fuensalida to Carlos II, 12 Aug. 1690.

[116] For Spanish losses at Marsaglia, see the account sent by Don Juan Carlos Bazan, Carlos II's envoy to the court of Turin, in AGS Estado 3656/3.

[117] Cf. Leganes to Carlos II, 11 Feb. 1692, informing of his having anticipated 400 000 *lire* of the salt revenues of the Milanese to meet the urgent cost of recruiting the infantry and remounting the cavalry. For similar proceedings, see *consulta*, 30 Nov. 1693, AGS Estado 3418/189.

ish troops were so highly prized by all observers,[118] and why successive governors of Milan generally sought them in preference to other troops. In the winter of 1694–5 Leganes sent some of his captains, and one of his senior officers, Don Felipe de Araujo, to recruit in Spain, hoping to raise 1000 men there (including 500 in Araujo's native Galicia).[119] The 1690s did see a big increase in the number of Spanish troops in the Milanese. By October 1690 there were four Spanish *tercios* there (Savoy, Lombardy, Naples and that of the duke of San Pedro), a total of 2365 men.[120] By June 1691 this had risen to six *tercios*, totalling 4290 men.[121] Leganes hoped to increase this to eight *tercios*, but by November 1691 the number had fallen to five tercios, with only 3899 men.[122] During the winter of 1691–2 the numbers recovered to 4214 men in six *tercios*;[123] but by June 1692 they had again fallen to five *tercios* (Savoy, Lombardy, Naples, Duke of San Pedro, Lisbon), totalling 3280 men.[124] Leganes was able to 'compose' these (i.e. maintain them) in the winter of 1692–93 only by 'reforming' them into two other Spanish *tercios* which had been sent to Milan.[125] The situation remained much the same for the rest of the Nine Years War, the end-of-campaign review of November 1695 revealing the same five *tercios* with a total of 4106 officers and men.[126]

Given that there were nearly 12 200 infantry in total in the army of Lombardy in November 1695, it is clear that the highly prized Spanish infantry were never a majority (and in fact generally a minority) of the troops available to the governor of Milan. This was true throughout Carlos II's reign.[127] The bulk of the army of Lombardy was made up of Italians, Swiss and Germans. The second biggest contingent, in 1695 and generally, were the Italians, i.e. local Lombard regiments and to a lesser extent units from other parts of Spanish Italy, although these might be recruited in the territories of Spanish Milan's more compliant neighbours. Milanese officials were therefore understandably concerned at French recruitment in neighbouring Parma and Lucca in 1671. In 1678 the army of Lombardy had included 400 men recently levied from Franche-Comté, a source which was effectively closed in the 1680s and 1690s. The neighbouring Grisons, however, supplied 400 men in 13 companies in 1689, and in the spring of 1690 17 compa-

[118] Cf. Vittorio Amedeo II to Operti, 15 July 1691, Moncalier, copy in AST, Lettere Ministri, Olanda, mazzo 1.
[119] Leganes to Carlos II, 14 Dec. 1694, Milan, ASG Estado 3421/6.
[120] AGS Estado 3413/68.
[121] *Relacion*, AGS Estado 3415/28.
[122] *Relacion*, AGS Estado 3416/39.
[123] *Relacion*, AGS Estado 3416/131.
[124] *Relacion*, AGS Estado 3417/53.
[125] *Consulta*, 20 Dec. 1692 on attached documents, AGS Estado 3418/138.
[126] *Relacion*, AGS Estado 3423/?
[127] In 1678 only half of the 7265 infantry in Milan were Spanish; *Relacion*.

nies (the additional four providing a garrison for Finale).[128] By 1689 the Swiss cantons were no longer a major source of recruits for the army of Lombardy, having moved into the French orbit (in 1663). However, in the 1690s Spanish and allied diplomacy in Switzerland succeeded in recovering some lost ground there. The Spanish field army in Piedmont in 1692 included two Swiss regiments, totalling 1600 men, while there were 2200 Swiss in the army of Lombardy in November 1695. By 1695 the army of Lombardy also included a regiment of Irish deserters from the French service.[129] Finally, the army of Lombardy continued in the 1690s, as in previous decades, to depend on supplies of German troops. In the spring of 1690 German infantry provided 22 of the 178 companies which made up that army (2638 soldiers and 280 officers).[130] In 1691 the emperor agreed to the levy of more German troops (for the Milanese). Applying the same sort of analysis to the much smaller cavalry complement of the army of Lombardy is less revealing, partly because there was a less clear-cut distinction between Spanish and Italian units. However, perhaps the most obvious development between 1690 and 1696 was the growth in the German element, notably the cavalry of the Elector of Bavaria and the Duke of Württemberg, taken into his pay by the King of Spain.[131]

Many of these soldiers were raised voluntarily, by recruiting captains supplied with the necessary commissions and money. But this 'official' method was by no means the only one. The cavalry troop raised by the Milanese Prince Trivulzio, in the 1670s, is typical of the extent to which local noblemen still played an important part in raising (and leading) troops after the so-called 'Military Revolution', particularly in areas where they had estates and influence.[132] Alternatively, foreign princes and others (the Swiss cantons and the Grisons) might conclude a capitulation whereby they assumed responsibility for supplying and maintaining a troop at a certain level (i.e. levying and recruiting) in

[128] *Relacion*. In the winter of 1691–2 Leganes ratified a capitulation with the Grisons for (another) 500 men in his efforts to increase the army of Lombardy; *London Gazette* 2732 (Milan, 2 Jan. 1692).

[129] They were among those transported to Catalonia; Stanhope to Hopkins, 27 Apr. 1695, Madrid, SP 94/74, fo. 26.

[130] *Relacion*.

[131] Cf. *Relacion*, AGS Estado 3416/132. For the Wurttemberg troops, see P.H. Wilson, *War, State and Society in Wurttemberg 1677–1793* (Cambridge, CUP, 1995), pp. 114–15.

[132] See C. Storrs and H.M. Scott, 'The Nobility and the "Military Revolution" 1600–1800', *War in History* III (1996), pp. 1–41. The reviews of the army of Lombardy reveal that many of its officers were drawn from the great families of Lombardy and from the nobility of Spain. The casualties at Marsaglia in 1693 included the marquis of Solera, eldest son (and heir) of the count of Santisteban, who was granted *grandeza* as the only appropriate reward and consolation for this loss; *consulta* of 12 Dec. 1693, AGS Estado 3418/194. For Prince Antonio Trivulzio's appointment as lieutenant general of the Milanese cavalry, see the thanks from Milanese in *consulta*, 10 Apr. 1694, AGS Estado 3419/78. For numerous appointments of members of the leading Milanese noble families (the Borromeo *et al.*) to commands in the Milanese militia, see A. Gonzalez Vega and A.M. Diez Gil, *Titulos y privilegios de Milan siglos XVI–XVII* (Valladolid, 1991).

return for a fixed sum.[133] Private individuals continued to offer corps on their own account. In 1695 Don Carlos Bononi offered a cash sum for a vacant captaincy of horse, half to be paid immediately and half on receiving a declaration from Carlos II that he would not be 'reformed' before being promoted.[134] The terms of these offers were not always acceptable. In 1696 Don Gaetano del Pozo, captain in the Milanese cavalry, offered to raise four companies of infantry (200 men) in the kingdom of Valencia, but on conditions the council of state would not accept.[135] In a rather different way, in 1696–96 officials found a way to pass on the costs of 'remounting' the cavalry in the winter months. This was a time when the king's horses were neglected by their riders, who were on leave, necessitating expensive purchases of new horses by the military authorities before the next campaign. In what might be regarded as a further abandonment by the central administration of its 'absolutist' monopoly of military provision – by contrast with the process of centralized state control regarded as such a marked feature of the so-called 'Military Revolution' – the Duke of Sesto decided to allow home for the winter only those cavalrymen who provided their own mounts. The move worked: 300 men who rode the king's horses decided to provide their own, making a great saving.[136]

*University of Dundee*

(The concluding part of this study will be published in the next issue.)

[133] See the capitulations for the Wurttemberg troops (1690), AGS Estado 3415/93; and for troops from the Grisons (1692) in *London Gazette* 2732 (Milan 2 Jan. 1692).
[134] *Consulta*, 2 Aug. 1695, AGS Estado 3422/34.
[135] *Consulta*, 28 Feb. 1696, AGS Estado 3423/20–2.
[136] *Consulta*, 19 Feb. 1696, AGS Estado 3423/14, 15.

# [14]

# The Army of Lombardy and the Resilience of Spanish Power in Italy in the Reign of Carlos II (1665–1700) (Part II)

*Christopher Storrs*

## IV

The Milanese could not, particularly in wartime, meet all its extensive military obligations alone. In 1678, in time of peace, anticipations and debt repayments meant that Milan's ordinary revenue, a total of 4.5 million *lire*, could not cover expenditure, while in 1690 the *Congregazione* of Milan, a leading organ of government dominated by the local nobility, claimed that the army cost 500 000 *lire* a month. The Milanese alone could not bear the cost of the army of Lombardy, particularly in wartime when costs soared. The 1690s saw just such a massive increase in expenditure associated with the war. Apart from the army, from the end of 1690 the Milanese was obliged to pay the Duke of Savoy a subsidy in lieu of allowing his troops to take their winter quarters in the duchy of Milan. Not surprisingly, the governor was obliged to ask the Milanese for more money, to a level not known since the Thirty Years War. He was also obliged to anticipate revenues,[137] and to increase the tax burden,[138] prompting repeated complaints to Madrid from the Milanese. Since the council of state in Madrid was always anxious about the implications for the monarchy as a whole of discon-

[137] Typically, in the winter of 1695–6 Leganes ordered the Milanese authorities to assign 25 000 *escudos* of the next year's salt farm to the artillery train (prompting the magistrates to take the matter up with the council of Italy); *consulta*, 6 Dec. 1695, AGS Estado 3422/131.

[138] In 1693 Leganes sent an agent to Rome to secure papal consent to an ecclesiastical contribution to the Milanese war finances; Leganes to Carlos II, 5 Apr. 1693, AGS Estado 3418/97. The correspondence in the Estado series throughout the Nine Years War is replete with financial problems, the governors' expedients and complaints from the Milanese.

2 **Christopher Storrs**

tent in the Milanese, and since it was very soon apparent that the Milanese alone could not supply the revenues to support a greatly increased army of Lombardy,[139] it was clear that the latter must be subsidized by the other Italian possessions, and ultimately, if necessary, by Spain itself.

It has long been thought that the declining population of Naples in the later seventeenth century made it difficult for that realm to continue to function, as during the previous century and a half, as a major recruiting ground for the Monarchy.[140] Successive viceroys of Naples complained that they could not supply what was constantly demanded and expected of them, and feared the disturbances provoked in Naples by forcible levies for service outside the kingdom.[141] However, these complaints were neither entirely new nor well founded. Fewer men were probably 'exported' from Naples to the monarchy as a whole between 1665 and 1700 than between 1618 and 1648–59, not least because the scale of warfare was not the same. However, although mroe work needs to be done to establish reliable totals, broadly speaking Naples seems to have remained a vital source of troops for the Milanese throughout the reign of Carlos II. Faced with a pressing need for troops in north Italy, the council of state invariably advised the king to order the viceroys of Naples and (to a lesser degree) Sicily to provide them. In 1678, with the Messina revolt over, a newly raised regiment left Naples for Finale, *en route* for Catalonia. In 1680 a *tercio de napoletanos* was formed for service in Milan and served there throughout the 1690s. Another new regiment was raised in Naples in 1690, in which year (following the breach with France) 1800 men were sent to Milan. In September 1690 14 galleys reached Liguria with 600 soldiers for Milan.[142] In addition to these forces, the viceroy issued commissions in the autumn of 1690 for the levy of another regiment for service in Milan.[143] By the autumn of 1691, following this substantial exodus, the council of state was anxious about further denuding the kingdom of Naples.[144] However, the traffic continued. In May 1693 five Spanish galleys reached Liguria from Naples with 500 Spanish troops;[145] and in November 1693, after the heavy losses at Marsaglia, more than 3000 Neapolitan troops were *en route* or waiting to leave for

[139] See Vittorio Amedeo II to Operti, 15 July 1691, Moncalier, copy in AST, Lettere Ministri, Olanda, mazzo 1.

[140] Stradling, *Europe and the Decline*, p. 182; G. Coniglio, *Il viceregno di Napoli nel secolo XVII* (Rome, 1955), pp. 23–4. For the Neapolitan military establishment in the seventeenth century, see Ribot Garcia, 'Las provincias', pp. 105ff.

[141] Fearing French attack in the spring of 1692, and popular disorder in Naples, the viceroy of Naples sought troops from Milan; *consulta*, 7 Apr. 1692, AGS Estado 3416/120.

[142] They were to serve in the cavalry. However, their horses were delayed as the right vessels could not be found; Consul Kirk to Nottingham, 16 Sept. 1690, Genoa, PRO SP 79, fo. 173.

[143] *London Gazette* 2411 (Naples, 17 Oct. 1690).

[144] *Consulta*, 3 Sept. 1691, AGS Estado 3415/89.

[145] Kirk to Blathwayt, 10 May 1693, Genoa, Add. 21486, fo. 30.

Milan. By December 1693, 2000 troops had reached north Italy from Naples.[146] Another 2000 left Naples in the spring of 1694 (although some of these were bound for Catalonia).[147] Indicative of the extent to which the effectiveness of the army of Lombardy depended on this flow of troops is the governor of Milan's complaint in the summer of 1690 that he could not send the 11 000 men promised the duke of Savoy in the treaty of 1690 because the infantry promised from Naples and Sicily still had not arrived.[148] Significantly, too, in the winter of 1695–6 Leganes sought to have the new Mallorcan *tercio* (above), which was inevitably delayed, sent instead to Naples, and for the viceroy of Naples to send an equivalent force to the Milanese.[149] The Italian leg of the Spanish 'system' was therefore still functioning in the last decades of Habsburg Spain, i.e. it could still supply from the south of Italy men for service in the north. There was no doubt that it sometimes functioned imperfectly, but it did not necessarily perform any worse than other state structures found wanting by the demands of constant warfare.

In addition Naples, for long the Spanish paymaster in Italy, to the detriment of its own finances, remained obliged to supply Milan with cash long after the extraordinary efforts of the Thirty Years War.[150] Throughout Carlos II's reign, the kingdom was obliged to remit 10 000 ducats a month to pay the contractors supplying the army of Lombardy's *pan de municion*. In times of emergency, or expected French attack (e.g. 1668) the viceroy of Naples was ordered to send more money to Milan. Inevitably, constant warfare in the 1690s increased the long-term commitment and burden for the kingdom of Naples. In the spring of 1693 the viceroy of Naples claimed that the costs of fitting out the galley squadron prevented him from remitting Naples' share of the subsidy paid to the Duke of Savoy by Carlos II. However, such laments were not new and heroic efforts were still made. I have no reliable totals for the reign as a whole, or for the 1690s in particular. However, it seems clear enough that, although the kingdom of Naples may not have been exporting the sort of sums it did at the height of the Thirty Years .War, Coniglio's conclusion that by the end of the

[146] [?] to Medinaceli, 5 Dec. 1693, Turin, copy in AGS Estado 3085.

[147] Morandi, 'Torino e Napoli durante la guerra della Grande Alleanza nel carteggio diplomatico di G-B. Operti (1690–97)', in *Archivio per le provincie napoletane* (Naples, 1935), p. 349.

[148] *Consulta*, July 1690, AGS Estado 3412/2. In fact they arrived very soon after.

[149] *Consulta*, 8 Feb. 1696, AGS Estado 3423/13. The difficulties encountered and raised by the viceroy of Mallorca in levying this force underline the real problems faced by the council of state in attempting to articulate (operating through a number of intermediary institutions, including the council of Aragon) a Monarchy-wide strategy in the face of local fears and preoccupations.

[150] For Naples' contribution to Spanish imperial finance in Italy between the middle of the sixteenth and the middle of the seventeenth centuries, and its impact on Neapolitan public finance, see A. Calabria, *The Cost of Empire: The Finances of the Kingdom of Naples in the Time of Spanish Rule* (Cambridge, 1991), which (despite its title) ignores the last 60 years of Spanish dominion.

1680s the kingdom of Naples was exhausted and unable to contribute as in the past is not entirely true.[151] That said, successive viceroys and the council of Italy in Madrid justifiably continued to worry about the long-term damage to Neapolitan finances caused by short-term measures to raise money during both the Messina revolt and the Nine Years War.[152] The continued importance of Naples and its contribution also explains Spanish and Neapolitan fears of a French assault on the realm.[153] If this had materialized, the Spanish (and allied) war effort in northern Italy would have been seriously undermined.

By the 1690s, too, Sicily, a net consumer of the military and financial resources of the monarchy during the Messina revolt, was again a contributing part of the 'system'.[154] In the summer of 1690 the Sicilian galleys carried 500 Spanish troops from the island for service in Milan – the Viceroy, the Count of Uceda, arranging for the remittance of sums to the Milanese to pay for those troops.[155] In August 1690 the recently voted Sicilian *donativo* was directed to be sent to the governor of Milan, although the latter was subsequently ordered to send 100 000 ducats to the Duke of Savoy. In total, Sicily remitted at least 250 000 ducats to Milan and 130 000 ducats to Turin between 1688 and 1696.[156] As with the kingdom of Naples, these figures do not compare with the sums remitted from Sicily earlier in the seventeenth century. The earthquake of 1693 undoubtedly reduced Sicily's ability to contribute more,[157] while Madrid was also unwilling to provoke another revolt. However, Sicily too continued to supply the army of Lombardy, and so to sustain Spanish power in Italy.

Naples, Sicily and, to a lesser extent, Sardinia[158] also continued to supply grain, which had long been an instrument of Spanish power and influence in Italy.[159] Grain was essential for the *pan de municion* prepared by the contractors for the army of Lombardy, and which was occasionally supplied to allied troops, as in November 1690 to the Emperor's troops in Italy. Late in 1695, Leganes requested 40 000 *tumulos* of wheat for this purpose from the viceroy of Sicily, the Count of Santisteban. Grain could also aid recruiting for the army of Lombardy. In the winter of 1693–4 Leganes allowed the Grisons to import 4000 measures of corn from the Milanese, in return for permission for

[151] G. Coniglio, *Il viceregno*, pp. 321–2.

[152] *Consulta*, 6 July 1690, AGS Estado 3412/6.

[153] See R.M. Filamondo, *Il genio bellicoso di Napoli* (Naples, 1694) for fears of a French attack in the summer of 1692.

[154] For the Sicilian military establishment in the seventeenth century, see Ribot Garcia, 'Las provincias', p. 108.

[155] *Consulta*, 29 Aug. 1690, AGS Estado 3412/89.

[156] L. Ribot Garcia, 'La hacienda real de Sicilia en la segunda mitad del siglo XVII', *Cuadernos de Investigacion Historica* II (1978), pp. 401–2.

[157] See Duke of Uceda (Viceroy of Sicily) to Bazan, Palermo, 21 Jan. 1694, AGS Estado 3656/33.

[158] See Count of Monterrey to Carlos II, 28 Nov. 1694, AGS Estado 3420/94.

[159] For the arrival at Finale (for Milan) of grain from Sicily, see Leganes to Carlos II, 30 Nov. 1695, Milan, AGS Estado 3421/3.

6000 German troops to cross their territory;[160] and the prospect of Spanish grain undoubtedly influenced the Helvetic Confederation to disregard French efforts to have them refuse the governor permission to recruit in the Confederation.[161] Finally, in 1695–6, Carlos II's ally, the Duke of Savoy, and other Italian princes turned to Spain after poor harvests, and it could have been unwise to refuse them. Successive viceroys might object that exports increased prices and the risk of popular disorder (especially if the exports became public knowledge); but Spain's imperial and strategic needs invariably came first. The viceroy of Sicily therefore sought to satisfy both Leganes and the Duke of Savoy, the latter being allowed in 1695–6 to receive part of his growing subsidy arrears in the form of Sicilian grain.[162]

However, particularly in wartime, the rest of the Italian possessions could not meet all Lombardy's needs. In this case, efforts were made to supply the army of Lombardy with men and *matériel* from Spain itself. A number of *tercios* passed from Spain and Mallorca (invariably to be 'reformed') between 1668 and 1689,[163] but this traffic was most urgent in wartime.[164] The Nine Years War was no exception. In October 1690 the Spanish galley squadron carried 800 men from Barcelona to Finale for Milan.[165] In the winter of 1691–2 it was hoped to send substantial numbers of new levies from Castile and Estremadura, and from the kingdom of Aragon to Milan. Not all these plans were realized; nevertheless, nearly 1000 troops did reach the Milanese from Spain via Cadiz, Alicante and Barcelona.[166] Late in 1693, following the allied defeat in Piedmont and Leganes' urgent requests for help, Spanish infantry, originally destined for Milan but then diverted to Catalonia, were embarked on the Italian galleys and a search made in Spain for artillery for Milan.[167] Unfortunately two of the galleys carrying these troops sank, and only 400 men were put ashore.[168] In January 1694, in view of the need for men in all theatres, Carlos II ordered the creation of a number of new regiments.[169] In the autumn of 1695

[160] N. Luttrell, *A Brief Historical Relation of State Affairs from September 1678 to April 1714* (Oxford, 1857) III, p. 248.

[161] *London Gazette* 2950 (Milan, 3 Feb. 1694).

[162] Count of Santisteban to Carlos II, Palermo, 1 Nov. 1695 and 13. Jan. 1696; and *consulta*, 30 Aug. 1696, AGS Estado 3658/23, 59, 109.

[163] *Memoria*, AGS Estado 3418/69.

[164] In 1675 400 men were raised in Granada for service in Milan; AGS Contaduria Mayor de Cuentas [CMC], tercera epoca [3a], legajo 3163.

[165] *London Gazette*, 2613.

[166] Cf. *consulta*, 3 Sept. 1691, AGS Estado 3415/89; AGS CMC legajo 3172; Madrid Newsletter, 20 Jan. 1692, Add. 25448, fo. 28, and *London Gazette* 2742 (Madrid, 24 Jan. 1692); *Memoria*, AGS Estado 3418/69. In Nov. 1691 the seven galleys of the duke of Tursis's (Genoese) squadron arrived in north Italy with 500 troops from Barcelona; *London Gazette* 2721 (Geneva, 24 Nov. 1691) and 2728 (Genoa, 15 Dec. 1691).

[167] *Consulta*, 19 Dec. 1693, AGS Estado 3419/4; *consulta* of 2 Jan. 1694, AGS Estado 3419/1.

[168] *London Gazette* 2939 (Genoa, 19 Dec. 1693).

[169] De Soto de Clonard, *Historia organica* V/VI, p. 26.

6 Christopher Storrs

he decided to send to the Milanese a new *tercio* of 4000–4500 men being levied in Mallorca.[170]

Again particularly in wartime, Madrid also contributed towards the costs of the war effort in Milan (as elsewhere).[171] In 1691 Leganes took with him from Madrid to Milan 300 000 *escudos* (a sum only raised by promising the exalted status of *grandeza* to the Genoese banker Grillo). In the winter of 1691–2, for example, of the 2 000 000 *escudos* agreed for the *indulto* (levy) on the effects of the recently arrived Indies fleet, 600 000 were to be remitted to Milan.[172] In the summer of 1692, in reply to Leganes' frantic representations, another 100 000 *escudos* was sent to Milan (and additional sums to the Duke of Savoy) from Madrid.[173] In the winter of 1692–3 Madrid remitted 100 000 crowns for the fleet at Naples (and 150 000 to the Duke of Savoy).[174] Finally, in the winter of 1695–6, Grillo (one of the leading *asentistas* in the 1690s) agreed to remit 300 000 pieces of eight to Milan (and the same amount to Flanders).[175]

However, as has already been noted, ministers in Madrid could not consider the needs of Milan, or Italy as a whole, in isolation. In the spring of 1692, in view of the pressing need to reinforce the garrisons of both Oran and Ibiza, the council of war urged that the necessary men be found among the troops waiting at Alicante for transports to take them to Italy for Milan.[176] Ministers in Madrid were, understandably, more concerned about the defence of the peninsula, particularly Catalonia and – to a lesser degree – Navarre, the two provinces most vulnerable to risk from French attack.[177] In November 1693, following urgent demands for reinforcements from Milan after the second allied defeat in Piedmont, the Duke of Montalto declared in the council of state: 'si se pierde Milan es una grandissima perdida, pero si se pierde Cataluna se pierden Cataluna y Milan'.[178] In the spring of 1694 the Marquis of Villafranca argued in the council of state that more resources could only be sent to Milan (for a siege of Casale) if there was no threat to Catalonia.[179] Nearly a year later the Constable of Castile asserted in the council of state that their main concern must

[170] *Consulta*, 24 Sept. 1695, AGS Estado 3422/83.

[171] In 1680, a year of peace, Madrid did not (need to) budget for remittances to Milan; Kamen, *Historia de España Menendez Pidal*, p. 273.

[172] 1 000 000 was to go to Flanders and 400 000 to Catalonia; *London Gazette* 2735 (Madrid, 9 Jan. 1692). For a similar order of priorities in remittances in the 1670s, see Kamen, *Historia de España Menendez Pidal*, pp. 267ff.

[173] Leganes to Carlos II, 30 June 1692, AGS Estado 3417/48; Stanhope to Nottingham, 30 July 1692, Madrid, SP 94/73, fo. 76.

[174] Stanhope to Nottingham, 25 Feb. 1693, Madrid, SP 94/73, fo. 103.

[175] Stanhope to Shrewsbury, 29 Feb. 1696, Madrid, SP 94/74, fo. 73.

[176] *Consulta*, 13 Apr. 1692, AGS Estado 3416/122.

[177] See *London Gazette* 2355 for the transport of 1000 troops from Gibraltar to Catalonia by galley (1689); and AGS CMC 3a, legajo 3326 for the levy of troops in Madrid for Catalonia (1691–2).

[178] *Consulta*, 1 Nov. 1693, AGS Estado 3418/178.

[179] *Consulta*, 15 Apr. 1694, AGS Estado 3419/87.

be Catalonia.[180] Indeed, the council of state seemed to regard the army of Lombardy (and that of Flanders) as a pool of troops to be brought to Catalonia if the latter was threatened.[181] Besides these competing demands, ministers in Madrid increasingly regarded Spain itself as an exhausted recruiting ground.[182] These factors, and the greater proximity to the Milanese of Spain's other Italian realms, made these latter a far more important source than Madrid for men, *matériel* and funds for the army of Lombardy.

This crucial flow of men and supplies demanded secure communications. The overland journey from Naples to Milan was not impossible, but it offered ample opportunity for desertion *en route* and depended too much on the goodwill of princes (the Pope, the Grand Duke of Tuscany, the Duke of Mantua), who might be swayed by French promises and/or threats. Spain's possession since the 1550s of the Tuscan *presidios*, or garrisons, made the sea journey more practicable and attractive. These garrisons represented an extensive naval and military complex of major strategic importance to Spain, and were a crucial element in another, less celebrated Spanish imperial communications link than Geoffrey Parker's 'Road' to Flanders. Part maritime, part terrestrial (i.e. the overland route from Finale to Milan, which constituted a less well-known 'Spanish Road' than that to the Low Countries from Milan described by Parker), the route between Naples and Milan played a major part in the supply of the army of Lombardy in the later seventeenth century. The Tuscan *presidios* comprised the *Estado de los Presidios* proper in the south (Orbitello and Port'Ercole on the mainland and the offshore island of Giglio) and in the north the city of Piombino on the mainland and the island of Elba (apart from Porto Ferraio).[183] Together with Sardinia and Sicily, the whole dominated the Tyrrhenian Sea, making it a Spanish lake and, in the words of the Marquis of Ios Velez, viceroy of Naples (whose responsibility the *presidios* were) in 1678, acted as a 'brake on Italy'.[184] The *presidios* also lay at the end of a line of communications between Spain and Italy via the Balearic islands and Sardinia. The garrisons not only allowed the Spaniards to intervene militarily in central Italy if necessary; they also – as was made clear in the council of state in the spring of 1691 (in response to a request to send the galleys to northern Italy, rather than to the *presidios*) – offered a valuable strategic position

[180] *Consulta*, 28 Jan. 1695, AGS Estado 3421/17.

[181] See Stanhope to Galway, 2 Dec. 1694, and 24 Feb., 10 Mar. and 19 May 1695; Madrid, Kent Record Office U1590/0154; G. Maura Gamazo and Prince Adalberto of Bavaria, eds, *Documentos referentes a las postrimerias de la casa de Austria* (3 vols, Madrid, 1927–31) II, p. 324, Lancier to Max Emmanuel II, Madrid (intention to bring over 3000 troops from Low Countries to Catalonia); Van der Meer to Fagel, 1696, ARAH/SG, 8644/327.

[182] Cf. Concern in the council of state at the poor success of a recent levy in Madrid; *consulta*, 8 Jan. 1692, AGS Estado 3416/13.

[183] See map in Alcala Zamora, 'Razon de estado', p. 299.

[184] See Los Velez' account of the *presidios*, 23 Dec. 1678, published in Alcala Zamora, 'Razon de estado', pp. 355–58.

from which the galleys could be sent to wherever in Italy or the Mediterranean they were most needed.[185] Typically, at the end of the 1691 campaign, the galleys of Naples and Sicily returned to their home bases for the winter, with orders to return by March 1692 to the *presidios*, designated the general rendezvous for all the squadrons (see below) in the Spanish galley fleet.[186]

The importance of the *presidios* was apparent in the arsenal, docks and shipyards, the extensive fortifications whose upkeep was a constant preoccupation of successive viceroys of Naples (each contrasting his own vigour with his predecessor's neglect)[187] and the substantial garrison. The works required constant attention. As for the garrison(s), there were said to be 4000 men in Porto Longone alone in 1665, and 3000 men distributed throughout the *presidios* in the spring of 1696.[188] Not surprisingly, the request of the Grand Duke of Tuscany in the late 1670s that he be allowed to purchase or otherwise secure the *presidios* (which clearly threatened his states) was rejected by Carlos II, even though Spain seemed incapable (because of the Messina revolt) of maintaining its position in Italy. The council of state was unanimous that the *presidios* were too important to be left in non-Spanish hands.[189] Similarly, in 1685, following a suggestion from the Spanish envoy in Genoa, Don Juan Bazan, that Spain seek Porto Ferraio (used by the French as a naval base in the recent war with Spain) from the grand duke in exchange for Orbitello, the council of state was very clear that the loss of Orbitello would merely expose the other *presidios*. Fears of a French attack on the complex were a powerful influence upon Spanish policy during the 1690s. In the winter of 1691–2 frantic efforts were made from Naples to reinforce the *presidios*, and above all Porto Longone, a nerve centre of Spanish Italy.[190]

## V

The other major contribution to the defence of the sea route between Naples and Milan, and between Spain and Italy, and so to the continued functioning of the army of Lombardy, was sea power. The latter inevitably played a major part in a monarchy, which in many respects was vitally dependent on ships for imperial communications and for the movement of men and supplies. Unfortunately, traditional accounts, where they have not simply written off Spanish naval power

[185] *Consulta*, 6 Apr. 1691, AGS Estado 3654/40.
[186] *London Gazette* 2713 (Genoa, 25 Oct. 1691).
[187] See Los Velez, 1678, in Zamora, 'Razon de estado', pp. 355ff.
[188] In the spring of 1696 Leganes, desperate as ever for troops, suggested to the viceroy of Naples, the Duke of Medinaceli, that he (Leganes) should take 300 Neapolitans from the Tuscan garrisons, to be replaced by new levies already under way in Naples; Leganes to Medinaceli, 18 Apr. 1696, Milan, CPS.
[189] Alcala Zamora, 'Razon de Estado'.
[190] *Consulta* of 3 May 1685, AGS Estado 3621/32; Naples newsletter, 29 Feb. 1692 in Add. 25448.

after the failure of the 'Armada' of 1588, have largely ignored the reign of Carlos II.[191] This is understandable. The large Mediterranean galley fleet of the later sixteenth and early seventeenth centuries was certainly a thing of the past. By contrast with the numbers of galleys at Spain's disposal in the half century after 1560,[192] the monarchy's Mediterranean galley fleet hovered around a total of just 25–30 vessels throughout Carlos II's reign. It was composed of a number of squadrons of varying sizes. In 1679 the Neapolitan squadron totalled eight galleys, that of the Duke of Tursis (i.e. hired Genoese galleys) seven, the Sicilian squadron six, the Sardinian two and the Spanish squadron seven – a total of 30. Spain's galley forces fluctuated around this level for the rest of Carlos II's reign.[193]

On occasion, the galley force might be supplemented by Spain's other naval forces. In December 1691 Carlos II ordered that the captain general of Spain's *Armada del Oceano* be directed to transport the nearly 900 infantry assembled at Malaga and Alicante for service in Milan to Finale.[194] In the summer of 1692 the *flotilla de guerra* joined the galleys in the Mediterranean, following the departure of the Indies fleet.[195] Corsairs – particularly, in the Mediterranean, those of Mallorca and Naples – also supplemented the king's naval efforts, in what may represent yet another aspect of that 'privatization' of warfare in Habsburg Spain analysed by Thompson.[196] Sometimes, too, private vessels were freighted to carry men and *matériel*,[197] although they still required a convoy. Above all, Spain benefited from the presence of allied naval power. This clearly contributed to Spain's successful response to the serious French naval challenge in the Mediterranean from the 1660s. Dutch naval support in the war against Messina was overshadowed by the presence of the Anglo-Dutch fleet during the Nine Years War, especially in 1694 and 1695. In the summer of 1694, following the arrival of the main English and Dutch fleets at Cadiz, a combined

[191] Duro, *Armada Espanola* IV and V is a useful if not exhaustive exception.

[192] See Thompson, *War and Government*, appendix, table H, pp. 300–1.

[193] P. Bamford, *Fighting Ships and Prisons: The Mediterranean Galleys of France in the Age of Louis XIV* (Minneapolis, MN, 1973), p. 41; Duro, *Armada espanola* IV, p. 350; Garcia, 'Las provincias', pp. 110ff.; R. Mantelli, *Il pubblico impiego nell'economia del regno di Napoli* (Naples, 1986), pp. 144ff. (Neapolitan squadron). For an intended total of 30 galleys for the 1690 and 1691 campaigns, see *consultas* of 1690 in AGS Estado 3990.

[194] Carlos II to Leganes, 21 Dec. 1691, AGS Estado 3415/126.

[195] Lancier to Max Emmanuel of Bavaria, 9 July 1692, in Maura and Adalberto, *Postrimerias* II, p. 20. In Sept. 1692 a Spanish fleet comprising 19 galleys, 17 men of war, and 3 fireships arrived at Finale, landing 3500 men for Milan and capturing a Genoese vessel leaving Marseille *en route*; Kirk to Blathwayt, 28 Sept. 1692, Genoa, Add. 21486, fo. 27.

[196] For the Mallorcan corsairs, see Operti's memorial, complaining at their seizing a ship leaving Nice; no date, AGS Estado 3654/57, one of the many references to the corsairs in the Estado series. I know of no detailed study of the Mallorcan corsairs. On Spanish corsairs in the Atlantic, see E. Otero Lana, *Los corsarios españoles durante la decadencia de los Austrias. El corso español del Atlantico peninsular en el siglo XVII (1621–1697)* (Madrid, 1992).

[197] In 1692 it was hoped to send Spanish troops to Italy on Danish ships putting in at Cadiz; *consulta*, 24 Jan. 1692, AGS Estado 3416/42.

10 Christopher Storrs

English, Dutch and Spanish fleet was operating in the Mediterranean.[198] However, English and Dutch naval support was neither constant nor entirely reliable. Throughout the Nine Years War and Carlos II's reign as a whole, communications and defence in the Spanish Mediterranean depended essentially on the monarchy's own 25–30 galleys.

Despite its reduced size, the Spanish Mediterranean fleet, financed largely out of ecclesiastical revenues (the *subsidio, cruzada* and *excusado,* administered by the *Consejo de la Cruzada*), remained very expensive.[199] The Sicilian squadron absorbed 10 per cent of the island's budget between 1688 and 1696;[200] while the Neapolitan squadron cost between 150 and 200 000 ducats a year. As with the army of Lombardy, many of the services associated with the Mediterranean galley fleets – including the Tursis galley squadron – were effectively provided by private contractors.[201] However, that did not mean an absence of the administrative (especially financial, accounting) cadres also present in Lombardy.[202] The chief commands were equally a matter of dispute and rivalry in Madrid.[203] Apart from the cost, the problems created for the galley squadrons by the failure to pay promptly the contractors[204] and by the state of the galleys themselves,[205] perhaps the biggest headache was the need to supply and replenish the large number of oarsmen needed to man the galleys. The seven galleys of the squadron of Spain alone required more than 2000 oarsmen in 1668. The supply problem was exacerbated by a high death rate. Most oarsmen were convicted criminals, sentenced to the galleys (*forzados*), although the proportion may have been falling throughout the seventeenth century, partly because of increased demand for convict labour elsewhere. Con-

198 Details in J.C. De Jonge, *Geschiedenis van het Nederlandsche Zeewezen* (6 vols. Haarlem, 1860) III, p. 425.

199 Thompson, *War and Government,* pp. 81, 91ff.

200 Calculation based on figures in Ribot Garcia, 'Hacienda'.

201 Cf. *asiento* (1662) with Duke of Tursis for four years; BL Egerton MSS 352, fos. 180ff.; and *asiento* (1681) with Don Francisco de Monserrat y Vives, Marquis of Tamarit, to supply eight galleys of the squadron of Spain for five years; Egerton 352, fos. 131ff.

202 The structure of *pagadores,* etc. is evident from the extensive records relating to the financing of the galleys in AGS CMC 3a. Cf. memorial of *pagador* of galleys of Spain, Mar. 1699, promising to make good 6000-plus *reales* missing from his last accounts; AGS Guerra y Marina 3908.

203 Cf. the appointment of Oropesa's candidate, the Marquis of Camarasa, to command the Neapolitan galleys, and the defeat of the Queen's candidate, in Dec. 1686; *CODOIN* LXXIX, p. 375.

204 For the failure of the contractors supplying the Duke of Tursis's squadron to receive the sums assigned them by the *comisaria general de la cruzada,* see AGS Estado 3629 (1695). The accounts of individual contractors, e.g. Lorenzo Justiniano, who supplied galleys of the Spanish squadron between the 1660s and 1680s, are in AGS CMC, 3a.

205 See the Duke of Albuquerque, viceroy of Sicily, to the regent (Carlos II's mother), 8 Nov. 1668, Palermo, AGS Estado 3492/17, on the poor state of the '*capitana*' (flagship) of the Sicilian galley squadron and the need to replace it (and the lack of funds for this); and Carlos II's order to the viceroy of Naples, 29 Oct. 1691, AGS Estado 3322/178, to supply the Spanish galleys with wood for 2000 oars, the lack of oars threatening to render that squadron useless in the next year's campaign.

victs remained the single most important source of oarsmen, half the complement of the Spanish squadron in 1668.[206] Fortunately, peninsular Spain and Spain's Italian dominions could be called on for their convicts,[207] while some of the lesser Italian princes sought to gain favour with the King of Spain (and to relieve themselves of the burden) by offering him their convicts for his galleys.[208] If these were insufficient, convicts who had completed their sentences might be retained, sometimes forcibly,[209] or slaves purchased.[210] There were occasional windfalls. The suppression in 1695 of the privateer stronghold of Ponza netted a number of Carlos II's Sicilian and Spanish subjects, who were sent to the galleys.[211]

Spain's Mediterranean galley forces were much greater than those of princes like the Duke of Savoy (whose fleet was negligible) or the (more considerable) Grand Duke of Tuscany,[212] and than that of the republic of Genoa, with six galleys in 1689.[213] The growth of the French Mediterranean fleet clearly represented a challenge of a very different order.[214] However, the fundamental problem of Spanish naval power and strategy in the Mediterranean in Carlos II's reign was the stark contrast between the relatively small size of the galley fleet and its vast range of responsibilities, and its crucial role in maintaining

[206] R. Pike, *Penal Servitude in Early Modern Spain* (Wisconsin, 1983), pp. 13–14.

[207] For the system as it operated in Spain, see I.A.A. Thompson, 'A Map of Crime in Sixteenth Century Spain', *Economic History Review*, 2nd ser., XXI (1968), pp. 244–67. For lists of convicts supplied to the Neapolitan galley squadron from that realm between 1667 and 1669, see Add. 20924, fos. 155ff. In Dec. 1694 Leganes was ordered, in view of the shortage of *forzados* in Spain's Genoese galley squadron, to send as many as he could, in time for the 1695 campaign; AGS Estado 3420/173. In 1699, Carlos II ordered the transport of convicts to Sardinia to supply the Sardinian galleys which were running short; Carlos II to Duke of Najera, 20 Jan. 1699, AGS Guerra y Marina 3908.

[208] In Dec. 1692 Vincenzo, the recently installed Prince of Guastalla, supplied twelve 'condenados al remo' and promised more; Leganes to Carlos II, 14 Dec. 1692, Milan, AGS Estado 3418/23. In 1694 Leganes justified his efforts to resolve the differences between the Prince of Masserano (bordering the Milanese and a vassal of Carlos II as Duke of Milan) on the grounds of the need to support a prince loyal to Spain and who – among other things – gave his *condenados* for the King's galleys; Leganes to Carlos II, 31 May 1694, AGS Estado 3419/164.

[209] For an abortive mutiny on one galley in 1698, see AGS Estado 3852/41–45.

[210] In his contribution to a *consulta*, 31 Mar. 1691, on the war in Italy, and emphasizing that it was no easy matter to put the galley fleet in motion, the Marquis of Los Velez pointed out that orders must be sent both to local magistrates (to supply their convicts) and to the viceroy of Mallorca to buy slaves for the galleys from the corsairs, and that the money to pay for the latter must be made available by the *consejo de cruzada*; AGS Estado 3654/34.

[211] Lambert Blackwell to Trenchard, 30 May 1695, Livorno, SP 98/18. Cf. Stanhope to Nottingham, 7 Mar. 1691, SP 94/73 fo. 25, for the English envoy's efforts to secure the release of English subjects condemned (in the Spanish Monarchy) to the galleys.

[212] For the activities of the Tuscan galleys, see *London Gazette* 2404 (1688).

[213] For Genoa, see the instructions given the French envoy there, 1689, in *Recueil des instructions données aux ambassadeurs et ministres de France depuis les traités de Westphalie jusqu'à la révolution française* (Paris, Gênes, 1912) XIX, p. 216.

[214] For the growth of French naval power in this era, see G. Symcox, *The Crisis of French Sea Power 1688–1697* (The Hague, 1974), pp. 12ff; Bamford, *Fighting Ships*; A. Zysberg, *Les Galériens* (Paris, 1987), p. 66.

12 **Christopher Storrs**

the strategic links between the Mediterranean elements of the monarchy: ferrying troops and officials, money, munitions and other supplies between Spain, southern Italy, the *presidios* and Liguria,[215] and carrying Spanish viceroys[216] and Spanish (and allied) diplomats to Italy.[217]

Not surprisingly, these issues and the burdens they imposed prompted a long-running debate in the council of state as to the best use and disposition of the Mediterranean galley fleet. Typical is the discussion in the council of state in the summer of 1690, against the background of a worsening international situation which posed the inevitable problems of defence priorities. In a *consulta* of 27 May the Constable of Castile reminded his fellow councillors that he had always urged that half the Italian galleys should be stationed in Italy and half in Spain, and now proposed that the Neapolitan, Sicilian and Sardinian squadrons remain in Italy and that three galleys of the Genoese squadron should join them. This would ensure sufficient vessels to transport troops and to defend the crucial Finale (see below). However, the Admiral of Castile argued that the galleys were not as necessary in Italy as they were in Catalonia.[218] A month later the members of the council of state still disagreed about how best to use the monarchy's galley forces. The constable now agreed that the galleys were not needed in Italy, following the French Toulon fleet's departure from the Mediterranean for the Channel. The admiral largely agreed, suggesting that the two galleys of the Sardinian squadron should suffice in Italian waters. However, the Count of Chinchon thought that the galleys of Naples and Sicily should remain around Genoa because there was now no threat to Catalonia (Louis XIV making his main effort in the south in Piedmont): therefore the Spanish galleys and the Genoese galleys in Spanish service should suffice in Spanish waters. The Marquis of Los Velez took yet another view, urging that all the galleys should remain together (in Spanish waters): in view of reports that 16 French galleys were fitting out at Marseille, it seemed foolish to him to oppose them with two separate, weaker squadrons. As for the marquis of Mancera, he believed that the two Sardinian galleys were insufficient to provide the transports necessary in Italian waters,

[215] In 1694 Borgmanero objected to a proposal to besiege Nice on the grounds that the necessary artillery must come from Naples; Borgomanero to the emperor, 5 June 1694, AGS Estado 3937. (Of course the alternative, the siege of Casale, better suited Spanish interests.) Cf. details of troops carried from Naples for Porto Longone, and enjoying rations on board, June 1694; AGS Varios/Galeras, 153; and ferrying of powder and men from Naples to Catalonia in 1695; Gastañaga to Carlos II, 29 Apr. 1695, Barcelona, AGS Estado 3657/65.

[216] The Marquis of Leganes travelled from Spain to his governorship of Milan via Genoa, on two galleys of the Tursis squadron, in the spring of 1691; *London Gazette* 2667 (Genoa, 19 May 1691).

[217] The English envoy, William Aglionby, was shipwrecked off Corsica when travelling from Spain on the Tursis galleys *en route* for Turin; Aglionby to Nottingham, 19 Dec. 1693, Genoa, SP 92/26, fo. 59.

[218] *Consulta*, 27 May 1690, AGS Estado 3411/116.

and suggested that one galley should be detached from each of the Neapolitan and Sicilian squadrons to reinforce them.[219] These sessions of the council of state reveal the choices facing Spanish policy-makers and the variety of options available to deal with them. This old debate was inevitably sharpened during years of warfare such as the 1690s, being founded upon basically inadequate resources to cope with a major defence commitment, and in face of an enemy who could attack the monarchy on a wide front and who always seemed to hold the initiative.

The imbalance between the wide range of functions outlined above and Spain's exiguous naval resources in the Mediterranean, particularly following the growth of French naval power there, imposed an often inglorious strategy, one which has no doubt helped confirm the erroneous impression of the complete eclipse of Spanish naval power in the Mediterranean in this era. Typically, in the summer of 1693, the entire Spanish Mediterranean fleet (galleys and men of war) fled to the safety of the virtually impregnable harbour of Port Mahon to avoid the French fleet which had descended on the Spanish coast.[220] In the council of state later that year, in an anxious atmosphere following the second defeat in Piedmont, the constable of Castile suggested that, once it was known for certain that the French fleet had either headed for the Atlantic or back to its Toulon base, the galleys should be ordered to Catalonia to carry reinforcements for the Milanese.[221] In January 1695 Leganes complained that the ferrying of troops from Lombardy to Catalonia would weaken the galley force in Italian waters.[222] In the spring of 1696 he informed the viceroy of Naples that, following the departure of the French fleet from the Mediterranean for the Atlantic, the viceroy could safely send Neapolitan troops to north Italy.[223] Louis XIV fully understood the role and strategy of the Spanish Mediterranean galleys. Instructing his own galley commanders, in the summer of 1696, to seek out and destroy the Spanish galleys, he observed that Spain had always regarded its galleys as a bond between its scattered Mediterranean possessions. It was precisely for this reason that Louis wanted to destroy those galleys.[224]

Just as the army of Lombardy performed successfully enough on land during the Nine Years War to reverse the defeats of the 1680s, so Spain's Mediterranean galleys successfully fulfilled their role in evading the French and maintaining the communications and supply links which underpinned the military successes in north Italy. In 1690 the prospect of Spanish naval support in the defence of his vulnerable

[219] *Consulta*, 26 June 1690, AGS Estado 3411/179.

[220] Stanhope to Blathwayt, 5 and 12 Aug. 1693, Madrid, Add. 21489, fos. 19, 21; Lancier to Prielmayer, 6 Aug. 1693, Madrid; Maura and Adalberto, *Postrimerias* II, p. 122.

[221] *Consulta*, 26 Sept. 1693, AGS Estado 3655/55.

[222] Leganes to Carlos II, 25 Jan. 1695, AGS Estado 3657/19.

[223] Leganes to the Duke of Medinaceli, 18 Apr. 1696, Milan, CPS.

[224] Bamford, *Fighting Ships*, p. 43.

14 Christopher Storrs

maritime territories (Nice, Oneglia) helped decide the Duke of Savoy to break with Louis XIV. It would be wrong to suggest that the Mediterranean was a Spanish lake in the 1690s. Vittorio Amedeo II's trust proved misplaced, the Spanish galleys being unable to prevent the French conquest of Nice (1691). Between 1692 and 1694, too, Spain's position in Italy and throughout the western Mediterranean seemed at times on the verge of collapse before the threat posed by the Toulon and Marseilles fleets. In part it was saved by the weather, Naples's saviour in 1693, and in part by the arrival of the Anglo-Dutch fleet in 1694–5. However, the Spanish Mediterranean galley fleet also survived because of the monarchy's impressive geographical and strategic resources, including a string of excellent bolt-holes stretching across the western Mediterranean (above all the excellent harbour on the island of Minorca, part of the Balearic islands)[225] and a clear-sighted strategy which gave priority to communication over fighting. This may not have been glorious, but it ensured that the fleet played its part in the Nine Years War, contributing to the articulation, preservation and resurgence of Spanish power in Italy. From this point of view, the Spanish galleys were more successful in the Mediterranean than Louis XIV's vessels.[226] Nor should we forget that, for all its failings, the Spanish galley fleet (each galley carrying its own 'garrison' of regular troops) was the only real allied naval force in Italian waters for much of the Nine Years War. In October 1690 the Neapolitan galleys pursued a number of French merchant ships into Leghorn, breaching the neutrality of the Grand Duchy of Tuscany, while the Neapolitan and Sardinian galley squadrons preyed on allied (including English) and enemy shipping alike.[227] Those galleys also achieved some striking successes in isolated incidents. In 1695 the viceroy of Naples successfully sent some of his galleys against Ponza, a port to the east of Livorno, under the dominion of the Duke of Parma, which was being used by French privateers.[228] Finally, although – like most of the belligerent powers, Spain allowed its military and naval strength to decline with peace after 1696 – Philip V inherited a fully operational fleet of 27 galleys in 1700.[229]

Sea power contributed to the defence of Finale, in Liguria, west of

[225] In the spring of 1695 1000 Neapolitan troops, who embarked at Finale for Catalonia, were caught by a violent storm; 140 were drowned but the rest were able to put into the friendly harbour of Port Mahon; Stanhope to Hopkins, 27 Apr. 1695, Madrid, SP 94/74, fo. 26.

[226] See Symcox, *Crisis.*

[227] Cf. AGS Estado 3689, 3858.

[228] Lambert Blackwell to Trenchard, 23 and 30 May 1695, Livorno, SP 98/18. This represented an extension of Spanish dominion in Italy, which the viceroy of Naples was inclined to retain. However, the Duke of Parma (supported by the pope) successfully pressed Carlos II to return Ponza at the end of the Nine Years War; AGS Estado 3684.

[229] Kamen, *War of Succession*, p. 58. From what has gone before it should be clear that Kamen's criticism, that Spain lacked an effective striking force in the 28 galleys inherited by Philip V, ignores their true role.

Genoa, the key point for the landing of troops and other supplies from Spain, Naples and elsewhere for Lombardy. An imperial marquisate, Finale had been occupied by Spanish troops in 1602 and formally granted to Philip III by Emperor Matthias in 1619, specifically to provide a landing-place for Spanish troops. Although substantial fortifications were built at Finale, the 1st Marquis of Leganes' proposal in 1634 to build port facilities to ease the landing of men and supplies does not seem to have been acted upon. It was reconsidered in the late 1660s, and permission for the improvements secured from the emperor.[230] However, the proposed works were too expensive at a time of economies, and again nothing was done. This somewhat reduced the value of Finale, which was not always easy to use, necessitating the occasional continued use of facilities in the territory of the republic of Genoa. However, Finale remained far too important for the council of state to agree to the proposal from the Duke of Savoy, Carlo Emanuele II, in 1674 that Finale be sold to him. Following the loss of Nice to the French in 1691, Finale was the only allied naval base in north Italy for the rest of the Nine Years War. This explains why Finale's normal garrison, which totalled just under 300, was on occasion substantially increased – as in the spring of 1691 (see above).

Once at Finale it was just a 50-mile march to the borders of the Milanese – although this was enough to allow significant rates of desertion.[231] There was no military road as such, another of Leganes' proposals in the 1630s for such a construction also getting nowhere. The route taken by the 'Spanish Road' between Finale and Milan ran in a north-easterly direction, across Mantuan Monferrato (above) and passing through Cairo, Spigno and Bistagno,[232] before crossing into the Milanese just below Alessandria. From there it was another 50 miles to Milan itself, although the troops might in fact be destined for one of the other fortresses of the Milanese. Unfortunately, the Duke of Mantua's switch to the French camp (and the French presence in Casale) seriously threatened the viability of this route in the 1680s. This obliged the Spanish forces landed at Finale to take a rather different, more roundabout route to the Milanese, across Genoese territory, entering the Milanese at Serravalle either after an overland march or after embarking again and landing at Sestri Levante (in Genoese territory, west of Genoa itself), and then marching to Serravalle. Significantly, almost immediately after the French entry into Casale, Spanish policy-makers sought to discover, from diplomats and archivists, whether the Genoese republic was legally bound to allow the transit

[230] J.L. Cano de Gardoqui, *La incorporacion del marquesado de Finale (1602)* (Valladolid, 1955), pp. 1ff.; D.J.A. de Abreu, *Coleccion de los tratados de paz . . . de Espana* (12 vols, Madrid, 1752) x, p. 454.

[231] Cf. Leganes' efforts to recover 80 soldiers who had deserted from the *tercio* of the Duke of San Pedro *en route* from Finale to the Milanese and taken refuge in Genoese territory; Leganes to Carlos II, 30 June 1692, Turin, AGS Estado 3417/49.

[232] See map in Parker, *Army of Flanders*, p. 71 (Parker otherwise says little about this Spanish 'Road').

16 Christopher Storrs

of Spain's troops. The contrary was the case. However, and despite the Genoese banning the Spanish fleet from their harbour (1683) for the rest of the 1680s, the republic granted this right of passage – so crucial to both the Milanese and Finale – on a yearly basis. Ensuring that this system worked (and arranging transports) was the job of the Spanish minister in Genoa. In the autumn of 1685, for example, the envoy, Bazan, sought specific permission (and Genoese commissaries – to help recover deserters and ensure trouble-free provisioning *en route*) for passage along the 'usual' route (i.e. Milan–Serravalle–Sestre–Finale) of troops sent from Milan to relieve the garrison of Finale, of 500 *desmontados*, going from Milan to Catalonia, and of 200 Spanish infantry recently arrived at Finale for Milan. This detour seems to have worked well until 1691, when the Republic, clearly anxious about its neutrality in the Nine Years War, evaded Bazan's request for transit rights for the whole year – though passage was granted on an *ad hoc* basis thereafter. By then the problems of both the Duke of Mantua and Casale were anyway largely resolved, making the Monferrato route less risky. Whichever route was used, Finale remained the linchpin of the Milanese supply network. In May 1685, the execution at last of the long-discussed works there was suggested by the Prince of Astillano, in the council of state, as crucial to prevent complete French mastery in north Italy. Similarly (and equally fruitlessly), following the conclusion of the Nine Years War, Leganes' successor as governor of Milan, the Prince de Vaudemont, proposed in 1699 the construction of a new harbour and arsenal at Finale which would have enabled it to play more effectively its proper role in the imperial communications and supply system.[233]

The ambitions of other north Italian princes were also a source of great anxiety in Madrid and Milan. This meant above all the Duke of Savoy, eager to implement his rights in Monferrato as embodied in the Treaty of Cherasco (1631). The issue was complicated by the great number of small imperial fiefs in Monferrato. As early as 1669 there was concern in Milan that Carlo Emanuele II was attempting to attach to himself some of the feudatories of the Langhe region of Monferrato.[234] The council of state learned with some concern in the spring of 1690 that the Emperor (desperate for money to finance his war effort) had agreed to invest Vittorio Amedeo with a number of fiefs in the Monferrato, and to grant him the imperial vicariate (a post of some dignity and influence in north Italy) in return for a substantial

[233] For the Sestre and Serravalle route, see Bazan to Carlos II, 12 Apr. 1685, Genoa, AGS Estado 3622/39 (for grant for 1685); same to same, 27 Sept. and 25 Oct. 1685, Genoa, E3621/152; same to same, 31 Jan. and 5 Dec. 1686, Genoa, AGS E3622/29, 73; Bazan's general account of his mission to Genoa (1685–93) and his duties, AGS Estado 3633/206. For Astillano's view, see *consulta* of 3 May 1685, AGS Estado 3621/32; and for Vaudemont's proposals, see *consulta* of 3 Oct. 1699, AGS Estado 3427/88.

[234] See AGS Estado 3380.

sum. Spanish ministers were concerned about the implications for the links between Milan and Finale and the wider monarchy.[235]

The fact that Vittorio Amedeo II was an ally of Madrid between 1690 and 1696 did not make Spanish ministers any the less anxious about the duke's ambitions. Savoyard ministers could not but be aware of these anxieties. Given the extent to which the Duke of Savoy himself depended upon Spanish military, naval and financial support during the Nine Years War, and Spain's greater influence within the Grand Alliance, Vittorio Amedeo and his ministers recognized the need to soothe Madrid's anxieties if their own schemes of aggrandizement were to succeed. In 1692 the Savoyard ambassador in Vienna, the Marquis de Prie, devised a project aimed at gaining Geneva and the Swiss cantons for the Grand Alliance by means of a renunciation of the traditional claims on the former by the house of Savoy.[236] Prie intended that his master should be compensated in Monferrato for his renunciation. To improve the scheme's chances of success, Prie made special provision for Spain's military highway through the area. Spain would be allocated a road through Monferrato from Milan to Finale, while Vittorio Amedeo would promise not to erect any fortifications in its vicinity (which might threaten its security). Spain's views were never canvassed, as the scheme never really took off. Nevertheless, the proposal reveals contemporary awareness of the importance to Spain of its 'Milanese Road'. When the Duke of Savoy sent a minister to Madrid in 1695 to propose that he receive territory from Spain in north Italy in lieu of his substantial subsidy arrears, he also offered guarantees to protect the Milan–Finale route, but again to no avail.[237] In the summer of 1696 Spanish ministers were very concerned to learn of proposals in Vienna to grant Vittorio Amedeo Monferrato in order to keep him in the Grand Alliance.[238] The strategic argument was not the only consideration in Madrid. (Leganes' response, when consulted by the council of state on Vittorio Amedeo's 1695 proposal, was thought to be too narrowly concerned with military communications.)[239] Nevertheless, it was an important one and continued after 1696 to cause concern about Savoyard ambitions. In 1697 there was renewed anxiety in Milan at Vittorio Amedeo's ambitions on the Langhe fiefs in Monferrato, and at a rumoured treaty between the Dukes of Savoy and Modena concerning the latter. In the summer of 1697 Leganes had to countermand orders from the governor of Finale to seize the castle of Gorzegno, which the Duke of Savoy had designs on, and possession of which would enable him to threaten communications between Finale and Milan. Although Vittorio Amedeo offered the Spanish king what he claimed were territories (unidentified) much better placed for the

[235] See AGS Estado 3411/37–42 (spring 1690).
[236] Details in Storrs, 'Diplomatic Relations', pp. 144ff.
[237] *Consulta*, 30 Dec. 1695, AGS Estado 3657/165.
[238] Don Joseph de Arce to Carlos II, 18 Aug. 1696, Vienna, AGS Estado 3939.
[239] *Consulta*, 25 Jan. 1696, AGS Estado 3658/31.

road to Finale, in exchange for a free hand in the Langhe, Madrid was not convinced; and in the summer of 1699 the Prince de Vaudemont sent to Madrid an agreement concluded with Marquis Giovanni Francesco del Carretto di Gorzegno, whereby the latter acknowledged the feudal superiority of the King of Spain (as Duke of Milan) in return for a cash sum.[240]

Spanish ministers were equally suspicious of Imperial ambitions in north Italy. After a period of relative weakness, the 1690s saw the Emperor making a new reality of imperial power in north Italy, not least by sending considerable forces there which obliged the various princes and republics to pay contributions or supply winter quarters for their maintenance.[241] While in the longer term the Emperor was undoubtedly seeking to strengthen his position in any forthcoming struggle over the Spanish Succession, in the short term his troops contributed to Spain's military revival in north Italy, the Milanese reaping the benefits of being an Imperial fief.[242] But Spanish ministers were increasingly suspicious of the way those troops were used. Their suspicions were heightened by the inclination of imperial commanders to divert forces to bring some of the Italian princes to heel. In 1693 Leganes refused the request of the imperial commander, Caprara, for troops to execute a recent imperial decree against the Duke of Modena. Leganes justified his refusal to Carlos II on the grounds of his unwillingness to divide and weaken his own force.[243] However, Spanish ministers were undoubtedly also reluctant to see the further extension into Spanish Italy of effective imperial authority. The governor's concern was less the justice or morality of Caprara's action, and more its effect on attitudes to the King of Spain among his Italian neighbours. Whereas intervention against the Duke of Mantua between 1689 and 1692 had been necessary, Leganes feared that intervention against the Duke of Modena in 1693 would erode faith in both the King of Spain and the claim of the allies to be defending the liberty of the Italian princes (against French oppression). In 1694 Borgomanero was urged to discover just what the imperialists were up to in north Italy. Spanish suspicions were aroused further by the reluctance of the Imperial commanders to agree to the demolition of the fortress of Casale following its surrender in 1695.[244] Demolition, and a peace in 1696 which obliged Imperial as well as French troops to leave Italy, thus removed

[240] Cf. *consultas*, 24 July 1697, AGS, Estado, 3425/183; and of 5 Feb. and 22 Mar. 1698, AGS Estado 3426/4 and 25.

[241] The growth of imperial power in Italy during the War of the Spanish Succession is described by Ingrao, *In Quest*, pp. 79ff. The situation in the 1690s is less well covered; but see Braubach, *Eugen* I.

[242] The extent to which Carlos II was an imperial vassal (for Milan, Finale, Piombino, Siena and much more in north Italy) is emphasized by the various investitures recorded in Abreu, *Coleccion de los tratados* X, pp. 386, 441, 454, 458, 467 and 481.

[243] *Consulta*, 27 May 1693, AGS Estado 3418/101–2.

[244] Carlos II to Borgomanero, 28 May 1694 and *consulta*, 12 Aug. 1694, both in AGS Estado 3937; Bazan to Carlos II, 18 June 1695; Turin, AGS Estado 3657/89.

another, if more recent and less obviously hostile, threat to Spanish predominance there.

## VI

What was the function of the army of Lombardy? Most Spanish policy-makers and officials saw Spanish policy as pacific, concerned merely with the *conservacion* of reputation and territory.[245] In this light, the army's main function was undoubtedly the defence of the Milanese, although on occasion it contributed to the defence of the monarchy's wider Mediterranean interests. In the spring of 1692 Leganes sought to send troops to Naples, where the viceroy feared a French attack and wanted troops to prevent popular disorder, and to the Spanish outpost on the Ligurian coast, Finale, which also feared a French assault.[246] In 1695, with Catalonia expected to bear the brunt of France's offensive, troops were switched from Lombardy to Catalonia.[247]

The army might also be used, as we have seen, in support of Spain's allies and clients among the lesser princes and feudatories and other Italian powers in north Italy, against rebellious subjects or external foes. In the late 1680s, units of the army of Lombardy were lent to the republic of Venice for the war against the Turks (in addition relieving the Milanese of their financial burden).[248] In wartime, as we have seen in the Nine Years War, the army of Lombardy might take the offensive. However, Leganes and most of the members of the council of state in Madrid were not entirely happy about participating in the invasion of Dauphiné in 1692. This was above all because of the threat to the size and quality of an army whose numbers were always too low, and both expensive and difficult to replace, and whose defeat or ruin might leave the Milanese exposed.[249] Spanish commanders were horrified at the proposal that they take their winter quarters in Dauphiné, so far from their home base. Leganes was also very concerned at the loss of good, especially experienced troops that any adventurous strategy or demanding campaign involved.[250] This inevitably created difficulties with allies, who suspected rightly that Fuensalida, Leganes and Spanish ministers generally were interested primarily in 'local' concerns (the defence of Milan, the expulsion of the French from Casale and

[245] See Lancina, *Comentarios.*

[246] Leganes to Carlos II, 9 Mar. 1692, AGS Estado 3416/121.

[247] Leganes to Carlos II, 25 Jan. 1695, AGS Estado 3657/19.

[248] Details in AGS Estado 3411/24.

[249] Strikingly, in the *consulta* of the council of state of 19 Aug. 1696, on the implications of the Duke of Savoy's desertion of his allies, the Count of Monterrey thought that an allied defeat in north Italy might provoke 'unas vespras sicilianas' – presumably either another anti-Spanish revolt in Sicily or in Milan itself; AGS Estado 3423/150.

[250] In part this was because whereas the Milanese was not obliged to support the army of Lombardy when it operated outside the Milanese, Dauphiné was incapable of supporting them; Leganes to Carlos II, 12 Oct. 1692, Genoa, AGS Estado 3417/106.

Pinerolo) and not keen to carry the war into France[251] – although the Spanish commanders' doubts about the wisdom of the sort of risky battle strategy favoured by Vittorio Amedeo II were shared by other allied commanders. Such battles might, for no very obvious advantage (to Spain and its Monarchy), jeopardize the existence of that army of Lombardy which was the key to the survival of Spanish Milan and the focus of the Spanish system in Italy. As with Spain's Mediterranean galley force, it was crucial to ensure that this remained intact as a deterrent rather than risk it attempting anything more ambitious. That was not to say that Spanish policy-makers were not ready to mount major offensives: they did so against Guastalla (1689) and Casale (1695). However, they preferred to pursue their own strategies and ambitions. Such concerns confirmed a view, held by a number of senior Spanish soldiers and policy-makers, that Spain should have a large force of its own in north Italy in order to be able to undertake the sort of operations it preferred there, rather than having to do as her allies wished. This was, effectively, the *raison d'être* of the continued existence of the army of Lombardy.[252]

## VII

Like any system, the Spanish Monarchy in the 1690s had its weaknesses and failings. In May 1692, 1300 men assembled at Alicante since the winter for service in Milan were still there awaiting transports, and did not reach Milan that year.[253] The previous month, Leganes had complained that the bread contractor in Milan could not fulfil his obligations because he had received no remittances from Naples, where the viceroy had used the funds to fit out galleys ordered to Spain.[254] These examples suggest that the term 'system' may be incorrect, implying smooth structure when the reality was frantic juggling with inadequate resources and constant frustration of plans. However, the Spanish system in north Italy continued to work well and to fulfil its essential purpose: the supply of the army of Lombardy and the maintennce of territory, power and reputation, which were greater in the closing years of Carlos II's reign than they had been in 1680 or 1690. Spain's success in Italy and elsewhere in the Nine Years War obviously owed something to the diversion of French resources in other theatres and to the military and naval efforts in Italy and the Mediterranean. Equally, the breakdown of the Grand Alliance in Italy in 1696 owed something to Spanish failures: to pay subsidies and to provide military

[251] Coloma to Carlos II, 21 Nov. 1690, Hague, AGS Estado 3989. Cf. D. McKay, *Prince Eugene of Savoy* (London, 1977), p. 33.

[252] Cf. *consultas*, 26 Sept. 1692, and attached correspondence, AGS Estado 3417/94–98.

[253] Bazan to Leganes, 8 May 1692, Genoa, AGS Estado 3416/178. The men at Alicante were diverted to Catalonia, to Leganes' chagrin, Leganes to Carlos II, 17 July 1692, Camp at San Segundo, AGS Estado 3417/75.

[254] *Consulta*, 3 May 1692, AGS Estado 3416/141.

and naval help either as promptly or as much as promised. Nor, finally, can we ignore the probability that Louis XIV offered Spain much better peace terms than it merited in 1697 in order to advance the Bourbon cause in the diplomatic struggle for the Spanish Succession. However, without the efforts and resources of Spain the Grand Alliance could not have halted the apparently unstoppable progress of Louis XIV. This owed a great deal both to a dogged will to conserve the Monarchy and to the relative coherence and articulation of its structures (plus some very able soldiers, diplomats and others).[255] The 1690s were, at least by contrast with the 1660s, 1670s and 1680s, a great success for the Spanish Monarchy, both in general and in Italy in particular. Having weathered the storm of these earlier decades, the Spanish system remained operational and was used to great effect in the 1690s. It remained intact on Carlos II's death, when an entirely new political situation was created which led to the break-up of that system.

The reign of Carlos II was not therefore one simply of bleak and inexorable decline. Spanish structures were certainly tested and sometimes found wanting, but that was true of all those states involved in major warfare. Allied leaders were frequently exasperated (and even hindered) by the precedence quarrels between the Spanish and imperial forces in Italy,[256] but there was some justification for the insistence of the army of Lombardy on its separate identity, both as a recognition of its own role and achievement and as ensuring an independent instrument of policy for Madrid. As we have seen, the army of Lombardy in the later seventeenth century was by no means fully integrated into a highly centralized, bureaucratic state structure as in the Military Revolution model of Michael Roberts, although at the same time the Italian dominions may have been more integrated into the overall monarchy, partly at least because of the pressures of war and the seriousness of the foreign, above all French, threat. We should above all be impressed that the supposedly moribund Spanish Monarchy had survived and in the final phase of Carlos II's reign was able to participate in a major European struggle and reverse some major recent losses. This may represent the positive aftermath of a Monarchy-wide equivalent to the 'last Castilian crisis' identified by Antonio Dominguez Ortiz and Kamen.[257] Whether this is so or not, in European terms the Spanish Monarchy was stronger and in a better position in 1700 than it had been in 1678 and even in 1688.

*University of Dundee*

[255] Allied leaders in Italy in the 1690s generally admired Leganes' zeal and ability, cf. Vittorio Amedeo II to Operti, 15 July 1691, Moncalier, AST, LM, Olanda, mazzo 1.

[256] Vittorio Amedeo II to de la Tour, 5 Dec. 1691, Turin, AST, LM, Olanda, mazzo 1.

[257] A. Dominguez Ortiz, 'La Crisis de Castilla en 1677–1687', in ibid., *Crisis y Decadencia de la Espana de los Austrias* (Barcelona, 1973), pp. 197ff.; H. Kamen, 'The Decline of Castile: The Last Crisis', *Economic History Review* XVII (1964), pp. 63ff.

22 Christopher Storrs

## Acknowledgements

I should like to thank Dr Derek McKay of the London School of Economics and Dr H.M. Scott of the University of St Andrews for their comments on an earlier version of this article.

# [15]

# War in German Thought from the Peace of Westphalia to Napoleon

*Peter H. Wilson*

The study of ideas about war is dominated by discussion of military theory, philosophical commentary and international law. Nowhere is this more the case than for Germany, where it seems impossible to move without encountering the towering figure of Carl von Clausewitz (1780–1831). Dissections of his seminal work *On War*, along with those of other major figures like Frederick the Great, King of Prussia (1740–86), predominate.[1] The wider social and cultural context in which such ideas took shape and the political purposes to which they were applied often disappear into the background. It is upon this 'background' that I intend to focus my attention.

In doing so I will commit what to many will appear heresy and ignore Clausewitz; not because I regard him as insignificant, but because the intellectual origins and importance of his thought have already been documented elsewhere.[2] Instead, I wish to concentrate on German attitudes to two key aspects of war and how these related to political theory and practice. These are the purposes of war, the nature of the instrument fashioned to wage it and the association of both with the rise of the centralizing, absolutist German territorial state. While narrowing the focus somewhat with regard to the issues, I intend to widen the selection of individual views to include not only major military and political theorists, but also rulers, statesmen and, where possible, ordinary soldiers and civilians. Further, the investigation will touch on, but not discuss in detail, three related areas. The first is the question of what motivated men[3] to fight. This can only be answered adequately by investigating matters like recruitment practices, conditions of service and the social composition of armed forces, all of which lie largely beyond the scope of this study. These problems also limit discussion of military–civil relations which constitute a second important area.[4] The third is the thorny question of militarism, any discussion of which must confront the complex problem of definition which also cannot be resolved here.[5] In the following I shall use the term militarism in a largely cultural sense, denoting the glorification of war and the warrior and the diffusion of military ways of thinking and acting among non-military sections of society. I regard this as distinct from, though related to, the process of militarization by which I mean the accumulation of coercive means in the form of organized physical force. Any discussion of war in German thought must be set in the context of this essentially political development which took a distinct course within the Holy Roman Empire, or Reich.

Elsewhere in Europe, militarization accompanied and indeed propelled the formation of 'national states', meaning government of multiple contiguous regions by a centralized, differentiated and autonomous political structure, rather than the narrower 'nation-state' with its connotations of a distinct symbolic identity.[6] This process was characterized by monopoly formation whereby a ruler and his allies centralized coercive powers, eliminating domestic rivals and excluding external jurisdictions.[7] The most important monopolies were those of violence and taxation, supported by an increasingly sophisticated bureaucratic infrastructure designed to extract war-making resources from the local networks of trade and production. One of the major distinguishing features between early modern and modern Europe is the transformation of these structures from private to public monopolies. The state took on a form which transcended the life of the individual ruler while control of the fiscal-military apparatus shifted to broader sections of society. Both the Glorious Revolution (1688) and the French Revolution (1789) have been identified as important stages in these transformations for Britain and France respectively.[8]

Monopoly formation took a different course in the Reich.[9] Political centralization by the emperor was prevented by a complex system of practical and constitutional checks on his power, developed since the late fifteenth century and consolidated in the period 1648–84. An internal equilibrium emerged to regulate inner-German politics, preserving the traditional status quo by a combination of collective security and domestic conflict resolution. 'Imperial absolutism', so far as Habsburg emperors had ever attempted it, was prevented, but at the cost of stunting monopoly formation at national level. While the emperor was left with formal war-making powers, he was denied an infrastructure to put these into effect, beyond what he could establish in his own hereditary lands. There was no permanent imperial army (*Reichsarmee*), just a fairly slow mobilization system, last reformed in 1681–2. Provision of the actual forces was devolved to the princely territories and autonomous cities which made up the Reich. Monopoly formation thus took place at territorial level and involved local disputes between princes and their estates (*Landstände*) which claimed to represent the wider interests of the inhabitants. National coordination was dependent on the shifting balance between emperor and princes, while that at regional level rested on the system of *Kreise*, or imperial circles, which operated with varying effectiveness across the Reich.

Permanent territorial armies emerged slowly from the bodyguard and garrison companies established in the larger principalities in the later sixteenth century to provide a professional core for the militia forces which were periodically restructured and retrained to bring them into line with military developments. Contrary to the general view of German military history which emphasizes Prussia, Austria was at the forefront of this process, as the Habsburgs' greater resources enabled them to maintain sizeable numbers of professional soldiers permanently from the 1580s. Several other territories like Saxony and Bavaria mobilized large forces during the Thirty Years War (1618–48), but it was not until the 1650s that these achieved the permanence and inner coherence of the Habsburg army. The prolonged wars against France and the Turks from the 1660s encouraged medium and smaller territories to militarize so that even comparatively minor states like Bamberg or Mainz had the equivalent of one percent or more of their populations under arms by the end of the century. Wartime mobilization, which generally saw the activation of the militia, could push this proportion to well over 5 percent.

These levels were sustained by a mixture of voluntary enlistment and modifications of militia recruitment to provide either temporary or permanent drafts into regular formations. All armies recruited a significant population of their soldiers beyond their frontiers, though most of these 'foreigners' actually came from other German territories. The emperor enjoyed considerable prerogatives in this respect, particularly in the imperial cities, but any prince could recruit elsewhere provided he had the permission of the relevant authorities.

Individually, the territorial armies remained small, but collectively they equalled or surpassed that maintained by France, which in 1678 possessed the largest single force seen in Europe since the Roman Empire. This high degree of militarization was associated with a political shift towards absolutism, but, as this article will show, it also coexisted with a widespread abhorrence of war.

## I

The mid-seventeenth century saw a shift in German attitudes to war that was fundamental in forming the rhetoric of political centralization at territorial level. The traditional idea that war was a natural disaster or sent by God as divine punishment was gradually giving way to a more mechanistic view of conflict governed by rational rules pursued for rational ends. In itself, the notion that war should adhere to rules was nothing new. What changed was that these rules were increasingly defined in secular terms associated with the centralizing absolutist territorial state.

Like that elsewhere in Christian Europe, German thought had long maintained that combatants should follow the laws of war (*bellum iustrum*), dating back to the writings of St Augustine. These laws had two elements. The *ius in bello*, provided rules for the conduct of hostilities, specifying for instance guidelines for the treatment of prisoners and civilians. The *ius ad bellum* concerned itself with establishing criteria by which conflicts could be considered 'just' and reconciled with the Christian commandments prohibiting killing and hostility to neighbours. The first criterion was the 'principle of authority' (*auctoritas principis*) that war could only be waged by a recognized, legally constituted authority. Second, there had to be 'just cause' (*iusta causa*) to begin a conflict, such as self-defence or upholding a legal right. Finally, belligerents should follow the 'right intention' (*recta intentio*) defined by St Augustine as promoting good and avoiding evil. In short, the purpose of any just war should be to promote peace. If few had difficulty accepting these basic concepts, their precise definition always provoked intense controversy, not only among theorists, theologians and rulers, but also among a wider public.[10]

It is in these debates that the rhetoric surrounding German territorial militarization took shape. Despite the traumatic experience of the Thirty Years War, few German theorists seem to have shared the bleak view of human nature elaborated in Hobbes' *Leviathan*. However, most tended to agree with Samuel Pufendorf (1632–94) that kinship between men was 'a rather weak force'. Though 'natural law' provided common ground, Pufendorf believed that people should regard their fellow beings 'not indeed as our enemy, but as a friend we cannot wholly rely on'. It followed that 'a cautious man who loves his own security will believe all men his friends but liable at any time to become his enemies; he will keep peace with all, knowing that it may soon be exchanged for war. This is the reason why that country is considered happy which even in peace contemplates war'.[11]

Practical men of war and politics concurred. Count Raymondo Montecuccoli (1609–80), the imperial general, believed that friendship depended solely on convergence of interest. It followed that princes made and broke alliances as it suited them, their actions belying the expression of perpetual friendship that prefaced their treaties. The lesson was clear: 'statesmen cannot doubt that there can be no real peace between powerful competing states; one must suppress or be suppressed, one must either kill or perish'.[12] The Great Elector, Friedrich Wilhelm of Brandenburg-Prussia (1640–88), advised his successor in a similar vein that 'alliances to be sure are good, but one's own forces are better still. One can rely on these with more security.'[13]

Increasingly, the same military and political conclusions were drawn from this conception of interpersonal and international relations. The best defence was a permanent army. 'Whoever wants peace', wrote Montecuccoli in 1641, 'prepares himself for war. The most important preparation is the assembly of a strong numerous army, because great things are only achieved with great power.'[14] To Pufendorf and others, this had clear political implications for only a state was capable of organizing such a force. War became 'the true and principle cause' why people came together and submitted themselves to the common authority of the state. Natural law might encourage general benevolence but in practice it needed states to uphold it:

> It is therefore a duty of sovereigns to take measures to develop military virtue and skill with weapons in the citizens, and to make ready in good time all that is needed for repelling force: fortified places, weapons, soldiers and — the sinews of action — money.[15]

The philosophical underpinnings of the military and fiscal monopolies were in place. Whether they liked it or not, theologians and theorists found that the princes were closing their debate on what constituted the right 'authority' to wage war. The *bellum iustum* concepts were being reworked so that only the sovereign state had a legitimate monopoly of violence. A key element of this was in place by the mid-seventeenth century with the defusion of Bodin's concept of indivisible sovereignty. 'Declaring war or making peace is one of the most important points of majesty, since it often entails the ruin or preservation of a state.'[16]

Most German political theorists were uncomfortable with such inflexible notions which conflicted so obviously with the fragmented sovereignty of the Reich. Leibniz penned his lengthy tract *Caesarinus Fürstenerius* in 1677 precisely to redefine indivisible sovereignty and permit princes like his employer, the Duke of Hanover, a role in international relations alongside the emperor.[17] Though there was general agreement that war and peace-making powers rested in the sovereign ruler, the idea that these should be absolute was rejected in favour of some form of limited participation in executive control of the monopoly of violence by representative institutions such as the estates. Hermann Conring (1606–81) was probably the most extreme in his rejection of absolutism, arguing that the introduction of mercenaries into the Reich in the previous century had profoundly altered its political character by promoting princely 'despotism'. Others like Pufendorf looked across the Rhine to France. In his history of European states written in 1682, Pufendorf argued that French military success did indeed derive from its absolutist structure but saw this as a creation dating back to Louis XI. France was widely regarded as a military despotism, the ruler of which was effectively satirized by Leibniz in 1683 as *Mars Christianissimus*, or 'the Most Christian War God'. Few endorsed France as a model solution to the religious and civil strife of Germany's recent past.[18]

Princes and their apologists were ambivalent towards these ideas, accepting their validity for national politics where few wished to endorse imperial absolutism, but rejecting them at territorial level as unacceptable infringements on princely prerogatives. Although few in number, German advocates of absolutism were influential. Wilhelm Freiherr von Schröder's (1640–88) widely-read *Fürstliche Schatz- und Rentkammer (Princely Treasury and Exchequer*, 1686) became virtually a textbook for territorial rule. The traditional contractual concepts underpinning German late medieval constitutionalism were reworked entirely in the princes' favour. Ruler–ruled relations had been regarded as a two-sided bargain. Subjects submitted to their rulers' authority and provided the necessary assistance in return for protection and privileges. The most important of these was the right to be consulted on matters of common concern and importance. The territorial estates provided the forum for such consultation and the cement for the contractual bargain. Acting as the custodians for all territorial laws and privileges, the estates simultaneously prevented the tyranny of the prince and the anarchy of the subjects. Schröder rejected this. Based on a reading of Roman history which emphasized the imperial rather than the republican phases, and backed up by ample but selected Biblical references, he argued that the prince was only morally obliged to fulfil his side of the contract whereas the subjects were bound always to be obedient regardless of the actions of their ruler. Moreover, Schröder was explicit on the sources of princely power. This rested in the twin monopolies of violence and taxation from which institutions like the estates were to be excluded.[19]

War-making became part of the 'mysteries of state' over which only the prince, elevated by God above the selfish squabbles of his subjects, had the mastery. Wars were complex matters considered beyond the comprehension of ordinary subjects who were expected to suffer in silence. As August Count Styum, Bishop of Speyer (1770–97), put it in 1785: 'Why indeed, should they judge and talk about them at all? It is best for them to neither judge nor talk, for they cannot be adequately informed about the true state of affairs: and chatter can easily confuse the common people.'[20]

Such ideas fed into a general shift in the literature on princely power and government. Developing in the sixteenth century, this emphasized either the personal qualities necessary for rule in the so-called 'mirror of princes' works (*Fürstenspiegel*), or discussed 'practical government' (*Regimentslehre*). While retaining an emphasis on moral correctitude and practical advice, the tone became more obviously authoritarian after the mid-seventeenth century. The most famous of these books, Veit Ludwig von Seckendorff's *Vom teutschen Fürstenstaat* (*Concerning the German Princely State*, 1655) advocated the type of benevolent authoritarianism later known as cameralism. By the late seventeenth century, this 'science of government' was firmly entrenched in the curricula of German universities which were more concerned with turning out trained administrators than speculative enquiry.[21]

However, there were limits to how far even princely servants were prepared to take their advocacy of absolutism. Schröder was one of the few proponents of divine-right monarchy which most saw as an alien French concept associated with despotism. Even German Catholics, generally more favourable to absolutism than Protestants, avoided explicit references to it as it infringed Papal supremacy. The majority restricted themselves to conventional statements that all political power derived ultimately from God and practical advice on how to rule more effectively.[22]

Despite its association with reasons of state (*Staatsraison*) ideology, this German literature differed substantially from its more famous Italian variety. Machiavelli was not only attacked by enlightened rulers like Frederick the Great of Prussia (1740–86), but before that by seventeenth-century advocates of absolutism. The German prince was to be an authoritarian, but he was to be a morally upright one. The image of the prince as benevolent father to his people (*Landesvater*) persisted until the end of the Reich. While his subjects were indeed often denied the right to challenge or criticize his decisions, the prince remained bound by a complex bundle of moral guidelines that varied according to local circumstances. The Catholic rulers of the south and west were strongly influenced by the culture of baroque piety (*pietas*), stressing the duties of the monarch to promote the common good and defend the 'true faith'. Protestant absolutism tended to be fused with Lutheran paternalism or with neostoic influences, especially strong in Calvinist territories or those with Calvinist rulers like Brandenburg. All were important because effective rule depended on the widespread acceptance of the prince's actions as legitimate.[23]

Finally, advocacy of absolutism remained restricted to the princely territories. Though some argued for an extension of the emperor's military and fiscal powers, the consensus persisted that monopoly formation should take place at territorial rather than national level. It is worth remembering that though Schröder was in the emperor's service, he applied his ideas to Austria rather than the Reich. Absolutism and militarization were to serve Habsburg dynastic ambitions, not promote a revival of imperial power.

Meanwhile, other aspects of the traditional Christian *bellum iustum* were reworked to support such pretensions. The so-called New Humanism of the late sixteenth century played a significant role in this by advocating the direct application of ideas from classical antiquity to solve contemporary technical problems. There was considerable interest in the military literature of ancient Greece and Rome, particularly Tacitus, that was assisted by the availability of new translations and editions. Much of this was already well disseminated before the chaos of the Thirty Years War engulfed the Reich. Its influence extended well beyond providing models of militia organizations for the short-lived Orangist army reforms adopted by the Nassau relations of the Dutch stadholder and other minor Rhenish rulers. In particular, it made a major impact through the neostoicism of Justus Lipsius (1547–1606) who showed a truly stoic disregard for sectarian emotions by holding university chairs successively in Lutheran Jena, Catholic Louvain and Calvinist Leiden. Regarding human passions as the chief source of strife, Lipsius advocated their suppression in favour of discipline, patience and fortitude in adversity.[24] Profoundly influenced by Tacitus, Lipsius elaborated a concept of discipline of great political and military significance. While soldiers had always been trained in the art of weapons handling, Lipsius' emphasis on *exercitium* elevated drill to the primary means of instilling discipline and building unit cohesion. Perfection in the exercise of arms became not merely a sign of military efficiency but also subordination to authority. Soldiers lost their individuality in the greater whole of their regiment. Second, command was tied to a strict hierarchical order (*ordo*) exercised by *coertio* implying self-discipline as well as coercion, and held together by the *exempla* of punishment and reward.

By integrating the command structure into the same system of control as the ordinary soldiers, Lipsius provided the rhetorical underpinning for the territorial state's efforts to transform the early modern military enterpriser into the modern officer.[25] Moreover, his theory of discipline injected a new secularism into the Christian ethics governing war's conduct (*ius in bello*). Alongside traditional prohibitions of immoral conduct and ill-treatment of civilians that dominate sixteenth-century articles of war, came new rules designed to enforce an increasingly well-defined hierarchical command structure. Collective discipline replaced individual conscience and personal honour as guides for the behaviour of most military personnel.[26]

Perhaps most importantly, Lipsius redefined war, transforming it from uncontrolled violence into the orderly application of force, directed by a legitimate and competent authority in the interest of the state. Not only did this reinforce the growing consensus that only the sovereign ruler should have war-making powers (*auctoritas principis*), but it altered the other two criteria governing the legitimacy of conflict. Both the question of the just cause (*iusta causa*) and intention (*recta intentio*) came to be seen in more secular terms based on dynastic interest, prestige and dignity, with the projection of the resultant conflicts with other powers as the consequence of necessity (*necessitas*) and public utility (*utilitas publica*). The previous emphasis on self-defence and the preservation of peace was replaced by a new appreciation of the political potential of armed force. No longer a natural disaster to be avoided at all costs, war became a legitimate means to advance princely policy. Of course this was not solely due to Lipsius. It is important to remember that the emergence of the new conception of the political role of violence was driven by events and not the other way around. Much of the new language of 'necessity', like the rhetoric surrounding state building in general, was adopted by princes and advisors to justify what they were doing. Nonetheless, it did add a new ruthlessness to princely belligerence and set rulers apart from their estates which clung to more traditional notions about the role of war.[27]

Any assessment of these issues is complicated by the difficulty of disentangling true motive from rhetorical justification. Given the nature of the Reich, defence was simultaneously an imperial obligation and a territorial duty for any ruler. However, the precarious international and inner-German situation after 1648 also made it a political necessity. Rulers seeking to justify one form of defence often referred to the obligations of another. This was particularly true of those princes whose involvement in German and international politics endangered their territories' defence. The requirement to provide troops for imperial collective security was frequently used to justify forces intended for territorial and dynastic policies.

Defence was central to these policies. The ability to protect the territory and maintain public order was one of the major justifications for absolutism. An effective defence was also essential to safeguard the ruler's resource base and dynastic possessions. The logic of German territorialization necessitated separate territorial armies in addition to the system of collective security. The fact that this system was both inadequate and based on territorial contingents only reinforced this trend. This found expression in the statements of princes and their advisors. For example, since its establishment in 1600 the Hessen-Kassel militia was consistently justified on the grounds of territorial defence, despite the continued development of the imperial defence structure. Württemberg bureaucrats constantly stressed the need that, as the leading Swabian prince, the duke needed an appropriate military establishment to maintain order in the region and meet his obligations to the Reich. The duke frequently used this as an excuse for additional forces that in fact were intended to further dynastic objectives. Other rulers also argued that their inflated territorial armies were required to assist the ineffective *Reichsarmee* in imperial defence.[28]

The growing rhetoric of absolutism now went beyond this to see the army as integral to the structure of the territorial state. In 1675 the Saxon publicist Christian Gastel advocated absolutist fiscal-military monopolies and related German princely prestige expressly to military and financial power rather than the traditional hierarchy based on status and titles.[29] Count Waldeck agreed stating simply that 'troops and money give power'. His patron, the Great Elector, was also in no doubt about advising his successor that 'a lord is of no consideration unless he has troops and means of his own, for this is what has made me considerable from the time that I have had them'.[30] A consensus emerged among princes, statesmen and professional soldiers that 'a large and well-schooled army is the best rampart of the state'.[31] This found frequent expression in secret 'political testaments', confidential memoranda and public statements. Maxmilian I of Bavaria (1597–1651) advised his son that 'after God and the love of the people, an efficient army, permanently available money and good fortresses are the best supports for the principality'.[32] Kaunitz was even more emphatic when he advised Maria Theresia in 1761 that 'no one would disagree, that the mainstay of the monarchy, the security and prosperity of the land and loyal subjects, rests principally in the quality and strength of the military'.[33] Similarly, Duke Carl Leopold of Mecklenburg announced in 1718 that he regarded the army as 'the pillar and foundation of a secure and peaceful state'.[34]

From here it was only a short step to see the army as essential for the expansion of the state. Contemporaries were in no doubt that a powerful military establishment increased a ruler's prestige and influence. Though this was regarded partly as a defensive deterrent, examination of princely aims reveals that increased influence was intended to bring additional lands and titles.[35] Political and military opinion concurred that a permanent army was required. 'What makes a monarch powerful and respected', wrote a southwest German officer in 1739, 'is a strong army that he maintains in peacetime and is thereby able to confront his enemies at any time'.[36] Even Pufendorf was prepared to endorse offensive wars provided 'a perfectly safe opportunity occurs and the country's condition can easily bear it'.[37]

These statements indicate that the contemporary response to external threats was closely related to arguments for internal political consolidation and outward expansion. All required a level of military preparedness. Up till now, however, there has been a tendency to argue that this only led to militarization in the larger territories. The smaller ones were allegedly content with the imperial defence structure and could dispense with forces of their own.[38] This is misleading. The principal difference was only one of scale. The resources of the smaller territories were more limited and their political ambitions more modest, but they still needed troops. At the very least, even the smallest territories wanted to fulfil their commitments to imperial defence. Failure to do so left the territory open to exploitation by the larger 'armed estates' who could plunder its resources and infringe its sovereignty by manipulating the system of collective security. Though the smaller bishoprics and imperial cities often pressed for a reduction in their obligations in peacetime they rarely advocated total disbandment. Retention of a contingent even on a reduced establishment, was a practical demonstration of territorial sovereignty and *Reichsstandschaft* (status of imperial estate). It helped mark the crucial distinction between those princes and cities who were full estates of the Reich and those who were merely territorial nobles and towns. Moreover, even the smallest territory was not immune from the same external and internal political pressures that operated in their larger neighbours. They too required soldiers for domestic policing and to uphold their territorial integrity.

However, war was far from being 'little more than a seasonal variation on hunting' for the princes and their courts as often portrayed by subsequent literature on absolutism.[39] Despite the new emphasis on princely glory and honour, much of the language of baroque belligerence was primarily defensive. Leibniz's famous dictum that 'weapons are the true instruments of peace' was not merely an advocacy of a standing army, but a reminder that the true purpose of war was to sustain peace.[40] At one level this was simple deterrence, expressed by Waldeck in his advice to the Great Elector late in 1654 that 'if his electoral highness is armed, the desire [of his neighbours] to breakfast upon him will pass'.[41] At another, it extended to the reasons rulers themselves gave for opening hostilities. These manifestos indicate that war was still regarded as an extension of a legal battle in which the resort to violence came only after all efforts at peaceful resolution had foundered on the obstruction and culpability of the other side. That this cannot be dismissed entirely as an exercise in cynicism and hypocrisy is clear from the considerable lengths to which princes were prepared to go to portray their actions as legitimate. No less than 287 pamphlets were published during the brief War of the Bavarian Succession (1778–9) defending the actions of the two protagonists. Significantly, such efforts extended beyond attempts to sway the opinions of neutral rulers and statesmen to include concerted campaigns to win the hearts and minds of a broader public. Moreover, this began well before the Enlightenment made it fashionable to criticize war as an instrument of policy and included a wide variety of written and symbolic means of communication designed to influence even illiterate sections of the population.[42]

It should also be remembered that the goals of glory and honour were conveniently flexible concepts which a prince could as easily, and as illustriously, achieve by making peace as by waging war. Johann Philip von Schönborn, Elector-Archbishop of Mainz (1647–73), provides a good example. Known as the

'German Solomon', Schönborn had been instrumental in easing the negotiations leading to the Peace of Westphalia. He then led the other two ecclesiastical electors (Cologne and Trier) as self-appointed mediators to resolve major international crises, trying in 1658–9 to end the Franco-Spanish War, tackling the Northern War in 1660, Louis XIV's dispute with the Papacy after 1662, the War of Devolution in 1667–8 and dying amid efforts to halt the Dutch War in 1672–3. Meanwhile, within imperial politics Schönborn led the French-sponsored Rhenish Alliance (*Rheinbund*) (1658–68), expressly constituted to resolve inner-German conflict and preserve the internal equilibrium of the Reich by checking the power of the emperor. These efforts were partly motivated by self-interest since the electors' territories lay in or close to the war zones. Schönborn also had no qualms about using violence within his own territories, bombarding the recalcitrant city of Erfurt into submission in 1664. Nonetheless, participation on the international stage helped raise the profile of the electors and consolidate their newly-confirmed right to make alliances with foreign powers (*ius foederis*) guaranteed in the Peace of Westphalia, provided they did not violate the security of the Reich. It is also significant that their assistance was often requested since both Christian ethics and Natural Law theories encouraged warring parties to accept mediation so as to avoid the stigma of appearing the aggressor. Needless to say, Schönborn and his colleagues were often marginalized once negotiations had begun, but this did not stop others following their example, while the ideal of imperial mediation (*Reichsmediation*), or collective action to resolve German and international conflict, persisted throughout the eighteenth century as the preferred policy of the great majority of the weaker princes.[43]

Indeed, it was often in the princes' own interests to pursue peace, for absolutism rested on its claim to preserve domestic tranquillity. Glorification of peace was as integral to princely symbolism as images of war. Charles VI, for instance, was portrayed as the hero of Austrian trade, benevolently promoting schemes for the common good. Heroism was conveniently transformed for this purpose, becoming depersonalized so that only the prince was capable of attaining it while ordinary mortals were reduced to bit players in his grand actions.[44] In short, German rulers may well have monopolized the means to war, but they certainly did not embark on it lightly.

## II

Popular attitudes to war are less easy to determine. From the available evidence it appears that the older belief persisted that war was a product of events beyond human control. Most soldiers expressed resignation before death rather than enthusiasm for action and glory. Few felt able to describe events on paper, preferring instead to wait for an opportunity to give a verbal account on their return home. Combat was seen as a fearful experience which most were simply pleased to have survived without injury. 'Better dead than captured or injured' wrote Prussian trooper Nicolaus Binn prior to the battle of Kunersdorf in 1759. Musketeer Riemann commented on the death of his brother three years later 'that it is for the best that he is delivered from his dangerous wound which would have left him a wretched cripple for the rest of his days'.[45] While ordinary soldiers clearly respected their rulers, it was left to the officers to tell them that 'what could be more glorious for us than for our lifeless bodies to be counted amongst corpses sacrificed on those fields for the advantage of our Most Gracious King, the utility of his states and our own fame and that of the dead'.[46]

Religion provided a refuge from the horrors of active service in pointed contrast to its role in peacetime where piety was not only part of official efforts to enforce discipline, but itself had to be enforced by coercive means: Friedrich Wilhelm I of Prussia (1713–40) had sentries posted outside churches on Sundays to ensure nobody left prematurely.[47] Bishop Styrum of Speyer admonished his soldiers to cheerfully suffer the hardships of military life, remembering that, like civilians, 'they have deserved these temporal evils as a punishment for their sins . . . and must humbly submit themselves to the will of God'. Such words are perhaps not surprising from an authoritarian who even tried to forbid his subjects from keeping dogs.[48] Nonetheless, they did reflect beliefs widely held by the ruling elite. If anything, discipline was tightened on campaign. Prussian regiments met twice daily for prayer, Holy Communion was held once every other week and the entire army held thanksgiving services after each victory.

However, this clearly met a need among the soldiers. The famous incident where the exhausted Prussians spontaneously broke into the Lutheran hymn 'Now thank we all our God' after the battle of Leuthen in 1757 was far from unique. The poet Ewald von Kleist noted that on 'mornings on the march, before the soldiers strike up songs about the king of Prussia, they sing hymns'.[49] Private Baarthel Linck wrote to his wife, after hearing the Te Deum Laudamus sung after Lobositz in 1756, that, 'I can rightly say that I have never before felt such reverence in our entire army'. The NCO J.S. Liebler attributed the Prussian victory snatched from a near defeat on that day solely to divine intervention, pouring scorn on those who believed success was possible without God's help. Binn also believed 'victory comes solely from God'. Such sentiment was common and even officers like Captain Barsewisch attributed the army's success to 'God and the king'. The Austrian field marshal Daun blamed his defeat at Torgau in 1760 on divine will. Both officers and men frequently praised God for their own survival in battle. Servicemen wrote home urging their wives and families to pray for their safety and a quick peace.[50]

Such attitudes were encouraged by the authorities partly from conviction and partly as a means of social control. The first action taken by Landgrave Carl of Hessen-Kassel upon the outbreak of the Nine Years War in 1688, in addition to mobilizing his troops and calling the estates for money, was to schedule a general day of prayer and penance. It was simply standard procedure in an emergency. The population was also expected to participate in the war effort through regular church attendance and living a pious and obedient life. In this way princes sought to preserve their reputations in the face of possible defeat, offloading responsibility for the outcome on to God's will and blaming reverses on the sins of their subjects.[51]

## III

Increasingly, however, rulers themselves took refuge in more mechanistic views of war and international relations. This was part of a broader shift in European thought which, it has been suggested, came about in response to the destruction of the previous intellectual certainties by the upheavals of the Reformation and Counter Reformation.[52] Philosophers, military theorists and statesmen came to believe that there were natural laws governing war and politics just as scientific laws regulated the rest of the universe. Discovery of these laws became the object of enquiry in an effort to banish the doubt and anxiety caused by the apparent unpredictability of events. Complex problems were rationalized as a series of geometrical patterns allocating each factor a precise place and prescribed role in a greater whole. The terrors of untamed nature were reduced to elegant order in the baroque garden. Wild human passions were subdued by the grace of the galliard, pavane and minuet danced by the refined, sophisticated and self-disciplined courtier. Similarly, the violence and turbulence of early modern politics were made to conform to the order and regularity of a machine, most famously by J.H.G. von Justi (1717–71):

> A properly constructed state must be exactly analogous to a machine, in which all the wheels and gears are precisely adjusted to one another; and the ruler must be the foreman, the mainspring or the soul — if one may use the expression — which sets everything in motion.[53]

In the same way as God was clockmaker and clockwinder of a mechanical universe, the territorial prince supervised the smooth running of domestic politics while his bureaucrats and advisers rushed about like mechanics and engineers making all manner of beneficial adjustments.[54] Given their preference for interpreting imperial politics as a system of rational checks and balances it is not surprising that many Germans regarded international relations in a similar way. Seventeenth-century theorists were fond of comparing European politics with the Newtonian universe where states acted like planets in perfect equilibrium. From this stemmed a mechanistic conception of 'national interests', dictated by impersonal factors like geography, strategic position and the largely static 'national character' of the inhabitants. Together, these provided a set of strategic, territorial and, to a lesser extent, commercial interests to form what Louis XIV termed the 'maxims of state' which should guide each ruler's policy. These ideas were given greater coherence by the evolution of international law and the decline of universalist pretensions of individual rulers like the Habsburgs, allowing for a more balanced interaction of states. Not surprisingly, statesmen like Kaunitz believed that this 'balance of power' functioned to some extent automatically, guided by its inherent system.[55]

The same framework provided an explanation for the interaction between domestic and foreign policy. The maxims of state could alter depending on the actions of other elements in the international equilibrium. Similarly, changes to the internal balance within a state could have international repercussions. Nicolaus Hieronymus Gundling, Professor at Halle University, noted in 1713 that 'where there are estates there is no effective military administration'.[56] Absolute regimes, in other words, had better armies. Frederick the Great also believed that states led by ambitious princes were more successful in the hostile international environment, while those with parliamentary systems degenerated into sloth like Sweden and the Dutch Republic. States which had accumulated coercive means had a natural tendency to expand; those that had not went under. Such beliefs permitted a further development of Lipsius' rationalization of violence as a legitimate instrument of state policy. Fuelled by the Enlightenment concept of utility applied to military and political efficiency, war became an acceptable means of advancing the common good, leading Voltaire to welcome the partition of the militarily ineffective and politically backward Poland by the apparently more progressive and enlightened monarchies of Austria, Prussia and Russia in 1772.[57]

Practical politics, of course, was fond of throwing spanners into these mechanical utopias. Attempts to discover underlying laws only produced a bewildering variety of conflicting theoretical systems and models. Access to accurate data remained difficult, despite efforts at surveillance, cataloguing and recording, extending by the mid-eighteenth century even to regular census returns in some territories.[58] Even when information was available, human prejudices often intruded to prevent it from being exploited effectively. Mitchell, the British Ambassador accompanying Frederick the Great on the ill-fated Olmütz campaign of 1758, wrote disparagingly that 'in this army the spies are paid too sparingly, consequently the intelligence is none of the best, and when there comes intelligence, which does not agree with the hypothesis we have formed, that intelligence is little regarded'.[59]

## IV

In any case, by this stage the rationalization of war and politics was coming under widespread criticism from new intellectual currents associated with the Enlightenment.[60] This has often been misinterpreted as a novel departure in the last third of the eighteenth century. In fact, enlightened thought merely widened the scope of existing criticism of absolutism and its conflicts. What was new was the way these ideas led to a transformation of attitudes to war and the rhetoric used to legitimize it.

While mainstream religious thought had limited its opposition to unjust wars, minority groups had long been more radical in their pacifism. Protestant fundamentalism known as Pietism led many to question the morality of violence. Johann Neubauer, a theology student impressed into the Prussian army against his will in the 1720s, expressed concern at being made to fire live ammunition even during drill.[61] Others refused to perform any military service. The German Mennonites had long rejected war in all its forms and had been made to suffer for these beliefs, even in the Swiss cantons which periodically threatened to expel them for not serving in the militia. Mennonites in the smaller territories like Zweibrücken, Mömpelgard and the Palatinate, were generally permitted to pay fines in lieu of service. Keen to encourage emigration to East Prussia depopulated by plague in 1709, Friedrich I (1688–1713) granted exemption from military duties to the persecuted Swiss Mennonites. His successor, Friedrich Wilhelm I, quickly reversed this policy, trying to coerce not only the new immigrants but also existing communities into submitting to his conscription laws. By threatening to leave the country, the Prussian Mennonites persuaded Frederick the Great to restore their freedoms in 1746. This was extended to Mennonites living in West Prussia, annexed in 1772, though exemptions were now hedged with certain restrictions and dependent on payment towards the upkeep of a military school. Similar groups fared worse in the Habsburg territories, though the surviving Hutterite craftsmen in Moravia refused even to make weapons.[62]

Outside such minority groups criticism of armies as instruments of war was muted prior to the later eighteenth century. Popular resentment of soldiers was widespread, but stemmed from what they did rather than what they represented. Everywhere they went soldiers were associated with unpaid bills, extortion, wilful damage to property, crime and disorder. Villagers in Tamm in Württemberg complained in August 1737 that soldiers refused to listen to them and simply did whatever they liked.[63] Fights between soldiers and civilians were common, while young officers often ran amok attacking people on the street.[64] The arrival of recruiting parties could spark serious trouble. In early eighteenth-century Mecklenburg church bells were rung to warn of the soldiers' approach, whereupon peasants and local civil officials turned out armed with farm implements to drive them off. Students of Halle University fought pitched battles between 1717 and 1719 with the local Prussian regiment which was notorious for duping men into service. Parishioners in Prussian Westphalia even killed several soldiers who had come to seize them as recruits during Sunday service in 1720.[65]

Such cases were fairly common, though it should be stressed that for the most part soldiers and civilians coexisted relatively peacefully. The main cause of the animosity was not a principled rejection of militarism, but the social composition of the armies and the general poverty of most of the personnel. Though the number of criminals in the ranks has been greatly exaggerated in subsequent literature, contemporaries did acknowledge that the long-standing practice of territories like Bavaria of sentencing men to military service brought 'the whole army into disrepute'.[66] More generally, soldiers became an object of ridicule. Whereas Prussian personnel at least received a new uniform annually, many others were less fortunate with those in Hohenlohe being expected to make theirs last up to four years. Some men could no longer turn up for parade because they had no trousers.[67] The men of Württemberg Grenadier Regiment von Augé were so old that by 1780 the phrase *er kommt zu Augé* had entered the popular vocabulary as the equivalent of 'he's past it'.[68] The Stuttgart city authorities petitioned Duke Carl Eugen of Württemberg (1744–93) to change the recruiting practices of their Civic Watch Company so that it would consist of 'fitter men and thereby not become an object of general laughter and derision'.[69] Later the duke was compelled to issue free firewood to the garrison of the Hohentwiel fortress after the inhabitants of neighbouring Austrian villages had poked fun at soldiers scavenging in the countryside.[70] Significantly, such problems were not restricted to the armies of the smaller territories. Prussian soldiers stationed in Saxony during the Seven Years War were so poorly paid that they were often seen begging and the entire army became known as *Sechsgröschler* or 'six pence men'.[71]

The traditionally low opinion of soldiers was joined from the mid-eighteenth century by a more politicized criticism focusing particularly on the armies of the smaller territories. Part of this originated in the enlightened attack on petty particularism as havens for unreconstructed despotism. The decisions of some of the lesser princes to hire troops to help suppress the American Revolution triggered a storm of protest. Apart from the not inconsiderable novelty of service on the other side of the Atlantic, these arrangements were not different from other subsidy treaties signed by German princes since the 1660s. It was the intellectual climate that had changed, leading to charges that the princes were selling their subjects like slaves in a 'soldier trade' (*Soldatenhandel*) to help a 'tyrant' suppress the type of social experiment many intellectuals wanted to see in Europe. Immortalized in Schiller's *Kabale und Liebe* and other works of fiction, this became a convenient weapon with which to attack the old regime for those championing social and political reform.[72]

To many progressive thinkers, the armies of the smaller states were simply an opportunity for the petty princes to play at soldiers (*Soldatenspielerei*). Goethe dismissed the Weimar soldiers (for whose welfare he was responsible as head of the territory's Military Commission) as 'military macaronis'.[73] Visiting Anhalt-Zerbst in September 1763 Boswell noted that the prince,

> . . . has got his troops, forsooth, to the number of 150 foot and 30 horse, and, during the last war, he took a fancy that the king of Prussia was coming to attack him. So he put in readiness his little battery of cannon, and led out his 180 to make head against the armies of Frederick.[74]

Such comments often carried a clear political message. The publicist Johann Pezzl used such images to attack the 'misery of polycracy' when he condemned the,

> . . . government of a great band of petty princes and all the autonomous priests and lay [rulers] of the Holy Roman Empire! One hears here of edifying policies of the government of such square-mile monarchies and miniature courts, and elsewhere of some princeling who sits on a throne though he is scarcely able to rule twelve chickens. Nonetheless, he is determined to shine, following each move with one greater still. He has to have his cooks, his horses, his dogs, his vizier and his troops, an entire army consisting of only four grenadiers, six musketeers and two hussars. And in order to get all this going, he takes everything from his small herd of peasants bar their shirts. This is only part of the horror of German multiple rule. For the good of the nation, I hope that it will at last come under a single ruler, the sooner the better.[75]

While painting an unduly black picture of conditions in the smaller territories,[76] such opinions did reflect one aspect of the political developments taking place within the Reich. The armies of the smaller territories did appear increasingly irrelevant. Since the mid-eighteenth century, the lesser territories had been marginalized by the disproportionate growth in Austrian and Prussian political and military power. Already during the Seven Years War Bavarians objected to their ruler's participation on the grounds that the territory was too small to get involved in the squabbles of the major powers.[77] After 1763 such ideas gained ground throughout Europe. Most famously, Leopold of Tuscany (1765–90) disbanded his army except for a regiment stationed in Florence whose primary purpose seems to have been providing urine for his chemical experiments.[78] However, it is easy to forget that imperial politics made disarmament extremely difficult. The principality of Reuss had attempted to stay out of the Seven Years War by posting signs along its frontier declaring its neutrality. The Prussians invaded anyway and treated it as an occupied country.[79] Even though most territories scarcely possessed sufficient troops to protect themselves, maintenance of a force was a practical demonstration of their continued determination to uphold their sovereignty in the face of encroachments from German and foreign powers. While many territories did reduce their forces after 1763, this was dictated by financial stringency as well as a growing sense of political powerlessness, rather than a desire for total disbandment. Indeed, we should be careful not to overexaggerate the extent of anti-military sentiment in the later eighteenth century. There was growing criticism of the stifling martial atmosphere at Potsdam after the death of Frederick the Great. Both his successors showed less inclination to stay there while the princesses at court complained that there was nothing but coarse soldiers and the din of arms drill.[80] Even Captain Archenholz wrote that Friedrich Wilhelm I had turned Berlin into 'a copy of Sparta, the like of which has never been seen on this earth. The residence resembled a camp, only soldiers were honoured', so that the capital became 'a city dedicated to Mars where despotism showed its teeth in the most abominable form'. Nonetheless, Prussian monarchs continued to devote considerable time to their army after 1786 with Friedrich Wilhelm III (1797–1840) personally collecting militaria and spending hours designing new uniforms, while Archenholz was full of praise for Frederick the Great and the bravery of his forces.[81] Enthusiasm for things military extended to other sections of society. Tobacco boxes engraved with martial emblems and battle scenes became a commercial success during the Seven Years War, along with 'victory ribbons' (*Vivatbänder*) which civilians could buy to pin on their clothes. Though sales declined after 1763, engravings of military subjects remained popular, with Daniel Chodowiecki's (1726–1801) picture of the hunched figure of Frederick riding out to inspect his troops representing one of the most reproduced images of the great king.[82]

Nonetheless, critical voices were becoming more strident. Significantly, both the opponents and defenders of traditional forms of military organization adopted the metaphor of the machine. Previously this had been seen as a symbol of perfection, and many, like Montecuccoli, had expressed the hope that if warfare could be subordinated to fixed rules, it would become more predictable and hence less costly. Now, the obsession with discipline and order was condemned for reducing war to a mathematical equation, obscuring the fact that human lives were at stake.[83] The Prussian army, was, in Herder's words, a 'hired, thoughtless, strengthless, will-less machine' whose soldiers had become dehumanized and incapable of independent action. It only took one man to step out of line for the whole artificial apparatus to collapse. Johann Gottlieb Fichte condemned discipline 'written in blood' as the only thing holding it together. Immanuel Kant went further by echoing earlier comments that the very existence of permanent armies made war more likely since they provided both the means and the excuse for conflict.[84]

If it took until the late eighteenth century for criticism of armies to take a more political tone, attacks on war itself were well-established before the Enlightenment. No part of the German press of the early eighteenth century advanced arguments in favour of war. On the contrary, peace was regarded as more rational and beneficial. Rulers — always foreign ones due to government censorship — were regarded as irrational beings, pursuing irrational objectives of personal power and glory with disastrous consequences for their subjects. Where they could comment on events, journalists tended to go beyond simply condemning war to advocate peaceful resolution to conflict. Diplomacy was expected to bring results and most papers welcomed the international congresses of the 1720s summoned to sort out the problems left after the Peace of Utrecht (1713).[85] This represented a major change in attitudes since the mid-seventeenth century. Whereas peace had been seen as simply the absence of war, obtainable only as a gift from heaven, it was now considered the normal state of affairs that could be achieved by human action. By mid-century this had become commonplace. In the opinion of Kaunitz, war was now an illness which disturbed 'the natural order of things'.[86]

Many were concerned after 1713 that there should be no return to the almost continual warfare that had plagued western Europe since 1667. Mechanistic models of a balance of power seemed increasingly unattractive. The rise of new powers like Britain and Russia disturbed the previous bipolar balance between France and Habsburgs making the system apparently less predictable. German solutions to this tended to resemble the famous project for perpetual peace of Abbé de St Pierre in that they rejected alliance systems in favour of some form of international regulation. Indeed, St Pierre's proposal would have effectively transformed Europe into an enlarged version of the Reich with rulers surrendering part of their sovereignty to a single court of arbitration. Most writers were realistic enough to appreciate that few monarchs would willingly submit to this, but still viewed the prospect of permanent peace with optimism. German rulers remained unconvinced, and Frederick the Great was quick to dismiss such schemes as utopian daydreaming. Nonetheless, they provide evidence for a well-articulated pacifist sentiment long before the Enlightenment and represent a genuine enthusiasm for defensively-oriented political systems like the Reich. Significantly, peace projects resurfaced in the 1790s, precisely when both the Reich and European peace were under renewed attack.[87]

There was also a growing literature from within military circles urging an end or at least a limit to war. Count Wilhelm von Schaumburg-Lippe (1748–77), otherwise known as the 'cannon count' on account of his passion for artillery, wrote in 1775 that war should only be defensive. Jakob Friedrich Baron von Bielfeld (1717–70), tutor to the princes at the Prussian court, argued that war was simply unnecessary because God had endowed the earth with resources sufficient to meet everyone's needs. Co-operation not conflict was the best way to exploit these. War was increasingly seen as absurd and contrary to reason.[88] The brief and inconclusive War of the Bavarian Succession played a major role in fostering these beliefs. Ridiculed as the 'Potato War' on the grounds that the plundering of that crop by the Prussians in Bohemia constituted the main action, the entire conflict struck many as completely unnecessary. Even such a veteran opponent of Prussia as Kaunitz argued it was pointless and unjustifiable to 'spill blood, ruin states and spend money for such minor causes'. The success of the negotiated settlement, partly initiated by Maria Teresia behind Joseph II's back, seemed to confirm the hopes of those who believed diplomacy was the best way to defuse tension.[89]

Consideration of how to prevent war led some to draw radical political conclusions. Pezzl was typically polemical and worth quoting at length:

> The European princes call each other cousin. This title is very edifying and flattering, but has dreadful consequences. All these cousins are mortal. Their cooks and ladies of pleasure have ensured that some occasionally quit this earth without heirs. The other cousins see that it's worth acting quickly. A few genealogists and diplomats prove to whoever pays the most that he is the nearest cousin with the best legal claim. The other cousins also have genealogists. It now depends on whoever can find the most lawyers . . . and marches into the field. Neighbouring princes learn that a campaign is in the offing. Everyone gets in on the act, determined to seize his share of the cake so far as his powers permit.[90]

Such attacks were part of a prolonged assault on princely prerogatives that struck at the heart of absolutist ideology. From being celebrated as *prudentia civilis*, the mysteries of state were increasingly attacked as a dangerous deception. German Pietism had long encouraged the idea that public behaviour should correspond to private morality. Similarly, the growth of court criticism in bourgeois circles since the 1680s had exposed the 'politeness' of the courtier as a façade to hide immorality and deceit. Champions of the territorial estates had long argued that these played a vital role in ensuring public accountability and preventing rulers from plunging their lands into unnecessary conflict.[91] This is an argument that has found favour with later historians sympathetic to the estates, but which obscures the fact that most territorial assemblies had no clear solution to the problem of defence.[92] What was significant was the growing number of theorists who, while critical of the estates as unrepresentative oligarchies, nonetheless proposed some form of constitutional control over the rulers' war-making powers. Horst Dreitzel's analysis of the writings of Gottlieb Samuel Treuer (1683–1743) and Johann Justi indicates that the key elements of liberal constitutionalism were already well worked before the so-called 'Pre-March' (*Vormärz*) era of 1815–48.[93] The nature of the political debates had changed fundamentally. Previously, domestic politics had involved a struggle over the existence of the military and fiscal monopolies. Now it centred on a fight to control these, in the process forcing a transition from a private to a public monopoly regulated by some kind of constitution.[94]

## V

Naturally, such criticism provoked a response. Defence of the standing army on economic and social grounds was well established by the early eighteenth century. Pastor Röder wrote in 1787 that a large army 'brought state revenue into circulation [and] sustained and clothed many poor citizens without the state suffering thereby'. Scharnhorst wrote in similar vein three years later that it would be impossible for the Prussian state to extract 22 million taler annually from its population if expenditure on the army did not circulate over half this sum. 'If this state reduced its army, its revenue would also decline' and major sections of the economy would suffer adversely.[95] Others argued that defence expenditure represented a good investment. Failure to maintain a serviceable army, wrote one Swabian officer, was 'a false economy and misconception', because if the country was invaded, such an army would not only have to be raised anyway, but would now be 'from untrained peasants at twice the cost'. In the meantime large tracts of land would have to be abandoned to the enemy and the country and its inhabitants ruined for 'twenty and thirty or more years'.[96] This was the kernel of the 'armed estate' argument developed by many princes in the 1680s to persuade their subjects to fund permanent armies with regular taxation.[97] Others pointed to the useful work on public projects carried out by soldiers, ranging from laying out the 'English Garden' in Munich to pulling down the medieval town walls during the modernization of Kassel.[98] Generally, this has been seen as a phenomenon of the later eighteenth century resulting from the need to find soldiers something to do in the long peace after 1763 and to justify their upkeep to enlightened critics.[99]

While the rhetoric did become more common, the use of soldiers as a state workforce stemmed from a practical need for cheap labour and had been common since the late seventeenth century.[100]

Justification of standing armies on social grounds also had a long heritage. The classic argument was that they provided valued employment to the poor and needy. Often this was given a political dimension. Röder believed that 'the subjects will be improved [by military service] in body and soul and accustomed to discipline, cleanliness and better activity'. Baron Adolph von Knigge wrote confidently in 1793 that Germany need not fear revolution because most of the 'rabble' had been recruited into the armies and had no interest in acquiring greater freedoms, 'because it matters little to them whether they earn their money by creating havoc and shooting, or chopping wood'.[101] However, while obviously welcomed by the state, this should not be taken as evidence for a conscious policy of 'social militarization'. It is true Friedrich Wilhelm I ordered furloughed soldiers to wear military emblems to prevent them 'reverting to peasants', but in most cases the so-called military values endorsed by the state were not different from those already promoted by cameralist social disciplining of civil society.[102]

The more strident tones of the later Enlightenment did elicit a different response from the more open-minded officers. Many began to argue that soldiers should be treated with greater respect and sought to silence the critics by moderating military disciplinary codes. Others encouraged improved education for officers and the founding of enlightened military academics. While they remained a minority, these men were influential during the Reform Era (1807–19). Nevertheless, they, like most critics, only addressed what were regarded as abuses in the existing system.[103]

For some this was not enough. By the 1790s there was a growing realization that military matters could not be seen in isolation, but had to be viewed in their wider social, political and economic context. Limited reforms were bound to fail. The entire system should be abolished and replaced by one linking the army to a new socio-political order. The Prussocentric view of German history has tended to relate these arguments exclusively to the late eighteenth-century reform work of Scharnhorst, Gniesenau and Yorck.[104] In fact, while the French Revolution did throw the issues more sharply into focus, the essential elements of the debate were already rehearsed before 1789 or even 1776.

Soldiers, bureaucrats and philosophers had long wrestled with the problem of integrating the army into society. No clear idea had emerged by the late eighteenth century, but most saw some form of militia as a potential solution. Early thinkers had tended to derive their projects from the classical past like Machiavelli or Lipsius who promoted variants on the 'every citizen a soldier, every soldier a citizen' model. Lipsius' ideas had already proved hugely influential and it is significant that his new conception of drill and discipline was first implemented in the territorial militia schemes of the late sixteenth century. Thereafter, his belief that every inhabitant had a duty to serve remained the cornerstone of the absolutist measures to adapt militia organizations as a means to recruit men into the army. Most princes talked of their desire for a 'well-exercised militia' (*wohl exercirte Miliz*) as a supplement to their professional soldiers. In wartime, militiamen were often drafted directly into the permanent regiments or used to create additional field units. Some states, like Prussia and Hessen-Kassel, adapted the system to provide a regular flow of conscripts into the army who were then released for most of the year into the civilian economy to save the government the cost of their upkeep. Even though Friedrich Wilhelm I famously banned the use of the word 'militia' when creating this 'canton system' (*Kantonverfassung*) in 1713–33, he still emphasized the subject's duty to serve.[105] The same emphasis appeared in the work of more enlightened thinkers. Rousseau advocated that 'every citizen shall be a soldier from duty, none by profession' and Thomas Abbt in his book *Vom Tode* (*On Death*, 1761) also saw an idealized form of citizens-in-arms without regarding a republican form of government as a requisite.[106]

The chief advantages were practical rather than emotional or ideological. Frederick the Great noted in his *Anti Machiavel* that 'experience has generally shown that the best troops of any state are the national ones' and preferable to foreign mercenaries unless the country had insufficient population.[107] Native conscripts were 'not as apt to abandon each other in battle' because they came from the same region.[108] Likewise, when discussing his officers, the king claimed he had tried 'to hammer the name Prussia into them so that all officers learn that regardless which province they come from or where they are stationed, they constitute a single interdependent body'.[109] Abbt was more idealistic but still concerned with matters of efficiency. Patriotism was treated as a panacea for all that he regarded as wrong with existing armies, believing that it would replace discipline as the chief motivating factor. Count Rumford, the American-born Bavarian reformer, used language similar to Abbt when in 1795 he argued that 'it is necessary to make soldiers citizens, and citizens soldiers'. However, his aim was essentially conservative, hoping 'to establish a respectable standing military force, which should do the least possible harm to the population, morals, manufacturers, and agriculture of the country'.[110] Rumford was not alone. Indeed, all the princes and their generals were attempting the same: to maximize the military potential of their territory with the minimum social and economic disruption. These concerns lay behind the Prussian canton system as much as lesser known schemes such as those in Württemberg for a combination of regulars and militia in the 1730s and 1740s.[111] Recruitment of foreigners was continued, and even extended, by Frederick the Great, in spite of his own views, precisely because their use did not damage the local economy. The problems that were to preoccupy American revolutionary generals and later political economists had long been discussed in German princely cabinets.[112]

Not all reformers viewed the greater integration of army and society with enthusiasm. Kaunitz and Maria Theresia identified Prussia with a dangerous new form of militarism expressly because its army was recruited by a form of conscription which, they believed, necessitated the subordination of all aspects of state and society to supporting an inflated military establishment. The Prussian 'military state' broke all previous rules of conflict, pursuing war with unparalleled ruthlessness in 'that the king does not just exploit his own population, money and military potential, but also all the inhabitants, money, food and other materials of innocent and neutral neighbours as far as force enables him'.[113] Not only did this make Prussia a major challenger to Austrian political interests, but a danger to the whole of civilization. Kaunitz was convinced that Prussian militarism was 'incompatible with the happiness of humanity'.[114] Though he recognized that it had certain technical advantages, he consistently opposed its adoption in Austria, fighting a losing battle throughout the 1760s and 1770s against Joseph II and the military reformers who wanted to implement Prussian-style conscription. Whereas Joseph II believed it would have positive benefits by making every citizen a soldier, Kaunitz argued it was precisely this which made 'the Prussia system so repulsive'. He thought a proposal from the Austrian war ministry in 1769 to weigh and measure young men as potential conscripts particularly odious and inhuman.[115]

Accordingly, Kaunitz and Maria Theresia aimed at nothing less than 'the total destruction of Prussia' as written into the military alliance with France in 1756.[116] Ironically, these aims were themselves a novel departure. As Christof Dipper argues, Frederick the Great's intentions upon invading Saxony in August 1756 were limited to the fairly conventional desire to defend himself against a hostile coalition while grabbing a little extra territory where possible. Austrian aims, on the other hand, pointed towards 'total war', involving nothing less than the dismemberment of the Prussian state and the destruction of its war machine.[117]

The militia schemes generally envisaged that soldiers would be motivated by a sense of patriotism. However, it is clear that servicemen's attachment to their German identity was far from simple. For most, notions of 'nation' and 'fatherland' blended loyalty to a territorial ruler with a wider sense of cultural belonging. Ansbach soldiers serving in America celebrated their ruler's birthday with cries of 'Hyroh for Alexander, God save our prince. Hyroh to Germany!'[118] Soldiers of larger territories often applied the term nation to their own state. Barsewisch talks of 'the general national characteristics of the Prussian troops' and 'the Prussian nation', using the word nation interchangeably to refer to the entire army and personal attributes.[119] Similarly, when Wilhelm IX became Landgrave of Hessen-Kassel in 1785 and eradicated all French influence from the court at Kassel he was not acting in a straightforward 'German' manner, but was promoting a more specifically Hessian identity.[120] Regional identities could influence soldiers' attitudes. Eighteenth-century Austrians fired at practice targets shaped like Prussian grenadiers while Lessing's play *Minna von Barnhelm* provides evidence for Prusso-Saxon hostility.[121] However, loyalty to 'Germany' was simultaneously loyalty to the Reich; an idealized traditional community providing space for different identities within a greater whole. Sometimes this could be truly cosmopolitan, exemplified by Carl Abraham Zedlitz's lecture on patriotism to the Prussian Académie Royale (!) which was given in French.[122]

## VI

These ideas appeared deficient to a small but growing number of angry young men who began to challenge both the established order and the existing criticism of it. The idea of perpetual peace was dismissed not only as utopian but actually harmful to civilization. War was now attributed a positive role in human development, providing a means for individual and collective self-fulfilment. From the late 1760s onwards a number of writers were already drawing on arguments that were to become standard in the nineteenth- and twentieth-century glorification of war. They included most notably Frederich Wilhelm von Meyen (1759–1829), an Austrian officer, Johann Valentin Embser (1749–83), a teacher in Zweibrücken, and Johann Friedrich Wilhelm Jerusalem (1709–89), the Brunswick court preacher. All wanted to take war away from the privileged sphere of princes and cabinets and 'reunite' it with the whole of society.[123]

Such sentiment gained ground after 1789, especially in the wake of German defeats at the hands of Revolutionary and Napoleonic France 1792–1806. In pointed contrast to Kaunitz's metaphor of war as an illness, Kant, Grave, Fichte and Arndt all saw it as a 'medicine' for a weak and weary generation. War would cleanse and revive moral strength, sapped by the long peace since 1763 and by life under the dead hand of the absolutist princelings. A new German national identity would be forged in battle just as a new art would emerge through storm and stress (*Sturm und Drang*). Violence appealed to Romanticism's celebration of human passions and emotions. The enlightened concept of the anti-hero[124] was rejected along with absolutism's claim that heroism was the monopoly of the prince. In Romantic egalitarianism, all were equal before death. Courage and bravery were no longer attributes of a privileged birth. War encouraged virtues that peace could not foster, calling forth new heroes for a new age, symbolized in the issue of medals to ordinary soldiers rather than the previous cash rewards.

A sharp distinction was now drawn between the 'old regime' and the Romantic brave new world; a distinction largely endorsed by subsequent historians.[125] The 'cabinet' or 'dynastic wars' of the princes, fought for arbitrary, unnecessary reasons, were contrasted with the glorious struggle to evict the hated French and found a nation-state. The battlefield as the place of slaughter had been transformed into the field of freedom and honour.[126] For some this transformation was personal. Johannes Kunisch has drawn attention to this change in Heinrich von Kleist (1777–1811), one of the leading figures in the German literary revival. In 1799 Kleist resigned his commission in the Prussian army because he found his position as an officer incompatible with his humanity. By 1809 he enthusiastically embraced war as reviving a demoralized generation and giving hope for a brighter future for all Germans.[127]

In practice this transition was not so simple, nor as beneficial as the radicals hoped. The old order, however discredited in their eyes, did not collapse, nor did the resumption of prolonged European warfare from 1792 to 1815 transform slaves into brave men as Arndt and others had prophesied. The so-called 'War of Liberation' (1813–14) did indeed foster a wider sense of German nationalism, providing examples of genuine popular enthusiasm and a desire to expel the French. However, the actual task was completed by conscript armies provided by Russia, Prussia, Austria and those German states which defected from Napoleon's Confederation of the Rhine.[128] Ironically, it was this degree of compulsion rather than the more celebrated presence of volunteer units that encouraged broader national sentiment. The conscription systems implemented in Prussia, Austria and the surviving smaller territories were far more universal than anything experienced under the old regime. Moreover, they extended the traditional duty to defend the homeland to an obligation to serve the national interest wherever that might be. Conscription, like universal taxation, broke down privilege and particularism, easing the identification of the individual with the wider community.[129]

In fact the reality lagged considerably behind the rhetoric prefacing the conscription decrees. Many young soldiers returned disillusioned with experience of actual combat which proved to be less than glorious. Their attitudes came very close to the general feeling of helplessness in the face of death which had overwhelmed men of the absolutist armies. However, it is significant that these negative feelings did not remain in the collective memory after 1815. The situation was similar to that after the Wars of German Unification (1866–71) which left society preconditioned for future conflict.[130]

Though often unwilling to accept it, princes and military men came to see advantages in the new conception of war. This had begun already prior to the French Revolution with the rise of political realism (*Realpolitik*). In the spirit of the enlightened attack on tradition and custom, political realism jettisoned the baggage of past justifications for conflict, legitimizing war on the basis of 'interests of state'. In the hands of skilful statesmen, this concept proved even more flexible than the previous notion of princely glory as it could be redefined to suit circumstances. New trends in historical scholarship assisted this development. As historians moved away from a dogmatic representation of the past to one of critical distance, statesmen no longer felt bound to act as their predecessors had done. The relatively static maxims of state of the mechanistic model of international relations were replaced by more organic metaphors embracing wider social and economic as well as political interests. Johannes Burkhardt has demonstrated how this changed conception of history assisted the Franco-Austrian rapprochement that preceded the Seven Years War in 1756. Enlightened revisionism of the previous account of Franco-Austrian relations provided new ways for statesmen to manipulate the past to justify an alliance between two formerly inveterate enemies.[131] Combined with the concept of nationalism, political realism opened up new possibilities for German governments to exploit the military potential of their populations and legitimize belligerence well into the next century.

## VII

Surveying the period from the Peace of Westphalia to Napoleon it is possible to identify a clear relationship between shifts in attitudes to war and changes in political and military practice. It is easiest to see this from the perspective of the development of the German territorial state. The completion of monopoly formation at territorial level during the later seventeenth century was accompanied by a rationalization of violence as a means of advancing state policy. Traditional Christian theological and moral approaches were reworked to support political centralization and permanent armies. The laws governing the conduct of war were rewritten, emphasizing discipline and a hierarchical command structure. Simultaneously, the criteria used to justify conflict were reconstructed. The state assumed the position of sole authority with legitimate control over physical violence. All other forms were gradually criminalized as rebellion, piracy, banditry and murder. Nonetheless, these justifications continued to refer to notions of legality, providing guidelines to which even princes were expected to adhere. In this sense the conflicts of the old regime were in fact limited. German princes made war for specific 'legitimate' ends, not as an end in itself. Martial deeds were glorified, not war as such. Peace and conflict resolution remained integral elements of princely aims and absolutist ideology.

Popular attitudes, so far as they can be ascertained, remained more firmly rooted in traditional beliefs. War was still regarded as an event largely beyond the control of ordinary mortals, if not princes and statesmen. While princes considered war a rational policy instrument, their subjects continued to view it as an unmitigated evil. Peace was what the majority desired. These differences are not surprising and have long been commented upon. What has tended to go unremarked is the fact that princes were compelled to take account of popular opinion. They did try to turn it to their advantage to reinforce these systems of rule. They promoted the idea that war was part of the mysteries of state and as such should remain outside the domain of public discussion. Simultaneously, it was emphasized that all subjects had a part to play, not only in shouldering the fiscal-military burden, but also in enlisting divine protection through leading pious and obedient lives. Contrary to both these intentions and the subsequent image of general lack of interest in 'cabinet wars', it is clear that war remained a topic of public debate. Princes were compelled to adjust their actions if they wanted to retain the sense of legitimacy upon which, ultimately, their rule depended.

The public debate provided the context for the growth of two new distinct but related critiques of war and its political uses. Mainstream Enlightened thought extended traditional Christian condemnation of unjust war to include all conflict and the instruments for waging it. Though radical in many respects, this critique remained within the existing intellectual framework. It simply transformed the rationalization of violence into one of peace. This was in tune with prevailing popular enthusiasm for peace and the measures to achieve it which dated back to the early eighteenth century. Romantic criticism emerged from and partly in reaction to these ideas. In arguing that war could not be divorced from its wider context, it radicalized an element of Enlightened thought from a critique of abuses in the existing system to a sustained attack on the system itself. In the process it abandoned key elements of continuity linking Enlightened criticism to absolutist ideology, transforming a glorification of peace into one of war.

This intellectual shift coincided with a political transformation originating in the debate on the nature of princely rule and extending well beyond the collapse of the Reich in 1806. The crucial issue in territorial politics had ceased to be whether absolutism could be reversed, whether the fiscal-military monopolies could be dismantled. It now centred on the control of those monopolies and their conversion from private to public institutions. The German territorial state proved surprisingly resilient throughout these upheavals, transforming itself and refounding its social basis to coopt wider sections of society into its systems of control. In doing so, it also adopted many of their attitudes to conflict which then became fused with existing beliefs in the validity of violence as a policy instrument. The two strands of criticism were reconciled in a way that ensured the survival of monarchical government into the nineteenth century. The Romantic ideal of war provided a new justification for its political use and the extension of coercive measures to obtain the manpower to wage it through more universal forms of conscription. The critique of the selfish, pointless wars of princes was smothered by the new notion of the public good, now defined as national and state interests. Though the nationalist ideology was to conflict with the still particularist nature of territorial government, it contained a mythology of violence that was to prove far more intoxicating than the earlier mechanistic concepts.

Whether these ideas helped propel German history along a special path (*Sonderweg*), distinct from the rest of Europe, cannot be determined here. What is certain, however, is that belligerence and militarism were far from the predominant characteristics of German thought prior to the early nineteenth century.

## Notes

1. C v Clausewitz, *On War* (ed. and trans M. Howard and P. Paret, Princeton 1976); J. Luvaas, ed., *Frederick the Great on the Art of War* (New York 1966); P. Paret, ed., *Makers of Modern Strategy from Machiavelli to the Nuclear Age* (Princeton 1986); P. Airas, *Die geschichtlichen Wertungen Krieg und Friede von Friedrich dem Grossen bis Engels* (Rovanierni 1978)

2. A. Gat, *The Origins Of Military Thought from the Enlightenment to Clausewitz* (Oxford 1989); P. Paret, *Clausewitz and the State* (Oxford 1976), both with good bibliographies. See also P. Paret, *Understanding War: Essays on Clausewitz and the History of Military Power* (Princeton 1992).

3. I use the word 'men' here deliberately because the overwhelming proportion of German soldiers in this period were male. See my 'German Women and War, 1500–1800', *War in History*, 3 (1996), 127–60.

4. For guidance in these areas see F. Redlich, *The German Military Enterprizer and his Workforce. A Study in European Economic and Social History* (2 vols, *Vierteljahreshefte für Sozial- und Wirtschaftsgeschichte*, Beihefte 47 and 48, Wiesbaden 1964–5); M. Messerschmidt, 'Preussens Militär in seinen gesellschaftlichen Umfeld' in H.J. Puhle and H.U. Wehler, eds, *Preussen im Rückblick*, special issue of *Geschichte und Gesellschaft*, 6 (1980), 43–88; R. Pröve, *Stehendes Heer und ständische Gesellschaft im 18. Jahrhundert. Göttingen und seine Militärbevölkerung 1713–1756* (Munich 1995), with an excellent bibliography, and his 'Zum Verhältnis von Militär und Gesellschaft im Spiegel gewaltsamer Rekrutierungen (1648–1789)', *Zeitschrift für historische Forschung*, 22 (1995), 191–224.

5. For varied attempts see E. Willems, *A Way of Life and Death: Three Centuries of Prusso-German Militarism — an Anthropological Approach* (Nashville 1986); A. Vagts, *A History of Militarism* (London 1938); V.R. Berghahn, *Militarismus* (Cologne 1975); L. Dehio, 'Um den deutschen Militarismus', *Historische Zeitschrift*, 180 (1955), 43–64; H. Herbell, *Staatsbürger in Uniform 1789 bis 1961* (Berlin [DDR] 1969); E. Obermann, *Soldaten, Bürger. Militaristen. Militär und Demokratic in Deutschland* (Stuttgart 1958); G. Ritter, *The Sword and the Sceptre: the Problem of Militarism in Germany* (4 vols, London 1972–3); P. Bachmann and K. Zeisler, *Der deutsche Militarismus* (2nd edn, Cologne 1986).

6. Here I follow C. Tilly, *Coercion, Capital and European States A.D. 990–1992* (Oxford 1992), 2–3.

7. For the following, see N. Elias, *The Civilizing Process* (Oxford 1994) esp. 312–14, 346–55; M. Mann, *The Sources of Social Power* (2 vols, Cambridge 1986–93); A. Giddens, *The Nation–State and Violence* (Berkeley 1985); H. Gerth and C.W. Mills, eds, *From Max Weber. Essays in Sociology* (London 1948), 77–83; J.E. Thomson, *Mercenaries, Pirates and Sovereigns. State-Building and Extra-Territorial Violence in Early Modern Europe* (Princeton 1994). These ideas are discussed at greater length in my *German Armies. War and German Politics 1648–1806* (London 1998), esp. 5–25.

8. J. Brewer, *The Sinews of Power. War, Money and the English State 1688–1783* (New York 1989); Mann, *Social Power*, Vol. II, 167–253.

9. K.O. Aretin, *Das alte Reich 1648–1806*, Vol. I *Föderalistische oder hierarchische Ordnung (1648–1684)* (Stuttgart 1993); H. Duchhardt, *Deutsche Verfassingsgeschichte 1495–1806* (Stuttgart 1991); P.H. Wilson, *War, State and Society in Württemberg, 1677–1793* (Cambridge 1995) and the literature cited there.

10. K. Repgen, 'Kriegslegitimationen in Alteuropa. Entwurf einer historischen Typologie', *Historische Zeitschrift*, 241 (1985), 27–49; J.T. Johnson, *Ideology, Reason and the Limitation of War. Religious and Secular Concepts 1200–1740* (Princeton 1975), 28–149; E. Luard, *The Balance of Power. The System of International Relations, 1648–1815* (London 1992), 321–9.

11. S. Pufendorf, *On the Duty of Man and Citizen* (1st edn 1673, ed. J. Tully, Cambridge 1995), 119.

12. Montecuccoli's attitude to alliances can be found in his *Trattato della guerra* (1641) printed in A. Veltzé, ed., *Ausgewählte Schriften des Raimund Fürsten Montecuccoli* (Vienna 1899). The quote comes from his *Della guerra col Turco* (1670) cited in G.E. Rothenberg, 'Maurice of Nassau, Gustavus Adolphus, Montecuccoli and the "military revolution" of the 17th century', in Paret, ed., *Makers*, 32–63 cf. 60–1. For further discussion of his ideas see T.M. Barker, *The Military Intellectual and Battle: Raimondo Montecuccoli and the Thirty Years War* (Albany 1975), and Gat, *Origins*, 13–24.

13. The Great Elector's comments from 1667 were printed in R. Dietrich, ed., *Die Politische Testamente der Hohenzollern* (Munich 1981), 191–2.

14. Montecuccoli, *Trattato*, 72–3.

15. Pufendorf, *On the Duty*, 133, 154.

16. Jean Bodin's ideas are most accessible in *Bodin on Sovereignty* (ed. J.H. Franklin, Cambridge 1992) which has a good introduction.

17. The key passage of this tract is printed in English translation in *Leibniz: Political Writings* (ed. P. Riley, Cambridge 1988) 111–20. For the background see G. Schnath, *Geschichte Hannovers im Zeitalter der neunten Kur und der englischen Sukzession 1674–1714* (5 vols, Hildesheim 1938–82), Vol. I, 104–6.

18. Conring and Pufendorf's ideas are discussed in H. Dreitzel, *Absolutismus und ständische Verfassung im Deutschland. Ein Beitrag zu Kontinuität und Diskontinuität der politischen Theorie in der frühen Neuzeit* (Mainz 1992), 60–6, 70–4. *Mars Christianissimus* is printed in *Leibnitz*, 121–45.

19. Dreitzel, *Absolutismus*, 82–4; H. Gross, 'The Holy Roman Empire in Modern Times: Constitutional Reality and Legal Theory', in J.A. Vann and S.W. Rowan, eds, *The Old Reich. Essays in German Political Institutions 1495–1806* (Brussels 1974), 1–29.

20. Quoted in K. Epstein, *The Genesis of German Conservatism* (Princeton 1966), 267. For the mysteries of state see the excellent discussion in A. Gestrich, *Absolutismus und Öffentlichkeit. Politische Kommunikation in Deutschland zu Beginn des 18. Jahrhunderts* (Göttingen 1994), 34–56.

21. V.L. v. Seckendorff, *Teutscher Fürstenstaat* (reprint of the 1737 edn Aalen 1972); J. Gagliardo, *Germany under the Old Regime 1600–1790* (Harlow 1991), 114–22; K. Tribe, 'Cameralism and the Science of Government', *Journal of Modern History*, 56 (1984), 263–84.

22. Dreitzel, *Absolutismus*, 48–54, 88–90. Interestingly, the exception to this was Lorraine where the dukes embraced French concepts of divine right.

23. Frederick of Prussia, *Anti-Machiavel* (trans. P. Sonnino, Athens, OH 1981); R. Birley, 'Antimachiavellianism, the Baroque and Maximilian of Bavaria', *Archivum Historicum Societas Jesu*, 103 (1984), 139–48; H. Münkler, *Im Namen des Staates. Die Begründung der Staatsraison in der frühen Neuzeit* (Frankfurt/M. 1878), esp. 321–7; M. Braubach, 'Politik und Kultur an den geistlichen Fürstenhöfen Westfalens gegen Ende des alten Reichs', *Westfälische Zeitschrift*,

105 (1955), 65–82; C. Hinrichs, *Preussentum und Pietismus. Der Pietismus im Brandenburg Preussen als religiös-soziale Reformbewegung* (Göttingen 1971); O. Hintze, 'Calvinism and raison d'état in Early Seventeenth-century Brandenburg', in F. Gilbert, ed., *The Historical Essays of Otto Hintze* (New York 1975), 88–154.

24. There are good discussions of Lipsius' ideas in G. Oestreich, *Neostoicism and the Early Modern State* (Cambridge 1982), reprinting his key articles; Rothenberg, 'Maurice of Nassau', 35–45. For the militia reforms see H. Ehlert, 'Ursprünge des modernen Militärwesens. Die Nassau-oranischen Heeresreformern', *Militärgeschichtlichen Mitteilungen*, 38 (1985), 27–56; G. Papke, *Von der Miliz zum stehenden Heer. Wehrwesen im Absolutismus* (Vol. I of *Deutsche Militärgeschichte 1648–1939*, Munich 1983), 122–38; H. Schnitter, *Volk und Landesdefension* (Berlin [DDR] 1977); W. Schulze, 'Die deutschen Landesdefensionen im 16 und 17 Jahrhundert', in J. Kunisch and B. Stollberg-Rillinger, eds, *Staatsverfassung und Heeresverfassung in der europäischen Geschichte der frühen Neuzeit* (Berlin 1986), 129–50.

25. See Redlich, *Enterprizer*, Vol II and R. Wohlfeil, 'Ritter-Söldnerführer-Offizier. Versuch eines Vergleichs', in J. Bärmann et al., eds, *Geschichtliche Landeskunde* (Vol. 3, Wiesbaden 1966), 45–70.

26. Numerous articles of war are printed in J.C. Lünig, *Corpus iuris militaris des Heiligen Römischen Reiches* (Leipzig 1723, reprinted Osnabrück 1968); J.G. Kulpis, *Eines hochlöbl. schwäbischen Crayses alte und neue Kriegsverordnungen* (Stuttgart 1737); E. v. Frauenholz, *Entwicklungsgeschichte des deutschen Heerwesens* (6 vols, Munich 1936–48). (Vol. 3 of this work also prints material on the militia reforms). They are discussed by W. Erben, 'Ursprung und Entwicklung der deutschen Kriegsartikeln', *Mitteilungen des Instituts für österreichische Geschichtsforschung*, supplement to Vol. 6 (1901), 473–529. As the composition of the officer corps grew more aristocratic in the early eighteenth century, officers were increasingly exempted from the disciplinary codes of the rank and file and expected instead to conform to a code of conduct based on self-discipline and a sense of personal honour: see K. Demeter, *The German Officer-Corps in Society and State 1650–1945* (London 1965), 111–56; V.G. Kiernan, *The Duel in European History. Honour and the Reign of Aristocracy* (Oxford 1989) and the theoretical discussion in Elias, *Civilizing Process*, 441–99.

27. M. Behnen, 'Der gerechte und der notwendige Krieg. "Necessitas" und "utilitas reipublicae" in der Kriegstheorie des 16. und 17. Jahrhunderts', in Kunisch and Stollberg-Rillinger, eds, *Staatsverfassung und Heeresverfassung*, 43–106. For the estates' attitude see P.H. Wilson, 'The Power to Defend, or the Defence of Power: the Conflict between Duke and Estates over Defence Provision, Württemberg 1677–1793', *Parliaments, Estates and Representation*, 12 (1992), 25–45 and *War, State and Society*, 54–73.

28. H-G. Böhme, *Die Wehrverfassung in Hessen-Kassel im 18 Jahrhundert bis zum siebenjährigen Kriege* (Kassel and Basle 1954), 35–7; Hauptstaatsarchiv Stuttgart (hereafter HSAS), A28: Bü. 99 16 January 1720; J.A. von Bandel, *Auf eine Lüge eine Maultasche!* (1766) 52–6.

29. Dreitzel, *Absolutismus*, 66–9.

30. Waldeck cited in W. Jannen Jr, '"Das Liebe Teutschland" in the 17th Century — Count Georg Frederick von Waldeck', *European Studies Review*, 6 (1976), 165–95 at 191; The Great Elector in Dietrich, ed., *Politische Testamente*, 191–2.

31. A Prussian officer quoted in C. Duffy, *The Military Experience in the Age of Reason* (London and New York 1987), 15.

32. Cited in E. von Frauenholz, *Die Eingliederung von Heer und Volk in den Staat in Bayern 1597–1815* (Munich 1940), 14

33. W.A. von Kaunitz-Rietberg, 'Votum über das Militare 1762', in H. Bleckwenn, ed., *Zeitgenössische Studien über die altpreussische Armee* (Osnabrück 1974), 3.

34. Preamble to Mecklenburg articles of war cited in G. Tessen, *Mecklenburgisches Militär in Türken- und Franzosenkriegen 1648–1718* (Cologne and Graz 1966), 188.

35. For princely aims see Wilson, *War, State and Society* 10–25 and the literature cited there.

36. HSAS, C14: Bü. 330 15 June 1739.

37. Pufendorf, *On the Duty*, 154.

38. This view is expressed by C.W. Ingrao, *The Hessian Mercenary State. Ideas, Institutions and Reforms under Frederick II, 1760–1785* (Cambridge 1987), esp. 6–7. For the following see HSAS, C14: Bü. 332.; L.5.22.6.1; R. Gebauer, *Die Aussenpolitik der schwäbischen Reichskreises vor Ausbruch des spanischen Erbfolgekrieges (1697–1702)* (Marburg, PhD, printed 1969), 16–25; R. Graf. von Neipperg, *Kaiser und schwäbische Kreis (1714–1733)* (Stuttgart 1991), 15–31; P.-C. Storm, *Der schwäbische Kreis als Feldherr 1648–1732* (Berlin 1974), 110–11, 258–63, 268, 330–48; B. Sicken, *Das Wehrwesen des Frankischen Reichskreises. Aufbau und Struktur (1681–1714)* (2 vols, Nuremberg 1967), I, 167–235, R. Fester, *Die armirten Stände und die Reichskriegsverfassung 1681–1697* (Frankfurt am Main 1886).

39. M. Howard, *The Causes of Wars and Other Essays* (Oxford 1983), 13.

40. Cited by Schnath, *Geschichte Hannovers*, Vol. I, 339.

41. Quoted in S.B. Fay, 'The Beginning of the Standing Army in Prussia', *American Historical Review*, 22 (1917), 763–77 at 769 n. II. On the essentially defensive character of the Great Elector's foreign policy see E. Opgenoorth, 'Der Grosse Kurfürst, das Reich und die europäischen Mächte', in O. Hauser, ed., *Preussen, Europa und das Reich* (Cologne 1987), 19–31.

42. Repgen, 'Kreigslegitimationen', 39–43; Gestrich, *Absolutismus und Öffentlichkeit*, esp. 79–81, 194.

43. G. Mentz, *Johann Philipp von Schönborn, Kurfürst von Mainz, Bischof von Würzburg und Worms 1605–1673* (2 vols, Jena 1896–9); O. Meyer, *Johann Philipp von Schönborn: Fürstbischof von Würzburg, Erzbischof von Mainz, Bischof von Worms 1605–1673* (Würzburg 1973); F. Jürgensmeier, 'Johann Philipp von Schönborn', *Fränkische Lebensbilder*, 6 (1975), 161–84; M.L. v. Pragenau, 'Johann Philipp von Mainz und die Marienburger Allianz von 1671–1672', *Mitteilungen des Instituts für Österreichische Geschichtsforschung*, 16 (1895), 582–623; F.J. Krappmann, 'Johann Philipp von Schönborn und das Leibnizsche Consilium Aegyptianum', *Zeitschrift für die Geschichte des Oberrheins*, NF45 (1932), 185–219; W. Frhr. v. Tettau, 'Erfurts Unterwerfung unter die Mainzische Landeshoheit', *Neujahrsblätter herausgegeben von der Historischen Kommission der Provinz Sachsen*, 11 (1887), 3–56; K.P. Decker, *Frankreich und die Reichsstände 1672–1675* (Bonn 1981), esp. 11–15; R.H. Thompson, *Lothar Franz von Schönborn and the Diplomacy of the Electorate of Mainz* (The Hague 1973); H. Duchhardt, 'Friedenswährung im 18. Jahrhundert', *Historische Zeitschrift*, 240

(1985), 265–82 and his 'International Relations, the Law of Nations, and the Germanies. Structures and Changes in the Second Half of the Seventeenth Century', in C. Ingrao, ed., *The State and Society in Early Modern Austria* (West Lafayette 1994), 286–97.

44. Gestrich, *Absolutismus und Öffentlichkeit*, 49–53; J. Kunisch, *Fürst-Gesellschaft-Krieg. Studien zur bellizistischen Disposition des absoluten Fürstenstaates* (Cologne 1992), 1–42; D. Kaiser, *Politics and War. European Conflict from Philip II to Hitler* (Cambridge, MA 1990), 416; Gidden's *Violence*, 114–5.

45. H. Bleckwenn, ed., *Preussische Soldatenbriefe* (Osnabrück 1982), quotes from Part II, 7, 34. See also the discussion in K. Latzel '"Schlachtbank" oder "Feld der Ehre"? Der Beginn des Einstellungswandels gegenüber Krieg und Tod 1756–1816', in W. Wette, ed., *Der Krieg des kleinen Mannes* (Munich 1995), 76–92.

46. Preface addressed to the rank and file in C.H.C.L. v. Geispitzheim, *Historische Nachrichten von dem Koenigl. Preusisch. Hochloeblichen Füsilier-Regiments . . . von Erlach* (2 parts, 1778–9), Part II.

47. Hinrichs, *Preussentum und Pietismus*, 155–66; R.L. Gawthrop, *Pietism and the Making of Eighteenth-Century Prussia* (Cambridge 1993), 225–7; C. Jany, 'Die Kantonverfassung Friedrich Wilhelm I', *Forschungen zur Brandenburgischen-Preussischen Geschichte*, 38 (1926) 225–72 at 266–7; F.K. Tharau, *Die geistige Kultur des preussischen Offiziers von 1640 bis 1806* (Mainz 1968), 23–7, 41, 49–50.

48. Quotes from Epstein, *Genesis* 267–8. On Styrum see J. Arndt, *Das Niederrheinisch-Westfälische Reichsgrafenkollegium und seine Mitglieder (1653–1806)* (Mainz 1991), 291–2.

49. Cited in W. Hubatsch, *Frederick the Great. Absolutism and Administration* (London 1975), 200.

50. J.J. Dominicus, *Aus dem Siebenjährigen Krieg. Tagebuch des preussischen Musketiers Dominicus* (ed. D. Kerler, Munich 1891), esp. 6–7, 61–3; E.F.R. v. Barsewisch, *Von Rossbach bis Freiberg 1757–1763. Tagebuchblätter eines friderizianischen Fahnenjunkers und Officiers* (ed. J. Olmes, Krefeld 1959), 27, 44, 88, 103–4, 116, 121, 171, 202, 247. Quotations from Bleckwenn, ed., *Soldatenbriefe*, 11–15, 22.

51. H. Philippi, *Landgraf Karl von Hessen-Kassel*, (Marburg 1976), 114; Gestrich, *Absolutismus und Öffentlichkeit*, 127–8, 153.

52. T.K. Rabb, *The Struggle for Stability in Early Modern Europe* (New York 1975).

53. Quoted in T.C.W. Blanning, *Reform and Revolution in Mainz 1743–1803* (Cambridge 1974), 19. Justi's metaphor has been generally misunderstood. It is not in fact a plea for excessive regimentation of every aspect of life but expression of the hope that if a state adjusted its actions according to law it would run smoothly without the need for authoritarian direction. See B. Stollberg-Rillinger, *Der Staat als Maschine. Zur politischen Metaphorik des absoluten Fürstenstaates* (Berlin 1986).

54. H. Eichberg, 'Geometrie als barocke Verhaltensnorm. Fortifikation und Exerzitien', *Zeitschrift für historische Forschung*, 4 (1977), 17–50, and his 'Ordnen, Messen, disciplinieren. Moderner Herrschaftsstaat und Fortifikation', in Kunisch and Stollberg-Rillinger eds, *Staatsverfassung und Heeresverfassung*, 347–75; J. Kunisch, *Absolutismus* (Göttingen 1986), 9–19.

55. M.S. Anderson, *The Rise of Modern Diplomacy 1450–1919* (London 1993),

149–80; J. Black, *The Rise of the European Powers 1679–1793* (London 1990), 154–62; Luard, *The Balance of Power*, 1–29, 57–99; K.J. Burkhardt, 'Der Dreissigjährigen Krieg als Staatsbildungskrieg', *Geschichte in Wissenschaft und Unterricht*, 45 (1994), 487–99; A. Lossky, 'Maxims of State in Louis XIV's Foreign Policy in the 1680s', in R. Hatton and J.S. Bromley, eds, *William III and Louis XIV. Essays 1680–1720* (Liverpool 1968), 7–23; F. Bosbach, 'Die Habsburger und die Entstehung des Dreissigjährigen Krieges. Die '*Monarchia Universalis*', in K. Repgen, ed., *Krieg und Politik 1618–1648* (Munich 1988), 151–68.

56. Quoted in Dreitzel, *Absolutismus*, 75.

57. R. Vierhaus, 'Militärische Macht im Kalkül der europäischen Staatengemeinschaft des 18. Jahrhunderts', in B.R. Kroener, ed., *Europa im Zeitalter Friedrichs des Grossen* (Munich 1989), 23–34; Kaiser, *Politics and War*, 208–10.

58. M. Raeff, *The Well Ordered Police State: Social and Institutional Change through Law in the Germanies and Russia 1600–1800* (New Haven 1983) provides considerable detail on this.

59. Mitchell to Holdernesse 14 July 1758, A. Bisset, ed., *Memoirs and Papers of Sir Andrew Mitchell K.B.* (2 vols, London 1850), II, 418–19.

60. The following omits discussion of how the rejection of the 'scientific approach' to war affected tactical and strategic thinking. This area is well covered by Gat, *Origins*, 54–135 and W. O. Shanahan, 'Enlightenment and war: Austro-Prussian Military Practice', in G. Rothenberg et al., eds, *War and Society in East Central Europe* (New York 1982), II, 82–111.

61. 'Curriculum vitae militaris Dom. Neubauer', reprinted in H. Bleckwenn, ed., *Kriegs- und Friedersbilder 1725–1759* (Osnabrück 1971), 248. For the influence of Pietism see, in addition to works cited in n. 47 above, M. Fulbrook, *Piety and Politics. Religion and the Rise of Absolutism in England, Württemberg and Prussia* (Cambridge 1983).

62. P. Brock, *Pacifism in Europe to 1914* (Princeton 1972), 213–54; L.J. Baack, 'Frederick William III, the Quakers and the Problem of Conscientious Objection in Prussia', *Journal of Church and State*, 20 (1978), 305–13.

63. P. Sauer, *Tamm. Geschichte einer Gemeinde* (Ulm 1980), 187. The complaints of the Württemberg estates in HSAS L5 Tomi Actorum Provincialium Wirtembergicorum give numerous other examples, especially for the 1730s and 1750s.

64. Examples in E. Hagen, 'Die fürstlich würzburgische Hausinfanterie von ihren Anfängen bis zum Beginne des Siebenjährigen Krieges 1636–1756', *Darstellungen aus bayerischen Kriegs- und Heeresgeschichte*, 19 (1910), 69–203 at 169.

65. Tessin, *Meckklenburgisches Militär*, 153; Hinrichs, *Preussentum und Pietismus*, 135–7, 145–8; Jany, 'Kantonverfassung', 236–7.

66. B. Thompson, Count Rumford, *Collected Works* (ed. S.C. Brown, 5 vols, Cambridge, MA 1968–70), V, 404–5 (from 1788).

67. F.K. Erbprinz zu Hohenlohe-Waldenburg, 'Über hohenlohisches Militärwesen', *Württembergisch Franken*, NF 40 (1966), 212–41 at 224.

68. R. Weltrich, *Friedrich Schiller* (Stuttgart 1899), 329.

69. HSAS, A202: Bü. 863 9 January 1751.

70. K. V. Martens, *Geschichte von Hohentwiel* (Stuttgart 1857), 194. See also 176–7.

71. H. Schlechte, ed., *Das geheime politische Tagebuch des Kurprinzen Friedrich Christian 1751 bis 1757* (Weimar 1992), 361, 387.

72. See P.H. Wilson, 'The German "Soldier Trade" of the Seventeenth and Eighteenth Centuries: A Reassessment', *International History Review*, 18(1996), 757–92.

73. Cited by W.H. Bruford, *Germany in the Eighteenth Century* (Cambridge 1935), 33.

74. F.A. Pottle, ed., *Boswell on the Grand Tour. Germany and Switzerland 1764* (Melbourne 1953), 102.

75. Quoted in H. Möller, *Fürstenstaat oder Bürgernation: Deutschland 1763–1815* (Berlin 1989), 70.

76. On these see C. Ingrao, 'The Smaller German States', in H.M. Scott, ed., *Enlightened Absolutism* (London 1990), 221–44.

77. A. Schmid, *Max III Joseph und die europäischen Mächte* (Munich 1987), 399.

78. K.O. v. Aretin, *Das Reich. Friedensordnung und europäisches Gleichgewicht 1648–1806* (Stuttgart 1992), 14, n.9.

79. A. Brabant, *Das heilige römische Reich teutscher Nation im Kampf mit Friedrich dem Grossen* (3 vols, Berlin 1904–34), I, 146.

80. D. Kotsch, *Potsdam. Die preussische Garnisonstadt* (Brunswick 1992), 112.

81. J.W. v. Archenholz, *Gemälde der preussischen Armee vor und in dem Siebenjährigen Kriege* (Berlin 1791), 7; K.P. Merta, *Uniformen der Armee Friedrich Wilhelms III* (Berlin 1993), 18–20.

82. *Die Bewaffnung und Ausrüstung der Armee Friedrichs des Grossen* (exhibition catalogue, issued by the Wehrgeschichtliches Museum Rastatt, 1986); K. Vanja, *Vivat- Vivat- Vivat! Widmungs- und Gedenkbänder aus drei Jahrhunderten* (Berlin 1985); F. v. Conring, *Das deutsche Militär in der Karikatur* (Stuttgart 1907).

83. Rothenberg, 'Maurice of Nassau', 57–63; Kunisch, *Fürst-Gesellschaft-Krieg*, 138–46.

84. Vagts, *Militarism*, 78, 81. More examples in R. Höhn, *Revolution, Heer, Kriegsbild* (Darmstadt 1944), 55–120. See Gestrich, *Absolutismus und Öffentlichkeit*, 227–8 for an anonymous pamphlet from 1702 arguing that since soldiers depended on war for their livelihoods, they tended to agitate for it.

85. Gestrich, *Absolutismus und Öffentlichkeit*, 214–27.

86. Cited in F.A.J. Szabo, *Kaunitz and Enlightened Absolutism 1753–1780* (Cambridge 1994), 294. On the change of attitude see Duchhardt, 'Friedenswährung', 265, 282.

87. L. Krieger, *The German Idea of Freedom* (Chicago 1957), 46–85; K.v. Raumer, '1648/1815. Zum Problem internationaler Friedensordnung in älteren Europa' in *Forschungen und Studien zur Geschichte des Westfälischen Friedens* (Münster 1965), 109–26; A. and W. Dietze, *Ewiger Friede? Dokumente einer deutschen Diskussion um 1800* (Munich 1989); Gestrich, *Absolutismus und Öffentlichkeit*, 228–33. According to Behnen, 'Der gerechte und der notwendige Krieg', 106 n. 233, at least 43 German dissertations between 1626 and 1719 were concerned with the problem of conflict resolution.

88. Kunisch, *Fürst-Gesellschaft-Krieg*, 131–59, 215–16; H.H. Klein, *Wilhelm zu Schaumburg–Lippe* (Osnabrück 1982).

89. P.B. Bernard, *Joseph II and Bavaria* (The Hague 1965); K.O. v. Aretin, *Heiliges Römisches Reich 1776–1806* (2 vols, Wiesbaden 1967), I, 110–30. The

quote comes from Kaunitz's memorandum on Austria's political and military situation 7 September 1778 printed in ibid., II, 1–2.

90. From Möller, *Fürstenstaat*, 22.

91. Gestrich, *Absolutismus und Öffentlichkeit*, 57–74, 227 and the works listed in n. 61.

92. F.L. Carsten, *Princes and Parliaments in Germany from the Fifteenth to the Eighteenth Century* (Oxford 1959). For a contrary interpretation see the literature in n. 27.

93. Dreitzel, *Absolutismus*, 92–142 and his 'Ständestaat und absolute Monarchie in der politischen Theorie des Reiches in der frühen Neuzeit', in G. Schmidt, ed., *Stände und Gesellschaft im alten Reich* (Stuttgart 1989), 19–50. See also Epstein, *Genesis*, 253–76 for further discussion of these debates.

94. See Elias, *Civilizing Process*, 349–50, 390–2 for a theoretical elaboration of this point.

95. P.L.H. Röder, *Geographie und Statistik Wirtemberg* (2 vols, Laibach im Krain/Ulm 1787–1804), I, 159. Scharnhorst cited in Kunisch, *Fürst-Gesellschaft-Krieg*, 205. For similar comments by Frederick the Great see Duffy, *Military Experience*, 15–16.

96. HSAS, C14: Bü. 330 15 June 1739.

97. Fester, *Armirten Stände*; W. Grube, *Der Stuttgarter Landtag 1457–1957* (Stuttgart 1957), 369.

98. S.C. Brown, *Benjamin Thompson Count Rumford* (Cambridge, MA 1979), 117–40; C. Ingrao, *The Hessian Mercenary State* (Cambridge 1987), 168.

99. Papke, *Von der Miliz*, 185–6.

100. For some examples see documents relating to the use of soldiers as construction workers in Ludwigsburg in the 1720s to 1730s in HSAS, A6: Bü. 65 and L6.22.6.28 11 April 1722 and 13 April 1722. Troops also helped build the town of Erlangen in 1686, see A. Jakob, *Die Neustadt Erlangen. Planung und Entstehung, Erlanger Bausteiner zur Fränkischen Heimatforschung*, 33 (1986) special issue, 191. See also Wilson, 'German Women', 157–8.

101. Röder, *Geographie*, 159; A. Frhr. v. Knigge, 'Über die Ursachen, warum wir vorerst in Teutschland wohl keine gefährliche politische Haupt-Revolution zu erwarten haben', in T. Stammen and F. Eberle, eds, *Deutschland und die Französische Revolution 1789–1806* (Darmstadt, 1988), 254–62 at 261.

102. See J.J. Sheehan, *German History 1770–1866* (Oxford 1989), 32. For social militarization see O. Büsch, *Militärsystem und Sozialleben im alten Pressen 1713–1807. Die Anfänge der sozialen Militärisierung des preussisch–deutschen Gesellschaft* (Berlin 1962) now available in English translation as *Military System and Social Life in Old Regime Prussia 1713–1807* (Atlantic Highlands 1997)

103. D. Hohrat and R. Henning, *Die Bildung des Offiziers in der Aufklärung* (Stuttgart 1990); R. Uhland, *Geschichte der Hohen Karlsschule in Stuttgart* (Stuttgart 1953); Gat, *Origins*, 56–66.

104. W.O. Shanahan, *Prussian Military Reforms 1786–1813* (New York 1945); P. Paret, *Yorck and the Era of Prussian reform 1807–1815* (Princeton 1966); G.A. Craig, *The Politics of the Prussian Army 1640–1945* (2nd edn, Oxford 1954), 22–65; C.E. White, *The Enlightened Soldier: Scharnhorst and the 'Militärische Gesellschaft' in Berlin 1801–1805* (New York 1989).

105. For Machiavelli see Behnen, 'Der gerechte und der notwendige Krieg', 50–63, and H. Delbrück, *History of the Art of War* (4 vols, Lincoln, NE 1990,

English translation of 1920 edn), IV 101–13. For militia systems and recruitment practices see in addition to the works cited in n. 24 above: Büsch, *Militärsystem*; Jany, 'Kantonverfassung'; M. Lehmann, 'Werbung, Wehrpflicht und Beurlaubung im Heere Friedrich Wilhelm I', *Historische Zeitschrift*, 67 (1891), 254–89, R. Frhr. v. Schroetter, 'Die Ergänzung des preussischen Heeres unter dem ersten Könige', *Forschungen zur Brandenburgischen und preussischen Geschichte*, 23 (1910), 81–145; W. Thum, *Die Rekrutierung der sächsischen Armee unter August dem Starken (1694–1733)* (Leipzig 1912); B. Sicken, 'Die Streitkräfte des Hochstifts Würzburg gegen Ende des Ancien Régime', *Zeitschrift für bayerische Landesgeschichte*, 47 (1984), 691–744; P.K. Taylor, *Indentured to Liberty. Peasant Life and the Hessian Military State 1688–1815* (Ithaca 1994); Klein, *Schaumburg–Lippe*, 35–41; R. Harms, 'Landmiliz und stehendes Heer in Kurmainz nametlich im 18. Jahrhundert', *Archiv für hessische Geschichte und Alterumskunde*, NF6 (1909), 359–430; A. v. Pfister, *Die Militizgedanke in Württemberg und die Versuche zu seiner Verwirklichung* (Stuttgart 1883); Wilson, *War, State and Society*, 115–17, 139–40, 158, 171–2, 176–8 and the archival sources cited there.

106. Vagts, *Militarism*, 77–86 quote from 77–8; Kunisch, *Fürst-Gesellschaft-Krieg*, 204–7.

107. Frederick, *Anti-Machiavel*, 84.

108. Luvaas, ed., *Frederick the Great*, 75 citing the *Military Testament* of 1768.

109. *Political testament* of 1752 in Dietrich, ed., *Politische Testamente*, 310–11.

110. Rumford, *Collected Works*, V,5.

111. Plans of Privy Councillor Georg Bernhard Bilfinger in HSAS, L6.22.7.5a (1738); A202: Bü. 1993 (1741); A202: Bü.2244 (1747).

112. G.J. Neimais, 'Militia vs. the Standing Army in the History of Economic Thought from Adam Smith to Friedrich Engels', *Military Affairs*, 44 (1980), 28–32; P.D. Nelson, 'Citizen Soldiers or Regulars. The views of American General Officers on the Military Establishment, 1775–1781', *Military Affairs*, 43 (1979), 126–31.

113. W.A. Kaunitz, *Staats-Betrachtungen über gegenwärtigen Preussischen Krieg in Teutschland* (Vienna, 1761) printed J. Kunisch, *Das Mirakel des Hauses Brandenburg* (Munich 1978), 101–41 at 105.

114. Quoted in Szabo, *Kaunitz*, 266–7.

115. Kaunitz, 'Votum'. For further discussion see Szabo, *Kaunitz*, 278–94. On Joseph II's militarism see T.C.W, Blanning, *Joseph II*, (London 1994), 125–9. For Austrian conscription measures see J. Komlos, *Nutrition and Economic Development in the Eighteenth Century Habsburg Monarchy* (Princeton 1989), esp. 225–39.

116. Kunisch, *Mirakel*, esp. 17–43. There is a striking similarity between the views of Prussian militarism expressed in these documents from the eighteenth century and the subsequent opinions advanced by the Allied Control Commission after 1947 and incorporated into the standard historical interpretation of German military history by Anglo-Saxon and German writers: Craig, *The Politics of the Prussian Army*; M. Kitchen, *A Military History of Germany* (London 1975), esp. Ch. 1; H.U. Wehler, *Deutsche Gesellschaftsgeschichte*, Vol. 1 (Munich 1987), 244–54. This is a point that requires a fuller discussion than is possible here but to which I intend to return.

117. C. Dipper, *Deutsche Geschichte 1648–1789* (Frankfurt am Main 1991), 305–9.

118. J.C. Döhla, *A Hessian Diary of the American Revolution* (ed. B.E. Burgoyne, Norman 1990), 218.

119. Barsewisch, *Von Rossbach*, 12, 113, 119.

120. K.E. Demandt, *Geschichte des Landes Hessen* (Kassel 1980), 284–5.

121. J.C. Allmayer-Beck, *Das Heer unter dem Doppeladler. Habsburgs Armeen 1718–1848* (Munich 1981), 56; G.E. Lessing, *Minna von Barnhelm oder das Soldatenglück*, written in 1763.

122. Jannen, 'Das Liebe Teutschland', 187–73; Duffy, *Military Experience*, 10. For further discussion of German national sentiment in this period see H. James, *A German Identity 1770–1990* (London 1990); M. Walker, *German Home Towns. Community, State and General Estate 1648–1871* (Ithaca 1971); M. Hughes, *Nationalism and Society. Germany 1800–1945* (London 1988) and his *Early Modern Germany 1477–1806* (London 1992), 149–50, 159–62.

123. Kunisch, *Fürst-Gesellschaft-Krieg*, 161–226; Epstein, *Genesis*, 291–3; Gat, *Origins*, 139–49.

124. On this see H. Speier, 'Militarism in the Eighteenth Century', *Social Research*, 3 (1936), 304–36 at 322–3.

125. For example E.R. Huber, *Heer und Staat in der deutscher Geschichte* (2nd edn, Hamburg 1943); E. Luard, *War in International Society* (London 1986).

126. Phraseology from Latzel, '"Schlachtbank"'.

127. Kunisch, *Fürst-Gesellschaft-Krieg*, 203–26. See Paret, *Understanding War*, 155–65 for a comparison between Kleist and Clausewitz with similar conclusions.

128. Though concentrating on the 1809 campaign, J.H. Gill, *With Eagles to Glory* (London 1992) provides a good overview of the extensive literature on the armies of the smaller German states in this period.

129. Paret, *Understanding War*, 39–74. For the measures see Shanahan, *Prussian Military Reforms*, 127–224; Paret, *Yorck*, 111–53; C. Jany, *Geschichte der preussischen Armee* (4 vols, Osnabrück, 1967), IV 1–102.

130. On the negative experience of combat see Latzel '"Schlachtbank"', and J. Walter, *The Diary of a Napoleonic Foot Soldier* (ed. M. Raeff, Moreton-in-Marsh 1991) which also prints letters from soldiers in the Westphalian army. For the legacy of war see G.L. Mosse, *The Nationalization of the Masses* (New York 1975); D.E. Showalter, 'Army, State and Society in Germany, 1871–1914: an Interpretation', in J.R. Dukes and J. Remak, eds, *Another Germany* (London 1988), 1–18.

131. J. Burkhardt, 'Geschichte als Argument in der habsburgisch-französischen Diplomatie. Der Wandel des frühneuzeitlichen Geschichtsbewusstseins in seiner Bedeutung für die Diplomatische Revolution von 1756', in R. Babel, ed., *Frankreich im europäischen Staatensystem der frühen Neuzeit* (Sigmaringen 1995), 191–217. Such historicism involved a rejection of the earlier conviction that classical antiquity could provide answers to contemporary questions. For further discussion of this see Gat, *Origins*, 8–9.

*Peter H. Wilson*

is Lecturer in Early Modern European History at the University of Newcastle. His publications include *War, State and Society in Württemberg, 1677–1793* (Cambridge University Press, 1995) and *German Armies: War and German Politics 1648–1806* (UCL Press, 1998). He is currently writing on absolutism and war.

# [16]

# *Tactics and Recruitment in Eighteenth Century Prussia*

**Dennis E. Showalter**

The new military history, with its focus on the political and economic, the social and intellectual matrices of war, has found one of its most fruitful areas of study in eighteenth-century Prussia. The interpretive structure is familiar. A succession of rulers pursued interrelated policies of aggression and absolutism, expanding alike the state's influence abroad and its control at home. Their most important instrument in both cases was the military. In order to sustain armed forces strong enough to support Brandenburg-Prussia's assertive power politics, the entire spectrum of material and moral resources had to be mobilized and focussed to a single end. In the process, what began as a jumble of discrete political entities was firmly welded into a solid striking instrument, the wonder of Europe and the terror of its neighbors even in its decline. At the same time this emerging Prussia incorporated into its civic philosophy a set of postulates elevating martial and military virtues, extending their application into virtually every aspect of public and private life. While the exact consequences of this process may still be debated, their essentially negative nature is overwhelmingly conceded.[1]

In the process of developing and refining this structure, the Prussian army itself has been oddly neglected. Curt Jany's three monumental volumes, first published in the 1920's, appear to have satisfied most scholarly demands for material on the army as a military instrument. Christopher Duffy's work is essentially a literate update. A recent upsurge of antiquarian interest, most notably fostered by Hans Bleckwenn, has provided reprints of a broad spectrum of contemporary memoirs, histories, *Ranglisten* and drill regulations. Material on everything from the army's military music to its techniques for pitching camp is now readily available. Unfortunately, most of it is presented with a mixture of nostalgia and tunnel vision that has so far limited its use.[2] As a result, Prussia's army tends to be fitted into assorted procrustean beds, used to illustrate such general concepts as dynastic absolutism, limited war, or the evolution of the bureaucratic state. Among military historians it frequently becomes a negative example of the dangers inherent in resting on laurels however well-earned, of following systems however well-developed.[3] This approach is strengthened by eighteenth-century attitudes on the subject of military science and military institutions. Every era defines ultimate truth in its own way. The biological determinism of the nineteenth century gives way before the computer printout of the twentieth. The eighteenth century's intellectual life in general was dominated by a concern for first principles, for integrating social phenomena into an order borrowing its essential rationale from the world of mathematics. It is hardly surprising that military theorists and practical soldiers alike sought to tame that process which is above all the province of confusion, not so much to put the conduct of war and the behaviour of armies under artificial restrictions, but to express them in terms comprehensible and acceptable to the societies and systems the military establishments existed to serve. The Thirty Years' War had marked the end of the temporary ascendancy of the military enterpriser and his *soldateska.* Whatever the financial and moral costs of bringing armies under the control of governments, the alternatives were perceptively worse. The process generated a certain reciprocity, as soldiers in turn sought to justify their existence to their now-permanent paymasters in universal rather than craft-specific terms.[4]

Following this pattern too closely, however, incorporates a significant intellectual risk. Armies exist to fight, prepare themselves to win, and develop internal dynamics as a response to their perceptions of the demands of battle. These perceptions may be, and often are, spectacularly inaccurate. They may be, and often are, significantly influenced by prejudices and preconceptions reflecting everything from social origins to personal antagonisms. But they are the prism through which all the objective considerations so dear to the social-scientific historian are filtered. The Prussian army of the eighteenth century was certainly a product of the greater world of political, social, and economic developments. But it was also part of a lesser world of material changes in the craft of war—changes which in turn generated doctrinal and attitudinal changes that did at least as much to shape its nature as any applications of *l'ésprit geometrique.*

## I

The Prussian army's approach to war was shaped by a fact so obvious that it is correspondingly easy to overlook: Prussia functioned in an international environment that did not wish her well. General descriptions of eighteenth-century international relations as manifesting an increasing moderation reflecting a growing harmony of interests overlook the fact that a balance of power is intended to prevent empire rather than preserve peace. It incorporates, moreover, a bias in favour of decision, as opposed to balance: a desire to form or participate in dominant, rather than blocking, coalitions. Nor does a balance of power guarantee the position of lesser elements. Eighteenth-century international politics commonly featured plans for the dismantling even of such great powers as Spain or Austria. Sweden and the Ottoman Empire underwent significant territorial losses. Poland disappeared from the map altogether.[5] In such an environment it was scarcely unreasonable for the Great Elector and his successors to accept the case that Prussia must be either hammer or anvil; that, to borrow a phrase subsequently ascribed to Bismarck, the pike in Europe's fishpond prevented her from ever becoming a carp. Nor was it unreasonable for Prussia's soldiers to strive for the most efficient military instrument possible in the circumstances.

Achieving this required a certain concern for first principles. Aside from any moral questions, Prussia's geographic vulnerability and economic weakness condemned her to a defensive grand strategy whenever she chose to play an independent role. This point, conceded by the Great Elector, was overtly affirmed by his two successors and ultimately conceded by Frederick the Great as well.[6] But it is precisely states with such a limitation that must pay close attention to the offensive on strategic operational and tactical levels. An army thinking only in defensive terms sacrifices both moral and physical initiative. Doomed always to react, it observes, waits, ripostes—and ultimately retreats. Even the argument, based primarily on experiences from 1861 to 1918, that the offensive costs lives to no purpose, can be significantly misleading. Hesitating and overcaution can produce effects similar to those generated by repeatedly testing the speed of a buzz-saw with the bare hand: a series of small-scale losses for correspondingly small gains that can rapidly mount to a distressing total.

These truisms had been reinforced significantly in Prussia by the experiences gained in the reign of the Great Elector and King Frederick I. In addition to furnishing contingents for the Empire's wars with the Turks, and for the great coalitions against France, Brandenburg's army had fought first Poland, then Sweden, in the east. Where the distances were so extensive relative to the forces deployed, defensive-mindedness was a gateway to disaster. Sweden depended for her Baltic empire on the ability of her armies to move fast and strike hard. Even in Poland's decline, its aggressive cavalry could embarrass any but the steadiest infantry. Nor, for that matter, were the experiences of the Prussian contingents who served under the Duke of Marlborough likely to encourage commitment to the concept of "little war" as ultimately a less costly alternative to decisive action.[7]

The question then became how best to prepare for that circumstance. It received additional emphasis around the turn of the century as the matchlock and the pike, standard weapons of the infantry for over a hundred years, gave way in Europe's armies to the flintlock musket and its socket bayonet. Introduced in the late seventeenth century, the flintlock and bayonet marked the reintroduction for the first time since the decline of Rome's legions of the all-purpose infantryman, combining in his own person fire and shock power enabling him once more to assume the decisive role in battle. Indeed the weapon's relative potential was so great that it generated a corresponding change in tactical formations. Matchlock and pike infantry, however flexible it might become in the hands of a master like Turenne or Gustavus, was essentially a defensive instrument, able to wear an enemy down, to protect cavalry and prepare its charges, but unable, save by accident, to decide battles on its own. To be effective, both the clumsy pike and the slow-firing matchlock had to be employed in masses—though again the relative size of these masses was susceptible of significant reduction as leadership, training, and discipline improved in the course of the nineteenth century. Ultimately, however, these were weapons of attrition, depending for this effect on cumulative effort as opposed to an overwhelming blow.[8]

The flintlock for its part offered a military virtue unknown to date in the Age of Gunpowder: technically-reliable rapid fire. The musket's relative inaccuracy has been especially highlighted for North American readers by a tendency to compare it with the hunting rifles of the Appalachian frontier. Contemporaries were often equally critical. Thus Gerhard von Scharnhorst and Carl von Clausewitz alike dismissed the musket carried for over a quarter-century by the Prussian infantry as the worst in Europe. A junior officer with more direct experience of the weapon described it as neither firearm, pike nor club.[9] Tolerances for the *Infanteriegewehr* M1782 were wide enough to be almost nonexistent. The caliber of individual muskets ranged between 20.4 and 18 mm. Weapons varied as much as 8 cm in length. The windage, the clearance between ball and barrel, was so great that a musketeer who pointed his loaded weapon toward the ground ran some risk of having the ball roll out by itself. Apart from its ballistic deficiencies, the M1782 was so constructed as to make aiming nearly impossible. It was badly balanced. It weighed over ten pounds. The butt was in almost straight line with the stock. Long years of peace made it as much an object for drill and parade as a weapon. Many of the older barrels were ultimately polished so thin that they could no longer take a full powder charge. Certain regiments also made a practice of loosening screws and bands whenever possible in order to achieve a martial rattle while performing the manual of arms—a practice not entirely foreign to more modern armies, but one which did nothing to improve the weapon.[10]

Critics overlooked the fact that the smoothbore flintlock musket was never regarded by its most enthusiastic advocates as a precision weapon suitable for individual feats of marksmanship. Instead it was refined and developed along the lines of the modern submachine gun, or more recently, the assault rifle. Instead of improving its ballistic qualities, gun designers and practical soldiers alike sought to enhance its rate of fire. The *Infanteriegewehr* M1782 was the culmination of a century's effort. Its ramrod was made of iron—more durable than the wooden versions favored elsewhere in Europe until the middle of the 18th century, less likely to swell and stick in a barrel heated by rapid fire. The ramrod was also cylindrical, eliminating the necessity of reversing it in order to ram down a charge. Unlike any other military musket of its era, the M1782 had a cone-shaped touchhole which carried the spark directly to the charge. The great windage also contributed to easier loading.[12]

In its developed form, in short, the Prussian musket was designed not to minimize its limitations of accuracy but to maximize its advantages as a quick-firing weapon. Aiming was not only discouraged, but forbidden. The musketeer was simply ordered to point his weapon in the general direction of the enemy's crossbelts, fire on command, and reload as quickly as possible. And the musket's very imbalance, specifically a muzzle-heaviness caused by the iron ramrod and the heavy bayonet, enhanced the effectiveness of this process by limiting the normal tendency of excited men in combat to shoot too high. Foreign observers at peacetime maneuvers might laugh as whole battalions fired volleys into the ground. Men who faced Prussian musket fire in the field found it much less amusing.

Whatever its form, the musket ultimately remained a single-shot weapon with a complicated loading drill. Specially-selected detachments under carefully-regulated conditions might be able to get off six, even seven rounds a minute. In battle, three was a practical limit.[13] The key to the musket's proper employment, therefore, was to bring as many barrels as close to the target as possible. At Blenheim, for example, Row's Brigade, 2400 muskets strong, had advanced to within thirty paces of the village itself when it was struck by a single volley from 4,000 French muskets. Eight hundred men were killed or wounded—an effectiveness rate of 20%. Four decades later, at Fontenoy, five British battalions, a force just less than 2500 men, inflicted over 600 casualties with one volley at thirty paces. These high figures were from closely controlled fire, at the beginning of an action, and at point-blank range. Later exchanges of fire, affected by smoke, excitement, and casualties, were likely to be substantially less effective. However, the best available evidence suggests that eighteenth century infantry could hit live targets with anywhere from ten to twenty per cent of the shots fired—given a functioning blend of discipline and confidence.[14]

The ultimate challenge for any eighteenth-century army lay in creating and sustaining these closely-related military virtues. The sixteenth-century reforms of Maurice of Nassau had begun a long-term process of raising the demands, human and professional, made on the ordinary soldier. A modern army could be neither "a brute mass, in the Swiss style, nor a collection of bellicose individuals, in the feudal style." And the modern soldier, correspondingly, could be neither a heroic warrior nor a mindless automaton.[15] Contemporary military historians remain significantly, if often subliminally, influenced by attitudes formed in the nineteenth and early twentieth centuries. From the French Revolution to the Second World War and beyond, soldiers and scholars alike have asserted the martial virtues of the citizen in arms. Fighting, like Cromwell's plain russet-coated captain for a cause he knows and loves, or at least accepts, he compensates for any lack of specific skill by enthusiasm and intelligence. Ultimately he is a better military bet than the professional, the man who substitutes technique for commitment.[16]

The shortcomings of this line of argument became apparent as early as World War I. Every man in uniform lacked not moral qualities, but technical skills. War had become so exacting in its demands, so alien to the normal routines of western society that only a miniscule number of men could cope effectively with its demands in the absence of extensive, systematic preparation.[17] This pattern has become even more familiar since 1945, as an increasingly-technical weaponry enhances demands made on the men at the cutting edge.[18] In this context it is useful to establish parallels between the modern tank crewman, gunner, or rifleman and his eighteenth-century ancestors. Both faced the requirement of mastering a broad spectrum of arcane physical skills—not only to satisfy a drill instructor, but as a literal matter of life and death. The complicated loading drill of an eighteenth-century musket can excite amusement even when described by scholars who take it seriously. Yet a major reason for its apparent complexity involved the purpose of simplifying the process, as opposed to making it more complex. Eighteenth-century Prussia was by no means completely disarmed, but familiarity with hunting weapons did not prefigure competent handling of a military musket, particularly under the stresses of battle. The recruit must therefore not merely be taught, but conditioned, to perform by the numbers. Each procedure was distinctly described; each procedure was inculcated by constant repetition, reinforced when necessary—and often on general principles—by the vicious sanctions characteristic of the Prussian military system. The fact, however, was that good will was by itself insufficient, even when it could be presumed to make a musketeer fit to stand in a Prussian firing line any more than it qualifies a modern soldier as a tank or assault helicopter crewman. Observers of the Prussian army in the wars of the French Revolution described with a mixture of pity and contempt men loading and firing mechanically, as their comrades were shot down by French skirmishers, until whole lines were reduced to isolated individuals still pointlessly blasting away into their own powder smoke. To some extent, of course, this was due to fear of the corporal's stick or the file closer's pistol. It also reflected the power of habit. But while the eighteenth-century common soldier might not have been exactly a Benthamite Utilitarian, he was nevertheless capable of developing his own form of felicific calculus. And that capacity, whether based on personal experience or the osmotically-distributed wisdom of older comrades, suggested that the most effective survival mechanism in battle was to stand one's ground and keep firing.

In *The Face of Battle,* John Keegan repeatedly raises the question why men fight when the common sense of self-preservation urges running away.[20] Even in an eighteenth-century context, when vigorous pursuit of a defeated enemy was an exception, flight was often likelier to be a more dangerous reaction than aggression or passivity—simply remaining in place. *Homo sapiens* appears to have no significant biological inhibitions against killing a submitting fellow—on the contrary, he is quite capable of enjoying the process. The ultimate purpose of the tactical offensive is not to kill the enemy in place, a costly task, but to force or frighten him into running, and *then* kill him. This latter was the particular function of eighteenth-century cavalry, one which contributed not a little to the long-standing antagonism between the two branches of service. If casualties for an infantry force that stood its ground could be murderous, the results of breaking in the face of an enemy might well prove annihilating—particularly at the end of a hard-fought day, when individual surrenders of common soldiers were not likely to be as strictly observed as the laws of war demanded. Individual mastery of musket drill, and the offensive approach implied in that mastery, was for over a century a survival mechanism whose utility surpassed the obvious alternative of flight.

Skill at arms was only half the process, and arguably the least half. Bringing as many muskets as possible against an enemy required two things. First, it demanded that the mass formations of the matchlock-and-pike era be extended—that lines be no deeper than necessary to maintain a consistent rate of fire. Second, it demanded that patterns of drill be so adapted that these lines could sustain cohesion while moving about under fire. Any doubts as to the difficulty of this process can be dispelled by viewing the modern cinema's efforts at reproducing an eighteenth-century infantry attack; (the uniformed extras rippling across the fields in *Barry Lyndon* are only one obvious example). And third, the morale of the individual soldier must be strong enough to sustain the demands made on him by the new tactics. In each case recruitment was a major factor. The familiar argument that the mercantilist, absolutist economies of early modern Europe were unwilling or unable to spare productive elements for military service must be balanced by a narrower, more technical point. Eighteenth-century battle drill, with its blend of complexity and flexibility, favoured the professional, and not merely for the obvious reason that he could spend his lifetime paying homage to its complexities. Drill increasingly functioned as a social bond for men whose recruitment had severed most of their peacetime connections. Anthropologists may debate whether common movement of major muscles does in fact rouse echoes of primitive hunting groups. Certainly the process as applied to eighteenth-century armies had its own communities and its own status structures. The private soldier who mastered the apparent arcanae of military bearing and military movements tended to take pride in the accomplishment. If he did not generate the feeling positively, the relative absence of blows and curses improved his sense of wellbeing. His chances for tangible signs of approval from his superiors, even promotion to noncommissioned rank, depended essentially on his ability to perform in the context of his new community. These standards were no less artificial than their counterparts in the civilian world, and arguably much more survival-oriented. The well-being of a military community depended essentially on the skill of each of its members. The clumsy, awkward, or unwilling soldier in an eighteenth century line of battle endangered his comrades perhaps more than himself. A musket held inches out of alignment when firing by ranks could mean a burst eardrum for the man in front of the muzzle blast. A man out of alignment during an advance could be the first link in a chain ending with enemy troopers cutting down an entire battalion. Eighteenth century discipline is generally presented as imposed from above, reflecting

Frederick the Great's aphorism that the common soldier should fear his officers more than the enemy. But it must also be remembered that for the man in the ranks, mastery of the drill book was a battlefield survival mechanism. Any sympathy for the torment suffered by the inexperienced or the incompetent was likely to be significantly diminished by the knowledge that their clumsiness put their fellow-soldiers at risk. Thus the sanctions imposed by superiors were reinforced, directly or indirectly, by the rank and file.[21]

The tactical concepts Frederick the Great initially took to war were at once a response to and an extension of his infantry's professional skills. Like their European counterparts, Prussian tacticians generally favored bringing as many muskets as possible into the firing line by lengthening the frontage of infantry formations. By 1740, a Prussian battalion deployed in four ranks.[22] In that year Frederick introduced the three-rank line to the units invading Silesia; in 1742, this disposition was extended to the rest of the army. The ranks themselves became looser. Until 1748, regulations prescribed that the right arm of each man fit behind the left arm of his next in rank—a position impossible to maintain away from the drill ground and still load a musket. The elbow-to-elbow spacing introduced in that year, though still dense by modern standards, at least facilitated reloading under stress.[23]

These innovations reflected a high level of confidence in both the individual Prussian soldier's training and the Prussian army's discipline. Controlling these attenuated lines, much less moving them forward into enemy fire, could not be done entirely by force and threats. Even during maneuvers it was considered noteworthy when colonels and company officers were able to move a line of twenty or more battalions forward a few thousand paces without losing direction and touch.[24] The possibilities and risks of confusion in battle though most clearly illustrated at Kunersdorf, were manifested in every action Frederick fought. As a result, wise peacetime instructors stressed method over speed. However ponderous Prussian movements might seem initially, experience indicated that they were also precise. No time needed to be lost in repetition, in catching up, in restoring dress or distance sacrificed for time. A Prussian infantry assault was intended to be a battle-winning hammer blow—nothing else. Frederick the Great might ultimately be more traditionalist than innovator. He was also more consistently willing than any of his contemporaries to seek decisions through offensive operations. And in the eighteenth century, this meant that the infantry must sooner or later go forward and do the ultimate dirty work of war: close with the enemy, force him off his ground, and kill him or facilitate his being killed by someone else. The questions to be resolved were how and in what order these related tasks were best accomplished.

Frederick began by insisting on maintaining a steady rate of advance. Once a line of men halted for any reason, experience indicated that it was extremely difficult to start it moving again. This had less to do than is commonly supposed with the absence of patriotism and enthusiasm—neither quality remarkable for making its possessors bullet-proof. Rather, the noise level of a modern battlefield rendered it extremely difficult to pass commands along a line of advance. The problem was exacerbated because the tactical and the administrative organizations of a battalion rarely coincided. Instead of forming for action by companies, a battalion was closed up and divided into eight platoons of essentially equal strength. The platoons in turn were grouped by twos into divisions. The resulting juggling of command assignments meant that soldiers often went into battle led by officers they barely knew and, more to the point, whose voices they were unlikely to recognize. These were not circumstances to be overcome by any amount of punishment.

The infantry's fire tactics further complicated the situation. Prior to 1740, Prussian battalions were intensively trained in "platoon fire." This system, developed by the turn of the century, theoretically enabled infantry formations to maintain continuous fire while maintaining a reserve of loaded weapons. The eight platoons of a battalion delivered volleys in turn in a complicated order that proved far more difficult to sustain in battle than on the drill grounds.[25] In practice it tended to collapse into "rolling fire," every man reloading and pulling trigger as fast as he could on his own hook, with officers unable to halt the process in the general din. The carefully-inculcated small arms drill designed to make the process virtually automatic also significantly inhibited controlling it, once begun. The musketeer was caught up in a mechanical process that gave some purpose to his presence and dulled because of its complexity the desire to run away. Distracting him from it by any means short of striking up his gun muzzle was difficult at best.[26]

When infantry was expected to combine movement and fire, the challenge grew even more complex. The drill regulations prescribed a method for "fire while advancing." Successive platoons took three giant steps forward, fired, and reloaded while the rest of the battalion closed on them "with short and slow steps." Individual musketeers were taught how to reload on the move.[27] Results of both techniques in battle were too often similar to those achieved by the hypothetical individual unable to chew gum and walk simultaneously. A battalion was likely to disrupt itself by its own evolutions long before the enemy's muskets or artillery could do it any significant damage.

This possibility was indicated even as the Prussian infantry saved Frederick's reputation, and perhaps his throne, at Mollwitz. Their platoon volleys shattered the Austrian cavalry just as the drill instructions predicted. When the Austrian infantry moved forward, it too was halted in its tracks, mowed down by the steady Prussian fire. But when the order to advance was given, musketry proved less decisive than the steady advance, almost in slow motion, of the long, blue-coated lines with their bayonets fixed. The Austrian infantry included large numbers of inexperienced men. Its fire discipline and its fire techniques were alike among the worst in Europe. In particular, its volleys on the day of Mollwitz were slow, irregular, and above all too high.[28] As the Prussians closed in, enveloping the deeper Austrian formations, frightened men began breaking ranks, clustering around their colors in masses thirty or forty deep, perfect targets for point-blank volleys. The next step was a general flight, encouraged by platoon volleys that could now be delivered in relative safety, expedited by a few squadrons of Prussian hussars.[28]

A general with more combat experience than Frederick might well have been pardoned for assuming that the bayonet, or more accurately its threat, was the key to victory. The 1740's witnessed a general revival of interest in the potential of infantry shock action. Partly this reflected a new interest in classical military history, in particular an appreciation of the use Macedonia's phalanx had made of the sarissa and Rome's legions of the combination of pilum and gladius. Partly it manifested growing concern for the cost of battles which required firing lines to exchange volleys at point-blank range. The effect resembled pushing two candles into a blowtorch and seeing which melted more quickly. Thousands of essentially-irreplaceable, highly-trained infantry were slaughtered at places like Dettingen and Fontenoy for results that too often proved indecisive.[29]

Given Prussia's combination of essentially limited resources and a geopolitical position impelling her to the offensive, some way out of this tactical dead end seemed imperative. Frederick's decision was rendered easier by his conviction, shared by such distinguished field soldiers as Marshal Saxe, that fire action was significantly overrated. At worst it made noise without doing damage; at best it broke wills before it killed men. The key to victory lay not in overwhelming an enemy where he stood, but in destroying the cohesion of his formations, in convincing each individual in his ranks that his survival was better assured through flight than by fighting. In 1741 Frederick ordered his infantry to keep its bayonets permanently fixed on duty. The revised drill regulations of 1743 proclaimed that no enemy could stand before a charge properly delivered. On the outbreak of the Second Silesian War in 1744, the King asserted that his infantry had to do only two things in battle: form line quickly and precisely, then keep advancing when ordered.

This did not mean that Frederick had fallen victim to the mystique of cold steel that was to obsess so many generals in a later century. He insisted it was "against all human expectation" that an enemy would withstand a determined and steady advance. But if he did, a volley at twenty paces, or better yet ten, should change his mind. Various forms of platoon fire were retained in the drill manual for their value against cavalry or the light troops of the Austrian army, the *Grenzer*. Increasingly, however, doctrine and expedience alike favored full battalion volleys—as many as 600 muskets firing at once, ideally into the whites of an enemy's eyes, followed immediately by a bayonet charge. More generally, each battalion had two or three light cannon or howitzers assigned to it to provide covering fire. And above all, Frederick stressed battlefield mobility. Much of the Prussian army's drill was designed to facilitate moving from columns of march into lines of battle even in the face of an enemy, thereby enabling rapid concentration against the weakest point of a position—and correspondingly facilitating that collapse of morale Frederick expected to result from a Prussian attack.[30]

II

Frederick's acceptance of assault tactics was also facilitated by the composition of his infantry. Until 1733, the Prussian army was recruited from volunteers. An original focus on Prussian territory expanded with the accession of Frederick William I, partly because of the landlords' continued reluctance to sacrifice their labor force, partly because of the king's insistence on tall, well-built soldiers. His original reasoning was not quite as deranged as his critics suggest. Big men could more readily handle and more quickly reload the long-barreled infantry musket. Linking size and fitness was reasonable in an economic environment where malnutrition was common, and a military environment where colonels were often more concerned with the number of warm bodies in the ranks than with the suitability for the field.

Given this pressure to be more selective, recruiting parties tended to develop the nature of press gangs. Open racketeering in the pattern of Shakespeare's Falstaff was common even in the early years of Frederick William I's iron rule. A man would be forcibly held, claimed to have enlisted, and released only on payment of a bribe whose recipients were not always NCO's and senior privates. Confident of their king's support, even less corrupt recruiters embarked on open manhunts across the frontiers of the smaller German states. Hanover came close to declaring war in 1729 over the alleged misbehavior of Prussian agents on her territory. In other states, recruiting for the Prussian service became a capital offense alongside witchcraft and parricide.[31]

Yet the men obtained by these dubious methods were a durable lot. One of the most pervasive and misleading myths of Prussian military history is that the army suffered an average loss of twenty per cent of its manpower annually through desertion or death—the latter, it is strongly implied, usually being a result of ill-treatment. Willerd Fann has traced the source of this high attrition rate to an error made by Max Lehmann, and repeated enough times by enough soldiers to acquire a life of its own—repeated not least because it fit nineteenth- and twentieth-century conceptions of life in the Prussian army as poor, nasty, brutish, and short. Fann goes on to show that the overall desertion rate from 1713 to 1740 was actually a modest 1.9 per cent per year. The death rate was even lower: under 1.4 per cent.[32]

These statistics support the argument that desertion was not necessarily the last resort of desperate men. Indeed, it might well indicate neither a generalized distaste for military life nor a horror of conditions in Prussia. If the duty was demanding, the pay was regular and the uniforms durable. Deserters not infrequently reenlisted in other Prussian regiments for the sake of the relatively high bounties. Others might spend a season or two on the tramp, then find their way back to the colors from hunger or habit under new names. Officers and sergeants were unlikely to be excessively inquisitive if a recruit seemed unusually familiar with the manual of arms. Camp myths even told of martial spirits who enlisted under the colors of other states as a kind of paid vacation, then returned to Prussian service when they felt the need to do real soldiering again. The veteran rebuked by a hometown militia colonel, who answered that *he* had once served the King of Prussia, had more than a few counterparts throughout the lands of Germany.

The Prussian army's obsession with desertion was an essential form of preventive maintenance. Trained, experienced soldiers were commodities scarce enough and valuable enough to be worth taking pains to preserve. An increasingly-familiar system of sanctions—men set to watch each other, saddled horses kept ready for instant pursuit, generous rewards for anyone contributing to a deserter's capture—combined with the growing bureaucratization of Prussian society to limit any propensity to desert from peacetime garrisons. Not only were the risks disproportionately high; the opportunities to disappear even long enough to develop a new martial identity were significantly limited. But positive reinforcements existed as well. During Frederick William's reign the right of furlough was steadily extended, particularly during the harvest season. Soldiers, whether foreign or native, were encouraged to seek employment outside of duty hours—partly to contribute their mites to Prussia's economic development, partly because Frederick William believed that busy hands were happy, or at least contented, hands. Boredom and anomie, both likely to flourish in Prussia's isolated garrison towns, contributed as much to desertion and unrest as did direct ill-treatment.[33] His son too consistently sought to increase the number of foreigners in the Prussian service by making that service more attractive, by increasing bounties, and above all by improving standards of treatment in the line regiments. Thus an order of October 28, 1740, recommended that "physical" means of instruction be used only when appeals to the common soldier's "better nature" proved in vain.[34]

Whatever might have been their images to the king they served, the civilians among whom they lived, or the historians who write about them, Prussia's foreign soldiers did not regard themselves as the dregs of humanity. Instead they saw themselves as cosmopolitans with pasts if not necessarily futures, men who followed the honorable profession of arms by their own choice. Native Prussians in their ranks appeared by comparison as crude and unsophisticated boors.[35] The sword each Prussian infantryman carried was more than a useless piece of ironmongery. It symbolized his status and his honor. Deprived of them, even a regiment full of men impressed from Saxony was capable of breaking an Austrian line of battle almost single-handed at Liegnitz in 1760. The shout of "honor or death" with which they attacked was neither invented nor inspired by their officers.[36]

This did not mean Prussia's foreign infantrymen were fanatical warriors. Their general attitude seems rather to have prefigured that of Britain's Indian army prior to 1947. Volunteers all, in the service of a system which by its nature could engage nothing but their martial loyalties, they would fight for honor, comradeship, and pride of craft within the terms of a contract no less firm for being unwritten and implied. Once the demands of service significantly exceeded the familiar, the expected, Indian soldiers required judicious handling if they were to be used as first-line troops.[37] By no means all of Prussia's mercenaries were misled victims or simple snowbirds, ready to desert, like the Swiss memoirist Ulrich Bräher, at the first smell of powder. But all armies possess a sense of what is acceptable and expected under given circumstances. The familiar and apocryphal tale of a desperate king being informed by an old soldier, "Fritz, we've earned our eight groschen for today," incorporates a fundamental truth. The blindfold slaughterhouses into which Frederick repeatedly led his men amounted for many of them to breach of contract, both legitimating desertion and making it increasingly acceptable as a survival mechanism.[38]

Whatever the shortcomings and advantages of professionals even in times of profound peace, the kings of Prussia could not expect to attract and retain enough of them to provide more than a nucleus of the kind of army that would enable Prussia to maintain and enhance her position in central Europe's power structure. Almost from the beginning of his reign, Frederick William I faced contradictory challenges. His was a poor kingdom, made even poorer by the spending habits of Frederick I—which in turn had enhanced Prussia's vulnerability by suggesting she was richer than was in fact the case. At the same time, Frederick William's essentially non-assertive foreign policy made it highly unlikely that a large regular army would pay for itself by conquest. The most obvious solution involved tapping Prussia's own manpower resources on a long-term, systematic basis—not to make good high death and desertion rates, but to enlarge the number of men under arms.

This process offered still another advantage. Since the days of the Great Elector, rulers of Brandenburg-Prussia had energetically sought to break the independent power of their landed aristocracy—not least by bringing them into state service as army officers. Conscripting peasants from noble estates was a significant means of outflanking the still largely intransigent Junkers, limiting their traditional freedoms by asserting state authority over their traditional subjects—perhaps even encouraging a greater degree of identification with the crown. The ultimate grounds for developing and implementing a conscription system were military rather than social. As finally introduced in 1733, it divided the kingdom into districts based on the number of "hearths". Each regiment was assigned a specific district, which was in turn subdivided into as many "cantons" as the regiment had companies. All able-bodied men between the ages of eighteen and forty were registered and eligible for enrollment. This structure was not merely a method of recruitment. From its inception, it strongly prefigured the Selective Service system practiced in the United States in the 1950's and 60's. Whatever might be the theoretical value of universal service, practical considerations made it impossible. No subsistence agricultural economy could stand to lose its most physically-vigorous elements for several of their most productive years. Nor, more concretely, could the army afford to absorb and properly train every eligible man—and experience everywhere in Europe indicated that half-trained men in an infantry firing line were positively dangerous. A process of random selection seemed as irrational to King Frederick William as it did to General Lewis Hershey and the U.S. Congress. Therefore numerous social and economic groups were exempted—or more properly, occupationally deferred. Nobles and businessmen, landowners, apprentices in a broad spectrum of crafts, textile workers, theology students, first-generation colonists—the list grew with the years, each category having its own rationale. The argument that this left the burdens of military service entirely on small-scale farm laborers, poor peasants, and urban workers is accurate, but misleading if for no other reason than its applications of nineteenth-century standards to an earlier period. In eighteenth-century Prussia, all owed service to the state. Those who had only their bodies provided accordingly. Those who could provide other than physical service were not merely expected but required to do so. The military system of Prussia increasingly expanded to influence the entire life of peasant and townsman alike. Taxes and quarterings, feeding army bases and providing one's own teams for military purposes, compulsory labour on the new network of fortresses built throughout Prussia—all contributed to the process of integrating state and subject.

The "cantonist" himself was scarcely a free agent. His landlord and his company commander, if not necessarily the same individual, might well be brothers or cousins. The landed aristocrat, himself suffering the enhanced financial and personal burdens of state service, was likely to respond by enhancing the demands on his peasants—not least by transferring systems of army discipline and army administration to his estate. Yet at the same time Prussia's peasant conscript was by no means a necessary object of pity. He spent eighteen months to two years with the colors learning his new craft, then was "furloughed"—returned to the civilian life and the civilian economy for nine or ten months each year, then recalled for a brief refresher course. Neither soldier nor peasant, he walked a fine line between his dual existence. Yet at worst the new system made it possible to plan futures as individuals and families were freed from the pressures of haphazard and uncontrolled domestic recruiting. Moreover, between 1727 and the system's abolition in 1801, less than half of the 8,700,000 registrants actually donned uniform—a percentage allowing ample margin for *Bauernschlauheit* in all its variant forms. For the assertive or the fortunate, military service could mean a degree of protection. Furloughed privates successfully appealed to the military authorities, and even the crown itself, against the abuses of local bureaucrats. They obtained permission to marry from their colonels when their landlords were stubborn. The emancipating aspects of military service must not be exaggerated. As the aristocracy became more completely integrated into the military and civil system in the course of the century, a corresponding number of loopholes disappeared. Nevertheless a significant element in that popular militarism so often described as characteristic of the Prussian experience seems, paradoxically, to have been the ability of even common soldiers to challenge the oppressively deferential society in which they lived.[39]

From the regimental perspective, the canton system had significant advantages. It provided a manpower pool deep enough to allow some selectivity. Compared to their mercenary counterparts, the cantonists were big, well-set-up youngsters, able physically to meet the demands of both drill and active service.[40] As a class they were steady and reliable. This may have owed something to a Lutheran faith which in its northeast German version particularly stressed obedience, subordination, and performance of assigned duties.[41] The army's piety, however, probably should not be exaggerated. If Prussian troops sang hymns on the march, this reflected not so much religious enthusiasm as the familiarity of the songs. Similarly, the British armies of World War I used hymns as the basis for many of their parodies less from a sense of class-conscious blasphemy than because these were the tunes everyone knew. More useful in securing the cantonist's compliance was the fact that he was commanded in battle, essentially and often literally, by the same men who ordered his civilian destiny. This gave him every practical reason to manifest a positive attitude—particularly since a shirker or a deserter left more hostages to fortune than did an alien.[42]

Positive factors, however, were also involved. While national identification lay far in Prussia's and Germany's future, the cantonal structure did generate significant parish and regional solidarity in the companies and regiments. The presence of cantonists in the ranks also appealed to a sense of feudal obligation far from dead in the officer corps. It was far easier to identify with the welfare of men whose fathers and grandfathers had served yours than with the rootless cosmopolitans brought in at random by the recruiting parties. Intellectually, an increasing number of Prussian officers were influenced by Enlightenment concepts of the dignity and rationality of all men. On a more practical level, even the rawest and most arrogant of subalterns was unlikely to rejoice at the prospect of marching into battle in front of a hundred loaded muskets borne by men who hated him.[43]

None of this meant that the Prussian army of Frederick the Great was evolving into a *Wehrgemeinschaft* held together by moral force.[44] Yet its mix of cantonists and mercenaries, a mix that hardened into a solid, professional blend in the course of the Silesian wars, did encourage the development of an alternative to the by-now traditional fire tactics. To advance without returning an enemy's volleys, to sustain casualties without returning them in the confidence that one's own skill, and the skill of one's battalion, would either intimidate the enemy or destroy him—these were tasks not likely to be performed effectively either by terrified automata or zealous amateurs.

## III

Tested in battle, Frederick's concepts seemed to work brilliantly. They reached their apogee during the Second Silesian War. At Hohenfriedberg in 1745, three grenadier battalions and two battalions of the Anhalt-Dessau Regiment advanced against the Saxons without firing a shot, drums beating and bands playing. At 30 paces the Saxons' nerve broke, and subsequent claims that the defenders were blinded by powder smoke or sunlight failed to obscure the fact that the Prussians wound up in possession of the ground. Later in that same year, at Kesselsdorf, six Prussian battalions carried a Saxon battery in the teeth of canister fire that dropped over half the attackers. On another part of the field, Prince Moritz of Anhalt-Dessau saw his wing of the army halt in its tracks and open fire as soon as they saw their targets. He promptly ordered and led a charge which led the Prussians into the middle of the Saxon positions. Ten days later the war was over and Prussia's possession of Silesia was confirmed.

Christopher Duffy exaggerates in asserting that "after Kesselsdorf . . . the belief took root that no power could withstand a body of Prussian infantry advancing with shouldered muskets."[45] That particular myth probably owed more to the German General Staff's official history of the wars of Frederick the Great. This multi-volume work, as present-minded as it is comprehensive, tends generally to describe attacks in terms of the late nineteenth-century ideal of relentless closing with an enemy until he was destroyed at bayonet point. In fact, such performances were relatively few. The Saxon army, victim of the most remarkable assaults, was hardly considered a first-rate force by either its allies or its enemies. Even at Hohenfriedberg its beaten battalions had not run away, but instead fell back into a woods, reformed behind a deep ditch, and continued to inflict casualties until outflanked and forced to retreat. If before the Seven Years' War, Prussian infantry training continued to stress advancing at the expense of firing, this reflected the King's confidence in his ability so to manage all three arms in battle that his foot soldiers could normally count on striking an enemy in overwhelming force at his most vulnerable point. In this context it was important above all that the momentum of an advance be sustained, that no battalion stop to fire without orders—which, Frederick expected, would never be necessary to issue.[46]

The doctrine made sense as a rational construction. It ignored, however, the enemy. Frederick's first contacts with the revitalized army of Maria Theresa might well have inspired him to anticipate Napoleon in affirming that "these animals have learned something." Intensive training had improved their infantry's fire discipline. Bitter experience had shown the risks of breaking in the presence of a Prussian cavalry that was by now the most formidable shock instrument in Europe. And while Frederick had concentrated on his infantry, the Austrians had significantly improved their artillery, creating in particular an efficient force of heavy guns and using them effectively to support their infantry's firing lines.[47]

The results of these improvements were quickly and painfully apparent. In front of Prague, fourteen Prussian battalions, muskets at the shoulder, got to within 200 paces of the Austrian position before being stopped by cannon and musket fire, then driven back in rout by a sharp counterattack. Two months later, at Kolin, nine Prussian battalions overran two battery positions in heroic style before being checked by Austrian fire, then overridden by a cavalry charge. Over 14,000 Prussians fell at Prague, over 13,000 more at Kolin—and if Frederick could count both battles as victories, he was nevertheless haunted by images of Pyrrhus.[48] Casualties were hard to replace in any eighteenth-century army, but Prussia's mixture of recruiting practices and tactical doctrine gave her a specific problem.

The logic of eighteenth-century linear warfare demanded an infantry essentially uniform in quality, each battalion not significantly better or worse than the next because all performed an essentially identical task. This in turn reflected the normal composition of infantry formations everywhere in Europe—recruited haphazardly, with regional or provincial identities tending to be nominal.[49] The practice of drawing up lines of battle on the basis of regiments' or colonels' seniorities was more than a concession to aristocratic pride. It reflected the interchangeability of the building blocks. In Prussia, however, the growth of regional and provincial identities referred to earlier had created a corresponding pecking order. At its head were the grenadiers, the company of picked men from each battalion, who were organized in homogeneous independent battalions in wartime. Within the line infantry itself, sharp differences also existed. Frederick and most of his generals regarded men from Pomerania and the Mark of Brandenburg as superior to those from East Prussia or Westphalia. After the occupation of Silesia, the King created what amounted to a new category of line infantry, the fusiliers, recruited primarily in areas where the population was considered less reliable, less fit, or less warlike than that of the old provinces.[50]

There are two ways of using elites. One is as first-line shock troops, a spearhead in the pattern of the Wehrmacht's Panzer divisions. The other is as an insurance policy, like Napoleon's Guard: to complete a victory or avert a disaster prepared by lesser troops. Frederick, with his concern for decision, placed his best men in the first waves. Thus the losses of Prague and Kolin were sustained by the grenadiers and the crack provincial regiments—the army's core, whose erosion inevitably affected the morale of the rest. But a great part of Frederick's genius lay in his adaptability. Early in the war he began considering the possibility of drawing an enemy's teeth with expendable troops—the hostilities-only free battalions raised from and commanded by anyone available.[51] Adjustment to reality was also facilitated by the fact that the Prussian infantry had never abandoned fire tactics and fire training. It was merely a question of adjusting battlefield practice to bring traditional skills once more to the fore.

Leuthen is generally considered the greatest of Frederick's victories, the ultimate triumph of the oblique order. It was also a triumph for the Prussian musketeers. For the first time in Frederick's reign they took their ammunition wagons into battle with them. In the course of the day some men fired three times the regulation allowance of 60 cartridges. When the 26th Meyerinck Regiment, hard pressed, was ordered into reserve, a shout went up from the ranks that all they needed was more ammunition. Pouches refilled, the mixture of cantonists from Pomerania and mercenaries from everywhere continued in the first line, winning its officers no fewer than fifteen awards of the *Pour le merite.*[52]

In victory or defeat, Frederick never again neglected infantry fire power. The grenadiers who opened the battle of Torgau advanced "with the for the royal Prussian troops usual unceasing musket fire."[53] Not the least shock of Zorndorf was the Russians' seeming imperviousness to battalion volleys delivered at point-blank range. Kunersdorf degenerated into a disaster when Frederick's infantry began running out of ammunition. His musketeers were increasingly supplemented not only by battalion guns but by batteries of heavy 12-pounders, the famous *Brummer*. But the Seven Years' War left the King convinced that victory belonged to the infantry able to fire faster than its opponents over a longer time.[54] Where he had once spoken of one or two volleys deciding the issue, his battalions were now expected to deliver as many as half a dozen in succession, and only then push forward over any remaining opposition. Ideally they were moving batteries, able to maneuver as swiftly and efficiently as the oblique order demanded, yet equally able to deliver two thousand rounds a minute on command.

In this context the complex geometric evolutions perfected in Prussia between the Peace of Hubertusberg and the French Revolution were less absurd than their critics suggested. All were designed ultimately to facilitate quick deployment into battle formation and disciplined execution of small arms drill under the worst circumstances. The infantryman and his musket were intended to become, in modern parlance, a weapons system. In that context the question of whether his ideal march pace was 75 or 76 steps to the minute was no more ridiculous than the efforts of contemporary research and development agencies to determine whether the optimal crew of a tank should be two, three, or four.[55] Similarly, the increasingly-fanatical rigor of postwar Prussian discipline reflected Frederick's response to the steep and irreversible decline in the quality of his infantry after the initial battles of the Seven Years' War. The cantons, under increasing pressure, continued to deliver recruits with the potential to become excellent soldiers. But long-service professionals and trained cantonists could not be replaced by impressed deserters and hastily-conscripted peasants. Engaging their enthusiasm, appealing to their patriotism, did not simply deny basic postulates of the absolutist system. These were unimportant exercises relative to the essence of the problem. Technique, not emotion, was the ultimate criterion in forming a modern infantryman. The King's relative neglect of light troops similarly reflected an enduring conviction that they were military pawns: minor pieces, to be checked and taken by their equivalents, but nothing more.[56]

The Prussian army's relative decline under Frederick William

II was in many aspects arrested during the wars of the French Revolution.[57] It might well be accused of learning its lessons too well. Thus the collapse of army and government alike in the aftermath of Jena and Auerstädt represented in good part a logical, almost a natural reaction to the Frederician concept of a decisive battle waged by the state's cutting edge: its armed forces. Yet at the same time it represents no concession to a later century's patrioteers to agree that Prussia faced in 1806 a French army at the peak of its efficiency, commanded by one of history's greatest captains at the height of his powers. Defeat at such hands, while it pitilessly exposes weaknesses, is by no means *prima facie* evidence of irreversible dry rot. The Prussian army had concentrated excessively on a single aspect of battle: developing maximum firepower from an infantry line. This did not mean that Frederick, his generals, and their successors necessarily erred in principle. Even during the Napoleonic Wars, the French combination of skirmishers and columns demonstrated significant limitations in the face of disciplined firing lines properly screened by their own light troops. Specifically, Wellington's infantry in the Peninsula won its greatest victories by combining fire and movement, in Prussian fashion, completing the effect of their musketry by attacks the French rarely awaited much less withstood.[58]

A developing weapons technology would soon render exposed mass formations of any kind, line, or column obsolete. Eighteenth-century Prussia's enduring military legacy was its emphasis on professionalism, as opposed to enthusiasm, as the key to victory in an era of war by machine. Liberalism, nationalism, and Marxism have combined to develop a powerful set of myths regarding motivation in battle. The experience of the previous century suggests in fact that rather than being a portent for the future, the era of the military amateur which began with the French Revolution was in fact a temporary anomaly. It was ended by an increasingly-sophisticated technology which in turn generated a spectrum of physical and emotional demands too great to be met by citizens in uniform, no matter how enthusiastic. An army's fighting power in an industrial age rests less on abstract principles than on skill at arms produced by training and discipline, skill in turn fostering confidence and small-group cohesion. Above all it depends on toughness, a willingness to fight and if necessary to die.[59] The ability of the Frederician system to inculcate and sustain these qualities deserves careful, systematic investigation—particularly by societies increasingly uncomfortable with the concept of public interest imposing general civic obligations.

FOOTNOTES

1. Günter Wollstein, "Preussen-Literatur zur Geschichte des 'aufgehobenen' Staates im 'Preussenjahr' und in dessen Umfeld," *Militärgeschichtliche Mitteilungen* XXXIII (1983), 91-116, is an excellent critical analysis of recent German scholarship on the "Prussian problem" in general.
2. Cf. Curt Jany, *Geschichte der Preussischen Armee vom 15. Jahrhundert bis 1914*, rev. ed., Vols. I-III (Osnabrück, 1967); and Christopher Duffy, *The Army of Frederick the Great* (Newton Abbott, 1974).
3. Blechwenn's multi-volume series, *Das altpreussische Heer,* Vols. I- (Osnabrück, 1971- ) is summarized in his beautifully-illustrated *Unter dem Preussen-Adler* (Munich, 1978). *Biblio-Verlag's Altpreussischer Kommiss, offiziell, offizös und privat,* 42 vols. (Osnabrück, 1971-1978), is an even richer fund of reprinted sources on the eighteenth-century army.
4. As in, among recent general works, Geoffrey Best, *War and Society in Revolutionary Europe, 1770-1870* (New York 1982), pp. 150 ff.; John Gooch, *Armies in Europe* (London, 1980), pp. 16 ff.; and Martin Kitchen, *A Military History of Germany* (Bloomington, Ind., 1975), pp. 27 ff.
5. G. Lee Kennett, "Tactics and Culture: The Eighteenth-Century Experience," Commission Internationale d'Histoire Militaire, *Acta,* V (Bucarest, 1981), 152-159; and more generally, W.O. Shanahan, "Enlightenment and War: Austro-Prussian Military Practice, 1760-1790," *War and Society in Central Europe,* Vol. II, *East-Central European Society and War in the Pre-Revolutionary Era,* eds. G. Rothenberg, B. Kiraly, P. Sugar (New York, 1983), pp. 83-111.
6. These points are briefly and brilliantly established in Paul Schroeder, *Austria, Great Britain and the Crimean War* (Cornell, 1971), pp. 402-403. Cf. also Derek McKay and H.M. Scott, *The Rise of the Great Powers, 1648-1815* (London and New York, 1983), pp. 20 *passim.*
7. Gerhard Ritter, *Frederick the Great: A Historical Profile,* tr. with intro. by P. Paret (Berkeley and Los Angeles, 1968), pp. 95 ff., makes the strongest modern case for Frederick's positive acceptance of this possition. I. Mittenzwei's DDR biography, *Friedrich II von Preussen* (Berlin, 1979), is a good recent example of the argument that it was forced on him by bitter experience.
8. David Chandler, *Marlborough as Military Commander,* 2nd ed. (London, 1979), pp. 63, 324 ff.
9. See particularly Michael Roberts, "Gustav Adolf and the Art of War," *Essays in Swedish History* (London, 1967), pp. 56-70.
10. Carl von Clausewitz, *Nachrichten über Preussen in seiner grossen Katastrophe,* Kriegsgeschichtliche Einzelschriften, ed. Grosser Generalstab, vol. 10 (Berlin, 1888), p. 426; G.H. Peitz and Hans Delbrück, *Das Leben des Generalfeldmarschalls Grafen Neithardt von Gneisenau,* Vol. I (Berlin, 1864), pp. 525 ff.; and F. Meinecke, ed., "Aus den Akten der Militärreorganisationskommission von 1808," *Forschungen zur brandenburgischen und preussischen Geschichte,* V (1892), 139.
11. W. Eckardt and O. Morawietz, *Die Handwaffen des branden-burgisch-preussisch-deutschen Heeres, 1640-1945* (Hamburg, 1957), pp. 43 ff.
12. Curt Jany, *Die Gefechtsausbildung der preussischen Infanterie von 1806, Urkundliche Beiträge und Forschungen zur Geschichte des preussischen Heeres,* ed. Grosser Generalstab, Vol. V (Berlin, 1903), pp. 33 ff.; Eckhardt and Morawietz, 38 ff.; Peter Paret, *Yorck and the Era of Prussian Reform* (Princeton, 1966), pp. 14-15.
13. Hans Delbrück, *Geschichte der Kriegskunst im Rahmen der politischen*

*Geschiche*, Vol. IV, *Neuzeit* (Berlin, 1920), 329 ff. incorporates the best discussion of rates of fire. Physical exhaustion was a major limiting factor; experienced officers frequently complained that their men were fit for nothing after delivering artificially-rapid bursts. Jany, III, 86.

14. These calculations are from B.P. Hughes, *Firepower. Weapons Effectiveness on the Battlefield, 1630-1850* (New York, 1974), pp. 81-83.
15. Cf. Michael Roberts, "The Military Revolution, 1556-1660," *Essays in Swedish History*, 195-225; and the critique by Geoffrey Parker, "The Military Revolution, 1550-1660—A Myth?" *Journal of Modern History* XLVII (1976), 195-214. The quotation is from Roberts, 198.
16. The aftermath of Vietnam has generated salutary and systematic questioning of this dogma in U.S. military circles. See particularly the essays in Sam C. Sarkesian, ed., *Combat Effectiveness: Cohesion, Stress and the Volunteer Military* (Beverly Hills, Cal., 1980).
17. A point especially well established in Shelford Bidwell and Dominick Graham, *Fire-Power: British Army Weapons and Theories of War, 1904-1945* (London, 1982), pp. 116 ff.
18. See in particular Richard Simpkin, *Human Factors in Mechanized Warfare* (Elmsford, NY, 1983).
19. Most spectacularly in the destruction of Grawert's division by French skirmishers at Jena in 1806. Cf. Ross, 98, and David G. Chandler *The Campaigns of Napoleon* (New York, 1966), p. 484.
20. John Keegan, *The Face of Battle* (London, 1976), *passim.*
21. William H. McNeill, *The Pursuit of Power: Technology, Armed Force and Society since A.D. 1000* (Chicago, 1982), pp. 130 ff., stresses the psychological, as opposed to the pragmatic, aspects of the drill process.
22. A Prussian battalion at full strength consisted of five musketeer and one grenadier companies, each 114 rank and file. The grenadier company, however, was almost inevitably detached for separate service.
23. Cf. Duffy's summary, 82-83, with the more detailed account in Jany I, 813 ff.
24. See G.H. Berenhorst's sarcastic description in *Betrachtungen über die Kriegskunst*, 3 vols. (Leipzig, 1798-1799), I, 424-425.
25. David G. Chandler, "Variations in Infantry Tactical Method in English and Other Armies, and their Influence on the Level of Battlefield Success, 1688-1713," Commission Internationale d'Histoire Militaire, *Acta*, II (1975), 45-51; describes the evolution of platoon fire in detail; Jany, I, 820 presents its Prussian version.
26. Berenhorst, I, 255; Hyppolite J.R. de Toulongeon, *Une Mission militaire en Prusse en 1786*, ed. J. Finot, R. Golmiche-Bouvier (Paris, 1881), 197.
27. Jany, *Preussische Armee*, 820-821.
28. See the treatment in Christopher Duffy, *The Army of Maria Theresa* (New York, 1977), pp. 78-79; and the Austrian commander's narrative in K. Duncker, "Militärische und politische Actenstücke zur Geschichte des ersten Schlesischen Krieges," *Mittheilungen des K.K. Kriegs-Archivs* (Vienna, 1887), p. 205.
29. Hew Strachan, *European Armies and the Conduct of War* (London, 1983), 23 ff., is a good, recent survey from a French perspective. Steven Ross, *From Flintlock to Rifle. Infantry Tactics, 1740-1866* (Cranbury, NJ, 1979) pp. 33 ff., is technically-oriented. Cf. for more detail Jean Colin, *L'infanterie au XVIIIe siècle: la tactique* (Paris, 1907) and Robert Quimby, *The Background of Napoleonic Warfare* (New York, 1957).
30. See his "Disposition für die Sammtlichen Regimenter Infanterie, wie solche sich bei dem vorfallenden Marsche gegen den Feind . . . zu verhalten haben,"

*Oeuvres,* 30 vol. (Berlin, 1846-1857), XXX, 74-77.

31. John Childs, *Armies and Warfare in Europe, 1648-1789* (New York, 1982), pp. 52 ff., summarises Prussian recruiting practices. Kurt Schützle, "Über das Rekrutierungssystem in Preussen vor und nach 1806/07 und seine Auswirkung auf die geistig moralische Haltung der Soldaten," *Die Preussische Werbung unter Friedrich Wilhelm I und Friedrich dem Grossen bis zum Beginne des Siebenjährigen Krieges mit besonderer Berücksichtigung Mecklenburg-Schwerins* (Schwerin, 1887), remains useful.
32. Willerd Fann, "Peacetime Attrition in the Army of Frederick William I, 1713-1740," *Central European History* XI (1978), 323-334.
33. Duffy, 57 ff., is a good modern summary emphasizing the negative aspects of Prussian service. Jany, *Preussische Armee* I, 700 ff., strikes a more positive note. For purposes of comparison cf. J.A. Houlding, *Fit for Service: The Training of the British Army, 1715-1795* (Oxford, 1981); and Rodney Atwood, *The Hessian Mercenaries from Hessen-Kassel in the American Revolution* (New York, 1980). Without attempting to whitewash Frederician discipline, two points are worth noting. Hans Bleckwenn (*Preussen-Adler,* 72) is only the latest of the old army's defenders to point out that a relatively small number of hard cases received a disproportionate number of the most draconic punishments, and that such men gave foreigners, indeed soldiers in general, a bad name. Moreover, the vivid accounts of the system's horrors were likely to be composed by critics: officers like the author of "Versuch von der Kriegeszucht," *Kriegsbibliothek* I (1755), who favored a discipline based on honor and mutual respect, or soldiers distinguished from the common run by their literacy, who perceived themselves as having been enlisted by guile or force. That they hated the Prussian army is understandable, but deserters and malcontents are seldom a reliable guide to the internal dynamics of any armed force. Such works as Ulrich Bräher's *Der arme Mann im Tockenburg* (Zürich, 1789; reprint ed. Munich, 1965), often cited for the army's routine on the eve of the Seven Years' War, are best taken at a certain critical distance. Willerd Fann, "On the Infantryman's Age in Eighteenth Century Prussia," *Military Affairs* XLI (1977), 165-170, stresses the rootedness foreigners and old soldiers generally had in their regiments.
34. Cited in Jany, *Preussische Armee,* II, 10.
35. F.C. Laukhard, *Magister F. Ch. Laukhards Leben und Schicksale von ihm selbst beschrieben* 13th ed., 2 vols. (Stuttgart, 1930), I, 248-249.
36. The incident is described without glosses in *Army of Frederick the Great,* 143.
37. Jeffrey Greenhut, "The Imperial Reserve: The Indian Infantry on the Western Front, 1914-15," Ph.D. Dissertation, Kansas State University 1978, is a good case study of the problem of implied contracts in the Indian Army. His "Sahib and Sepoy: An Inquiry into the Relationship between the British Officers and Native Soldiers of the British Indian Army," *Military Affairs,* XLVIII (1984), 15-18, stresses anthropological at the expense of practical factors in the Indian soldier's attitude. More general studies include T.A. Heathcote, *The Indian Army: The Garrison of British Imperial India, 1822-1922* (New York, 1974), pp. 104-105; and Stephen P. Cohen, *The Indian Army. Its Contribution to the Development of a Nation* (Berkeley, 1971), pp. 35 ff.
38. The problem of preventing desertion in the field increasingly pervades, if not dominates, Frederick's military writings. See in particular Jay Luvaas, ed., *Frederick the Great on the Art of War* (New York, 1966), pp. 114, 121-122.
39. The most comprehensive treatment of the cantonal system and its consequences remains Otto Büsch, *Militärsystem und Sozialleben im alten*

*Preussen*, rev. ed. (Frankfurt, 1981). Cf. also Klaus Schweiger, "Militär und Bürgertum. Zur gesellschaftlichen Prägkraft des preussischen Militärsystems in 18. Jahrhundert," *Preussen in der deutschen Geschichte*, ed. D. Blasius (Königstein, 1980), pp. 179-199; and Manfred Messerschmidt, "Preussens Militär in seinem gesellschaftlichen Umfeld," *Preussen im Rückblick*, ed. H.J. Puhle, H-U Wehler, *Geschichte und Gesellschaft, Sondernummer* VI (1983), 46-53.

40. Toulongeon, 170.
41. A point particularly stressed by Ritter, 133.
42. Büsch in particular emphasizes the growing strength and comprehensiveness of this connection.
43. See in particular Werner Gembruch, "Menschenführung im preussischen Heer von Friedrich dem Grossen bis 1806," *Menschenführung im Heer*, Vol. III of *Vorträge zur Militärgeschichte, ed. MCFA (Herford, 1982), pp. 41-61; and F.K. Thurau, Die geistige Kultur des preussischen Offiziers* (Mainz, 1968).
44. As asserted in Reinhard Höhn, *Der Soldat und das Vaterland während und nach dem Siebenjährigen Krieg* (Weimar, 1940).
45. Duffy, *Army of Frederick the Great*, 164.
46. For the development of Frederick's tactical thinking, see *Die taktische Schülung der preussischen Armee durch König Friedrich den Grossen während der Friedenszeit 1745 bis 1756*, Kriegsgeschichtliche Einzelschriften, ed. Grosser Generalstab, vols. 28-30 (Berlin, 1900), esp. pp. 440 ff. This work suffers from the present-mindedness common to its genre, tending in particular to exaggerate the King's distrust of fire action.
47. Duffy, *Army of Maria Theresa*, 76 ff.; 105 ff.
48. A particularly scathing indictment of Frederick's new tactics by an officer of Hussars is Warnerey, *Campagnes de Frederic II, Roi de Prusse, de 1756 a 1762* (Amsterdam, 1788), p. 113. General Hans Karl von Winterfeldt, one of Frederick's most trusted officers, bluntly informed the monarch in the aftermath of Prague and Kolin that "with shouldered muskets and without firing we aren't going to make it *(kommen wir nicht durch)*." A. Janson, *Hans Karl von Winterfeldt, des Grossen Königs Generalstabschef* (Berlin, 1913), p. 372.
49. The most comprehensive analysis of this pattern is Andre Corvisier, *L'Armée française de la fin du XVII*[e] *siècle au ministère de Choiseul*, Vol. I, *Le Soldat* (Paris, 1964), esp. pp. 410 *passim*.
50. Duffy, *Army of Frederick the Great*, 72; Jany, *Preussische Armee*, II, 5-6.
51. Olaf Groehler, *Die Kriege Friedrichs II* (Berlin, 1966), 156. Cf. Major von Schnackenburg, "Die Freikorps Friedrich des Grossen," *Militar-Wochenblatt*, 1883, *Beiheft* VI.
52. The incident is summarized in Jany, *Preussische Armee*, II, 456.
53. From the report of the Swedish military plenipotentiary with the Austrians, in *ibid.*, 587.
54. "Das Militärische Testament von 1768 in: *Militärische Schriften Friedrichs des Grossen*, ed. A.V. Taysen (Dresden, 1893), p. 205.
55. A good technical account of this process is Max Jähns, *Geschichte der Kriegskunst vornehmlich in Deutschland*, Vol. III, *Das XVIII. Jahrhundert seit dem Auftreten Friedrichs des Grossen, 1740-1800* (Munich and Leipzig, 1891), pp. 2523 ff.
56. Paret, *Yorck*, is the best critical analysis of this issue.
57. John E. Stine, "King Frederick William II and the Decline of the Prussian Army, 1786-1797," Ph.D. Dissertation, University of South Carolina, 1980.
58. A point recently established in Paddy Griffith, *Forward into Battle: Fighting*

*Tactics from Waterloo to Vietnam* (New York, 1981), pp. 13 ff.

59. Martin von Creveld, *Fighting Power: German and U.S. Army Performance 1939-1945* (Westport, CT, 1982), *passim*, is an important comparative analysis; Max Hastings, *Overlord. D-Day and the Battle for Normandy* (New York, 1984), offers a perceptive case study.

# [17]

# THE RELATIONSHIP BETWEEN THE REVOLUTIONARY WAR AND EUROPEAN MILITARY THOUGHT AND PRACTICE IN THE SECOND HALF OF THE EIGHTEENTH CENTURY

Peter Paret

What I should like to do in this paper is to compare the war in America with other conflicts of the period, to consider these wars as discrete military episodes—separate entities that combine into a broad stream of military experience—and to ask what these wars attempted to do, how they went about doing it, and how we might characterize the relationship between effort and achievement in each. By comparing the Revolutionary War with other conflicts, we not only fit it more accurately into the overall picture of eighteenth-century warfare, but we may also come to understand some of its unique phenomena more clearly than we would if we were to immerse ourselves in its particulars to the exclusion of what soldiers and governments were doing elsewhere.

Let me begin with two statements that in one form or another pervade the literature: First, in essential respects the Revolutionary War differed from other wars of the period; and, second, the elements that differentiated it from other conflicts were of seminal significance—that is, the Revolutionary War, at least as it was fought on the American side, pointed toward the future. Don Higginbotham, in his book *The War of American Independence,* expressed the idea in this way: "The American

Revolution did more than prove the validity of Enlightenment ideals; it ushered in yet another revolution—in the aims and nature of warfare.''[1] It should be added that the passage in which this statement occurs contrasts wars waged by mercenaries for aims to which they are indifferent—dynastic or state policy—with wars fought by patriots, defending, in Washington's words, ''all that is dear and valuable in life.'' Another scholar, the English historian Piers Mackesy, in his book *The War for America* states that ''the struggle that opened at Lexington was the last great war of the *ancien régime.*''[2] That sounds like a contradiction of Higginbotham's statements; but it need not be one. Mackesy may be saying that Great Britain fought the war in a traditional manner, or perhaps he uses the term *ancien régime* not to characterize behavior but to define a period of time—as a synonym for the eighteenth century before the French Revolution. He continues with a statement that certainly seems to be in complete accord with Higginbotham's view: ''In the American War there first appeared the fearful spectacle of a nation in arms.'' But the second part of his sentence immediately qualifies and restricts this assertion: ''In the American War there first appeared the fearful spectacle of a nation in arms; and the *odium theologicum*'' (which, for our purposes, we might translate as the ''bane of ideology'') ''which had been banished from warfare for a century returned to distress the nations.'' I don't mean to go on with textual analyses of recent scholarship; I have cited these passages from two admirable works simply to illustrate the difficulty historians face in bringing out the particularity of a specific event while giving an accurate account of its larger context. And furthermore, the second half of Mackesy's sentence points to a not unimportant analytic failing that is frequently encountered in the literature on the American Revolution. Mackesy rightly observes that the bane of ideology, which had been banished for a century, returned. That is, ideologically motivated war, in which many of the participants even at the lowest levels are emotionally involved—rather than detached impassive professionals—was not introduced at Lexington, but *re*introduced.

That suggests that the Revolutionary War should be compared to the European military experience of the seventeenth, rather than of the eighteenth, century: to the Dutch struggle for independence; to certain phases of the Thirty Years' War; to the English Civil War. It might be useful to resist the tendency of bracketing the Revolutionary War with the conflicts of the mid-eighteenth century, a time when Europe had temporarily shed the *odium theologicum,* when many states had achieved relative political stability, and when the European community had devised a nonideological balance-of-power system as the basis for its international relations. Political development proceeded at different rates of speed on the two sides of the Atlantic; and rather than contrast the military behavior of an emerging nation with those of developed states, it might be more appropriate to compare the Revolutionary War with some seventeenth-century episodes and then perhaps compare the Mexican War, which was hardly waged "for everything that is dear and valuable in life," with the War of the Austrian Succession or with some other eighteenth-century attempt at territorial aggrandizement. I am not suggesting that we disregard differences in time in favor of constructing historically disembodied models of civil and military behavior. The passage of time and the uniqueness of the specific event must always be the first determinants of historical analysis; but I do want to raise the question whether comparisons should be based solely on proximity in time or whether stages of social, ideological, and political development should not be taken into account as well.

Let me return once more, briefly, to the statements quoted above in order to trace one or two of their implications further. It is, of course, true that European armies in the eighteenth century were essentially mercenary and professional in character—at least so far as the rank and file are concerned. But many—including the Prussian, Austrian, and Russian armies—were in fact made up of a mix of mercenaries, who might be foreign or native volunteers, and of native conscripts.[3] Certainly the Prussian conscript or the Austrian Grenzer was not a free citizen who fought for a policy that he understood or in some manner identified with: he was a peasant, more likely than not illiterate, who was forcibly enrolled. But there can be no question that he was not only motivated by compulsion and, after a period of service, by *esprit de corps* but also by loyalty to his local environment—the patriarchal conditions of his existence—and by a regional patriotism. Soldiers may not yet have been conscious of fighting for a nation—Frederick the Great's grenadiers thought of themselves as Pomeranians, Silesians, men of the Mark Brandenburg, rather than as Prussians; their peers across the Rhine may already have dimly sensed that beyond their native Normandy or Poitou there was a more comprehensive abstraction called France—but everywhere in Europe the idea of nation was announcing itself, and here and there it was already cracking the shell of the absolute monarchy and of corporate society. Governments and commanders employed the concept of nation to justify their actions, appealed to their men in its name, and in turn were influenced by it. The military institutions of eighteenth-century Europe contained within their native cadres the seed of the future nation in arms.

But just as we cannot regard the armies of the *ancien régime* simply as institutions of uninvolved mercenaries, so we should not assume that the military future belongs wholly to the nation in arms. Once more we must ask what time frame should contain our analysis. Fifty years ago it was easier than it is today to view modern history as a process toward the nation-state and the nation in arms. Now, with separatist movements at work in such ancient political entities as Great Britain and Spain and with the emergence of new multinational empires, we can no longer be quite so certain. And even in the early stages of the process that may now have passed its peak, the trend was far from uniform. In the wars of the French Revolution and of the Napoleonic Age we can, on the one hand, point to what might be called the "sentiment of military nationalism" in the French armies and at least to the force of military patriotism—if not yet nationalism—in the reformed Prussian army and the modernized Austrian army, though to a lesser extent. But such developments scarcely affected the rank and file of the British and Russian armies, which do not differ radically from their eighteenth-century predecessors. The English and German professionals who were defeated in America decisively beat the Grande Armée and the *Grande Nation* in Spain and at Waterloo three decades later. The European military future was mixed; and so, of course, was that of the United States.

I have made these comments, which go over familiar ground, merely to suggest the kind of evidence that ought to be considered when we try to fit the Revolutionary War into its historical environment—that is, place it among the wars that immediately precede and follow it. When we come to analyze the war in America as one conflict among several, we will find it useful to divide our inquiry into two parts: first we must take a closer look at the hypothesis of the war's seminal nature, which on the one hand refers to motivation and organization. Having sorted out the matter of influence, we should then consider some other elements in the war—

number of men involved, size of the theater of operations, the relationship between effort and goal—and compare these with analogous factors in the three major wars that were waged in Europe between 1756 and the 1790s.

To begin with: motivation. The politico-military characteristics of the Revolutionary War find no parallel in eighteenth-century Europe. Part civil war, part struggle against an external opponent, the conflict was waged by a political authority organized as an assembly representing states that possessed by themselves a measure of sovereignty. Its army was composed of state militias and of a central force, the Continental army, originally made up of volunteers enlisting for varying periods of time but soon enrolling some men through a compulsory quota system, which, however, accommodated a range of exemptions. Except for the ill-conceived Canadian expedition, the policy of the Revolutionaries was one of enduring, of maintaining an independent political authority and an armed force in being, regardless of territorial losses. In this they succeeded magnificently; but it is equally impressive that in the course of the war they consolidated the political resources of their society and created a new system of government.

Nothing similar can be found in Europe in the hundred years preceding Lexington: "A revolutionary struggle which involved an armed insurgent population was unique in the memory of the age."[4] And, indeed, a significant element of American resistance consisted not in regular operations but in thousands of episodes of civil disobedience and active opposition throughout the vast area of the thirteen states—what we today mean when we use the term "revolutionary warfare" in a generic sense.[5] And it was entirely appropriate that as a counterstrategy the British repeatedly chose a policy of pacification—long-range penetrations, breakup of the rebel infrastructure, reestablishment of a loyal administration and society.

But the War of American Independence was not only highly innovative in its political features, it was also unique in the sense that it did not set a trend. It inspired some Europeans, but it was not a model that European societies followed. The political and military upheavals of the age of the French Revolution and of Napoleon contained nothing like it. The French Revolution itself was from the start a highly centralized movement whose task was not to create a new nation, but to replace one social system and ideology with another and a relatively inefficient system of centralized government with a stronger one. After a brief transitional period its military institutions, too, progressed from a lower to a higher level of standardization and uniformity and fought in support of policies that almost immediately changed from the defense of the Revolution to aggressive national expansion on the order of Louis XIV's assault on the balance of power.

Other revolutionary movements, such as the Polish insurrection of 1794, followed a different pattern: they neither possessed America's relative social homogeneity, her economic and diplomatic resources, or her strong, yet flexible, political traditions, nor were they able to pursue a strategy of delay and attrition because of the size of their territories and the distance separating them from the enemy base. The occupation of one or two of their urban centers meant the end of the struggle. Nor, finally, can we trace similarities in the popular movements against French imperialism during the second half of Napoleon's reign. Resistance in Spain, in the Tyrol, in Russia was characterized not by democratic tendencies but by traditional loyalties and hatred of the foreigner. In 1823 the Spanish peasant, who had helped make life unbearable for the French between 1808 and 1813, welcomed a French expeditionary force, which occupied Madrid with the blessing of the other major powers and overthrew the constitutional, mildly liberal, anticlerical system that had gained power by a coup d'état.

Probably the closest European parallel to the American Revolutionary War was provided by the anti-revolutionary movements in France during 1793 and 1794: the insurrection of Lyon, that of Toulon, and the uprising in the Vendée.[6] These were true armed insurrections, incorporating a significant proportion of the population, fighting for such traditional liberties as freedom of worship and freedom from conscription against the double tyranny of centralization and a hostile, activist ideology. The comparison doesn't bear too much weight, but in passing let me refer to the difficulties England experienced in supporting her allies in the French civil war of the 1790s. The troubled course of naval operations off Toulon and in Quiberon Bay, both relatively near to major British bases, suggests that waging a war across the Atlantic posed almost insuperable obstacles to the command structure and technology of the period and to the social and economic preconceptions on which all eighteenth-century logistic systems were based.[7]

Let me now turn to the area of tactics and of operational organization.

The view that in the Revolution Americans pioneered a new type of warfare that influenced the next generation of European soldiers, once widely accepted among American historians, is no longer tenable today.[8] Again we must look both at what came before and what followed the Revolutionary War. The assertion of American tactical and operational innovation rests almost entirely on the issue of infantry tactics. But it is a misconception to hold that eighteenth-century armies fought only in tightly packed linear formations. Since the beginning of the century each major force had units trained for reconnaissance—and combat patrols, raids, ambushes, outposts—for the so-called war of detachments, or the little war, and the relative proportion of these units increased in each generation. A crucial element of the military revolution that occurred in the 1790s was the fusion of these specialists of the light service with specialists of the line, the heavy infantry, so that henceforth at least in some armies—first in the French, then particularly in the Prussian army—the same men could fight in line, fire volleys, form attack columns, and skirmish. Integrated infantry tactics were not the result of American stimulus, but a development that occurred throughout. It might be added that rifles were introduced as military equipment in the middle of the eighteenth century in Europe. Elite light infantry units, *Jäger,* in the Prussian and Hessian services were armed with rifles and acted as tactical models for other light infantry, equipped with the cheaper and in some respects more efficient smoothbore musket. Here too the campaigns in America at most confirmed a trend that was already well under way.

Infantry tactics were only one area of war that saw significant development at the end of the *ancien régime.* Leaving aside the introduction of universal conscription in some societies, we see at least four other vital changes that occurred to varying extent in the European services. Army structure was recast into divisions or brigades, relatively self-sufficient, standardized operational commands. In 1812, for instance, the reformed Prussian field army consisted of six brigades, each of which permanently combined two infantry regiments, a grenadier battalion, three cavalry regiments, engineer, supply, and reserve units, and a small staff. Restrictions imposed by France and the poverty of the state prevented the organization of artillery and light infantry units in sufficient number to permit their permanent integration in the brigade structure; they were assigned according to operational needs. But basically the former haphazard assemblage of regiments and battalions into ad hoc commands, whose composition was constantly changing, had given way to permanently integrated combat groups, whose components had learned to work together and which, as a whole, could be part of the line of battle one day and perform an independent mission the next. The gain in flexibility and rapidity of operations, as well as in their more securely articulated overall control, is obvious.

Second, the traditional system of fixed supply-points was modified in favor of greater logistic flexibility. Third, artillery was made more mobile and powerful, the number of guns was increased, and new tactics were evolved to exploit the army's new potential. Finally, the Napoleonic period witnessed significant changes in strategic doctrine. They were made possible by some of the developments just mentioned—the division organization, for instance, and the development of a more comprehensive and authoritative general staff. The essential characteristics of the new strategic style—which, of course, was by no means universally understood or followed—may be summarized as speed, the effectively coordinated action of sometimes widely separated commands, and a greater readiness to risk battle—a belief that destroying an army might bring greater advantages than outmaneuvering it.

The war in America contributed little or nothing to these developments. There is no evidence of standardized divisional organization on either side, though it can be argued that independent commands, which were more significant than in Europe, point in that direction. In logistics, too, the war in America taught the use of improvisation. On the other hand, the scarcity of roads and the great expanse of the theater of war increased the value of depots and forts. So far as artillery goes, overseas influence on its design, manufacture, and tactics did not exist. Finally, operations in America were not distinguished from wars on the Continent by greater speed or a more urgent insistence on physical decision. They did, however, include coordinated actions of a kind that had no true parallel in central Europe. An extensive strategic pattern such as that formed by British operations in 1777 was determined by geographic factors and the location of bases to which no equivalents existed in Europe; nevertheless it might be interpreted as a harbinger of the coming cooperation of divisions and army corps. But on the generation of commanders of the Revolution and the Napoleonic Age, who were brought up on the campaigns of Maurice de Saxe and Frederick, the American campaigns made little impression. In the military education of

Napoleon they appear not to have figured at all. And in general that holds true of every military aspect of the war in America. The war does not figure prominently in the professional literature of the 1780s and 1790s. Even the numerous publications that now deal with the little war, partisan warfare, or the war of detachments rarely draw on American experiences; most of their tactical examples are taken from the Seven Years' War and, after 1792, from the Wars of the French Revolution.

If this still seems surprising, it may be useful to ask what the concept of influence can and cannot mean in relation to our subject. Similarities of doctrine, equipment, actions need not be the result of one society or army learning from another; they may be determined by attitudes general to the times or by its technology. The point might become clearer if we reverse the direction that influence is conventionally assumed to have taken in the Revolutionary War and look at instances of Americans referring to European patterns. I suppose that the adopting of Steuben's simplified drill could be interpreted as exerting a Prussian influence on the Continental army; but really all that is at work here is a commonsense response to fundamental conditions imposed by the basic infantry weapon of the time, the smoothbore musket, which requires volleys—in short, linear formations—to be effective. For Washington to be concerned about precedence in the order of battle, about ceremonial, the correct manner of mounting guard in camp, and other paraphernalia associated with the forces of European absolutism is no more than to think in the common military idiom of his generation—and perhaps also to respond, as leaders of revolutionary forces often do respond, to the attraction of regularization, of demonstrating of one's legitimacy by appearing as much like the enemy as possible. Similarly, for Washington to read Bland's *Treatise on Military Discipline* and Guibert's *Essai général,* and to be stimulated by these works to think about organizational and tactical issues in his command and reach his own conclusions, is not to become a link in a chain of influence—especially since these authors had nothing startlingly new to say to him. On the other hand, if Wellington had chosen the Battle of the Cowpens as model for a new defensive doctrine, or if Scharnhorst had based the training of Prussian skirmishers on American patterns, we could realistically speak of an American influence on Europe.

To have meaning in our context, "influence" must be a process leading to the adoption of something significantly different from prevailing ideas or methods. It must mean more than similar actions determined by common economic and technological conditions and more than the gradual accretion of professional expertise. Every war, after all, affords lessons; they may be the result of observing one's own forces at work and of recognizing that this or that aspect could be improved—logistic arrangements, promotion policies, for example—or they may be learned from the enemy, which in the Revolutionary War could mean no more than confirmation of matters that were already known. But this process of experience and of learning, which certainly occurred on both sides, has no relation to the hypothesis that Americans fighting for their independence necessarily fought in a manner different from that of traditional European societies and that subsequently these societies adopted the more modern style of the patriots. To sum up, European armies acquired very little that was new to them from the American War—in some areas because social and political conditions differed too greatly and remained too dissimilar, even after the French Revolution, to make borrowings possible; in others because every European army already contained significant innovative elements, which enabled each service to adapt—sometimes with great reluctance—to new military challenges.

Let me now proceed to the second and final part of our analysis: a comparison of numbers of men involved, size of the theater of operations, and the relationship between aim and achievement in the Revolutionary War and the three major European wars of the second half of the eighteenth century. No more than the most fragmentary outline of the opening phases of these conflicts can be given here, but even that may prove enlightening. While I trace events in Europe, the reader may want to keep in mind the first stages of the war in America, beginning with the engagements in April 1775 between 4,000 patriots and 1,800 British troops at Lexington and Concord and during the British return to Charleston. On May 10, Fort Ticonderoga surrendered. Five weeks later the Battle of Bunker Hill was fought between 2,000 patriots and 2,500 British soldiers; after this no significant confrontation between land forces occurred until November, when the British surrendered their post at St. Johns in Canada.

When we consider the outbreak of the Seven Years' War, we must first of all dismiss the common half-truth that wars in the eighteenth century were always limited wars. That belief is due in large part to a failure of clearly distinguishing methods of fighting and reasons for fighting and also to the tendency of forgetting that "limited," "unlimited," and "total" are relative terms. Total war meant something quite different in 1812 from what it was to mean in 1917, let alone in 1944. Actually these terms are not very useful as analytic devices unless they are combined with a study of the relationship between effort and aim. It would certainly be difficult to interpret the Seven Years' War as a limited war. The aim of the anti-Prussian alliance was to destroy Prussia as the second major power in Central Europe, which, though not the same as destroying her altogether, is far more than depriving her of some relatively insignificant territory.[9] Prussia's aim was the maintenance of the status quo, and the method that Frederick employed to achieve it was a preventive attack. Between June and August 1756 he mobilized a field army of 120,000 men. On August 29 he invaded Saxony, the weakest member of the hostile alliance. On October 1 the opening battle of the war was fought between 28,000 Prussians and 33,000 Austrians, resulting in a Prussian victory at a cost to both sides of some 5,600 casualties. Two weeks later 18,000 Saxons surrendered to Prussian forces. The main result of the campaign was that Frederick gained Saxony as an operational base for the war. During the winter he increased his army to 180,000 and the following April opened the new campaign in a theater of operations about the size of Massachusetts.

In contrast to the Seven Years' War, the second conflict in our sample, the War of the Bavarian Succession, was a limited war. Very little fighting took place—most of it small-unit actions in hilly and wooded terrain, raids, ambushes, harassment of marching columns and transport. But while the intensity of violence, in Frederick's words, was insipid, the limited war actually settled a major political issue.

In the last days of 1777 the elector of Bavaria died. He left no direct successor, and Austria used the occasion to claim the country. If the coup succeeded, it would alter the European balance of power by significantly strengthening the Austrian empire. Consequently Frederick objected, mobilized, and, when his threat was dismissed as a bluff, invaded Bohemia and Moravia in July 1778. In effect that spelled the end of Austria's coup, which was predicated on the absence of serious opposition. Austria was not prepared to fight a major war and eventually withdrew from Bavaria.

This brief and uneventful episode provides an illuminating contrast to events taking place at the same time in America. The theater of operations measured about 220 miles by 60 miles. Two Prussian armies of some 160,000 men advanced into this area and were opposed by an equivalent Austrian force, which adopted a fairly passive defense. Prussian strategy was to push both armies forward; the one that met major resistance would fix the enemy, permitting the other to maneuver. For a time Frederick hoped to swing his left flank through Moravia and to threaten Vienna. But supply difficulties, epidemics, and the absence of the need to seek a military decision caused the Prussians after some months to withdraw through the Bohemian mountains, retaining only a few bases for operations in the coming year, which turned out to be unnecessary.[10]

Finally, the Wars of the French Revolution opened in April 1792 when France declared war on Austria and Prussia largely for internal political reasons. The Girondins, the party for the moment dominating the revolutionary government, believed that a war would unite the nation behind their leadership. The allies, on the other hand, hoped that by invading France they would strengthen the domestic opposition to the Revolution and pressure Paris to modify its policies. To achieve these goals they were prepared to commit only a fraction of their strength—Prussia mobilized no more than one-fourth of her field army—and the 170,000 men that the allies deployed along a 300-mile front proved to be insufficient.

What conclusions can we draw from our survey? It seems apparent that the War of American Independence and the three contemporary European conflicts are of entirely different character, different not only in their political features but also in the fundamental elements of space and of force. In America small armies operated over a very large area that lacked a single center of crucial administrative and social importance, such as Paris or Vienna. In Europe far more powerful forces operated in a fraction of that space. The difference is of a magnitude that has qualitative significance. Staff-work, logistics, strategic and operational concepts, even tactics—all functioned in different ways on the two sides of the Atlantic.

That is the basic reason why neither really affected the other. The concentrated battle-tactics of Europe lost much of their validity in the territorial expanse and among the political dispersion of the thirteen states. The few thousand soldiers moving back and forth between Canada and Georgia, whose climactic encounters would hardly be considered battles in Europe, could not teach the commander much that would be of value in Germany or France. Or so, at least, Europeans thought. And that, obviously, explains what would otherwise be the puzzling absence of thorough treatment of the American War and its lessons in the European literature.

Of all European services, the British was best suited by experience, doctrine, and understanding of naval power to fight overseas. But England was hamstrung by the impact that domestic opposition to the war had on strategic planning and by the political and social character of her army's and navy's command structure and organization. Besides, her efforts and her aims were never fully in accord. No doubt at the beginning it was expected that a show of strength would restore order, but even if the policy of pacification had succeeded, it would not have brought back the political conditions of the 1760s. After the first two years of fighting, England could hope only that a military victory would enable her to treat from strength and to conclude a settlement that would have denied the thirteen states total independence, but surely would have granted everything short of it. That was perhaps not a sufficiently compelling motive to help her overcome the obstacles to fighting a war across 3,000 miles of ocean.

In this respect, incidentally, the American War is like the others to which we have compared it: in each case, the side whose interests were most profoundly affected emerged as the victor. That holds true for the Seven Years' War, in which Prussia's political autonomy was at stake; for the war of 1778, fought to prevent a shift in the balance of power that would have damaged Prussia more than it would have benefited Austria; and for the campaign of 1792, in which the allies, like the British before them, hoped that a show of force would bring the other side to its senses.

And it is crucial to remember that the stronger political motive of the American Revolutionaries was held not by a small elite; it expressed attitudes, a sense of what was possible and desirable, that could be found throughout society. Furthermore, these feelings and ideas had been shaped by their having developed in a unique environment—the American environment, which was defined by remoteness from Europe and by territorial expansiveness. It was this setting that made American political ideals very different, not only from European concepts of the centralized state, but also from European republican ideologies in the 1770s and 1780s (as well as in the two centuries since then). And it was the same remoteness and openness of the American military environment—so unlike that of the community of European states, smaller, far more densely developed, immediately abutting, pushing against each other—that in the final analysis enabled the patriots to succeed in their political experiment and also to triumph in its defense.

## 1 Notes

1. Don Higginbotham, *The War of American Independence.* (New York, 1971), p. 103. See also ibid., p. 57.

2. Piers Mackesy, *The War for America, 1775-1783* (Cambridge, Mass., 1964), p. 4.

3. Some Prussian examples: In 1776 the rank and file were evenly divided between natives and foreigners (most of whom were non-Prussian Germans)—78,767 to 78,280—a relationship that remained unchanged to the end of Frederick's reign. In 1787 new regulations called for a slight preponderance of natives in all branches except the hussars, where natives and foreigners were to be equal in number. At the outbreak of the Wars of the French Revolution natives outnumbered foreigners by some 20,500 men in the infantry and by some 4,000 men in the cavalry. In the officer corps the percentage of natives was still higher, although as late as 1805, as many as one-third of all infantry officers holding the rank of lieutenant colonel or higher were foreigners. For additional statistics, and remarks on the politically significant appeal that Prussian service had for foreigners, see Peter Paret, *Clausewitz and the State* (New York, 1976), p. 59. Austrian manpower policies of the period aree analyzed in Jürg Zimmerman, *Militärverwaltung und Heeresaufbringung in Osterreich bis 1806,* vol. 3, *Handbuch zur deutschen Militärgeschichte* (Frankfurt, 1965).

4. Mackesy, *War for America,* p. 31.

5. On this aspect of the war, see John Shy, "The American Revolution: The Military Conflict Considered as a Revolutionary War," in *Essays on the American Revolution,* ed. Stephen J. Kurtz and James H. Hutson (Chapel Hill, 1973), pp. 121-56.

6. I have discussed the revolutionary elements on both sides of the conflict in the Vendée in Peter Paret, *Internal War and Pacification: The Vendée, 1789-1796,* Center of International Studies, Research Monograph no. 12 (Princeton, 1961).

7. For analyses of English and Continental conditions, see R. Arthur Bowler, *Logistics and the Failure of the British Army in America, 1775-1783* (Princeton, 1975), and *Heeresverpflegung,* vol. 6, *Studien zur Kriegsgeschichte und Taktik,* ed. Military History Section I of the Great General Staff (Berlin, 1913), pp. 2-73.

8. The following discussion is based on Peter Paret, "Colonial Experience and European Military Reform at the End of the Eighteenth Century," *Bulletin of the Institute of Historical Research* (1964): 47-59.

9. It is nevertheless notable that such a balanced, critical interpreter of Prussian history as Hajo Holborn defines the aim of the Austro-French alliance as "the total destruction of Prussia" *(A History of Modern Germany* [New York, 1964], pp. ii, 235).

## Notes 2

10. Since the military aspects of this conflict have been largely ignored in the literature, it may be useful to mention the two best brief accounts: Curt Jany, *Geschichte der Preussischen Armee,* rev. ed. (Osnabrück, 1967), pp. iii, 107-29; and far superior analytically, Colmar von der Goltz, *Von Rossbac bis Jena* (Berlin, 1906), pp. 408-17. The chapter dealing with the war in Paul B. Bernard, *Joseph II and Bavaria* (The Hague, 1965), is better on the diplomatic maneuvers than on the course of operations.

# [18]

# THE DEVELOPMENT OF THE COMBAT DIVISION IN EIGHTEENTH-CENTURY FRENCH ARMIES

By

STEVEN T. ROSS

The development of the infantry division as a tactical combat unit was a major step forward in the evolution of modern armies. Although historians agree in placing this development during the second half of the eighteenth century, they are at odds as to its cause.

The most common assertions concerning the evolution of the infantry division fall into two broad categories. One group of historians asserts that the division was developed by the armies of the *ancien régime* and that the forces of the Revolution simply adopted this innovation.[1] A second group of scholars maintains that the division was a creation of the First Republic and was a response to the necessity of organizing extraordinarily large numbers of troops. The armies created by the Committee of Public Safety were, these historians argue, simply too large to be directed by a single field commander issuing orders directly to regimental units. It therefore became necessary to create intermediate commands, and the division was designated to meet this need.[2] Actually both of these positions are accurate up to a point, but neither takes into account the great complexity of this development. The innovations of both the monarchy and the revolutionary republic must be considered in order fully to understand the complexities of the problem.

In modern terms, the division is defined as the elementary organic unit of the combined arms, marching and fighting

[1] Jean Colin, *L'éducation militaire de Napoleón* (Paris: R. Chapetot, 1900); Robert S. Quimby, *The Background of Napoleonic Warfare* (New York: Columbia University Press, 1957); and Spencer Wilkinson, *The French Army Before Napoleon* (Oxford: Clarendon Press, 1915) are representative of this point of view.

[2] Lynn Montross, *War Through the Ages* (New York: Harper and Brothers, 1960); Robert R. Palmer, *Twelve Who Ruled* (Princeton: Princeton University Press, 1941); and Theodore K. Ropp, *War in the Modern World* (Durham: Duke University Press, 1959) adhere to the view that the creation of the combat division was a response to circumstances.

together under the command of a general officer. Initially, however, it meant something quite different. The word itself was employed early in the eighteenth century. During the War of the Austrian Succession, the word meant literally what it implied: any part of a field army not operating under the direct control of the commander-in-chief. Frequently sections of the main army marching by different roads would be designated as divisions, but such units would revert to the direct control of the army commander once they rejoined the central force. They were not permanent commands, and usually did not consist of units drawn from all arms of the service. These early divisions were not commanded by a general officer but by a senior regimental commander or by an aide to the commander-in-chief. In other words, the division of the early eighteenth century was not a standing unit; it was an ad hoc formation, more accurately a column.[3]

The French continued to employ this term during the Seven Years' War, and in the course of this conflict the word began to take on a more specific connotation. Armies operating in Germany were with increasing frequency divided into units, each comprising infantry, calavry, and artillery. These units marched and fought together but were still only temporary formations—expedients created by field commanders for specific missions and dissolved upon the completion of a campaign. The French army did not make provision for the existence of a division within its table of organization, and it was left to the individual army commands whether or not they would create such units.[4]

Between the end of the Seven Years' War and the outbreak of the Revolution, the infantry division went through still another stage of development. After 1763, Louis XV and his war ministers instituted a general reform program with the goal of improving the army's combat efficiency. In March 1776, the war minister, the Count Saint Germain, divided France into sixteen geographical areas known as divisions. These divisions were basically administrative zones rather

[3] Marechal Maurice Saxe, *Mémoires sur l'art de la guerre* (Dresden, 1757), pp. 53-54.

[4] Colin, *op. cit.*, p. 45 and p. 57.

than combat commands. They were placed under the direction of a lieutenant general who was responsible for recruiting, logistics, discipline, internal security and inspection of units.[5] In addition to these administrative functions, the divisions and their commanders were assigned roles which prefigured those of the future combat division. For example, each command had a permanent garrison: The Flanders division had a cadre of twenty-four battalions of infantry; and six infantry battalions and fifty squadrons of cavalry were stationed in Lorraine.[6] At the same time the battalions were organized into permanent regiments each of two battalions.[7] Finally, the lieutenant generals were given the authority to hold inter-arm maneuvers in order to accustom the various branches of the armed services to operating and fighting together.[8]

Shortly after the introduction of these reforms, Saint Germain was dismissed as a result of court intrigues, and efforts to improve the French army were halted for many years. Under Louis XVI, however, a new series of reforms was introduced when on March 17, 1788, the number of divisional zones was expanded to eighteen. In addition, the line regiments were organized into permanent brigades, and the brigades in turn were formed into twenty-one combat divisions.[9] These units were not precisely identical with the modern division, however, for they did not contain any of the specialist units such as pioneers, artillery, or cavalry. On the other hand, the commander of the administrative division could call upon the commander of the infantry division to hold joint maneuvers with other arms of the service.

Generally, then, the *ancien régime* in France did not witness the development of the division as a permanent unit comprising all arms and operating under a single tactical command. Nevertheless, many elements of the modern di-

[5] Leon Mention, *Le comte de Saint Germain et ses réformes* (Paris: A. Clavel, 1884), pp. 86-89.
[6] *Ibid.*
[7] *Ibid.*, p. 132.
[8] *Ibid.*, p. 89.
[9] Albért Duruy, *L'armée royale en 1789* (Paris: C. Lévy, 1888), pp. 59, 62-63.

vision were originated prior to the outbreak of the Revolution. Furthermore, many non-commissioned officers and enlisted men who had been trained by the royal army would later become officers in the republican forces and would put into practice on the field of battle much of what they had learned in the army of the Bourbons. The armed forces of the revolutionary republic would also retain the administrative division and expand the combat division composed exclusively of infantry into an organic unit comprising all arms.

The revolutionaries of 1789 had no intention of making drastic changes in the composition of the state's armed forces and instituted relatively few military reforms during the first few years of revolutionary activity. The old militia was replaced by a National Guard, and entrance into the officers corps of the regular army was opened to all on a basis of talent rather than social rank. But at first relatively few outside of the aristocracy took advantage of this opportunity; most of them who became officers prior to the outbreak of the war did so by way of the National Guard, where officers were elected rather than appointed by the crown.[10]

The outbreak of war in 1792 changed this situation drastically, although the revolutionaries were slow to recognize the need for the drastic innovations circumstances imposed upon them. Two factors appear outstanding as causative factors in the reorganization of the nation's armed forces: the large-scale emigration of trained officers, and the rapid expansion of the army's manpower.

In 1789, the majority of the regular army officers were of noble extraction.[11] Concentrations of officers drawn from the middle class did appear in specialist units such as the artillery and engineers, but the other branches of the service were led almost exclusively by nobles. In fact, the ratio between noble and middle class officers had been increasing steadily in favor of the nobles ever since 1781.[12] As the Revolution became progressively more democratic, large numbers of

[10] Georges Six, *Les généraux de la Révolution et de l'Empire* (Paris: Bordas, 1947), p. 25.

[11] *Ibid.*, p. •29.

[12] The Ségur Law of 1781 in effect prevented non-nobles from entering the officer corps.

noble officers began to join their fellow aristocrats in leaving France and in joining counterrevolutionary groups in the Rhineland and Piedmont. The rate of emigration grew steadily after 1789, and with the onset of war it proceeded even more rapidly until by 1793 two-thirds of the officers—some 6000 out of approximately 9000—had left the country.[13] This emigration appears even more serious when it is recalled that most of the officers who emigrated came from the infantry and cavalry, leaving these arms of the service practically denuded of leaders. To fill the gaps, the government had to draw new officer material from the National Guard and from the noncommissioned officers of the regular army.[14] For the most part the new officers were unfamiliar with the rather complicated drill system which characterized the eighteenth-century army, and for this reason alone, some change in the organization and tactics of the army became immediately necessary. An obvious solution was to make more effective use of the trained artillery and engineer officers by promoting a greater integration of the various service arms. At the same time, innovations became even more necessary since untrained officers had to handle ever larger number of untrained troops.

Originally the government had made no plans for great increases in troop strength; consequently in 1792, the French went to war with about the same number of troops they had under arms before the outbreak of the Revolution—about 210,000 men.[15] Initial defeat plus large-scale desertion of officers favorable to the royalist cause forced the government to take drastic measures. Since it could not increase the number of trained men and experienced officers, the revolutionary leaders had no alternative other than to substitute mass and élan for training and discipline and to make even greater use of the officers remaining.

As early as 1792, National Guard units were directed to

[13] Wilkinson devotes much space to the large-scale emigration of royalist officers, although it appears to contradict his view that the reforms of the republic were essentially extensions of reforms initiated by the Bourbons.

[14] Six, conclusion, *passim*.

[15] Duruy, p. 7.

send volunteers to the field armies, and by the following spring a limited form of conscription had been introduced. In March, 1793, the government called for 300,000 conscripts, and at the end of August, the Committee of Public Safety introduced a general conscription act—the *leveé en masse*—which the Convention enacted on the 23rd. Vast numbers of raw recruits rushed or were forced into cadre units, and by September the Convention had at its disposal fourteen field armies numbering about 660,000 men.[16]

With such great numbers of troops led by such unexperienced officers, it became vital to reorganize the army in such a manner as to make the most effective use of both officers and enlisted men. Such reorganization, however, was not immediate. Rather, it came slowly as the field commanders and finally the Committee of Public Safety gradually came to realize the necessity for it.

In the campaigns of 1792, the army was still led by officers of the royal army who had chosen to side with the Revolution, and as a result the army fought in the old, indeed, reactionary style. In fact, the more recent innovations of the Bourbon Monarchy were ignored, and generals reverted to the use of the two-regiment brigade instead of employing the two-brigade division. Artillery and other specialist units were not attached to the brigades but were retained under the direct control of the army commanders.[17] There were two reasons for this arrangement: First, there were not enough officers who could command infantry and artillery in combination, and second, the infantry was so poorly trained that the generals placed a great deal of reliance on their artillery and preferred to keep it under their direct control. At the decisive battle of the Valmy, for example, the infantry never fired a shot. The Prussians were halted entirely by the French artillery, and Kellerman had the batteries directly subject to his orders rather than to those of the brigade commanders.

[16] Ministère de la guerre, État-Major de l'armée, Archives historiques, Paris, Octobre 1793. Estimated strengths of the various field armies were drawn up in September and in the following month were published in the various army bulletins.

[17] Arthur Chuquet, *Guerres de la Révolution*, I *La première invasion prussienne* (Paris, Plon, 1887), Chapter II.

As more and more recruits began to enter the ranks in the spring and summer of 1793, the problems of a lack of trained officers and a surplus of uninstructed manpower began to hamper the effectiveness of the field armies. The commanders on the spot first had to grapple with this problem. Their solution was to place one or two battalions of new men into a brigade containing an equal number of veteran units. This alternative provided only a temporary solution for there were still insufficient veteran units to go around. Gradually the commanders began to reduce their brigades from four to three battalions, placing two new and one veteran together and using the other trained battalion as a cadre for a new brigade. Other commanders, instead of reducing the size of their brigades, expanded the size of their regiments. One veteran and two volunteer battalions would be placed in a regiment and the brigade raised to a total of six battalions.[18] At first, neither alternative was universally attempted. When they were carried out, it was on an ad hoc basis at the whim of the individual general.

The continuing influx of recruits throughout 1793 and 1794 eventually made the Committee of Public Safety aware of the need for a general reorganization of the armed forces. Carnot, the member in charge of military affairs, working in close co-operation with Bouchotte, the War Minister, finally devised rules for the amalgamation of new with veteran battalions. Early in 1794, army commanders were ordered to adopt the three-battalion regimental system. They were directed to place two new and one veteran battalion into a regiment that was redesignated as a demi-brigade. Two regiments or demi-brigades were to constitute a brigade, and two brigades constituted a division.[19] However, because this reorganization was carried out while campaigns were still in progress, and because trained officers were still lacking, the brigade never came into existence. Instead, a number of demi-brigades were placed under the command of a general officer who was given the title of general of division. The

[18] *Ibid.*, II, *Valmy*, pp. 71-73.

[19] Ramsay Phipps, *The Armies of the First French Republic*, I (London, Humphrey Milford, 1926), p. 31.

number of demi-brigades varied from division to division as did the size of the battalions in each demi-brigade. In 1794, a division might range in size from seven to sixteen battalions, and the battalions numbered from 500 to 1300 men.[20] The effectives in a division varied anywhere from 7800 to 13,400 troops, but despite the great diversity in size and composition, the divisions of 1794 were organized on the same general basis as those of 1788.[21]

The main difference between the royal and republican divisions was that the latter contained combined artillery and cavalry units. Just as with the number of demi-brigades and battalions, the distribution of specialist units was highly irregular. It was not uncommon for a division totally to lack artillery, but it was more frequent to have both foot and horse-artillery batteries assigned to divisional generals, and at times, demi-batteries were given to the demi-brigades.[22] Cavalry units usually of squadron size were often distributed among the divisions for purposes of reconnaissance. The cavalry, however, was distributed less freely than was the artillery, for the republican commanders preferred to keep their cavalry in separate divisions to which horse-artillery batteries were attached.[23]

In the first months of 1795, efforts were made to regulate the distribution of specialist units, and various army commanders directed that each division's artillery was to be turned over to the army command for use as a general reserve. Like other plans made while the armies were still engaged in active fighting, this order was only partially fulfilled. Field armies simply did not have the time to carry out this reorganization; furthermore, divisional commanders were reluctant to part with their extra weapons.[24] Thus, by the end of 1795, though the divisional system had not yet been fully elaborated, the concept of a unit which consisted of all service arms had been generally accepted. Nonetheless, the

[20] Matti Lauerma, *L'artillerie de campagne française pendant les guerres de la révolution* (Helsinki: Soumalien Tiedeakatemia, 1956), pp. 149-150.
[21] *Ibid.*
[22] *Ibid.*
[23] *Ibid.*
[24] *Ibid.*, p. 150.

precise composition of this unit continued to vary greatly from place to place.

The defeat of Holland, Spain, and Prussia, in addition to the English evacuation of the continent, gave the French still another opportunity to reorganize their forces. Although campaigns were still being waged in Germany and Italy against the Austrians, conditions now allowed the government to institute reforms. By this time too the French had developed a body of battle-hardened veteran officers who could lead the contemplated units.

A new army organization law was completed on January 7, 1796. It provided for an army of 110 demi-brigades of the line, ten of which were to form colonial garrisons. Each demi-brigade was to consist of three battalions of 1100 men. A battalion in turn was divided into eight fusilier and one grenadier company. Thitry light demi-brigades were also created. They were constituted like the line units except that chasseurs replaced grenadiers. Eight artillery regiments of 1787 men each and eight horse artillery regiments of 466 men were also established. The cavalry was organized into twenty-six regiments of 532 men, and twenty-one dragoon regiments, twenty-five chasseur, and thirteen hussar regiments each with a complement of 944 troops.[25]

In peacetime, the various demi-brigades and regiments were stationed in military divisions identical in function to those of the *ancien régime.* New zones were added when Belgium and Rhineland were incorporated into the Republic. Thus the total number of these administrative, training, and replacement center zones was raised to twenty-two.[26]

The division as a combat unit still had no place in this table of organization, but its use had become a standard procedure in time of war. The French had sufficient officer material able to direct units consisting of troops drawn from all arms of the service. When organizing a campaign, demi-brigades, artillery batteries, and cavalry squadrons were drawn to-

[25] Report of the Minister of War to the Directory on the size and strength of the army according to the law of Jan., 1796, in Archives nationales, AF3*14.

[26] *Ibid.* Eventually the number of administrative zones was raised to twenty-four.

gether as required and placed under the command of one of these officers. As a result, divisions were not designated by a number but by the name of the commanding officer.[27]

Individual demi-brigades were still used for certain special assignments. They were, for example, employed against royalist guerrilas in the Vendée, Southern France, Beligum, and Luxemburg. In such cases, they were placed under the control of the departmental civil authorities or of the commander of one of the administrative divisions, but the use of the combat division had become the standard method for all major operations.[28]

The combat division after 1796 also tended to take on a fairly standard form. Generally it consisted of three demi-brigades with light and line units being used more or less interchangably. The division usually contained several artillery batteries with horse and foot batteries assigned according to local conditions. Pioneer and cavalry units were also assigned according to the type of mission a division had to perform. The French, however, continued to retain much flexibility in the size and composition of their combat divisions. For example, in the campaigns of 1799, which were the last battles fought by the Republic, Masséna's Army of the Danube had a division numbering 11,232 men, with two horse artillery and two foot artillery batteries. He also had a division with but 4668 troops and no artillery.[29] The divisions of the Army of Italy varied in strength from 8000 to 10,000 men, with one or two horse artillery batteries and some 200 foot artillerymen.[30] In the Army of Naples, divisions ranged from 3500 to 6000 troops with from 23 to 321 artillerists.[31] Since there were as yet no corps commands, the

---

[27] All of the field armies designated their divisions in this manner. See Archives historiques, État-Major de l'armée, Armée du Danube Correspondance as an example.

[28] See the orders of battle for any of the major field armies. The order of battle of the Army of the Danube for September 22, 1799, in Archives historiques, État-Major de l'armée, Armée du Danube Correspondance, septembre 1799, carton B²77, provides an excellent example.

[29] Ministère de la guerre, Archives historiques, État-Major de l'armée, Armée du Danube Correspondance, Mai 1799, carton B²73.

[30] *Ibid.*, Armée d'Italie Correspondance, octobre 1798, carton B³56.

[31] *Ibid.*, Armée de Naples Correspondance, de Macdonald mai-octobre 1799, carton B³322*.

army commanders issued orders directly to the generals of division and at times to the demi-brigade commanders. Nevertheless, the principle that the combat division consist of troops drawn from all branches of the service operating under the control of a general officer had been firmly established. The armies of the Consulate, Empire ,and Restoration would adopt, utilize, and elaborate upon this system which had become a permanent part of the French military structure.

The armies of the *ancien régime* took the first steps in the creation of the modern divison. By 1789, the Bourbons had created permanent brigades, units consisting of two infantry brigades, and administrative zones with permanent cadres in which an inspector general could order units from all arms to carry out maneuvers in common. The leaders of the Revolution had no desire to make drastic changes in this system, but under the pressure of war, increased numbers, and the flight of veteran officers they had little choice but to elaborate upon the innovations of the old royal army. Combat divisions in the early years of the Republic were basically ad hoc formations created in response to circumstances. Later, the combat division, having proven its utility, became an integral part of the organization of the French army. These divisions were not permanent units maintained in time of peace, for the old administrative divisions served as training and replacement centers for the field armies. Yet for all campaigns after 1793, the combat division was the major tactical unit of the French armed forces. Thus it was during the *ancien régime* that the foundations for the modern combat divisions were laid, and it was the Republic, responding to circumstances, which built upon these foundations and completed the structure.

*University of Nebraska*

# Part V
# Technology

# [19]

# FLINT AND STEEL: A STUDY IN MILITARY TECHNOLOGY AND TACTICS IN 17TH-CENTURY EUROPE

GORDON R. MORK

*The famous Three Musketeers always fought with swords because in the early part of the 17th century a sword was more convenient than a musket that required several minutes to load, aim, and fire. In battle musketeers fought the offensive, with pikemen standing by to defend them against an enemy charge. This dichotomy of functions made even simple maneuvers difficult. During the century improvements in the musket lock lessened firing time, and the invention of the bayonet enabled musketeers to defend themselves. The pikeman became obsolete. In a comprehensive study, Mr. Mork discusses how the century's technical improvements created major changes in tactics.*

A MILITARY REVOLUTION was completed in the first decade of the 18th century. It began in the late middle ages when foot soldiers, armed with lengthy pikes and hand guns, proved their superiority over feudal cavalry. In spite of developments during the next two hundred years, however, infantry often remained clumsy and ineffective. But the royal fusiliers who fought the wars of the 18th century were modern soldiers fighting in modern armies. With flint in their gun locks for spark and the steel of the bayonet for shock, the battlefield was theirs. For nearly a century and a half after the Duke of Marlborough's "famous victory" at Blenheim in 1704, soliders would still be armed as his had been and would still use tactics much like his.

The social implications of the new army, which are beyond the scope of this study, were immense. No longer did independent feudal nobles in heavy armor rule the field of battle and thus all of society. No longer were monarchs forced to call upon undependable and unruly mercenaries to maintain themselves against their nobility or one another. The armies created by this revolution carried the king's weapons, wore the king's coat, ate his bread, and—most important—acted at his command. They were the servants of a bureaucratic state which imposed its rule, and its peace upon society.[1]

## WITH PIKE AND MUSKET

The pike was introduced into western warfare by the Swiss infantry of the 15th century. The pikeman wore considerable armor and carried a stout spear which was at least three times his height. Formed into large squares, pikemen were disciplined to move together as a phalanx and soon proved the value of an organized and well-armed infantry. Surely the first knights who found themselves confronted with the solid squares of bristling pikes thought the use of such weapons was, at best, unchivalrous. But age brings respectability, even nobility, and the pike eventually gained a place of honor as the "queen of the battlefield." [2]

Figure 1.—The pikeman's offensive position, presenting the pike.

By the mid-17th century the pikeman had discarded some of his armor, but still bore the weight and protection of considerable steel, as can be seen in Figures 1 and 2.[3] There were three basic positions for the pike in battle. At the first position—attention—the pike was rested on the ground with the point extending straight up. In the second —presenting the pike—the soldier held his weapon horizontally just below shoulder level, aiming the point of the pike at the height of a horse's breast (Figure 1).[4] This was the pikeman's offensive position, though it could also be used to meet the charge of hostile infantry or even cavalry. Presenting their pikes, a block of soldiers would march forward in the "push of the pike" which made the Swiss and the Spanish squares so much feared. In formation the pikes of the first several ranks would extend beyond the first rank of men. The men in the rear would often keep their pikes pointed high in the air, above the heads of their comrades, while during the "push" they would lower them just as the formation met the enemy. The third position was the defense against the cavalry charge (Figure 2). The pike was held in the left hand, braced against the right foot, and extended forward at such an angle that the point would be aimed at the breasts of the oncoming horses. The pikeman partially drew his sword with his right hand to be prepared for close combat. It was as hard for charging cavalry to pierce a square of seasoned pikemen in this defensive position as it would be to jab an angry porcupine with one's bare finger.[5]

Hand firearms appeared on European battlefields not long after the pike. The earliest hand gun was a sort of miniature cannon, fired by touching a lighted match to a hole at the rear of the barrel. But soon stocks and gun locks were developed and the arquebus was born. The weapon was so slow and clumsy that its firepower was at first considerably below that of the crossbow and the longbow, both of which continued to be used well into the 16th century. But little by little the power of hand firearms was demonstrated.[6]

The early arquebus was equipped with a matchlock, like that in Figures 3 and 4, shown in detail in Figure 16. A lever beneath the stock of the gun lowered a piece of slowly burning linen rope soaked in saltpeter (the match) into a pan at the rear of the gun barrel. The fine flash powder in the pan was thus ignited; it, in turn, set off the main powder charge to which it communicated by a small hole in the barrel, and the gun was fired. The musket, a larger weapon which used the same matchlock firing mechanism, was introduced in the mid-16th century and soon replaced the lighter and less powerful arquebus. The musket was more cumbersome, could be used only with a forked rest, and took longer to load and fire. But its superior range and power made it a much more formidable weapon.[7]

The musketeer shed his armor, and by the mid-17th century, even replaced his helmet with a rakish hat. As can be seen in Figure 3, he carried a bandoleer over his shoulder with about twelve wooden tubes, each of which held a measured charge of powder. A larger tube carried the fine powder for the pan. Musket balls were carried in a pouch at his waist or, in battle, in his mouth. Also at his waist were the coils of a slow match which he needed to fire the weapon. At his side he carried a sword, for use as a last resort, but in hand-to-hand combat some musketeers preferred simply to use the butts of their muskets as clubs.[8] The musketeer in Figure 4 is about to fire. He has clipped one end of the match to the serpentine, propped the musket on his rest, and is squeezing the lever which is lowering the serpentine into the pan. He holds the stock against his chest rather than his shoulder and makes no attempt to aim along the barrel. If highly skilled, this musketeer could probably have gotten off one shot every three or four minutes.

The introduction of the pike and musket greatly strengthened the infantry. Feudal cavalry no longer ruled the battlefield, but either pikemen or musketeers, fighting alone, had serious weaknesses. A block of charging pikes could be immobilized by a cavalry charge on its flanks and then cut to pieces with firearms. The 17th-century cavalrymen could still defeat the pikemen because, as William Barriffe wrote in 1643, "the Horseman carries fiery weapons and can kill the Pikeman at a distance, they neither being able to defend themselves nor offend their enemies." [9] Musketeers caught in the open by cavalry, on the other hand, were equally unable to defend themselves effectively. In the late 16th century it was a maxim that cavalry could successfully charge any number of unprotected muskets; their fire was too slow and inaccurate to drive off the horsemen.[10]

Figure 2.—The defensive position against charging cavalry.

Figure 3.—Although the musketeer used no armor, he was seriously encumbered by the size and weight of his weapon, its rest, and a long match.

Figure 4.—A musketeer firing.

Therefore, in the 16th century the musket found its place along the edges of the squares of pikemen. From the safety of their comrade's lowered pikes they could fire on the enemy, and simultaneously provide firepower to protect an immobilized square of pikemen from the opposing shot. The Swiss and the Spanish emphasized depth of rank and file, and great squares of three or four thousand men would go into battle together. Early in the century one musket to five pikes became the standard ratio; but as the firepower of the musketeers became more dependable and its potential was grasped by both officers and men, the ratio of shot to pikes grew, until Maurice of Nassau, in the final decade of the century, brought it up to one musket per pike. He also improved the arrangement of battle order. The huge Swiss and Spanish squares were completely inflexible and wasted a great deal of manpower. Maurice arranged his men in battalions with several hundred pikes in

Figure 5.—A sixteenth-century battalion.

the center and equal blocks of muskets on each side, somewhat as shown in Figure 5. In this engraving musketeers flank the block of pikemen in the basic formation. Notice that the officers carry shorter weapons called partisans or spontoons. Thus Maurice emphasized extension rather than depth. His basic formations were only six ranks deep so they did not waste the fire of musketeers at the rear of a great square. When threatened by a charge of hostile cavalry or pikes the musketeers could fall back in close order behind the lowered pikes of their comrades.[11]

Gustavus Adolphus introduced more improvements in infantry tactics. Using Maurice's basic formation, he developed a system of doubling the number of files to move his musketeers into a file six men deep, a major maneuver would have been necessary to defend against a cavalry charge on one of the flanks.

As the ratio of shot to pikes grew, and as the great captains developed ways to maximize the effectiveness of their fire, the push of the pike became less frequent. The offensive role was being taken over by the musketeer, and the pikeman was becoming only a guard to protect him from the cavalry charge. The days when the charge of the pikemen had struck fear into the hearts of their enemies, apparently, were over. Hans von Grimmelshausen, whose character Simplicissimus was both a wily observer and practitioner of 17th-century military techniques, opined that whoever killed a pikeman whose life could have been

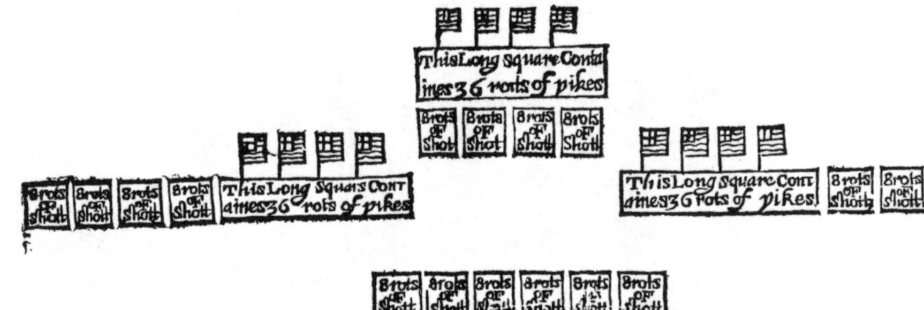


Figure 6.—Gustavus Adolphus' Swedish brigade.

firing position only three ranks deep. By exploiting the flexibility of the smaller battle groups he created such formations as the Swedish brigade (Figure 6) which proved very effective with his well-trained troops.[12] Gustavus had many variations on his basic formation; Figure 6 shows a brigade of just over 1500 men. He often interspersed cavalry with his units. (Barriffe wished that Gustavus had developed something like the bayonet so that he could have advanced tactical ideas even further.) In this figure, where a *rot* is a spared, murdered an innocent man. Pikemen bothered nobody but those who voluntarily threw themselves onto the pikes.[13]

By the middle of the 17th century a classic style of pike and musket tactics was developed. The formation of the battalion was basically the same as that of Maurice of Nassau, with muskets on the wings and pikes in the center. For improved firing the musketeers would march out by ranks, forming in front of the block of pikes. The musketeers would then be only three ranks deep (or occa-

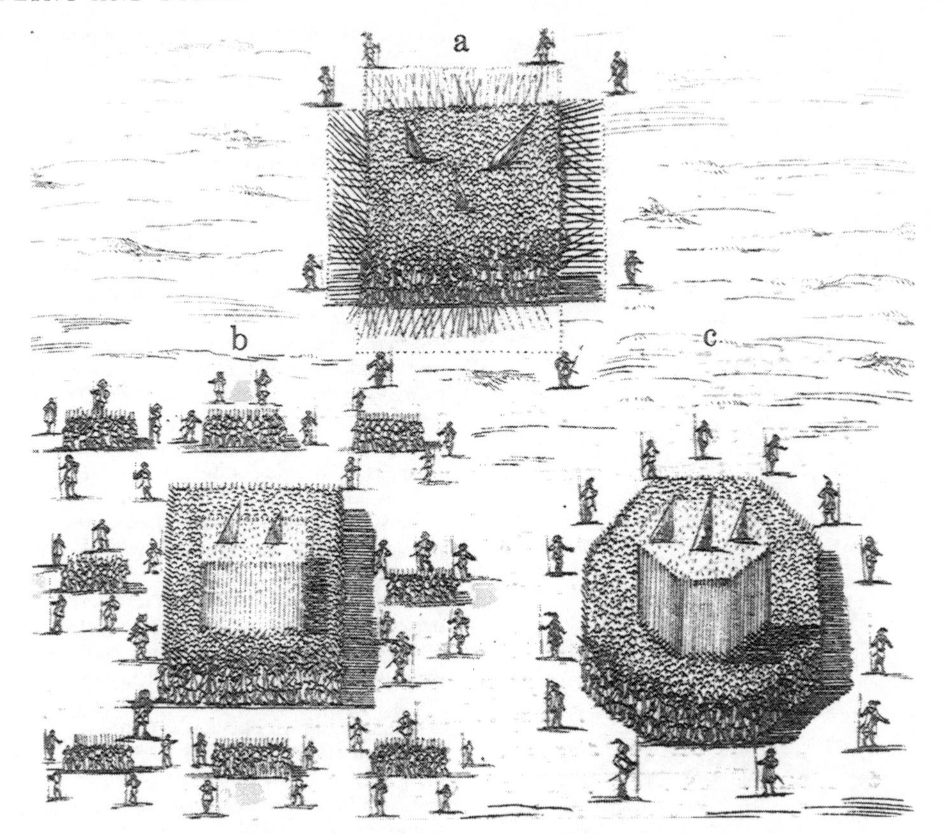


Figure 7.—Several defensive formations. 7a.—The basic block formation ready to receive a charge. 7b.—Block formation at attention. 7c.—The hollow octagon.

sionally four, if the standard formation had a depth of eight ranks), and could either fire in a volley, the first rank kneeling, or could lay down a rolling fire, with one rank firing and pausing to reload as each of the other two fired. For a protective formation in the face of a charge or a hostile push of pikes, the musketeers would fall back into the block of pikemen in formations such as those in Figure 7. Blocks of officers carrying smaller pikes and halberds could gather on the corners of the square for further protection. The pikemen could then lower their pikes between the musketeers and ward off a charge, while the musketeers could continue firing. The basic formation was the square, ready to receive a charge (Figure 7a); and at attention (7b). An improvement of this defensive position was the hollow octagon, with a double rank of musketeers on the circumference under the protection of the pikes, and a baggage train, or reserve of musketeers, inside the formation (Figures 7c and 8). This formation presented a face in each direction and no sharp corners vulnerable to attack. Such a formation was a good defensive posture and was used by certain regiments of the French in the Battle of Rocroi, 1643.[14]

In spite of the development of these formations,

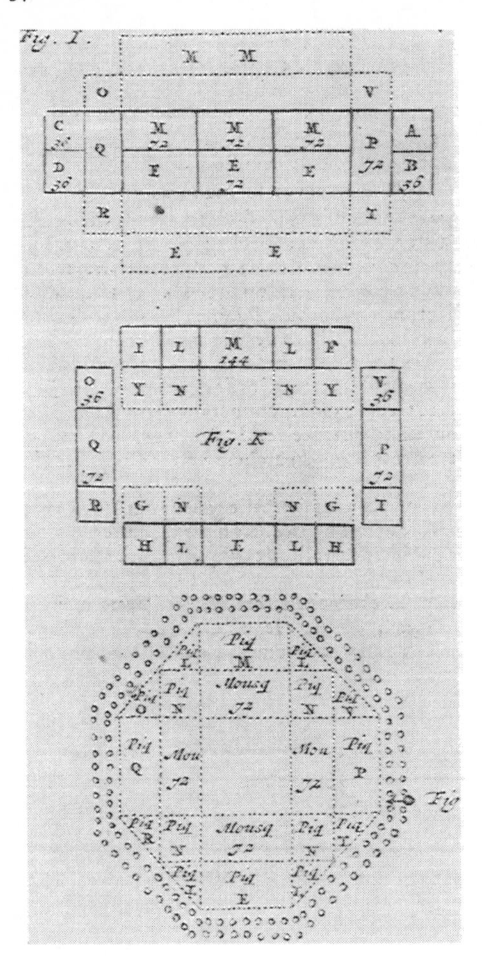


Figure 8.—Diagram showing the formation of the hollow octagon.

pike and musket tactics remained terribly inefficient. Basically the problem was this—the musket was of real use only as an offensive weapon, while the pike was generally used only in defense. The offensive push of the pike was rare and the defensive use of the musket, once it had been fired, was almost nil. Of course musketeers carried swords, but fencing was greatly encumbered when the soldier was supposed to hold a musket, and perhaps a rest as well, in the other hand. Thus, only half of the army would be of use at any one time, the musketeers for offense and the pikemen for defense. Moreover, the problems of changing from offensive to defensive positions made incredibly complex marching maneuvers necessary. First the musketeers were put in ranks facing the enemy so that their firepower could be most effectively used, then they retreated into a defensive position like the hollow octagon in case cavalry threatened to attack. Figure 8 shows in three steps how a battalion could move from marching order to the octagonal defensive formation. The figure appears to contain 720 men. If an officer's commands to the men forming the figure were as confusing as the lettering of the diagram, it is doubtful if the figure could have been used in battle. Yet it, or very similar figures, were actually used. Complicated wheeling, countermarching, and right and left flanking movements were necessary, often with different ranks and files moving in different directions at the same time. It would seem that only a highly skilled drill team could have performed the maneuvers required—from batallion formation, to firing position, to defensive position—for this classic style of pike and musket tactics.

William Barriffe, in his manual of 1643, provided well over two hundred pages of detailed marching instructions necessary to form the many figures he recommended for proper deployment of troops. He included such diverse arts as facing, reducement, inversion, conversion, doubling ranks, doubling files, doubling the rear, and even doubling by bringers up, and half-files by bringers up. He recognized that the standards of training in 17th century England were abysmally low, and one wonders how he could have believed his drill manual to have been at all practicable. In a poetic aside he commented:

> So be there many Officers in Bands,
> That neither know themselves, nor care for those
> That skillful are in Postures and Commands,
> Nor are they careful which end foremost goes.
> They think to dice, to drab, to sweare and swill,
> Is skill enough for them, learn more that will.

And he noted that the common soldiers "are scarce called forth to exercise either Posture or Motion once in four or five years." [15]

Only rarely in the other European armies of the day, were things any better. The average foot soldier was a mercenary, hired for a campaign and dismissed at its close; standing armies, in so far as they did exist, made up only a small nucleus of the troops used in war. It is true that sometimes, as during the Thirty Years War for example, men would remain under arms for a considerable length of time. Thus they might have developed some basic discipline, at least with respect to their military duty, if not toward the civilian population. But standards could not have been very high. In the 17th century, European infantry was not even trained to march in cadenced step. A few picked troops may have drilled in step prior to 1650, but examples are rare and poorly documented. On the march a cadenced step, absolutely necessary to maintain some semblance of orderly spacing in an army, was not widely used until the time of Frederick the Great and Maurice de Saxe in the 18th century.[16]

Even on the parade ground, therefore, the performance of the basic maneuvers necessary for successful use of pike and musket tactics must have strained the abilities of officers and men to the very limits. In the heat of battle "when the roaring of cannon, the clashing of armes [sic], the neighing of horses, and other confused noises causeth, that neither captain nor other officer can be heard. . ." commands, such as "half-files double your front inward intire!" or "left flank, double your right flank by division!" could have produced only utter bewilderment and chaos among the vast majority of troops.[17]

The formations suggested by some writers reached the point of absurdity. Lostelneau, writing in 1647, dismissed the square and the octagon as commonplace. Instead, he offered intricate combinations of large and small squares, rectangles, triangles, and double files, arranged into gigantic formations of several thousand men, two of which are shown in Figures 9 and 10. Figure 9 is a diagram of a defensive formation of pikes and muskets. The shaded dots represent 2,304 pikes, the others represent 2,048 muskets. A double row of muskets surrounds the figure, while the muskets in the center are presumably held in reserve. Figure 10 is a diagram of a fanciful formation for 2,532 muskets and 1,600 pikes, the latter indicated

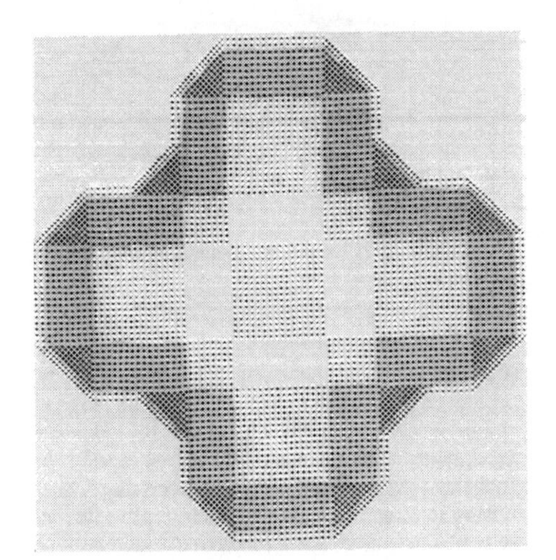

Figures 9 and 10.—Diagram for defensive formation of pikes (shaded dots) and muskets.

by the shaded dots. To form the figure the soldiers would have to be trained to march in files either ten or five deep. The normal depth of files, according to Lostelneau, was either eight or six men. Thus, to form this figure normal marching order would first have to be revised. Although these figures have a certain artistic charm, their military value must have been small. Not only were they complex and inflexible, but most of the muskets were tucked away in the center where their firepower was wasted. Certainly the average musketeer, if faced with a cavalry charge after he had spent his shot, could not have been expected to await calmly the command of a drum to signal which of several ornate figures he should form. The individualistic, unruly mercenary of the mid-17th century would have hastened to save his own skin by retreating behind the screen of pikes in as direct and rapid a manner as possible. Barriffe knew that in practice, when the musketeers were "forced to retire," there was inevitably "a great confusion and hindering those that are behind them." [18] One can imagine the disaster which would have ensued if someone had attempted to use Lostelneau's complicated figures in the heat of battle.

## FROM PIKE TO BAYONET

During the 17th century the ratio of shot to pike continued to grow. In the French army, for example, the standard was two muskets to one pike in 1651, three to one in 1677, and four to one in 1688.[19] To increase the mobility of the pikemen their armor was lightened. Thus the battalion, which had once been a solid block of pikes with musketeers gathered on its flanks, became a line of musketeers who scurried to the shelter of an ever-diminishing number of pikes when threatened with a charge. The pikemen were having a more and more difficult time serving their defensive role. The contemporary observer Jacques de Puységur complained that generally the pikes could protect only the center of the battalion and not the outer flanks. And if the flanks fell to a charge the pikes were of little use.[20] In spite of ever more complex formations then, the pikemen were often unable to fulfill their function.

Certain military men were experimenting to find some replacement for the pike so that all of the soldiers could be armed with firearms. In the mid-17th century small bands of elite troops discontinued the use of the pike and were provided with arrangements of portable stakes to be set up or driven into the ground in front of the musketeers to protect them from cavalry charges. An English manuscript of 1649 specified that dragoons should carry matchlock muskets and, in their belts, two "swyn-feathers or foot pallisados" about four feet in length.[21] Some of these stakes may also have served as musket rests. Others looked very much like a picket fence when assembled.[22]

Another defensive contraption was the *chevaux de frise* (Figure 11), first used by the armies fighting the Turks in eastern Europe. It was made of a wooden beam (B), ten to twelve feet long, which was drilled to receive a large number of small pikes

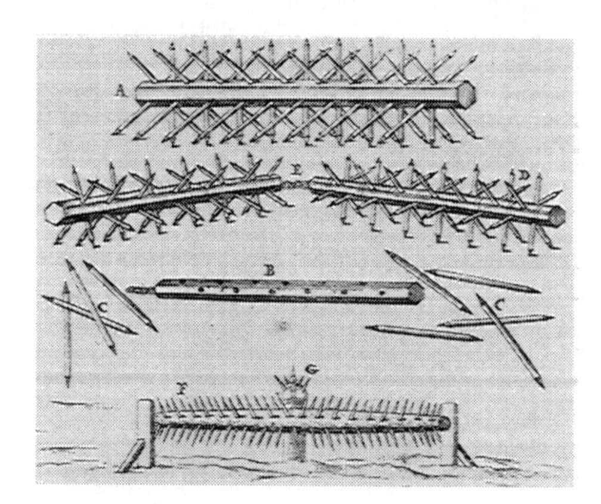


Figure 11.—The *chevaux de frise.*

(C) about half as long. In one variation it was placed on a pivot to block a gateway (F, G). The component parts could be carried into battle by musketeers and assembled when the need arose. But the instrument must have been far too unwieldy to have been useful in field battles. Instead, it seems to have been employed extensively for guarding camps, blocking roads, or protecting breaches in fortifications.[23]

These developments were eventually to be

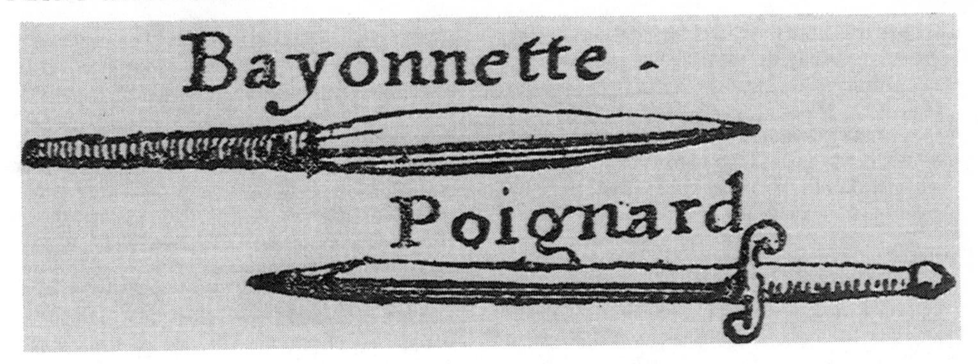


Figure 12.—A drawing of the plug bayonet.

superseded by the bayonet. Species of bayonets appear early in military literature. In 1625 a pamphlet was published in England recommending that English archers have half-pikes attached to their bows, much in the manner of a modern bayonet.[24] A decade later the converse suggestion was made, that pikemen ought to have bows attached to their pikes to give them some firepower. Within the next few years attempts were made to use the musket rest as a defense by unscrewing its head and sticking it into the muzzle of the musket. "But this was so tedious and troublesome that it fell without profit." The musketeers found that the weapons "proved extreme troublesome to themselves, dangerous to their fellows, and of no validity against the enemy." [25] William Barriffe, however, claimed to have "found out a way, to use the Half-pike and Musquet, with so much facility and ease, that it is farre lesse troublesome then the rest: and yet of a greater length then any of the former [musket] Rests, or Half-pikes; as being compleat ten foot in length, with the arming." His invention could be used as a rest, as a pallisado against horses, or as a half-pike in hand-to-hand fighting. Apparently the weapon could be used either independently of the musket or attached to it, but Barriffe provides no illustrations with his proposal. Armed with the new weapon, he wrote, the English musketeers would have a substantial advantage over their foes. After having "poured out a great volly or showre of Lead on the adverse Musquettiers; they may then nimbly with their Half-pikes, fall in amon[g] them." Also, if the musketeer found his firepower reduced by insufficient or poor quality shot or powder of if "haile, snow, or raine" rendered the "fiery weapon of no use," then the half-pike would be particularly important. Gustavus Adolphus' troops, he argued, with their flexible formations and relatively high degree of training, could have used the half-pike musket combination to great advantage. A number of gentlemen in England, some of whom brought back ideas from the Thirty Years War in Germany, were experimenting with the half-pike and musket at the time, but apparently their efforts were without practical consequences.[26]

The first real bayonet (Figure 12) was known as the plug bayonet because its handle was a tapered plug to be inserted into the muzzle of the musket. A small plug bayonet was a regular part of a hunter's equipment during the 17th century; two early hunting bayonets are in the collection of the Tower of London. Such hunting weapons must have been popular in France as well, because Louis XIV mentions in a proclamation of 1660 that accidents with them were common.[27]

Plug bayonets may have been used by British troops as early as 1633, but the documentation is imprecise.[28] Puységur mentions in his memoirs that he first observed soldiers using plug bayonets in 1647. He described them as "having blades one foot long" and "handles just as long as the blades, the ends of which were the right size to put into the barrel of the fusils." [29] His description of the bayonet is basically the same as that published by Gaya with his plate (Figure 12) in 1673. He describes it as having a blade about a foot long, with a wooden handle about eight or nine inches long tapered to fit into the muzzle of the fusil.

Gabriel Daniel wrote in 1724 that the first regular military use of the plug bayonet in France was by a regiment of fusiliers raised in 1671.[30] By that time bodies of elite troops—grenadiers, fusiliers, and dragoons—were beginning to be equipped with plug bayonets in several countries. These men were used for special guard and raiding duty rather than field battle. They were rarely accompanied by pikes on such duty and therefore needed the extra protection of the plug bayonet. Figure 13, which is an unsual drawing of an octagonal formation lacking pikemen, may show such a guard detatchment. In an order of April 1672, Charles II of England provided for a regiment of special dragoons whose arms were a musket and a "bayonett or greate knife." [31] Puységur reported the arming of a French grenadier company with fusils and plug bayonets in 1678; the Seventh Royal Fusiliers, among the first troops in Britain to use the bayonet regularly, were established in 1685.[32]

Figure 13.—An octagonal formation without pikes which may represent an elite guard armed with fusils and bayonets.

Some military men wanted to use the bayonet in field battle as well as on guard duty and in raiding parties. Sir James Turner's thoughts of 1670–1671 are perhaps indicative of the ideas of many of his contemporaries:

> When musketeers have spent their powder and come to blows, the butt-end of their musket may do an enemy more hurt than those despicable swords which most musketeers wear at their sides. In such medleys knives whose blades are one foot long made for both cutting and thrusting (the haft being made to fill the bore of the musket), will do more execution than either sword or butt of musket.[33]

The plug bayonet was not a very handy weapon. To insert or withdraw it, the soldier had to grasp it at or near the blade; if it fit the muzzle poorly, it was likely either to fall out easily or to become so badly stuck that it could hardly be removed. While the bayonet was fixed, the musket ceased to be a firearm. Because the musket was so heavy (between twelve and twenty pounds) fighting with the bayonet was cumbersome. Still, it was an improvement over the swordplay which Lostelneau and his contemporaries must have expected from their musketeers. And even if the musketeers were entirely routed, at least they would be encouraged not to discard their muskets.

The drawbacks of the plug bayonet for men in the field were soon realized, and attempts were made to develop reliable methods of attaching the bayonet beneath the barrel of the gun so that it could be loaded and fired with the bayonet in place. Bayonets equipped with two rings to secure them to the barrel were reported by Puységur about 1678. The British general Hugh Mackay claims to have invented the method while fighting the Scots in 1689. A third-hand report from a contemporary of Queen Anne (1702–1714) claimed that her horse grenadiers used ring bayonets, and as late as 1737 an English glossary defined the bayonet as a blade attached to the gun barrel by rings.[34]

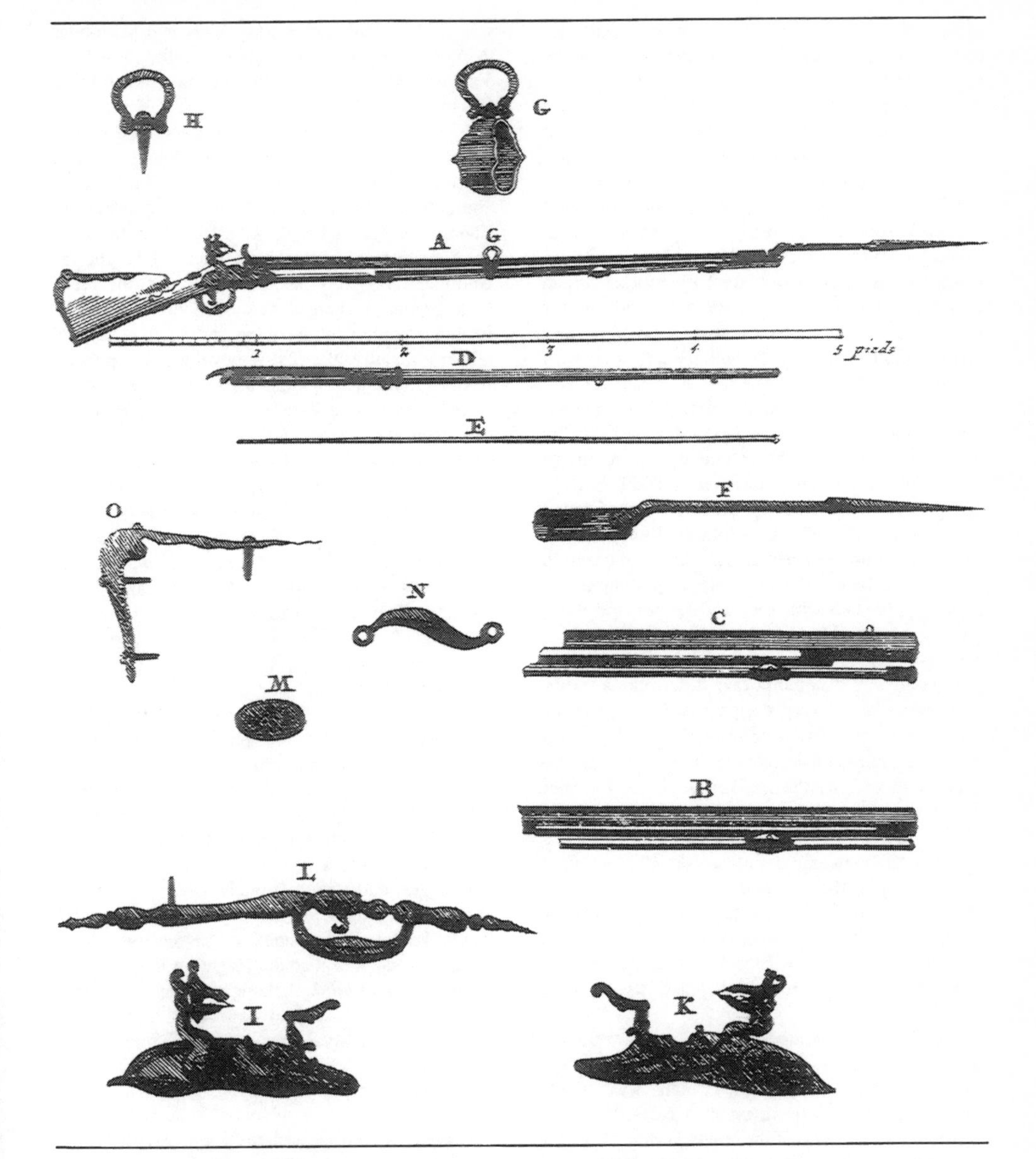


Figure 14.—The parts of a fusil and the socket bayonet. The fusil with its flintlock firing mechanism is drawn to the scale shown (in feet). The bayonet (F), the flintlock (I,K), the rings for holding the sling (G,H), and the other elements of the figure are not to scale. The muzzle of an ordinary fusil is shown in B, and a muzzle modified to receive the socket bayonet in C.

Authorities differ concerning who should receive credit for inventing the modern form of the bayonet, i.e., having it attached to the barrel by a sleeve or socket which passes over the muzzle and locks securely onto it. Quite likely a number of men were working on it independently. One military history gave credit to a certain Martinet, a *maréschal de camp,* who is said to have invented a socket bayonet in 1681 and perfected it in 1692.[35] A 19th-century catalogue of arms notes a wheel-lock musket of the late 16th century which was fitted with a socket bayonet. The author treated it as an anachronism, however, and credited Couhorn, a Dutch military engineer, with the invention around 1680.[36]

Sébastien de Vauban, the designer of French fortifications, probably has as good a claim to the invention as anyone. He first mentioned a sort of socket (or perhaps ring) bayonet in 1669, but did not perfect it immediately. In 1687 he informed the royal minister of war that he had developed a socket bayonet and asked that a demonstration be arranged before the king. He even went so far as to suggest that with the new weapon the army might dispense with pikemen entirely.[37]

The demonstration took place in 1688, but it did not go well. Contemporary descriptions testify that the bayonets were designed with a sleeve or socket to fit over the muzzle of the musket, with the blade slightly offset from the barrel so that one could load and fire the musket while the bayonet was in place. But the new weapons worked badly. The muzzles of the muskets varied so much in size that the bayonets could not be forced onto some of them, while they slipped off others as soon as they were used. Sometimes the musket ball struck the blade. Louis was displeased with the exhibition, and plans to rearm the French armies with socket bayonets were abandoned, at least for the time being.[38]

But Vauban continued to work on developing a reliable socket for the bayonet and is generally credited with the bayonet which was finally adopted in France. In an undated work, probably written during the 1690s Vauban described the bayonet as having a fifteen-inch blade with a socket five inches long, formed with a slot to insure a firm fit; the diameter of the socket could thus be adjusted to fit the muzzle of the particular firearm. When the bayonet was in place, the fusil-bayonet was six feet nine inches long. This is a bit longer than the one shown in Figure 14, but otherwise Vauban's description fits the bayonet shown there and in Figure 15.[39]

Figure 14 shows the fusil with a socket bayonet. The button on top of the barrel appears to be a locking device for the bayonet rather than a sight. Some fusils, however, like the one pictured in Figure 20, had sights. Figure 15 shows the fusilier's equipment, front and back. Though the equipment was still called a bandoleer, the tubes with prepared charges had been given up. The fusilier's equipment included the socket bayonet (E) in a sheath (D), priming powder (F), a powder flask (K), and a pouch (H) for shot and cartridges.

In spite of the developments in bayonets, pikes remained. The proportion of pikes to shot in European armies had been falling more or less steadily for almost two hundred years, but complete abolition of the pike was viewed as a drastic step which the military leadership was hesitant to take. The transition to the bayonet was made in the late 1680s by the Imperial and Prussian armies, a decade later by the English, and in 1703 by the French.[40] Part of the reason for the delay, particularly in the case of France, was a general conservatism on the part of the leadership. Military leaders are often loath to give up the arms which have won them glory on past fields of battle.[41] Barriffe, for example, was certain that his suggestions for the half-pike musket combination would be unjustly rejected by narrow minds.[42]

There was a great tradition of the pike as "la reine des armes à pied." Pikemen were usually the biggest and strongest of the troops. There was a feeling among some military men that anybody could be taught to shoot a musket, but that a pikeman was a real soldier, fighting hand to hand with pike and sword. Perhaps because the pikeman wore armor he seemed to retain some of the tradition of medieval chivalry. In 1677 an Englishman, the Earl of Orrery, expressed this almost nostalgic feeling very well.

> Our foot soldiers generally are two third Shot, and one third Pikes, which I have often lamented; for methinks the Pikes should be at least half . . . and without dispute, the Pike is the usefullest Weapon for the Foot. . . . The Swissers, generally, and justly esteemed ex-

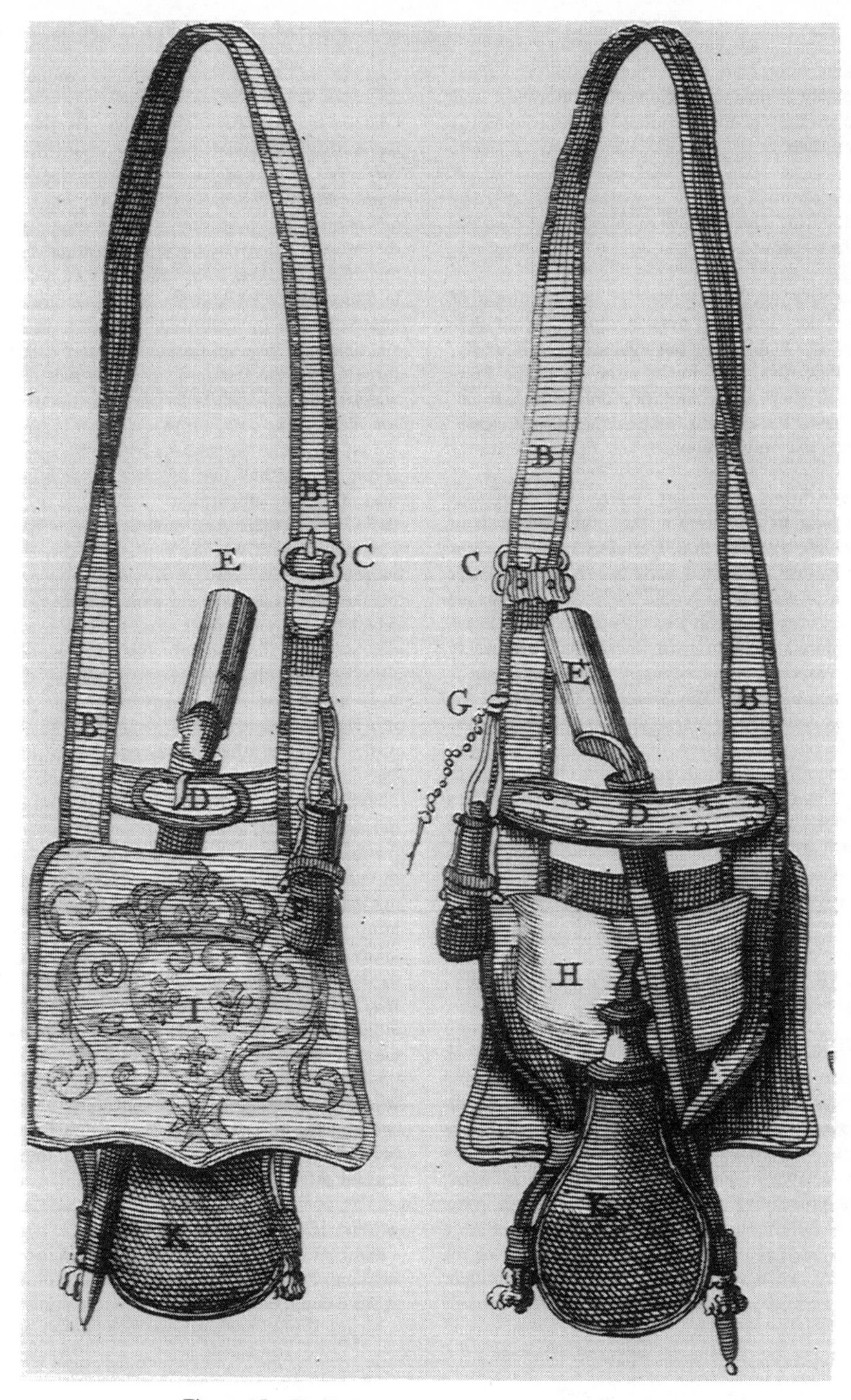


Figure 15.—Fusilier's equipment shown front and back.

> cellent Foot, have more Pikes than Shot; which, possibly as much as their Valor, Discipline, and the strength of their Bodies, has contributed to their Glory.

After recounting a battle in which he had participated, during which a push of pikes had carried the day, he continued:

> But what need I say more of the usefulness of the Pike above the musket, than that all Persons of Quality who put themselves voluntarily, or otherwise, into the Infantry, carry the Pike; which they would not do, unless it had adjudgedly the Honour to be the Noblest Weapon, since the bravest choose, and fight with it.[43]

Nevertheless, one must realize that there was something to be said for the pikeman, at least in his defensive function. Certainly a line of 17th-century fusiliers armed with bayonets, no matter how well disciplined, could not hold out against a direct charge of heavy cavalry as well as a block of armored pikemen with their fifteen to twenty foot weapons. And—perhaps more important—the firearms of that day were not far enough advanced to stop, or even materially reduce, the weight of a full charge through sheer firepower. Vauban, who was a hardy foe of the pike, admitted that until firepower was increased the pikes probably would continue to have a place in the French army.[44] More than a generation after pikes had disappeared from European battlefields some theorists steadfastly maintained that they should be re-introduced.[45]

## FROM MATCHLOCK MUSKET TO FLINTLOCK FUSIL

Throughout the 17th century the matchlock musket was slowly developing in efficiency, and thus providing enough firepower that the commanders wished to have more muskets and fewer pikes. After 1650 the awkward rest was generally done away with, and improvements in loading and firing procedures had increased the speed of firing. Good information on just how often a musket could be fired is lacking. At the beginning of the century, when as many as 100 separate motions were necessary to load and fire, muskets probably could be shot once every three to ten minutes. Barriffe (1643) had some sixty musket postures, and Lostelneau (1647) had thirty-five. By the end of the century a trained musketeer could fire about twice as fast as had his predecessor one hundred years earlier.[46] Vauban's calculation was one shot per minute, but it is likely that his figure was for the more efficient flintlock fusil rather than the matchlock musket.[47] Arrangements of musketeers in files six deep by Maurice of Nassau and Gustavus Adolphus indicate that loading took roughly six times as long as firing. A century later files three deep were standard, implying that the firing was twice as efficient.[48] Reports of effective range for the musket vary. Smythe (1590) claimed 200 yards; Gaya (1678) claimed 240 to 300 yards, but recommended half that distance for real effectiveness. Thus the admonition "don't shoot till you see the whites of their eyes" makes some sense.[49] The common musket was smoothbore and notoriously inaccurate. Only occasionally did elite troops carry muskets with rifled barrels, called "fowling pieces," which gave any real accuracy. In battle musketeers depended on the bulk of volley firing and cared little for individual aim.[50]

If one adds to these disadvantages the problems inherent in the matchlock, one can see why the 17th-century musketeer wished to hide behind a barrier of pikes whenever he was faced with the charging enemy. The match was difficult to keep burning; one had to blow on it several times during the loading procedure to keep it aglow. In the rain the problem was multiplied, and even if the burning match could be kept dry, the spare match that hung at the musketeer's belt would almost certainly be spoiled. Burning matches, giving odor by day and light by night, rendered surprise attack nearly impossible. Grimmelshausen's character Simplicissimus (1669) claimed that he could produce a match which would not give away the position of musketeers by smell and would burn when wet. He also claimed he had contrived "a special art to provide that no bullet may hit thee." [51] It is difficult to tell which of these feats was the more fantastic.

The constantly burning match was very dangerous. If, during drill or loading, a musketeer should let his match touch his powder or that of his comrades, there was usually only one result. A wind could blow a hot ash into some powder and create an equal disaster. The match had to be held in his hand (Figure 3) and was lighted at both ends; when the gun was to be fired it had to be attached to the serpentine clip (Figures 4 and 19) and then removed from it again after firing. Thus the match required his constant attention. The matchlock was entirely unsuited to use on horseback; it was all a musketeer could do to fire and reload while on solid ground. A detailed photograph of a matchlock is shown in Figure 16.

Nearly a century after the more efficient flintlock fusil had replaced the matchlock musket, some men still suggested that the old English longbow be substituted for the more modern weapon. In 1776 Benjamin Franklin recommended the longbow for American troops and gave the following reasons for favoring it: 1) the bow was as accurate as a common fusil; 2) the bow fired four arrows while the fusil fired only one ball; 3) the fusil gave out smoke which impaired vision; 4) the arrow was as lethal, and perhaps more often disabling than the ball; 5) bows were easier and cheaper to manufacture. The range of a musket or fusil and of a bow in the hands of a skilled archer were judged to be about the same.[52] Unfortunately there was no army of skilled bowmen to try their weapons against the fusiliers of the 18th century.

The first alternative to the matchlock was the wheel lock, shown in Figure 17. In use as early as 1517,[53] the wheel lock was a complex and delicate mechanism in which a wound spring spun a serrated steel wheel which came in contact with a chip of pyrites, giving a spark which set off the charge. Wheel locks were used for cavalry pistols and for many hunting arms, but they were too expensive and too easily broken for use by the common soldier.

Early flintlocks were generally known as snaphances; some of the first models probably used the pyrites of the wheel lock, snapping it against a steel plate, or battery, for spark. Exact dating is difficult, but snaphances were probably first made around the end of the 16th century. The stronger flint and the stiffer springs necessary for its use were added by the 1640s. Also the steel plate, or battery, was attached to the pan cover, so that the pan would be instantly and automatically uncovered when the flint struck the steel.[54] Figure 18 gives a detailed view of a late 17th-century snaphance lock. The mechanism can be understood by studying Figure 19 which shows the "Vauban lock," a combination of the flintlock and the matchlock. The weapon was called either a "fusil-musket" or "musket-fusil." The soldier could use either lock, depending on his preference, or the circumstances. To fire the matchlock the burning match was attached to the serpentine (M); the pan (K), which had to be kept covered to protect the priming powder, was exposed by sliding back a cover (I) allowing the serpentine and match to be lowered into the touch-hole (H) via the lever beneath the gun stock (which resembled a trigger guard). To fire the flintlock the soldier only had to cock the tightly sprung hammer (C) containing the flint (F) and release it with the trigger. As it sprang forward it struck the steel of the battery (G) creating sparks and knocking the battery forward (as shown in the diagram) to expose the pan, so that the sparks might ignite the priming powder. The flintlock was thus much more rapid and efficient than the matchlock, when it was working correctly, but many claimed the matchlock was more dependable.

The early flintlocks were not as reliable as the matchlock. When the burning match touched the flash powder in the pan, the musket was almost certain to fire. But the flint did not always strike enough sparks to ignite the powder in the pan. It tended to wear out quickly, sometimes after as few as ten shots, and, at times, the spring in the lock worked poorly. Thus, for a sustained fire the matchlock was judged superior. Though the matchlock long maintained its place in the rank and file of European armies, flintlocks were soon put into use by various elite troops. General Monck, writing in the 1640s, recommended that horsemen carry flintlock weapons, because so armed "... upon any Service in the night they may go undiscovered." Puységur wrote that he saw fusils in use in France in 1647, and elite troops there came to make regular use of them by 1670. A regiment of fusiliers was created in 1671 which was the favorite of Vauban, as it used neither pike nor musket. He complained, however, that it was never allowed to fight on its own, but was used only to guard artillery. The troops which were equipped with fusils during this period were usually also provided with plug bayonets.[55]

Louis XIV and his conservative generals had some difficulty in keeping the fusil from becoming

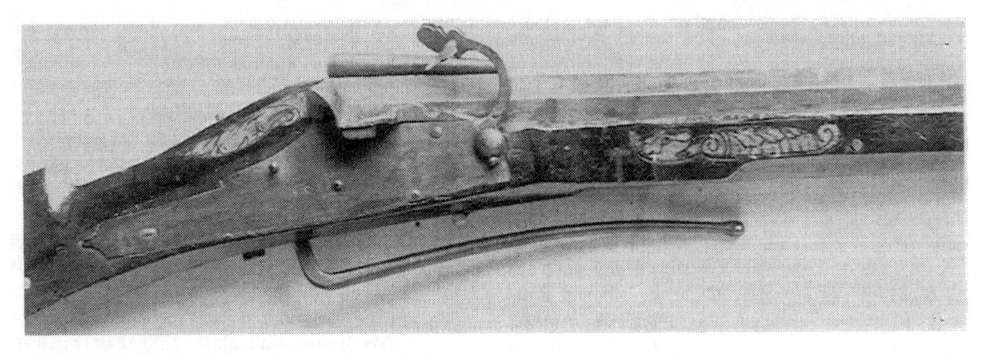

Figure 16

Figure 17

too popular. An ordinance of 1665 ordered that no regular soldier be allowed to use the fusil; only the pike and musket were approved weapons. The next year Louis' minister Louvois wrote to a subordinate:

> The king forbids, no matter what the circumstances, that soldiers be paid who are not armed either with the musket or the pike; that is to say that the intention of His Majesty is to entirely abolish the usage of fusils.

Evidently the orders were not entirely effective; the following is from an ordinance of 1670:

> As for the manner in which soldiers must be armed, although His Majesty, through divers regulations and ordinances, has ordered that there shall be always in each company one third pikes and that no one shall be armed with the fusil; nevertheless there are hardly any pikes in the company and most of the soldiers take it upon themselves to choose to carry fusils.

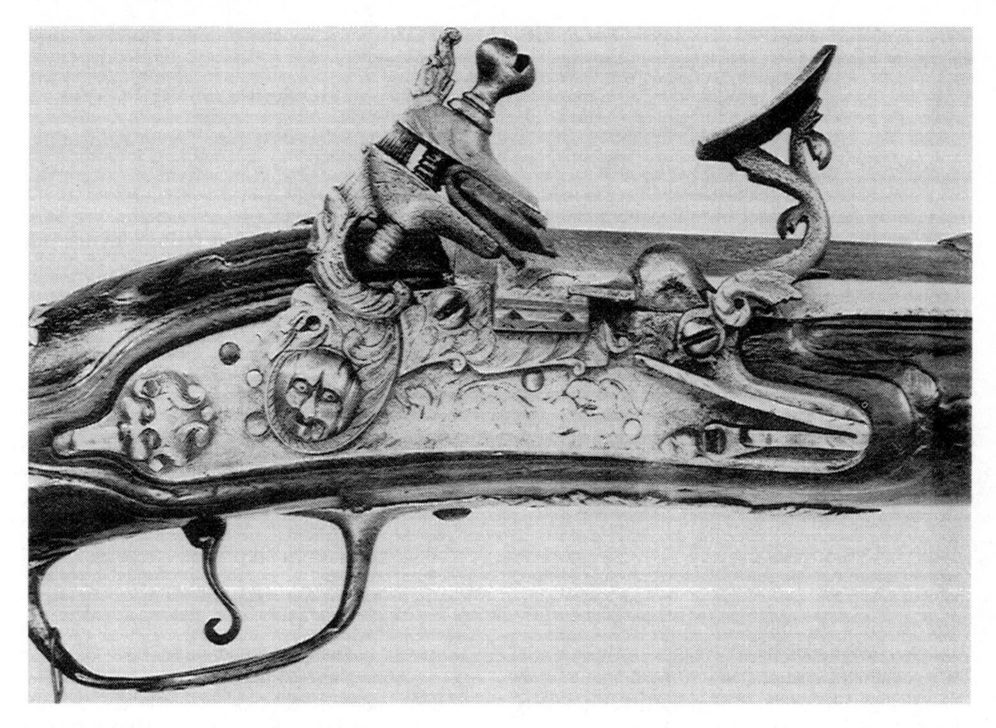

Figure 18.—Detail of a snaphance lock.

The ordinance yielded a bit to popular pressure and allowed four picked men out of each company of sixty to carry fusils, as long as they were of the same size and caliber as the muskets in use. The order was renewed in 1675.[56]

The controversy between the proponents of the musket and those of the fusil was spirited. Even the partisans of the fusil admitted that the musket had some few advantages. For example, Puységur noted that the fusil might misfire after several shots, whereas a matchlock could continue to fire for some time. Daniel added that the musket was often larger and more powerful than the fusil. But both Puységur and Daniel agreed that on balance the fusil was the better weapon. It was about twice as fast to load, and reliable enough so that the encumbrance of the match could be eliminated.[57]

Perhaps the most outspoken advocate of the fusil was Vauban. Writing in 1687 he listed five arguments "of a thousand" which he had against the musket. He gave only two which have not yet been mentioned. First, the use of a match made night loading very difficult. Second, the musket was shot from the breast, from right below the chin, while the fusil was designed to be shot from the shoulder; thus more accuracy could be obtained. Fusils often had sights for aiming, while muskets had not; see Figure 20.[58] Vauban's point is particularly significant; it illustrates that some of the advantages of the fusil were not inherent in the use of the flintlock, but rather were general improvements in firearms which could have been applied to either a flint or a match lock. Similarly, the fusil was often lighter in weight, was usually fitted with a sling for carrying, and was designed for use with the socket bayonet.

Figures 4 and 20 illustrate the position from

which a musket was fired. The musketeer in Figure 20 is equipped in basically the same way as was Lostelneau's thirty years earlier, except that he has no musket rest. He braces the musket butt against his chest just below his chin, and points it in the general direction of the enemy. The fusil, on the other hand, was held against the shoulder as are modern firearms, and was often equipped with front and rear sights, as shown on the fusil at the bottom of the figure. Two balls linked with a small bit of iron were sometimes fired by musketeers to increase their effectiveness.

Vauban made an attempt to please both sides in the match vs. flint dispute. About 1688 he designed a lock (Figure 19), which could be used with either match or flint. Other combination locks were used earlier in both the Empire and in England, but the device came to be known, nevertheless, as the "Vauban lock." [59] With such a lock a soldier could take his choice of flint or match, perhaps using the flint when on a surprise attack or in bad weather and the more dependable match when long periods of sustained fire were desired. It was soon seen, however, that the flintlock was generally superior and the combination lock became a rarity. Imperial troops shifted to general use of the flintlock about 1689, England about a year later, and France finally followed in 1699.[60]

Two other important innovations were the paper cartridge and the iron ramrod. The iron ramrod, replacing the more fragile wooden one, was introduced by the Prussians in the early 18th century. The paper cartridge was being developed throughout the 17th century. Instead of cartridges, most musketeers had used the bandoleer (Figures 3, 4, and 20). Paper cartridges of one kind or another had been known for some time; they had been used in the cavalry as early as the late 16th century. General Monck mentioned cartridges in the 1640s, but did not recommend them over bandoleers. Orrery, who looked back to the days of the pike, also looked forward to those of cartridges, strongly recommending their use in 1677. The Prussian infantry began using them in 1670. Cartridges were tried in 1677 in France, but were given up in favor of the bandoleer. The final move to cartridges in France was apparently made about 1690. In 1702 a French author, Saint Remy, showed the equipment of the fusilier (Figure 15), with a pouch for cartridges rather than with the prepared charges in tubes tied to the bandoleer.[61]

In the better organized, better equipped, and better trained armies of the 18th century the flintlock fusil found its place. With its many improvements it was a more sophisticated weapon than the matchlock musket and demanded high standards of technology and discipline to be effective. The highly trained fusiliers of the 18th century were able to fire between two and three shots per minute; their weapon was so satisfactory that it was to remain in use by Europeans in basically the same form until the 1840s.[62]

## THE FORCES OF CHANGE

Sometimes the historian finds a decisive day and hour when a technological advance revolutionizes the art of war and changes the direction of mankind. How glorious it would be to read accounts of a great battle in which the disciplined regulars of Frederick the Great met the feudal-mercenary army of Henry of Navarre, or even the semi-modern Swedes of Gustavus Adolphus. In an afternoon the valiant pike and musket would see its doom before the disciplined fire of the fusil. Such a battle never took place. Nevertheless, by looking at examples from several battles, we can see the forces at work which caused the new weapons, created by engineers and craftsmen, to be generally adopted.

In one case, at least, battlefield necessity was directly the mother of invention. In 1689 General Hugh Mackay was commanding British regulars, armed with muskets and plug bayonets, in a campaign against the Scottish Jacobites; the decisive battle was fought at Killiecrankie. Mackay's men were drawn up in close order when the Scots prepared to attack. The Highlanders discharged their firearms at the British line with little effect. Then they charged, screaming Gaelic oaths and swinging their great broadswords, breaking the British line and winning the day. Mackay tells of the battle and his subsequent invention in his memoirs:

> All our officers and souldiers were strangers to the Highlanders' way of fighting and embattailling, which mainly occasioned the consternation many of them were in; which, to remedy

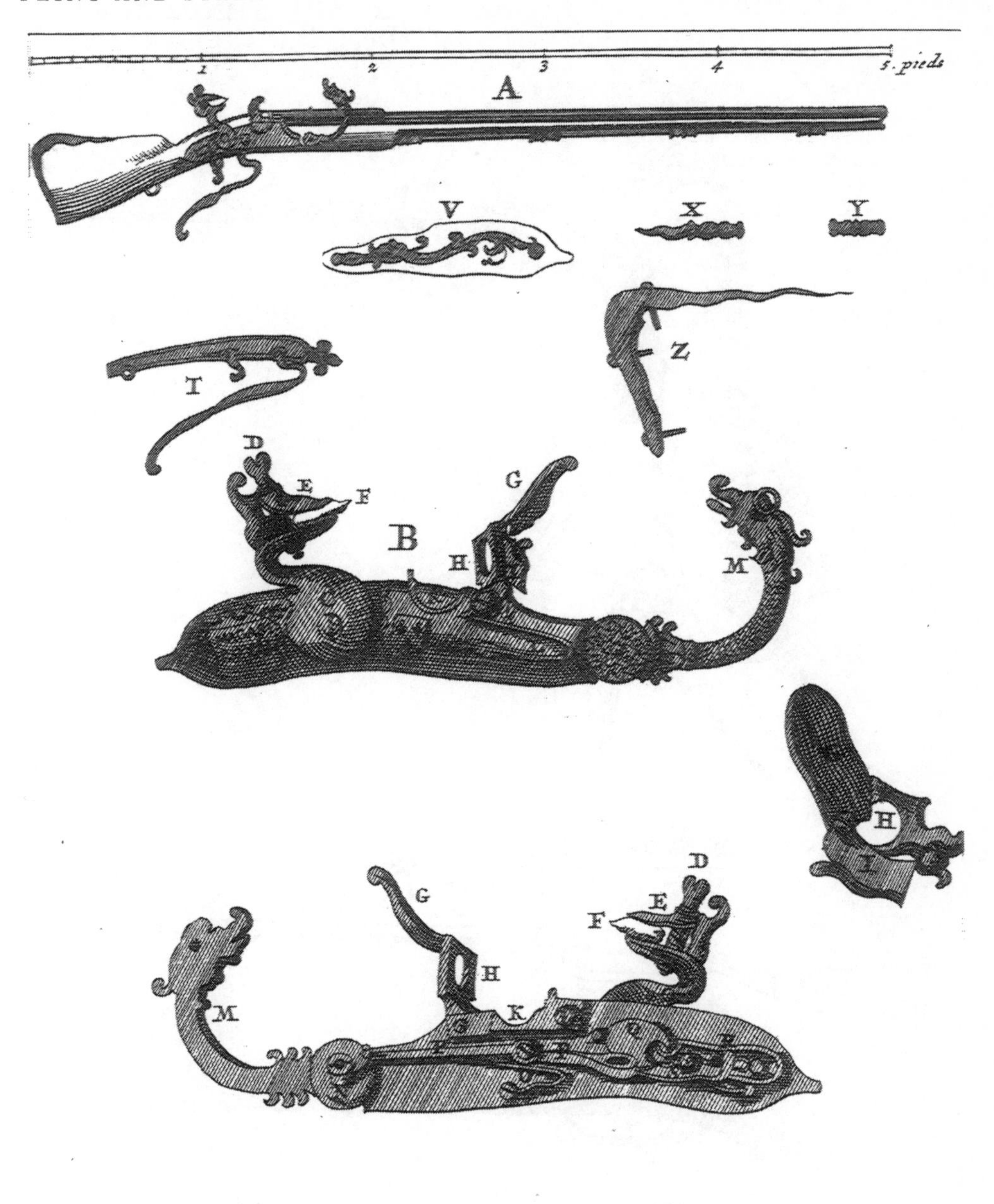


Figure 19.—The Vauban lock.

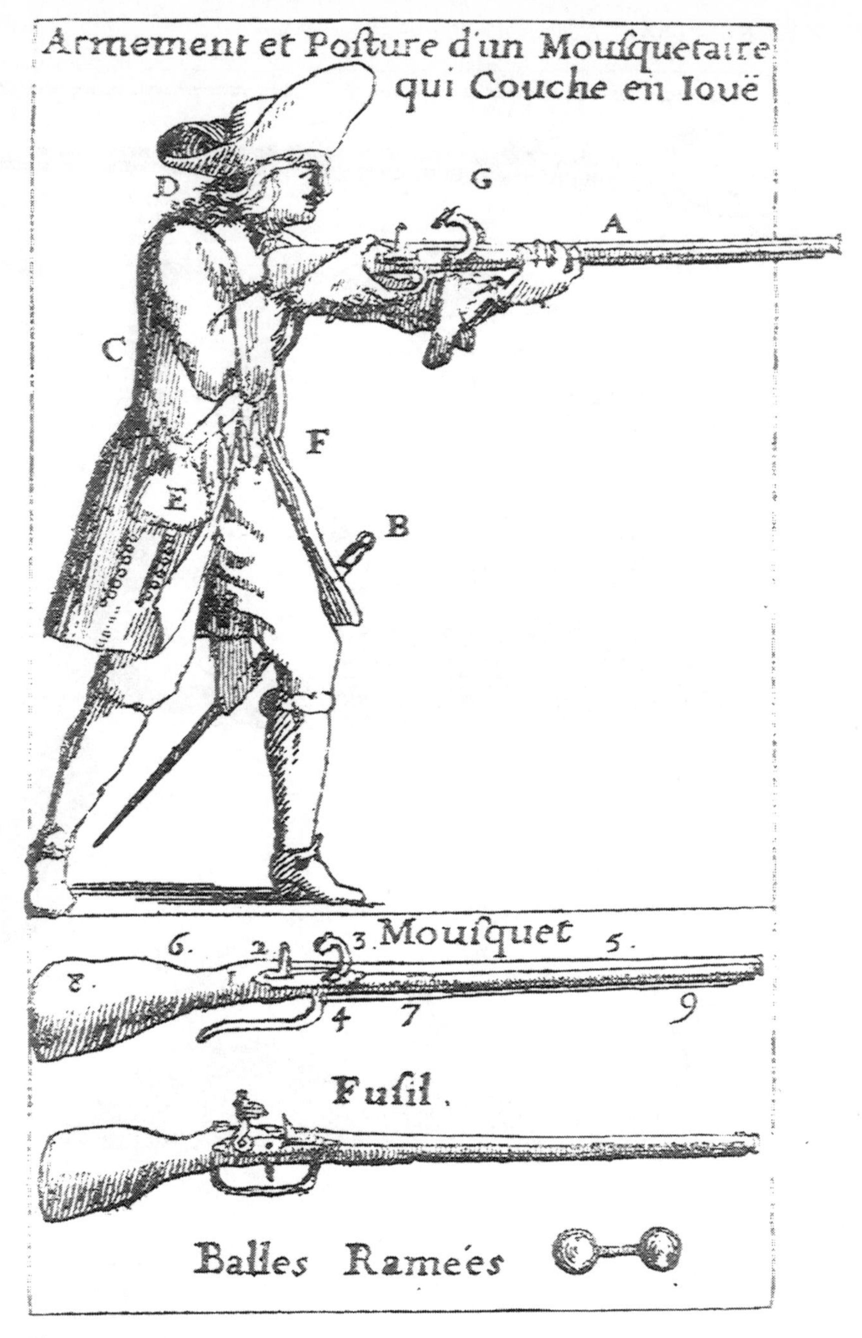


Figure 20.—A musketeer firing, and a comparison between the musket and the fusil.

> for the ensuing year, having taken notice on this occasion that the Highlanders are of such a quick motion that if a battalion keep up his fire till they be near to make sure of them, they are on it before our men can come to their second defense, which is the bayonet in the musle of the musket: I say, the general having observed this method of the enemy, he invented the way to fasten the bayonet so to the musle without, by two rings, that the soldiers may safely keep their fire till they pour it into their breasts, and then have no other motion to make but to push as with a pick.[63]

Mackay had served in the low countries from the mid-1670s to 1685, so perhaps he picked up his ideas for the ring bayonet there. In any event his story is an excellent illustration of the development of weapons by men in the field who knew just what they needed for effective fighting.

But the men in the field needed intelligent leadership to provide the necessary weapons for them. In the case of France, as has been demonstrated, the royal court was not anxious to see the new weapons adopted. It was the course of battle which overcame this resistance. Two battles which forced technological change upon the French army occurred in the 1690s. In 1692 the French general in the Netherlands, the Duke de Luxembourg, was not anxious for battle, but his opponent, William of Orange, recently made King of England, needed a victory for political purposes. Tricking Luxembourg through false intelligence, William launched a surprise attack on the French near Steenkerke in August 1692. The terrain was such that cavalry could not be used during the major portion of the battle. The superior firepower of the fusils with which most of William's men were armed, the fact that nearly all his men used firearms—pikes having been replaced by *chevaux de frise*—plus the factor of surprise, almost carried the day for the Anglo-Dutch army. Contemporary accounts speak of "un feu terrible" and the French losses were heavy. The day was saved, however, by a French charge "epée à la main", and the Anglo-Dutch fusiliers were forced to retreat before the French pikes and swords.[64]

One might suppose that the French victory—the defeat of fusil by sword and pike—would have solidified the opposition to the new weapons. But this was not the case. The French leadership realized that the opposing army had superior firepower and that only a slight hesitation in the Anglo-Dutch attack coupled with an extraordinary display of French valor had turned defeat into victory.

Luxembourg sent his son, the Count de Luxe, personally to report to Louis XIV on the battle. Louis replied immediately to Luxembourg as follows:

> The Count de Luxe talked to me a long time regarding muskets and fusils for my troops, and he assured me that the fire was sustained only by the fusiliers, and that the new soldiers were not able to handle their muskets. The great fire of the enemies must be attributed to their large proportion of fusils over muskets.[65]

Jean de Beaurain, in his contemporary military history, reported the lesson learned by the French at Steenkerke.

> The advantage which the enemies had had at the beginning of the action was attributed to the great number of fusils which they had, with which nearly all the foreign troops, especially the English, were armed. The troops of the king [of France] still were using muskets, which rendered the fire of the Allies so much superior to that of the French infantry. Such à test should have established in that campaign the time of the suppression of the musket; and actually the king planned to do so. Because of the account which M. de Luxembourg sent to His Majesty of that action, the king proposed the arming of all his infantry with fusils and with pikes. He wrote about the plan to the generals of his armies, and charged them to consult with their most competent officers about it, in order that he might resolve with them the question of what would be most useful to his services. But the difficulty of furnishing fusils during the winter to two thirds of the infantry, and an old prejudice for the musket, which appeared more useful for creating sustained fire, served to change the plans, so that only one third of each company would receive fusils, the rest being armed with muskets and pikes.[66]

The following year, 1693, at Neerwinden another battle took place in which Anglo-Dutch firepower showed its strength. This time the Allied fire forced back a charge of French heavy cavalry, quite an achievement, since it meant that the fusilier now had enough power of his own to hold off horsemen. Once again, however, a French infantry charge won the day. Luxembourg sent four battalions of infantry with muskets and bayonets on the Anglo-Dutch flank, while sending a Swiss pike push on their front line.[67]

In both of the battles, nevertheless, the power of the fusil was amply demonstrated. Though infantry shock tactics won the day in each case those victories were hardly more meaningful for the development of 18th-century warfare than was the victory of the claymore-swinging Highlanders at Killiekrankie. This is not to say that shock tactics were to be entirely abandoned. Indeed an entire French school of military tactics developed which put the major emphasis on infantry shock and on a formation in depth (*ordre profond*) to strengthen the shock. But such tactics were not to dominate the 18th century, even in France.[68] Firepower had come into its own; in 1699 fusils finally completely replaced muskets.

The days of the French pikeman were numbered. The use of firearms acting alone, without the cover of pikemen, was not a completely new concept in the 1680s and 1690s. Small groups of elite troops, operating in difficult country or attacking outposts, etc., had traditionally operated without pikes; such were the troops who had been among the first to be issued fusils and plug bayonets throughout the 1670s. Troops fighting in mountain regions, like those under Nicolas de Catinat in the Alps and under the Duke de Vendôme in Italy, gave up the pike almost entirely before the official orders were given to do away with it. By 1701 those French regiments which had retained pikes had at least four fusiliers for every pikeman. During the winter of 1703–1704 pikes were finally eliminated. The French army was in modern equipent, and ready to face the new century unencumbered with semi-feudal and Renaissance weapons.[69]

Some problems remained. During the War of the Spanish Succession officers trained in classic pike and musket tactics still used some of the traditional formations and movements. Intervals between men and between groups of men were rarely regular and ease of maneuver suffered accordingly. Armies did not yet march in cadenced step.[70]

But there was a great difference in basic tactics. The change had been made which freed armies from the complex wheelings and countermarches made necessary by the division of offensive and defensive weapons between two bodies of troops. Now each man carried a reliable firearm and an adequate arm of steel for either producing or meeting shock. No longer was it necessary to march musketeers into a forward line for firing and then arrange for them to retreat into a defensive posture under the sheltering pikes. The development from the great squares of Swiss toward an extended line, which Maurice of Nassau had begun a century before, could now culminate in the three-rank formations of the War of the Spanish Succession, Frederick the Great, and the "thin red line." The military revolution was complete.

## NOTES

Mr. Mork is a Lecturer in Modern European History at the University of California, Davis.

1. John B. Wolf, *The Emergence of the Great Powers, 1685–1715* (New York, 1951), 8–14. The author acknowledges his debt to Professor Wolf, who first interested him in the topic at hand. See also, Michael Roberts, *The Military Revolution, 1560–1660* (Belfast, n.d.), and Theodore Ropp, *War in the Modern World* (New York, 1962), 37–59.
2. Charles Oman, *A History of the Art of War in the Sixteenth Century* (London, 1937), 63ff.; Henry J. Webb, *Elizabethan Military Science* (Madison, Wisconsin, 1965), 87–91, 107; Roberts, *Military Revolution*, 5–6.
3. Charles Ffoulkes and E. C. Hopkinson, *Sword, Lance and Bayonet* (Cambridge, England, 1938), 113; Louis de Gaya, *Traité des armes* [Paris, 1678], reprint ed. Charles Ffoulkes (London, 1911), 156.
4. Le Sieur de Lostelneau, *Le maréschal de bataille: contenant le maniment des armes . . . divers ordres de batailles . . .* (Paris, 1647), 78; William Barriffe, *Military Discipline: Or the Young Artillery-man . . . whereunto is also Added the Postures and Beneficiall Use of the Halfe-Pike Joyned With the Musket* (4th ed.; London, 1643), 4–5.
5. Lostelneau, *Maréschal de bataille*, 98; William Garrard, *Arte of Warre* (n.p., 1591), 229, quoted in Webb, *Elizabethan Military*, 88. .
6. Oman, *Art of War in the Sixteenth Century*, 172ff.; Hans Delbrück, *Geschichte der Kriegskunst* (Berlin, 1920), IV, 102ff.
7. Oman, *Art of War in the Sixteenth Century*, 225; Webb, *Elizabethan Military*, 93–98. In the usage of the day *musket* always referred to a matchlock gun, while *fusil* referred only to the flintlock; in this paper I will follow that usage.
8. Lostelneau, *Maréschal de bataille, passim;* Gaya, *Traité des armes*, 21–24; George, Duke of Albemarle, Baron Mon[c]k, *Observations Upon Military and Political Affairs* (London, 1671), 103; Theodore A. Dodge, *Gustavus Adolphus . . .* (Boston, 1895), I, 37–39; Raimondo, duca di Melfi, Montecuccoli, *Mémoires . . .* (Strasbourg, 1735), 13.

## FLINT AND STEEL

51

9. Bariffe, *Military Discipline*, 231.
10. Webb, *Elizabethan Military*, 119; E. de la Barre Duparcq, *Elements of Military Art and History*... (New York, 1863), 45.
11. Allain M. Mallet, *Les travaux de Mars ou la fortification nouvelle*... (Paris, 1672), III, 15; Oman, *Art of War in the Sixteenth Century*, 568; Jean L. A. Colin, *L'infanterie au XVIII<sup>e</sup> siècle: La tatique* (Paris, 1907), 18.
12. Basil H. Liddell Hart, *Great Captains Unveiled* (Edinburgh, 1927), 115–118; Roberts, *Military Revolution*, 7–8.
13. Gaya, *Traité des armes*, 32; Delbrück, *Kriegskunst*, IV, 305.
14. Mon[c]k, *Military and Political Affairs*, 42–77; Lostelneau, *Maréschal de bataille*, 244.
15. Barriffe, *Military Discipline*, 1, 74.
16. Delbrück, *Kriegskunst*, IV, 291ff.; Robert S. Quimby, *The Background of Napoleonic Warfare* (New York, 1957), 23, 44; Roberts, *Military Revolution*, 11, points out in a bibliographical note that no one has properly answered the question of when marching in step was introduced.
17. Barriffe, *Military Discipline*, 5–6, 34, 40, 55.
18. *Ibid.*, 233; see also, Quimby, *Background of Napoleonic Warfare*, 19, and Webb, *Elizabethan Military*, 102.
19. Quimby, *Background of Napoleonic Warfare*, 9.
20. Jacques François de Chastenet, marquis de Puységur, *Art de la guerre* (Paris, 1749), I, 143.
21. Cited in Ffoulkes, *Sword, Lance, and Bayonet*, 42; they were also called "Swedish feathers" and "Spanish riders."
22. Mon[c]k, *Military and Political Affairs*, 26–27; Mallet, *Travaux de Mars*, III, 146–147; C. Jany, *Geschichte der königlichen-preussischen Armee bis zum Jahre 1807* (Berlin, 1928), I, 593; John Y. Akerman, "Notes on the Origin and History of the Bayonet," *Archaeologia: or Miscellaneous Tracts*, XXXVIII (1860), 429; Delbrück, *Kriegskunst*, IV, 306.
23. Mallet, *Travaux de Mars*, III, 148; Gaya, *Traité des armes*, 113–118. *Chevaux de frise* is usually used in the plural, though sometimes in the singular.
24. Charles Ffoulkes, *Arms and Armament* (London, 1945), 70–71.
25. Barriffe, *Military Discipline*, 241, 229.
26. *Ibid.*, 232–233, 260. Barriffe neither used the term *bayonet* nor any of its variations.
27. Ffoulkes, *Arms and Armament*, 72; Charles Ffoulkes, *Inventory and Survey of the Armouries of the Tower of London* (London [1916]), II, 315; James Sibbald D. Scott, *The British Army* (London, 1868), II, 316. Plug bayonets were used in Italy for boar hunting as late as 1835, Akerman, *Archaeologia*, 424.
28. Ffoulkes, *Sword, Lance, and Bayonet*, 108.
29. Quoted by Akerman, *Archaeologia*, 422; note that Puységur recalled that the soldiers were carrying fusils rather than muskets, rather unusual in 1647.
30. Gabriel Daniel, *Histoire de la milice française* (Amsterdam, 1724), II, 422.
31. Ffoulkes, *Sword, Lance, and Bayonet*, 43.
32. Puységur, *Art de la guerre*, I, 113; Ffoulkes, *Arms and Armament*, 73; Akerman, *Archaeologia*, 424, 430–431; Ffoulkes, *Sword, Lance, and Bayonet*, 105.
33. James Turner, *Pallas Armata* (London, 1683), 175, quoted by Akerman, *Archaeologia*, 423.
34. Puységur, *Art de la guerre*, I, 220; Hugh Mackay, *Memoirs of the War Carried on in Scotland and Ireland, 1689–1691* (Edinburgh, 1833), 52.
35. Ludovic Jablonski, *L'armée française à travers les ages* (Paris, 1890–1894), II, 64; he cites no sources. If he was referring to Jean Martinet, the drill master whose name became a part of military terminology, he was in error; that Martinet was killed in battle in 1672.
36. Auguste F. Demmin, *An Illustrated History of Arms and Armour* (London, 1877), 448–449; his assertion is also without citation.
37. Sébastien le prestre de Vauban, *Vauban: sa famille et ses écrits*..., ed. A. de Rochas d'Aiglun (Paris, 1910), I, 290, II, 285, 287–288. See also Pierre E. Lazard, *Vauban, 1633–1707* (Paris, 1934), 452–463.
38. Puységur, *Art de la guerre*, I, 148; Daniel *Milice française*, II, 421. Vauban might have been consoled in his disappointment by the fact that as late as 1843 British soldiers still reported that they were unable to attach their socket bayonets to their gun barrels properly, Ffoulkes, *Sword, Lance, and Bayonet*, 110.
39. Vauban, *Ses écrits*, I, 290, II, 228.
40. Jany, *Geschichte der Preussischen Armee*, I, 589–590.
41. See Peter Paret, *Innovation and Reform in Warfare* (U.S.A.F. Academy, Colorado, 1966), *passim*.
42. Barriffe, *Military Discipline*, 228. On conservatism in the French court see Camille Rousset, *Histoire de Louvois* (Paris, 1861–1863), III, 325–326.
43. Roger [Boyle], Earl of Orrery, *A Treatise on the Art of War* ([London], 1677), 24–25.
44. Vauban, *Ses écrits*, II, 286.
45. Maurice, comte de Saxe, *Rêveries*, trans. Thomas R. Phillips (Harrisburg, Pa., 1944), 39ff. Two other 18th-century French theorists wished to return to the use of pikemen, Jean-Charles de Folard and Jean de Mesnil-Durand; see Quimby, *Background of Napoleonic Warfare*, 31–36, 71.
46. Webb, *Elizabethan Military*, 92, 98.
47. Reginald Blomfield, *Vauban, Sebastian le Prestre de Vauban* 1633–1707 (London, 1938), 169.
48. Ropp, *War in the Modern World*, 49.
49. John Smythe, *Certain Discourses Military*, ed. J. R. Hale (Ithaca, N.Y., 1964), xxxix–xl; Gaya, *Traité des armes*, 22.
50. Alfred R. Hall, *Ballistics in the Seventeenth Century* (New York, 1952), 8; Mon[c]k, *Military and Political Affairs*, 103.
51. Hans von Grimmelshausen, *Simplicissimus the Vagabond*, trans. A. S. T. Goodrick (London [1924]), 375–376.
52. Benjamin Franklin to Major General Charles Lee, Philadelphia, Feb. 11, 1776, *Memoirs of the Life of the late Charles Lee, Esq.*... (London, 1792), 240–241. Ffoulkes (*Arms and Armament*, 54) incorrectly attributes Franklin's opinion to Lee.
53. Viscount Dillon, "On the Development of Gunlocks, from Examples in the Tower," *Archaeological Journal*, L (1893), 121.
54. *Ibid.*, 127–129; W. Y. Carman, *A History of Firearms* (London, [1955]), 100–101; Demmin, *Arms and Armour*, 522. Smythe, *Discourses Military* (1590), xcvi, mentions the "snaphaunce".
55. Mon[c]k, *Military and Political Affairs*, 24; Rousset, *Louvois*, I, 193, 238–239.
56. Rousset, *Louvois*, I, 190–191.
57. Puységur, *Art de la guerre*, I, 147; Daniel, *Milice française*, II, 423.

58. Vauban, *Ses écrits,* II, 286; Gaya, *Traité des armes,* 25–26.
59. Rousset, *Louvois,* III, 329; Dillon, *Archaeological Journal,* 129–130; Montecuccoli, *Mémoires,* 15.
60. Maxime Weygand, *Histoire de l'armée française* (Paris, 1953), 151; Colin, *L'infanterie,* 26; Ffoulkes, *Arms and Armament,* 54.
61. Demmin, *Arms and Armour,* 525; Jany, *Geschichte der Preussischen Armee,* I, 591; Delbrück, *Kriegskunst,* IV, 306; Mon[c]k, *Military and Political Affairs,* 102; Orrery, *Treatise,* 31; Rousset, *Louvois,* III, 325; Pierre Surirey de Saint Remy, *Mémoires d'artillerie* . . . (Amsterdam, 1702), I, 284ff.; Vauban, *Ses écrits,* I, 290–291.
62. Peter Paret, *Yorck and the Era of Prussian Reform, 1807–1815* (Princeton, 1966), 14, 271–273. De la Barre Duparcq (*Military Art and History,* 56) claims the Prussians of Frederick the Great could fire six rounds a minute.
63. Mackay, *Memoirs,* 52.
64. Edouard Hardÿ de Périni, *Batailles françaises* (Paris [1894–1908]), V, 304; Antoine de Pas, marquis de Feuquière, *Mémoires* . . . (Amsterdam, 1741), 233; Jean chevalier de Beaurain, *Histoire militaire de Flandre* . . . (Paris, 1755), III, 201–202; Armand de Mormés de Saint-Hilaire, *Mémoires* . . . (Paris, 1903–1916), II, 236–237.
65. Rousset, *Louvois,* III, 330–331.
66. Beaurain, *Flandre,* III, 208–209.
67. Hardÿ de Périni, *Batailles françaises,* V, 318.
68. Much of Quimby's *Background of Napoleonic Warfare* deals with the controversy of *ordre mince* vs. *ordre profond.*
69. Daniel, *Milice française,* II, 421; Hardÿ de Périni, *Batailles françaises,* VI, 26, 95–96; Puységur, *Art de la guerre,* I, 118.
70. Colin, *L'infanterie,* 27.



## PICTURE CREDITS

Figures 1–4: From Lostelneau (see note 4, above), 79, 99, 9, 29. Courtesy of the Walter Library, University of Minnesota.

Figure 5: From Mallet (see note 11, above). Courtesy of the University Library, University of California, Berkeley.

Figure 6: From Barriffe (see note 4, above), 259. Courtesy of the Walter Library, University of Minnesota.

Figures 7 and 8: From Mallet (see note 11, above), 33, 43. Courtesy of the University Library, University of California, Berkeley.

Figures 9 and 10: From Lostelneau (see note 4, above), 308–309, 365. Courtesy of the Walter Library, University of Minnesota.

Figure 11: From Mallet (see note 11, above), 149. Courtesy of the University Library, University of California, Berkeley.

Figure 12: From Gaya (see note 3, above), 16. Courtesy of the University Library, University of California, Berkeley.

Figure 13: From Mallet (see note 11, above), 33. Courtesy of the University Library, University of California, Berkeley.

Figures 14 and 15: From Saint Remy (see note 61, above), II, 279, 289. Courtesy of the Walter Library, University of Minnesota.

Figures 16–18: Guns from the collection of the Division of Military History, Smithsonian Institution. Smithsonian photographs 16210, 14499, and 61318.

Figure 19: From Saint Remy (see note 61, above), II, 281. Courtesy of the Walter Library, University of Minnesota.

Figure 20: From Gaya (see note 3, above), 24. Courtesy of the University Library, University of California, Berkeley.

# [20]

# *Muskets and Pendulums: Benjamin Robins, Leonhard Euler, and the Ballistics Revolution*

BRETT D. STEELE

Ballistics was revolutionized between 1742 and 1753 by Benjamin Robins (1707–51) and Leonhard Euler (1707–83). As one artillery officer wrote in 1789, "Before Robins, who was in gunnery what the immortal Newton was in philosophy, the founder of a new system deduced from experiment and nature, the service of artillery was a mere matter of chance, founded on no principles, or at best, but erroneous ones."[1] John Pringle, a president of the Royal Society, put it more simply in 1783 by stating that Robins created a "new science."[2] John Nef wrote in 1950 that Robins's work "provides a landmark in the interrelations between knowledge and war."[3] Two engineers more recently described him as being "one of the fathers of aerodynamics," while Thomas P. Hughes referred to him as "a founder of modern gunnery."[4] What did

MR. STEELE is in the Program for the History of Science and Technology at the University of Minnesota, writing his dissertation on 18th-century ballistics and gunnery and working on an economic theory of technological products. His research was supported by fellowships from the Smithsonian Institution's National Museum of American History and the Deutsches Museum and by the assistance of I. S. Weissbrodt. He thanks Ed Layton, Roger Hahn, Michael Segre, Mark Levinson, Maarten Heyboer, John Jackson, Don Opitz, and the *Technology and Culture* referees for their helpful comments and criticisms.

[1]Papacino D'Antoni, *A Treatise on Gunpowder; a Treatise on Fire-Arms; and a Treatise on the Service of Artillery in the Time of War,* trans. Captain Thomson of the Royal Regiment of Artillery (London, 1789), p. xvii.

[2]John Pringle, *Six Discourses . . . on occasion of Six Annual Assignments of Sir Godfrey Copley's Medal* (London, 1783), p. 273.

[3]John Nef, *War and Human Progress: An Essay on the Rise of Industrial Civilization* (Cambridge, Mass., 1950), p. 194.

[4]H. M. Barkla and L. J. Auchterlonie, "The Magnus or Robins Effect on Rotating Spheres," *Journal of Fluid Mechanics* 47 (1971): 437. See Thomas P. Hughes's commentary after David D. Bien's article, "Military Education in 18th Century France: Technical and Non-technical Determinants," in *Science, Technology and Warfare: Proceedings of the 3rd Military History Symposium, USAFA, 8–9 May 1969,* ed. Monte D. Wright and Lawrence J. Paszek (Washington, D.C., 1971), p. 73. No books devoted to the history of ballistics in the 18th century exist in English at present. In other languages, however, there are some useful intellectual histories that include the subject. See M. P. Charbonnier, *Essais sur*

such a seemingly obscure British mathematician and engineer do to generate such acclaim? Charles Hutton, the 18th-century artillery professor at Woolwich, said that Robins's research represents "the first work that can be considered as attempting to establish a practical system of gunnery, and projectiles, on good experiments, on the force of gunpowder, on the resistance of the air, and on the effects of different pieces of artillery."[5] More specifically, Robins invented new instruments which he used to discover and quantify the enormous magnitude of air-resistance force acting on high-speed projectiles and to make the first observations of the sound barrier. He also conducted a theoretical and experimental thermodynamic analysis of interior ballistics, discovered the Magnus (or Robins) effect of fluid mechanics, and established a rational understanding of the rifling phenomenon. Of all his aerodynamic discoveries, the enormous and complex function of air-resistance force encountered by high-speed projectiles caused the greatest sensation in the 18th century. This discovery quantitatively showed the inadequacy of Galileo's projectile theory, which neglected air resistance, and the oversimplification of Sir Isaac Newton's and Christian Huygens's air-resistance theory for projectile motion. Furthermore, Robins's air-resistance experiments made the practical mathematical analysis of high-speed ballistic motion possible.

Robins summarized his initial discoveries in *New Principles of Gunnery*, a short book that was first published in 1742.[6] Euler translated this work into German and added an extensive mathematical analysis in 1745. Using air-resistance values based on Robins's experimental measurements, Euler solved the equations of subsonic ballistic motion in 1753 and summarized some of the results into convenient numerical tables. This was the first published analysis of projectile trajectories to incorporate empirical air-resistance values.

In the short span of eleven years, Robins and Euler dramatically increased the predictive power of ballistics by constructing theoretical and empirical foundations. This effort also marks one of the first

---

*l'histoire de la balistique* (Paris, 1928); István Szabó, *Geschichte der mechanischen Prinzipien* (Basel, 1977), esp. the chapter "Die Anfänge der äußeren Ballistik"; and A. P. Mandryka, *Istoriia ballistiki* (Moscow, 1964). The more recent articles by engineers that focus on Robins's ballistics research include H. M. Barkla, "Benjamin Robins and the Resistance of Air," *Annals of Science* 30, no. 1 (March 1973): 107–22; W. Johnson, "Benjamin Robins (Eighteenth Century Founder of Scientific Ballistics): Some European Dimensions and Past and Future Perceptions," *International Journal of Impact Engineering* 12, no. 2 (1992): 293–323.

[5]Nef, p. 195.

[6]Benjamin Robins, *Mathematical Tracts of the Late Benjamin Robins*, ed. James Wilson (London, 1761). *New Principles of Gunnery* is contained in vol. 1.

significant applications of Newtonian mechanics to engineering analysis, as well as the coupling of differential equations with complex experimental measurements, the hallmark of 19th-century physics. Robins's and Euler's work therefore represents a scientific revolution. This revolution has had a strong effect on science, engineering, and warfare ever since. Significant branches of aerodynamics and thermodynamics grew from it. A cannon, after all, is an internal combustion engine, and a cannonball is a flying body. The ballistics revolution generated new theories that offered a rational understanding of gunnery, the technology of controlling gunfire. This made the teaching of calculus and mechanics to artillery and engineering officers increasingly profitable for Western governments during the second half of the 18th century. The increased precision and reduced uncertainty of their artillery fire in battlefields and sieges proved to be a generous return for this educational investment. This change in gunnery was also intimately linked to the simultaneous changes in artillery hardware, organization, and tactics.

Although the ballistics revolution has received little attention from professional historians, it challenges important claims in the history of 18th-century science and technology: that mathematical analysis and scientific experimentation had little interaction and that technology (with the exception of navigation) was not significantly influenced by rational mechanics. The ballistics revolution also highlights important characteristics regarding the historical role of engineering research. In addition to "merely" applying existing scientific knowledge to develop technologically useful theories, engineers have also created fundamental scientific knowledge in direct response to technological needs. By "science," I am specifically referring to that branch of knowledge exemplified by Newtonian celestial mechanics. In Robins's case, as in many others, the creation of scientific knowledge for engineering had profound consequences for science in general.

### *Ballistics before Robins*

Galileo's vacuum or parabolic trajectory theory was the only widely used ballistics theory before 1742. He presented it in *Two New Sciences* (1638), one of the key works of the scientific revolution. While often perceived to have no practical value because it neglects air resistance, Galileo's theory was nevertheless valid for certain gunnery problems. For heavy mortar shells fired at low speeds, the air-resistance force is too small to decelerate the projectile significantly during its relatively short flight.[7] Galileo admitted that his neglect of air resistance made his

[7]Paul-Lawrence Rose, "Galileo's Theory of Ballistics," *British Journal of Science* 4, no. 14 (1968): 156–59.

theory too inaccurate for high-velocity or "violent" shots. Nevertheless, he argued that his theory was valid for low-velocity mortar shells:

> This excessive impetus of violent shots can cause some deformation in the path of a projectile, making the beginning of the parabola less tilted and curved than its end. But this will prejudice our Author little or nothing in practicable operations, his main result being the compilation of a table of what is called the "range" of shots, containing the distances at which balls fired at (extremely) different elevations will fall. Since such shots are made with mortars charged with but little powder, the impetus is not supernatural in these, and the (mortar) shots trace out their paths quite precisely.[8]

While the vocabulary Galileo used sounds archaic, he demonstrated a qualitative comprehension of the effects of air resistance: it deforms the parabolic trajectory at high speeds but is negligible at low velocities. To suggest that one of Galileo's motivations for studying the dynamics of falling bodies was to solve a key problem in military technology may sound cynical. Nevertheless, it is important to remember the extent to which war dominated early modern European life. As Henry Guerlac wrote in his pioneering dissertation, "Science and War in the Old Régime":

> Those who doubt that war and pure science can ever be bedfellows would do well to consider the career and works of Galileo. Living in one of the most war-torn periods in European history, he saw during the course of his long life the civil wars of France, the struggle of the Dutch against their Spanish masters, the defeat of the Armada of Philip, and nearly the whole course of the Thirty Years' War. His work felt the impact of war, and he was no wise averse to capitalizing on the usefulness to the soldier of certain of his discoveries. His teaching, his inventions and his theoretical studies all reveal this tendency.[9]

The validity of the parabolic theory for low-velocity mortar shells helped convince many gunnery textbook authors in the 17th and 18th centuries to incorporate this theory.[10] After all, Western Europeans had recognized the value of uniting mathematical theory with technological practice in the education of military engineers and artillery

[8]Galileo Galilei, *Two New Sciences,* trans. Stillman Drake (Madison, Wisc., 1974), p. 229.

[9]Henry Guerlac, "Science and War in the Old Régime" (Ph.D. diss., Harvard University, 1941), p. 58.

[10]The most famous examples are Nicholas François Blondel, *L'art de jeter les bombes* (Amsterdam, 1669); Surirey de Saint Rémy, *Mémoires d'artillerie* (Amsterdam, 1702).

commanders since the 16th century.[11] The anonymous editor of *The Compleat Gunner* (first published in 1672), a collection of English translations of the most important artillery literature of that age, included a description of Galileo's projectile theory as developed by Evangelista Torricelli, as well as Marin Mersenne's account of his own ballistics experiments.[12] Bernard Forest de Bélidor, the prominent French military engineer, used Galileo's theory to derive extensive range tables for mortar fire in *Le bombardier français* in the 1730s.[13] To use these tables, a gunnery officer first had to determine the shell's range when fired at an angle of 15 degrees with a specific quantity of gunpowder. He then had to find the particular range table where the range for 15 degrees matched his shell's observed range. This range table would then provide the officer with the mortar's range at other elevation angles, provided he maintained the same gunpowder charge. A French military commission, as described in *Le bombardier français,* verified the utility of Galileo's theory for heavy mortar shells fired at low speeds and short ranges (less than 600 yards).[14] Numerous problems existed with maintaining uniform artillery hardware and gunpowder quality, as well as consistent aiming techniques, during the 17th century. Such problems often made it difficult for bombardiers to maintain the consistency assumed in Galileo's theory. Such limitations, however, far from weakening Galileo's influence on early modern gunnery, inspired efforts to improve the consistency of artillery fire in order to take full advantage of his theory's power.[15] Such work was reflected in the 18th-century military interest in mechanical uniformity and interchangeable parts, which culminated in the French artillery reforms of Jean Baptiste Vaquette de Gribeauval.

Although artillery officers did use Galileo's ballistics theory for particular problems, general ballistics theories valid for all artillery

[11]See William Bourne, *The Arte of Shooting in Great Ordnance* (Amsterdam, 1969), originally published in 1587. Also see Martha D. Pollak, *Military Architecture, Cartography and the Representation of the Early Modern European City* (Chicago, 1991).

[12]*The Compleat Gunner in Three Parts* (Yorkshire, 1971), pt. 3, pp. 3–75.

[13]B. Forest de Bélidor, *Le bombardier français, ou nouvelle méthode de jeter les bombes avec précision* (Paris, 1731).

[14]Ibid., pp. 15–18.

[15]The practical difficulty of shooting mortar shells consistently was addressed in de Resson, "Méthode pour tirer les bombes avec succès," *Mémoires de l'Académie Royale des Sciences* (Paris, 1716), pp. 79–86. Only by following the rigorous loading and firing techniques, outlined in this paper, could the necessary consistency be maintained to utilize the parabolic theory, according to de Resson. Perhaps some soldiers listened to de Resson's advice on loading mortars, because in 1717 at the Siege of Belgrade a confident young Polish bombardier literally bet his head to Prince Eugene that he could knock out the Turkish magazine with only three mortar shells. The first two missed, but the third succeeded, with horrendous consequences for the Turks. See C. Duffy, *Fire and Stone: The Science of Fortress Warfare, 1660–1860* (Newton Abbot, U.K., 1975), pp. 122–23.

pieces eluded the great natural philosophers and mathematicians of the scientific revolution. Huygens, Newton, and Johann Bernoulli attempted to analyze projectile motion in a resisting medium.[16] They failed to improve on Galileo's theory for solving gunnery problems for the following reasons. The basic differential equations of projectile motion in the atmosphere are nonlinear and do not have an exact solution.[17] Had these mathematicians succeeded in numerically integrating these equations or deriving linear approximations, their results would have remained worthless for gunnery. These equations also contain two numerical parameters that no one had accurately measured before Robins. These are the projectile's initial or muzzle velocity and the air resistance (the aerodynamic drag acting on a projectile in flight).[18] Without valid numbers for these parameters, the differential equations can yield analytical solutions that may be mathematically interesting but remain worthless for making quantitative scientific predictions. Galileo's idealized ballistics theory therefore remained the only useful ballistics theory for gunnery until the ballistics revolution. It had a similar appeal that basic neoclassical microeconomics theories have today: even though their direct applicability is limited, the rational thinking these theories stimulate is very powerful.

In the early 1950s, A. Rupert Hall made an influential argument that ballistics was useless for gunnery before the 19th century. One reason, he claimed, was that smoothbore artillery was too inaccurate to make a mathematical prediction of its performance possible. He wrote that "the gun itself was so inconsistent in its behavior that great accuracy in preliminary work, even in the lay of the gun itself, was labour in vain."[19] Hall concluded that "it was the engineering ingenuity of the nineteenth century, not the progressive elaboration of dynamical theories originating with Galileo and developed by Newton, that was responsible for the revolution which then, at last occurred, with the introduction of scientific ballistics to gunnery."[20] This idea is flawed regarding both the

[16]See Charbonnier (n. 4 above), chap. 3; A. Rupert Hall, *Ballistics in the Seventeenth Century* (Cambridge, 1952), chaps. 5 and 6; and Szabó (n. 4 above), pp. 199–211, for an analysis of these natural philosophers' ballistics analysis.

[17]A nonlinear differential equation refers to the lack of the additive property, $f(x+z) \neq f(x) + f(z)$, with respect to the dependent variable.

[18]Huygens and Newton demonstrated that air resistance was proportional to the projectile's velocity squared, but they did not establish a numerical proportionality factor appropriate for military projectiles.

[19]Hall, p. 55.

[20]Ibid., p. 71. Hall slightly modified his opinion that ballistics was not useful for gunnery before the 19th century in "Gunnery, Science and the Royal Society," in *The Uses of Science in the Age of Newton*, ed. John Burke (Berkeley, 1983). For example, he stated that "existing military art was incapable of adopting a mathematical theory of projectile flight and

timing and the cause of the ballistics revolution. The revolution was caused, in part, by the engineering ingenuity of the *18th* century *and* by the scientific revolution of Galileo and Newton.

During the 18th century, numerous technological innovations succeeded in increasing the efficiency and precision of artillery fire.[21] The artillery reforms of Austria's Prince Joseph Wenzel von Lichtenstein and France's General Gribeauval that began in the 1740s and 1760s, respectively, depended on numerous innovations to improve the precision of artillery fire. These innovations include Jean de Maritz's boring machine,[22] various aiming instruments including tangent sights, and accurate screws to control the cannon's elevation angle.[23] One indication of such reformed artillery's precision was the French artillerists' boast, at the Battle of Yorktown at the end of the American Revolutionary War, that they could shoot six consecutive shots through a small opening in the British fortifications.[24] B. P. Hughes has measured the accuracy of this artillery, determining that a 12-pound cannon could hit a 6-foot screen 100 percent of the time at 600 yards, 26 percent of the time at 950 yards, and only 15 percent of the time at 1,300 yards.[25] While it remains difficult to determine precisely the accuracy of late-18th-century smoothbore artillery, it was certainly consistent enough to make scientific gunnery calculations useful, not to mention being accurate enough to cause almost half the allied combat casualties suffered during the Napoleonic Wars.[26]

### *Benjamin Robins*

Benjamin Robins, the central figure of the ballistics revolution, has received little notice from professional historians.[27] This contrasts with

---

applying it to practice, nor [so far as one can tell] did it ever attempt to do so, at least before the death of Newton. Therefore, if the learned men developed the theory out of a desire to solve useful problems, they were mistaken" (p. 116).

[21]William H. McNeill, *The Pursuit of Power* (Chicago, 1982), pp. 167–74.

[22]These machines were designed to bore solid-cast cannon accurately enough to achieve consistently straight bores and to minimize windage, the difference between the diameter of the cannon bore and ball. Similar machines were adopted by John Wilkinson to machine James Watt's steam engine pistons and by Count Rumford to disprove the caloric theory of heat.

[23]C. Duffy, *The Army of Maria Theresa: The Armed Forces of Imperial Austria, 1740–1780* (Vancouver and London, 1977), pp. 106, 112.

[24]North Callahan, *George Washington: Soldier and Man* (New York, 1972), p. 243.

[25]B. P. Hughes, *Firepower* (London, 1974), pp. 36–38.

[26]Robert O'Connell, *Of Arms and Men* (New York, 1989), pp. 178–79.

[27]William Johnson, a prominent research engineer in impact mechanics, has done much to reverse this neglect with his recent biographical research on Robins. John Nef is one of the few historians to consider seriously Robins's military significance, in *War and Human Progress* (n. 3 above), while Seymour Mauskopf is the first to consider Robins's significance

his high reputation in the 18th century.[28] He initially attracted attention in mathematics.[29] In 1727, at the age of twenty, he published a demonstration of the last proposition of Newton's *Treatise of Quadratures*[30] in the *Philosophical Transactions of the Royal Society.* He published a refutation of Johann Bernoulli's impact theory the following year. Elected as a fellow to the Royal Society, Robins became a private mathematics tutor to prospective university students. Although he remained active in pure mathematics, a serious interest in military engineering quickly developed. In the 1730s, Robins began a study of fortifications, hydraulics, and ultimately ballistics.[31] He received the Royal Society's Copley Medal in 1747 for his work in ballistics. The depth of Robins's engineering ambition is also reflected in his trips to study Dutch fortifications and his invitation by the prince of Orange to assist in the Dutch defense of Bergen op Zoom in 1747. The French siege of this large fortress was a key conflict in the War of the Austrian Succession. Unfortunately for Robins's engineering career, the fortress fell shortly after his arrival.

During the mid-1730s, Robins demonstrated his mathematical abilities in a debate with James Jurin concerning the nature of limits and infinitesimals in the theory of fluxions. Their argument was ignited by Bishop Berkeley's famous critique of the logical foundations of Newtonian mathematics.[32] Robins also criticized Euler's use of Gottfried Wilhelm Leibniz's differential calculus, which increased his reputation as a staunch defender of Newton. Nevertheless, Robins did not hesitate to describe Newton's errors regarding air resistance. Active in politics as well, Robins wrote a number of political pamphlets in support of the Tories, as well as serving on various political committees. Sir Robert

---

for the history of chemistry, in "Gunpowder and the Chemical Revolution," *Osiris,* 2d ser. (1988), pp. 96–97.

[28]See Leonhard Euler's praise of Robins in H. Brown's English translation of Euler's critique and German translation (*Neue Grundsätze der Artillerie* [Berlin, 1745]) of Robins's *New Principles of Gunnery* titled *The True Principles of Gunnery Investigated and Explored* (London, 1777), p. 49; Charles Hutton's praise in *Tracts on Mathematical and Philosophical Subjects* (London, 1812), tract 34, 2:307; and Pringle's praise, delivered on the occasion of awarding the Copley Medal to Charles Hutton (n. 2 above).

[29]W. Johnson, "Benjamin Robins: New Details of His Life," *Notes and Records of the Royal Society of London* 46, no. 2 (London, 1992): 235–52.

[30]Isaac Newton, *Two Treatises of the Quadrature of Curves, and Analysis of Equations of an Infinite Number of Terms,* explained by John Stewart (London, 1745).

[31]Wilson wrote a short biography on Robins in his introduction to *Mathematical Tracts of the Late Benjamin Robins* (n. 6 above), the main source of the biographical information provided here.

[32]For a description of this controversy, see F. Cajori, *Conceptions of Limits and Fluxions in Great Britain, from Newton to Woodhouse* (Chicago, 1919), pp. 96–148; and Niccolò Guicciardini, *The Development of Newtonian Calculus in Britain* (Cambridge, 1989), pp. 45–46.

Walpole and his Whig supporters were sufficiently antagonized by Robins's critiques that they blocked his application for the professorship of mathematics at the recently established Royal Military Academy at Woolwich in 1741. Robins published *New Principles of Gunnery* in 1742, in part as a response to this rejection.[33] His literary career flourished with the publication of *A Voyage Around the World in the Years 1740–1744 by George Anson, Esq.*, a book Lord Anson commissioned him to ghostwrite.[34] A naval gunnery reformer, Anson aided Robins in his ballistics research.[35] Robins died of a fever in 1751 in India, where he had gone to serve as engineer general and captain of the Madras artillery for the East India Company. In addition to commanding the artillery batteries, he redesigned Fort St. David as a part of the East India Company's military buildup against the French after the War of the Austrian Succession.[36]

Robins's single most influential accomplishment was his invention of the ballistics pendulum, the first reliable instrument that measured projectile velocity.[37] (See fig. 1.) The ballistics pendulum, coupled with a sophisticated knowledge of mathematics and mechanics and a talent for experimentation, gave Robins the means to address fundamental experimental and theoretical ballistics questions. Like any pioneering effort, his work was imperfect, yet it provided a rigorous scientific foundation for ballistics. Robins's interest also extended to artillery design issues. In his article "Practical Maxims relating to the Effects and Management of Artillery, and the Flight of Shells and Shot," he argued for the tactical benefits of decreasing artillery weight and lowering gunpowder charges.[38] These arguments were remarkably similar to those adopted by General Gribeauval in his efforts to reform the French artillery following France's humiliating defeat in the Seven Years' War (1756–63).[39] Robins also published "A Proposal for Increasing the

[33]Robins, *New Principles of Gunnery* (n. 6 above).

[34]For a discussion of the controversy surrounding Robins's work on this book, see W. Johnson, "Benjamin Robins: Two Essays: Sir John Cope's Arraignment and Lord Anson's *A Voyage Round the World*," *International Journal of Impact Engineering* 11, no. 1 (1991): 121–34.

[35]Peter Padfield, *Guns at Sea* (New York, 1974), p. 102.

[36]For a discussion of Robins's life in India, see W. Johnson, "Benjamin Robins (1707–1751): Opting Not to Be a Commissary for Acadia but a Fortifications Engineer in East India," *International Journal of Impact Engineering* 9, no. 4 (1990): 503–25, "In Search of the End of the Life, in India, of Benjamin Robins, F.R.S," *International Journal of Impact Engineering* 11, no. 4 (1991): 547–71, and "Benjamin Robins: New Details of His Life" (n. 29 above).

[37]For a study of the attempts before Robins to use a pendulum to study ballistic motion, see W. Johnson, "The Origin of the Ballistic Pendulum: The Claims of Jacques Casini and Benjamin Robins," *International Journal of Mechanical Science* 32, no. 4 (1990): 345–74.

[38]Benjamin Robins, *New Principles of Gunnery* (London, 1805), pp. 245–78.

[39]For a historical account of the Gribeauval artillery reforms, see Howard Rosen, "The Système Gribeauval: A Study of Technological Development and Institutional Change in Eighteenth Century France" (Ph.D. diss., University of Chicago, 1981).

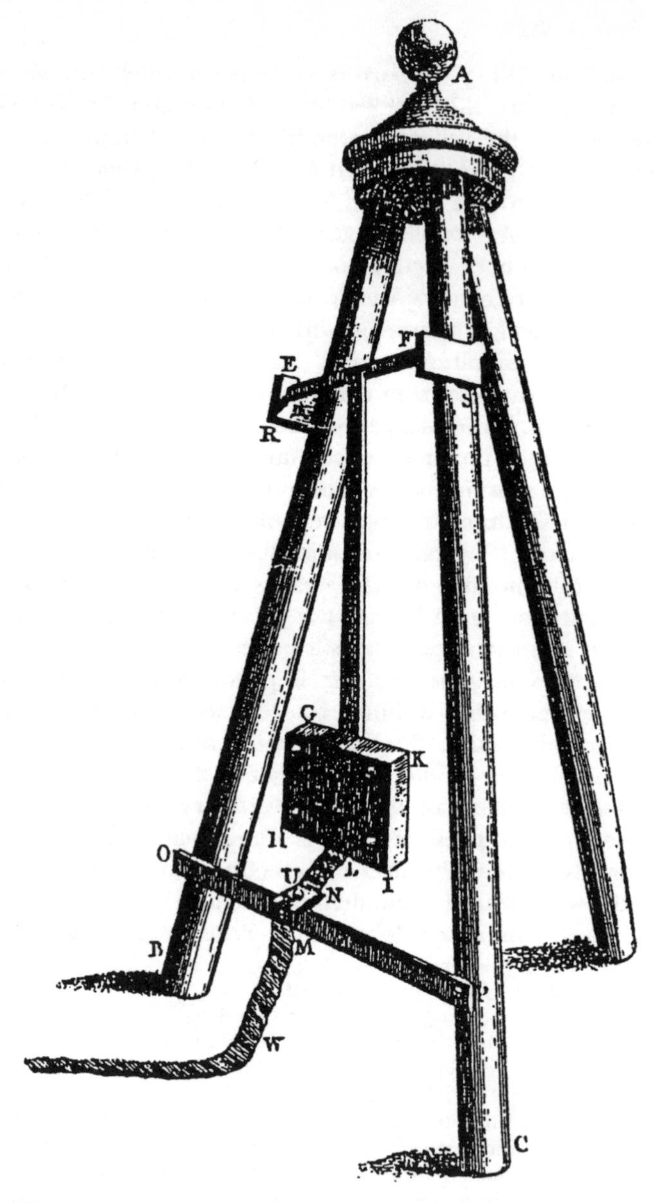


FIG. 1.—Benjamin Robins's 1742 ballistics pendulum. (Benjamin Robins, *Mathematical Tracts of the Late Benjamin Robins,* ed. James Wilson [London, 1761], 1:89.)

Strength of the British Navy," in which he argued for the effectiveness of a high-caliber, lightweight cannon in naval warfare.[40] This proposal helped inspire the invention of the carronade in the 1770s, a weapon the British Navy effectively used during the Napoleonic Wars.[41]

### *Robins's Interior Ballistics*

Robins devoted the first half of *New Principles of Gunnery* to the basic question of interior ballistics: what is a projectile's muzzle velocity as a function of its mass, gunpowder quantity, and barrel geometry? Building on the work of Daniel Bernoulli, who analyzed theoretically the muzzle velocity of a gun fired with compressed air,[42] and on the experimental work of Francis Hauksbee and Stephen Hales, Robins pursued this question by measuring the necessary empirical parameters, setting up the equations of motion, performing the mathematical analysis, and comparing his results with experimental observation. Robins first assumed that gunpowder is instantly transformed into an elastic fluid or compressible gas when ignited. Using high-quality military powder, he established empirically a relationship between gunpowder mass and the quantity of gas generated from the explosion. He also measured this gas's pressure at his estimation of the explosion temperature.[43] With these empirical relationships, Boyle's law (the isothermal law relating gas pressure to its volume), and the thirty-ninth proposition of book 1 of Newton's *Principia,* Robins obtained a solution.[44] He showed that the area beneath the pressure-volume curve representing the gas pressure that pushes the projectile through the barrel (the "work" performed by the gas on the projectile) is equal to the projectile's "kinetic energy" at the muzzle, in the modern definition of those terms.[45] (See fig. 2.) He then easily solved for the bullet's muzzle velocity. The work performed by the gas on the projectile, as Robins showed, depended on the initial gas pressure, which in turn depended on gas temperature—an early recognition of the connection between

[40]Benjamin Robins, "A Proposal for Increasing the Strength of the British Navy," in *New Principles of Gunnery* (n. 38 above), pp. 283–94.

[41]F. L. Robertson, *The Evolution of Naval Armament* (London, 1921), p. 126. Also see John E. Talbott, "The Rise and the Fall of the Carronade," *History Today* 39 (August 1989): 24–30, for a description of this military innovation.

[42]Daniel Bernoulli, *Hydrodynamics* (1738), trans. T. Carmody and H. Kobus (New York, 1968), pp. 264–74. Bernoulli showed that the "work" done by expanding air is equal to the "kinetic energy" of the projectile at the muzzle.

[43]Robins (n. 6 above), p. 70.

[44]The thirty-ninth proposition of book 1 of the *Principia* is an analysis of a body moving under the influence of centripetal forces. See Isaac Newton, *Mathematical Principles* (Berkeley, 1934), 1:125–27.

[45]Robins (n. 6 above), p. 76.

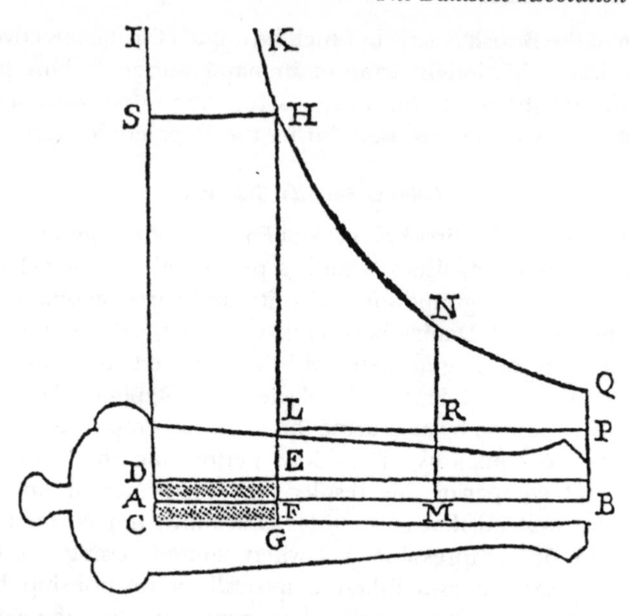


FIG. 2.—Robins's force-versus-displacement diagram, where lines *FH*, *MN*, and *BQ* represent the force acting on the projectile at the beginning, middle, and end of the barrel, respectively. Robins showed that the area *FHQB* is equal to the projectile's "kinetic energy" at point *B*. The area *DCGE* represents the volume of gunpowder. (Benjamin Robins, *Mathematical Tracts of the Late Benjamin Robins*, ed. James Wilson [London, 1761], 1:75.)

heat and mechanical work.[46] In spite of his numerous assumptions, Robins succeeded in demonstrating his theory's utility for muskets. He compared a musket's theoretical muzzle velocity with experimental observation by using the ballistics pendulum and achieved astonishingly close results.[47]

The ballistics pendulum is a simple instrument to build, but complex to use. It proved to be a revolutionary scientific instrument in the 18th century, because it allowed Robins and his successors to quantitatively measure both muzzle velocity and (by moving the pendulum at progressively greater distances from the gun) the air resistance of a projectile, the two fundamental parameters in the differential equations of ballistic motion. It was used by such prominent 18th-century ballistics researchers as Patrick D'Arcy, General Alessandro Vittorio Papacino D'Antoni, Hutton, and Count Rumford to investigate increasingly

[46]For a closer look at the mathematical analysis in this book, see W. Johnson, "Benjamin Robins' *New Principles of Gunnery*," *International Journal of Impact Engineering* 4, no. 4 (1986): 205–19; and Barkla (n. 4 above).

[47]Robins (n. 6 above), p. 91.

heavier projectiles with greater accuracy, and it remained the most popular ballistics research instrument until the 1850s.[48] Robins's ballistics pendulum, designed only to measure musket ball velocities, was a simple pendulum consisting of a flat plate connected to a rigid bar that swung from a tripod. Robins measured a musket ball's velocity by shooting the ball into the plate and observing the amplitude of the pendulum's swing. He derived an equation of the bullet's velocity just before impact as a function of the ballistics pendulum's swing angle. This calculation might seem elementary today, but it was sophisticated in the 1740s. It required insight into the conservation of linear momentum, angular momentum, and the dynamics of pendulums and falling bodies.[49]

Robins's theoretical analysis of a projectile's muzzle velocity represents a fundamental thermodynamic analysis of an internal combustion engine. This influenced John Robison's and possibly Sadi Carnot's subsequent thermodynamic analysis of the steam engine. Donald Cardwell credits Davies Gilbert with discovering in the 1790s that the area beneath a pressure-volume curve for a steam engine is equal to the work done by the steam against the cylinder.[50] While this claim may be valid for the steam engine, Robins's and Daniel Bernoulli's analysis shows that this knowledge was well established in the middle of the 18th century for another heat engine, the gun. Whether Davies Gilbert read *New Principles of Gunnery* is not known, but John Robison certainly did.[51] Robison was the author of the 1797 *Encyclopaedia Britannica* article on the steam engine where he essentially repeated Robins's analysis of the work done by expanding elastic fluids in a gun and then applied it to the steam engine.[52] He may have first read about it during his service in the Royal Navy during the Seven Years' War. It is also quite possible that Sadi Carnot, the founder of modern thermodynamics and a graduate of the École Polytechnique and the École d'Application de l'Artillerie et du Génie at Metz, was familiar with Robins's analysis. *New*

[48]Patrick D'Arcy, "Mémoire sur la théorie de l'artillerie, ou sur les effets de la poudre, et sur les conséquences qui en résultent par rapport aux armes à feu," in *Mémoires de l'Académie Royale des Sciences* (Paris, 1751), pp. 45–63; Benjamin Thompson, "New experiments upon gun-powder with occasional observations and practical inferences; to which are added, an account of a new method of determining the velocities of all kinds of military projectiles," *Philosophical Transactions of the Royal Society* (London, 1781), pp. 229–328; Charles Hutton, "The force of fired gun-powder and the initial velocities of cannon balls, determined by experiments," *Philosophical Transactions of the Royal Society* (London, 1778), pp. 50–85. Also see Hutton (n. 28 above), vols. 2 and 3.

[49]See C. Truesdell, *Essays in the History of Mechanics* (New York, 1968), pp. 239–71, for an essay on the history of rigid body dynamics.

[50]Donald Cardwell, *From Watt to Clausius* (Ithaca, N.Y., 1971), p. 79.

[51]John Robison, *A System of Mechanical Philosophy* (Edinburgh, 1822), 1:193–203.

[52]Cardwell, p. 81.

*Principles of Gunnery* was widely read by the technical officers of that age.[53] The full significance of Robins's thermodynamic analysis remains uncertain, however. Guillaume Amontons used the expansion of heated air to design a theoretical engine well before Robins.[54] Nevertheless, Robins appears to be the first to analyze the work performed by an internal combustion engine and to confirm his calculations by using rigorous experimental methods.

### *Robins's Exterior Ballistics*

Benjamin Robins's principal fame in the 18th century rested on his investigations of exterior ballistics or the mechanics of projectiles in free flight. By using the ballistics pendulum, he discovered the enormous and complex air-resistance forces acting on high-speed projectiles. These forces could initially be as high as 120 times the musket bullet's weight, a surprise to the scientific and engineering communities of the day. Conventional wisdom generally held that air resistance only slightly modified the parabolic trajectory. To validate his claims, Robins gave a demonstration of these air-resistance measurements before the Royal Society, showing how grossly distorted high-speed trajectories were from a parabola. According to the parabolic theory, a 24-pound solid shot fired from a cannon could reach 16 miles, should its actual initial velocity be used.[55] In practice, its maximum range was less than 3 miles because of air resistance. This disparity could not have been determined by simply observing projectile ranges. In Galileo's theory, the projectile's muzzle velocity is deduced from its observed range and elevation angle. The range, however, is affected by air resistance. For high-speed projectiles, this resistance is sufficient to cause a wide discrepancy between such deduced and actual muzzle-velocity values.

Newton and Huygens argued that air resistance was proportional to the square of the projectile's velocity. Robins showed that this was valid only at lower speeds. At velocities greater than 1,100 feet per second, approximately the speed of sound, he concluded that the resistance increased by a factor of three. Robins then commented that "as I have forbore to mix any hypothesis with the plain matters of fact deduced from experiment, I did not therefore animadvert on this remarkable circumstance, that the velocity, at which the moving body shifts its resistance, is nearly the same, with which sound is propagated through the air. . . . But the exact manner, in which the greater and lesser

[53]Even in the United States, much of *New Principles of Gunnery* was published in vol. 8 of the *Encyclopaedia; or, a Dictionary of Arts, Sciences and Miscellaneous Literature,* ed. T. Dobson (Philadelphia, 1798). See pp. 200 and 201 for Robins's thermodynamic analysis.

[54]Cardwell, p. 19.

[55]Robins (n. 6 above), p. 142.

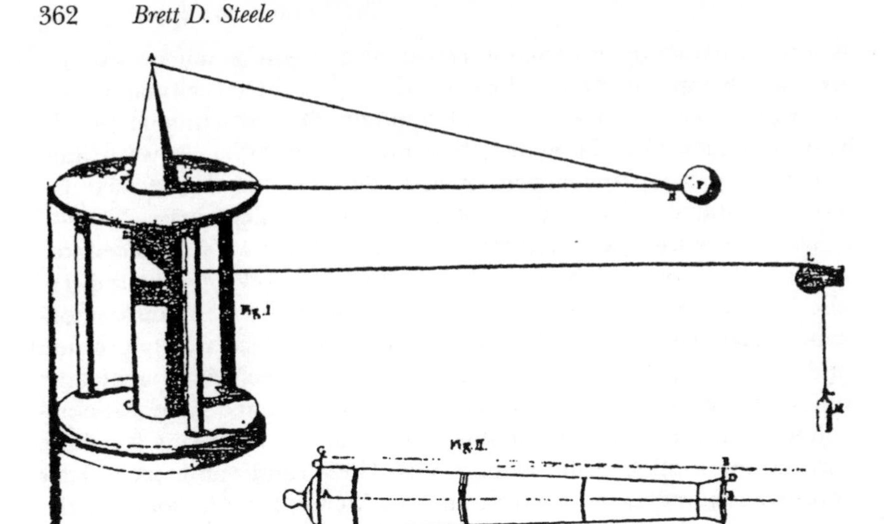

FIG. 3.—Robins's whirling arm. (Benjamin Robins, *Mathematical Tracts of the Late Benjamin Robins,* ed. James Wilson [London, 1761], vol. 1, between pp. 340 and 341.)

resistances shift into each other, must be the subject of farther experimental enquiries."[56] While it would be an exaggeration to suggest that Robins discovered the "sound barrier" in the modern sense of the word, he certainly made the first observations of the phenomenon while conducting the first supersonic aerodynamics experiments.[57]

In order to measure projectile air resistance at velocities too low for the ballistics pendulum, Robins invented the whirling arm (fig. 3). This consisted of a pivoted arm that rotated in the horizontal plane and was powered by a falling weight. The test object was placed at the outer end of the arm. While the results were less complicated to interpret than the ballistics pendulum, effective interpretation of its data also required a knowledge of mechanics.[58] Robins equated the product of the falling weight and its steady-state velocity (the "power" generated by the falling weight) with the "power" dissipated by the arm and projectile in the air. He then solved for the air-resistance force acting on the projectile alone. The whirling arm became the most widely used aeronautical research instrument until the development of the wind tunnel in the late 19th century.[59] John Smeaton adopted it for his windmill power measure-

[56]Ibid., p. 182.

[57]Hugh Dryden, "Supersonic Travel within the Last Two Hundred Years," *Scientific Monthly* (May 1954): 289–90.

[58]Robins (n. 6 above), p. 203.

[59]J. L. Pritchard, "The Dawn of Aeronautics," *Journal of the Royal Aeronautical Society* 61 (1957): 438.

ments.[60] Charles de Borda redesigned it to measure water-resistance forces.[61] George Cayley, the conceptual inventor of the airplane, used the whirling arm to measure both lift and drag forces acting on airfoils. F. W. Wenham, Otto Lilienthal, Horatio Phillips, W. H. Dines, Hiram Maxim, and S. P. Langley continued to develop the whirling arm for experimental airfoil analysis at the end of the 19th century.

With the whirling arm, Robins confirmed that the air-resistance force acting on subsonic spheres is proportional to its velocity squared. He also investigated the behavior of different geometries. Robins demonstrated that two different objects with the same surface area (a pyramid and an inclined plane) moving at the same velocities generated different air-resistance forces. Different air-resistance values also resulted when the short and the long side of an inclined plane faced the direction of motion at the same speeds. These results anticipated later investigations of aspect ratio in airfoils. Robins grasped some of the significance of his unexpected discovery that air resistance is not just a function of speed and surface area. He commented that "surely a matter, on the right knowledge of which all true speculations on ship-building and sailing must necessarily depend, cannot but be deemed, in this country at least, of the highest importance, both to the publick interest of the nation, and to the general benefit of mankind."[62]

Another aerodynamic property that Robins investigated was the lateral deflection of flying projectiles.[63] By firing musket balls into a series of evenly spaced tissue-paper curtains and by observing the resulting bullet holes, he demonstrated the enormous deflections of the bullet's trajectory from the initial direction of motion. At a range of 760 yards, for example, one musket ball deflected over 100 yards to the left of the gun barrel. Robins identified the spin imparted on the musket ball as it struck the musket barrel's side during firing as the cause of its deflection. He theorized that the rotation of the ball in flight disturbed the uniform flow of air past the ball. This rotation created a faster air flow on the side of the ball moving in the direction of the air flow than on the opposite side moving against it.[64] These conditions created a friction or "pressure" force that pushed the ball to the side where the air

[60]J. Smeaton, "Experimental enquiry concerning the natural powers of water and wind, to turn mills and other machines depending on circular motion," *Philosophical Transactions of the Royal Society* (London, 1759), pp. 138–74.

[61]C. de Borda, "Expériences sur la résistance des fluides," in *Memoires de l'Académie Royale des Sciences* (Paris, 1767), p. 495.

[62]Robins (n. 6 above), p. 217.

[63]For a detailed view of this aspect of Robins's work, see Barkla and Auchterlonie (n. 4 above). This phenomenon is readily observed while playing tennis or baseball.

[64]Robins (n. 6 above), pp. 207–8.

flow velocity was the greatest. To demonstrate this hypothesis, he hung a 4 ½-inch wooden ball from an 8-foot double string.[65] By winding up the string, Robins showed that the lateral deflection of the ball from its initial direction of motion coincided with the direction of spinning. The ball deflected to the side where the ball's side moved in the direction of the flowing air.

Robins offered further experimental proof of his theory with a musket.[66] In one of his experiments, he bent a fixed musket barrel a few degrees to the left. The bullet he shot had a trajectory that completely coincided with his theory. The bullet holes in the tissue-paper curtains showed that the bullet first began moving toward the left, in the direction of the musket's deflection. Eventually the bullet reversed its lateral direction of motion and crossed to the right side of the musket. Robins explained this apparent paradox by noting that the deflected musket forced the bullet to rotate from the left to the right. This would cause the air flow to be greater on the right-hand side; hence, the friction or "pressure" force pushed the projectile to the right, which its trajectory demonstrated. This phenomenon is now called the Magnus effect, named after a 19th-century German physicist who investigated it with full knowledge of Robins's work.[67] Barkla and Auchterlonie have argued that it should be renamed the "Robins effect" in recognition of Robins's prior discovery.[68]

Robins used his understanding of the "Robins effect" to explain theoretically why rifles have greater accuracy than muskets and why rifled bullets should not be spherical. He presented these ideas in a paper titled "Of the Nature and Advantage of Rifled Barrel Pieces," which he read before the Royal Society in 1747.[69] He initially critiqued the existing theories that explained the superior accuracy of rifles over smoothbore muskets, including the theory that the rotating motion of the rifles creates less air resistance because it bores through the air, just as a screw bores through wood, and that the rifled bullet receives a greater initial velocity because of its tight fit in the barrel, which causes it to fly straighter. This was utter nonsense, according to Robins. He argued that the rifled bullet's direction of forward motion coincides with its axis of rotation. Therefore, the flow of air passing around the bullet is uniform with respect to this axis. Such a uniform velocity could

[65]Ibid., p. 207.

[66]Ibid., p. 213.

[67]G. Magnus, *Über die Abweichung der Geschosse* (Berlin, 1860), p. 2.

[68]Barkla and Auchterlonie (n. 4 above), p. 438. Also see W. Johnson, "The Magnus Effect: Early Investigation and a Question of Priority," *International Journal of Mechanical Science* 28, no. 12 (1986): 859–72.

[69]Robins (n. 38 above), p. 328.

not create any lateral friction or "pressure" forces, according to Robins's theory. Robins also recognized a problem with using spherical bullets in a rifle. When the trajectory becomes curved, he feared the axis of the sphere's spin would not necessarily coincide with the direction of motion. He suggested using egg-shaped bullets to provide for the same stability seen in arrows. He then concluded this paper with an ominous prediction:

> I shall therefore close this paper with predicting, that whatever state shall thoroughly comprehend the nature and advantages of rifled barrel pieces, and, having facilitated and completed their construction, shall introduce into their armies their general use with a dexterity in the management of them; they will by this means acquire a superiority, which will almost equal any thing, that has been done at any time by the particular excellence of any one kind of arms; and will perhaps fall but little short of the wonderful effects, which histories relate to have been formerly produced by the first inventors of fire-arms.[70]

The use of smoothbore muskets as the standard infantry weapon until the second half of the 19th century was not due to an ignorance of their bullets' random trajectories but rather to the inability to manufacture desirable rifles and to the social lag that existed in military bureaucracies.[71]

### *Robins's and Euler's Ballistic Trajectory Analysis*

Leonhard Euler was the most accomplished mathematician of the 18th century. If he was not the greatest mathematician of all time, he was certainly the most productive. It was Euler, as Clifford Truesdell convincingly argued, who first derived what we now call "Newton's Second Law of Motion."[72] Euler was born in Basel in 1707 and attended the University of Basel with the initial ambition to become a minister. Johann Bernoulli held the chair in mathematics at Basel and gave Euler private lessons. In 1727 Euler accepted a position in physiology at the newly established Saint Petersburg Academy of Sciences but soon became the leading member of the mathematics section. He was extremely productive during his first stay in Russia, which lasted for fourteen years. He worked on a wide range of engineering research and mathematical problems, including problems related to navigation,

[70] Ibid., p. 341.

[71] See Merritt Roe Smith, *Harpers Ferry Armory and the New Technology* (Ithaca, N.Y., 1977), esp. chap. 7.

[72] C. Truesdell, *An Idiot's Fugitive Essays on Science* (New York, 1984), pp. 98–101.

shipbuilding, and pumps, and made fundamental contributions to number theory, mechanics, and differential and integral calculus. It would be difficult to find a topic in the mathematical sciences of the 18th century that Euler did not work on.

Euler's productive career at the Saint Petersburg Academy of Sciences came to an end when Empress Anna died in 1740 and the position of Germans in the Russian government became hazardous. Fortunately for Euler, Frederick the Great had just become king of Prussia and was in the process of reorganizing the Berlin Academy of Sciences. Frederick offered Euler a position, which he accepted in 1741. In addition to performing numerous administrative functions, including serving as the academy's acting president after the death of Pierre-Louis Moreàu de Maupertuis in 1759 and managing numerous technical projects, Euler generated an enormous quantity of research results, including fundamental work in elastic and rigid body mechanics, fluid dynamics, lunar theory, and optics. He also worked on such engineering subjects as water-turbine and gear design in addition to numerous mathematics topics including complex variables, differential equations, and the calculus of variations. An increasingly sour relationship with Frederick the Great and a specific disagreement regarding the financial management of the academy led to Euler's return to Saint Petersburg in 1766. Even total blindness failed to restrict his productivity during his second stay in Russia, which lasted until his death in 1783.

In 1745, in response to a request from Frederick the Great, Euler translated Robins's *New Principles of Gunnery* into German. He added an extensive mathematical commentary which criticized some of Robins's assumptions, pointed out his analytical errors, and addressed many additional areas of artillery and ballistics not covered by Robins. For example, Euler made an early analysis of a pressure vessel, while investigating the theoretical strength of a gun barrel. He derived the standard equation for a pressurized cylinder with unconstrained ends where the maximum stress is the product of the internal pressure and the ratio of the cylinder's radius to wall thickness.[73] Unfortunately, he made a mathematical error and obtained an additional factor of $\pi/2$ as a consequence. Euler also erred when he denied the existence of the Robins effect, arguing instead that the deflections occurred because of imperfections in the bullet's curvature. Nevertheless, in this work he derived the first proof of d'Alembert's paradox in fluid mechanics and also conducted a pioneering mathematical analysis of "supersonic" air resistance.[74]

[73]Euler (n. 28 above), pp. 85–91.

[74]Clifford Truesdell, *Rational Fluid Mechanics, 1687–1765* (Zurich, 1954), pp. 38–41.

Another significant part of Euler's commentaries was his analysis of a ballistic trajectory, which included air-resistance effects.[75] Euler used approximate methods to simplify his analysis of the complex nonlinear differential equations of ballistic motion. Unfortunately, his solution was valid only for military projectiles flying at low velocities. Yet he did obtain a partial solution relating launch angle to range when the air resistance is small. With this solution he proved that the angle required to launch a projectile at its maximum distance was not 45 degrees, as Galileo's theory held, but depended on the air-resistance magnitude instead.

Euler did not organize this analysis into useful gunnery tables. Rather, it was Robins who provided the first tabulated solutions of the differential equations of projectile motion in the atmosphere, thus permitting easy gunnery calculations.[76] Use of this table required only a knowledge of Galileo's ballistics theory. Robins presented these results to the Royal Society in 1746, just a year after Euler published his analysis of these equations of motion in his translation of *New Principles of Gunnery.* Unfortunately, Robins's table was not published until 1761 when James Wilson published *Mathematical Tracts of the Late Benjamin Robins,* a two-volume collection of Robins's research papers and books. Robins did not describe how he derived these ballistics tables; he seemed more concerned with demonstrating their utility, which he accomplished in an article titled "A Comparison of the Experimental Ranges of Cannon and Mortars, with the Theory contained in the preceding Papers," sent to the Royal Society from India in 1750.[77] Robins showed that his ballistics table, while admittedly approximate, was sufficiently accurate for the mortar and cannon pieces of his age.

Robins demonstrated his table's accuracy by comparing its predictions to experimental observations. A 13-inch sea mortar threw a 231-pound shell to a distance of 3,350 yards when loaded with 30 pounds of gunpowder, according to the Woolwich Arsenal reports. Robins's calculation of this range, after accounting for the change in atmospheric pressure, was 3,230 yards—a difference of 120 yards. For a 10-inch mortar firing a 96-pound shell to a distance of 3,350 yards, Robins's calculation was off by 160 yards. Robins pursued his argument by comparing his results with measurements of cannon ranges, as published by authors such as Surirey de Saint Rémy. He showed that, for a cannon firing a 24-pound shot at angles from 4 to 40 degrees and producing ranges from 820 to 2,050 toises (1 toise = 2 yards), respectively, the

[75]Euler (n. 28 above), pp. 294–320.
[76]Robins (n. 6 above), p. 179.
[77]Robins (n. 38 above), p. 231.

error of his theory varied from 46 to 122 toises. After comparing his calculations to a series of French experiments made at Metz in 1740, Robins concluded, that "Our theory differs less from the experiments, than the experiments do from each other."[78] For example, a 24-pound cannon effectively elevated to 5 degrees, loaded with 10 pounds of gunpowder, and fired repeatedly by the French had ranges of 834, 872, 851, 845, 871, and 838 toises. Robins's table for the same situation gives 850 toises. In spite of the approximate nature of this ballistics analysis, especially when Robins took into consideration the changes in air resistance due to atmospheric pressure changes, it represents the first adequate calculation of high-speed projectile range.

In 1753 Euler published the first complete analysis of the equations of ballistic motion in the atmosphere.[79] His basic assumption was that the projectile's air resistance was proportional to its velocity squared. Using Robins's quantitative measurements of muzzle velocity and air resistance, the key parameters essential for achieving any numerical results, Euler provided a fundamental method for handling this complex mechanics problem, a problem perhaps as difficult as the notorious three-body problem in celestial mechanics.[80] Both phenomena are nonlinear without an exact mathematical solution. For the ballistics problem, Euler numerically integrated the equations representing the trajectory's range, altitude, time, and velocity by using the trapezoidal rule.[81] He decided to divide the trajectories into sets of families or species to perform this integration. Each species represents those trajectories whose asymptotes of the ascending section are the same when the trajectory becomes infinitely extended. In other words, each species represents particular combinations of muzzle velocity and elevation angle. Euler calculated the ballistics table for a particular species as an example. With it he could determine velocity, range, maximum altitude, and flight time for a projectile fired at certain muzzle velocities and elevation angles. In 1764, Henning Friedrich, Graf von Graevenitz, a German infantry officer, provided a complete set of ballistics tables by calculating eighteen species of trajectories using

[78]Ibid., p. 239.

[79]L. Euler, "Recherches sur la véritable courbe que décrivent les corps jetés dans l'air, ou dans un autre fluide quelconque," *Mémoires de l'Académie de Berlin* (Berlin, 1753), pp. 321–52. H. Brown translated this paper and included it in *True Principles of Gunnery Investigated and Explored* (n. 28 above), pp. 322–66.

[80]For additional perspectives on Euler's ballistics work, see Szabó (n. 4 above), pp. 211–20; as well as Charbonnier (n. 4 above), pp. 118–41.

[81]The trapezoidal rule is a technique to integrate a function numerically or to find the area beneath a curve by approximating the area with a series of trapezoids. Integration is then a matter of calculating the area of each trapezoid and adding them up.

Euler's method.[82] (See fig. 4.) These ballistics tables proved to be especially valid for mortar fire in the 18th century.[83] (They remained in use at least until World War II for calculating ballistics tables for low-velocity and high-angle mortar fire.)[84] Numerous mathematicians and engineers expanded on Euler's work to analyze more complex ballistic trajectories and to derive simpler approximate theories. In the 18th century, these researchers included Johann Heinrich Lambert, de Borda, G. F. Tempelhoff, and Adrien-Marie Legendre. Vannevar Bush's differential analyzer and the ENIAC computer were developed in part to compute solutions of ballistics equations for high-speed and long-range artillery during the first half of the 20th century.

*The Military Response to Robins's and Euler's Ballistics*

The new scientific ground opened by Robins's and Euler's revolution in ballistics was rapidly utilized by the European military establishments. Euler's initial motivation to translate *New Principles of Gunnery* was provided by Frederick the Great, who wanted Euler to translate into German the best artillery theory book available in order to increase his artillery officers' competence in gunnery.[85] The French soon took notice of these Prussian and English ballistics developments.[86] *New Principles of Gunnery* was originally translated into French in 1751 by Jean-Baptiste Le Roy. According to Truesdell, Anne Robert Jacques Turgot wrote to Louis XVI in 1774 that "the famous Leonard Euler, one of the greatest mathematicians of Europe, has written two works which could be very useful to the schools of the navy and the artillery. One is a Treatise on the construction and Maneuver of Vessels; the other is a commentary on the principles of artillery of Robins. . . . I propose that Your Majesty order these to be printed."[87] It was 1783 before Jean-Louis Lombard translated Robins and Euler into French. The ballistics revolution offers

[82]H. F. Graevenitz, *Akademischen Abhandlung von der Bahn der Geschützkugeln* (Rostock, 1764).

[83]Jean-Louis Lombard, *Traité du mouvement des projectiles, appliqué au tir des bouches à feu* (Dijon, 1797), pp. 201–22.

[84]E. McShane, J. Kelley, and F. Reno, *Exterior Ballistics* (Denver, 1953), p. 258.

[85]See the introduction to Leonhard Euler, *Neue Grundsätze der Artillerie* (see n. 28), written by F. R. Scherrer for Euler's *Opera Omnia,* 2d ser., vol. 14 (Leipzig and Berlin, 1922). Also see Euler's letter to Frederick the Great regarding Robins's work and his translation plans, in *Correspondance de Leonhard Euler* (Basel, 1986), 4:309.

[86]For an overview of the relationship between science and warfare in 18th-century France, see Charles Gillispie, *Science and Polity in France at the End of the Old Regime* (Princeton, N.J., 1980); and Roger Hahn, "L'enseignement scientifique aux écoles militaires et d'artillerie," in *Écoles techniques et militaires au XVIII siècle,* ed. Roger Hahn and René Taton (Paris, 1986), pp. 514–45. The most extensive analysis of this relationship remains Guerlac's dissertation (n. 9 above).

[87]Truesdell (n. 72 above), p. 337.

33

## Die VIII. Art, $\gamma = 35°$, aufsteigender Bogen.

| Erhöh. Winkel β | Bogen AG = 2,302585c mult. mit | Weite AF = 2,302585c mult. mit | Höhe FG = 2,302585c mult. mit | Geschwind. in G $=\sqrt{2agc}$ mult. mit |
|---|---|---|---|---|
| 0° | 0, 0000000 | 0, 0000000 | 0, 0000000 | 1, 1517744 |
| 5° | 0, 0536504 | 0, 0535931 | 0, 0023402 | 1, 2298471 |
| 10° | 0, 1164065 | 0, 1158121 | 0, 0105315 | 1, 3372699 |
| 15° | 0, 1935934 | 0, 1911693 | 0, 0272378 | 1, 4901162 |
| 20° | 0, 2952450 | 0, 2881162 | 0, 0578050 | 1, 7219160 |
| 25° | 0, 4441013 | 0, 4256416 | 0, 1147698 | 2, 1190543 |
| 30° | 0, 7134214 | 0, 6645303 | 0, 2391278 | 3, 0237457 |

## Niedersteigender Bogen.

| Winkel in H | Bogen AH = 2,302585c mult. mit | Weite AE = 2,302585c mult. mit | Höhe EH = 2,302585c mult. mit | Geschwind. in H $=\sqrt{2agc}$ mult. mit |
|---|---|---|---|---|
| 5° | 0, 0477456 | 0, 0477002 | 0, 0020826 | 1, 0943354 |
| 10° | 0, 0916889 | 0, 0912676 | 0, 0078183 | 1, 0523529 |
| 15° | 0, 1334123 | 0, 1320020 | 0, 0168489 | 1, 0225533 |
| 20° | 0, 1741257 | 0, 1708310 | 0, 0290916 | 1, 0030180 |
| 25° | 0, 2149125 | 0, 2085131 | 0, 0447000 | 0, 9923740 |
| 30° | 0, 2568288 | 0, 2456933 | 0, 0640548 | 0, 9894922 |
| 35° | 0, 3010101 | 0, 2829554 | 0, 0877934 | 0, 9942320 |
| 40° | 0, 3487869 | 0, 3224633 | 0, 1181088 | 1, 0062590 |
| 45° | 0, 4008361 | 0, 3608380 | 0, 1532727 | 1, 0267250 |
| [illegible] | 0, 4624001 | 0, 4024300 | 0, 1986624 | 1, 0521799 |
| 55° | 0, 5336408 | 0, 4457985 | 0, 2551789 | 1, 0862895 |
| 60° | 0, 6202174 | 0, 4923160 | 0, 3281968 | 1, 1279210 |
| 65° | 0, 7295507 | 0, 5418005 | 0, 4251766 | 1, 1766132 |

E Die

Fig. 4.—One of Graevenitz's ballistics tables based on Euler's analysis of projectile motion where air resistance is considered. (H. F. Graevenitz, *Akademischen Abhandlung von der Bahn der Geschützkugeln* [Rostock, 1764], p. 33.)

one explanation of why the École Polytechnique provided such advanced scientific and mathematical education—to prepare cadets with sufficient knowledge to comprehend advanced ballistics textbooks such as the fourth volume of Etienne Bézout's *Cours de mathématiques, à l'usage du corps de l'artillerie* (first published in 1772) or Lombard's *Traité du mouvement des projectiles, appliqué au tir des bouches à feu.*[88] During the Napoleonic Wars, more École Polytechnique graduates served in the artillery than in any other branch of the French military.[89] One of the consequences of providing such an education was the mathematization of physics during the early 19th century, as the work of Augustin Jean Fresnel, Étienne Louis Malus, Joseph Louis Gay-Lussac, Sadi Carnot, and other École Polytechnique graduates so dramatically demonstrated.

Napoléon Bonaparte himself provides an example of the extent to which Robins and Euler influenced military thinking in the late 18th century. As a young artillery lieutenant at the regimental artillery school at Auxonne, he studied Lombard's translation of Euler's *Neue Grundsätze der Artillerie.* Lombard, incidentally, was Napoléon's artillery theory professor. Napoléon's thorough comprehension of such concepts as Robins's interior ballistics theories, the Robins effect, the limitation of Galileo's parabolic theory, the change in the air-resistance function at the speed of sound, and other fundamental ballistics concepts discovered by Robins is evident in his twelve-page summary of *New Principles of Gunnery,* written in 1788.[90] Napoléon's competence in ballistics was also demonstrated when Baron du Teil, the commander of the Auxonne artillery school, chose him to supervise a series of experiments designed to investigate the possibility of shooting mortar shells out of cannon.[91] Napoléon ultimately wrote two memoirs on this subject for du Teil.[92]

Even though an influence clearly exists, it is difficult to measure the precise impact that Robins and Euler had on Napoléon. It is possible to conclude, however, that their ideas contributed to Napoléon's success as a military commander, especially in his utilization of artillery. During the Siege of Toulon, the conflict that thrust Napoléon into national prominence during the French Revolutionary War, his scientific understanding of cannon and mortar fire was an important element in the development of his victorious strategy, which required precise

[88]Etienne Bézout, *Cours de mathématiques, à l'usage du corps de l'artillerie,* vol. 4 (Paris, 1797); Lombard (n. 83 above).

[89]Joachim Fischer, *Napoleon und die Naturwissenschaften* (Stuttgart, 1988), p. 199. According to Fischer, in the years 1804, 1807, 1808, 1809, 1810, 1812, and 1813, more than half the new École Polytechnique graduates served in the artillery. In 1814 and 1815, more than 70 percent served.

[90]N. Bonaparte, *Napoléon inconnu, papiers inédits (1786–1793) publiés par Fréderic Masson et Guido Biagi accompagnés de notes sur la jeunesse de Napoléon (1769–1793) par F. Masson* (Paris, 1895), 1:249–61.

[91]S. Wilkinson, *The Rise of General Bonaparte* (Oxford, 1930), p. 5.

[92]N. Bonaparte, "Mémoire sur la manière de disposer les canons pour le jet des bombes," in *Napoléon inconnu,* pp. 272–78.

information regarding his artillery's effectiveness at different ranges. At the beginning of the siege, Napoléon wrote to the Committee of Public Safety to request that it send an artillery general who can, "if only by his rank, demand respect and deal with a crowd of fools on the staff with whom one has constantly to argue and lay down the law in order to overcome their prejudices and make them take action which theory and practice alike have shown to be axiomatic to any trained officer of this corps."[93] Such a display of confidence from a young artillery officer with little previous combat experience certainly came in part from his theoretical understanding of ballistics.

A military historian likewise argued that one of Napoléon's advantages as a military commander lay in his education in ballistics:

> Trained in the artillery sciences, [Napoléon] had a keen grasp of the principles of physics and the concepts of energy and force. No one understood better than he the relationships of mass, time and the distance that went into the creation of energy. This much emerges from his methods of conducting a campaign or battle. . . . Once his plan developed, Napoleon's understanding of the concepts of energy and force would erupt again. Massive batteries, massive infantry columns and on occasion, massive cavalry columns could break a wall by the concentration of great energy and create rapid concentrations of force at this chosen point of attack, achieving local superiority even if he did not enjoy the overall advantages in numbers.[94]

Perhaps Napoléon referred to such reasoning when he stated, "I judge also that all officers ought to serve in the artillery, which is the arm which can produce the best generals."[95]

Great Britain was also inspired in part by the ballistics revolution to increase the scientific and mathematical education of artillery officers. The British established a military academy for the education of artillery and engineering officers in 1741. Its specific purpose, according to its warrant, was to instruct "the raw and inexperienced People belonging to the Military Branch of this (Ordnance) Office, in the several parts of Mathematicks necessary to qualify them for the Service of the Artillery, and the business of Engineers."[96] From the very beginning, the combina-

[93]John Eldred Howard, ed. and trans., *Letters and Documents of Napoleon*, vol. 1, *The Rise to Power* (New York, 1961), p. 40.

[94]R. Riehn, *1812: Napoleon's Russian Campaign* (New York, 1991), pp. 126–27.

[95]Quoted from F. Downey, *Cannonade: Great Artillery Actions of History* (New York, 1966), p. 333.

[96]O. F. Hogg, *The Royal Arsenal: Its Background, Origin, and Subsequent History* (London, 1963), p. 347.

tion of theory and practice was to be the means of instruction. The original rules for the new academy stated "that an Academy or School shall forthwith be established and opened at the Warren at Woolwich in Kent, for instructing the people of the Military branch of the Ordnance, wherein shall be taught, both in theory and practice, whatever may be necessary or useful to form good Officers of Artillery and perfect Engineers."[97] The quality of the scientific and mathematical education at Woolwich never reached the level of the French military schools. Nevertheless, the mathematics taught by Hutton, as demonstrated by his textbook *A Course of Mathematics, in Two Volumes: Composed and more Especially Designed, for the use of the Gentlemen Cadets in the Royal Military Academy at Woolwich,* shows the cadets had the opportunity to learn enough mathematics to comprehend Robins's and Euler's ballistics work.[98] Hutton seems to have used *New Principles of Gunnery* as a textbook when teaching ballistics during his thirty-four-year tenure at Woolwich beginning in 1773, and he edited a new edition in 1805.[99]

Henry Knox, the commander of the Continental army's artillery during the American War of Independence, was sufficiently impressed with Woolwich's graduates to send an urgent letter to the Continental Congress after the American defeat at Long Island in 1776: "As officers can never act with confidence until they are masters of their profession, an academy established upon a liberal plan would be of the utmost service to the continent, where the whole theory and practice of fortification and gunnery should be taught, to be nearly on the same plan as that at Woolwich—making allowances for differences of circumstances—a place to which our enemies are indebted for the superiority of their artillery to all who have opposed them."[100] Knox tried to maintain the quality of his artillery officers during the Revolution by requesting that "no officer should be appointed to the artillery who does not possess a proper knowledge of the mathematics and other necessary abilities for the nature of the service."[101] He specifically recommended the works of such military engineering and artillery

[97]Ibid., p. 348.

[98]Charles Hutton, *A Course of Mathematics, in Two Volumes: Composed and more Especially Designed, for the use of the Gentlemen Cadets in the Royal Military Academy at Woolwich* (London, 1798).

[99]Robins (n. 38 above). An edition of *New Principles of Gunnery* was published in Great Britain for almost every war in which that country fought from the mid-18th century to the beginning of the 19th century: 1742 (War of the Austrian Succession), 1761 (Seven Years' War/French and Indian War), 1777 (American Revolutionary War), and 1805 (Napoleonic Wars).

[100]William E. Birkhimer, *Historical Sketch of the Organization, Administration, Material and Tactics of the Artillery, United States Army* (Washington, D.C., 1884), p. 4.

[101]Ibid., p. 110.

authors as Sebastien le Préstre de Vauban, Baron Menno van Coehoorn, Nicholas François Blondel, Bélidor, John Muller, and Francis Holliday to John Adams, who was then serving in the Continental Congress.[102] Muller, the professor of artillery and fortifications at Woolwich, wrote *A Treatise of Artillery,* which contains a discussion of Robins's interior ballistics theory. Holliday, an English mathematics instructor, wrote *Introduction to Practical Gunnery, or, The Art of Engineering;* here, he discussed the effect of air resistance on projectiles and the analytical complexity such a phenomenon creates.[103] Even Alexander Hamilton had to demonstrate his mathematical competence to get his commission as an artillery captain from the colony of New York at the beginning of the Revolutionary War. He had learned how to apply his knowledge of mathematics to solve basic gunnery problems from a British army bombardier.[104] Hamilton therefore wrote with considerable authority in 1799 that an American military academy for military engineering and artillery officers should include such topics as calculus, conic sections, chemistry, hydraulics, hydrostatics, pneumatics, and the theory and practice of gunnery and fortification design.[105]

The German states in general and Prussia in particular took advantage of what the ballistics revolution had to offer. This was demonstrated by the ballistics research effort undertaken by Graevenitz, Tempelhoff, Legendre, and Lambert. Tempelhoff is a particularly good example of Robins's and Euler's influence on Prussian military thinking. In addition to his ballistics research and writings, Tempelhoff commanded the Prussian artillery during the French Revolutionary War and was the director of the Prussian Militärakademie der Artillerie from 1791 to 1807. Not only did he write a number of mathematics textbooks for the Prussian artillery corps, with subjects ranging from geometry to differential and integral calculus, but he also wrote *Le bombardier prussien,* a theoretical ballistics work that built on Robins's and Euler's analysis.[106] Frederick the Great praised the work, but he offered his sincerest compliment by restricting its distribution for national security reasons.[107]

The Austrians were also enlightened regarding the scientific education of artillery officers during the latter half of the 18th century. Prince Joseph Wenzel von Lichtenstein (1696–1772), whose reform of the

[102]North Callahan, *Henry Knox: General Washington's General* (New York, 1958), pp. 35–36.

[103]John Muller, *A Treatise of Artillery* (London, 1757), pp. 1–8; Francis Holliday, *Introduction to Practical Gunnery, or, The Art of Engineering* (London, 1756), p. 165.

[104]Robert Hendrickson, *Hamilton I (1757–1789)* (New York, 1976), pp. 92–93.

[105]John C. Hamilton, ed., *The Works of Alexander Hamilton* (New York, 1851), 5:380.

[106]G. F. Tempelhoff, *Le bombardier prussien* (Berlin, 1781).

[107]Oskar Albrecht, "Georg Friedrich von Tempelhoff," *Soldat und Technik* (September 1966), pp. 493–94.

Austrian artillery proved to be so shocking to Frederick the Great during the Seven Years' War and so motivating to General Gribeauval of France, set up an artillery research center at Moldauthein and an artillery school at Bergstadl in the 1740s during the War of the Austrian Succession.[108] The subjects taught included the standard mathematical topics such as arithmetic, geometry, and trigonometry, and such scientific engineering topics as mechanics, hydraulics, optics, fortifications, and ballistics.[109] Lichtenstein initially published the artillery books of Bélidor and others for his artillery school. In 1786, the Austrians set up a corps of bombardiers, who were especially trained to handle mortars, howitzers, and siege cannon.[110] One sees a direct influence of the ballistics revolution on this artillery corps as demonstrated by their textbook *Praktische Anweisung zum Bombenwerfen mittelst dazu eingerichteter Hilfstafeln,* which came from the third volume of *Mathematischen Vorlesungen des Artilleriehauptmanns und Professors der Mathematik bey dem kaiserl. köngl. Bombardierkorps Georg Vega.*[111] The first section of *Praktische Anweisung* addresses the effect of air resistance on military projectiles.

Finally, the Italians. General Alessandro Vittorio Papacino D'Antoni, a major general in the Sardinian army and chief director of the Royal Military Academies of Artillery and Fortification at Turin during the 1760s and 1770s, not to mention a highly regarded research engineer in interior ballistics, wrote extensively on theoretical, experimental, and practical aspects of ballistics and artillery. In his *A Treatise on Gunpowder; a Treatise on Fire-Arms; and a Treatise on the Service of Artillery in the Time of War,* D'Antoni devoted significant attention to Robins's interior ballistics analysis and measurements of air resistance, as well as the advances made in theoretical and experimental ballistics after the ballistics revolution.[112]

Although plenty of evidence exists that shows the influence of the ballistics revolution in 18th-century military education, this only indirectly indicates its influence on the actual battles and sieges of that age. Did artillery officers actually use Euler's and Robins's ballistics in combat, or did they do so only in classrooms to discipline their minds? This is a difficult question and will require considerable archival research to document fully. Nevertheless, some immediate evidence is already at hand. Graevenitz's book, *Akademischen Abhandlung von der*

[108]Duffy, *Army of Maria Theresa* (n. 23 above), p. 105.

[109]Ibid., p. 108.

[110]Anton Dolleczek, *Geschichte der Österreichischen Artillerie* (Graz, 1973). See the section titled "Das Bombardier Corps."

[111]*Mathematischen Vorlesungen des Artilleriehauptmanns und Professors der Mathematik bey dem kaiserl. köngl. Bombardierkorps Georg Vega* (Vienna, 1787).

[112]D'Antoni (n. 1 above), pp. 74–98.

*Bahn der Geschützkugeln,* where Euler's ballistics theory is presented with a complete set of numerical tables, was published in 1764. Perhaps the fact that Graevenitz took the trouble to numerically integrate the hundreds of equations required to create the tables is the best evidence for its practical utility in combat. What other rational motivation could exist to undertake such a tedious exercise? Graevenitz was not the first to calculate these tables, however. Paul Jacobi, a lieutenant in the Prussian artillery, calculated them and presented them to the Berlin Academy of Sciences soon after Euler published his solution in 1753. Unfortunately, Jacobi was killed in the Seven Years' War, and his manuscript was lost.[113]

Regardless of whether the ballistics revolution was directly felt on the battlefields and sieges of the Seven Years' War, it certainly made an impact on the combat of the French Revolutionary War in the 1790s. The most vivid evidence of this is Lombard's ballistics tables, published in 1787 as *Tables du tir des canons et des obusiers.*[114] French artillery officers used these tables in combat during both the French Revolutionary War and the Napoleonic Wars.[115] In his textbook *Traité du mouvement des projectiles, appliqué au tir des bouches à feu,* Lombard described the approximate interior and exterior ballistics theories he used to calculate the tables.[116] The difference between these tables and those of Bélidor from the 1730s is vivid proof of the ballistics revolution's influence on 18th-century warfare. Instead of using Galileo's parabolic trajectory theory to derive a simple relationship between elevation angle and range, Lombard's tables are all written in terms of muzzle velocity. Each type of cannon has four different tables. The cannon include siege (24-, 16-, 12-, 8-, and 4-pounders), field (12-, 8-, and 4-pounders), and howitzers (8- and 6-pounders). The weight refers to the cannonball. The first table shows the relationship between quantity of gunpowder and muzzle velocity for different strengths of gunpowder. The second table shows the relationship between muzzle velocity and impact velocity for different ranges, whereas the third and fourth tables show the relationship between muzzle velocity, range, and elevation angle below and above the natural point-blank range for the artillery piece in question.

The use of such tables in 18th-century warfare raises another question: if ballistics and range tables were available, why then did European governments take the trouble to provide artillery officers with a

[113]Graevenitz (n. 82 above); see the introduction.

[114]Jean-Louis Lombard, *Tables du tir des canons et des obusiers* (Auxonne, 1787).

[115]C. N. Amanton, *Recherches biographiques, sur le professeur d'artillerie, Lombard* (Dijon, 1802), p. 17. Also see Charbonnier (n. 4 above), p. 187.

[116]Lombard, *Traite' du mouvement des projectiles* (n. 83 above).

mathematical and scientific education? Is it really necessary to know ballistics theory in order to use numerical tables? Napoléon Bonaparte seemed to think so. He wrote in 1801 that some of Lombard's and Robins's ballistics theories are important for the artillery and should therefore be included in the textbooks for the proposed artillery and engineering school at Metz.[117]

Eighteenth-century gunnery tables were designed to speed up calculations, not to replace a solid grasp of the theory. Euler/Graevenitz's table, for example (fig. 4), is quite incomprehensible to someone who does not understand its derivation. Furthermore, there was much more to 18th-century gunnery than simply establishing the correct angle to launch a projectile to a desired distance. When supervising the firing of howitzer or mortar shells, an officer had to estimate the fuse's length to cause an explosion at an optimal point in the shell's trajectory. For example, a howitzer shell needed to explode at just the right point in the air in order to cause the greatest number of casualties.[118] Mortar shells, on the other hand, when used to destroy buildings, needed to explode after they crashed through a roof. Such calculations are relatively easy when using Euler's theory as presented in Graevenitz's tables. Lombard's tables seem much more straightforward than Graevenitz's, and gunners who had no knowledge of their derivation could potentially use them. These tables are based on certain simplifying assumptions, however, and could give misleading results if used under conditions that might violate these assumptions. Hence, only officers with a solid grasp of the theory could use these tables with full confidence, a quality not to be taken for granted during the tremendous confusion and uncertainty of combat. As Matti Lauerma wrote in *L'artillerie de campagne française pendant les guerres de la révolution,* "The lack of fundamental theoretical knowledge apparently diminished the accuracy of artillery fire to a considerable extent."[119]

General D'Antoni strongly believed that a sound knowledge of ballistics in particular, as well as mechanics in general, was essential for an artillery officer. For example, he wrote, "There are other methods of

[117]Napoléon Bonaparte, "Notes sur un project de réglement pour l'école d'artillerie et du génie," June 27, 1801 (no. 5621), *Correspondance de Napoléon I publiée par ordre de l'Empereur Napoléon III* (Paris, 1861), 7:232–33. Napoléon wrote, "Les ouvrages que l'on enseignait à l'école du génie avant la révolution existent et ne laissent rien à désirer. L'aide-mémoire, classé d'une manière convenable, et quelques principes de théorie qui se trouvent dans Lombard et dans Robins, fourniraient un bon ouvrage pour l'artillerie. On a aussi d'excellents traités sur les mines et sur l'art de lever les plans" (pp. 232–33).

[118]Hughes (n. 25 above), p. 34.

[119]Matti Lauerma, *L'artillerie de campagne française pendant les guerres de la révolution* (Helsinki, 1956), p. 57, or in the original French, "Le manque de connaissance théoriques de base diminuait apparemment dans une forte mesure la précision du tir de l'artillerie."

ascertaining the path described by projectiles, and the retarding force of the air; but it is to be presumed that the principles laid down in the course of this treatise will, from their practical utility and easy application, induce the students to exercise themselves in the theory of gunnery, whence they may derive from the use of fire-arms, particularly of mortars, advantages which can by no other means be obtained."[120] D'Antoni gave a specific example why theory was so useful.[121] He stated that there are two different types of mortar bombardments. The first is when the gunner's objective is to launch a shell at a particular target when the force of impact is not consequential, such as when the targets are enemy artillery pieces and troops or when the goal is to set fire to buildings. For such activity, bombardiers without any knowledge of ballistics can be taught to accomplish these goals. For bombardments when the force of the shell's impact is significant, the situation is different. "The second case, to break through casemated buildings, requires much theoretical knowledge in the officer charged with the execution of this piece of service, in order to determine the situation of the mortar, its proper charge and elevation; that the shell may impinge on the object with the greatest possible force."[122] D'Antoni then described the ballistics calculation required to determine the shell's impact velocity and how to calculate the force of impact. Clearly, there were some gunnery problems that could be solved by experience and practical training alone. Nevertheless, certain crucial problems demanded advance mathematical and scientific knowledge to solve effectively. This is just one similarity between 18th-century gunnery and 20th-century engineering.

The most direct evidence for the influence of the ballistics revolution on late-18th-century battlefields comes from the dramatically improved accuracy of ballistics theories that incorporated experimental air-resistance values. Bézout provided a series of tables in the fourth volume of his *Cours de mathématiques* that compared experimental measurements of artillery projectile ranges with calculations by using theories that were derived before and after the ballistics revolution, that is, Galileo's theory and air-resistance theories (fig. 5). The table for mortar-shell range and time of flight consists of columns (from left to right) of the launch angle, theoretical range without air resistance, theoretical range with air resistance, the experimental ranges, and the same division for time of flight. Although the difference between the range predicted by the air-resistance theory and average experimental range was as high as 37

[120] D'Antoni (n. 1 above), p. 98.
[121] Ibid., p. 225.
[122] Ibid., p. 226.

*TABLE des Portées de Bombes, calculées 1°. en supposant que l'air ne résiste pas; 2°. ayant égard à la résistance de l'air; & comparées aux Portées observées dans les épreuves faites à La Fère, au mois d'Octobre 1771, par les ordres de M.r le Marquis de Monteynard, Secrétaire d'État ayant le département de la Guerre, & sous la direction de M. de Beauvoir, Brigadier des armées du Roi, Commandant en chef l'école d'Artillerie.*

| ANGLES de PROJECTION. | PORTÉES CALCULÉES | | PORTÉES OBSERVÉES. | DURÉE DES PORTÉES | | | ANGLES de CHUTE. |
|---|---|---|---|---|---|---|---|
| | Sans égard à la résistance. | Eu égard à la résistance. | | Sans la résistance. | Eu égard à la résistance. | Selon l'Expérience. | |
| degrés. | toises. | toises. | toises. | secondes. | secondes. | secondes. | degrés. |
| 10 | 253 | 217 | 257. 249. 221, 228. | $4\frac{1}{5}$ | $4\frac{1}{20}$ | 4 | 14. |
| 20 | 476 | 396 | 440. 424. 394. 398. | $8\frac{3}{10}$ | 8 | $7\frac{1}{3}$ | 26. |
| 30 | 640 | 500 | 451. 516. 537. 492. | $12\frac{1}{5}$ | $11\frac{3}{10}$ | $10\frac{3}{4}$ | 36. |
| 40 | 728 | 547 | 569. 575. 574. 544. 577. | $15\frac{3}{5}$ | $14\frac{2}{5}$ | $14\frac{4}{5}$ | 48. |
| 43 | 738 | 549 | 506. 517. 543. 509. 544. | $16\frac{1}{2}$ | $15\frac{1}{5}$ | 14 | $50\frac{1}{2}$. |
| 45 | 739 | 547 | 490. 536. 505. 489. 554. | $17\frac{1}{5}$ | $15\frac{4}{5}$ | $15\frac{1}{5}$ | $52\frac{2}{3}$. |
| 50 | 728 | 534 | 481. 512. 488. 507. | $18\frac{1}{5}$ | $16\frac{9}{10}$ | 16 | $57\frac{1}{2}$. |
| 60 | 640 | 467 | 457. 424. 457. 448. | 21 | $19\frac{3}{10}$ | $19\frac{1}{5}$ | 68. |
| 70 | 476 | 348 | 349. 297. 349. 328. | $22\frac{4}{5}$ | $20\frac{7}{10}$ | 22 | 74. |
| 75 | 370 | 277 | 298. 265. 261. 256. | $23\frac{2}{5}$ | $21\frac{7}{10}$ | 22 | 78. |

Les bombes dont on a fait usage dans ces épreuves, étoient de 11 pouces 10 lignes de diamètre, du poids de 142$^{liv.}$, y compris la terre dont on les avoit remplies; & elles ont été chassées avec 3$^{liv.}$ $\frac{1}{4}$ de poudre.

Fig. 5.—Bézout's range and time-of-flight table comparing Galileo's ballistics theory, ballistics theory with air resistance considered, and experimental observations as a function of firing angle. (Etienne Bézout, *Cours de mathématiques, à l'usage du corps de l'artillerie* [Paris, 1797], p. 456.)

toises or 74 yards (at an angle of 50 degrees and range of about 500 toise or 1,000 yards), the theory failed in only three cases (43, 50, and 60 degrees) to provide a range within the area where the shells landed. Galileo's theory, in contrast, only succeeded at 10 degrees to provide a range within this area. Although Bézout did not provide enough experimental values for a proper statistical error analysis, this table suggests the power available to artillery officers after the ballistics revolution.

## *Conclusion*

The science of mechanics was a significant military technology during the 18th century; ballistics and its effect on gunnery is a case in point. This contradicts the perception that rational mechanics had little effect on early modern mechanical technology.[123] Beginning with Galileo in the 17th century and continuing with Robins and Euler in the 18th century, mechanics was developed, in part, to optimize artillery systems. Galileo's ballistics theory, a first-order approximation and valid only for a restricted set of gunnery problems, was nevertheless the foundation of the science of ballistics. Robins and Euler built on Galileo's work by using advanced theories of mechanics and mathematics coupled with experimental research. The inventor of the first aerodynamic instruments to measure successfully a projectile's velocity and air resistance, Robins discovered such fundamental aerodynamic phenomena as the enormous magnitude of air resistance at high speeds and the Robins effect, as well as making the first observations of the sound barrier. Furthermore, he conducted a pioneering theoretical and experimental study of the work generated by gunpowder gases within a gun barrel. Robins's experimental results made his own, as well as Euler's, analysis of the nonlinear differential equations of ballistic motion possible. They

[123]H. J. M. Bos, "Mathematics and Rational Mechanics," in *The Ferment of Knowledge: Studies in the Historiography of Eighteenth-Century Science,* ed. G. S. Rousseau and Roy Porter (Cambridge, 1980), p. 354. According to Bos, "The actual influence of theoretical results in the case of these (technological) problems is very difficult to assess. As regards the longitude problem the influence was certainly there; in the case of the other problems it is doubtful whether insights gained through mathematical theory effectively influenced practice before the nineteenth century." A corresponding view is found in Thomas L. Hankins, *Science and the Enlightenment* (New York, 1985), p. 23: "Only in astronomy did the new analysis show immediate practical results in the increased precision of astronomical tables and in the creation of new theories concerning the shape and motions of the earth and other heavenly bodies." Contrast this with Thomas Hughes and Gunther Rothenberg's comments regarding the practical utilization of mathematics and mechanics in 18th-century France and Austria (Hughes [n. 4 above], pp. 69–80). Hughes wrote that "science and technology were an integral and practical part of the military culture of eighteenth century France" (p. 74).

used the equation's solutions to construct useful gunnery tables. The ballistics revolution therefore contradicts the popular idea that the experimental and mathematical sciences remained essentially separate until the 19th century. Robins's and Euler's research revolutionized experimental and theoretical ballistics by transforming it into an aerodynamic and thermodynamic science, to use two admittedly anachronistic adjectives. This provided the benefit of increasing the effectiveness of ballistics theory for gunnery practice at the cost of increasing its analytical complexity. As a result, the military powers of 18th-century Europe had to improve their artillery officers' education in mathematics and science to compete effectively in warfare.

The historical development of ballistics demonstrates an important characteristic of engineering: the creation of fundamental scientific knowledge or basic research. As Steven Goldman recently argued, "The crucial point to appreciate is that engineering on its own activity generates knowledge. It does not passively wait for knowledge to be given to it from a different community of practitioners in order for it to attempt complex enterprises."[124] The role engineers have played in the development of the physical sciences before the 20th century has attracted significant, but limited, scholarly attention. Stephen Timoshenko outlined the basic theoretical and experimental research conducted by engineers in elasticity and strength of materials from the Renaissance until the beginning of the 20th century.[125] Terry Reynolds described the basic fluid dynamics theory developed by such 18th-century engineers as de Borda and Lazare Carnot.[126] The structural research conducted by certain U.S. engineers in the 19th century is discussed by Edwin T. Layton in "Mirror-Image Twins."[127] C. Stewart Gillmor's study of Charles-Augustin de Coulomb highlights an 18th-century engineer's contributions to physics and mechanics, while Cardwell shows the similar role engineers such as Sadi Carnot and Emile Clapeyron played in the creation of modern thermodynamics.[128] These authors demonstrate the often unacknowledged fact that scientific discoveries are not made solely by scientists studying natural phenomena and that the history of science is incomplete without taking engineering research into consideration.

[124]Steven L. Goldman, "Philosophy, Engineering, and Western Culture," in *Broad and Narrow Interpretations of Philosophy of Technology*, ed. Paul Durbin (Dordrecht, 1990), p. 141.

[125]Stephen Timoshenko, *History of Strength of Materials* (New York, 1953).

[126]Terry Reynolds, *Stronger than a Hundred Men* (Baltimore, 1983), pp. 231–48.

[127]Edwin T. Layton, "Mirror-Image Twins: The Communities of Science and Technology in 19th-Century America," *Technology and Culture* 12 (1971): 564–80.

[128]Cardwell (n. 50 above), pp. 186–211, 220–29; and C. S. Gillmor, *Coulomb and the Evolution of Physics and Engineering in Eighteenth Century France* (Princeton, N.J., 1971).

Benjamin Robins's ballistics work represents a prime example of engineering research because he deliberately set out to analyze a machine. Yet such research also provides an example of the paradoxical consequences of certain popular assumptions regarding engineering research. While investigating the behavior of bullets fired from muskets, Robins discovered fundamental aerodynamic principles. His study therefore also represents basic research. According to popular assumptions, engineering research should be classified only as applied research, the application of existing scientific ideas to solve technological problems. Since applied research cannot be basic research by definition, Robins's work presents a contradiction. This paradox is created by the rigid assumption that pure scientists hold a monopoly on generating basic research or that engineers can only apply scientific knowledge but that they do not create it. The traditional way to avoid this paradox is to classify any engineer who did especially influential basic research as either a scientist or a mathematician or to dismiss the significance of the discoveries. This is historically misleading, however. The labels of the pure sciences (e.g., "physics," "chemistry," and "biology") and engineering refer to the goals, motivations, values, and ideologies of particular intellectual groups. Such labels are social constructs and do not identify the way these groups generate desirable knowledge. In Robins's case we see an 18th-century mathematician and engineer who applied the science of mechanics, as developed by Galileo, Newton, Huygens, and others, to solve fundamental gunnery problems. Yet he did much more. Since significant parts of the scientific knowledge required to solve these technological problems did not exist, he performed the basic research himself and helped create the modern sciences of thermodynamics and aerodynamics in the process. This is not paradoxical; it reflects the very natures of science and engineering.

# [21]

## Thinking about Military Revolution

Dennis Showalter

From the relatively humble beginnings of a lecture delivered in what was a secondary British university, and a pamphlet published in a city then hardly noted as an intellectual center, the concept of "military revolution" has metastasized. It has metastasized semantically, subdividing into the "military technological revolution," which focuses on weapons systems; the "revolution in military affairs," involving related but not comprehensive bodies of innovation in warmaking; and the "military revolution" ***pur***, a comprehensive upheaval, "uncontrollable, unpredictable, and unforeseeable," that brings systemic changes not merely to armed forces but to states and societies. "Military revolution" has metastasized historically. From its original location in the late 16th and early 17th centuries it has been extended backward into the Middle Ages, and forward to the contemporary era with stopovers in the mid-19th and early 20th centuries. "Military revolution" has metastasized geographically. Its initial location in northern Europe, specifically the Netherlands and Sweden, has expanded first to most of the continent including the British Isles, then to Asia, Africa, and the Ottoman Empire. And finally, "military revolution" has metastasized conceptually. Its original paradigm of an episodic process with relatively clear beginnings and ends is being challenged by an alternate concept of development over centuries, with particular actions and reactions less significant than the underlying pattern of steady modernization. In the more extreme version of this thesis, military *revolution* becomes for practical purposes military *evolution*, and invites incorporation into the Whig/Marxist view of history as progress.

The *disputatio* between Jeremy Black and Geoffrey Parker presented here involves intellectual adversaries who invite preliminary categorizing in the context of Isaiah Berlin's famous dichotomy. Black is a fox: a wide-ranging investigator who in the context of war studies takes the world for his province and challenges traditional wisdoms regarding "the West and the Rest." Parker is a hedgehog. No less wide-ranging intellectually, his scholarship and his reasoning alike remain solidly based in the Western experience of the 16th and 17th centuries. Black's argument is that military revolution, however it is defined and wherever it appears, depends ultimately on military organization. Organization is institutional, by its nature favoring the long term and the slow hand. Its totemic gas is nitrogen. Parker, on the other hand, makes his case for the centrality to military revolution of technology-based innovations and the research bases and mentalities underpinning them. These innovations energize. They inspire "aha" moments. By their nature they are episodic, involving the kind of paradigm shifts discussed by Thomas Kuhn. They have the impact of oxygen.

Oxygen: the musket and the countermarch can both be more or less pinpointed in time. Nitrogen: the regiments that brought these innovations into battle effectively defy

**2**

such precise locating. Even the Spanish *tercio*, whose history has been so well delineated by Parker himself, was in good part a product of evolution, in the sense of dozens of modifications introduced in a basic structure over a *longue durée*. And thereby, perhaps, a way emerges not to reconcile the respective arguments presented here, but to synergize them—or perhaps, in Hegelian terms, present them in dialectical rather than confrontational contexts.

On the one hand, military organizations regard technical innovation, the entering edge of military revolution, instrumentally. Organizations can—and do—persist independently of material changes, sometimes for centuries. Limited space constrains me to offer a simplistic example, albeit one culturally appropriate for our two principal contributors: Britain's Household Cavalry traces an unbroken institutional history from the mid-17th century. Its primary technologies, however, have ranged from a half-dozen and more types of sword, through Lee-Enfield rifles and (in a brief World War I avatar as part of the Guards Machine-Gun Regiment) Vickers heavy machine guns, to wheeled scout and armored cars, to tracked reconnaissance vehicles. And through it all they have remained the Guards.

From Sweden to India, other armies can show similar long-running lineages. That stability in turn makes military organizations the counterpoint to military revolutions. Organizations are regularly perceived as antagonists by reforming individuals like the current U.S. secretary of defense, by agencies such as the U.S. Office of Net Assessment, and by scholars like Shelford Bidwell and Dominick Graham in their classic *Fire-Power*. Yet revolutions, military and otherwise, are not automatic processes. Without organization, innovation atrophies. The countermarch, for example, and all of its successive ramifications, might be mastered individually but could only be employed collectively—not even by groups of trained individuals, but by stable organizations, institutions whose members were positively committed to a common enterprise: the regiment. That did not mean literally every regiment in every army had to be a permanent fixture. Rather, the concept of permanence as an ideal state needed to replace the entrepreneurial mentality dominant in an earlier military era. And military permanence in turn was a function of stable state organization and the social stability it in turn fostered.

The reverse side of that coin is the fate of organizations, from regiments to states, failing to keep pace with the innovations of war, the military technical revolutions, and the concepts supporting and extending them. Particularly in the modern West, characterized if not defined by extensive civil-military interaction and widespread transfer of ideas and research, those members of an alliance that reduce their military effectiveness in favor of, let us say, domestic social programs tend to become clients. To pick up another of Parker's points, had the United States during World War II restricted, for the sake of alliance compatibility, developing its technological capacities vis-à-vis Britain, the principal daylight escort fighter of 1944 might well have been some variant of the Spitfire. D-Day would have been undertaken with an armored force depending on Cromwells, Grants, and perhaps a few Crusaders or Covenanters *faute de mieux*. To go back a step further, had Britain scaled its military preparation to France in 1939–40, the language of this dialogue might well be German.

Parker's related point about "singleton techniques" becoming isolated in cultures lacking a broad pattern of flexibility applies on the organizational as well as the technological side. Systems with unstable or incomplete organizations are also prone to "one-off" institutional changes that eventually atrophy for lack of reinforcement and absence of context. This holds for the West as well as the Rest. Nazi Germany's capacity to introduce even a "revolution in military affairs" was severely limited by its failure—in good part a deliberate decision on Hitler's part—comprehensively to dismantle or emasculate German secondary institutions. Soviet Russia was admirably adapted to the mass, low-tech, industrial form of war that culminated from 1941 to 1945. But it was unable to meet the specific military challenges of the technotronic era, much less the general ones posed by an emerging information/electronic age. The result was implosion: collapse not from imperial, but internal overstretch.

Even "military revolutions"—to say nothing of "military technological revolutions" and "revolutions in military affairs"—are to a significant degree susceptible to organizational control. It might even be argued that such control is necessary in their more specifically *military* aspects. The armies of the French Republic were manifestations of a military revolution in an early stage. But in their "revolutionary" format, they were regularly given all they could handle and more, from the Low Countries to Italy, by their unreformed and reactionary opponents. Only as the challenges and opportunities of the 1790s led to the organizing of the new forces in durable institutions with strong roots in the past (the demi-brigades of the *amalgame* come easiest to mind) did Napoleon's breakthroughs become possible.

To add examples would be to strain the framework of a general discussion. It seems worthwhile, however, to approach the subject of military revolution and its increasingly complex ramifications from a synthetic perspective, seeking to cross intellectual fault lines wherever possible if only for the sake of clearing a half-century's intellectual underbrush.

*Dennis Showalter is professor of history at Colorado College and a past president of the Society for Military History. His* Tannenberg: Clash of Empires *(Archon, 1991) won the Paul Birdsall Prize.*

(Original pagination p.9-10)

# Name Index